THE BIBLE

EXPOSITION
COMMENTARY

THE BIBLE

EXPOSITION

COMMENTARY

OLD TESTAMENT

WISDOM AND POETRY

JOB—SONG OF SOLOMON

WARREN W.
WIERSBE

David C Cook®
transforming lives together

THE BIBLE EXPOSITION COMMENTARY: OLD TESTAMENT WISDOM AND POETRY
Published by David C. Cook
4050 Lee Vance View
Colorado Springs, CO 80918 U.S.A.

David C. Cook Distribution Canada
55 Woodslee Avenue, Paris, Ontario, Canada N3L 3E5

David C. Cook U.K., Kingsway Communications
Eastbourne, East Sussex BN23 6NT, England

David C. Cook and the graphic circle C logo
are registered trademarks of Cook Communications Ministries.

LCCN 2008924758
ISBN 978-0-7814-4073-8

First edition published by Victor Books® in 2004 © Warren W. Wiersbe,
LCCN 00-043561, ISBN 0-7814-4073-4

Cover Design: John Hamilton Design
Cover Photo: iStockPhoto

Printed in the United States of America
Second Edition 2008

2 3 4 5 6 7 8 9 10

113009

CONTENTS

FOREWORD

The *Bible Exposition Commentary* had a modest beginning in 1972 when Victor Books published my commentary on 1 John and called it *Be Real*. Nobody remembers who named the book, but for me it was the beginning of three decades of intensive Bible study as I wrote additional commentaries, all of them with *Be* in the title. It took twenty-three books to cover the New Testament, and they were published in two bound volumes in 1989. Then I started the Old Testament *Be* series, and *Be Obedient*, on the life of Abraham, was published in 1991. Over twenty books are now available in the Old Testament series, and the Lord willing, I hope to complete the Old Testament within a year.

This volume on the Old Testament Wisdom and Poetry comprises the books covering Job through Song of Solomon. *The Bible Exposition Commentary* series is now complete in six volumes, the joyful work of over thirty years. During this time I have written books for several publishers, but "doing the next *Be* book" was always at the top of the agenda.

I owe a great debt of gratitude to the editorial staff for their encouragement and cooperation these many years, including Mark Sweeney, Jim Adair, Lloyd Cory, Greg Clouse, and Craig Bubeck. These men have been faithful to "shepherd" me through book after book, and I appreciate the friendship and ministry of each more and more. Every author should be as fortunate as I've been to work with such dedicated, skillful people who always take a personal interest in their authors. To the best of my knowledge, during these years we've ministered together, we've never had a cross word or a serious misunderstanding.

I especially want to thank the Lord for His kindness and mercy in allowing me to minister in this way through the printed page. I can think of many of my friends who could have done a far better job than I in this series, but the Lord graciously gave the privilege to me. He also gave me the wisdom and strength to get each book written on time—and sometimes ahead of time—in the midst of a very busy life as a husband and father, a pastor, a radio Bible teacher, a seminary instructor, and a conference speaker.

This leads me to say that I couldn't have done it without the loving care of my wife, Betty. She manages our household affairs so well and takes such good care of me that I've always had the time needed for studying and writing. When I started this series, our four children were all at home. Now they're all married, and my wife and I have eight wonderful grandchildren! Time flies when you're checking proofs!

The numerous readers of the *Be* series have been a great source of encouragement to me, even when they have written to disagree with me! I have received letters from many parts of the world, written by people in various walks of life, and they have gladdened my heart. Unless a writer hears from his readers, his writing becomes a one-way street, and he never knows if what he wrote did anybody any good. I want to thank the pastors, missionaries, Sunday school teachers, and other students of the Word who have been kind enough to write. We could compile a book of letters telling what God has done in the lives of people who have studied the *Be* series. To God be the glory!

As I close, there are some other people who ought to be thanked. Dr. Donald Burdick taught me New Testament at Northern Baptist Seminary and showed me how to study the Word of God. Dr. Lloyd Perry and the late Dr. Charles W. Koller both taught me how to "unlock" a Scripture passage and organize an exposition that was understandable and practical. I recommend their books on preaching to any preacher or teacher who wants to organize his or her material better.

For ten happy years, I was privileged to pastor the Calvary Baptist Church in Covington, Kentucky, just across the river from Cincinnati. One of my happy duties was writing Bible study notes for "The Whole Bible Study Course," which was developed by the late Dr. D.B. Eastep, who pastored the church for thirty-five fruitful years. No church I have ever visited or ministered to has a greater love for the Bible or a deeper hunger for spiritual truth than the dear people at Calvary Baptist. The *Be* series is, in many respects, a by-product of Dr. Eastep's kindness in sharing his ministry with me, and the church's love and encouragement while I was their pastor. I honor his memory and thank God for their continued friendship and prayer support.

To you who study God's Word with me, "I commend you to God, and to the word of his grace, which is able to build you up, and to give you an inheritance among all them which are sanctified" (Acts 20:32).

Warren W. Wiersbe

JOB

CHAPTER ONE
THE DRAMA BEGINS
Job 1–3

"You have heard of the patience [endurance] of Job" (James 5:11).

Yes, many people have heard about Job and his trials; but not many people understand what those trials were all about and what God was trying to accomplish. Nor do they realize that Job suffered as he did so that God's people today might learn from his experiences how to be patient in suffering and endure to the end.

When I decided to write about Job, I said to my wife, "I wonder how much suffering we'll have to go through so I can write this book." (I don't want to write or preach in an impersonal and academic way. The Word has to become real to me, or I can't make it real to others.) Little did we realize the trials that God would permit us to experience! But we can testify that God is faithful, He answers prayer, and He always has a wonderful purpose in mind (Jer. 29:11).

You, too, may have to go through the furnace in order to study the book of Job and really grasp its message. If so, don't be afraid! By faith, just say with Job, "But He knows the way that I take; when He has tested me, I will come forth as gold" (Job 23:10). Gold fears no fire. Whatever we have that is burned up and left behind in the furnace wasn't worth having anyway.

As we study the book of Job together, I trust that two things will be accomplished in your life: you will learn to be patient in your own trials, and you will learn how to help others in their trials. Your world is filled with people who need encouragement, and God may be preparing you for just that ministry. Either way, I hope this book helps you.

Lord Byron was on target when he wrote: "Truth is always strange; stranger than fiction."

The book of Job is not religious fiction. Job was a real person, not an imaginary character; both Ezekiel (14:14, 20) and James (5:11) attest to that. Because he was a real man who had real experiences, he can tell us what we need to know about life and its problems in this real world.

These first three chapters introduce us to the man Job and reveal four important facts about him.

Job's Prosperity
(Job 1:1-5)

The land of Uz was probably in or near Edom (Lam. 4:21). Eliphaz, one of Job's friends, came from Teman, which is associated with the Edomites (Job 2:11; Gen. 36:11).

His character (Job 1:1). Job was "perfect and upright" (Job 1:1). He was not sinless, for nobody can claim that distinction, but he was complete and mature in character and "straight" in conduct. The word translated "perfect" is related to "integrity," another important word in Job (2:3, 9; 27:5; 31:6). People with integrity are whole persons, without hypocrisy or duplicity. In the face of his friends' accusations and God's silence, Job maintained his integrity, and the Lord ultimately vindicated him.

The foundation for Job's character was the fact that he "feared God and shunned evil." "Behold, the fear of the LORD, that is wisdom; and to depart from evil is understanding" (28:28). To fear the Lord means to respect who He is, what He says, and what He does. It is not the cringing fear of a slave before a master but the loving reverence of a child before a father, a respect that leads to obedience. "The remarkable thing about fearing God," said Oswald Chambers, "is that when you fear God you fear nothing else, whereas if you do not fear God you fear everything else."

His family (Job 1:2). Job was prosperous in his family. The events in Job took place during the Patriarchal Age when a large family was seen as a blessing from God (Gen. 12:2; 13:16; 30:1). The children must have enjoyed each other's company since they met frequently to celebrate their birthdays. This speaks well of the way Job and his wife raised them. The fact that their father offered special sacrifices after each birthday feast does not prove their celebration was wicked. It only shows that Job was a pious man and wanted to be sure his family was right with God.

His material possessions (Job 1:3). In those days, wealth was measured primarily in terms of land, animals, and servants; and Job had all three in abundance. But being rich did not turn him away from God. He acknowledged that the Lord gave this wealth to him (Job 1:21), and he used his wealth generously for the good of others (4:1-4; 29:12-17; 31:16-32). Job would have had no problem obeying what Paul wrote in 1 Timothy 6:6-19.

His friends (Job 2:11). While it is true that his three friends hurt Job deeply and wronged him greatly, they were still his friends. When they heard about Job's calamities, they traveled a long distance to visit him, and they sat in silence as they sympathized with him. Their mistake was in thinking they had to explain Job's situation and tell him how to change it.

"My best friend," said Henry Ford, "is the one who brings out the best in me"; but Job's friends brought out the worst in him. However, in the end Job and his friends were reconciled (42:7-10), and I like to think that their relationship was deeper than before. To have true friends is to be wealthy indeed.

Job's Adversity
(Job 1:6-19)

In one day, Job was stripped of his wealth. One after another, four frightened messengers reported that 500 yoke of oxen, 500 donkeys, and 3,000 camels were stolen in enemy raids; 7,000 sheep were struck by lightning and killed; and all 10 of his children were killed by a windstorm. King Solomon was right: "Moreover, no man knows when his hour will come: As fish are caught in a cruel net, or birds are taken in a snare, so men are trapped by evil times that fall unexpectedly upon them" (Eccl. 9:12, NIV).

Job knew *what* had happened, but he did not know *why* it had happened; and that is the crux of the matter. Because the author allows us to visit the throne room of heaven and hear God and Satan speak, we know who caused the destruction and why he was allowed to cause it. But if we did not have this insight, we would probably take the same approach as Job's friends and blame Job for the tragedy.

Several important truths emerge from this scene, not the least of which is that *God is sovereign in all things.* He is on the throne of heaven, the angels do His will and report to Him, and even Satan can do nothing to God's people without God's permission. "The Almighty" is one of the key names for God in Job; it is used thirty-one times. From the outset, the writer reminds us that, no matter what happens in this world and in our lives, God is on the throne and has everything under control.

A second truth—and it may surprise you—is that *Satan has access to God's throne in heaven.* Thanks to John Milton's *Paradise Lost,* many people have the mistaken idea that Satan is ruling this world from hell ("Better to reign in hell, than serve in heav'n"). But Satan will not be cast into the lake of fire until before the final judgment (Rev. 20:10ff). Today, he is free to go about *on the earth* (Job 1:7; 1 Peter 5:8) and can even go into God's presence in heaven.

This third truth is most important: *God found no fault with Job, but Satan did.* God's statement in Job 1:8 echoes the description of Job in verse 1, but Satan questioned it. The word "Satan" means "adversary, one who opposes the law." This is a courtroom scene, and God and Satan each deliver different verdicts about Job. As you study this book, keep in mind that God said "Not guilty!" (1:8; 2:3; 42:7) There was nothing in Job's life that compelled God to cause him to suffer. But Satan said "Guilty!" because he is the accuser of God's people and finds nothing good in them (Zech. 3; Rev. 12:10).

Satan's accusation against Job was really an attack on God. We might paraphrase it like this: "The only reason Job fears You is because You pay him to do it. You two have made a contract: You protect him and prosper him as long as he obeys You and worships You. You are not a God worthy of worship! You have to pay people to honor You."

Job's three friends said Job was suffering because he had sinned, and that was not true. Elihu said that God was chastening Job to make him a better man, and that was partly true. But the fundamental reason for Job's suffering was *to silence the blasphemous accusations of Satan and prove that a man would honor God even though he had lost everything.* It was a battle "in the heavenlies" (Eph. 6:12), but Job did not know it. Job's life was a battlefield where the forces of God and Satan were engaged in a spiritual struggle to decide the question, "Is Jehovah God worthy of man's worship?"

Now we can better understand why Job was so unyielding as he resisted the advice of his friends. They wanted him to repent of his sins so that God would remove the suffering and make him prosperous again. Job was not going to "invent" sin in his life just so he could repent and "earn" the blessing of God. *To do that would be to play right into the hands of the accuser!* Instead, Job held fast to his integrity and blessed God even though he did not understand what God was doing. What a defeat for the prince of darkness!

A fourth truth emerges: *Satan can touch God's people only with God's permission, and God uses it for their good and His glory.* Phillips Brooks said, "The purpose of life is the building of character through truth." God is at work in our lives to make us more like Jesus Christ (Rom. 8:29), and He can use even the attacks of the devil to perfect us. When you are in the path of obedience and you find yourself in a severe trial, remind yourself that nothing can come to your life that is outside His will.

Some of the so-called tragedies in the lives of God's people have really been weapons of God to "still the enemy and the avenger" (Ps. 8:2). The angels watch the church and learn from God's dealings with His people (1 Cor. 4:9; Eph. 3:10). We may not know until we get to heaven why God allowed certain things to happen. Meanwhile, we walk by faith and say with Job, "Blessed be the name of the Lord."

Job's Fidelity
(Job 1:20-22)

The hosts of heaven and of hell watched to see how Job would respond to the loss of his wealth and his children. He expressed his grief in a manner normal for that day, for God expects us to be human (1 Thess. 4:13). After all, even Jesus wept (John 11:35). But then Job worshiped God and uttered a profound statement of faith (Job 1:21).

First, he *looked back* to his birth: "Naked came I out of my mother's womb." Everything Job owned was given to him by God, and the same God who gave it had the right to take it away. Job simply acknowledged that he was a steward.

Then Job *looked ahead* to his death: "and naked shall I return." He would not return to his mother's womb, because that would be impossible. He would go to "Mother Earth," be buried, and turn to dust. (The connection between "birth" and "Mother Earth" is seen also in Ps.

139:13-15.) Nothing that he acquired between his birth and death would go with him into the next world. Paul wrote, "For we brought nothing into this world, and it is certain we can carry nothing out" (1 Tim. 6:7).

Finally, Job *looked up* and uttered a magnificent statement of faith: "The Lord gave, and the Lord hath taken away; blessed be the name of the Lord" (Job 1:21). Instead of cursing God, as Satan said Job would do, Job blessed the Lord! Anybody can say, "The Lord gave" or "The Lord hath taken away"; but it takes real faith to say in the midst of sorrow and suffering, "Blessed be the name of the Lord."

"In all this Job sinned not, nor charged God with folly" (v. 22).

Job's Misery
(Job 2:1-3:26)

In this section, you hear four different voices.

The voice of the accuser (Job 2:1-8). Satan does not give up easily, for he returned to God's throne to accuse Job again. As in the first meeting (1:8), it is God who brings up the subject of His servant Job; and Satan accepts the challenge. We get the impression that God is confident His servant will not fail the test.

"Every man has his price," said Satan. "Job can raise another family and start another business because he still has health and strength. Let me touch his body and take away his health, and You will soon hear him curse You to Your face."

With God's permission (1 Cor. 10:13), Satan afflicted Job with a disease we cannot identify. Whatever it was, the symptoms were terrible: severe itching (Job 2:8), insomnia (v. 4), running sores and scabs (v. 5), nightmares (vv. 13-14), bad breath (19:17), weight loss (v. 20), chills and fever (21:6), diarrhea (30:27), and blackened skin

(v. 30). When his three friends first saw Job, they did not recognize him! (2:12)

Not all physical affliction comes directly from the evil one, though Satan's demons can cause (among other things) blindness (Matt. 12:22), dumbness (9:32-33), physical deformities (Luke 13:11-17), incessant pain (2 Cor. 12:7), and insanity (Matt. 8:28-34). Sometimes physical affliction is the natural result of carelessness on our part, and we have nobody to blame but ourselves. But even then, Satan knows how to use our folly to further his cause.

So abhorrent was Job's appearance that he fled society (Job 19:13-20) and went outside the city and sat on the ash heap. There the city garbage was deposited and burned, and there the city's rejects lived, begging alms from whoever passed by. At the ash heap, dogs fought over something to eat, and the city's dung was brought and burned. The city's leading citizen was now living in abject poverty and shame.

The voice of the quitter (Job 2:9-10). If ever a believer in Old Testament days shared in the fellowship of Christ's sufferings, it was Job. All that he humanly had left was his wife and his three friends, and even they turned against him. No wonder Job felt that God had deserted him!

"Curse God and die!" was exactly what Satan wanted Job to do, and Job's wife put the temptation before her husband. Yes, Satan can work through people who are dear to us (Matt. 16:22-23; Acts 21:10-14); and the temptation is stronger because we love them so much. Adam listened to Eve (Gen. 3:6, 12), and Abraham listened to Sarah (Gen. 16); but Job did not listen to the advice of his wife.

She was wrong, of course; but in all fairness, we must consider her situation. She had lost ten children in one day, and that would be enough to devastate any mother. The family wealth was gone, and she was no longer the "leading lady" in the land. Her husband, once the greatest man in the East (Job 1:3), was now sitting at the city garbage dump, suffering from a terrible disease. What did she have left? Rather than watch her husband waste away in pain and shame, she would prefer that God strike him dead and get it over with immediately. Perhaps if Job cursed God, God would do it.

In times of severe testing, our first question must not be, "*How* can I get out of this?" but "*What* can I get out of this?" Job's wife thought she had the problem solved; but if Job had followed her counsel, it would have only made things worse. Faith is living without scheming. It is obeying God in spite of feelings, circumstances, or consequences, knowing that He is working out His perfect plan in His way and in His time.

The two things Job would not give up were his faith in God and his integrity, and that's what his wife wanted him to do. Even if God did permit evil to come into his life, Job would not rebel against God by taking matters into his own hands. Job had never read *The Letters of Samuel Rutherford*, but he was following the counsel of that godly Scottish pastor who suffered greatly: "It is faith's work to claim and challenge loving-kindness out of all the roughest strokes of God." Job was going to trust God—and even argue with God!—and not waste his sufferings or his opportunity to receive what God had for him.

When life is difficult, it's easy to give up; but giving up is the worst thing we can do. A professor of history said, "If Columbus had turned back, nobody would have blamed him—but nobody would have remembered him either." If you want to be memorable, sometimes you have to be miserable.

In the end, Job's wife was reconciled to her husband and to the Lord, and God gave her another family (42:13). We don't know how much she learned from her sufferings; but we can assume it was a growing experience for her.

The voice of the mourners (Job 2:11-13). The term "Job's comforters" is a familiar phrase for describing people whose help only makes you feel worse. But these three men had some admirable qualities in spite of the way they persecuted Job.

For one thing, they cared enough for Job to travel a long distance to visit him. And when they commiserated with him, they didn't sit in a comfortable home or hospital room: they sat with him on the ash heap, surrounded by refuse. Because their grief was so great, they couldn't speak for seven days. (Of course, they made up for their silence afterward.) In fact, their expression of grief was like mourning for the death of a great person (Gen. 50:10).

The best way to help people who are hurting is just to be with them, saying little or nothing, and letting them know you care. Don't try to explain everything; explanations never heal a broken heart. If his friends had listened to him, accepted his feelings, and not argued with him, they would have helped him greatly; but they chose to be prosecuting attorneys instead of witnesses. In the end, the Lord rebuked them; and they had to ask Job's forgiveness (Job 42:7-10).

The voice of the sufferer (Job 3:1-26). After seven days of silent suffering, Job spoke, not to curse God but to curse the day of his birth. "Why was I ever born?" has been sobbed by more than one hurting child of God, including the Prophet Jeremiah (Jer. 20:14-18). This is not quite the same as saying, "I wish I were dead"; though Job did express that desire more than once (Job 6:9; 7:15-16; 14:13). *At no*

time did Job speak of ending his own life. Job's "birthday lament" is not a defense of suicide or so-called "mercy killing." It is the declaration of a man whose suffering was so intense that he wished he had never been born.

When you are hurting, you may say and do a lot of things that you later regret. Job's suffering was so great that he forgot the blessings that he and his family had enjoyed for so many years. Had he never been born, he would never have been the greatest man in the East! But pain makes us forget the joys of the past; instead, we concentrate on the hopelessness of the future. Job's friends heard his words but did not feel the anguish of his heart, and they took the wrong approach to helping him handle his trials. They argued with his words instead of ministering to his feelings.

Job cursed two nights: the night of his conception and the night of his birth (3:1-13). Conception is a blessing that comes from God (Gen. 30:1-2; Ps. 139:13-16); so when we curse a blessing, we are questioning the goodness of God. (Note that Job said a *child* was conceived, not "a mass of protoplasm" or "a thing." He was a *person* from conception.)

The key word here is *darkness*. When a baby is born, it comes out of darkness into the light; but Job wanted to stay in the darkness. In fact, he thought it would have been better if he had been born dead! Then he would have gone to the world of the dead (Sheol) and not had to face all this misery.

He closed his curse with four "why?" questions that nobody but God could answer. It is easy to ask why but difficult to get the right answer. There is nothing wrong with asking why, as long as we don't get the idea that God *owes* us an answer. Even our Lord asked, "Why hast Thou forsaken Me?" (Matt. 27:46) But if the Lord did tell us why things happen as they do, would that ease our pain or heal our broken hearts? Does reading the X ray take away the pain of a broken leg? We live on *promises,* not explanations; so we shouldn't spend too much time asking God why.

The last half of the lament is a description of the world of the dead, the place the Jews called Sheol (Job 3:13-26). That's where Job wanted to be! The Old Testament does not give a complete and final revelation of life after death; that had to await the coming of the Savior (2 Tim. 1:10). Job saw Sheol as a shadowy place where the small and great rested together, away from the burdens and sufferings of life on earth. Job would rather be dead and have rest than be alive and bear the misery that had come to him. After all, he was in the dark as far as his future was concerned (Job 3:23), so he might as well be in the darkness of Sheol.

Job shares a secret at the close of his lament (vv. 25-26): before all his troubles started, he had a feeling—and a fear—that something terrible was going to happen. Was it an intuition from the Lord? Sometimes God's people have these intuitions, and it motivates them to seek God's face and pray for His help. Is that what Job did? We don't know, but we do know that he was a broken man whose worst fears had now been realized.

It is unfortunate that the three friends laid hold of Job's lament instead of his statement of faith (1:21; 2:10). After hearing him curse his birthday, they felt it necessary to rebuke him and come to God's defense.

Now the discussion begins. Soon it will become a debate, then a dispute; and the Lord will have to intervene to bring matters to a head.

INTERLUDE

You will be spending a good deal of time with Job's three friends, so you had better get acquainted with them.

All three of the men were old (Job 32:6), older than Job (15:10), but we assume that *Eliphaz* was the oldest. He is named first (2:11), he spoke first, and the Lord seems to have accepted him as the elder member of the trio (42:7). He was associated with Teman, a place known for its wisdom (Jer. 49:7). Eliphaz based his speeches on two things: his own observations of life ("I have seen"—Job 4:8; 5:3, 27, NASB), and a frightening personal experience he had one night (4:12-21). Eliphaz put great faith in tradition (15:18-19), and the God he worshiped was an inflexible Lawgiver. "Who ever perished being innocent?" he asked (4:7); and a host of martyrs could have answered, "We have!" (And what about our Lord Jesus Christ?) Eliphaz had a rigid theology that left little or no room for the grace of God.

Bildad must have been the second oldest of the three since he is named second and spoke after Eliphaz. In a word, Bildad was a *legalist.* His life-text was, "Behold, God will not cast away a perfect man, neither will He help the evildoers" (8:20). He could quote ancient proverbs, and like Eliphaz, he had great respect for tradition. For some reason, Bildad was sure that Job's children died because they also were sinners (v. 4). The man seemed to have no feeling for his hurting friend.

Zophar was the youngest of the three and surely the most dogmatic. He speaks like a schoolmaster addressing a group of ignorant freshmen. "Know this!" is his unfeeling approach (11:6; 20:4). He is merciless and tells Job that God was giving him far less than he deserved for his sins! (11:6) His key text is, "Knowest thou not this of old ... that the triumphing of wicked is short, and the joy of the hypocrite but for a moment?" (20:4-5) Interestingly enough, Zophar speaks to Job only twice. Either he decided he was unable to answer Job's arguments or felt that it was a waste of time trying to help Job.

All three men said some good and true things, as well as some foolish things; but they were of no help to Job because their viewpoint was too narrow. Their theology was not vital and vibrant but dead and rigid, and the God they tried to defend was small enough to be understood and explained. These men perfectly illustrate Dorothy Sayers' statement, "There's nothing you can't prove if your outlook is only sufficiently limited."

Why would three men speak to their friend as these men spoke to Job? Why were they so angry? There is a hint of an answer in Job's words, "Now you too have proved to be of no help; you see something dreadful and are afraid" (6:21, NIV). *The three men were afraid that the same calamities would come to them!* Therefore, they had to defend their basic premise that God rewards the righteous and punishes the wicked. As long as they were "righteous," nothing evil could happen to them in this life.

Fear and anger often go together. By maintaining his integrity and refusing to say he had sinned, Job undermined the theology of his friends and robbed them of their peace and confidence; and this made them angry. God used Job to destroy their shallow theology and challenge them to go deeper into the heart and mind of God. Alas, they preferred the superficial and safe to the profound and mysterious.

Eliphaz, Bildad, and Zophar have many disciples today. Whenever you meet a person who feels compelled to explain everything, who has a pat answer

for every question and a fixed formula for solving every problem, you are back at the ash heap with Job's three friends. When that happens, remember the words of the Swiss psychologist Paul Tournier:

We are nearly always longing for an easy religion, easy to understand and easy to follow; a religion with no mystery, no insoluble problems, no snags; a religion that would allow us to escape from our miserable human condition; a religion in which contact with God spares us all strife, all uncertainty, all suffering and all doubt; in short, a religion without the Cross. (*Reflections* [New York: Harper & Row, 1976], 142)

We wonder how Job's three friends would have explained the Cross to the two Emmaus disciples! (Luke 24:13ff) Let's listen in on the first round of speeches.

CHAPTER TWO
DISCUSSION BEGINS
Job 4–7

"But what Satan could not do with all his Sabeans, and all his Chaldeans, and all his winds from the wilderness to help him, that he soon did with the debating approaches and the controversial assaults of Eliphaz, and Zophar, and Bildad, and Elihu. Oh, the unmitigable curse of controversy!"

—ALEXANDER WHYTE

T he three friends were silent for seven days (Job 2:13), and Job later wished they had stayed that way (13:5). "Then Eliphaz, the

Temanite, answered [Job]." But what did he answer? The pain in Job's heart? No, he answered the words from Job's lips; *and this was a mistake.* A wise counselor and comforter must listen with the heart and respond to feelings as well as to words. You do not heal a broken heart with logic; you heal a broken heart with love. Yes, you must speak the truth; but be sure to speak the truth in love (Eph. 4:15).

Eliphaz's Rebuke
(Job 4–5)

His approach (Job 4:1-4). Eliphaz's approach seems to start out positive enough, even gentle; but it was only honey to prepare Job for the bitterness that would follow. "If someone ventures a word with you, will you be impatient?" he asked (v. 2, NIV).

"Don't get upset, Job!" is what he was saying. "In the past, your words have been a help to many people; and we want our words to be a help to you."

Never underestimate the power of words to encourage people in the battles of life. James Moffatt translates Job 4:4, "Your words have kept men on their feet." The right words, spoken at the right time, and with the right motive, can make a tremendous difference in the lives of others. Your words can nourish those who are weak and encourage those who are defeated. But your words can also hurt those who are broken and only add to their burdens, so be careful what you say and how you say it.

His accusation (Job 4:5-11). Eliphaz then moved into his accusation. Job could "give it," but he couldn't "take it"! He could tell others how to handle their trials; but when trials came to his life, he didn't practice what he preached. "Is not your reverence your confidence?" asked Eliphaz. "And the integrity of your ways

your hope?" (v. 6, NKJV) If Job is living a godly life, Eliphaz argues, then he has nothing to fear; because God *always* blesses the righteous and judges the wicked.

This is the basic premise of all three friends: Do what is right and things will go well for you; do what is wrong and God will send judgment. That judgment may sometimes be gradual, like the growing of a crop for harvest (v. 8); or it may be sudden, like the coming of a storm or the attack of a lion (vv. 9-11). But you can be sure that judgment will come; for God is a righteous Judge.

Most people will agree that *ultimately* God blesses the righteous, His own people, and judges the wicked; but that is not the question discussed in Job. It is not the *ultimate* but the *immediate* about which Job and his three friends are concerned, and not only they but also David (Ps. 37), Asaph (Ps. 73), and even the Prophet Jeremiah (Jer. 12:1-6).

His arguments (Job 4:12–5:7). Eliphaz presented two arguments to prove his point: experience (4:12-21) and observation (5:1-7). The first argument is based on an eerie experience he had one night when he saw a "vision" and heard a voice. Two questions must be answered: What was the content of the message, and was the message a direct revelation from God?

Since there are no punctuation marks in the Hebrew manuscripts of the Old Testament, we are not always certain where quotations begin and end. Most English translations make 4:17-21 the complete statement of the "spirit"; but some students feel the statement is limited to verse 17, and the rest is commentary by Eliphaz. Either way, it's the same message: man's life is brief and frail, and he can never be righteous enough in himself to please God.

But was this statement a direct revelation from God? Probably not; the whole experience doesn't seem to fit God's pattern for revealing truth. For one thing, it lacks the authority of "The word of the Lord came to me saying" or "Thus says the Lord." And God doesn't usually "sneak up on" people and scare them. We don't know for sure, but it's possible that Eliphaz had a dream, meditated on it, and gradually transformed it into a vision.

One thing is sure: Eliphaz was not telling the whole story about God and man. Yes, man lives in a house of clay that eventually turns to dust; and man's life can be snuffed out like swatting a moth or pulling down a tent. But man is also made in the image of God, and the God who made him is a God of grace and mercy as well as a God of justice.

Eliphaz's second argument is based on his own personal observations of life (5:1-7). He has seen sinners prosper and take root, only to be destroyed and lose everything. This was a not-so-subtle description of Job's situation. It must have hurt Job deeply to hear that it was his sin that killed his children. But in Psalm 73, Asaph takes a wholly different view. He concludes that God allows the wicked to prosper in this life because it's the only "heaven" they will know. God will adjust things in the next life and see to it that His people are rewarded and the wicked are punished.

The problem with arguing from observation is that our observations are severely limited. Furthermore, we can't see the human heart as God can and determine who is righteous in His sight. Some sinners suffer judgment almost immediately, while others spend their lives in prosperity and die in peace (Eccl. 8:10-14).

Trouble doesn't grow out of the ground, like weeds; it's a part of man's birth, because man is born a sinner (Job 5:6-7). If Job is in trouble, concludes Eliphaz, he caused it himself because he sinned against God. Therefore, Job must repent of his sins and ask for God's forgiveness.

His appeal (Job 5:8-17). This lead to an appeal from Eliphaz that Job seek God and commit himself to Him. The God who does wonders and cares for His creation will surely help Job if he humbles himself and confesses his sins. Job should see his trials as discipline from God to make him a better man (vv. 17-18), a theme that will later be taken up by Elihu. Job must have been in bad shape for God to have to take away his wealth, his family, and his health in order to straighten him out! And isn't discipline a tool of God's love? (Prov. 3:11-12; Heb. 12:1-11)

His assurance (Job 5:17-27). Eliphaz closes his speech with words of assurance. The same God who wounds will also heal (Deut. 32:39; Hos. 6:1-2). He will deliver you from trouble, save you from your enemies, and give you a long and happy life and a peaceful death. "We have examined this, and it is true. So hear it and apply it to yourself" (Job 5:27, NIV).

But this is Satan's philosophy said in different words! "Does Job fear God for nothing? ... Skin for skin! Yes, all that a man has he will give for his life" (1:9; 2:4, NKJV). Eliphaz was asking Job to make a bargain with God: Confess your sins, and God will restore all that you have lost. If Job had done that, it would have disgraced Jehovah and vindicated Satan; and Job was not about to do it.

Job's Response (Job 6–7)

Job responded with two passionate appeals. First, he appealed to his three friends that they might show more understanding and sympathy (Job 6). Then he appealed to God, that He would consider his plight and lighten his sufferings before he died (Job 7).

Job's appeal to his friends (Job 6). Only Eliphaz had spoken so far, but Job could tell that Bildad and Zophar agreed with him. Not one of his friends identified with what Job was going through physically and emotionally. It was one thing for them to sit where he sat and quite something else for them to feel what he felt (Ezek. 3:15). The child who defined "sympathy" as "your pain in my heart" knew more about giving comfort than did these three.

To begin with, they didn't feel the *heaviness* of his suffering (Job 6:1-3). No wonder Job had spoken so impetuously! His friends would have done the same thing if they carried the load that he carried. Job didn't have the full revelation of heaven that believers have today, so his future was dim. We can read 2 Corinthians 4:16-18 and take heart.

Nor did his friends understand the *bitterness* of his suffering (Job 6:4-7). Job felt like a target at which God was shooting poisoned arrows, and the poison was making Job's spirit bitter. God had His army in array, shooting at one weak man; and Job's friends were adding to the poison. What Job needed were words of encouragement that would feed his spirit and give him strength, but all his friends fed him were words that were useless and tasteless. If his complaint sounded like the braying of a donkey or the lowing of an ox, it was because, like a starving animal, he was hungry for love and understanding.

Job tried to get them to feel the *hopelessness* of his situation (vv. 8-13). Prolonged and intense suffering can make a person feel powerless to handle life, and this can lead to hopelessness. If you can't control some of the elements that make up life, how can you plan for the future? Job asked, "What strength do I have, that I should still hope? What

prospects, that I should be patient?" (v. 11, NIV). In other words, "What am I waiting for? Life is only getting worse!"

Hopelessness can lead to a feeling of *uselessness*; and when you feel useless, you don't want to live. This explains why Job wanted God to take his life (3:20-23; 6:8-9; 7:15-16; 10:18-19; 14:13). Job didn't attempt this himself, for he knew that suicide was wrong; but he prayed that God might take him out of his misery. Job's friends were healthy and comfortable and didn't know the burden of waking up each morning to another day of suffering. Job's strength was gone, and he felt useless (6:12-13).

Courageously, Job pointed out the *ineffectiveness* of their ministry to him (vv. 14-30). They didn't pity him or try to meet his needs. They were like a dry brook in the desert that disappoints thirsty travelers. They were his "friends" as long as he was prosperous; but when trouble came, they turned against him.

Job made two requests of his friends: "Teach me" (v. 24) and "Look upon me" (v. 28). He didn't need accusation; he needed illumination! But they wouldn't even look him in the face and behold his plight. Physically, the three men were sitting with Job on the ash heap; but emotionally, they were like the priest and Levite, passing by "on the other side" (Luke 10:30-37).

In my pastoral ministry, I can recall visiting hospital patients who were difficult to look at because of disease, accident, or surgery; and sometimes they were difficult to listen to because they had become bitter. From my eye contact and my responses to their words, they could detect whether or not I really cared. It did little good for me to quote Scripture and pray unless we had first built a bridge between our hearts. Then we could minister to each other.

Job closed his address to his friends with a passionate appeal for them to reconsider his situation and take a more loving approach. "Relent, do not be unjust; reconsider, for my integrity is at stake" (Job 6:29, NIV). The three men were so intent on defending themselves that they forgot to comfort their friend!

Job's appeal to the Lord (Job 7). Job used several vivid pictures to describe the *futility* of life. He felt like a man who had been conscripted into the army against his will (v. 1a, "appointed time" in KJV), and like a laborer (v. 1b) or a hired man waiting for sunset and his daily wages (v. 2). At least these men had something to look forward to, but Job's future was hopeless. His nights were sleepless, his days were futile (Deut. 28:67), and the Lord didn't seem to care.

He then focused on the *brevity* of life. Time was passing swiftly; so, if God were going to do anything, He had better hurry! Job's life was like the weaver's shuttle (Job 7:6), moving swiftly with the thread running out. (The phrase "cut me off" in 6:9 means "to cut a weaving from the loom." See Isa. 38:12.) Life is like a weaving, and only God can see the total pattern and when the work is finished.

Job also saw his life as a breath or a cloud, here for a brief time and then gone forever, never to return (Job 7:7-10; James 4:14). God was treating him like a dangerous monster that had to be watched every minute (Job 7:11-12). No wonder Job was bitter against God for guarding him constantly. The fact that Job referred to *Yam* ("the sea") and *Tammin* ("a whale"), two mythological characters, didn't mean he was giving his approval to the teachings of Eastern myths. He used these well-known characters only to illustrate his point.

There was no way Job could escape God, the "watcher of men" (v. 20, NIV,

NKJV). If Job went to sleep, God frightened him in his dreams. If he was awake, he knew God's eye was upon him (10:14; 13:27; 31:4). He couldn't even swallow his spittle without God knowing about it! Why would God pay so much attention to one man? (7:17-18; Ps. 8:4)

Job closed his appeal with a request for forgiveness (Job 7:20-21). "If I have sinned, then forgive me. Why should I be a burden to You and to myself? Time is flying by swiftly, so let's settle things as soon as possible!" It was not a confession of sin, for Job still maintained his integrity; but it was an opportunity for God to deal with areas in Job's life that he knew nothing about (Ps. 19:12-14).

Then Job was silent. He had vented his pain and frustration and appealed to his friends for understanding and encouragement. Would he receive it?

Let's listen next to Bildad the Shuhite who gives a brief theological lecture on the justice of God.

CHAPTER THREE
THE DISCUSSION CONTINUES
Job 8–10

> "You may be as orthodox as the devil, and as wicked."
> —JOHN WESLEY

As the discussion continues, Bildad presents three logical arguments to prove Job is guilty; and Job counters with three painful questions to help his friends understand how perplexed and tormented he really is.

Three Logical Arguments
(Job 8:1-22)

"Your words are a blustering wind!" (Job 8:2, NIV) Can you imagine a counselor saying that to a suffering individual who wanted to die? Bildad did; in fact, he used the same approach in his next speech (18:2). Job had poured out his grief and was waiting to hear a sympathetic word, but his friend said that Job's speech was just so much hot air.

There is a reason for Bildad's approach: he was so concerned about defending the justice of God that he forgot the needs of his friend. "Does God subvert judgment? Or does the Almighty pervert justice?" (8:3, NKJV) Bildad preached a sermon on God's justice, and his text was taken from the "vision" of Eliphaz: "Shall mortal man be more just than God?" (4:17) In defending God's justice, Bildad presented three logical arguments.

The character of God (Job 8:1-7). It angered Bildad that Job even thought that God would do anything wrong. Had Job forgotten what God did to sinners at the Flood, or what He did to Sodom and Gomorrah? Isn't He the holy God, and doesn't His very nature demand that He do what is right? Job was blaspheming God by questioning Him and accusing Him of wrongdoing.

While Bildad's theology was correct—God *is* just—his application of that theology was wrong. Bildad was looking at only one aspect of God's nature—His holiness and justice—and had forgotten His love, mercy, and goodness. Yes, "God is light" (1 John 1:5; but don't forget that "God is love" (4:8, 16). His love is a holy love, and His holiness is exercised in love, even when He judges sin.

How are these two attributes of God reconciled? At the Cross. When Jesus died for the sins of the world, the righteousness of God was vindicated, for sin was judged; but the love of God was demonstrated, for a Savior was provided. At Calvary, God is both "just and the Justifier" (Rom. 3:24-26). God's law said, "The soul who sins shall die" (Ezek. 18:4, 20, NKJV); and God obeyed His own law in the sacrificing of His Son. In Christ's resurrection, the grace of God triumphed over sin and death; and all who repent and trust Jesus Christ will be saved.

In Old Testament times, believers looked forward to the Cross and were saved by faith in a Savior yet to come (John 8:56; Rom. 3:25; Heb. 11). Job was a believer; therefore, his sins had been dealt with by God. Even if Job had sinned against God in some great way, God would deal with His child on the basis of grace and mercy and not justice. When we confess our sins, God forgives us because He is faithful to His promise and just toward His Son who died for those sins (1 John 1:9).

It must have pained Job deeply when Bildad said that Job's children had died because they had sinned (Job 8:4). Bildad probably thought he was encouraging Job: "Perhaps they were not killed because of *your* sins but because of their own sins. They can't change anything now, but you can; so don't wait too long!"

Bildad's appeal in verses 5-7 is another echo of Satan's philosophy. "You say you have not sinned. Then plead with God to restore your prosperity. If you were right before God, He would do great things for you. Isn't prosperity better than pain?" Little did Bildad realize that his words would come true and Job's latter end would be greater than his beginning. However, in the end Job's prayer would be for Bildad and the others because *they* were the ones not right with God (42:7-13).

The wisdom of the past (Job 8:8-10). Eliphaz based his thinking on observation and experience, but Bildad was a traditionalist who looked for wisdom in the past. "What do the ancients say about it?" was his key question. To be sure, we today can learn from the past. "Those who do not remember the past are condemned to relive it," wrote George Santayana. But the past must be a rudder to guide us and not an anchor to hold us back. "How the past perishes is how the future becomes," said philosopher Alfred North Whitehead.

The fact that something was said or written years ago is no guarantee it is right. As one who enjoys reading the classics, I am impressed with the fact that they contain as much folly as wisdom; and they often contradict each other. Dr. Robert Hutchins, editor of *The Great Books of the Western World*, wrote in his preface: "In a conversation that has gone on for twenty-five centuries, all dogmas and points of view appear. Here are the great errors as well as the great truths."

"Tradition" and "traditionalism" are two different things. Historian Jeroslav Pelikan expresses this difference accurately when he says, "Tradition is the living faith of the dead; traditionalism is the dead faith of the living." To Bildad, the past was a parking lot; but God wants the past to be a launching pad. We *stand* with the ancients so that we can *walk* with them and *move* toward the goals that they were seeking. This includes our knowledge of God as well as our knowledge of man and the world. As John Robinson said to the Pilgrim Fathers when they left for the New World, "The Lord has more truth yet to break forth out of His Holy Word."

Bildad did not quote from the ancients; he knew that Job was as familiar with the past as he was. But Bildad made it clear that he respected the wisdom of the ancients more than the teachings of his contemporaries. The accumulated wisdom of the ages was bound to be worth more than the words of people who were "born only yesterday." Life is too brief for us to learn all they can teach us. We are fleeting shadows, so we had better learn wisdom while we have opportunity.

The evidence in nature (Job 8:11-22). In this "wisdom poem," Bildad may have summarized some of the sayings of the ancients as he argued from the law of "cause and effect." If this law applies in nature, why not in human life as well?

Take the papyrus plant as an example: If it doesn't have water, it withers and dies (vv. 11-13). Job was withering and dying, so there had to be a cause: he was a hypocrite, and his hope was perishing.

Bildad then moved from plants to spiders (vv. 14-15). Can you lean on a spider's web and be held up securely? Of course not! No matter how confident you may be, the web will break. Job's confidence was like that: In due time, it would break, and he would fall.

The third example came from the garden: If you pull up a plant, no matter how luxuriant it may be, it will eventually die (vv. 16-22). Something had happened to Job's "root system," and he was fading away; thus, sin was the cause. Nobody pulls up a *good* plant and destroys it, so there had to be something wrong with Job for God to so uproot him. God doesn't cultivate weeds and cast away the good plants! Bildad reaffirmed his earlier promise that God would restore Job's fortunes if he would only admit his sins and get right with God. It was the devil's invitation all over again!

Three Painful Questions (Job 9:1–10:22)

From this point on, the emphasis in the

discussion is on *the justice of God*; and the image that is uppermost in Job's mind is that of *a legal trial*. He wants to take God to court and have opportunity to prove his own integrity. A glance at some of the vocabulary indicates this:

contend (Job 9:3; 10:2) = enter into litigation
answer (9:3, 16) = testify in court
judge (v. 15) = an opponent at law, accuser
set a time (v. 19) = summon to court
daysman (v. 33) = an umpire, an arbitrator
reason (13:3) = argue a case
order my cause (v. 18) = prepare my case
plead (v. 19; 23:6) = dispute in court
hear me (31:35) = give me a legal hearing
adversary (v. 35) = accuser in court

In Job 9 and 10, Job asks three questions: [1] "How can I be righteous before God?" (9:1-13) [2] "How can I meet God in court?" (vv. 14-35) and [3] "Why was I born?" (10:1-22; see v. 18) You can see how these questions connect. Job is righteous, but he has to prove it. How can a mortal man prove himself righteous before God? Can he take God to court? But if God doesn't step in and testify on Job's behalf, what is the purpose of all this suffering? Why was Job even born?

"How can I be righteous before God?" (Job 9:1-13) This is not a question about salvation ("How may I be justified?") but about vindication ("How can I be declared innocent?"). If a man tried to take God to court, he would not be able to answer God's questions one time in a thousand! Yet Job doesn't know any other way to clear himself before his friends.

Most of this section is a declaration

focusing on the attributes of God, especially His invincible wisdom and power that control the earth and the heavens. Would anybody dare go to court with an opponent powerful enough to shake the earth, make the stars, and walk on the waves? (See Isa. 44:24 and Amos 4:13.)

But God is not only invincible, He is also *invisible*. Job couldn't see Him or stop Him to give Him a summons to court. God can do whatever He pleases, and nobody can question Him! Even the monster *Rahab* (Job 9:13, NIV, another mythological creature like *Yam* and *Tannin*, 7:12) has to bow before God's power.

"How can I meet God in court?" (Job 9:14-35) In order to prove himself righteous, Job had to take God to court. But suppose God accepted the summons? What would Job say or do? He discusses this by imagining several situations.

(1) "If God came, what would I say?" (vv. 14-19) How could Job answer God's cross-examination? How does one reason with God or present one's case before God? If God should answer, Job would not believe it was really His voice; and if Job should say the wrong thing, God would only afflict him more. When Job finally did meet God (Job 38–41), the Lord asked him seventy-seven questions! And Job couldn't answer one of them! His only response was to admit his ignorance and shut his mouth in silence.

(2) "If I could declare my innocence, what then?" (vv. 20-24) This is no assurance that God will set Job free. Both Eliphaz and Bildad claimed that God rewards the righteous and judges the wicked, but Job said that sometimes God destroys both the righteous and the wicked. Wicked judges condemn the righteous and help the ungodly, and God apparently does nothing about it. Job is accusing God of injustice, not only toward Job and his

family but also toward other innocent people in the land.

(3) "If I try to be happy, what good will it do?" (vv. 25-31) Time was running out for Job, like the king's messengers that hasten to their destinations, and the papyrus boats in Egypt that skim swiftly down the river, and the eagle that swoops down from the sky. Perhaps Job should take a more positive attitude toward his afflictions, forget his pain, and smile (v. 27). But would that change anything? No! He would still be guilty before God, rejected by his friends, and sitting on an ash heap in sickness and pain. Even if he took a bath and changed clothes as an act of public contrition and cleansing, he would still fear what God might do. Job is convinced that God is against him and that any steps he takes on earth will be nullified by heaven. The defendant can smile and put on a brave front in court, but that doesn't keep the judge from saying, "Guilty!"

(4) "If only I had a mediator!" (vv. 32-35) If God were a man, then Job could approach him and plead his case. Or if there were a "daysman" (mediator) between God and Job, he could take away the rod of judgment and bring Job and God together. But God is not man, and there is no mediator! *This is where Jesus Christ enters the picture!* Jesus is God and became man to reveal the Father (John 14:7-11) and to bring sinners to God (1 Tim. 2:5-6; 1 Peter 3:18). He is the "daysman" that Job was pleading for centuries ago (Job. 16:21).

"Why was I born?" (Job 10:1-22) Job's argument here is that God made him and gave him life (vv. 3, 8-12, 18-19), but God was not treating him like one of His own creations. After putting time and effort into making Job, God was destroying him! Furthermore, God was judging Job

without even telling him what the charges were against him (v. 2). No wonder Job was weary, bitter, and confused (vv. 1, 15). Note that in this chapter Job speaks directly to God and not to his friends.

God is not a man that He has to investigate things and fight against time (vv. 4-6). God is eternal and can take all the time He needs, and God is all-knowing and doesn't have to investigate like a private detective. Job had previously yearned for an umpire (9:33), but now he asks for a deliverer (10:7) so he can escape judgment. God was an ever-present Guard, watching Job's every move (v. 14). He was stalking Job like a lion (v. 16) and attacking him with His army (v. 17). Job was hemmed in, and there was no way out.

So Job's question seems reasonable: "Why then did You bring me out of the womb?" (v. 18, NIV) Job's existence on the earth seemed so purposeless he begged God to give him a few moments of peace and happiness before his life ended. He could see his life going by swiftly (7:6-7; 9:25-26), and there was not a moment to waste. "Let me alone," he prays, "so that I can have a little comfort before I go to the world of darkness."

Job could not understand what God was doing, *and it was important that he not understand.* Had Job known that God was using him as a weapon to defeat Satan, he could have simply sat back and waited trustfully for the battle to end. But as Job surveyed himself and his situation, he asked the same question the disciples asked when Mary anointed the Lord Jesus: "Why this waste?" (Mark 14:4) Before we criticize Job too severely, let's recall how many times we have asked that question ourselves when a baby has died or a promising young person was killed in an accident.

Nothing that is given to Christ in faith and love is ever wasted. The fragrance of Mary's ointment faded from the scene centuries ago, but the significance of her worship has blessed Christians in every age and continues to do so. Job was bankrupt and sick, and all he could give to the Lord was his suffering by faith; *but that is just what God wanted in order to silence the devil.*

When William Whiting Borden died in Egypt in 1913 while on his way to the mission field, some people may have asked, "Why this waste?" But God is still using the story of his brief life to challenge people to give Christ their all.

When John and Betty Stam were martyred in China in 1934, there were some who asked, "Why this waste?" But *The Triumph of John and Betty Stam* by Mrs. Howard Taylor has been a life-changing book since it was published in 1935. My girlfriend (now my wife) gave me a copy on my twenty-first birthday, and its message still grips my heart.

When the five missionaries were martyred in Ecuador at the hands of Auca Indians, some called the event a "tragic waste of manpower." But God thought differently, and the story of these five heroes of faith has been ministering to the church ever since.

Job asked, "Why was I born?" In the light of his losses and his personal suffering, it all seemed such a waste! But God knew what He was doing *then,* and He knows what He is doing *now.*

"You have heard of Job's perseverance and have seen what the Lord finally brought about," wrote James. "The Lord is full of compassion and mercy" (James 5:11, NIV). If you had told that to Job, he might not have believed it; but it was still true.

It was true for him, and it is true for us today.

Believe it!

INTERLUDE

The Hebrew word translated "daysman" in Job 9:33 means "to act as umpire." The "daysman" is the one with authority to set the day when competing parties come together to settle their dispute. In the East, the "daysman" put his hands on the heads of the two disputing parties to remind them that he was the one with the authority to settle the question. Job longed for somebody who could do this for him and God.

Job was serious about wanting to face God in court, even though he had nobody to represent him. "I desire to reason [argue my case] with God" (13:3). "I will defend mine own ways before Him" (v. 15). "Behold now, I have ordered my cause [prepared my case]; I know that I shall be justified" (v. 18). He felt that God was not treating him justly. "I cry aloud, but there is no justice" (19:7). God had "taken away" his "right" (27:2), and Job demanded an opportunity to be heard before the throne of God. But when the opportunity came, Job had nothing to say.

CHAPTER FOUR
AN ANGRY "YOUNGER" MAN
Job 11–14

"It is not why I suffer that I wish to know, but only whether I suffer for Your sake."
—LEVI YITZHAK OF BERDITCHER

Job's three friends were old men, so Zophar must have been the youngest since he spoke last. His first speech is not long; but what it lacks in length, it makes up for in animosity, for it reveals that Zophar was angry. There is a proper time and place for the display of righteous anger (Eph. 4:26), but Job's ash heap was not the place, and that was not the right time. "The wrath of man does not produce the righteousness of God" (James 1:20, NKJV). What Job needed was a helping hand, not a slap in the face.

Zophar makes three accusations against Job: Job is guilty of sin (Job 11:1-4); Job is ignorant of God (vv. 5-12); and Job is stubborn in his refusal to repent (vv. 13-20). In his reply, Job answers all three accusations: He affirms God's greatness (Job 12) and his own innocence (Job 13), but he has no hope, so why should he repent? (Job 14)

Zophar's Three Accusations (Job 11:1-20)

After listening to Eliphaz and Bildad accuse Job, Zophar should have had enough sense and compassion to take a new approach. Job would hold fast to his integrity no matter what God did or his friends said, so why continue that discussion? How sad it is when people who should share ministry end up creating misery. "Rejoice with them that do rejoice, and weep with them that weep" (Rom. 12:15) is good counsel to follow.

"Job is guilty!" (Job 11:1-4) Like Bildad (8:2), Zophar opened his address by calling Job a "windbag." How tragic that these three friends focused on Job's words instead of the feelings behind those words. A Chinese proverb says, "Though conversing face to face, their hearts have a thousand miles between them." How true that was at the ash heap!

After all, information is not the same as communication. Sidney J. Harris reminds us, "Information is giving out; communication is getting through."

Not only was Job's speech a lot of wind, but it was also chatter ("lies") and mockery (11:3). What Job said about God was not true and could only be compared to the idle chatter of people who speak without thinking. And what Job said about himself was an outright lie, for he was not pure before God. In maintaining his integrity, Job gave the impression that he was sinless, which, of course, was not true. (See 6:30; 9:20-21; 10:7.)

Job is ignorant of God (Job 11:5-12). Zophar's request in verse 5 was answered when God appeared (38:1); but it was Zophar and his two friends who were later rebuked by God, and not Job! Job was commended by the Lord for telling the truth. Beware of asking God to tell others what they need to know, unless you are willing for Him to show *you* what you need to know.

Zophar wanted Job to grasp the height, depth, breadth, and length of God's divine wisdom (11:8-9). In saying this, Zophar was hinting that he himself already knew the vast dimensions of God's wisdom and could teach Job if he would listen. It's too bad Zophar didn't know the vast dimensions of God's love (Eph. 3:17-19) and share some of that love with Job.

When Zophar said that the secrets of God's wisdom were "double" (Job 11:6), what did he mean? It could mean that God's wisdom is full and complete (Isa. 40:2), or that God has twice as much wisdom as Job thinks He has. The NIV says that "true wisdom has two sides" (Job 11:6). There is the small side that we see and the huge side that only God can see.

Since God knows everything, He knows all about Job and could punish him more than He has. "It could be worse!" is certainly no comfort to a man who has lost his family, his wealth, and his health, and is barely hanging on to life. You don't measure suffering in a quantitative way the way you measure produce at the supermarket. The flippant way in which Job's friends were speaking about his situation shows they lacked understanding. "The deeper the sorrow," says the Jewish *Talmud*, "the less tongue it has."

The two questions in verse 7 expect a negative answer. Nobody can "fathom the mysteries of God" or "probe the limits of the Almighty" (NIV). Of course, Job never claimed to know everything about God; but what he did know encouraged him to hold fast to his integrity and not give up.

God is not accountable to us. He can arrest and imprison anybody He chooses, convene the court and pronounce the sentence; and nobody can say a word in protest (v. 10; see 9:12). God knows who is wise and who is foolish, who is pure and who is sinful. Since God has passed judgment on Job, Job must be guilty.

Zophar closed this accusation by quoting a proverb (11:12). It's not easy to ascertain its meaning. The proverb may be saying that no matter how stupid a man is when he is born, even as dumb as a wild donkey, there is still hope for him to become intelligent. Or, the proverb might be saying just the opposite, as in the NIV: "But a witless man can no more become wise than a wild donkey's colt can be born a man." The NASB agrees: "And an idiot will become intelligent when the foal of a wild donkey is born a man." In view of Zophar's anger and insulting language, it is likely that the NIV and NASB translations are correct.

Job is stubborn and should repent (Job 11:13-20). "There is hope!" is Zophar's encouraging word to Job (v. 18), and he described what Job could experience. God would bless him abundantly, and his troubles would be over. Job could lift up his head again, and his fears would be gone (v. 15; 10:15). He would forget his misery like water gone over the dam (11:16). God would give him a long life, and it would be the dawning of a new day for him (v. 17). He would dwell in the light, not in the darkness of Sheol (10:20-22); and God's security would put an end to all his fears (11:19-20).

But if Job wanted these blessings, he had to get them on Zophar's terms. Yes, there was hope, but it was hope with a condition attached to it: Job must repent and confess his sins (vv. 13-14). *Zophar is tempting Job to bargain with God so he can get out of his troubles.* This is exactly what Satan wanted Job to do! "Doth Job fear God for nothing?" Satan asked (1:9). Satan accused Job of having a "commercial faith" that promised prosperity in return for obedience. If Job had followed Zophar's advice, he would have played right into the hands of the enemy.

Job did not have a "commercial faith" that made bargains with God. He had a confident faith that said, "Though He slay me, yet will I trust in Him" (13:15). That doesn't sound like a man looking for an easy way out of difficulties. "Job did not understand the Lord's reasons," said C.H. Spurgeon, "but he continued to confide in His goodness." That is faith!

Job's Three Affirmations (Job 12-14)

Zophar's speech was a brief one, but Job took a long time to answer each of Zophar's accusations. Job began with Zophar's second accusation that Job had no knowledge of God (Job 11:5-12). Job affirmed that he had wisdom and understanding just as they did (Job 12). Then he replied to Zophar's first accusation that Job was a guilty sinner (11:1-4). Job once again affirmed his integrity (Job 13). Job then closed his speech by challenging Zophar's third point, that there was still hope (11:13-20). In Job 14, Job admits that his hope is almost gone.

The greatness of God (Job 12). First, Job challenged his friends' declaration that they had more wisdom than he did. True, they were older than Job; but age is no guarantee of wisdom. There are old fools as well as young fools.

Then, Job rebuked them for being so unfeeling toward him and turning him into a laughingstock. He felt he was just and upright, which is the way God described him (1:1, 8; 2:3). "You who are at ease have no concern for people who are slipping. You say God is punishing me for my sins. Then why doesn't He punish robbers and other people who provoke God?" (12:5-6) Zophar claimed that wisdom was not accessible to man (11:7-9), but Job said that God's creatures could teach them what they needed to know (12:7-11; see Gen. 1:26-28). Even "dumb" creatures know that God's hand made everything and keeps everything going. In fact, the very breath they were using to accuse Job was God's gift to them; and He could remove it without their permission. God gave men and women the ability to taste and judge food. Would He not give them the even more important ability to evaluate words and assess truth? (Job 12:11)

In verses 12-25, Job describes the wisdom and power of God. Verse 12 likely refers to God, "the Ancient One" and "the One who lives long." These divine names are a rebuke to Job's aged friends who thought that their years of experience had taught them so much!

Job pointed out that God is completely sovereign in what He does with nature (vv. 14-15) and with people (vv. 16-25). What He destroys cannot be rebuilt, and what He locks up cannot be released (Rev. 3:6-8). He can send drought or flood, and nobody can stop Him (Job 12:15). He has the wisdom to know what to do, and He has the power to accomplish it (vv. 13, 16).

In His sovereignty over people, no matter what their status, God is in control. Job's argument is that all kinds of people experience difficulties in life because God can do what He pleases. He is no respecter of persons and is not impressed by a person's rank, wealth, or social status.

For example, if it is God's will, king's counselors will lose their authority and wealth, and judges will become confused and mad. In fact, kings themselves will lose their girdles (an insignia of authority), and priests ("princes," v. 19, KJV) will be stripped and become captives. Wise people like counselors and elders will be silenced (v. 20), and princes (nobles) and the mighty (v. 21) will lose their respect and strength.

But God is sovereign over nations as well as individuals (vv. 23-25; Dan. 2:20-22; Acts 17:24-28). He can enlarge a nation or destroy it, or give it freedom or bondage. All He has to do is take wisdom away from the leaders, and the nation's destruction is sure. Proud people don't like to hear this message. Ever since the city of Enoch (Gen. 4:16-18) and the Tower of Babel (11:1-9), mankind has been trying to build and manage things without God; and the end has always been failure and judgment.

The integrity of Job (Job 13). In this part of his defense, Job first expressed his *disappointment* in his three friends (vv. 1-12), then his *declaration* of faith in the Lord (vv. 13-17), and finally his *desire* that God come to him and get the issue settled once and for all (vv. 18-28).

(1) Disappointment (vv. 1-12). Job's friends had not been an encouragement to him. They had taken a superior attitude as judges, assuming that they knew God better than Job did. They did not identify with him in his grief and pain. Job called them "forgers of lies," "physicians of no value," and "deceitful defenders of God."

The word "forgers" (v. 4) also means "whitewashers." They smeared the whitewash of their lies over the discussion so that they avoided the difficult problems while maintaining their traditional ideas (Ps. 119:69). They stayed on the surface of things and never went deep into God's truth or Job's feelings. Counseling that stays on the surface will accomplish very little. If we are going to help people, we must go much deeper; but this demands love, courage, and patience.

As physicians, their diagnosis was wrong so their remedy was useless (Jer. 6:14; 8:11). And as "defenders of God," they would be better off silent; for they did not know what they were talking about. They had such a rigid and narrow view of God, and such a prejudiced view of Job, that their whole "case" was a fabrication of lies. What would they do when God turned the tables and examined them? (See Rom. 14:1-13.) "Your maxims are proverbs of ashes; your defenses are defenses of clay" (Job 13:12, NIV). What the three friends thought were profound statements of truth were only warmed-over ashes from ancient fires, clay pots that would fall apart. A good counselor needs much more than a good memory. He or she also needs wisdom to know how to apply the truth to the needs of people today.

(2) Declaration (vv. 13-17). This is one of the greatest declarations of faith found anywhere in Scripture, but it must be understood in its context. Job is saying, "I will take my case directly to God and prove my integrity. I know I am taking my life in my hands in approaching God, because He is able to slay me. But if He doesn't slay me, it is proof that I am not the hypocrite you say I am." Later, Job will take an oath and challenge God to pass judgment (Job 27). To approach God personally was a great act of faith (Ex. 33:20; Judg. 13:22-23), but Job was so sure of his integrity that he would take his chances. After all, if he did nothing, he would die; and if he was rejected by God, he would die; but there was always the possibility that God would prove him right.

(3) Desire (vv. 18-28). These words are addressed to God. Job has "prepared his case" (v. 18, NIV) and is sure that he will win. Job has two desires: that God would remove His chastening hand and give Job relief, and that God would come to Job in such a way that He would not frighten him. Job is asking God to meet him in court so they can talk over God's "case" against Job and Job's "case" against God. In verse 22, Job gives God the option of speaking first!

Why does Job want to meet God in court? So that God can once and for all state His "case" against Job and let Job know the sins in his life that have caused him to suffer so much. "Why should God pay so much attention to me?" asks Job. "He treats me like an enemy, but I'm just a weak leaf in the wind, a piece of chaff that is worth nothing. I'm a piece of rotting wood and a moth-eaten garment, yet God treats me like a prisoner of war and watches me every minute." Job felt the time had come to settle the matter, even if it meant losing his own life in the process.

The hopelessness of Job (Job 14). Zophar had assured Job that there was hope for him if only he would acknowledge his sins and repent (Job 11:13-20). But Zophar was not in Job's situation! From Job's point of view, his future was bleak. In verses 1-12, Job used several images to illustrate the hopeless condition of man in this world. He is like a flower that is soon cut down, a shadow that slowly disappears, a hired man that puts in his time and then is replaced. God knows the limits of our days (7:1; 14:5; Ps. 139:16). A suicide may foolishly hasten the day of death, but nobody will go beyond the limits that God has set for his or her life.

Since man is only a flower, a shadow, and a servant, why should God pay any attention to him? Since life is so short, why should God fill man's few days with grief and pain? "So look away from him and let him alone," prays Job (Job 14:6, NIV). "Let me have some peace before my brief life ends!" (paraphrase)

Job's strongest image is that of the tree (vv. 7-12). Chop it down, and its stump remains, and there is always a possibility that the tree might sprout again. The tree has hope, but man has no hope. When he dies, he leaves no stump behind. Man is more like water that evaporates or soaks into the ground; it can never be recovered again (v. 11; 2 Sam. 14:14). Man may lie down at night and awaken in the morning; but when he lies down in death, there is no assurance that he will be awakened again.

Early believers like Job did not have the revelation of future life as we now have it in Christ (2 Tim. 1:10). Passages in the Old Testament hint at future resurrection (Pss. 16:9-11; 17:15; Isa. 26:19; Dan. 12:2), but Job did not have any of these books to read and ponder. "If a man dies, shall he live again?" (Job 14:14) Job asked this important question but did not answer it. Later on, Job will make a great statement about future resurrection (19:25-26); but at this point he is vacillating between despair and hope.

In 14:13, Job asked God to give Himself a reminder to bring Job back from Sheol, the realm of the dead. Job was probably not thinking of resurrection, but of a brief return to earth so God could vindicate him before his accusers. Of course, a believer today is sealed by the Holy Spirit unto the day of redemption (Eph. 1:13-14); and God will not forget one of His children at the resurrection (1 Cor. 15:50-58).

Job reminded the Lord that he was the work of God's hands (Job 14:15), an argument he had used before (10:3). It seemed to Job that, instead of caring for His creature, God was doing nothing but keeping a record of his sins. What hope could Job have as long as God was investigating him and building a case against him? Instead of cleansing Job's sins, God was covering them and would not even tell Job what they were!

"Thou destroyest the hope of man," Job complained (14:19), and he used two illustrations to make his point. Man seems like a sturdy mountain, but the water gradually erodes the rock, and it eventually crumbles. Or an earthquake might suddenly move the rocks from one place to another and change the mountain. Death may come gradually or suddenly, but it will come; and man will go to a world where he knows nothing about what his family is doing. Job longed for that release from sorrow and pain.

When people are experiencing intense grief and pain, it is easy for them to feel that the future is hopeless and that God has forsaken them. The eminent American psychiatrist Karl Menninger called hope "the major weapon against the suicide impulse." Hopeless people feel that life is not worth living since they have nothing to look forward to but suffering and failure. They conclude that it is better for them to die than to live and be a burden to themselves and to others.

The German philosopher Friedrich Nietzsche called hope "the worst of all evils, because it prolongs the torments of man." But an individual who believes in Jesus Christ shares in a "living hope" that grows more wonderful every day (1 Peter 1:3ff).

Dead hopes fade away because they have no roots, but our "living hope" gets better because it is rooted in the living Christ and His Living Word. The assurance of resurrection and life in glory with Christ is a strong motivation for us to keep going even when the going is tough (1 Cor. 15:58).

Charles L. Allen has written, "When you say a situation or a person is hopeless, you are slamming the door in the face of God." Job had not yet slammed the door, but he was getting close to doing it; and his friends were not helping him at all.

"Now may the God of hope fill you with all joy and peace in believing, that you may abound in hope by the power of the Holy Spirit" (Rom. 15:13, NASB).

CHAPTER FIVE
DISCUSSION TURNS INTO DISPUTE
Job 15–17

"How rarely we weigh our neighbor in the same balance in which we weigh ourselves."
—THOMAS A KEMPIS

During this second round of speeches, the fire becomes hotter as the three friends focus more on proving Job wrong than on giving Job help. After all, their own peace of mind was at stake; and they were not about to surrender. If Job was not a sinner being punished by God, then the three friends' understanding of God was all wrong. *But that meant they had no protection against personal suffering themselves!* If obedience is not a guarantee of health and wealth, then what happened to Job might happen to them. God forbid!

An anonymous wit once described a theologian as "a blind man in a dark room searching for a black cat that isn't there—and finding it!" But a true theologian walks in the light of God's revelation in His Word, in history, and in creation; and he humbly accepts the truth, no matter what the cost.

Job's three friends were not true theologians because they saw only one side of the picture, the side they wanted to see. The longshoreman-philosopher, Eric Hoffer, wrote, "We are least open to precise knowledge concerning the things we are most vehement about." And also the things we are most fearful about!

Eliphaz: Two Warnings (Job 15)
In his first speech (Job 4–5), Eliphaz had displayed some kindness toward Job; but you find neither patience nor kindness in this second address. Nor do you find any new ideas: Eliphaz merely repeats his former thesis that man is a sinner and God must punish sinners (5:17-19). He issued two warnings to Job.

Job lacks wisdom (Job 15:1-16). How did Eliphaz know this? For one thing, he had listened to *Job's words* (vv. 1-6) and found them to be nothing but wind. Job's ideas were only "empty notions" and "useless words" (vv. 2-3, NIV). Job's words came from a belly filled with the hot desert wind (Jonah 4:8) and not from a heart filled with true wisdom. Eliphaz was using one of the oldest tactics in debate—if you can't refute your opponent's arguments, attack his words and make them sound like a lot of "hot air."

Samuel Johnson was the "literary czar" of eighteenth-century England, a man who loved to sit by the hour with his friends and discuss any and all topics. But Johnson always had to win the argument, whether he was right or not. The poet and playwright Oliver Goldsmith said, "There is no arguing with Johnson; for if his pistol misses fire, he knocks you down with the butt end of it!" Eliphaz was like that.

Eliphaz not only heard Job's words, but he *saw where those words led* (Job 15:4). "But you even undermine piety and hinder devotion to God" (v. 4, NIV). If everybody believed as Job believed—that God does not always punish the wicked and reward the godly—then what motive would people have for obeying God? Religion would not be worth it! *But this is the devil's theology, the very thing that God was using Job to refute!* If people serve God only for what they get out of it, then they are not serving God at all, they are only serving themselves by making God their servant. Their "religion" is only a pious system for promoting selfishness and not for glorifying God.

When God called Israel and established His covenant with her, the people's motive for obedience was fear of punishment. If they obeyed the law, God would bless them; if they disobeyed, He would punish them. But this was during the infancy of the nation, when God dealt with them as with children. Children understand rewards and punishments far better than

they do ethics and morality. But when the new generation was about to enter Canaan, Moses gave them a higher motive for obedience: their love for God (Deut. 6:4-5; 7:7; 10:12-16; 11:1, 13, 22; 19:9). They were no longer children, and God didn't need to frighten them (or "bribe" them) into obeying Him. Love is the fulfillment of the law (Rom. 13:8-10) and the highest motive for obedience (John 14:15).

Job's words told Eliphaz that Job had a *wicked heart* (Job 15:5-6). "Your sins are telling your mouth what to say!" (v. 5, TLB; see Matt. 12:34-37) Job was affirming his innocence, but Eliphaz interpreted his words as proving Job's guilt! What hope was there for Job when his friends would not even believe what he was saying?

Job lacked wisdom because *he lacked experience* (Job 15:7-10). At this point, Eliphaz turned on the sarcasm, another proof that he has run out of something intelligent to say. This is another debater's trick: when you can't refute the speech, ridicule the speaker. Job never claimed that he was the first man God created, that he was God's confidant, or that God had given him a monopoly on wisdom. Job knew that his friends were older than he was, but age is no guarantee of wisdom (32:9; Ps. 119:97-104).

According to Eliphaz, Job's attitude was wrong because he refused God's help (Job 15:11-16). Eliphaz saw himself and his friends as God's messengers, sent to bring Job the consolation he needed. Their words were "spoken gently" (v. 11, NIV), but Job's words were spoken in anger. The three friends were serving God, but Job was resisting God.

Then Eliphaz repeated the message he had given in his first speech (vv. 14-16; 4:17-19). Job had refused to accept it the first time, but perhaps he would accept it now that he had suffered more. If heaven is not pure before God, nor the angels that inhabit heaven, how can a mere man claim to be innocent? Man is born with a sinful nature and has a thirst for sin, and Job was no exception. All of this prepared the way for Eliphaz's second warning.

God judges the wicked (Job 15:17-35). In his first speech, Eliphaz had described the blessings of the godly man (5:17-26); but now he describes the sufferings of the ungodly man. Eliphaz was careful to remind Job that these were not his ideas alone, but that the ancients all agreed with him. If Job rejected what Eliphaz said, he was turning his back on the wisdom of their fathers. Eliphaz was a man who found great strength in tradition, forgetting that "tradition is a guide and not a jailer" (W. Somerset Maugham).

When you read this description of a wicked man, you realize that Eliphaz is talking about Job. Job was in pain, darkness, trouble, anguish, and fear. He was defying God and challenging God to meet him and prove him guilty. The fire had destroyed Job's sheep (1:16; 15:30, 34); invaders had stolen his camels (1:17; 15:21); he had lost all his wealth (v. 29); and his eldest son's house had been destroyed by wind and all Job's children with it (1:19; 15:28). Eliphaz was not at all subtle in his approach; everybody knew he was talking about Job.

But in his closing words (vv. 34-35), Eliphaz gave the hardest blow of all: He called Job a hypocrite and a godless man, and he blamed him for the tragedies that had befallen him and his family. Job had secretly "conceived" sin, and now sin had given birth to suffering and death (James 1:14-15; Isa. 59:4; Ps. 7:14). "Their womb fashions deceit" is the NIV rendering of Job 15:35, and the word translated "womb" is the same as "belly" in verse 1. According to Eliphaz, if you x-rayed Job,

all you would find would be hot air and sin! "Hypocrite" is a key word in the vocabulary of Job's three friends. Bildad suggested that Job was a hypocrite (8:13), and both Zophar and Elihu will take up the theme (20:5; 34:30; 36:13). Of course, Job denied the accusation (13:16; 17:8; 27:8) and argued that neither God nor his friends could prove it true.

The problem with Eliphaz's statement about the judgment of the wicked is that *it is not always true in this life.* Many wicked people go through life apparently happy and successful, while many godly people experience suffering and seeming failure. It is true that *ultimately* the wicked suffer and the godly are blessed; but, meanwhile, it often looks like the situation is reversed (Ps. 73; Jer. 12:1-4). Furthermore, God gives sunshine to the evil and the good and sends rain on the just and the unjust (Matt. 5:45). He is long-suffering toward sinners (2 Peter 3:9) and waits for His goodness to lead them to repentance (Rom. 2:4; Luke 15:17-19).

The greatest judgment God could send to the wicked in this life would be to *let them have their own way.* "They have their reward" (Matt. 6:2, 5, 16). The only heaven the godless will know is the enjoyment they have on earth in this life, and God is willing for them to have it. The only suffering the godly will experience is in this life, for in heaven there will be no pain or tears. Furthermore, the suffering that God's people experience now is working *for* them and will one day lead to glory (1 Peter 1:6-8; 5:10; 2 Cor. 4:16-18; Rom. 8:18). Eliphaz and his friends had the situation all confused.

Job: Three Requests (Job 16–17)

Job's response is to utter three heartfelt requests: first, a plea to his friends for sympathy (Job 16:1-14); then, a plea to God for justice (vv. 15-22); and finally, a plea to God to end his life and relieve him of suffering (17:1-16).

A plea for sympathy (Job 16:1-14). Job's friends still had not identified with his situation; they did not feel his agony or understand his perplexity. Job had already called them deceitful brooks (see 6:15) and "worthless physicians" (13:4, NIV), but now he calls them "miserable comforters" (16:2). All of their attempts to comfort him only made him more miserable! As the saying goes, "With friends like you, who needs enemies?"

Job assured them that, if they were in his shoes, he would treat them with more understanding than they were showing him. Instead of making long speeches, he would give them words of encouragement. He would listen with his heart and try to help them bear their burdens. Sometimes we have to experience misunderstanding from unsympathetic friends in order to learn how to minister to others. This was a new experience for Job, and he was trying to make the most of it. However, whether Job spoke or kept quiet, he was still a suffering man (v. 6).

In his appeal for loving sympathy, Job told his friends what he was receiving from the hand of God (vv. 7-14). Job is worn out; his family is gone; he is gaunt and weak. Both men and God attack him. Job feels like God has painted a target on his back and handed everybody bows and arrows! There is no relief—God keeps assaulting him like a relentless warrior. "I didn't attack God—He attacked me!" God was his enemy (16:9; 13:24), and nothing Job could do would bring about a truce. If Job looked up, God was against him. If he looked around, his friends were against him. Where could he turn?

A plea for justice (Job 16:15-22). How had Job responded to God's attacks? He put on sackcloth, wept in humiliation and contrition, and buried his face in the dust. In spite of the accusations of Eliphaz (15:4-6), Job knew he was right before God and that God would hear his prayers (16:17).

Job was caught on the horns of a dilemma. His suffering was so great that he longed to die, but he didn't want to die before he could vindicate himself or see God vindicate him. This explains his cry in verse 18: "O earth, do not cover my blood, and let my cry have no resting place!" (NKJV) The ancients believed that the blood of innocent victims cried out to God for justice (Gen. 4:8-15) and that the spirits of the dead were restless until the corpses were properly buried (Isa. 26:21). Even if Job died, he would be restless until he had been proved righteous by the Lord.

Job's repeated cry has been for a fair trial before the Lord (Job 9:1-4, 14-16, 19-20, 28-35; 10:2; 13:6-8, 19). He has lamented the fact that he had no advocate to represent him before God's throne (9:33). None of his friends would defend him, so his only hope was that God in heaven would defend him and bear witness to his integrity (16:19). But Job yearned for someone to plead with God on his behalf (v. 21).

The Christian believer has this heavenly Advocate in Jesus Christ (1 John 2:1-2). As our interceding High Priest, Christ gives us the conquering grace we need when we are tempted and tested (Heb. 2:17-18; 4:14-16). If we fail, then He is our Advocate to forgive us and restore us when we confess our sins to Him (1 John 1:5-2:2).

Of course, Job wanted a "lawyer" to plead his case before God and convince Him that he was innocent. Once Job had won his case, then God would vindicate him before his critical friends and restore Job's honor. God's people don't need that kind of intercession because the Father and the Son are in perfect agreement in their love for us and their plan for our lives. The Lord Jesus ever lives to make intercession for His people (Rom. 8:31-39; Heb. 7:25) and to perfect them in the will of God (13:20-21). We come to a throne of grace, not a throne of judgment; and we have confidence that our loving Father will do that which is best for us.

A plea for death (Job 17:1-16). One reason Job wanted his heavenly Advocate to act quickly was because he sensed that death was very near, "the journey of no return" (Job 16:22, NIV). When people suffer so much that their "spirit is broken" (17:1, NIV, NASB), then they lose their "fight" and want life to end.

Job's friends were against him and would not go to court and "post bond" for him (vv. 3-5). People treated Job as if he were the scum of the earth (v. 6). His body was only the shadow of what it had been (v. 7), and all of his plans had been shattered (v. 11). His friends would not change their minds and come to his defense (v. 10). In fact, they would not face his situation honestly, but they kept telling him that the light would soon dawn for him (v. 12). Is it any wonder that Job saw in death the only way of escape?

However, at no time did Job ever consider taking his own life or asking someone else to do it for him. Life is a sacred gift from God, and only God can give it and take it away. On the one hand, Job wanted to live long enough to see himself vindicated; but on the other hand, he didn't know how much more he could endure. Once he was in Sheol, the realm of the dead, he could not be vindicated on earth unless God brought him back.

Job pictured Sheol as his home, where he would lie down in the darkness and be at rest (v. 13). Since he had no family, he would adopt the pit (or "corruption") as his father and the devouring worm as his mother or sister. They would give him more comfort than his friends!

But would there be any hope in the grave? Could Job take his hope with him to Sheol? Paul answers the question: "If in this life only we have hope in Christ, we are of all men the most pitiable. But now Christ is risen from the dead, and has become the firstfruits of those who have fallen asleep" (1 Cor. 15:19-20, NKJV). *Our hope does not die, nor is it buried and left to decay; for our hope is a "living hope" because Christ has won the victory over death and the grave!* Christians sorrow, but they must not sorrow "as others who have no hope" (1 Thess. 4:13).

God did not answer Job's plea for death because He had something far better planned for him. God looked beyond Job's depression and bitterness and saw that he still had faith. When I was a young pastor, I heard an experienced saint say, "I have lived long enough to be thankful for unanswered prayer." At the time, I was shocked by the statement; but now that I have lived a few more years myself, I know what she was talking about. In the darkness of despair and the prison of pain, we often say things that we later regret; *but God understands all about it and lovingly turns a deaf ear to our words but a tender eye to our wounds.*

If only the next speaker would have expressed compassion to this hurting man! But Bildad is all primed to frighten Job out of his wits with the most vivid pictures of death found anywhere in Scripture.

INTERLUDE

The best way to help discouraged and hurting people is to listen with your heart and not just with your ears. It's not what they say but *why they say it* that is important. Let them know that you understand their pain by reflecting back to them *in different words* just what they say to you. Don't argue or try to convince them with logical reasoning. There will be time for that later; meanwhile, patiently accept their feelings—even their bitter words against God—and build bridges, not walls.

In his book about his wife's death, *A Grief Observed*, C.S. Lewis wrote from his own painful experience: "Talk to me about the truth of religion, and I'll listen gladly. Talk to me about the duty of religion, and I'll listen submissively. But don't come talking to me about the consolation of religion, or I shall suspect you don't understand" (p. 23).

There is true consolation in our faith, but it is not dispensed in convenient doses like cough medicine. *It can be shared only by those who know what it's like to be so far down in the pit that they feel as though God has abandoned them.* If you want to be a true comforter, there is a price to pay; and not everybody is willing to pay it. Paul wrote about this in 2 Corinthians 1:3-11.

John Henry Jowett said, "God does not comfort us to make us comfortable, but to make us comforters." God's comfort is never *given*; it is always *loaned*. God expects us to share it with others.

CHAPTER SIX
WILL THE REAL ENEMY PLEASE STAND UP?
Job 18–19

"Death is the great adventure, beside which moon landings and space trips pale into insignificance."
—JOSEPH BAYLY

Bildad opened his second speech with the same words he used in his first speech: "How long?" (Job 18:2; 8:2) and Job said the same thing when he replied (19:2). The friends were growing impatient with each other because their conversation seemed to be getting nowhere. George Bernard Shaw compared the average conversation to "a phonograph with half-a-dozen records—you soon get tired of them all."

Bildad blamed Job for the stalemate and admonished him, "Be sensible, and then we can talk" (18:2, NIV). It never dawned on Bildad that he and his two friends were playing the same tunes over and over again: (1) God is just; (2) God punishes the wicked and blesses the righteous; (3) since Job is suffering, he must be wicked; (4) if he turns from his sins, God will again bless him. They were going around in circles.

Bildad said that Job was not being sensible, nor was he being respectful. He was treating his friends like dumb cattle instead of like the wise men they really were (v. 3). Job was also being irritable and displaying anger instead of humility (v. 4). "Is God supposed to rearrange the whole world just for you?" Bildad asks. "Should He ravage the land with war or even send an earthquake just because of you?" Eliphaz wasn't the only one who knew how to use sarcasm!

However, Bildad planned to use a stronger weapon than sarcasm. His weapon was *fear*. If the three friends could not reason with Job, or shame Job into repenting, perhaps they could frighten Job by describing what happens when wicked people die.

Before we study Bildad's terrifying speech, we should note that fear is a normal human emotion and there is nothing wrong with it. We use the fear of sickness, injury, or death to teach children to wash their hands, stay away from power lines, and look carefully before crossing the street. Fear of financial loss motivates people to buy insurance, and fear of death encourages them to have an annual physical checkup.

Fear of death (and the judgment that follows) is a legitimate motive for trusting Jesus Christ and being saved. "And do not fear those who kill the body but cannot kill the soul," said Jesus. "But rather fear Him who is able to destroy both soul and body in hell" (Matt. 10:28, NKJV). Jesus preached a gracious message of love, but He also preached a stern message of judgment. Paul wrote, "Knowing, therefore, the terror of the Lord, we persuade men" (2 Cor. 5:11). When Jonathan Edwards preached his sermon "Sinners in the Hands of an Angry God," he did not violate any psychological or biblical principles. The emotions of nonbelievers must be stirred before their minds can be instructed and their wills challenged.

However, Bildad made two mistakes when he gave this speech about the horrors of death. To begin with, he preached it to the wrong man; for Job was already a believer (Job 1:1, 8). Second, he preached it with the wrong motive, for there was no love in his heart. Dr. R.W. Dale, the British preacher, once asked evangelist D.L. Moody if he ever used "the element of terror" in his preaching. Moody replied that he usually preached one sermon on heaven and one on hell in each of his campaigns, but that a "man's heart ought to be very tender" when preaching about the doom of the lost. Bildad did not have a tender heart.

The Terrors of Death
(Job 18:5-21)

In this address, Bildad painted four vivid pictures of the death of the wicked.

A light put out (Job 18:5-6). Light is associated with life just as darkness is associated with death. Since God is the author of life, He alone can "light our lamp"; for "He gives to all life, breath, and all things," and "in Him we live and move and have our being" (Acts 17:25, 28, NKJV). The picture here is that of a lamp hanging in a tent and a fire smoldering in a fire pot. Suddenly, the lamp goes out, and the last spark of the fire vanishes, and the tent is in total darkness (Prov. 13:9; 24:20).

Like the flame of the lamp or the spark in the coals, life is a precious but delicate thing. It doesn't take a very strong wind to blow it out. "There is but a step between me and death" (1 Sam. 20:3).

The American newspaper magnate William Randolph Hearst would never permit anybody to mention death in his presence. Yet on August 14, 1951, the flame of his life went out, and he died. "The spirit of man is the candle of the LORD" (Prov. 20:27), and God can blow out that lamp whenever He pleases.

A traveler trapped (Job 18:7-10). Frightened, the man leaves his tent and starts down the road, looking for a place of safety. But the road turns out to be the most dangerous place of all, for it is punctuated by traps. Bildad used six different words to describe the dangers people face when they try to run away from death:

a net—spread across the path to catch him

a snare—branches covering a deep pit

a trap—a "gin" (snare) with a noose that springs when touched; he is caught by the heel *a robber*—another pitfall

a snare—a noose hidden on the ground

a trap—any device that catches prey

These devices were used to catch birds and animals, not people; but the wicked person is like a beast because he has left God out of his life.

No matter what schemes the traveler invents, he cannot escape the traps; and the more he tries, the weaker he becomes (Job 18:7). Darkness and danger surround him, and there is no hope.

A criminal pursued (Job 18:11-15). Death is "the king of terrors" (v. 14), determined to arrest the culprit no matter where he is. If the escaped criminal runs on the path and escapes the traps, then death will send some of his helpers to chase him. Terror frightens him, calamity eats away at his strength, and disaster waits for him to fall (vv. 11-12, NIV).

The frightened criminal gets weaker and weaker but still tries to keep going. If he goes back to his tent to hide, the pursuers find him, arrest him, drag him out, and take him to the king of terrors. They take everything out of his tent, burn the tent, and then scatter sulfur over the ashes. The end of that man is fire and brimstone!

A tree rooted up (Job 18:16-21). Sometimes death is not as dramatic and sudden as the arresting of a criminal. Death may be gradual, like the dying of a tree. The roots dry up, the branches start to wither, and the dead branches are cut off one by one. Soon the tree is completely dead, and men chop it down. The death of a tree illustrates the extinction of a family, a "family tree." Not only is the wicked man himself cut down, but all the branches are cut down too; and he leaves no descendants to carry on his name.

(Remember, all of Job's children had been killed by the great wind.) In the East, the extinction of a family was viewed as a great tragedy.

Job had used a tree as an illustration of the hope of resurrection (14:7-11), but Bildad did not agree with him. According to Bildad, once the tree is down, that is the end; the wicked man has no future hope.

Though Bildad was talking to the wrong man and with the wrong motive, what he said about death should be taken seriously. Death is an enemy to be feared by all who are not prepared to die (1 Cor. 15:26), and the only way to be prepared is to trust Jesus Christ (John 5:24).

For the Christian believer, death means going home to the Father in heaven (John 14:1-6), falling asleep on earth and waking up in heaven (Acts 7:60; Phil. 1:21-23), entering into rest (Rev. 14:13), and moving into greater light (Prov. 4:18). None of the pictures Bildad used should be applied to those who have trusted the Lord for salvation.

The Trials of Life
(Job 19:1-29)

When Bildad finished describing the terrors of death, Job replied by describing the trials of life, *his own life.* "I don't have to *die* to experience trials," he said to his friends. "I'm experiencing them right now, and you don't seem to care!"

Insults (Job 19:1-4). Our words either hurt others or heal them; we either add to their burdens or help them bear their burdens with courage. Job's friends crushed him with their words; they made him feel worthless and helpless in the face of all his suffering. How sensitive we should be to the needs and struggles of others! Even if people do need rebuke, we should do it in love; and our words should hearten them and not weaken them.

"Even if I have sinned," Job said in 19:4, "it's *my* sin and not yours. God and I can work things out, so leave me alone." The word Job used ("erred") means "an unintentional sin." Job still defended his integrity and claimed that he had committed no sins worthy of all the suffering he had endured.

Illustrations (Job 19:5-12). Bildad had given four frightening pictures of the terrors of death, so Job countered with seven vivid pictures of the trials of his life, what he was experiencing right then and there!

He felt like *an animal trapped* (v. 6). Job saw himself caught in God's net, not because of his sins but because God had trapped him. Bildad described six different kinds of traps that would catch a fleeing criminal (18:7-10), but Job did not put himself into that picture. He was not running away from God, nor was he guilty of sin. It was God who had suddenly caught him for reasons Job did not understand.

He also felt like *a criminal in court* (19:7). God had wronged him by arresting him and bringing him into judgment. What had he done? Why were the charges not read to him? Why was he not permitted a defense? "Though I call for help, there is no justice" (v. 7, NIV). Throughout the book, Job pleads for justice and cries out for an advocate to defend him before God. What Job did not realize was that *he was the advocate defending God!* It was Job's faith and endurance that proved Satan wrong and brought glory to the Lord.

Job saw himself as *a traveler fenced in* (v. 8). Satan had complained that God had "walled in" Job and his family so that they were protected from trouble (1:9-12). Now Job is complaining because God has blocked his path, and he cannot move. Job could not see what lay ahead because God had shrouded the way with darkness.

At times God permits His children to experience darkness on a dead-end street where they don't know which way to turn. When this happens, *wait for the Lord to give you light in His own time.* Don't try to manufacture your own light or to borrow light from others. Follow the wise counsel of Isaiah, "Who among you fears the Lord? Who obeys the voice of His Servant? Who walks in darkness and has no light? Let him trust in the name of the Lord and rely upon his God" (Isa. 50:10, NKJV).

Dr. Bob Jones, Sr. used to say, "Never doubt in the darkness what God has taught you in the light." In fact, what God teaches us in the light will become even more meaningful in the darkness.

"Oh, the unspeakable benediction of the `treasures of darkness'!" wrote Oswald Chambers. "It is not the days of sunshine and splendor and liberty and light that leave their lasting and indelible effect upon the soul, but those nights of the Spirit in which, shadowed by God's hand, hidden in the dark cleft of some rock in a weary land, He lets the splendors of the outskirts of Himself pass before our gaze."

Job's suffering left him feeling like *a king dethroned* (Job 19:9). Before his calamities came, Job had been the leading man in Uz and the greatest man in the East (1:3; 29:1-25); but now all that honor and authority were gone. God had taken from him his royal robes and crown, and now he was the lowest instead of the highest. What humiliation!

His fifth picture is that of *a structure destroyed* (19:10). It could be a wall or a building that God's "troops" swooped down on and left in ruins. Job may have been looking back at his business affairs or his household; or perhaps he was contemplating his emaciated body. In any event, what was once strong and useful was now useless and destroyed. Bildad had spoken about a tent being destroyed (18:15), and Job knew what this meant.

In the sixth picture, Job borrowed the image of *a tree uprooted* (19:10; see 18:16). Job had used the tree as a picture of hope (14:7), but now he sees it as a symbol of *lost* hope. But in Job 14, Job was speaking about a tree that was chopped down, while here the tree is *uprooted.* Without a root system, the tree cannot live.

Job's final picture is that of *a besieged city* (19:11-12). God has declared war on Job (13:24) and is treating him like an enemy. His troops have attacked him and settled down for a long, hard siege. Imagine a large army building a ramp just to attack a tent! Once again, Job cannot understand why God has sent so much suffering. Why use an atomic bomb just to destroy a tent?

Isolation (Job 19:13-22). Job went on to explain how his suffering affected his relationship with people. We must recognize that extreme and prolonged pain often isolates sufferers from people and circumstances around them. When people really hurt, they may tend to withdraw and give the impression that others don't really understand what they are going through. Job felt alienated from those left in his family, from his friends, and even from his servants.

But there was more to this alienation than Job's pain. He was now bankrupt and ill, living at the city dump; and nobody wanted to be identified with him. Furthermore, people were convinced that Job was a guilty sinner suffering the judgment of God; so why be his friend? His appearance was repulsive, and people avoided looking at him. He was being treated like a leper, an outcast who was not wanted by family or friends.

One evidence of our Lord's compassion is the way He identified with outcasts. He ate with "publicans and sinners" (Matt. 9:9-13), touched the lepers (Matt. 8:1-4), accepted gifts from prostitutes (Luke 7:36-50), and even died between two criminals (23:32-33). Jesus knew what it was like to be "despised and rejected of men, a man of sorrows, and acquainted with grief" (Isa. 53:3). How important it is that we, His disciples, have this same kind of compassion. It's easy to identify with people we know and like when they are going through trials, but we tend to overlook the helpless, the poor, and the neglected in their sufferings.

Job's statement in Job 19:20 has become a familiar but misunderstood proverb: "I am escaped with the skin of my teeth." This is usually quoted, "I escaped *by* the skin of my teeth," that is, "I just barely escaped!" (If there were skin on our teeth, how thick would it be?) But the Hebrew text says "with" and not "by," and interpreters don't agree on the meaning.

Some suggest that Job meant, "I'm so far gone that only my gums are left!" But the gums are not usually referred to as "the skin of the teeth." Others say that he meant, "If there were skin on my teeth, that's how close I am to death!" Or, "My body is so emaciated that all I have left is the skin of my teeth!" (He was exaggerating, of course.) Whatever Job had in mind, the image clearly shows one thing: it was a miracle that Job was alive.

Job closed this part of his defense by appealing to his friends for pity (vv. 21-22; 6:14). God was against him, his family and friends had deserted him, and all he had left were his three intimate friends who were now pursuing him like wild beasts after their prey. Couldn't they stop and try to help him? Why must they have such hard hearts?

Insight (Job 19:23-29). Why did Job want his words to be recorded permanently? He thought he was going to die before God would vindicate him, and he wanted people to remember how he suffered and what he said. Bildad warned him, "The remembrance of him [a wicked man] shall perish from the earth" (18:17), and Job wanted his record to remain.

At this point, Job uttered another of his statements of faith that in this book punctuate his many expressions of grief and pain. It is significant that Job would go from the depths of despair to the heights of faith, and then back into the depths again. *This is often the normal experience of people experiencing great suffering.* The skies will be dark and stormy, a ray of light will suddenly shine through, and then the storm will come again.

In spite of what some preachers say, very few people can maintain a constant high level of faith and courage in times of severe pain and trial. John Henry Jowett, at one time known as "the greatest preacher in the English-speaking world," wrote to a friend: "I wish you wouldn't think I am such a saint. You seem to imagine that I have no ups and downs, but just a level and lofty stretch of spiritual attainment with unbroken joy and equanimity. By no means! I am often perfectly wretched, and everything appears most murky" (*John Henry Jowett*, by Arthur Porrit, p. 290).

In 19:25-27, Job expressed confidence that, even if he died, he would still have a Redeemer who one day would exercise judgment on the earth. Furthermore, Job affirmed that he himself expected to live again and see his Redeemer! "And after my skin has been destroyed, yet in my flesh I will see God" (v. 26, NIV). It was an affirmation of faith in the resurrection of the human body.

The Hebrew word translated "Redeemer" in verse 25 refers to the kins-man redeemer, the near relative who could avenge his brother's blood (Deut. 19:6-12), reclaim and restore his brother's property (Lev. 25:23-24, 39-55), and set his brother free from slavery (25:25). The kinsman redeemer could also go to court on behalf of a wronged relative (Prov. 23:10-11). In the book of Ruth, Boaz is the kinsman redeemer who was willing and able to rescue Ruth and give her a new life in a new land.

Previously, Job had talked about his need for an umpire (Job 9:33-34) and an Advocate in heaven (16:19). Now he takes it a step further: his Redeemer will one day vindicate him, and Job will be there to witness it! When you consider how little God had revealed in Job's day about the future life, these words become a remarkable testimony of faith. And when you add to this the discouragement expressed by Job's friends and his own intense suffering, Job's witness becomes even more wonderful.

Of course, this kinsman redeemer is Jesus Christ. He took upon Himself a human nature so that He might reveal God to us, experience all that we experience, die for our sins, and then return to heaven to represent us before the Father. He is *willing* to save and *able* to save. One day He shall stand upon the earth and exercise judgment; and He will vindicate His own people.

Job closed his speech with a word of warning to his three critical friends (19:28-29): They too will stand at God's judgment throne, so they had better be ready. They accused Job of being a sinner, but were *they* not also sinners? They said that God was judging Job for his sins, but will He not judge them as well? One day they will have to answer to God for the way they have spoken to and about Job, so they had better beware. Job's words remind us of Paul's counsel in Romans 14:10-13 and our Lord's warning in Matthew 7:1-5.

Abraham Lincoln once said, "He has a right to criticize who has a heart to help."

Do you qualify?

CHAPTER SEVEN
IT ALL DEPENDS ON YOUR POINT OF VIEW
Job 20–21

"The truest help we can render an afflicted man is not to take his burden from him, but to call out his best strength that he may be able to bear it."

—Phillips Brooks

Zophar is next in line to speak, but he has nothing new to say. It's the same old story: God punishes the wicked, so Job had better get right with God. His key text is Job 20:5, "The triumphing of the wicked is short, and the joy of the hypocrite but for a moment." This theme has already been discussed by Bildad (8:11-19; 18) and Eliphaz (15:20-35), but Zophar is so disturbed by Job's last speech that he feels he must speak. "I hear a rebuke that dishonors me, and my understanding inspires me to reply" (20:3, NIV). Zophar felt insulted by Job and decided to defend himself.

The Awful Fate of the Wicked (Job 20:4-29)
Zophar makes three affirmations to prove that the fate of the wicked is indeed terri-

ble: their life is brief (Job 20:4-11), their pleasure is temporary (vv. 12-19), and their death is painful (vv. 20-29).

Their life is brief (Job 20:4-11). Zophar declares that from the beginning of human history the triumphing ("mirth") of the wicked has been short. We wonder where he got his information, for the Lord waited 120 years before sending the Flood (Gen. 6:3), and God gave the wicked Canaanites at least four centuries before He judged them (15:13-16).

Most of the people in Scripture who pondered the problem of evil in the world started from a different premise—the wicked enjoy long life and freedom from trouble, while the righteous suffer much and die young (Pss. 37; 73; Jer. 12:1-4). Zophar was deliberately blocking out a lot of data to prove his point.

According to Zophar, the higher the wicked man climbs in his success, the farther down he will fall when his judgment comes. When he falls, he will go down the drain like his own dung; and people will ask, "Where is he?" (Job 20:6-7) He will vanish like a forgotten dream or like a night vision that cannot be called back (v. 8).

Not only will the wicked man's person and name vanish, but so will his wealth. After his death, the truth about his crimes will become known; and his children will have to use their inheritance to pay back the people their father has robbed. Their father was still in "youthful vigor" when he died (v. 11, NIV), but now he lies lifeless in the grave. According to Zophar, the wicked die young, when they least expect it.

When you survey both sacred and secular history, you discover that there are no ironclad rules that govern when either the wicked or the righteous will die. Generally speaking, people who ignore God's laws are more vulnerable to problems that could lead to an early death. Sexual promiscuity, the use of narcotics (including alcohol and tobacco), and a reckless lifestyle can all help shorten a person's life; *but there is no guarantee that this will happen.* It's amazing how some godless people live to an old age. Perhaps this is the grace of God in giving them time to repent.

Zophar was not talking about the natural consequences of a wicked life, but the judgment of God on sinners. Zophar and his two friends were certain that Job was a hypocrite, that his pious life was only a veneer to cover his secret sins. In his second speech, Eliphaz will even name some of the sins that Job committed! (22:5-9) But God does not always judge hypocrites and other sinners immediately, and the death of a young person is no evidence that he or she was a hypocrite.

The godly Scottish Presbyterian minister Robert Murray McCheyne died when he was only twenty-nine years old, and missionary William Whiting Borden ("Borden of Yale") was only twenty-five years old when he died in Egypt. David Brainerd, saintly missionary to the Native Americans, was twenty-nine when he died. According to Zophar, these men must have been guilty of secret sin, and God took them at an early age.

Their pleasure is temporary (Job 20:12-19). Zophar uses *eating* as his basic image here. The wicked man enjoys sin the way people enjoy food, keeping it in his mouth where he can "taste it" before swallowing it. In fact, he enjoys sin so much, he can't make himself swallow it! But eventually that delicious food in his mouth becomes poison in his system, and he becomes ill and vomits everything up. While enjoying his sin, he hasn't noticed that he's been bitten by a poisonous

viper and is destined for death. In other words, sin carries with it both enjoyment and punishment; and if you want the one, you must also accept the other. The pleasures of sin are only for a season (Heb. 11:25).

But God's judgment involves much more: the wicked man not only gets sick from his sin, but he does not enjoy the everyday blessings of life (Job 20:17). "He will not see the streams, the rivers flowing with honey and cream" (NKJV). The land of Canaan was a land "flowing with milk and honey" (Ex. 3:8; Lev. 20:24). Milk and honey were staples, not luxuries; and a land "flowing with milk and honey" would be productive and able to support the people. But the wicked man has lost his taste for basic foods, and nothing satisfies him anymore. His taste for sin has ruined his enjoyment of the fundamental blessings of life.

Using the image of *eating,* Zophar has made two points: what the wicked man swallows will make him sick and will take away his desire for the good things of life. He makes a third point in Job 20:18-19: the wicked man will not be able to enjoy (swallow down) some of the things he labored for. Because he acquired his wealth through sinning, that wealth will not satisfy him.

This certainly has been reflected in the lives of many people who have rejected Christ and devoted themselves to the pleasures of sin. The more they indulge, the more they crave; and the more they satisfy that craving, the less they enjoy. The less they enjoy, the more they have to sin in order to recapture the old thrills; and the more they sin, the more they destroy their ability to enjoy anything. To change the image, they have "blown all their fuses"; and the machinery of life no longer functions as it once did.

Their death is painful (Job 20:20-29).
Not even his riches will be able to prevent
death from coming to the wicked man
(Job 20:20; see Ps. 49). While he is enjoying his prosperity, the wicked man will
experience distress, misery, and God's
burning anger. God will "rain down His
blows upon him" (Job 20:23, NIV). The evil
man will try to run away, but God will
come at him with a sword and shoot at
him with a bronze-tipped arrow that will
pierce him.

At this point in his speech, Zophar
starts to sound like Bildad (Job 18). He
describes the wicked man trying to
escape God's judgment. The arrows come
at him as he runs through the darkness,
and the fire falls around him. Then a flood
catches up with him and destroys everything. But that's not the end: The wicked
man is finally dragged into court where
heaven and earth testify against him and
find him guilty (20:27).

The Actual End of the Wicked Man (Job 21:1-34)

After appealing once more for their
understanding and sympathy (Job 21:1-
6), Job replied to Zophar's statements and
refuted each of them. Job stated that, from
his point of view, it appears that the
wicked have long lives (vv. 7-16), they are
not often sent calamity (vv. 17-21), and the
death of the wicked is no different from
the death of other men (vv. 22-34). Point
by point, Job took Zophar's speech and
shredded it into bits.

But first, listen to Job's appeal to his
friends that they try to understand how
he feels. "If you really want to console me,
just keep quiet and listen" (v. 2, paraphrase). The Greek philosopher Zeno
said, "The reason why we have two ears
and only one mouth is that we may listen
the more and talk the less." The friends

thought their words would encourage
Job, but he said that their silence would
encourage him even more (13:3).

Job pointed out that his complaint was
not against men but against God. Men
had not caused his afflictions, and men
could not take them away. If he was impatient, it was because God had not
answered him (v. 3). The longer God
waited, the worse Job's situation became.
"Look at me and be astonished; clap your
hand over your mouth" (21:5, NIV).

As Job contemplated what he was
about to say, it stirred him to the depths
(v. 6). This was no speech from "off the
top of his head," for it had to do with
the basic facts of life and death. If Job's
friends were in his situation, they
would see things differently and *say*
things differently.

*The life of the wicked may be long (Job
21:7-16).* In contrast to Zophar's text
(20:5), Job said, "Why do the wicked still
live, continue on, also become very powerful?" (21:7, NASB) They have security on
every side: their children and homes are
safe (vv. 8-9, 11-12), their business pros-
pers (v. 10), and they have long lives in
which to enjoy their prosperity (v. 13).
They also have many descendants who
share the family wealth and enjoy it. The
death of the wicked is sudden; they don't
linger in agony and long for deliverance.
Of course, Job's situation was just the
opposite: His family had been destroyed,
his wealth was gone, and he was suffering greatly as he waited for death to
come.

But the saddest thing about the wicked
is the way they leave God out of their
lives *and still prosper* (vv. 14-15). They
want nothing to do with the Lord; in fact,
they say to Him, "Get away from us!
Leave us alone!" They refuse to pray to
the Lord, obey Him, or give Him credit

for their success. This is the philosophy of most unsaved people today; you might call it "practical atheism" (see Ps. 10). God is not in their thoughts, let alone in their plans (James 4:13-17). They are self-sufficient as they do what they want to do, and they do it "their way." Jesus described such a person in Luke 12:13-21.

Job hastened to say that this was not *his* philosophy of life. "But I refuse even to deal with people like that" (Job 21:16, TLB). The wicked take credit for their wealth, but Job acknowledged that everything comes from God (1:21). How, then, can Job's three friends classify him with the wicked?

Before considering Job's second point, we must face the disturbing fact that too many professed Christians actually admire and envy the lifestyle of the rich and famous. In one of his books, Dr. Kenneth Chafin tells about a pastor and deacon who were visiting prospects and stopped at a beautiful suburban home. The lawn looked like it was manicured, and two expensive cars sat in the driveway. Furthermore, the pastor and deacon could see the man of the house comfortably seated in his spacious living room, watching television. Everything about the place reeked of affluence. The deacon turned to his pastor and asked, "What kind of good news do we have for this fellow?"

In over forty years of ministry, I have performed many weddings and watched many young Christian couples get started in their homes. What a joy it has been to see homes where couples set the right priorities and resist the temptation to "follow the crowd" and live for material possessions. Unfortunately, some have lost their spiritual vision and succeeded in this world—without acknowledging the Lord. Alas, they have their reward.

The wicked do not often experience calamity? (Job 21:17-21). "Yea, the light of the wicked shall be put out," Bildad affirmed (18:5); but Job asked, "How often does that happen?" How often do you actually see God's anger displayed against the godless people of the world? "How often are they like straw before the wind, like chaff swept away by a gale?" (21:18, NIV) The wicked seem to be secure in this world, while the righteous suffer (but see Ps. 73).

But if God doesn't judge the wicked, He will judge their children (Job 21:19). Zophar had argued that point (20:10), and so had Eliphaz (5:4). Of course, both of them were aiming at Job, who had lost all of his children. "But what kind of judgment is that?" asked Job. "If a man lives in sin, let him suffer for his sin. After he dies, why should he care about what happens to his family? In Sheol, he will never know what is happening on earth."

Scripture makes it clear that the fathers are not punished for the sins of the children or the children for the sins of the fathers (Jer. 31:29-30; Ezek. 18:1ff). Certainly parents may be deeply hurt by the sins of their children, and children may suffer from the *consequences* of their parents' sins, but the judgment of God is always just (Deut. 24:16). It was cruel for the three friends to suggest that Job's sins had caused the death of his children.

Zophar had said that the life of a wicked man was brief, but Job refuted him by affirming that wicked people often live a long time. Zophar claimed that the pleasures of the wicked were temporary because God's judgment suddenly fell upon them, but Job asked, "How often have you seen that happen?" Now Job answers Zophar's third argument that the death of the wicked is painful.

The wicked die just like other people (Job 21:22-34). Life and death are in the hands of God, so what is mere man that he should teach God or claim to be able to explain God's ways? (v. 22) God will ask Job a similar question when He finally appears and gives Job his long-awaited opportunity to defend himself. Instead of Job questioning God, it will be God who questions Job and humbles Job with His questions!

Observation tells Job that some people die when they are in the fullness of life and apparently in excellent health, while others die after long and painful illnesses. Some people enjoy a long and happy life while others spend their days in misery, *but death is the same for all of them.* Strictly speaking, there is no such thing as "infant death" or "tragic death" or "unexpected death" because *death is death no matter when or how it comes.* The rich man dies, the poor man dies; the believer dies, the unbeliever dies; and "side by side they lie in the dust, and worms cover them both" (v. 26, NIV). Of course, Job is talking about the *physical* side of death and not the *spiritual.* When death comes, it obviously makes a great deal of difference *in the next life* whether or not the person had faith in Jesus Christ (Heb. 9:27).

Many people—including some Christian believers—hesitate to speak about death in general or their own death in particular. They have hospitalization and life insurance, but they prefer to avoid the subject and act as though death were not coming. "The idea of death, the fear of it, haunts the human animal like nothing else," wrote sociologist Ernest Becker. "It is a mainspring of human activity—activity designed largely to avoid the fatality of death, to overcome it by denying in some way that it is the final destiny for man" (*The Denial of Death*, Free Press p. ix)

"Behold, I know your thoughts," Job told his friends (Job 21:27). He could tell that his speech had not convinced them,

and he knew just what they were going to say when he finished speaking—exactly what they had said before! In verse 28 he quoted two of their statements that he had already refuted (see 18:13-21 and 20:20-29), but he expected to hear similar statements again.

Job asked his friends if they had ever investigated the situation in places other than their own homeland. As Dorothy Sayers wrote, "There's nothing you can't prove if your outlook is only sufficiently limited." He asked them, "Have you never questioned those who travel?" (21:29, NIV) People who travel are usually not provincial in their outlook but have wide experience in the things of the world. With all of their wisdom, Job's three friends might still be narrow in their outlook because they haven't seen what life is like in other places. If Job's friends inquired of well-traveled people, they would learn that in every part of the world, wicked people seem to escape the calamities that fall on the righteous.

Then Job became very personal and asked his friends, "If you really believe that the wicked are destined for an early death, *have you ever warned them?* Have you ever denounced them to their face?" (v. 31, paraphrase) If his friends had replied, "No, we have never talked to the wicked about their future," then Job could have said, "Then why are you warning *a righteous man* about his future?" How inconsistent can you get?

Job's closing words in 21:34 let the three friends know that he had no confidence in what they said. Their comfort was in vain ("nonsense," NIV), and their answers were nothing but falsehood. The Hebrew word translated "falsehood" means "a deliberate violation of God's Law, an act of treachery." It is often translated "trespass." When the three friends attacked Job, they were breaking faith and trespassing against God. Instead of helping Job, they were leading him astray.

I have a friend who prays daily, "Lord, help me today not to add to anybody's burdens."

It's too bad Bildad and Zophar and Eliphaz didn't pray that prayer!

Perhaps all of us should start praying it!

INTERLUDE

If you want to be an encouragement to hurting people, try to see things through their eyes. Be humble enough to admit that there might be other points of view. Job's three friends had a narrow experience of life. They held fast to their dogmatic assumptions and refused to budge. In a letter to some people who disagreed with him, Oliver Cromwell wrote, "I beseech you, in the bowels of Christ, think it possible you may be mistaken."

Someone has defined fanatics as "people who can't change their minds and won't change the subject." Samuel Johnson once said of a man, "That man has only one idea, and it is wrong."

There is always something new to learn about God, the Bible, people, and life. Let's be good learners—and good listeners!

CHAPTER EIGHT
ORDER IN THE COURT!
Job 22–24

"The God of Israel, the Savior, is sometimes a God that hides Himself, but never a God that absents Himself; sometimes in the dark, but never at a distance."
—MATTHEW HENRY

What should have been an encouraging discussion among friends had become an angry and painful debate. Instead of trying to calm things down, Eliphaz assumed the office of prosecuting attorney and turned the debate into a trial. It was three against one as Job sat on the ash heap and listened to his friends lie about him. According to the Jewish Talmud, "The slanderous tongue kills three: the slandered, the slanderer, and him who listens to the slander." At the ash heap in Uz, it was death all around!

**Three False Accusations
(Job 22:1-30)**
Like any effective attorney, Eliphaz had the case well in hand and his brief all prepared. He made three serious accusations against Job: he is a sinner (Job 22:1-11), he is hiding his sins (vv. 12-20), and he must confess his sins and repent before God can help him (vv. 21-30).

Job is a sinner (Job 22:1-11). Eliphaz can't resist shooting a sarcastic barb at Job. "Is it for your piety that He [God] rebukes you and brings charges against you?" (v. 4, NIV) Courts don't try people for their righteousness but for their lawlessness! Therefore, since God has sent terrible judgments upon Job, he must be guilty of sin. "Is not your wickedness great? Are not your sins endless?" (v. 5, NIV) But Eliphaz missed the point that Job had been making: "Why does God send the punishment *before He arrests me, reads the indictment, and conducts the trial?*" It all seemed unfair.

Eliphaz first accused Job of the sin of

pride (vv. 1-3). Job was acting as though his character and conduct were important to God and beneficial to Him in some way. Eliphaz's theology centered around a distant God who was the Judge of the world but not the Friend of sinners.

But Job's character and conduct *were* important to God, *for God was using Job to silence the devil.* Neither Job nor his three friends knew God's hidden plan, but Job had faith to believe that God was achieving some purpose in his life and would one day vindicate him. Furthermore, the character and behavior of God's people *are* important to the Lord because His people bring Him either joy or sorrow (1 Thess. 4:1; Heb. 11:5; Gen. 6:5-6; Ps. 37:23). He is not a passive, distant God who does not identify with His people but the God who delights in them as they delight in Him (Ps. 18:19; Isa. 63:9; Heb. 4:14-16).

As God's children, we should follow the example of Jesus who said, "I do always those things that please Him" (John 8:29). Then the Father will be able to say of us as He said of Jesus, "This is My beloved Son, in whom I am well pleased" (Matt. 3:17).

Along with pride, Eliphaz accused Job of *covetousness* (Job 22:6). He was a greedy man who abused people to acquire more wealth. He used his power and reputation (v. 8) to intimidate people and rob them. In the Mosaic Law, a creditor could take security from a debtor but not anything that would jeopardize his work, his health, or his dignity as a human being (Ex. 22:25-27; Deut. 24:10-13). Eliphaz accused Job of taking security from his brothers when none was needed, and he left people naked because he took their clothing from them until they paid their debts!

Eliphaz didn't even live in Job's territory, so how would he know how Job had treated people in his business dealings? Had some of Job's enemies passed these stories to Eliphaz? If so, he should have investigated the charges before announcing them publicly. The whole thing was pure fabrication, a feeble attempt to discredit a godly man who had helped many people (Job 29:11-17).

Job's third great sin was *lack of mercy and compassion* (22:7-9), which was a sin of omission. No wonder the Lord was not answering Job's prayers! "Whoever shuts his ears to the cry of the poor will also cry himself and not be heard" (Prov. 21:13). Job had turned away the weary, the hungry, the widows, and the orphans, instead of sharing with them out of his rich resources. Since showing hospitality is one of the first laws of the East, Job's sin was especially heinous.

Throughout Scripture, God shows a great concern for the poor, especially widows and orphans, and expresses anger at those who oppress the poor and exploit them (Ex. 22:22; Deut. 24:17, 26:12). The prophets scathingly denounced leaders, both political and religious, who oppressed the needy and robbed the poor (Isa. 1:17; Jer. 7:6; 22:1-4; Amos 4:1; 5:11; 8:4-10). Jesus had a special concern for the poor (Luke 4:16-19; Matt. 11:5), and the early church followed His example (Gal. 2:10; James 1:27; 2:1-9; Acts 6:1; 1 Tim. 5:1-16). The church *today* needs to follow that example.

Eliphaz clinched his first point with evidence anybody could see: Job was suffering great trials, which were the consequences of his many sins (Job 22:10-11). Why else would he be in darkness, danger, and the depths of suffering? This was the hand of God indicating that Job was a godless man.

The people who were standing around and listening to the discussion must have been shocked when they heard these accusations against their neighbor Job. They must have looked at each other and asked, "How can this be? Why didn't we know about Job's wickedness?" Eliphaz's next point answered their question.

Job is hiding his sins (Job 22:12-20). In other words, Job was a hypocrite, a statement that was made—or hinted at—more than once since the discussion began. "The hypocrite's hope shall perish," said Bildad (8:13). "For the congregation of hypocrites shall be desolate," said Eliphaz (15:34). And Zophar said, "The joy of the hypocrite [is] but for a moment" (20:5).

A hypocrite is not a person who fails to reach his desired spiritual goals, because all of us fail in one way or another. A hypocrite is a person who doesn't even try to reach any goals, *but he makes people think that he has.* His profession and his practice never meet. The Puritan preacher Stephen Charnock said, "It is a sad thing to be Christians at a supper, heathens in our shops, and devils in our closets."

Eliphaz advised Job to *look up* (22:12-14) and realize that nobody can hide anything from God. A hypocrite encourages himself in his sin by saying, "The Lord doesn't know and doesn't care" (see Ps. 10). But God sees and knows all things, and the hypocrite can't hide his sins from the Lord. God may not judge immediately, but eventually judgment will fall.

Then Eliphaz advised Job to *look back* (vv. 15-18) and remember what has happened to sinners in the past. Job had made it clear that he had nothing to do with "the counsel of the wicked" (21:16), but Eliphaz accused him of walking on that very path (22:15). History shows that hypocrites can hide their sins for only so long, and then their sins find them out. God is not only patient with them, but He

is good to them and fills their houses with good things (v. 18). The fact that Job was a very wealthy man was evidence of God's kindness and not Job's righteousness.

Poor Job! No matter which way he turned or how he tried to reason with his accusers, he was wasting his time and energy. First they said that God blesses the righteous and punishes the wicked, and now Eliphaz claims that God blesses the hypocrite and fills his house with good things!

The tragedy of hypocrisy is not only that God sends judgment, but that hypocrisy brings its own judgment. It destroys character; and when character is gone, when the salt has lost its flavor (see Matt. 5:13), what does a person have left?

It has well been said that the highest reward for a faithful life is not what you get for it but what you become by it. Bishop Brooke Westcott said, "Great occasions do not make heroes or cowards; they simply unveil them to the eyes of men. Silently and imperceptibly, as we wake or sleep, we grow strong or we grow weak, and at last some crisis shows what we have become."

Job must repent of his sins (Job 22:21-30). Eliphaz was sincere in his appeal to Job, just as Zophar was sincere when he asked Job to return to God (11:13-20). "Submit to God and be at peace with Him; in this way prosperity will come to you" (22:21, NIV). The word translated "prosperity" means "good of every kind." Of course, a hypocrite should return to God, not just to get out of trouble and restore his or her fortunes, but to please and glorify God in the rebuilding of character and service.

What does it mean to "submit to God"? It means to stop fighting God and accept His terms of peace (James 4:1-10). It also means to listen to His Word and obey what God says (Job 22:22). A sinner must put away sin (v. 23) and make God his greatest treasure (v. 25); he must pray and seek God's face (v. 27).

What does God promise to those who repent and return to Him? God will restore them (v. 23) and make Himself precious to them (v. 25) so that all their delight will be in the Lord and not in earthly wealth or pleasure (v. 26). God will answer their prayers and enable them to do His will (v. 27) as He gives direction and light (v. 28). Because they are restored to fellowship with God, they can help others who have fallen (vv. 29-30).

Eliphaz says some excellent things in this appeal, but he says them to the wrong man. When we get to the end of the book, we will discover that it is Eliphaz and his two friends who are out of fellowship with God. They will need Job to intercede for them so they can be restored (42:7-10).

If you were Job, how would you respond to this appeal?

Three Bitter Complaints
(Job 23–24)

Instead of arguing with his friends, or compromising his integrity by giving in to Eliphaz's appeal, Job ignores them completely and speaks to and about the Lord. Job has already made it clear that his dispute was not with men but with God, and he emphasizes this fact in his speech.

We may paraphrase Job 23:2, "My complaint today is bitter, and I have to keep a heavy hand on myself to keep from doing nothing but groaning." Job's three friends did not understand how much discipline Job needed just to be able to talk with them. Instead of giving in to his pain and doing nothing but groan, Job sought to master his pain and not give in to self-pity. The next time you

visit somebody in pain, keep in mind that suffering drains a person's energy and makes great demands on his strength and patience.

Job said that he had three complaints against the Lord.

"God is hiding from me" (Job 23:1-12). "Oh, that I knew where I might find Him, that I might come even to His seat [throne]!" (v. 3) This was another appeal to meet God in court and have a fair trial. Job was prepared to state his case, present his arguments, and let God give the verdict. Job was confident that, despite God's great power as a Lawgiver, he would win his case for he was an upright man, and God could not condemn the upright in heart. "There an upright man could present his case before Him, and I would be delivered forever from my judge" (v. 7, NIV).

But how does a mere man go about finding God? If Job went forward or backward (east or west), to the left or to the right (north or south), he could not see God or even catch a quick glimpse of Him. Of course, God is present everywhere (Ps. 139:7-12); but Job wanted a *personal* meeting with God. He had questions to ask and arguments to present!

God knew where Job was—in the furnace! (Job 23:10) But it was a furnace of God's appointment, not because of Job's sin; and God would use Job's affliction to purify him and make him a better man. This is not the only answer to the question, "Why do the righteous suffer?" but it is one of the best, and it can bring the sufferer great encouragement.

Scripture often uses the image of a furnace to describe God's purifying ministry through suffering. "See, I have refined you, though not as silver; I have tested you in the furnace of affliction" (Isa. 48:10, NIV). Israel's suffering in Egypt was like that of iron in a smelting furnace (Deut. 4:20), and her later disciplines were also a "furnace experience." "For You, O God, tested us; You refined us like silver" (Ps. 66:10, NIV). This image is used in 1 Peter 1:6-7 and 4:12 of believers going through persecution.

When God puts His own people into the furnace, He keeps His eye on the clock and His hand on the thermostat. He knows how long and how much. We may question why He does it to begin with, or why He doesn't turn down the heat or even turn it off; but our questions are only evidences of unbelief. Job 23:10 is the answer: "But He knows the way that I take; when He has tested me, I shall come forth as gold" (NKJV). *Gold does not fear the fire.* The furnace can only make the gold purer and brighter.

It's important to note that Job's life was pleasing to God *before he went into the furnace* (vv. 11-12). Eliphaz had warned Job to receive God's words and obey them (22:22), but Job had already been doing that. God's Word was his *guide* as he walked the path of life, and he was careful not to go on any detours. But even more, God's Word was his *nourishment* that was more important to him than his daily meals. Like Jeremiah (Jer. 15:16) and Jesus (Matt. 4:4; John 4:31-34), Job found in God's Word the only food that satisfied his inner person. (See Pss. 1:2; 119:103; 1 Peter 2:1-3.)

Some people go into the furnace of affliction, and it burns them; others go in, and the experience purifies them. What makes the difference? *Their attitude toward the Word of God and the will of God.* If we are nourished by the Word and submit to His will, the furnace experience, painful as it may be, will refine us and make us better. But if we resist God's will and fail to feed on His truth, the furnace

experience will only burn us and make us bitter.

Job had a second complaint.

"God is frightening me" (Job 23:13-17). "But He stands alone, and who can oppose Him? He does whatever He pleases" (v. 13, NIV). Job had no other gods to turn to for help, and no way to oppose God or change His mind. God runs the universe by decree, not by consensus or democratic vote. His thoughts and ways are far above ours, but He knows what is best, and we must accept His will and rejoice in it (Isa. 55:8-11).

Those who resist or deny the sovereignty of God rob themselves of peace and courage. "There is no attribute of God more comforting to His children than the doctrine of divine sovereignty," said Charles Haddon Spurgeon. "On the other hand, there is no doctrine more hated by worldlings." Why? Because the human heart is proud and does not want to submit to Almighty God. People want to "do their own thing" and "do it their way," rather than find delight in doing the will of God.

If this doctrine is such a source of strength, then why was Job so frightened when he thought about the sovereignty of God? It was because he suffered so much and wondered what Almighty God would send to him next. It's one thing to submit to God when you can see His face and hear His voice in His Word. But when, like Job, you are in darkness and pain, it is easy to "fall apart" and become frightened. "He carries out His decree against me, and many such plans He still has in store" (Job 23:14, NIV). What will happen next?

But Job 23:14 must be contrasted with Jeremiah 29:11—" `For I know the plans I have for you,' declares the Lord, `plans to prosper you and not to harm you, plans to give you hope and a future' " (NIV). *The future is your friend when Jesus Christ is your Lord, and you need not be afraid.* Psychologist Rollo May writes, "The most effective way to ensure the value of the future is to confront the present courageously and constructively." And the best way to do that is to submit to the Lord and realize that He is in control. "Alleluia! for the Lord God omnipotent reigneth" (Rev. 19:6).

"God perplexes me" (Job 24:1-25). This entire chapter focuses on the seeming injustices that God permits in this world. Job opens his speech by asking in effect, "Why doesn't God have specific days to hold court? Then I could attend and tell Him what I think of the way He is running the world!"

Job starts with *injustices in the country* (vv. 1-11), and then moves to *crimes in the city* (vv. 12-17). He closes his speech with *a curse on the wicked* (vv. 18-25). If God won't judge them, Job will!

(1) Injustices in the country (vv. 1-11). For the most part, no walls or fences separated the farmlands; each family had its plot, and people respected the landmarks ("boundary stones," NIV; see Deut. 19:14; Prov. 22:28; 23:10). God promised to curse those who moved the landmarks and stole property (Deut. 27:17), but wicked men did it just the same.

But they didn't stop there. They not only claimed the land, but also the animals that grazed on the land! They took flocks and donkeys and oxen from widows and orphans and left them in poverty. Job 24:5-11 gives one of the most graphic pictures of the plight of the poor found anywhere in the Bible. See them foraging for food like wild animals in the desert (vv. 5-6), freezing because they have no clothing (v. 7), drenched by the rain because they have no houses to live

in (v. 8), weeping because their children have been snatched from their arms until they pay their debts (v. 9), and forced to work for the rich and yet not allowed to eat any of the food that they harvest (vv. 10-11). Even the oxen are permitted to eat the grain that they thresh! (Deut. 25:4)

"Now," says Job to his friends, "if God judges the wicked, why hasn't He judged those who have treated the poor so unjustly and inhumanely?"

(2) Crimes in the city (vv. 12-17). Job begins with *murders* (vv. 12-14); he hears the groans of the wounded and sees the death of the innocent. On the average, 60 Americans are murdered every day, a total of nearly 22,000 people annually. That's like wiping out an entire city about the size of Fairbanks, Alaska; or El Cerrito, California; or Augusta, Maine. Some of these murderers are never identified, arrested, or convicted; and Job says, "But God charges no one with wrongdoing" (v. 12, NIV). Job had never murdered anybody, yet his friends said he was under the judgment of God!

In verse 15, Job mentions *sexual sins,* which are certainly rampant in some parts of our cities. The adulterer and the rapist wait for the darkness before they sneak out to satisfy their desires. Also waiting for the darkness is *the thief,* who breaks into houses (vv. 16-17). "There is crime in the city," said Job, "and God seems to be doing nothing about it."

(3) A curse on the wicked (vv. 18-25). This passage may be seen as a *description,* telling what will happen to the wicked (KJV, NIV, NASB); or it may be interpreted as a *denunciation,* a curse on the wicked (NKJV). I think it refers to Job's personal curse on the wicked, who seem to escape judgment.

Job's malediction can be summarized like this: "May the wicked vanish like foam on the water or snow that melts in the heat of the sun (vv. 18-19). May they be forgotten by everyone, even their own mothers, as they rot in the grave (v. 20). May their wives be barren and give them no heirs (v. 21). May their sense of security and success vanish quickly as they are brought low, mowed down like wheat in the harvest" (vv. 22-24).

"Now," says Job to his three critics, "if what I've said is not true, prove me wrong!" (v. 25) But they never did.

Job is to be commended for seeing somebody else's troubles besides his own and for expressing a holy anger against sin and injustice. Too often, personal suffering can make us selfish and even blind us to the needs of others, but Job was concerned that God help others who were hurting. His three friends were treating the problem of suffering in far too abstract a fashion, and Job tried to get them to see *hurting people* and not just philosophical problems. Jesus had the same problem with the Jewish lawyer who wanted to discuss "neighborliness," but not discover who his neighbor was and then try to help him (Luke 10:25-37).

Injustices in society cause a good deal of pain in people's lives, and we should certainly do all we can to uphold the law and promote justice. But those who make the laws and those who enforce them are only human and can't deal with everything perfectly. One of these days, the Lord Jesus Christ will return, judge the wicked, and establish His righteous kingdom. Till He comes, we will have to accept the reality of evil in this world and keep praying, "Even so, come, Lord Jesus" (Rev. 22:20).

CHAPTER NINE
HOW FAINT A WHISPER!
Job 25–28

"Every year makes me tremble at the daring with which people speak of spiritual things."
—BISHOP BROOKE F. WESTCOTT

Bildad's speech in Job 25 is the shortest in the book and focuses on God's power (vv. 1-3) and justice (vv. 4-6). It is disturbing to see how Job's friends speak so knowingly about God when, in the end, God revealed that they really didn't know what they were talking about. Too often, those who say the most about God know the least about God.

God's power is inherent in His nature (vv. 1-3): He has all dominion and fear ("awe") and reigns sovereignly in the heavens. He has everything under control and sees what is going on in all places. His army of angels is at His command and ready to obey His will. Who can resist Him?

God's justice is the outworking of His holy nature (vv. 4-6), for "God is light, and in Him is no darkness at all" (1 John 1:5). Since God is holy and just, how can mere man claim to be righteous before Him? (Remember, Job was holding fast to his integrity and refusing to confess that his sins had brought God's judgment on him.) Since man is born of woman, he is born with a sinful nature (Ps. 51:5). In the East, the moon and stars shine with great brilliance; but even they are not pure in God's sight. How can a mere man claim to be righteous before God, man who is nothing but a maggot and a worm? (See Job 4:17-18; 8:20; 9:2.) Now, we listen to Job's reply.

Job Acknowledges God's Power (Job 26)

Before magnifying God's great power in the universe, Job first rebuked Bildad for giving him no help (Job 26:1-4). Job had no power, but Bildad didn't make him stronger. According to his friends, Job lacked wisdom; yet Bildad didn't share one piece of wisdom or insight. "Who has helped you utter these words? And whose spirit spoke from your mouth?" (v. 4, NIV) If Bildad's words had come from God, then they would have done Job good; for Job had been crying out for God to speak to him. The conclusion is that Bildad's words came from Bildad, and that's why they did Job no good.

Then Job extolled the greatness of God (vv. 5-13). God sees everything, even the realm of the dead (vv. 5-6). Job used three different names for the place of the dead: the waters, Sheol, and "destruction" (Abaddon, Rev. 9:11). If God sees what's going on in the world of the dead, then surely He knows what is happening in the world of the living!

God not only sees everything, but He made everything and controls it (Job 26:7-13). Job began his hymn of praise with a statement about God's power in *the heavens* (vv. 7-9), and he described the earth with remarkable scientific accuracy (v. 7). God also controls the clouds and the rain.

Job then moved his attention to *the earth* (vv. 10-11) and praised God for marking out the horizon where the sun rises and sets. He is the God who controls day and night, land and water. The "pillars of heaven" is a poetic phrase for the mountains; they rest on earth, but they seem to hold up the heavens. All God has to do is speak, and the mountains tremble (9:6).

The last stanza of Job's hymn centers on God's power in *the waters* (26:12-13). God can stir up the sea or still it as He desires, and He has power over sea creatures ("Rahab" and "the gliding serpent," NIV). He can blow the storm clouds away and clear the sky after the storm.

The three friends must have listened impatiently because they already knew the things Job was talking about; *but they hadn't drawn the right conclusion from them.* Because they saw God's handiwork in nature, they thought they knew all about God; therefore, they could explain God to Job.

Job said that just the opposite was true. "Behold, these are the fringes of His ways; and how faint a word we hear of Him! But His mighty thunder, who can understand?" (v. 14, NASB) What we see of God in creation is but the fringes of His ways, and what we hear is but a whisper of His power! You may read The Book of Nature carefully and still have a great deal more to learn about God. Knowing a few facts about the creation of God is not the same as knowing truths about the God of Creation.

The fourteenth-century British spiritual writer Richard Rolle said, "He truly knows God perfectly that finds Him incomprehensible and unable to be known." The more we learn about God, the more we discover how much more there is to know! Beware of people who claim to know all about God, for their claim is proof they know neither God nor themselves.

Job Questions God's Justice (Job 27)

Bildad had made it clear that since God is holy, no man can stand righteous in His sight (Job 25:4-6). The corollary to this proposition is that God is obligated to punish people for their sins; otherwise, He would not be a righteous God. If Job is suffering, it must be that Job is sinning.

Job takes an oath (Job 27:1-6). Once again, Job stood fast in affirming his integrity (10:1-7; 13:13-19; 19:23-27; 23:2-7); but this time, he gave an oath: "As God lives" (27:2). Among Eastern people in that day, taking an oath was a serious matter. It was like inviting God to kill you if what you said was not true. Job was so sure of himself that he was willing to take that chance.

Job also repeated his charge that God was not treating him fairly ("[He] has denied me justice," v. 2, NIV). Job had asked God to declare the charges against him, but the heavens had been silent. Job had called for an umpire to bring him and God together, but no umpire had been provided.

So, Job declared that, as long as he lived, he would defend himself and maintain his integrity. He would not lie just to please his friends or to "bribe" God into restoring his fortunes. (Satan would have rejoiced at that!) Job had to live with his conscience ("heart," v. 6) no matter what his friends said or his God did to him.

Job utters a curse (Job 27:7-10). In the East, it was not enough for accused people simply to affirm their innocence; they also felt compelled to call down the wrath of God on those who said they were guilty. Job's words remind us of the "imprecatory psalms" (Pss. 58, 69, 137, etc.) in that they are a prayer for God's judgment on his enemies.

Who were Job's enemies? Anybody who agreed with Job's three friends that he was guilty of sin and deserved to be punished by God. While this conversation had been going on, many people had likely gathered around the ash heap and

listened to the debate; and most of them probably sided with Bildad, Zophar, and Eliphaz. Job could see the spectators nod their heads in agreement with his friends, and he knew that he was outnumbered.

Job's words sound cruel to us, especially in light of what we are taught about forgiving our enemies by both Jesus (Matt. 5:38-48) and Paul (Rom. 12:17-21). But Job lived even before the Mosaic Law was given, let alone the Sermon on the Mount; and we must not expect him to manifest the kind of spirit that was seen in Jesus (Luke 23:34) and Stephen (Acts 7:60).

However, in the sight of God, *Job was right.* God had *twice* declared before the court of heaven that Job was "a blameless and upright man, one who fears God and shuns evil" (Job 1:8; 2:3, NKJV). Therefore, Job's enemies were wrong; and Job had the right to ask God to vindicate him. In fact, *God was the only one who could prove Job right and his enemies wrong.* Where else could Job turn for help?

The three friends had repeatedly warned Job about the terrible destiny of the wicked, so Job threw their words right back at them. "May my enemies be like the wicked, my adversaries like the unjust" (27:7, NIV). Job saw his enemies experiencing great distress, calling out to God for help but getting no answer, and then being suddenly cut off by death. But isn't that the very judgment Job's friends predicted for him *and probably hoped would come?*

Bildad had affirmed that God is just and punishes those who disobey Him. But this does not mean that everybody who suffers is being punished for his or her sins. Sometimes we suffer because of the sins of others (e.g., Joseph) or because God is keeping us from sin (e.g., Paul in 2 Cor. 12). Jesus suffered, not for His own sins, for He had none, but for the sins of the world (1 Peter 2:22-24; 3:18); and because of His suffering and death, sinners can believe and receive eternal life.

Job teaches a lesson (Job 27:11-23). "I will teach you about the power of God" (27:11, NIV), says Job; and he describes God's judgment of the wicked. On the day when God vindicates Job, this is what will happen to his enemies.

They will die, and their widows will not mourn for them, a terrible insult in the Eastern world. Their children will be slain by the sword or the plague; and if any survive, they will spend the rest of their lives begging for something to eat. The wicked will lie down rich and wake up poor. Their silver and expensive clothing will be gone. Their houses will be destroyed like cocoons (or spiders' webs), or like the temporary shacks of the watchmen in the fields. The death of the wicked will not be peaceful. Terrors will come in at night like a flood and carry them away. Even if the wicked try to flee, the storm will follow them and destroy them.

You can recognize in this description many of the images that Job's friends used in their "judgment" speeches against him. Job did this deliberately to remind them that they had better be careful what they say *lest they declare their own punishment*. "Judge not, that you be not judged. For with what judgment you judge, you will be judged; and with the same measure you use, it will be measured back to you" (Matt. 7:1-2, NKJV).

Scripture records several instances where the judgment planned by an enemy was brought home to that enemy by the Lord. Pharaoh ordered the newborn Jewish boys to be drowned, and his own army was drowned in the Red Sea (Ex. 1:15-22; 14:23-31). Haman built a gallows on which to hang Mordecai, but Haman and his sons were hanged there instead

(Est. 7:10; 9:25). Daniel's enemies tried to have him destroyed, but they and their families ended up in the lions' den in the place of Daniel (Dan. 6:24). (See Prov. 11:8.)

Scholars do not agree on the interpretation of Job 27:23. The NASB reads, "Men will clap their hands at him, and will hiss him from his place," and most translations agree with that; but the word *men* is not in the original text. It simply reads, "He claps his hands against him." Who is "he"? Elmer B. Smick in *The Expositor's Bible Commentary* suggests that it might be God, and that verse 23 should be connected with verse 13 where "God" is the subject of the sentence (vol. 4, p. 972). He translates verse 23, "He claps his hands against them and hisses at them from his dwelling [heaven]." Whether God or men, there is rejoicing at the destruction of the wicked.

Job Seeks God's Wisdom
(Job 28)

"But where shall wisdom be found?" (Job 28:12) "Where then does wisdom come from? Where does understanding dwell?" (v. 20, NIV) Job asked these questions because he was weary of the cliches and platitudes that his three friends were giving him in the name of "wisdom." His friends were sure that their words were pure gold, but Job concluded they were tinsel and trash. The three men had *knowledge*, but they lacked *wisdom*.

"Wisdom is the right use of knowledge," said Charles Spurgeon. "To know is not to be wise. Many men know a great deal, and are all the greater fools for it. There is no fool so great a fool as the knowing fool. But to know how to use knowledge is to have wisdom."

In this poem about wisdom, Job gives three answers to his question, "Where shall wisdom be found?"

You cannot mine wisdom (Job 28:1-11).

Job takes us deep into the earth where brave men are mining gold, iron, copper, and precious stones. Precious metals and precious stones are often used in Scripture as symbols of wisdom (Prov. 2:1-10; 3:13-15; 8:10-21; 1 Cor. 3:12-23). Once you have found it, you must "refine" it in the furnace and "mint" it for practical use. Paul said that the opposite of God's wisdom is man's wisdom—"wood, hay, and stubble"—materials that are not beautiful, durable, or valuable (1 Cor. 3:12). You can find wood, hay, and stubble on the surface of the earth; but if you want real treasures, you must dig deep.

Job describes how men work hard and face great danger to find material wealth. They tunnel through hard rock and risk their lives to get rich. *Why will men and women not put that much effort into gaining God's wisdom?* The Word of God is like a deep mine, filled with precious treasures; but the believer must put forth effort to discover its riches. It takes careful reading and study, prayer, meditation, and obedience to mine the treasures of the Word of God; and the Holy Spirit of God is willing to assist us. Why are we so negligent when this great wealth lies so near at hand?

Though man can dig deep into the earth and find great wealth, though he can go places where birds and beasts would not dare to go, though he can even find the hidden sources of the great rivers, *man cannot find God's wisdom by mere human efforts.* It takes more than courage and native intelligence; it demands humility and spiritual perception.

The fact that a person succeeds admirably in one area of life doesn't mean he or she is qualified to speak about other areas of life. Advertisers use athletes to sell razors and automobiles, or actors and actresses to sell medicine. When famous scientists (who have never studied the Bible) speak authoritatively about spiritual things, their opinion is as valuable as that of any other untrained amateur theologian.

You cannot buy wisdom (Job 28:12-19). Modern society thinks that anything can be obtained or accomplished if only you have enough money. Government agencies ask for a bigger slice of the annual budget so they can do a better job of fighting crime, ending pollution, providing jobs, and building a better environment. While a certain amount of money is necessary to survive in modern society, money is not the do-all and be-all that the world says it is. It's good to enjoy the things money can buy (1 Tim. 6:17) *if you don't lose the things that money can't buy.*

In these verses, Job mentions gold five times, silver once, and names seven different precious stones; yet none of these treasures individually, nor all of them collectively, can purchase the wisdom of God. The real problem is that *man doesn't comprehend the price of wisdom and thinks he can get it cheaply* (Job 28:13). "[Wisdom] is more precious than rubies, and all the things you may desire cannot compare with her" (Prov. 3:15, NKJV). True wisdom is expensive. It is not received automatically just because you listen to a cassette tape, attend a seminar, or listen to a dynamic speaker.

Wisdom comes only from God (Job 28:20-28). Go as high as the birds can fly, and you won't find wisdom there. Go as deep as Abaddon and death, and wisdom is not there. Only God knows where to find wisdom, for God sees everything. (He doesn't have to dig into the earth to see what's there!) God has the wisdom to adjust the pressure of the wind and measure the amount of water in the atmosphere. If these proportions were changed, what disturbances in nature might result!

God knows how to control the rain and guide the storm as it moves across the earth. Flashes of lightning and peals of thunder may seem arbitrary to us, but God controls even the lightning and thunder.

Job answers his where-is-wisdom question in Job 28:28: "Behold, the fear of the Lord, that is wisdom; and to depart from evil is understanding" (see Ps. 111:10; Prov. 1:7; 9:10). This was God's description of Job (Job 1:8; 2:3); so, in spite of what his friends said about him, *Job was a man of wisdom.*

What is "the fear of the Lord"? It is loving reverence for God, who He is, what He says, and what He does (Mal. 2:5-6). It is not a fear that paralyzes, but one that energizes. When you fear the Lord, you obey His commandments (Eccl. 12:13), walk in His ways (Deut. 8:6), and serve Him (Josh. 24:14). You are loyal to Him and give Him wholehearted service (2 Chron. 19:9). Like Job, when you fear the Lord, you depart from evil (Prov. 3:7-8). The "fear of the Lord" is the fear that conquers fear (Ps. 112); for if you fear God, you need not fear anyone else (Matt. 10:26-31).

So, the first step toward true wisdom is a reverent and respectful attitude toward God, which also involves a humble attitude toward ourselves. *Personal pride is the greatest barrier to spiritual wisdom.* "When pride comes, then comes shame; but with the humble is wisdom" (Prov. 11:2, NKJV).

The next step is to ask God for wisdom (James 1:5) and make diligent use of the means He gives us for securing His wisdom, especially knowing and doing the Word of God (Matt. 7:21-29). It is not enough merely to study; we must also obey what God tells us to do (John 7:17). As we walk by faith, we discover the wisdom of God in the everyday things of life.

Spiritual wisdom is not abstract; it is very personal and very practical.

As we fellowship with other believers in the church and share with one another, we can learn wisdom. Reading the best books can also help us grow in wisdom and understanding. The important thing is that we focus on Christ, for He is our wisdom (1 Cor. 1:24), and in Him is hidden "all the treasures of wisdom and knowledge" (Col. 2:3). The better we know Christ and the more we become like Him, the more we will walk in wisdom and understand the will of the Lord. We must allow the Holy Spirit to open the eyes of our heart so we can see God in His Word and understand more of the riches we have in Christ (Eph. 1:15-23).

Job's speech is not yet finished. In the next three chapters, Job will review his life and then challenge God to either vindicate him or judge him. That will end the debate and usher in two new participants—Elihu and the Lord.

CHAPTER TEN
I REST MY CASE!
Job 29–31

"As long as we want to be different from what God wants us to be at the time, we are only tormenting ourselves to no purpose."
—GERHART TERSTEEGEN

Job and his friends had shared three rounds of speeches, and now Job felt it was time for him to sum up his defense. The phrase "Moreover, Job continued his parable [discourse]" (Job 29:1) suggests that Job may have paused and waited for Zophar to take his turn to speak, but Zophar was silent. Perhaps Zophar felt it was a waste of time to argue with Job anymore.

In these three chapters, Job recalled the blessings of the past (Job 29), lamented the sufferings of the present (Job 30), and challenged God to vindicate him in the future (Job 31). He climaxed his speech with sixteen "if I have ..." statements and put himself under oath, challenging God either to condemn him or vindicate him. It was as though Job were saying, "We've talked long enough! I really don't care what you three men think, because God is my Judge; and I rest my case with Him. Now, let Him settle the matter one way or another, once and for all."

Job Looks Back at Life's Joys
(Job 29)

Job had opened his defense by saying that he wished he had never been born (Job 3). Now he closed his defense by remembering the blessings he and his family had enjoyed prior to his crisis. This is a good reminder that we should try to see life in a balanced way. Yes, God permits us to experience difficulties and sorrows, but God also sends victories and joys. "Shall we receive good at the hand of God, and shall we not receive evil?" (2:10) C.H. Spurgeon said that too many people write their blessings in the sand but engrave their sorrows in marble.

"Oh, that I were as in months past, as in the days when God preserved me!" (29:2) When we are experiencing trials, it's natural for us to long for "the good old days"; but our longing will not change our situation. Someone has defined "the good old days" as "a combination of a

bad memory and a good imagination." In Job's case, however, his memory was accurate, and "the good old days" really were good.

There is a ministry in memory if we use it properly. Moses admonished Israel to remember the way God had led them and cared for them (Deut. 8:2). In fact, the word "remember" is found fourteen times in Deuteronomy and the word "forget" nine times. In days of disappointment, it's good to "remember the years of the right hand of the Most High" (Ps. 77:10-11; see 42:6). But the past must be a rudder to guide us and not an anchor to hold us back. If we try to duplicate today what we experienced yesterday, we may find ourselves in a rut that robs us of maturity.

It is significant that Job mentioned as his number-one joy *the presence of God in his home* (Job 29:2-6). God watched over him and shared His "intimate friendship" with him (v. 4, NIV). The light of God was upon Job, and God's presence was with him and his children. God was the source of all of Job's wealth and success, when his "path was drenched with cream and the rock poured out ... streams of olive oil" (v. 6, NIV). (Zophar promised Job "honey and cream" if he would repent. See 20:17, and note Deut. 32:13-14; 33:24.)

There is one especially poignant note in this opening statement: Job wished he were back in the prime of life (Job 29:4). While this is a natural desire, it is also a dangerous one. *If we focus so much on the glories of the past that we ignore the opportunities of the present, we may end up unprepared to meet the future.* That future will come whether we like it or not. Few people eagerly anticipate old age and the special problems that it brings, but we can't avoid it. It's a proven fact that those who have the most birthdays live the longest, and those who live the longest become the oldest; and old people eventually die.

Remember the "never die" jokes? Old skiers never die: they just go downhill. Old bakers never die: they just fail to rise. Old football players never die: they just fumble away. Old golfers never die: they just lose their drive. We may think *we* will never die, but we will, unless the Lord returns to take us to heaven; and this means that we must prepare for old age and death. It is futile to look back with regret; it is faith to look ahead with rejoicing.

"To know how to grow old is the master work of wisdom," wrote Henri Amiel, "and one of the most difficult chapters in the great art of living."

Job next listed the joy of *respect from others* (vv. 7-11). When he walked through the city, the young men stepped aside to let him pass. He had his seat at the city gate with the leading men of the city, and even they ceased their speaking when he arrived. Wherever he went, he was treated with respect. "Whoever heard me spoke well of me, and those who saw me commended me" (v. 11, NIV).

His third source of joy was *ministry to others* (vv. 12-17). What God gave to him, Job shared with others. Eliphaz had accused Job of exploiting the poor and needy (22:5-9), but Job denied it. These verses describe the ministry of a compassionate man who brought help and happiness to many. Job strengthened righteousness and justice in the city (29:14; Isa. 59:17) as he helped the handicapped, provided for the needy, and even defended the strangers. But Job did not stop with assisting the needy; he also confronted the wicked and broke their power (Job 29:17). Job compared the wicked to fierce animals that were ready to devour the weak, but he came and snatched the victims from their very jaws.

Confidence in the future (vv. 18-20) was another source of joy to Job before his calamities came upon him. God was blessing Job, and Job was sharing those blessings with others; so he had every reason to believe that life would continue that way for many years. He was confident that he would stay fresh and vigorous, live to an old age, and die in peace and glory. He saw himself as a deeply rooted tree that would go on bearing fruit (v. 19; Ps. 92:12-14). Since children are sometimes pictured as arrows (127:3-5), Job 29:20 suggests that Job expected to maintain his physical vigor and beget many children.

His final source of joy was the *privilege of speaking words of encouragement and help* (vv. 21-25). He was indeed a Barnabas, "a son of encouragement" (Acts 4:36, NKJV), whose words were respected and appreciated. When he spoke, it was as gentle and refreshing as the rain. When he smiled, it lit up the whole situation and gave people hope. Job's approval was like the dawning of a new day! He was a leader who helped the perplexed make wise decisions and gave the mourners fresh comfort and hope.

Yes, Job had enjoyed a rich and rewarding life; but now all of that was gone.

Job Looks Around at God's Judgment (Job 30)

From the delightful past, Job is suddenly thrust back into the dismal and disappointing present. You can almost hear him groan his first words, "But now" (Job 30:1; see vv. 9, 16). Job was wise enough to know that he had to face the reality of the present and not escape into the memory of the past. People who refuse to come to grips with life are in danger of losing touch with reality, and soon they lose touch with themselves.

"In their unsuccessful effort to fulfill

their needs, no matter what behavior they choose," writes psychiatrist William Glasser, "all patients have a common characteristic: *They all deny the reality of the world around them*" (*Reality Therapy,* p. 6). By refusing to live in the past and by honestly facing reality, Job took a giant step in maturity and integrity. In his lament, Job contrasted his present situation with the past and showed how everything had been changed by the judgment of God. His five "complaints" parallel the joys that he named in chapter 29:

"I have no respect" (30:1-15,
see 29:7-11)
"I have no blessing" (30:16-23,
see 29:2-6)
"I have no help" (30:24-25,
see 29:12-17)
"I have no future" (30:26-28,
see 29:18-20)
"I have no ministry" (30:29-31,
see 29:21-25)

"I have no respect" (Job 30:1-15). Young men who once stepped aside for Job (Job 29:8) now mocked him and even spit in his face (30:1, 9-10). But the worst part of this experience was that these young men were the sons of men so despicable that Job compared their fathers to donkeys wandering in the desert. He called them "children of fools, yea, children of base men" (v. 8). They were outcasts from society who had to forage in the wilderness to find food and fuel for their fires. At one time, Job had been the greatest man in the East; and now he was the song of the rabble (v. 9).

These men were unworthy to carry Job's sandals, and now they were openly ridiculing him. What made the difference? *Job was now an outcast like themselves.* When Job's bow was "renewed in

[his] hand"—a symbol of vigor and success (29:20)—these men respected him. But God had "loosed" his cord and afflicted him, so these rebels set aside their restraint and despised him (30:11). When formerly they had honored Job, it was not because they respected his character and integrity. It was because they respected his position and wealth and hoped to benefit from his favor. Their friendship was fickle, and their respect was hypocritical.

Because this rabble had "thrown off restraint" (v. 11, NIV), they made life miserable for Job. Job pictured them as a ruthless army, building siege ramps, laying traps for his feet, breaking down his defenses, and attacking him (vv. 12-14). They were also like a storm that frightened Job, blew away all his dignity, and destroyed his safety like the wind blows a passing cloud (v. 15).

Job experienced sufferings similar to those of our Lord Jesus Christ. The basest of people falsely accused Him (Matt. 26:59-64), spat upon Him (v. 67), and ridiculed Him while He was suffering (Luke 23:35-39); and He became "the song of the drunkards" (Ps. 69:12). Job didn't know it, but he was being honored by God to share in "the fellowship of His [Christ's] sufferings" (Phil. 3:10). Though sitting in an ash heap, Job had been promoted in the highest possible way!

"I have no blessing" (Job 30:16-23). "And now ... the days of affliction have taken hold upon me," groaned Job (v. 16). What a contrast to the days of cream and oil! (29:6) Instead of enriching him with blessing, God was robbing him of even the basic enjoyments of life. In the daytime, Job endured unbearable suffering; and at night, God wrestled with him, made his clothing like a straitjacket, and threw him in the mud (30:16-19, NIV).

Every night, God wrestled with Job; and Job lost.

Job prayed to God. He even stood up and cried out for deliverance; but his prayers were unanswered (v. 20). Instead of God's hand bringing help, it only attacked Job ruthlessly and tossed him about like a feather in a storm (vv. 21-22). Job begged for his life, but death seemed inevitable (1:23).

"I have no help" (Job 30:24-25). Job had faithfully helped others in their need (29:12-17), but now nobody would help him. They wouldn't weep with him or even touch him. He was treated like a leper who might contaminate them, or like a condemned man whom God might destroy at any time. It just wasn't wise to get too close.

Where were the people that Job had helped? Surely some of them would have wanted to show their appreciation by encouraging their benefactor in his time of need. But nobody came to his aid. Mark Twain wrote, "If you pick up a starving dog and make him prosperous, he will not bite you. This is the principal difference between a dog and a man."

Our motive for serving others is certainly not to obligate them to serve us (Luke 14:12-14). We help others because we love Christ and want to glorify Him (Matt. 5:16), and because we sympathize with their needs and want to help them (Rom. 12:15; Luke 10:25-37). Missionary doctor Wilfred Grenfell said, "The service we render for others is really the rent we pay for our room on this earth."

"I have no future" (Job 30:26-28). During the days of his prosperity, Job had expected to enjoy a long and comfortable life and a peaceful death (29:18-20); but now that was all changed. He looked for good, but God sent evil; he looked for light, but God sent darkness. Instead of comfort and peace, he experienced constant turmoil within. "The churning inside me never stops; days of suffering confront me" (30:27, NIV).

The British essayist William Hazlitt wrote, "Hope is the best possession. None are completely wretched but those who are without hope, and few are reduced so low as that." Job was, and even the Lord seemed not to care. Job's body was weak and feverish, and his skin was black from disease.

"I have no ministry" (Job 30:29-31). In the past, Job's words had brought encouragement and hope to many (29:21-25); but now his words were like the howling of the jackals and the moaning of the owls and ostriches (Mic. 1:8). Because his hope was dead, Job's song was a funeral dirge. His harp and flute were tuned to a minor key. How could he speak encouraging words to others when he himself was in the pit of discouragement? "And where is now my hope?" he had asked earlier in the debate. "As for my hope, who shall see it?" (Job 17:15)

Job Looks Ahead for God's Justice (Job 31)

This chapter records Job's final defense. It is like a legal document in which Job puts himself under oath before God and asks for judgment to fall if God can prove him wrong (Job 31:35-37). Job's only hope was that God would hear his cry and vindicate his name. He could die in peace if he knew that his enemies had been silenced and his reputation restored. In sixteen "if I have …" statements, Job reviews his life and relationships and asks God to pass judgment. "I sign now my defense" (v. 35, NIV), said Job as he made the oath official and signed the document. "I rest my case!"

In verses 33-37, Job asked God ("my

adversary" = judge) to give him three things: a hearing, an answer to his charges, and a document to prove his innocence. If God couldn't do these things, then Job was willing that God send the curses included in Job's oath. Job was prepared to give God an accounting of his every step if that's what it would take to bring the case to an end. Job had nothing to hide; he was not a hypocrite, cringing for fear of the people (vv. 33-34).

Job the man (Job 31:1-12). Job mentions three specific sins that could trip up any man: lust (vv. 1-4), deceit (vv. 5-8), and adultery (vv. 9-12).

(1) Lust is the first step toward sin, and sin is the first step toward death (James 1:13-16). It is one thing to see and admire an attractive person, but it is quite something else to look *for the purpose of lusting in the heart.* Jesus said, "Everyone who is looking at a woman in order to indulge his sexual passion for her, already committed adultery with her in his heart" (Matt. 5:28, WUEST). While sin in the heart is not as destructive as sin actually committed, it is the first step toward the act; and you never know where a polluted imagination will lead you. Furthermore, God above looks down and sees both our actions and "the thoughts and intents of the heart" (Heb. 4:12-13); and He will judge both. "Is it not ruin for the wicked, disaster for those who do wrong?" (Job 31:3, NIV)

(2) Deceit is the second sin that Job denies (vv. 5-8). He never used deception in his business dealings in order to make more money. In fact, he wouldn't even walk with those who did such things. His scales were honest (Lev. 19:35-37; Prov. 11:1), and he was not afraid for God to weigh him! (Dan. 5:27) His heart had not been covetous nor were his hands defiled because he had not taken what was not his. If he were guilty of covetousness and

deception, then Job was willing for his next season's crops to be taken by others.

(3) Adultery (Job 31:9-12) begins with lust in the heart (v. 1) that leads to furtive attempts to satisfy sinful desires. Job had never lurked about to see when his neighbor's wife would be alone. If he was guilty, then he was willing for his own wife to become another man's slave and mistress! Adultery is a heinous crime that brings shameful and painful consequences in this life, and judgment in the next (Prov. 6:27-29; Eph. 5:3-7; Heb. 13:4).

Job the employer (Job 31:13-15). So careful was Job in his self-examination that he even included his treatment of his servants. Most masters in that day would have ignored this aspect of life. Job treated his servants generously and settled their grievances fairly because he knew that one day he would have to give an account to God (v. 14; Eph. 6:9). He also knew that he was created by the same God who created them and that he was born in the same way.

Job the neighbor (Job 31:16-23, 29-32). In reply to the false accusations of Eliphaz (22:6-9), Job had already told how he had cared for the poor and needy (29:12-17); but now he repeated it as a part of his oath. He was not boasting; he was defending himself before men and seeking vindication from God. If he had lifted his hand in court against any man, Job hoped that God would rip that arm from its socket.

Job was concerned for the needs of widows, orphans, and the poor. He provided them with food and clothing and came to their defense in court. He even treated them like members of his own family and cared for them until they could care for themselves. God had given Job his wealth, and God could take it away from him if he didn't share it with others (31:23). But Job was also a good neighbor to his enemies (vv. 29-31) and to strangers passing through town (v. 32). Because Job was a wealthy and powerful sheik, no doubt there were many people who envied him and hated him; yet Job was kind to them. He didn't gloat over their misfortunes (Ex. 23:4-5; Prov. 24:17-18; Matt. 5:43-47) or ask God to curse them (Rom. 12:17-21).

Job was also generous to strangers, giving them food to eat and a place to spend the night. None of Job's servants could ever accuse their master of being selfish (Job 31:31, NIV). His home was open to all, and he was generous with his gifts.

Job the worshiper (Job 31:24-28). Job worshiped God with a sincere heart. He didn't worship his wealth or trust it for his security, nor did he take credit for earning it (Deut. 8:17-18). Eliphaz had accused Job of making gold his god (Job 22:24-25), but Job denied it. He did not worship gold nor did he worship the heavenly bodies and secretly "throw them a kiss of homage" (1 Kings 19:18, NIV). If Job committed such a sin, men might not see it; but God would see it and would judge Job for being unfaithful to Him.

Job the steward (Job 31:38-40). In verses 35-37, Job had completed his "official demand" for a hearing and signed the document. Then he remembered one more area that needed to be covered: his stewardship of the land God had given him. Job treated the land as though it were a person. If he had abused the land, it would have cried out against him and wept in pain (v. 38). If Job's field hands had been overworked and underpaid, then God would have had every reason to give Job a harvest of weeds instead of wheat and barley.

Review Job's oath and you will discover that he has asked God to send some terrible judgments if he is guilty of any of these sins: others will eat his harvest and uproot his crops (v. 8); his wife will become another man's servant and mistress (v. 10); his arm will fall from his shoulder (v. 22); his harvest will be weeds and thistles (v. 40). He made it clear that he was willing to face the righteous judgment of God (vv. 14, 23, 28) along with these other judgments.

When the words of Job were ended, everybody sat in silence, wondering what would happen next. Would God send immediate judgment and prove Job guilty? Or would He accept Job's challenge, appear to him, and give Job opportunity to defend himself? Perhaps God would speak from heaven and answer Job's questions.

Job had challenged God because he was sure God would vindicate him. Job's three friends were sure that God would condemn him.

What will God do? The answer may surprise you!

CHAPTER ELEVEN
ELIHU HAS THE ANSWERS
Job 32–33

"A vain man may become proud and imagine himself pleasing to all when he is in reality a universal nuisance."

—BENEDICT SPINOZA

Job was silent. He had ended his defense and given oath that he was not guilty of the sins he had been accused of by his friends. Job had challenged God either to vindicate him or pass sentence on him. The trial had gone on long enough, and it was time for the Judge to act.

Job's three friends were silent, appalled that Job had dared to speak so boldly *to* God and *about* God. They were sure that God's judgment of Job was the next thing on the agenda.

God was silent. No fire came from heaven, and no voice spoke in divine wrath. The silence was God's eloquent witness to the three friends that they were wrong in what they had said both about Job and about God. It was also God's witness to Job that the God of the universe is not at the beck and call of His creatures. God doesn't appear just because somebody thinks it's time for a showdown.

At the famous "Speaker's Corner" in London's Hyde Park, a man denouncing Christianity issued this challenge: "If there is a God, I will give Him five minutes to strike me dead!" He took out his watch and waited. After five minutes, he smiled and said, "My friends, this proves that there is no God!"

A Christian believer in the crowd called to him, "Do you think you can exhaust the patience of Almighty God in five minutes?"

However, in the crowd around the ash heap, one person was not silent. It was Elihu, a man so unknown that his full pedigree had to be given so people could identify him (Job 32:2). Neither Job (1:1) nor his three friends (2:11) needed that kind of detailed identification for others to know them.

Elihu gave a long speech—six chapters in our Bible—in which he explained the character of God and applied this truth to Job's situation. One way to outline his speech is as follows:

1. God is speaking through me (Job 32; note v. 8)
2. God is gracious (Job 33; note v. 24)
3. God is just (Job 34—35; note 34:10-12)
4. God is great (Job 36—37; note 36:5, 26)

While Elihu said some of the same things as the other speakers, his purpose was different from theirs. He was not trying to prove that Job was a sinner, but that Job's view of God was wrong. Elihu introduced a new truth into the debate: that God sends suffering, not necessarily to punish us for our sins, but to keep us from sinning (33:18, 24) and to make us better persons (36:1-15). Paul would have agreed with the first point (2 Cor. 12:7-10) and the writer of Hebrews with the second (Heb. 12:1-11).

Let's consider the first two of Elihu's affirmations about God.

God is Speaking Through Me (Job 32)

Elihu emphasized that he had waited patiently before speaking, and he gave two reasons. For one thing, he was younger than Job and the three friends; and youth must respect age and experience (Job 32:4, 6-7). It would have been a terrible breach of etiquette had Elihu interrupted his elders.

His second reason was because he wanted to hear the complete debate and have all the arguments before him (v. 11; Prov. 18:13). The fact that Elihu quoted from their speeches indicates that he had listened closely and remembered what each man said (Job 32:12). Like many "young theologians," Elihu had a bit of youthful conceit in his speeches ("Hear what I know!"—vv. 6, 10, 17; 33:1-3); but for the most part, he was a sincere young man who really thought he could help Job find answers to his questions.

Having introduced himself into the discussion, Elihu then gave four reasons to explain why it was important for him to speak and for them to listen. After all, he was a "nobody"; and he had to convince them that what he had to say was worth hearing.

He was indignant (Job 32:1-3, 5). Four times in these verses we are told that Elihu was angry. He was angry at the three friends for not refuting Job, and he was angry at Job for justifying himself rather than God. Job claimed that God was wrong, and the three friends couldn't prove that Job was wrong! Bildad, Zophar, and Eliphaz had given up the cause (v. 15) and were waiting for God to come and deal personally with Job (vv. 12-13). Elihu was disgusted at their failure.

"It is easy to fly into a passion—anybody can do that," wrote Aristotle. "But to be angry with the right person to the right extent and at the right time and with the right object and in the right way—that is not easy, and it is not everyone who can do it."

He was inspired (Job 32:8-10). Age should bring wisdom, but there is no guarantee that it will (Prov. 16:31). Alas, there are old fools as well as young fools! As a younger man, Elihu couldn't claim to have wide experience in the ways of God and men; but he claimed to have something better: the insight of the Spirit of God. The Holy Spirit had instructed Elihu's spirit (1 Cor. 2:11) and revealed God's truths to him. Elihu didn't need the wisdom that comes with experience, for he had been taught by God (Ps. 119:97-100).

This explains why Elihu repeatedly exhorted Job and his friends to listen to him (Job 32:10; 33:1, 31, 33; 34:2, 10, 16; 37:14). It also explains why he emphasized the phrases "mine opinion" (32:6, 10, 17; "what I know" in the NIV) and "my words" (33:1-3). It isn't every day that you can hear a man who has been inspired by God, so you had better listen!

He was impartial (Job 32:14, 21-22). "Now he has not directed his words against me, so I will not answer him with your words" (v. 14, NKJV). Elihu made it clear that he had no reason for taking sides since neither Job nor any of the three friends had attacked him personally. Elihu also said that he would avoid rehashing the same arguments that they had used, though he didn't fully live up to that promise.

Elihu may have been impartial but he was by no means neutral. He was too angry for that! He promised to deal only with issues, but some of the things he said in his anger were more personal than philosophical. But he did keep his promise and not flatter anyone (vv. 21-22). As you read his speech, you will notice that six times he addressed Job by his first name (33:1; 34:5, 7, 35, 36; 35:16), something that even Job's three closest friends had not done in their many speeches. In the East, it was most unusual for a younger man to address his elders in such a familiar way.

He was impelled (Job 32:16-20). Elihu had waited a long time for the opportunity to speak; and while he was waiting, the pressure within him had built up to the bursting point. He was full of words like a wineskin full of wine. As the new wine ferments, it produces gas that inflates the wineskin; and if the skin is old and dry, it will break (Matt. 9:17). If anybody had suggested that Elihu was "full of gas," he would have been offended; because to him, it was God's Spirit compelling him to speak. Elihu had a mandate from God to tell everybody what he knew. Little did he know that, when God finally appeared on the scene, He would completely ignore Elihu and all that he said.

God is Gracious
(Job 33)

This is a remarkable speech because it introduces into the debate a new insight into the purpose of suffering. Job's friends had argued that his suffering was evidence that God was punishing him for his sins, but Elihu now argues that sometimes God permits us to suffer *to keep us from sin.* In other words, suffering may be *preventive* and not *punitive.* (See Paul's experience recorded in 2 Cor. 12:7-10.) God does all He can to keep us from sinning and going into the pit of death, and this is evidence of His grace (Job 33:24).

Before launching into his argument, Elihu assured Job that his words were sincere and given by God's Spirit, so Job had no reason to be afraid (vv. 1-7). Elihu didn't claim to have any "inside track" with God; he was made of clay just like Job. He promised not to be heavy-handed in his speaking, and he invited Job to feel free to reply. Elihu didn't want this to be a monologue, but that's exactly what it turned out to be. Either Job was silenced by what Elihu said, or Elihu didn't pause long enough for Job to speak (see vv. 31, 33), or Job didn't think it was worthwhile to respond.

Having assured Job that his words would be helpful and not hurtful, Elihu then proceeded to quote what Job had said about himself (vv. 8-11). Job's words will form the premise for Elihu's argument.

First, Elihu said that Job had claimed to be sinless (v. 9), *which was not what Job had said.* That Job claimed to be sinless was Zophar's interpretation, not Job's

declaration (11:4). Job did say that he did not lie (6:30), that he was not wicked (10:7), that he was just and upright (12:4), and that he had not disobeyed God (23:11-12); but he never said he was sinless. He consistently maintained his integrity (2:3; 27:4-5), but never said he was perfect. In fact, he denied perfection (9:20-21). Elihu's basic premise was weak because he confused Zophar's words with Job's words. It may have sounded like Job was claiming to be *sinless,* but he was only saying that he was *blameless,* which is an entirely different thing.

Second, Elihu quoted Job as saying that God was unjust and was treating him like an enemy (33:10-11). This quotation was true (13:24, 27; 16:9; 19:7, 11). In his speeches, Job had repeatedly asked God why He was attacking him and why He didn't give him a fair trial. Elihu's great concern was not to debate what Job said about himself but to refute what Job said about God.

This "young theologian" knew something about public speaking because Job 33 is a model address. First, he stated his thesis in verses 12-14: God is greater than man and speaks to him in ways that he may not always recognize. He then described three different ways that God may speak to man: dreams and visions (vv. 15-18), suffering (vv. 19-22), and the ministry of the mediating angel (vv. 23-33).

The word "pit" is used five times in verses 14-33. God's purpose in discipline is to save people from death (James 5:19-20) by breaking their pride and bringing them back to the place of obedience (Job 33:17-18). God seeks to keep them from the pit (v. 18), but rebellious sinners *draw near* to the pit (v. 22), then *go down* to the pit (v. 24), and *into* the pit (v. 28). When it is almost too late, the Mediator brings them *back from* the pit (v. 30), and they are rescued. "God does all these things to a man—twice, even three times—to turn back his soul from the pit, that the light of life may shine on him" (vv. 29-30, NIV). God is "not willing that any should perish" (2 Peter 3:9).

Dreams and visions (Job 33:15-18). In Bible times, God sometimes spoke to people through dreams and visions; today His Spirit directs us primarily through His Word (Heb. 1:1-2). If sinners have frightening visions or dreams, it might shock them and keep them from committing the sins they had planned. Job himself experienced terrifying dreams (Job 7:13-14), and Eliphaz had an unforgettable night vision (4:12-21). God sends dreams and visions in order to "open the ears of men," which gets them to listen to God's Word and obey. If they don't humble themselves, they may go down to the pit of death.

A man stopped a stranger on a New York City street and said, "Can you share a dream with me? I'm on my way to my psychiatrist, and I haven't slept for a week. I desperately need a dream to tell him!"

Not all dreams have hidden meanings, and not all dreams come from God with special messages in them. More than one nightmare has been caused by improper diet! People who plan their lives around what they learn from the "dream book" are asking for confusion rather than direction. God can use dreams to shake the confidence of a proud sinner, but this is not His normal approach today.

Suffering (Job 33:19-22). In *The Problem of Pain*, C.S. Lewis says, "God whispers to us in our pleasures, speaks in our conscience, but shouts in our pains: it is His megaphone to rouse a deaf world." God sometimes uses pain to warn us, humble us, and bring us to the place of submission (Heb. 12:1-11). Elihu describes a sick man, suffering on his bed, wasting away because he has no appetite. (Is this a picture of Job? See 6:7; 7:3-6; 16:8; 17:7; 19:20.) But this man is suffering because God wants to get his attention and prevent him from breaking God's law.

It is a mistake to say that all suffering comes from God, because we cause some suffering ourselves. Careless driving may lead to an accident that will make many people suffer. Improper eating may upset the body and cause abused organs to protest with pain. There is pleasure in sin (Heb. 11:25), but sin causes suffering. "The way of transgressors is hard" (Prov. 13:15). If people defy the Law of God, there is a price to pay.

And we must not say that all suffering is a punishment for sin. Elihu argues that sometimes God permits suffering *in order to keep people from sinning and going to the pit*. God gave Paul a "thorn in the flesh" to keep him from getting proud, and Paul learned to thank God for it (2 Cor. 12:7-10). Elihu hoped that Job would submit to God, accept his painful situation, and get from it the blessings God had for him.

Nobody wants to be sick; everybody prays for healing. But the British Congregational theologian P.T. Forsyth said, "It is a greater thing to pray for pain's conversion than its removal." That's what Paul learned to do with his thorn in the flesh. What might have been a weapon to tear him down became, by the grace of God, a tool to build him up! Had he lost that messenger of pain, Paul might have become proud of his spiritual achievements; and that pride might have led him into sin.

Elihu has presented two ways that God speaks to people in order to keep them from the pit: visions and dreams, and sickness and pain. Now he presents the third.

The ministry of the mediating angel (Job 33:23-33). The book of Job opens with a description of God's heavenly court where the angels ("sons of God") report for duty (Job 33; 1:6ff; 2:1ff). Eliphaz mentions the angels in 4:18 and possibly in 5:1 ("holy ones"), and angels are also mentioned in 38:7 as rejoicing at the creation of the world. Except for this present passage, these are the only references to angels in the book.

Elihu paints an awesome picture. The sinner has been warned by dreams and visions and has been chastened by sickness and suffering. He is drawing near to the grave, and "the destroyers" ("messengers of death," NIV) are about to capture him (33:22). Then a special messenger suddenly stands up ("one among a thousand") and pleads his case. This messenger has a twofold ministry: he tells the sufferer what he ought to do (v. 23), and he intercedes with God to have the person restored.

It seems likely that this interceding angel is the Angel of the Lord, our Lord Jesus Christ, the Mediator who gave His life as a ransom for sinners (1 Tim. 2:5; Mark 10:45). As the Angel of the Lord, the Son of God visited the earth in Old Testament times to deliver special messages and accomplish important tasks (Gen. 16:9; 22:11; Ex. 3:2; Judg. 6:11). But Elihu saw this Angel not only as a Mediator between God and men, but also as the Provider of the ransom for sinners.

This is the heavenly "mediator" that Job has been asking for throughout the debate! Job wanted an "umpire" to bring him and God together for a trial (Job 9:33), a heavenly "witness" to argue his case before God (16:19), a "redeemer" who would vindicate him even after his death (19:25). The ministry of this Angel is purely an act of God's grace (33:24). "Spare him from going down to the pit; I have found a ransom for him" (v. 24, NIV). That sounds like our Lord Jesus Christ, who is both our Mediator and our Ransom (1 Tim. 2:5-6).

The concept of "the ransom" is woven into the fabric of biblical theology. The Hebrew word means "to atone for sin by the offering of a substitute." The condemned sinner can't be set free by the paying of some cheap price such as money (Ps. 49:7-9), good works, or good intentions. It must be a ransom that God will accept, and God asks for the shedding of blood (Lev. 16–17). Job didn't ask his three friends to ransom him because he knew they couldn't (Job 6:21-23). Only God can provide the ransom, and He did. If God has provided a ransom for lost sinners about to go down into the pit, *how foolish of them not to receive it!*

Elihu promised Job that God would radically alter his situation if only he would humble himself. It would be like a "new birth"! (33:25; see John 3) He would once more enjoy prayer and fellowship with God (Job 33:26). He would confess his sins and admit that God had punished him far less than he deserved (v. 27). Job would move out of the darkness into the light and gladly bear witness of God's redemption (v. 28).

Job 33:31-33 suggests that Elihu wanted Job's response, but at the same time Elihu wanted Job to keep quiet! Elihu was filled to the brim with his subject and didn't want to stop talking. But Job didn't reply *because he was waiting for God to speak.* Job had already stated his case and thrown down the gauntlet. What Elihu thought about him or said to him made little difference to Job.

Job had taken his case to a much higher court; and when Elihu finishes speaking, the Judge will appear.

CHAPTER TWELVE
ELIHU EXPLAINS AND DEFENDS GOD
Job 34-37

"What, then, is the God I worship?
… You are the most hidden from us
and yet the most present among us,
the most beautiful and yet the most
strong, ever enduring; and yet we
cannot comprehend you."
—St. Augustine

Theology ("the science of God")
used to be called "the queen of
sciences" because it deals with
the most important knowledge
we can have, the knowledge of God.
Theology is a necessary science, but it is
also a difficult science; for it is our attempt
to know the Unknowable (Rom. 11:33-36).
God has revealed Himself in creation, in
providence, in His Word, and supremely
in His Son; but our understanding of
what God has revealed may not always
be clear.

"The essence of idolatry," wrote A.W.
Tozer, "is the entertainment of thoughts
about God that are unworthy of Him"
(*The Knowledge of the Holy*, Harper & Row,
p. 11). So, whoever attempts to explain
and defend the Almighty must have the
humble heart of a worshiper; for "knowledge puffs up, but love builds up" (1 Cor.
8:1, NIV).

As you read Elihu's speeches, you get
the impression that he was not growing;
he was swelling. You also get the impression that his listeners' minds were wandering, because he kept exhorting them to
listen carefully (Job 33:1, 31, 33; 34:2, 10,
16). In the last two thirds of his speech,

Elihu explained and defended *the justice
of God* (Job 34–35) and *the greatness of God*
(Job 36–37).

God is Just
(Job 34–35)
Elihu had promised not to use flattery
(Job 32:21), but he came close to it in 34:2
when he addressed his audience as "wise
men" and "men of learning" (NIV).
Actually, he was flattering himself;
because if these "learned wise men" were
willing to listen to him, they must have
thought that he was more learned and
wise than they! Quoting Job's words (v. 3;
12:11), Elihu urged them to use discernment as they "tasted" his words, so that
he and they might "learn together what is
good" (34:4, NIV). Elihu compared his
speaking to the enjoyment of a tasteful
and nourishing meal.

Elihu listed two of Job's complaints to
be discussed: "God is unjust" (vv. 5-6)
and "There is no profit in serving God"
(vv. 7-9). He answered the first complaint
in verses 10-37 and the second in Job 35.

"God is unjust" (Job 34:5-6, 10-37).
The injustice of God was one of the major
themes in Job's speeches. He felt that he
was being treated like a sinner, and yet
God would not "come to court" and tell
Job what he had done wrong. (See 9:2, 17-
20; 19:6-7; 27:2.) Elihu recalled Job saying
that he was innocent and had been denied
justice (34:5; 10:7; 6:29), and that God was
shooting arrows at him (34:6; 6:4).

Elihu presented three arguments to
prove that there is no injustice with God.
To begin with, *if God is unjust, then He is
not God* (34:10-15). "Far be it from God,
that He should do wickedness, and from
the Almighty, that He should commit
iniquity" (v. 10). "It is unthinkable that
God would do wrong, that the Almighty
would pervert justice" (v. 12, NIV).

Abraham asked, "Shall not the Judge of all the earth do right?" (Gen. 18:25) and the obvious answer is yes!

If God is truly God, then He is perfect; and if He is perfect, then He cannot do wrong. An unjust God would be as unthinkable as a square circle or a round triangle. According to Elihu, what seems injustice to us is really justice: God is paying sinners back for what they do (Job 34:11). In fact, God is so just that He has ordained that *sin itself will punish the evildoer.* (See Pss. 7:15; 9:15-16; 35:8.) There is no way to escape the justice of God.

Elihu emphasized that God is sovereign, and a sovereign God can be indicted by no law or judged by no court. The king can do no wrong. God was not *appointed* to His throne, so He can't be taken from it (Job 34:13). To say that God is unjust is to say that He is not God and therefore has no right to be on the throne. But God controls our very breath and can take our lives away in an instant (vv. 14-15; Acts 17:25, 28). "It is of the LORD's mercies that we are not consumed, because his compassions fail not" (Lam. 3:22).

The book of Job magnifies the sovereignty of God. From the very first chapter, it is obvious that God is in control; for even Satan is told what he can and cannot do. During the debate, it appears that God is absent; but He is aware of how Job feels and what Job and his friends say. Thirty-one times in the book of Job, God is called "the Almighty." Elihu was right on target: God is sovereign and cannot do wrong.

His second argument is that *if God were unjust, there could be no just government on earth* (Job 34:16-20). As a respected elder, Job had participated in local government and had helped to bring justice to the afflicted (29:7-17). But all human government was established by God (Gen. 9:1-7;

Rom. 13:1-7); so if mortal man can execute justice on earth, why can't a holy and sovereign God execute justice from heaven? He can dethrone kings and remove nobles, and He shows no partiality (Dan. 4:25, 32, 35). If the God who rules the world were unjust, there could be no order or harmony; and everything would fall apart.

However, Elihu made a big mistake in singling out and emphasizing only one divine attribute, the justice of God; for God is also loving and gracious. (Bildad had made the same mistake in his speeches.) In His wisdom, God devised a plan of redemption that satisfies both His justice and His love (Rom. 3:21-31). Because of the Cross, God can redeem sinners and still magnify His righteousness and uphold His holy law.

Elihu's third argument is that *if God were unjust, then He must not see what is going on in the world* (Job 34:21-30). But God is omniscient and sees all things! A human judge, with his limitations, hears a case and makes the best decision he can, and sometimes he's wrong. But God sees every step we take, and there is no place where we can hide from Him (Ps. 139:7-12). Job wanted God to meet him in court so he could present his case, but what could Job tell God that God didn't already know? "God has no need to examine men further, that they should come before Him for judgment" (Job 34:23, NIV). Unlike human officials, God is not obligated to conduct an inquiry and gather evidence; He knows everything and can judge with perfect wisdom.

One of Job's complaints was that God was silent and had hidden His face from him (9:11; 23:1-9), but Elihu had an answer for that: "But if He remains silent, who can condemn Him? If He hides His face, who can see Him?" (34:29, NIV) In

Job 24, Job had accused God of ignoring men's sins; but what right had he to judge the Judge? God waited four centuries before judging the wicked nations in Canaan (Gen. 15:13-16) and 120 years before sending the Flood (6:3). Sinners should be grateful that God gives them time to repent (2 Peter 3:9).

God rules over nations and individuals (Job 34:29), but He is not responsible for their sins; for He gives them freedom to make decisions. They also have the freedom to turn from their sins and trust God. Because of this, Elihu closes this part of his speech with an appeal to Job that he confess his sins and repent (vv. 31-33). "Ask God to teach you what you don't know," he counsels, "and promise not to sin like this again" (see v. 32). God rewards us on *His* terms, not our terms; and one of His requirements is that we repent and turn from our sins.

Elihu paused and gave Job opportunity to speak (v. 33), but Job said nothing. This may have angered Elihu even more because he ended this part of the address with a terrible accusation against Job. He said that Job lacked knowledge and insight, that he was rebellious and spoke proudly against God. Clapping the hands is today a sign of approval, but in that day it was a gesture of mockery and contempt (27:23; Lam. 2:15). Elihu concluded that Job needed *even more testing!* (Job 34:36) Perhaps that would bring him to his senses.

Having disposed of Job's first complaint, Elihu turns to the second one. *"There is no profit in obeying God" (Job 34:7-9; 35:1-16).* Again, Elihu tries to throw Job's own words back in his face: "I am innocent" (10:7; 12:4; 27:6), and "What have I gained by obeying God?" (9:29-31; 21:15) Job did make the first statement, but the second is not an accurate quota-

tion of his words. *Job never did bargain with God as Satan said he would* (1:9, 21; 2:9-10). Eliphaz had discussed this topic (Job 22) and had come to the conclusion that neither man's piety nor his iniquity could make any difference to the character of God. But Elihu felt it was important to deal with the theme again.

Elihu asked his listeners to look up to the heavens and see how far away the clouds were, and then imagine how far God's throne was from the earth (35:5-7). Can a man's sins or good deeds on earth exert such power that they will travel all that distance and change the Almighty in heaven?

Then Elihu asked them to consider human society (vv. 8-16). Our sins or good works may affect people around us (v. 8), but God is not affected by them. Certainly God grieves over man's sins (Gen. 6:6) and delights in the obedience of the faithful (Ps. 37:23); but our good deeds can't bribe Him, and our misdeeds can't threaten Him. God's character is the same whether men obey Him or disobey Him. God can't change for the better because He is perfect, and He can't change for the worse because He is holy.

God cares for the birds and beasts, and they trust Him (Job 35:11; Matt. 6:25-34); but men made in the image of God don't cry out to God until they are under a terrible burden of oppression (Job 35:9). They forget God until trouble comes. But God knows that their prayers are insincere, so He doesn't answer them (vv. 12-13). This explains why Job's prayers haven't been answered: his heart was not right with God (v. 14).

But even if God doesn't relieve the burden, He can give the trusting sufferer "songs in the night" (v. 10; Ps. 42:8; 77:6). "Any man can sing in the day," said Charles Spurgeon. "It is easy to sing when we can read the notes by daylight; but he is the skillful singer who can sing when there is not a ray of light by which to read." The Lord gave "songs in the night" to Jesus before He went to the cross (Matt. 26:30) and to Paul and Silas in the prison in Philippi (Acts 16:25). If God doesn't see fit to remove our burdens, He always gives strength to bear them—and a song to sing while doing it!

Elihu dismisses Job's complaint that he can't see God. The important thing is that *God sees Job* and knows his case completely (Job 35:14). Job's situation won't be changed by his empty talk and many words (v. 16), so the only thing for Job to do is wait and trust (v. 14).

God is gracious (Job 33), and God is just (Job 34–35); but God is also great and mighty (Job 36–37), and Elihu thought that Job needed to recognize how great God is.

God is Great
(Job 36–37)

"Behold, God is mighty" (Job 36:5). "Behold, God exalteth by His power" (v. 22). "Behold, God is great" (v. 26). In these two chapters, Elihu magnifies the greatness of God in His *merciful purpose for man* (vv. 1-25) and in His *mighty power in nature* (36:26–37:13). He concludes his speech by making one last appeal to Job to fear the Lord and repent (vv. 14-24).

God's merciful purpose for man (Job 36:1-25). Elihu's self-importance reaches new heights as he introduces the last third of his speech (vv. 1-4). His listeners must have been getting restless; otherwise, why did he have to say, "Bear with me a little [longer]"? (v. 2) The statement "I will fetch my knowledge from afar" (v. 3) suggests that either he is boasting of wide knowledge or of getting his knowledge right from heaven. And to call himself

"one perfect in knowledge" (v. 4, NIV) is hardly an evidence of humility!

(1) Explanation (vv. 5-15). The fact that God is great and mighty does not mean that He ignores man or has no concern for individuals. "God is mighty, but does not despise men; He is mighty and firm in His purpose" (v. 5, NIV). What is that purpose? To punish the wicked and help the afflicted ("poor," vv. 6, 15, KJV). Elihu contrasts God's dealings with the arrogant wicked and the afflicted righteous. "He does not keep the wicked alive, but gives justice to the afflicted" (v. 6, NASB).

Job thought that God was ignoring him, but God keeps His eyes on the righteous (v. 7; 1 Peter 3:12) and eventually transforms their circumstances. He lifts them from the ash heap to the throne (Luke 1:52-53) and sets them free from their chains (Job 36:7-8). He chastens us that He might correct us and teach us the right way to live. If we learn our lesson and obey, He will bless us once again. But if we rebel, He will destroy us (vv. 9-12).

The response of the heart is the key. The hypocrites ("godless in heart," NIV) only heap up wrath as they harden themselves against God. No matter how much God disciplines them, they refuse to cry out for help. But the humble in heart get God's message ("He speaks to them in their affliction," v. 15, NIV) and turn from their sins. The phrase "the unclean" in verse 14 refers to the male prostitutes at the various idolatrous shrines (Deut. 23:17). Elihu chose this image as a picture of the very depths of shame and sin. The wicked not only die young (Job 36:14; 20:5, 11), but they die in disgrace.

(2) Application (vv. 16-25). Job must make a decision. "He [God] is wooing you from the jaws of distress to a spacious place" (v. 16, NIV; Ps. 18:19). Job's table was laden with suffering when it could be

laden with the choicest of foods. How would Job respond?

Elihu saw several dangers ahead for Job and tried to warn him. The first was that Job might look for some "shortcut" for getting out of trouble and thereby miss the message God had for him. Job might agree to let somebody "buy his way out," but no amount of money could do that (Job 36:18-19). *The Wall Street Journal* said it best: "Money is an article which may be used as a universal passport to everywhere except heaven, and as a universal provider for everything except happiness."

The second danger was that Job might consider taking his own life (v. 20). "The night" and "darkness" are images of death, and Job often expressed a longing to die (3:1-9, 20-23; 7:21; 10:18-22). Many sufferers have committed suicide in order to escape their hopeless situations, but there was not much danger that Job would take this route. Job was a man of faith and was not about to go into God's presence uninvited.

Elihu saw a third danger, that Job might give up all hope and turn to a life of sin (36:21). In my own pastoral ministry, I have counseled people who were so bitter against God that they abandoned their professions of faith and went back into the world. "If life is going to be this tough," they say, "then we might just as well enjoy ourselves while we can." They forget that there can be no true enjoyment without God, and that sin eventually brings its own harvest of suffering and sorrow.

Finally, Elihu urged Job to catch a new vision of the greatness of God and start praising Him (vv. 22-25). God wants to teach us through our sufferings (v. 22), and one evidence that we are learning our lessons is that we praise and thank Him,

even for trials. "Glorify Him for His mighty works for which He is so famous" (v. 24, TLB). "Praise changes things" just as much as "prayer changes things."

God's mighty power in nature (Job 36:26–37:24). "Behold, God is great, and we know Him not" (36:26). This is the theme of the last part of Elihu's speech; and he illustrated it with the works of God in nature, specifically, God's control of His world during the seasons of the year.

(1) Autumn (36:27–37:5). In the East, after the heat and drought of summer, both the land and the people welcome the autumn rains. It is interesting to discover Elihu's insight into the "water cycle" of nature (evaporation, condensation, precipitation) and the need for electricity (lightning) to help the "system" work.

With the mind of a scientist but the heart of a poet, Elihu describes the storm. He begins with the formation of the clouds (36:26-29), then the release of power by the lightning (vv. 30-32), and then the sound of the thunder (36:33–37:5). To Elihu, the lightning is the weapon of God (36:32), and the thunder is the voice of God (37:2, 4-5). In the East, you can see a storm brewing miles away and with fascination watch as it approaches.

What was Elihu's response to the drama of the storm? For one thing, the storm reminded him of God's sovereignty and God's goodness. "This is the way He governs the nations and provides food in abundance" (36:31, NIV). It also aroused in him a sense of awe at the mighty power of God (37:1). David recorded a similar experience in Psalm 29.

(2) Winter (vv. 6-10). At some point, the autumn rains become winter ice and snow. Workers must stop their labor, and wild animals retreat to the protection of their

dens. God breathes on the waters, and they freeze. What the weatherman calls "meteorological phenomena," Elihu calls the miracle work of Almighty God. Isaac Watts agreed with Elihu when he wrote:

I sing the goodness of the Lord
That filled the earth with food;
He formed the creatures with His word,
And then pronounced them good.

There's not a plant or flower below
But makes Thy glories known;
And clouds arise and tempests blow
By order from Thy throne.

(3) Spring (vv. 11-13). Eventually the warmer winds start to blow, the snow and ice melt, and the rain clouds appear once again. Elihu knew that the wind plays a most important part in the world's weather. Nobody can predict exactly what the wind will do (John 3:8), but God is in complete control (Ps. 148:8). The "water cycle" operates effectively: the clouds are full of water, the lightning flashes, and the rain falls. Sometimes God sends the storms for discipline (Job 37:13; Gen. 6–8; Ex. 9:13-26; 1 Sam. 12:16-19); but for the most part, the rain is the gift of His love and mercy (Job 37:13).

(4) Summer (vv. 14-18). Now the clouds "hang poised" (v. 16, NIV), and everything is still. The summer sun heats the air, the south wind (the "sirocco") blows from the desert, and people start to "swelter in [their] clothes" (v. 17, NIV). The sky is like a brass mirror, and nobody feels like doing anything but resting.

But Elihu was doing much more than delivering a poetical, scientific lecture on the four seasons. He wanted Job to consider the greatness of God and the wonders of nature *and realize how little Job really knew about God and His working in this world.* Elihu asked Job three rhetorical questions—about the clouds, the lightning, the wind, and the rainless skies. "Can you explain these things?" he asked. "Can you control them?"

This led to Elihu's final thrust: "If you can't explain to us the everyday things of nature, then how will you ever prepare a court case to defend yourself before God?" He then warned Job that to challenge God might lead to Job's being swallowed up by God's judgment (v. 20). Verses 21-22 describe the "clear shining after rain" (2 Sam. 23:4), the blue sky, the bright sun, the "golden splendor" and "awesome majesty" of God (NIV). "You can't even look at the sun," says Elihu, "and yet you want to meet God face to face!"

Elihu's closing words remind us that, even though we can't fully understand God, we know that He is great and just and does not afflict men to no purpose. What should our personal response be? "Therefore, fear Him!" Job had come to that same conclusion after pondering the works of God in the world (Job 28:24-28).

It is possible that while Elihu was speaking, an actual storm was in the making in the distance; and when he finished, the storm broke—*and God was in the storm!*

Job will now get what he'd been asking for: a personal meeting with God. Was he ready? *Are we ready?*

INTERLUDE

With all his verbosity and lack of humility, Elihu did say some good things that Job needed to hear. Elihu's use of rhetorical questions in Job 37:14-18 prepared Job for the series of questions Jehovah would ask him in Job 38–41. Unlike the three friends, Elihu assessed Job's problem accurately: Job's *actions* may have been right—he was not the sinner his three friends described him to be—but his *attitude* was wrong. He was not the "saint" Job saw himself to be. Job was slowly moving toward a defiant, self-righteous attitude that was not at all healthy. It was this "know-it-all" attitude that God exposed and destroyed when He appeared to Job and questioned him.

So, even though God said nothing about Elihu, the man did have a helpful ministry to Job. Unfortunately, Job wouldn't accept it.

CHAPTER THIRTEEN
THE FINAL EXAMINATION
Job 38–42

"I had a million questions to ask God; but when I met Him, they all fled my mind; and it didn't seem to matter."

—CHRISTOPHER MORLEY

The storm that Elihu had been describing finally broke, and God spoke to Job out of the storm. The answer to Job's problems was not an *explanation about God*, such as the three friends and Elihu had given, but a *revelation of God*. The four men had declared and defended the greatness of God but had failed to persuade Job. When God displayed His majesty and greatness, it humbled Job and brought him to the place of silent submission before God. That was the turning point.

Swiss psychologist Dr. Paul Tournier wrote in his book *Guilt and Grace* (Harper & Row, p. 86), "For God's answer is not an idea, a proposition, like the conclusion of a theorem; it is Himself. He revealed Himself to Job; Job found personal contact with God."

We prefer that God speak to us in the sunshine, but sometimes He must speak out of the storm. This is how He spoke to Israel on Mount Sinai (Ex. 19:16-19; Heb. 12:18) and centuries later to Elijah (1 Kings 19:8-11). Ezekiel saw the glory of God in a storm and heard the voice of God speaking to him (Ezek. 1–2). Experiencing this majestic demonstration of God's power made Job very susceptible to the message God had for him.

God's address to Job centered on His works in nature and consisted of seventy-seven questions interspersed with divine commentary relating to the questions. The whole purpose of this interrogation was to make Job realize his own inadequacy and inability to meet God *as an equal* and defend his cause.

"Then summon me, and I will answer," Job had challenged God, "or let me speak, and You reply" (Job 13:22, NIV). God had now responded to Job's challenge.

God's address can be summarized in three questions:

1. "Can you explain My creation?" (38:1-38)
2. "Can you oversee My creation?" (38:39–39:30)
   Job's first response (40:1-5)
3. "Can you subdue My creation?" (40:6–41:34)
   Job's second response (42:1-6)

The first question dealt with God's power and wisdom in bringing the universe into being. The second dealt with His providential care of His creatures, and the third centered on two creatures (probably the hippopotamus and the crocodile) that defy man's ability to subdue them. When Job repented of his self-righteousness, God restored him (vv. 7-17).

God is now called "the Lord," that is, Jehovah God, a name that (except for 12:9) has not been used in the book of Job since the first two chapters. In their speeches, the men have called Him "God" and "the Almighty" but not "Jehovah." This is the name that God revealed to Israel centuries later (Ex. 3:13ff), the name that speaks of His self-existence ("I AM THAT I AM") and His personal covenant relationship to His people.

"Can You Explain My Creation?" (Job 38:1-38)

Job was sure that his speeches had been filled with wisdom and knowledge, but God's first question put an end to that delusion: "Who is this that darkens My counsel with words without knowledge?" (Job 38:2, NIV) *The Living Bible* paraphrases it, "Why are you using your ignorance to deny My providence?" (TLB) God didn't question Job's integrity or sincerity; He only questioned Job's ability to explain the ways of God in the world. Job had spoken the truth about God (42:7), but his speeches had lacked humility. Job thought he knew about God, but he didn't realize how much he *didn't* know about God. Knowledge of our own ignorance is the first step toward true wisdom.

God began with *the Creation of the earth* (38:4-7) and compared Himself to a builder who surveys the site, marks off the dimensions, pours the footings, lays the cornerstone, and erects the structure. Creation was so wonderful that the stars sang in chorus and the angels (1:6; 2:1) shouted for joy, *but Job wasn't on the scene!* Then, how can he claim to know so much about the works of God?

From the beginning, God planned His Creation to be a garden of joyful beauty; but sin has turned Creation into a battlefield of ugliness and misery. Man in his selfishness is wasting natural resources, polluting land, air, water, and outer space, and so ravaging God's Creation that scientists wonder how long our planet will support life as we know it. Mahatma Gandhi was right: "There is a sufficiency in the world for man's need but not for man's greed."

The Lord then moved to a consideration of *the seas* (38:8-11). The image here is not *building* but *birth:* The seas were "knit together" in secret (v. 8; see Ps. 139:13) and then burst forth like a baby emerging from the womb. They were clothed with clouds and darkness, and their limits were set by God. "Who did all of this?" asked God of Job, and Job knew the answer.

The next aspect of Creation that God mentioned was *the sun* (Job 38:12-15). Here God pictured Himself as a general commanding His troops (the heavenly host). Had Job ever told the sun to rise and dispel the darkness? As the light spreads across the world, it reveals the details of the landscape, like the impression of a seal on clay or the unfolding of a beautiful garment taken out of a dark closet. But the light also puts an end to the evil deeds done in the darkness (John 3:19-21) and stops the criminal from attacking his victim.

The next eleven questions (Job 38:16-24) relate to the *vast dimensions of creation.*

The average child today knows more about the heights and depths of the universe than Job and his friends could ever have imagined. Had Job ever taken a walk in the depths of the sea and visited "the gates of Sheol"? Did he know how far down he had to go to find the ocean's floor? (The greatest depth measured so far is in the Pacific Ocean—35,810 feet or 6.78 miles.) And as for the reaches of space, *Voyager 2* spent twelve years going 4.4 billion miles, and in 1989 passed within 3,000 miles of Neptune's cloudbank!

In verses 19-21, God asked Job if he could calculate the reaches of east and west, or if the horizons were too much for him to measure. Then God inquired if Job understood the heights where the snow and hail were stored until God needed them (vv. 22-23; Ex. 9:18-26; Josh. 10:11) or the places where God kept His lightning and winds (Job 38:24). To be sure, God's words are full of irony; but that's what Job needed to puncture his pride and bring him to his knees in repentance.

How much did Job know about *the rain?* (vv. 25-28) Did he know how to plot its course so that it would accomplish God's purposes? Could he tell the lightning where and when to flash? Was he able to "father" rain and dew so that the land would have the water that it needed? Can he explain why God sends rain to the places where nobody lives? Then God turned from the spring and autumn rains to the winter *hail and frost* (vv. 29-30). If Job didn't know how the rain was "fathered," did he understand how the ice was "born"?

By this time, Job was probably wishing for a reprieve; but the Lord kept right on. He centered Job's attention on the heavens—the Pleiades, Orion the hunter, the various constellations ("Mazzaroth," KJV),

and the Bear ("Arcturus" with his cubs). Did Job understand the laws that governed their movements, and could he control these stars and planets and make them appear in their proper seasons? Man may study the heavens, but he can't control them.

The question "Canst thou set its dominion in the earth?" (v. 33) is translated in the NASB, "Or fix their rule over the earth?" The NIV reads, "Can you set up God's dominion over the earth?" and *The Living Bible* says, "Do you know ... how the heavens influence the earth?" Is there a suggestion here that the stars and planets have a direct influence over events on earth as the advocates of astrology maintain? Not at all. The statement can be paraphrased: "Job, if you understand so much about the heavenly bodies that are thought by some to affect the earth, then why don't you use that authority to change your situation?" The Lord was speaking with "holy sarcasm" and not revealing some profound truth.

In verses 34-38, the Lord called Job's attention to the clouds. Since Job knew the laws of the heavens, could he order the clouds to give rain? Was the lightning his servant, reporting for duty? Could Job take inventory of the clouds and "tip them over" like jars to make the rain come?

Creating all these things is one thing; maintaining them for man's good is quite something else. The Lord moved next into a series of questions about His providential working in the world. He moved from the inanimate world to the animate.

"Can You Oversee My Creation?" (Job 38:39–39:30)

The Lord brought before Job's imagination a parade of six beasts (lioness, goat, hind [deer], wild donkey, wild ox, and horse) and five birds (raven, ostrich, stork, hawk, and eagle). As he contemplated these creatures, Job had to answer the question, "Do you understand how they live and how to take care of them?" Obviously, Job's reply had to be no.

The providence of God is certainly remarkable (see Ps. 104). In His wisdom and power, God supervises the whole universe and makes sure that His creatures are cared for. "You open Your hand and satisfy the desire of every living thing" (Ps. 145:16, NKJV). We humans have a difficult time keeping the machinery of life operating successfully, but God runs the whole universe with such precision that we build our scientific laws on His creation.

Did Job know how to feed the lion cubs or the young ravens? (Job 38:39-41) Would he even know that they were hungry? Where could he find food for them? The ravens would know to find the carcasses left behind by the lions because God taught the birds (even unclean ravens!) how to find food.

God then moved from the topic of death to the subject of birth. Did Job know the gestation periods for the goats and deer and how the young are born? (39:1-4) How do the little ones grow up safely, and how does the mother know when they are ready to leave home? Shepherds and farmers assist their animals during pregnancy and birth, but the wild beasts bring forth their young alone.

The wild donkey (vv. 5-8), also known as the *onager*, roamed the wilderness freely and refused to be domesticated. It survived without human assistance because God taught it how to take care of itself. The wild ox (the *aurochs*) was another "loner" in the animal kingdom (vv. 9-12), refusing to yield to the authority of men. You couldn't keep him in your barn, harness him to your plow, or force him to do your threshing.

"Now, Job," asked the Lord, "if you can't succeed with these animals, how do you expect to succeed when you meet Me in court? How strong do you think you are?"

God then turned to a description of two birds, the stork ("peacock," KJV) and the ostrich (vv. 13-18). God asked Job no questions in this paragraph; He simply reminded him of the bizarre anatomy and behavior of the ostrich and suggested that perhaps Job could explain it.

The stork has beautiful wings that are very serviceable, but all the ostrich can do with her wings is fan the air! Why did God make a bird that couldn't fly but that could run faster than a horse? Why did He make a bird that puts her nest in such a vulnerable place where her eggs might be destroyed or eaten by a predator? Unlike most birds, why does she seem to be unmindful of her young?

The horse was next in line (vv. 19-25), an animal that was greatly admired and valued for strength and courage. This is a description of a war horse, not a farm horse; and you can visualize it prancing and pawing and eager to rush into the battle. When he hears the trumpet, he can't stand still, but runs so fast that he seems to be "eating up the ground." It was God, not Job, who made the horse with the strength and ability it needed to face danger and serve effectively on the field of battle.

The parade ended with two birds, the hawk and the eagle (vv. 26-30). Who gave the birds the instinct to migrate and the knowledge to build nests? Not Job! Eagles build their nests high on the cliffs; but God gave them keen eyesight so they can see their prey from afar, swoop down, and capture it. Eagles can also find corpses on which to feed themselves and their young because God made them that way.

Job's First Response
(Job 40:1-5)

God uses language that reflected Job's desire to take God to court and argue his case. "Will the faultfinder contend with the Almighty? Let him who reproves God answer it" (Job 40:2, NASB). God presented His case; now He gave Job opportunity to present his case. But Job has no case to present! His first words were, "Behold, I am vile!" which means, "I am insignificant and unworthy. I have no right to debate with God." Job had told his friends to cover their mouths (21:5), and others had covered their mouths when Job appeared (29:9); but now Job had to put his hand over his mouth lest he say something he shouldn't say (Prov. 30:32; Rom. 3:19). *Until we are silenced before God, He can't do for us what needs to be done.* As long as we defend ourselves and argue with God, He can't work for us and in us to accomplish His plan through us.

But Job was not quite broken and at the place of sincere repentance. He was silent but not yet submissive; so, God continued His address.

"Can You Subdue My Creation?"
(Job 40:6–41:34)

Instead of confronting Job again with the broad sweep of His creation, God selected only two creatures and asked Job to consider them. It's as though God were saying, "My whole universe is too much for you to handle. However, here are two of My best products. What can you do with them?"

The issue now is not the *power* of God but the *justice* of God (Job 40:8). Job had said that God was unjust in the way He treated him (6:29; 27:1-6) and in the way He failed to judge the wicked (21:29-31; 24:1-17). In 40:9-14, God asked, "Job, do you have the strength and holy wrath it takes to judge sinners? If so, then start judging them! Humble the proud sinners and crush the wicked! Bury them! You claim that you can do a better job than I can of bringing justice to the world, so I'll let you do it!"

However, before God turned Job loose on the sinners of the world, He asked him to put on his majestic robes and "practice" on two of His finest creatures, the hippopotamus (vv. 15-24) and the crocodile (41:1-34). If Job succeeded in subduing them, then he would qualify to execute judgment against a sinful world.

The hippopotamus (Job 40:15-24). Most students agree that the animal described is the hippopotamus, although some prefer the elephant or the water buffalo. The word "behemoth" is the transliteration of a Hebrew word that means "super-beast." Today's big-game hunter with his modern weapons would probably not be deterred by the hippo's size or strength, but this beast was a formidable enemy in the days of arrows and spears.

God reminded Job that He was the Creator of both the hippo and man (v. 15), and yet He made them different. The hippo eats grass and is strong and mighty; Job ate a variety of fine foods and was weak and unable to fight with the hippo. The hippo has a powerful body, with strong muscles and bones like iron rods; while man's body is (comparatively speaking) weak and easily damaged. The hippo lounges in the river, hidden under the water, and feeds on the vegetation that washes down from the hills; while man has to toil to earn his daily bread. A raging river doesn't frighten the hippo, and hunters don't alarm him. In Job's day, it was next to impossible to capture the hippopotamus; but how easy it is to capture a man!

"Now, Job," asks the Lord, "can you

capture and subdue this great creature? If so, then I'll believe that you have the power and wisdom to judge the world justly."

The crocodile (Job 41:1-34). The word "leviathan" is the transliteration of a Hebrew word, the root of which means "to twist, to writhe." People used the word to describe the "sea monsters" that were supposed to inhabit the Mediterranean. Psalm 104:25-26 may refer to whales or dolphins. The Jews used the word to describe their enemies (Isa. 27:1), especially Egypt (Ps. 74:13-14). Revelation 12:9 refers to Satan as "that old serpent." In mythology, the leviathan was a many-headed monster that ruled the waters and feared no man.

"Can you capture the leviathan?" asked the Lord. "And if you can, what will you do with him?" (see Job 41:1-11). Well, what can you do with a captured crocodile? You can't make a pet out of him, no matter how agreeable he seems to be (vv. 3-5); and the merchants won't want to buy him from you (v. 6). If you try to train him, you'll quit in a hurry and never try to do it again! (vv. 8-9) God drew a practical conclusion: "If you can't come to grips with the crocodile, how will you ever be able to stand before Me?" (vv. 10-11).

In verses 12-24, God gave a poetical description of this great creature's mighty limbs, fierce teeth and strong jaws, and impregnable covering (vv. 12-17). When the crocodile churns up the river and blows out water, the sun reflects from the vapor; and it looks like fire and smoke from a dragon's mouth (vv. 18-21). His armor is so strong that he can go anywhere without fear (vv. 22-24).

The chapter closes with a description of the leviathan's anger and courage (vv. 25-34). People flee from him in fear (v. 25), but he doesn't flee from them. In verses 26-29, God named eight different weapons that the leviathan laughs at and treats like pieces of straw or rotten wood. Just as this creature fears nothing *around* him, so he fears nothing *under* him; for his underside is protected with a covering like sharp pieces of pottery (v. 30). He fears no enemy on the land or in the water (vv. 31-32), for he makes the water to foam like the ingredients in the apothecary's mixing pot. And when he swims through the water, the wake looks like the white hair of an old man!

Job's Second Response
(Job 42:1-6)

Job knew he was beaten. There was no way he could argue his case with God. Quoting God's very words (Job 42:3-4), Job humbled himself before the Lord and acknowledged His power and justice in executing His plans (v. 2). Then Job admitted that his words had been wrong and that he had spoken about things he didn't understand (v. 3). Job withdrew his accusations that God was unjust and not treating him fairly. He realized that whatever God does is right and man must accept it by faith.

Job told God, "I can't answer Your questions! All I can do is confess my pride, humble myself, and repent." Until now, Job's knowledge of God had been indirect and impersonal; but that was changed. Job had met God personally and seen himself to be but "dust and ashes" (v. 6; 2:8, 12; Gen. 18:27).

"The door of repentance opens into the hall of joy," said Charles Spurgeon; and it was true for Job. In the climax of the book, Job *the sinner* became Job *the servant of God* (Job 42:7-9). Four times in these verses God called Job by that special Old Testament title "My servant" (see 1:8; 2:3). How did

Job serve God? By enduring suffering and not cursing God, and thereby silencing the devil! Suffering in the will of God is a ministry that God gives to a chosen few.

But Job the servant became Job *the intercessor.* God was angry with Job's three friends because they hadn't told the truth about Him (42:7), and they had to be reconciled to Job so he could pray for them. *Job became the umpire between God and his three friends!* By forgiving his friends and praying for them, Job brought back the blessing to his own life (v. 10). We only hurt ourselves when we refuse to forgive others.

Job ended up with twice as much as he had before. He had twenty children, ten with God and ten in his home. (He and his wife were also reunited.) Friends and relatives brought money for a "restoration fund," which Job must have used for purchasing breeders; and eventually, Job had twice as much livestock as before. He was once again a wealthy man. If the "double" formula also applied to Job's age, then he must have been seventy when the story began (Ps. 90:10), and God allowed Job to live twice as many years (Job 42:16).

In the East, parents are especially proud of beautiful daughters, and Job had three of them: Jemimah ("dove"), Keziah ("cinnamon") and Keren-Happuch ("horn of eye paint"). Jemimah had quietness, Keziah had perfume, and Keren-Happuch had the cosmetics!

To die "old and full of years" was the goal of every person. It means more than a long life; it means a rich and full life that ends well. This is the way Abraham and Isaac died (Gen. 25:8; 35:29), and also King David (1 Chron. 29:28).

POSTLUDE

We must not misinterpret this final chapter and conclude that every trial will end with all problems solved, all hard feelings forgiven, and everybody "living happily ever after." It just doesn't always happen that way! This chapter assures us that, no matter what happens to us, *God always writes the last chapter.* Therefore, we don't have to be afraid. We can trust God to do what is right, no matter how painful our situation might be.

But Job's greatest blessing was not the regaining of his health and wealth or the rebuilding of his family and circle of friends. His greatest blessing was *knowing God better and understanding His working in a deeper way.* As James wrote, "You have heard of the perseverance of Job and seen the purpose of the Lord, that the Lord is very compassionate and merciful" (James 5:11, NKJV). And Hebrews 12:11 reminds us: "Now, no chastening seems to be joyous for the present, but grievous; nevertheless, afterward it yields the peaceable fruit of righteousness to those who have been trained by it" (NKJV).

"In the whole story of Job," wrote G. Campbell Morgan, "we see the patience of God and endurance of man. When these act in fellowship, the issue is certain. It is that of the coming forth from the fire as gold, that of receiving the crown of life" (*The Answers of Jesus to Job,* Baker, p. 117).

No matter what God permits to come into our lives, He always has His "afterward." He writes the last chapter—and that makes it worth it all.

Therefore, BE PATIENT!

PSALMS

The book of Psalms has been and still is the irreplaceable devotional guide, prayer book, and hymnal of the people of God. The Hebrew title is "the book of praises" (*tehillim*). The Greek translation of the Old Testament (the Septuagint) used *psalmos* for *tehillim*; the word means "a song sung to the accompaniment of a stringed instrument." The Vulgate followed the Septuagint and used *psalmorum*, from the Latin *psalterium*, "a stringed instrument." *The King James* adopted the word, and thus we have the book of Psalms.

Writers. The writers of about two-thirds of the psalms are identified in the superscriptions. David leads the way with 73 psalms. He was Israel's "beloved singer of songs" (2 Sam. 23:1, NIV) and the man who organized the temple ministry, including the singers (1 Chron. 15:16; 16:7; 25:1). The sons of Korah, who served as musicians in the temple (1 Chron. 6:31ff; 15:17ff; 2 Chron. 20:19), wrote 11 psalms (42-49, 84, 85, 87), Asaph 12 psalms, King Solomon two (Pss. 72 and 127), Ethan wrote one (Ps. 89), and Moses one (Ps. 90). However, not all scholars give equal value to the titles of the psalms.

Organization. The book of Psalms is divided into five books, perhaps in imitation of the Five Books of Moses (Gen.-Deut.): 1-41, 42-72, 73-89, 90-106, 107-150. Each of the first three books ends with a double "amen," the fourth ends with an "amen" and a "hallelujah," and the last book closes the entire collection with a "hallelujah." The book of Psalms grew over the years as the Holy Spirit directed different writers and editors to compose and compile these songs and poems. David wrote 37 of the 41 psalms in Book I, so this was the beginning of the collection. Books II and III may have been collected by "the men of Hezekiah" (Prov. 25:1), a literary guild in King Hezekiah's day that copied and preserved precious Old Testament manuscripts. Hezekiah himself was a writer of sacred poetry (Isa. 38). Books IV and V were probably collected and added during the time of the scholar Ezra (Ezra 7:1-10). As with our modern hymnals, there are "collections within the collection," such as "The Songs of Degrees" (120-134), the writings of Asaph (Pss. 73-83), the psalms of the sons of Korah (42-49), and the "hallelujah psalms" (113-118, 146-150).

Poetry. Hebrew poetry is based on "thought lines" and not rhymes. If the second line repeats the first line in different words, as in Psalm 24:1-3, you have *synonymous parallelism.* If the second line contrasts with the first, as in Psalms 1:6 and 37:9, it is *antithetic parallelism.* When the second line explains and expands the first, the writer has used *synthetic parallelism* (Ps. 19:7-9), but when the second line completes the first, it is *climactic parallelism* (Ps. 29:1). With *iterative parallelism,* the second line repeats the thought of the first (Ps. 93), and in *alternate parallelism,* the alternate lines carry the same thought, as in Psalm 103:8-13. You don't bring these technical terms into the pulpit, but knowing what they mean can give you great help when you study. To interpret Psalm 103:3 as God's promise to heal every sickness is to ignore the synonymous parallelism of the verse: the forgiveness of sins is like the healing of disease (see Ps. 41:4).

Some of the psalms are laments to the Lord, written by people in dire circumstances. There are also messianic psalms that point forward to the Lord Jesus Christ. There are also psalms of praise and thanksgiving, royal psalms, wisdom psalms, psalms of affirmation and trust, penitential psalms, and even imprecatory psalms calling down God's wrath on the enemy. We will consider each of these categories as we meet them in our studies.

Value. There are over four hundred quotations or allusions to the Psalms in the New Testament. Jesus quoted from the book of Psalms (Matt. 5:5/Ps. 37:11; 5:36/Ps. 48:3; 6:26/Ps. 147:9; 7:23/Ps. 6:8; 27:46/Ps. 22:1; John 15:25/Ps. 69:4). The Lord gave guidance from the book of Psalms when the church in Jerusalem chose a new apostle (Acts 1:15ff; Pss. 69:25; 109:8). The early church also used the Psalms to buttress their preaching

(Acts 2:31; Ps. 16:10) and to find encouragement in times of persecution (Acts 4:23-31; Ps. 2). Singing selected psalms was a part of their worship (Eph. 5:19; Col. 3:16; 1 Cor. 14:26) and should be a part of the church's worship today. It's helpful and interesting to study Bible history from the viewpoint of the psalmists: creation (8), the flood (29), the patriarchs (47:9, 105:9, 47:4), Joseph (105:17ff), The Exodus (114), the wilderness wanderings (68:7, 106:1ff), the captivity (85, 137).

But primarily, the psalms are about God and His relationship to His creation, the nations of the world, Israel, and His believing people. He is seen as a powerful God as well as a tenderhearted Father, a God who keeps His promises and lovingly cares for His people. The psalms also reveal the hearts of those who follow Him, their faith and doubts, their victories and failures, and their hopes for the glorious future God has promised. In this book, we meet all kinds of people in a variety of circumstances, crying out to God, praising Him, confessing their sins and seeking to worship Him in a deeper way. In the book of Psalms, you meet the God of creation and learn spiritual truths from birds and beasts, mountains and deserts, sunshine and storms, wheat and chaff, trees and flowers. You learn from creatures of all sorts—horses, mules, dogs, snails, locusts, bees, lions, snakes, sheep, and even worms. The psalms teach us to seek God with a whole heart, to tell Him the truth and tell Him everything, and to worship Him because of Who He is, not just because of what He gives. They show us how to accept trials and turn them into triumphs, and when we've failed, they show us how to repent and receive God's gracious forgiveness. The God described in the book of Psalms is both transcendent and immanent, far above us and yet personally with us in our pilgrim journey. He is "God Most High" and "Immanuel—God with us."

Note: In these expositions, references to verses in the psalms will not be marked Ps." (psalm) or "Pss." (psalms). References to verses in other Bible books will be identified in the usual manner. When referring to the book of Psalms, I will use "The Psalms."

BOOK I
Psalm 1

The editor who placed this jewel at the beginning of The Psalms did a wise thing, for it points the way to blessing and warns about divine judgment. These are frequent themes in The Psalms. The images in this psalm would remind the reader of earlier teachings in the Old Testament. In Genesis, you find people walking with God (5:21, 24; 6:9; 17:1), the life-giving river (2:10-14), and trees and fruit (2:8-10). The law of the Lord connects the psalm with Exodus through Deuteronomy. Finding success by meditating on that law and obeying it reminds us of Joshua 1:8. The psalm presents two ways—the way of blessing and the way of judgment—which was the choice Israel had to make (Deut. 30:15, 19). Jesus used a similar image (Matt. 7:13-14). Bible history seems to be built around the concept of "two men": the "first Adam" and the "last Adam" (Rom. 5; 1 Cor. 15:45)—Cain and Abel, Ishmael and Isaac, Esau and Jacob, David and Saul—and Bible history culminates in Christ and Antichrist. Two men, two ways, two destinies.

Psalm 1 is a wisdom psalm and focuses on God's Word, God's blessing on those who obey it and meditate on it, and God's ultimate judgment on those who rebel. Wisdom psalms also wrestle with the problem of evil in the world and why God permits the prosperity of the wicked who reject His law. Other wisdom psalms include 10, 12, 15, 19, 32, 34, 37, 49, 50, 52, 53, 73, 78, 82, 91, 92, 94, 111, 112, 119, 127, 128, 133, and 139. While this psalm depicts two ways, it actually describes three different persons and how they relate to the blessing of the Lord.

The Person Who Receives a Blessing from God (vv. 1-2)
God's covenant with Israel made it clear that He would bless their obedience and judge their disobedience (Lev. 26; Deut. 28). The word "blessed" is *asher*, the name of one of Jacob's sons (Gen. 30:12). It's plural: "O the happinesses! O the blessednesses!" The person described here met the conditions and therefore God blessed him.[1] If we want God's blessing, we, too, must meet the conditions.

We must be directed by the Word (v. 1). Israel was a unique and separate people; they were among the other nations but not to be contaminated by them (Num. 23:9; Ex. 19:5-6; Deut. 32:8-10; 33:28). So it is with God's people today: we are in the world but not of the world (John 17:11-17). We must beware of friendship with the world (James 4:4) that leads to being spotted by the world (James 1:27) and even loving the world (1 John 2:15-17). The result will be conforming to the world (Rom. 12:1-2) and, if we don't repent, being condemned with the world (1 Cor. 11:32). Lot looked toward Sodom, pitched his tent toward Sodom, and soon moved into Sodom (Gen. 13:10-12; 14:12). Though he was a saved man (2 Peter 2:7-8), Lot lost all that he had when the Lord destroyed the cities of the plain (Gen. 18-19; 1 Cor. 3:11-23). We move into sin and disobedience gradually (see Prov. 4:14-15 and 7:6ff). If you follow the wrong counsel, then you will stand with the wrong companions and finally sit with the wrong crowd. When Jesus was arrested, Peter didn't follow Christ's counsel and flee from the garden (Matt. 26:31; John 16:32; 18:8), but followed and entered the high priest's courtyard. There he stood with the enemy (John 18:15-18) and ultimately sat with them (Luke 22:55). The result was denying Christ three times. The "ungodly" are people who are willfully and persistently evil; "sinners" are those who miss the mark of God's standards but who don't care; the "scornful" make light of God's laws and ridicule that which is sacred (see Prov. 1:22; 3:24; 21:24).[2] When laughing at holy things and disobeying holy laws become entertainment, then people have reached a low level indeed.

We must be delighted with the Word (v. 2). We move from the negative in verse 1 to the positive. Delighting in the Word and meditating on the Word must go together (119:15-16, 23-24, 47-48, 77-78), for whatever we enjoy, we think about and pursue. "Meditate" in the Hebrew means "to mutter, to read in an undertone," for orthodox Jews speak as they read the Scriptures, meditate and pray. God's Word is in their mouth (Josh. 1:8). If we speak to the Lord about the Word, the Word will speak to us about the Lord. This is what is meant by "abiding in the Word" (1 John 2:14, 24). As God's people, we should prefer God's Word to *food* (119:103; Job 23:12; Jer. 15:17; Matt. 4:4; 1 Peter 2:2), *sleep* (119:55, 62, 147-148, 164), *wealth* (119:14, 72, 127, 162), and *friends* (119:23, 51, 95, 119). The way we treat the Bible is the way we treat Jesus Christ, for the Bible is His Word to us. The

verbs in verse 1 are in the perfect tense and speak of a settled way of life, while in verse 2, "meditate" is the imperfect tense and speaks of constant practice. "He keeps meditating."[3]

The Person Who Is a Blessing (v. 3)

God blesses us that we might be a blessing to others (Gen. 12:2). If the blessing stays with us, then the gifts become more important than the Giver, and this is idolatry. We are to become channels of God's blessing to others. It's a joy to *receive* a blessing but an even greater joy to *be* a blessing. "It is more blessed to give than to receive" (Acts 20:35).

The tree is a familiar image in Scripture, symbolizing both a kingdom (Ezek. 17:24; Dan. 4; Matt. 13:32) and an individual (52:8; 92:12-14; Prov. 11:30; Isa. 44:4 and 58:11; Jer. 17:5-8; Matt. 7:15-23). Balaam saw the people of Israel as a "garden by a river" with trees in abundance (Num. 24:6). Like a tree, the godly person is alive, beautiful, fruitful, useful, and enduring. The most important part of a tree is the hidden root system that draws up water and nourishment, and the most important part of the believer's life is the "spiritual root system" that draws on the hidden resources we have in Christ (Eph. 3:17; Col. 2:7). This is known as "abiding in Christ" (John 15:1-9).

In Scripture, water for drinking is a picture of the Spirit of God (John 7:37-39; 1 Cor. 10:4), while water for washing pictures the Word of God (Ps. 119:9; John 15:3; Eph. 5:26). Thirst for water is an image of thirst for God (42:1; 63:1; 143:6; Matt. 5:6; Rev. 22:17), and the river is often a picture of God's provision of spiritual blessing and help for His people (36:8; 46:4; 78:16; 105:41; Ex. 17:5-6; Num. 20:9-11; Ezek. 47; and Rev. 22:1-2). We can't nourish and support ourselves; we need to be rooted in Christ and drawing upon His spiritual power. To meditate on the Word (v. 2) is one source of spiritual energy, as are prayer and fellowship with God's people. "Religion lacks depth and volume because it is not fed by hidden springs," wrote Alexander Maclaren.

Trees may wither and die, but the believer who abides in Christ stays fresh, green, and fruitful (see 92:12-14). "Fruit" speaks of many different blessings: winning people to Christ (Rom. 1:13), godly character (Rom. 6:22, Gal. 5:22-23), money given to the Lord's work (Rom. 15:28), service and good works (Col. 1:10), and praise to the Lord (Heb. 13:15). It's a tragedy when a believer ignores the "root system" and begins to wither. We must remember that the tree doesn't eat the fruit; others eat it. We must also remember that fruit isn't the same as "results," because fruit has in it the seed for more fruit. Fruit comes from life, the life of God flowing in and through us.

The godly person described in verses 1-3 is surely a picture of our Lord Jesus Christ, who, according to John 14:6 is the way (v. 1), the truth (v. 2), and the life (v. 3).

The Person Who Needs a Blessing (vv. 4-6)

The first half of the psalm describes the godly person, while the last half focuses on the ungodly, *the people the godly must seek to reach with the gospel.* How desperately these people need to know God and receive His blessings in Christ! The wicked are pictured in many ways in Scripture, but the image here is *chaff.* In contrast to the righteous, who are like trees, the ungodly are dead, rootless, blown about, and destined for the fire. Chaff is worth nothing. When the grain is winnowed, the wind blows the chaff away, and what chaff remains is thrown

into the fire. John the Baptist used these same images of the tree, fruit, and chaff to warn sinners to repent (Matt. 3:7-12). The wicked of this world seem rich and substantial, but from God's point of view, they are cheap, unsubstantial, and destined for judgment. (See Ps. 73.) No wonder Jesus used the garbage dump outside Jerusalem (gehenna) as a picture of hell, because that's where the cheap waste ends up in the fire (Mark 9:43-48). The chaff is so near the grain, but in the end, the two are separated, and the chaff is blown away or burned. But until that happens, we have the opportunity to witness to them and seek to bring them to Christ.

There is a coming day of judgment, and the Lord, the Righteous Judge, will separate the wheat from the tares, the sheep from the goats, and the trees from the chaff, and no unbeliever will be able to stand in the assembly of the righteous. The verb *knows* in verse 6 doesn't mean that God is aware of them intellectually and has the godly in his mind. Rather, it means that God has chosen them and providentially watched over them and brought them finally to His glory. The word *know* is used, as in Amos 3:2, to mean "to choose, to enter into covenant relationship with, to be personally acquainted with."[4] The Jewish Publication Society translation of Amos 3:2 is: "You alone have I singled out of all the families of the earth." That same translation gives verse 6 as "For the Lord cherishes the way of the righteous ... ." At the last judgment, Jesus says to the wicked, "I never knew you; depart from Me, you who practice lawlessness" (Matt. 7:23, NKJV).

This psalm begins with "blessed" and ends with "perish." True believers are blessed in Christ (Eph. 1:3ff). They have received God's blessing, and they ought to be a blessing to others, especially to the chaff that will one day be thrown into the fire. Let's seek to win as many of them as we can.

Psalm 2

Psalm 1 emphasizes God's law while Psalm 2 focuses on prophecy. The people in Psalm 1 delight in the law, but the people in Psalm 2 defy the law. Psalm 1 begins with a beatitude and Psalm 2 ends with a beatitude. Psalm 1 is never quoted in the New Testament, while Psalm 2 is quoted or alluded to at least eighteen times, more than any single psalm. (See Matt. 3:17; 7:23; 17:5; Mark 1:11; 9:7; Luke 3:22; 9:35; John 1:49; Acts 4:25-26; 13:33; Phil. 2:12; Heb. 1:2, 5; 5:5; Rev. 2:26-27; 11:18; 12:5; 19:15). It is a Messianic psalm, along with 8, 16, 22, 23, 40, 41, 45, 68, 69, 102, 110, and 118. The test of a Messianic psalm is that it is quoted in the New Testament as referring to Jesus (Luke 24:27, 44). But this is also a royal psalm, referring to the coronation of a Jewish king and the rebellion of some vassal nations that hoped to gain their freedom. Other royal psalms are 18, 20, 21, 45 (a royal wedding), 72, 89, 101, 110 and 144. According to Acts 4:25, David wrote this psalm, so it may have grown out of the events described in 2 Samuel 5:17-25, 8:1-14, and 10:1-19.

Israel was ruled directly by the Lord through His prophets and judges until the nation asked for a king (1 Sam. 8). The Lord knew this would happen (Gen. 17:6, 16; 35:11; Num. 24:7, 17) and made arrangements for it (Deut. 17:14-12). Saul was not appointed to establish a dynasty, because the king had to come from Judah (Gen. 49:10), and Saul was from Benjamin. David was God's choice to establish the dynasty that would eventually bring the Messiah into the world (2 Sam. 7). However, both Psalm 2 and 2 Samuel 7 go far beyond David and his successors, for both the covenant and the psalm speak about a universal kingdom and a throne established forever. This can be fulfilled only in Jesus Christ, the Son of David (Matt. 1:1).

Some psalms you *see* (114, 130, 133), some psalms you *feel* (22, 129, 137, 142), but this one you *hear*, because it is a record of four voices.

Conspiracy—The Voice of the Nations (vv. 1-3)

David didn't expect a reply when he asked this question, because there really is no reply. It was an expression of astonishment: "When you consider all that the Lord has done for the nations, how can they rebel against Him!" God has provided for their basic needs (Acts 14:15-17), guided them, kept them alive, and sent a Savior to bring forgiveness and eternal life (Acts 17:24-31; see Dan. 4:32). Yet, from the tower of Babel (Gen. 11) to the crucifixion of Christ (Acts 4:21-31) to the battle of Armageddon (Rev. 19:11ff), the Bible records humanity's foolish and futile rebellions against the will of the Creator. The kings and minor rulers form a conspiracy to break the bonds that the Lord has established for their own good. The picture is that of a stubborn and raging animal, trying to break the cords that bind the yoke to its body (Jer. 5:5; 27:2). But the attempt is futile (vain) because *the only true freedom comes from submitting to God and doing His will*. Freedom without authority is anarchy, and anarchy destroys. I once saw a bit of graffiti that said, "All authority destroys creativity." What folly! Authority is what releases and develops creativity, whether it's a musician, an athlete, or a surgeon. Apart from submitting to the authority of truth and law, there can be no true creativity.

The British theologian P. T. Forsythe wrote, "The first duty of every soul is to find not its freedom but its Master."

But the nations' rebellion isn't against "God" in some abstract way; they defy the Messiah, Jesus Christ, the Son of God. The one thing the nations can agree on is "We will not have this man to reign over us" (Luke 19:14). The word "Messiah" comes from the Hebrew word meaning "to anoint"; the Greek equivalent is "Christ." In the Old Testament, kings were anointed (1 Sam. 10:1; 2 Kings 11:12), as were prophets (1 Kings 9:16) and priests (Ex. 28:41). Jesus said that the world hated Him and would also hate those who followed Him (John 7:7; 15, 18-19, 24- 25; Matt. 24:9; Luke 21:17). The phrase "set themselves" means "get ready for war." The consequences of this defiance against the Lord and His Christ are described in Romans 1:18ff, and it isn't a pretty picture.

Mockery—The Voice of God the Father (vv. 4-6)

The peaceful scene in heaven is quite a contrast to the noisy scene on earth, for God is neither worried nor afraid as puny man rages against Him. He merely laughs in derision (37:8-13; 59:1-9). After all, to God, the greatest rulers are but grass to be cut down, and the strongest nations are only drops in the bucket (Isa. 40:6-8, 12-17). Today, God is speaking to the nations in His grace and calling them to trust His Son, but the day will come when God will speak to them in His wrath and send terrible judgment to the world (Rev. 6-19). If people will not accept God's judgment of sin at the cross and trust Christ, they will have to accept God's judgment of themselves and their sins.

It was God who gave David his throne on Zion, and it was God who gave David victory after victory as he defeated the enemies of Israel. But this was only a picture of an even greater coronation: God declares that there is but one legitimate King, and that is His Son who is now seated on the throne of glory (Mark 16:19; 1 Cor. 15:25; Eph. 1:19-23). Jesus Christ is both King and Priest after the order of Melchizedek (Heb. 5:5-6; 7:1ff). Today, there is no king in Israel (Hos. 3:4), but there is a King enthroned in the heavenly Zion (Heb. 12:22-24). If we fail to see Jesus Christ in this psalm, we miss its message completely: His death (vv. 1-3, Acts 4:23-28), resurrection (v. 7, Acts 13:33), ascension and enthronement in glory (v. 6), and His return and righteous rule on earth (vv. 8-9, Rev. 2:9, 27; 12:5).

Victory—the Voice of God the Son (vv. 7-9)

The enthroned King now speaks and announces what the Father said to Him. "I will declare the decree" informs the rebels that God rules His creation on the basis of sovereign decrees. He doesn't ask for a consensus or take a vote. God's decrees are just (7:6), and He never makes a mistake. According to Acts 13:33, verse 7 refers to the resurrection of Christ, when He was "begotten" from the tomb and came forth in glory. (See Rom. 1:4 and Heb. 1:5 and 5:5.) In the ancient Near East, kings were considered to be sons of the gods, but Jesus Christ is indeed the Son of God. (See 89:26-27; 2 Sam. 7:14.) At our Lord's baptism, the Father alluded to verse 7 and announced that Jesus was His beloved Son (Matt. 3:17; Mark 1:11; Luke 3:22).

The Father has promised the Son complete victory over the nations, which means that one day He will reign over all the kingdoms of the world. Satan offered Him this honor in return for His worship, but Jesus refused (Matt. 4:8-11). Christ's rule will be just but firm, and if they oppose Him, He will smash them like so many clay pots. The Hebrew word translated "break" can also mean "shepherd," which explains the *King James Version* translations of Revelation 2:27, 12:5, and 19:15. Before going to battle, ancient eastern kings participated in a ritual of breaking clay jars that symbolized the enemy army, and thus guaranteed the help of the gods to defeat them. Jesus needs no such folly; He smashes His enemies completely (Rev. 19:11ff; Dan. 2:42-44). Jesus is God, Jesus is King, and Jesus is Conqueror.

Opportunity—the Voice of the Holy Spirit (vv. 10-12)

In view of the Father's decree and promised judgment, and the Son's victorious enthronement in heaven, the wise thing for people to do is to surrender to Christ and trust Him. Today, the Spirit of God speaks to mankind and pleads with sinners to repent and turn to the Savior.

Note that in verses 10 and 11, the Spirit speaks first to the kings and leaders, and then in verse 12, He addresses "all" and urges them to trust the Son. The Spirit starts his appeal with the world leaders, because they are accountable to God for the way they govern the world (Rom. 13). The people are enraged against God mainly because their leaders have incited them. They are ignorant because they follow the wisdom of this world and not the wisdom that comes from God (1 Cor. 1:18-31). They are proud of what they think they know, but they really know nothing about eternal truth. How can they learn? "Be instructed" (v. 10) from the Word of God. The word also means "to be warned." How gracious the Lord is to save sinners before His wrath is revealed!

Once the Spirit has instructed the mind, He then appeals to the will and calls the rebels to serve the Lord and stop serving sin (v. 11). True believers know what it means to have both fear and joy in their hearts. Love for the Lord casts out sinful fear (1 John 4:18) but perfects godly fear. We love our Father but still respect His authority. The third appeal is to the heart and calls for submissive love and devotion to the King. In the ancient world, vassal rulers would show their obedience to their king by kissing his hand or cheek. Judas kissed Jesus in the garden, but it meant nothing. This is the kiss of submission and even reconciliation. The Spirit ends with a word of warning and a word of blessing. The warning is that this loving King can also become angry and reveal His holy wrath suddenly and without warning (1 Thess. 5:1-4). The theme of wrath is connected with the Father (v. 5) and the Son (vv. 9, 12).[5]

Psalm 1 opens with "blessed" and Psalm 2 concludes with promised blessing for all who put their trust in the Son of God. That promise still stands (John 3:16-18; 20:31).

Psalm 3

This is the first time we find the word *psalm* in the book. The Hebrew word is *mizmor* and means "to pluck strings." This is also the first prayer in the Psalms, and the first psalm attributed to David. All the psalms in Book I (Pss. 1-41) are attributed to David except 1, 10, and 33. (Ps. 2 is assigned to him in Acts 4:25.) Psalm 3 is categorized as a "personal lament," and there are many of these in the collection (Pss. 3-7, 13, 17, 22, 255-28, 35, 38-40, 42-43, 51, 54-57, 59, 61, 63-64, 69-71, 86, 88, 102, 109, 120, 130, 140-143).[6] David wrote the psalm after he had fled Jerusalem when his son Absalom took over the throne (2 Sam. 15-18). The king and his attendants had crossed the Jordan River and camped at Mahanaim. This is a morning psalm (v. 5); Psalm 4 was written during the same events and is an evening psalm (4:8). It's possible that Psalm 5 also fits into the same time period, as well as 42, 43, 61, 62, 63, 143. (See 5:3, 8-10.)

Conflict: He Admits His Troubles (vv. 1-2)

The prayer begins very abruptly with "Lord." Like Peter sinking into the sea (Matt. 14:30), David didn't have time to go through a long liturgy, for his own life was at stake and so was the future of the kingdom. David knew that God is a "very present help in trouble" (46:1). Absalom had taken a long time to build up his support for taking over the kingdom and the number increased day by day (2 Sam. 15:12-13; 16:7-8; 17:11; 18:7). Absalom was handsome, smooth-spoken, and a gifted liar who knew how to please the people and steal their hearts (2 Sam. 15:1-6). British statesman James Callaghan said, "A lie can be halfway around the world before the truth has got its boots on." There's something in the heart of mankind that enjoys feeding on lies.

Not only were David's enemies increasing but the news was getting worse. People were saying, "The king is beyond help." (See 31:13; 38:19; 41:4-9; 55:18; 56:2; 69:4 and 71:10-11.) The word "help" in the Hebrew (yeshua) is translated "save" in verse 7 and "salvation" in verse 8 and gives us the names "Jesus" (Matt. 1:21) and "Joshua." It's used 136 times in the Psalms.

Why had God permitted this dangerous and disgraceful uprising? It was part of David's chastening because of his sins of adultery and murder (2 Sam. 12:1-12).

God in his grace forgave David when he confessed his sins (2 Sam. 12:13-14; Pss. 32 and 51), but God in his government allowed David to reap the bitter consequences of those sins. He experienced painful family problems (2 Sam. 12-14), including the death of the son Bathsheba bore him, the rape of his daughter Tamar, and the slaying of his sons Amnon, Absalom, and Adonijah.

This is the first use of "Selah" in Scripture (vv. 2, 4, 8); it is used seventy-one times in the Psalms and three times in Habakkuk 3. Hebraists aren't agreed whether it comes from words meaning "to lift up" or "to be silent." If the first, then it might be a signal for louder voices or the lifting and blowing the trumpets, perhaps even the lifting of hands to the Lord. If the second, it could signal a pause, a moment of silence and meditation.

Confidence: He Affirms His Trust in the Lord (vv. 3-4)

But David wasn't a man easily beaten. Without ignoring his problems, he lifted his eyes from the threatening situation around him and looked by faith to the Lord. David knew he was in danger, but God was his shield (see Gen. 15:1). Israel's king was referred to as a "shield" because he protected the nation (84:9; 89:18), but David depended on God as his shield (7:10; 18:2; 47:9; 59:11; 84:11; Deut. 33:29). David was in disgrace because of his own sins and his son's treachery, but God was the source of David's glory. Absalom turned his father's "glory into shame" (4:2), but one day that glory would be restored. The situation was discouraging, but the king knew that God would lift up his head and restore him to his throne (27:6; 2 Sam. 15:30). His faith was in the promises God had made to him in the covenant recorded in 2 Samuel 7, and he knew God would not forsake him.

The temple had not yet been built on the "holy hill of Zion," but the ark was there (see 2 Sam. 15:25) and that was God's throne (80:1, NASB). David may have been forced off his throne, but Jehovah was still on the throne and in control, and Absalom had attacked God's anointed king (2:2). That was a dangerous thing to do. David kept crying out to God in prayer, knowing that God had not forsaken him in the past and would not forsake him now. "This poor man cried out, and the Lord heard him, and saved him out of all his troubles" (Ps. 34:6, NKJV).

Celebration: He Anticipates the Victory (vv. 5-8)

When David awakened the next morning, his first thought was of the Lord and how He had protected him and his attendants during night. This was a sign to him that the Lord was with them and would see them through the crisis. It reminds us of Jesus asleep in the storm (Mark 4:39) and Peter asleep in the prison (Acts 12). If we trust Him and seek to do His will, God works on our behalf even while we're asleep (121:3-4; 127:2). David affirmed that he would not be afraid if tens of thousands of people were set in battle array against him, for God would give him victory (Deut. 32:30).

The morning was the most important time of day for David, as it should be for us today.

It was in the morning that he met with the Lord and worshiped Him. It was his time to pray (5:3), to sing (57:7-8; 59:16) and to be satisfied by God's mercy (90:14). "For His anger is but for a moment, His favor is for life; weeping may endure for a night, but joy comes in the morning" (30:5, NKJV). Abraham arose early in the morning (Gen. 19:27; 21:14; 22:3), and so

did Moses (Ex. 24:4; 34:4), Joshua (Josh. 3:1; 6:12; 7:16; 8:10), Samuel (1 Sam. 15:12), Job (Job 1:5), and our Lord (Mark 1:35).

God not only rested David but He also rescued him. David's prayer in verse 7— "Arise, O Lord"—takes us back to the years when Israel was in the wilderness, as David was at that time. When the guiding cloud of glory began to move and the camp set out, Moses would say (or sing): "Rise up. O Lord! Let Your enemies be scattered, and let those who hate You flee before You" (Num. 10:35, NKJV). David had sent the ark back to Jerusalem (2 Sam. 15:24-29), but he knew that the presence of a piece of sacred furniture was no guarantee of the presence of the Lord (see 1 Sam. 4). David had no access to the tabernacle or the ministry of the priests, but he was spiritual enough to know that *the love and obedience of His heart was what God wanted*. He didn't have the ark of God, but he had the God of the ark! He couldn't offer animal sacrifices or incense, but he could lift his hand to worship God (141:2). The glory of God was with him (v. 3) and so was the blessing of God (v. 8). Let the enemy arise! (v. 1). God will also arise and give victory!

Some translations render the verbs in verse 7 as past tense (KJV, AMP, NASB), indicating that David was looking back at the many past victories God had given him. "You saved my life many times in the past, so why would you abandon me now?" The *New International Version* sees this as a prayer for present and future victories. Either way, David had the faith to trust God to go before him and defeat the army of Absalom, and God did. Striking the enemy on the cheek—a "slap in the face"—was an act of humiliation. David saw the rebellious army as a pack of animals that needed their teeth broken (7:2; 22:12-13, 16, 20-21; 10:9; 17:12; 35:17; 57:4; 58:6).

Jonah quoted verse 8 when he was in the great fish (Jonah 2:9) and then experienced that salvation. Though he had used brilliant strategy in opposing Absalom's plans, David refused to take the credit. It was the Lord who alone would receive the glory. David also refused to carry a grudge against his people, but asked the Lord to bless them. This reminds us of our Lord's prayer on the cross (Luke 23:34) and Stephen's prayer as he was being stoned to death (Acts 7:60). God restored David to his throne and enabled him to prepare Solomon to succeed him. David was also able to bring together his wealth so that Solomon would have what he needed to build the temple. (See 1 Chron. 22-29.)

Psalm 4

When you compare the wording in this psalm with Psalm 3, you cannot but draw the conclusion that they deal with the same situation in David's life: foes/distress (v. 1), many/many (vv. 6, 2), glory (vv. 2, 3), call/answer (vv.1, 4), lie down/sleep (vv. 8, 5). Psalm 3 is a morning psalm (v. 5) and Psalm 4 an evening psalm (v. 8). For the historical setting, review the introduction to Psalm 3. This is the first mention of "the chief musician," who is included in the titles of fifty-three psalms. He was the "minister of worship" and custodian of the sacred psalms at the tabernacle and then the temple (1 Chron. 6:31-32; 15:16-22; 25:1, 7). The Hebrew word *neginoth* means "accompanied by stringed instruments" (4, 6, 54, 55, 61, 67, 76) and refers to the harp and lyre (1 Chron. 23:5; 25:1, 3, 6). It's a wonderful thing that David could turn this distressing experience into song, to the glory of God. His example shows us what our responses ought to be in times of crisis.

Look to the Lord (v. 1)

"Hear me" is a passionate and concerned call that means "Answer me!" David had been praying for God's help and was desperate to receive an answer. (See 18:6; 50:15; 55:16; 145:18.) During his youthful days of exile, he had a priest with him to consult the Urim and Thummim and determine God's will, but not during Absalom's rebellion. "God of my righteousness"[7] implies not only that God is righteous and will do what it best ("my righteous God"), but also that David's righteousness came from God, and therefore God should vindicate him ("God of my innocence"). Yes, David was being chastened because of his disobedience, but God had forgiven his sins. God had called David to be king, and God alone could vindicate him.

David reminded the Lord that He had often delivered him in times past, so He was able to deliver him now. "Distress" means "pressed into a corner, in a tight place." But God "enlarged him" or "set him in a broad place," for David grew spiritually in difficult situations (18:19, 36; 25:17; 31:8; 118:5; 119:32). David knew he didn't deserve any help from the Lord, but he prayed on the basis of God's mercy and favor. God in His grace gives us what we don't deserve, and God in His mercy doesn't give us what we do deserve.

Confront the Enemy (vv. 2-3)

David wasn't at the scene of the revolt, but he spoke out to those who had turned against him and made Absalom king. The phrase "sons of men" refers to the leading men of rank who had been seduced by Absalom and with him were leading the people astray. David understood their thinking and how Absalom had deceived them. David had no glory of his own, for all his glory came from the Lord (3:3). The enthusiastic mob was following vanity and would pay dearly for their sins. When you follow vain things and believe falsehood, you can only go astray. The people weren't just deposing a king; they were fighting against the Lord Jehovah who had placed David on the throne. Absalom certainly wasn't a man of God, nor was he God's chosen one to rule over Israel. The rebels were actually following a false god when they listened to Absalom's flattery and lying promises (2 Sam. 15:1-6). David didn't try to compromise with the rebels; he knew what they were, and he rejected them.

Encourage Your Friends (vv. 4-5)

In these verses, David speaks to his own followers, some of whom were so overcome by their emotions that they were about to get out of hand. David gave them six instructions, all of which are useful to us today when we find ourselves getting angry.

Tremble before the Lord (4a). Believers who fear the Lord need not fear anything else. Absalom's followers neither trembled before the Lord nor before their rightful king.

Don't sin (4b). Sinful anger leads to sinful words and deeds, and even to murder (Matt. 5:21-26). Paul quoted this verse in Ephesians 4:26, using the Septuagint (Greek Version of the Old Testament). It reads, "Be angry, and do not sin" (NKJV), which reminds us that not all anger is sinful. There is a holy anger against sin that ought to be in the heart of every believer (Mark 3:5), but we must be careful not to be guilty of unholy anger.

Search your own hearts (4c). It's easy to get angry at the sins of others and ignore our own sins (Matt. 7:1-5). In fact, David himself was guilty of doing this (2 Sam. 12:1-7). Some translate this phrase "Speak

to your own heart" (see 10:6, 11, 13). Instead of tossing and turning in bed because of the things others are doing, take inventory and see if there aren't sins in your own heart that need to be confessed.

Be still (4d). The *Amplified Bible* translates this, "Be sorry for the things you say in your heart." Another translation is "say so in your own heart," that is, "Say to your own heart, Sin not." The honest searching of the heart should lead us to confess our sins to the Lord and claim His gracious forgiveness (1 John 1:9).

Offer right sacrifices (5a). They couldn't offer them there in the wilderness, but they could promise the Lord they would do so when they returned to Jerusalem. This is what Jonah did (Jonah 2:9). Absalom was offering insincere and hypocritical sacrifices to impress the people (1 Sam. 15:12), but God didn't accept them. (See Ps. 50:14-15.)

Trust the Lord (5b). Absalom was trusting his leadership, his army, his clever strategy, and his popularity with the people, but he wasn't trusting the Lord. His plans were destined to fail.

David was not only a great king and military strategist, but he was also a loving shepherd who cared for his people and wanted them to walk with the Lord. David knew that the spiritual condition of his people was far more important than their military skill, for the Lord gives victory to those who trust and obey (Ps. 51:16-19).

Praise the Lord (vv. 6-8)

David's leaders reported to him what many of the people were saying, so he knew that there was discouragement in the ranks (see also 3:2). "Who will show us any good?" means "O that we might see some good!" (AMP), or "Can anything good come out of this?" or "Who can get us out of this plight?" The tense of the verb indicates that this discouraging statement was repeated again and again by the complainers, and the more they complained, the more others took up the strain. The Jewish Publication Society version reads, "O for good days!" It's well been said that "the good old days" are a combination of a bad memory and a good imagination. What kind of "good" were the people looking for—material wealth, peace and security at any price, a godly king, a successful new king?

David knew what kind of good he wanted: the light of God's smile upon him and his people. To see the glorious face of God and know that He was well pleased would take care of everything. This statement refers to the priestly blessing in Numbers 6:24-26, and see also 31:16; 44:3; 67:1; 80:3, 7, 19; and 119:135. There was no priest present to bestow this blessing, but David knew that God would answer the prayer of his heart. The king wanted to see the Lord change darkness into light, and that's exactly what He did. But not only did David's darkness become light, but his discouragement was replaced by joy (v. 7). The Israelites experienced great joy at weddings and bountiful harvests (Isa. 9:3; Jer. 48:33); but the joy God gave David exceeded even those times. (See Rom. 15:13 and John 16:24.) Finally, David praised God for the peace the Lord placed in his heart before the battle had been fought and won (v. 8; see 3:5). God had given him rest the night before, and now he would rest again, knowing that God was his shield (3:3). The Hebrew word for "peace" (*shalom*) means much more than the absence of conflict. It carries with it the ideas of adequacy for life, confidence and fullness of life. Perhaps the Lord brought Deuteronomy 33:12 to David's mind— "The beloved of the Lord shall dwell in safety by Him, who shelters him all day

long ..." (NKJV). This promise is even more meaningful when you recall that David's name means "beloved."

Psalm 5

Like Psalm 3, this is a morning psalm (v. 3). David may have written it during the crisis caused by Absalom, but we have no indication that he did. However, the description of David's enemies given in verses 4-6 and 9-10 suggests the period prior to David's flight from Jerusalem. The *New International Version* translates verse 10, "Let their intrigues be their downfall," and there was certainly a great deal of deception and intrigue going on at that time.[8] The Hebrew words for "house" and "holy temple" (v. 7) are also used for the tabernacle in Exodus 23:19, Deuteronomy 23:18, Joshua 6:24, 1 Samuel 1:9, 3:3, and 3:15, so we don't have to date the psalm from the time of Solomon. "Nehiloth" in the title is a musical instruction that probably means "for flutes."

Because of the prayer in verse 10, Psalm 6 is classified as one of the "imprecatory psalms" (see 12, 35, 37, 58, 59, 69, 79, 83, 109, 139, and 140). In these psalms, the writers seem to describe a God of wrath who can hardly wait to destroy sinners. The writers also seem to picture themselves as people seeking terrible revenge against these enemies. But several facts must be considered before we write off the psalmists as pagan brutes who cannot forgive, or God as a "dirty bully." To begin with, the enemies described are rebels against the Lord (5:10), and in some instances, against the Lord's anointed king. The Jews were a covenant people whom God promised to protect as long as they obeyed Him (Lev. 26; Deut. 27-29). In His covenant with Abraham, God promised to bless those who blessed Israel and to curse those who cursed them (Gen. 12:1-3). When the Jews asked God to deal justly with their wicked enemies, they were only asking Him to fulfill His covenant promises. "God is love" (1 John 4:8, 16), but God is also "light" (1 John 1:5), and in His holiness, He must deal with sin. Ever since the fall of man in Genesis 3, there has been a battle going on in the world between truth and lies, justice and injustice, and right and wrong; and we cannot be neutral in this battle. "If the Jews cursed more bitterly than the Pagans," wrote C. S. Lewis in *Reflections on the Psalms*, "this was, I think, at least in part because they took right and wrong more seriously. For if we look at their railings we find they are usually angry not simply because these things have been done to them but because these things are manifestly wrong, are hateful to God as well as to the victim" (p. 30).

Those who have difficulty accepting the "imprecations" in The Psalms must also deal with them in Jeremiah (11:18ff; 15:15;l 17:18; 18:19ff; 20:11ff) and in the preaching of John the Baptist (Matt. 3) and Jesus (Matt. 23), as well as in the requests of the martyrs in heaven (Rev. 6:9-11). However, no one will deny that these servants of God were filled with the Spirit and wanted the Lord's will to be accomplished. Perhaps our problem today is what C. S. Lewis pointed out: we don't hate sin enough to get upset at the wickedness and godlessness around us. Bombarded as we are by so much media evil and violence, we've gotten accustomed to the darkness.

If this psalm did grow out of the time in the wilderness when David was fleeing from Absalom, then he teaches us an important lesson: no amount of danger or discomfort should keep us from our time of morning fellowship with the Lord. In this psalm, David gives us three valuable instructions to encourage our daily fellowship with the Lord.

We Prepare to Meet the Lord (vv. 1-3)

If we had an invitation to enjoy a private visit with the President of the United States, or perhaps Queen Elizabeth, we would certainly prepare for it; yet many believers rush into their morning devotional time as if no preparation were necessary. David was open with the Lord and admitted his inward pain ("meditation" can be translated "groaning") and his prayer was a cry for help. David was King of Israel, but he saw the Lord alone as his King (Ex. 15:18). David was a man with a broken heart, but he knew that the Lord understood his sighs and groanings (see Rom. 8:26). We may come to God's gracious throne with "freedom of speech" ("boldly" in Heb. 4:16, and see 10:19, 35) because the Father knows our hearts and our needs and welcomes us. Like our Lord Jesus Christ (Mark 1:35), David kept this appointment "morning by morning" and allowed nothing to interfere. (See 55:18, 59:17; 88:14 and 92:3.)

David was not only *faithful* in his praying each morning but he was also *orderly* and *systematic*. The word translated "direct" in verse 3 was used to describe the placing of the pieces of the animal sacrifices in order on the altar (Lev. 1:8). It also described the arranging of the wood on an altar (Gen. 22:9), the placing of the loaves of bread on the table in the tabernacle (Lev. 24:8), and the setting of a meal before the guests (Ps. 23:5). David wasn't careless in his praying; he had everything arranged in order. The word also has a military connotation: a soldier presenting himself to his commander to receive orders, and an army set in battle array on the field. In past years, many soldiers had presented themselves to David to get their orders, but David first presented himself to the Lord. In order to exercise authority, leaders must be under authority. "I will look up" conveys the idea of waiting expectantly for God to come and bless (see NIV). In our daily morning meetings with the Lord, we should come like priests bringing sacrifices to the altar and soldiers reporting to our Captain for duty.

We Seek to Please the Lord (vv. 4-6)

God has no pleasure in wickedness nor can He be neutral about sin; therefore, rebel sinners couldn't enter into His presence (15:1ff; 24:3-6). God delights in those who fear Him (147:11) and who offer sincere praise to Him (69:31). To please God, we must have faith (Heb. 11:6) and be identified with His Son in whom He is well pleased (Matt. 3:17). When you read verses 5-6 and 9-10, you meet a crowd of people who deliberately and repeatedly disobey God and think nothing of the consequences. It's the crowd John describes in Revelation 21:8, the people who are going to hell. God loves the world of lost sinners (John 3:16) and sent His only Son "to be the Savior of the world" (1 John 4:14, and see 1 Tim. 2:3-4 and 2 Peter 3:9). Jesus died on the cross for the sins of the world (1 John 2:1-2), and His invitation to salvation is sent to all who will believe and come (Matt. 11:28-30; Rev. 22:17). Such are the vast dimensions of God's grace and love (Eph. 3:18-19).

But the glorious truth of God's love doesn't change the fact that God hates sin and punishes sinners. He has no pleasure in them, and they cannot dwell with Him (v. 4) or stand before Him as they are (v. 5; see 1:5-6). He abhors murderers and liars and destroys them if they don't trust His Son (v. 6). It isn't necessary to dilute the word "hate" in verse 5 because you find it also in 11:5 and 45:7, and see 7:11. In fact, the Lord expects those who love Him to love what He loves and hate what He hates (97:10; 119:113; 139:21; Prov. 6:16-17; Amos 5:15; Rom. 12:9). There is no such thing as "abstract evil" except in dictionaries and philosophy books. Evil is not an abstraction; it's a terrible force in this world, wrecking lives and capturing people for hell. God's hatred of evil isn't emotional; it's judicial, an expression of His holiness. If we want to fellowship with God at His holy altar, then we need to feel that same anguish (anger plus love) as we see the evil in this fallen world.

We Submit to the Lord (vv. 7-12)

When he wrote "But as for me," David contrasted himself with the wicked crowd that rebelled against the King. David had come to pray, and he had three requests.

He prayed for guidance (vv. 7-8). Because he wasn't a member of the tribe of Levi, David couldn't actually enter the tabernacle as could the priests, but he used that phrase to describe his approach to the Lord. David was in the wilderness, but he came to the Lord with the kind of awe that the priests and Levites displayed in the tabernacle. In the worship of our great God, there's no place for cuteness and flippancy. For believers to enter into the presence of God to worship and pray, it cost Jesus His life (Heb. 10:19-20), and to treat this privilege lightly is to cheapen that sacrifice. David knew he needed guidance from God, for he had to put the kingdom back together again. (See James 1:5.)

He prayed for justice (vv. 9-10). David didn't issue orders to his officers to go out and slaughter his enemies; instead, he turned them over to the Lord. During that tragic battle in which Absalom was slain, "the forest devoured more people that day than the sword devoured" (2 Sam. 18:8). David's prayer was answered: "let them fall by their own counsels" (v. 10). But it was not because they rebelled against David; their great sin was that they had rebelled against God. "The Lord loves righteousness and justice" (Ps. 33:5, NIV; and see 36:6; 58:11; 97:2; Isa. 30:18; Luke 18:7-8; Rom. 1:32). Anybody who resents this kind of praying can't honestly pray, "Hallowed be Thy name. Thy kingdom come, Thy will be done in earth, as it is in heaven" (Matt. 6:9-10). In Romans 3:13, Paul quoted "their throat is an open sepulcher" as part of his proof that the whole world is guilty before God (Rom. 3:19)— and that includes all of us! Instead of being upset over God's treatment of David's enemies, we need to examine our own relationship with the Lord!

He prayed for God's blessing (vv. 11-12). David didn't rejoice because some of God's covenant people were evil and were judged by the Lord, but because Israel's God had been glorified and His king vindicated. The future of God's great plan of salvation rested with Israel, and if the Davidic dynasty was destroyed, what about God's gracious Messianic covenant with David (2 Sam. 78)? The outcome of our fellowship with the Lord should be joy in His character, His promises, and His gracious answers to prayer. Even though some of his own people had turned against him, David prayed that God would bless and protect them! This sounds like our Lord on the cross (Luke 23:34) and Stephen when he was stoned to death (Acts 7:60). Note that verse 11 emphasizes faith and love, and verse 12 gives the assurance of future hope. The shield in verse 12 is the large rectangular shield, like a door, and not the smaller round shield of 3:4.

David began his devotions seeking help for himself but ended by seeking blessing for all the people, including his enemies. That's the way our devotional times ought to end.

Psalm 6

The inscription tells us that David wrote this psalm but we aren't sure when he wrote it. It could have been composed during the time of Absalom's rebellion when David was old, sick, and unable to handle all the complex responsibilities of the kingdom. David's gradual failure as a visible leader was one of Absalom's "selling points" as he stole the hearts of the Israelites (2 Sam. 15:1-6). But the psalm might have been written at any time during David's reign when he was ill and being attacked by his enemies. He describes his plight—"foes without, fears within"—and cries out to God for mercy. He was sure he was facing death (v. 5), which indicates that his experience was real and that he wasn't using sickness and war only as metaphors for his personal troubles. Neginoth means "stringed instruments," and Sheminith means "eighth," which may refer to the number of a familiar melody, a lower octave for men's voices or the number of strings of the instrument to be played. You find Sheminith also in the title of Psalm 12 (see 1 Chron. 15:21). Psalm 6 is the first of seven "penitential psalms" in which the writers are being disciplined by God and experiencing suffering. The other psalms are 32, 38, 51, 102, 130, and 143, and all of these psalms are helpful to us when we need to confess our sins and draw closer to the Lord. In this psalm, David records the stages in his difficult experience of moving by faith from trial to triumph.

The Pain of Discipline (vv. 1-3)
Eight times in the psalm David addresses

God as "LORD—JEHOVAH," the covenant name of God, and the address in verse 1 is repeated in 38:1, and see Jeremiah 10:24. When God deals with His children, usually He first rebukes and then chastens, just as parents first warn disobedient children and then discipline them (Heb. 12:5-6; Prov. 3:11-12). According to Hebrews 12:1-13, chastening is not punishment meted out by an irate judge but discipline given by a loving Father to help His children mature (see Rev. 3:19). Sometimes God chastens us in order to deal with our disobedience, but at other times, He chastens us to prepare us for what lies ahead. It's like the training of an athlete for a race. David thought God was angry with him, but that wasn't necessarily true. However, when you consider that he was surrounded by foes (v. 7), evildoers (v. 8), and enemies (10), and that his body was weak and in pain and his soul troubled, you can see why he felt like he had a target on his back.

Three times he used the Hebrew word *bahal*, which means "faint, weak, troubled, terrified." It is translated "vexed" in the *King James Version* (vv. 2, 3, 10), but in the 17th century, the word "vex" was much stronger than it is today. The translators of the Greek Old Testament used *tarasso*, which is the word used in the Greek of John 12:27, "Now is my soul troubled …" (and see Matt. 26:38 and Mark 14:34). Knowing that he deserved far more than what he was enduring, David begged for mercy (see 103:13-14) and asked God to send help speedily. The painful question "How long?" is asked at least sixteen times in The Psalms (6:3; 13:1-2; 35:17; 62:3; 74:9-10; 79:5; 80:4; 82:2; 89:46; 90:13; 94:3). The answer to the question is, "I will discipline you until you learn the lesson I want you to learn and are equipped for the work I want you to do." According to Hebrews 12, when God disciplines us, we can despise it, resist it, collapse under it and quit, or accept it and submit. What God is seeking is submission.

The Futility of Death (vv. 4-5)

David felt that God had turned His back on him and deserted him, so he asked Him to return; and then he began to reason with Him. Every Jew knew that the Lord was "merciful and gracious" (Ex. 34:6-7), so David asked God to manifest that mercy to him and spare his life. Furthermore, what would the Lord gain by allowing David to die? (See 30:9-10; 88:10-12). King Hezekiah used a similar approach when he prayed for deliverance from death (Isa. 38:18-19). The word "grave" in verse 5 (KJV) is *sheol*, a word that can mean "the grave" or "the realm of the dead." Here it means the latter. In Old Testament times, people didn't have the clear revelation of the after-life that was brought through Jesus (2 Tim. 1:10), although there were glimpses of what God had in store for His people (16:9-11; 17:15; 49:14-15; 17:24). A body in the grave can't praise or serve God, and David wasn't certain what his spirit could do for the Lord in sheol. Conclusion: it would be wiser for the Lord to deliver him and let him live. David still had work to do.

The Strain of Despair (vv. 5-7)

We have gone from a morning psalm (3:5) to an evening psalm (4:8) and back to a morning psalm (5:3). Now we have another evening psalm (6:6). But whereas in the previous psalms, the Lord gave sleep and peace to David, here we find the king sleepless because of fear and pain. He was worn out from groaning, tossing and turning, and he spent a good deal of time weeping. "I soak my pillow … I drench my couch" (v. 6, AMP; see 38:9-10). Sleeping had been replaced by suffering. Sleep is important for healing (John 11:11-12), so David's lack of sleep only made the condition worse. David's weakened condition was revealed by the dullness of his eyes (v. 7; see 1 Sam. 14:27, 29). It's remarkable how much physicians can discover about our physical condition by looking into our eyes.

A man I considered to be a godly spiritual leader once said, "I hear Christians say that their pain and sickness brought them closer to God, but in my case, that didn't always happen." That encouraged me! From my own experience and pastoral ministry, I've learned that sickness and pain either make us better or bitter, and the difference is *faith*. If we turn to God, pray, remember His promises and trust Him, we will find His grace sufficient for our needs (2 Cor. 12:9). The Lord may not do what we ask, when we want it, but He will do what needs to be done and help us glorify His name. The question we should ask isn't "When will I get out of this?" but "What can I get out of this?"

The Joy of Deliverance (vv. 8-10)

At this point, there's a sudden and surprising change from suffering to joy, an experience recorded in other psalms (22:22; 56:10; 69:30). It doesn't matter whether this change occurred later or immediately after David prayed, but he felt healing in his body and peace in his heart and mind. Perhaps word came to him that the enemy had retreated or, better yet, had been defeated, and he knew God had heard his cries. Or maybe his circumstances hadn't changed at all, but David felt God's witness in his heart that all would be well. The Lord had heard his weeping and requests and had accepted his prayer.

He used this experience to glorify the Lord as he witnessed to his enemies. How this message was conveyed to them, we

don't know; but David was quick to honor the Lord for what had occurred. Perhaps the words in verses 8-10 are an apostrophe, a speech addressed to persons not present but meaningful to those people hearing or reading it. His enemies said that David was done for, but the failure of their prediction would leave them ashamed and defeated. The phrase "Depart from me" is quoted in Matthew 7:23 and Luke 13:27 and seems quite final.

Psalm 7

Cush the Benjamite was among King Saul's fawning flatterers. He was one of a group of evil men from Saul's tribe who reported what they heard about David during those years when Saul was out to capture and destroy his rival. Saul played on the sympathy of his leaders and bribed them into serving as spies (1 Sam. 22:6ff; 23:21; 24:8ff; 26:18-19). To earn the king's approval and rewards, they even lied about David, and Saul believed them. We don't know what lies Cush told Saul, but David was concerned enough to cry out to God for deliverance and vindication. "Shiggaion" is used only here in the Psalms (but see Hab. 3:1) and could mean "a passionate psalm with strong emotion." Some believe it comes from a word meaning "to wander, to cry aloud." The theme is God's vindication of His servant and judgment on his enemies (vv. 6, 8, 11). The psalm described four different judgments.

Other People Judge us Wrongly (vv. 1-2)

Cush lied about David; therefore, Saul persecuted and pursued David (vv. 1, 5, 13). David fled to the Lord for refuge (see 11:1; 16:1; 31:1; 57:1; 71:1l; 141:8) because the Lord knew that David was innocent of

Saul's accusations. David had saved his father's sheep from the attacks of dangerous beasts (1 Sam. 17:34-37), and now he felt like he was the victim. (For animals as symbols of enemies, see 10:9; 17:12; 22:12-13, 16, 20-21; 35:17; 57:4; 58:6; 124:6.) David saw himself as a "dead dog," a "flea," or a hunted bird (1 Sam. 24:14; 26:20). Note that the *King James Version* and the *New American Standard Bible* move from the plural (v. 1) to the singular (v. 2), from Saul's men to Saul himself. Saul's judgment of David was false, and David trusted the Lord to protect and save him. When today, people falsely accuse us and create problems for us, we should follow David's example and find refuge in the Lord. But let's be sure that we are suffering *wrongfully* and not because of our own foolishness or disobedience (Matt. 5:11-12; 1 Peter 3:13-17).

We Judge Ourselves Honestly (vv. 3-5)

David affirmed his integrity before the Lord and asked the Supreme Judge to vindicate him because his hands were clean. David wasn't claiming to be sinless; he was stating that he was blameless in his motives and actions (v. 8; see 18:16-26; Phil. 2:12-15). If indeed David was guilty of sin, he was willing to accept God's discipline; but he knew that his hands were pure. David had two opportunities to kill King Saul and refused to do so (1 Sam. 24, 26). This was proof enough that his heart was not filled with personal malice and a desire for revenge. How important it is that we are open and honest with both our Lord and ourselves. If he was proved guilty, then David was willing for his own honor to be laid in the dust; but David knew that his hands were clean (Isa. 1:15; 59:3; Ezek. 23:37, 45; Acts 20:26).

God Judges Sinners Righteously (vv. 6-13)

David didn't take the situation into his own hands; rather, he turned Saul and his scheming men over to the Lord. Only God's holy anger could truly vindicate David (Rom. 12:17-21). "Arise, O Lord" reminds us of the words of Moses when the camp of Israel began their march with the ark leading the way (Num. 10:35; see also 2 Chron. 6:40-42). David knew that danger was near, and he wanted the Lord to move into action. (See 3:7; 9:19; 10:12; 17:13; 44:26; 68:1.) It's during those times when God seems inactive that we get impatient and want to see things happen immediately. But God is more longsuffering than we are, and we must wait for Him to work in His time. "Let God convene the court! Ascend Your throne on high! Let all the people gather together to witness the trial! Let the Lord try me and prove to all that I am innocent!" David knew that Almighty God could test the minds and the hearts (v. 9; see Rev. 2:23), and he wanted to see the wickedness of his enemies exposed and stopped. David's defense was with the Lord.

How can God both love the world (John 3:16) and hate the wicked? (On God's hatred of evil, see 5:5.) The *King James Version* puts "with the wicked" in italics, which means the phrase was added by the translators, but both the *New International Version* and the *New American Standard Bible* translate the text without it. Their emphasis is that God expresses His anger at sin every day, so He doesn't have to summon a special court to judge sinners. He allows sinners to reap the sad consequences of their sins day by day (v. 16; see Rom. 1:24, 26-27, 32), but sometimes their persistent rebellion causes Him to send special judgment when His longsuffering has run its course

(Gen. 6:5ff). God's love is a holy love, and if God loves righteousness, He must also hate wickedness.

Note that God is called "God Most High" (vv. 8, 10, 17), which is El Elyon in the Hebrew. This divine name is used twenty-three times in the Psalms and goes back to Genesis 14:18-22. (See also Deut. 32:8; 2 Sam. 22:14 and 23:1.) Jesus was called "Son of the Most High" (Mark 5:7; Luke 1:32, 35; 8:28).

Sin Itself Judges Sinners Ultimately (vv. 14-17)

The image of sin as pregnancy is frequently found in Scripture (Job 15:35; Isa. 33:11; 59:4, 13; James 1:13-15). Sinners "conceive" sin that, like a monstrous child, eventually grows up and destroys them. They dig pits and fall into them themselves (see 9:16; 37:14-15; and 57:6; 1 Sam. 25:39; Prov. 26:27; Ecc. 10:8; Ezek. 19:4). The trouble they cause comes back on their own heads (Gal. 6:7). There is a work of divine retribution in this world, and nobody can escape it. "Though the mills of God grind slowly, yet they grind exceeding small" (Friedrich von Logau).

God abandoned King Saul to his own ways (1 Sam. 15), and ultimately both the arrow and the sword caught up with him (vv. 12-13; 1 Sam. 31:3-4). He wanted to kill David, but his own sword killed him. Pharaoh ordered the male Jewish babies to be drowned in the Nile, and his own army was drowned in the Red Sea. Haman built a gallows on which to hang Mordecai, and Haman himself was hanged on it (Est. 7).

The psalm closes with David extolling the Lord, not for the fact that sinners have been judged, but because the righteousness of God has been magnified. The fact that people are ensnared by their own sins and ultimately judged brings no joy to the hearts of believers, but the fact that

God is glorified and His righteousness exalted does cause us to praise Him. God judges sin because He is holy, and His decrees are just (v. 6). "Even so, Father, for so it seemed good in Your sight" (Luke 10:21). Finally, keep in mind that God gave His own Son to die for the sins of the world, so that He might uphold His own holy law and at the same time offer His mercy and grace to all who will believe. People may not like the way God runs His universe, but, as Dorothy Sayers expressed it, "for whatever reason God chose to make man as he is—limited and suffering and subject to sorrows and death—He had the honesty and the courage to take His own medicine" (*Christian Letters to a Post-Christian World* [Eerdmans, 1969], p. 14).

Psalm 8

In this beautiful expression of praise to God, David stands amazed that the God of creation, the great and glorious Jehovah, would pay any attention to frail people on earth. David understands that God glorifies Himself in the heavens, but how can He glorify Himself on earth through such weak, sinful people? This is a "nature psalm" (see 19, 29, 65, 104), but it is also a Messianic psalm (Matt. 21:16; Heb. 2:6-8; 1 Cor. 15:27; Eph. 1:22). The answer to the question "What is man?" is ultimately answered by Jesus Christ, the "Last Adam," through whom we regain our lost dominion. "Gittith" means "winepress" and may identify a vintage tune (see 81 and 84). As they worship and serve Him (Matt. 5:13-16), the faithful people of God glorify His name on earth (vv. 1, 9) and help to defeat His enemies (v. 2). That God, in His remarkable condescension, should focus attention on us is proof of our dignity as creatures made in the image of God. The grandeur of men and women is found only there. Apart from knowing God, we have no understanding of who we are or what we are to do in this great universe.

God Created Us (vv. 1-2, 5a)

The phrase "our Lord" is a threefold confession of faith: there is but one God, all people were created by God, and the Jewish people in particular are "his people and the sheep of his pasture" (100:3). They can call Him "our Lord." See 135:5, 147:5, and Nehemiah 10:30. However, Jehovah was not a "tribal god" who belonged only to Israel, for He wanted His name (character, reputation) to be known "in all the earth" (66:1; 83:18; Ex. 9:14, 16; Josh. 3:11). Not only has the Lord set His glory "above the heavens" (beyond the earth's atmosphere), but He has also deigned to share His glory with His creatures on earth. The glory of God dwelt with Israel in the tabernacle and temple, and it was especially revealed in the person and work of Jesus Christ (John 1:14). Wicked people crucified "the Lord of glory" (1 Cor. 2:8), but He was raised from the dead and has returned to heaven in honor and great glory (Phil. 2:5-11).

In verse 2, David moved from God's transcendence to His immanence. Jehovah is so great that He can entrust His praise to infants and children and still not be robbed of glory! Jesus quoted this verse after He cleansed the temple (Matt. 21:16). Words are only sounds plus breath, two very weak things. Yet words of praise even from sucklings (not yet weaned) and babes (children able to play in the streets) can defeat God's enemies! The cry of baby Moses ultimately brought Egypt to her knees, and the birth of Samuel was used by God to save Israel and bring David to the throne. Of course, it was the birth of Jesus that brought salvation to this world. Indeed, God has used the weak and helpless to praise Him and help defeat His enemies (1 Cor. 1:27). David himself was but a youth when he silenced Goliath and defeated him (1 Sam. 17:33, 42-43), and he brought great glory to the name of the Lord (17:45-47). God didn't need us, yet He created us and prepared a wonderful world for us. As the Westminster Catechism states it, our purpose is to "glorify God and enjoy Him forever," and if we leave God out of our lives, we miss life's greatest opportunity.

God Cares for Us (vv. 3-4)

The sun rules the day, but its blinding light usually blots out anything else we might see in the heavens, but at night, we are overwhelmed by the display of beauty from the moon, stars, planets, and galaxies. Ralph Waldo Emerson wrote that if the stars came out only once in a century, people would stay up all night gazing at them. What we know today about the size of the universe makes the earth and its inhabitants look even more insignificant than they appeared in David's day. Our knowledge of light years and the reaches of outer space gives us even more reason for appreciating our insignificance in the solar system and God's wonderful concern for us. In His great love, the Lord chose the earth for Himself (Ps. 24:1) and created us in His own image. "Man" in verse 4 is *enosh*, "weak man," and "son of man" is "son of *adamah*—son of the earth, earth-born" (Gen. 2:7). Both titles emphasize the weakness and frailty of humankind.

God spoke the worlds into existence, but David saw creation as coming from God's fingers (v. 3; see Ex. 8:19 and 21:18) and hands (v. 6), the work of a Master

Craftsman. It was evil for the Jews to worship the heavenly host (Ex. 20:4-6; Deut. 4:15-19; 17:2-7), but they understood that creation was proof of a caring Creator who prepared the world for the enjoyment and employment of mankind. God is mindful of us ("remembers," see Gen. 8:1; 19:29; 30:22) and cares for us ("visits," see Jer. 29:11; Job 10:12). God completed His creation before He made Adam and Eve and placed them in the garden, so everything was ready for them, to meet their every need.

God Crowns Us (vv. 5-8)

Why does God pay attention to "frail creatures of dust"? Because He has made them in His own image, and they are special! Instead of humans being "a little higher than animals," as science believes, they are actually "a little lower than God." The word *elohim* can mean angelic creatures (see Heb. 2:7), but here it definitely means "God." The Lord crowned Adam and Eve and gave them dominion over the other creatures (Gen. 1:26-27). We are co-regents of creation with the Lord! The angels are servants (Heb. 1:14), but we are kings, and one day, all who have trusted Christ will be like Him (1 John 3:1-3; Rom. 8:29).

People today live more like slaves than rulers, so why aren't we living like kings? Because our first parents sinned and lost their crowns, forfeiting that glorious dominion. According to Romans 5, sin is reigning in our world (v. 21) and death is also reigning (vv. 14 and 17), but Jesus Christ has regained the dominion for us and will one day share it with us when He reigns in His kingdom (Heb. 2:6-8). When Jesus ministered here on earth, He exercised the dominion that Adam lost, for He ruled over the beasts (Mark 1:13; 11:1-7), the fowl (Luke 22:34), and the fish (Luke 5:4-7; Matt. 17:24-27; John 21:1-6). Today

He is on the throne in heaven and all things are "under his feet" (1 Cor. 15:27; Eph. 1:22; Heb. 2:8). The phrase means "completely subjected to Him" (47:4; Josh. 10:24; 1 Kings 5:17). Through the exalted Christ, God's grace is reigning today (Rom. 5:21) so that God's children may *"reign in life"* through Jesus Christ (v. 17). He has made us "kings and priests to His God and Father, to Him be glory and dominion forever and ever. Amen" (Rev. 1:6). By faith, "we see Jesus" (Heb. 2:8-9), crowned in heaven, and that assures us that one day we will reign with Him and receive our crowns (Rev. 20:1-6).

To summarize: God the Father created us to be kings, but the disobedience of our first parents robbed us of our crowns. God the Son came to earth and redeemed us to be kings (Rev. 1:5-6), and today the Holy Spirit of God can empower us to "reign in life by one, Jesus Christ" (Rom. 5:17). When you crown Jesus Christ Lord of all, you are a sovereign and not a slave, a victor and not a victim. "O Lord, our Lord, how excellent in your name in all the earth!"

Psalm 9

The emphasis is on joyful praise (vv. 1,2, 11, 14), especially for God's care of Israel and His righteous judgment on the nations that attacked His people. You find the theme of judgment and justice in verses 4, 7-8, 16 and 19-20, and note the mention of the throne of God (vv. 4, 7, 11, NIV). For a parallel passage, see Isaiah 25:1-5. "Muth-labben" means "death of a son," but we don't know how it relates to the psalm. Perhaps it was the name of a familiar melody to which the psalm was to be sung. Ever since the Lord spoke the words recorded in Genesis 3:15 and 12:1-3, there has been a war going on between the forces of Satan and the forces of God, and the focus has been on the nation of Israel. (See Rev. 12.) That battle goes on today.

Personal Praise: God Saves the King (vv. 1-8)

David offers whole-hearted praise to the Lord (Matt. 15:8) for delivering him and his army from the enemy nations that attacked Israel. His aim was to honor the Lord, not to glorify himself. His joy was in the Lord, not just in the great victory that He had been given (Phil. 4:4), and he wanted to tell everybody about God's wonderful works. See verses 14 and 103:1-2, 117:1, 138:1, 1 Peter 2:9, and Ephesians 2:7. "God Most High" is *El Elyon*; see 7:8, 10, 17; 18:13; 21:7. This was the name that Abraham honored after God gave him victory over the kings (Gen. 14).

David describes the victory in verses 3-6, verses that should be read in the past tense: "Because my enemies were turned back ..." Note the repeated "You have" in verses 4-6. God turned the enemy back, and in their retreat, they stumbled and perished before the Lord. Why did the Lord do this? To maintain the right of David to be king of Israel and accomplish God's purposes in this world. God's rebuke is an expression of His anger (2:5; 76:6). To "blot out" a name meant to destroy the person, place or nation completely (83:4; Ex. 17:14; Deut. 25:19; 1 Sam. 15; and see Deut. 9:14, 25:19, 29:20). In contrast to the wiping out of the nations, the Lord and His great name stand forever. His throne cannot be overthrown. In fact, in the victory God gave David, the king saw a picture of the final judgment and victory when God will judge the world, and Paul referred to verse 8 in his address in Athens (Acts 17:31).

National Praise: God Shelters the People (vv. 9-20)

The focus now centers on the people of the land, whom David calls the oppressed (v. 9), the humble ("afflicted" v. 12), and the needy and the poor (v. 18). These are the faithful worshipers of the Lord who have been persecuted, abused, and exploited by local rulers for being true to the Lord. See 10:17; 25:16; 40:17; 102:1; Zephaniah 2:3 and 3:12-13. David praises the Lord for His faithfulness in caring for His sheep.

The refuge—God will not forsake them (vv. 9-10). The first word means "a high safe place" and the second "a stronghold." During his years of exile, David found the wilderness strongholds to be places of safety, but he knew that the Lord was the safest refuge (46:1). The phrase "times of trouble" means literally "times of extremity" (see 10:1; 27:5; 37:39; 41:1; 73:5; 107:6, 13, 19, 26, 28). To "know God's name" or "love God's name" means to trust Him and be saved (5:11; 69:36; 91:14; 119:132; 1 Sam. 2:12). God forsook His own Son (Matt. 27:46) that He might never forsake His own people.

The avenger—God will not fail them (vv. 11-17). David calls upon the suffering remnant to sing praises to God because He is on their side and fights their battles. He will not fail to hear their cries and execute justice on their behalf. Israel's calling was to bear witness to the nations that Jehovah is the only true and living God (18:49; 44:11; 57:9; 106:27; Isa. 42:6; 49:6). The ark was now in Jerusalem so Jehovah was on His throne in Israel. "Inquisition for blood" refers to the official investigation of murder, to see who was guilty of the crime, symbolized by having blood on the house (Deut. 22:8), the hands (Ezek. 3:17-21; 33:1-9), or the head (Acts 18:6). See Genesis 9:5 and 10:13. There was no police force in Israel, but a near kinsman could avenge the murder of a family member. This is why God assigned the six "cities of refuge" to provide havens for people who accidentally killed someone (Num. 35). But when God is the avenger, He has all the evidence He needs to find and punish rebellious sinners. The suffering remnant prays to God in verses 13-17 and asks to be taken from the gates of death (sheol, the world of the dead; see 107:18; Job 17:16; 38:17; Isa. 38:10) and put at the gates of Zion (v. 14). From death to life! They also ask God to catch their enemies in their own traps (vv. 15-16; see 7:14-16) and finally consign them to the grave (sheol). "Higgaion" could mean "meditation," or it may refer to a solemn sound on the accompanying instruments.

The conqueror—God will not forget them (vv. 18-20). "Arise, O Lord" reminds us of the conquering march of Israel (Num. 10:35), when God went before His people to defeat their enemies. "Man" in verse 19 is *enosh*, "weak frail man," a fact that sinners don't want to admit. (This we will see in Ps. 10.) One day the Lord will put the rebels in their rightful place and they will discover that they are only—dust!

Psalm 10

The problem in Psalm 9 is the enemy invading from without, while the problem in Psalm 10 is the enemy corrupting and destroying from within.[9] There were wicked nations around Israel (9:5), but there were also wicked people within the covenant community (10:4), people who claimed to know God, but whose lives proved they did not know God (Titus 2:16). They know there is a God, but they live as though there is no God or no final judgment. They are "practical atheists" who are their own gods and do whatever they please.

Questioning God (v. 1)

The psalmist wrestles with the age-old problem, "Why doesn't God do something about the prosperity of the wicked (vv. 2, 3, 4, 7, 10, 15) and the misery of the afflicted (vv. 2, 8-10, 12, 14, 17, 18)?" It's also discussed in 13:1-3; 27:9; 30:7; 44:23-24; 73; and 88:13-15, as well as Job 13:24ff and Jeremiah 14. The wicked are marching through the land, but the Lord seems to be distant and unconcerned. During the past century, millions of godly people have lost their homes, jobs, possessions, families, and even their lives because of the ruthless deeds of evil leaders, and where was God? (See 22:1, 11; 35:22; 38:21; 42:9; 43:2; 71:12; 74:1; 88:14.) God has expressed a special concern for widows, orphans, and the helpless (68:5; 82:3; Deut. 10:18; 24:17-21; 26:12-13; 27:19), yet He is not to be found. He "covers His eyes" as though nothing is happening (see Lev. 20:4; 1 Sam. 12:3; Prov. 28:27).

Rejecting God (vv. 2-13)

The psalmist now describes these wicked people, what they do, and why they do it. He gives four statements that express what they believe, because what they believe determines how they behave.

"There is no God" (vv. 2-4, see v. 4, NASB). Believing this lie frees the wicked to do whatever they please, for they become their own god. "You shall be as God" (Gen. 3:5 and 6:5). The wicked cleverly plot against the righteous and hotly pursue them until they get what they want. These evil workers live to please themselves and fulfill their selfish desires, and then brag about their sins! (Phil. 3:18-21). They revile the Lord (vv. 3, 13, NIV) and "stick their nose up" when anybody challenges them.

"I shall not be moved" (vv. 5-7). This arrogant attitude comes from an igno-

rance of the laws of God, because unconverted people have no understanding of the Word of God or the ways of God (1 Cor. 2:10-16). Because God is longsuffering, they think they're getting away with their sins (Eccl. 8:11). Peace and prosperity give them a false sense of security that will end very suddenly. See Luke 12:13-21 and 1 Thessalonians 5:1-3. Telling lies and swearing oaths they have no plans to keep, they escape the penalties of the law and pursue their devious ways. Like people savoring tasty food, they keep lies under their tongues and enjoy them (Job 20:12-15; Prov. 4:17). Paul quoted verse 7 in Romans 3:14. It is the godly who have God's promise of true security (15:15; 16:8; 21:7; 62:2; 112:6).

"God doesn't see me" (vv. 8-11). Like ferocious lions, wicked people hide and watch for opportunities to pounce on the helpless prey, and like hunters or fishermen, they catch their prey in their nets. They are sure that the law won't catch up with them or the Lord notice what they do. The lion is often used as a picture of ruthless sinners who attack others (17:12; 37:32; 56:6; 59:3; 64:4).

"God will not judge me" (vv. 12-13). At this point, the psalmist cries out to God for help, and he uses three different names for God: Jehovah, the God of the covenant, and El and Elohim, the God of power. The wicked boast that God will not investigate their sins or judge them, but God says, "Be sure your sin will find you out" (Num. 32:23). The Lord will keep His covenant promises to His people, and there will be a day of reckoning when sinners will be judged by a righteous God. "Arise, O God" takes us back to Numbers 10:35 and the triumphant march of Israel.

Read those statements again and see if they don't express the outlook of lost sinners today.

Trusting God (vv. 14-18)

As the psalm draws to a close, the writer expresses his full confidence that God is on His throne and has everything under His control. The Lord may not explain to us why some people seem to get away with their evil deeds, but He does assure us that He will judge sinners and ultimately defend His own. In this paragraph, the Lord answers all four of the statements of the wicked that are quoted in verses 2-13.

God sees what is going on (v. 14). This answers the claim in verses 8-11 that the Lord pays no attention to what the wicked are doing. Even more, God sees the trouble (outward circumstances) and grief (inward feelings) caused by the wicked as they persecute the helpless, and He will take the matter in hand. The poor and needy can safely commit themselves into the hands of the Lord (55:22; 1 Peter 5:7).

God judges sin (v. 15), and this answers the false claim of verses 12-13. The psalmist prays that the Lord will carefully investigate each sinner's life and works, until every evil deed is exposed and judged. But he asks that the sinners be judged in this life and their power removed ("break the arm"). This prayer isn't always answered. (See Rev. 6:9-11.)

God is King (v. 16). The wicked claim that there is no God (vv. 1-4), but the truth is that God *is* and *He rules over all!* (See 2:6; 5:2; 24:7-10; 29:10; 1 Sam. 8:6-7.) After their deliverance from Egypt, the Israelites sang praises to their King: "The Lord shall reign forever and ever" (Ex. 15:18).

God defends His own people (vv. 17-18). The wicked boast that they will not be moved (vv. 5-7), but God has other plans for them. He hears the prayers of the persecuted, He sees their plight, He strengthens their hearts for whatever trials He permits (Rom. 8:28), and He eventually judges those who abuse them. People of faith can depend on the God of heaven, but the self-confident and arrogant "people of the earth" have no future with the Lord. Life without the Lord is empty and vain (49:12-20; 62:9). Christians have their citizenship in heaven (Phil. 3:20), and their names are written down in heaven (Luke 10:20). They don't belong to this world, although their ministry is in this world. God's people have been "redeemed from the earth" (Rev. 14:3) and have heaven as their home. The phrase "them that dwell on the earth" is found often in the book of Revelation (3:10; 6:10; 8:13; 11:10; 12:12; 13:8, 12, 14; 14:6; 17:2, 8) and describes not only where these unbelievers live but what they live for—the things of the earth. The "earth dwellers" may seem to have the upper hand today, but wait until the Lord reveals His hand!

Psalm 11

It's difficult to determine the historical background of this psalm. David was often in danger, whether in the court of Saul (1 Sam. 19:1), in the wilderness being chased by Saul, or during the rebellion of Absalom, his son. David did flee from Saul's court and hide in the wilderness for perhaps ten years, and he did abandon Jerusalem to Absalom and take refuge over the Jordan, both of which proved to be wise moves. But during the crisis described in this psalm, David did not flee his post but remained on duty, trusting the Lord to protect him, and He did. Whatever the crisis, the psalm teaches us that we must choose between fear (walking by sight) or trust (walking by faith), listening to human counsel or obeying the wisdom that comes from the Lord (James 1:5).

What David Should Do (v. 1)

When the crisis arose, David's counselors immediately told him to leave Jerusalem and head for the safety of the mountains. They didn't seem to have faith that the Lord could see him through (see 3:2 and 4:6). David used the imagery of the bird in 55:6-7. But David didn't need wings like a dove; he needed wings like an eagle (Isa. 40:31) so he could rise above the storm by faith and defeat his enemies. The verb "flee" is in the plural and refers to David and his court. It's right for us to flee from temptation (2 Tim. 2:22) as Joseph did (Gen. 39:11-13), but it's wrong to flee from the place of duty, as Nehemiah was invited to do (Neh. 6:10-11). The leader who flees needlessly from the crisis is only a hireling and not a faithful shepherd (John 10:12-13). Beware of listening to unwise counsel. Put your faith in the Lord, and He will protect you and direct your paths.

What the Enemy Does (v. 2)

"For, look" (NIV) suggests that these counselors are walking by sight and evaluating the situation from the human perspective. (See 2 Kings 6:8-23.) It's good to know the facts, but it's better to look at those facts in the light of the presence and promises of God. There was a secret plot afoot, not unusual in an eastern palace. The bows and arrows may have been literal, but it's more likely they are metaphors for deceptive and destructive words (57:4; 64:3-4; Prov. 26:18-19; Jer. 9:3, 8; 18:18). Perhaps this psalm was written during the early days of Absalom's campaign (2 Sam. 15:1-6). David was upright before God (v. 2) and righteous (vv. 3, 5), and he knew that the Lord was righteous and would do the right thing (v. 7).

What Can the Righteous Do? (v. 3)

David was God's appointed king, so anything that attacked him personally would shake the very foundations of the nation. God had abandoned Saul as king, and Absalom had never been chosen king, and both men weakened the foundations of divine government. (See 75:3 and 82:5.) Society is built on truth, and when truth is questioned or denied, the foundations shake (Isa. 59:11-15). The question "What can the righteous do?" has also been translated, "What is the Righteous One doing?" God sometimes "shakes things" so that His people will work on building the church and not focus on maintaining the scaffolding (Heb. 12:25-29; Hag. 2:6). But the traditional translation is accurate, and the answer to the question is, "Lay the foundations again!" Each new generation must see to it that the foundations of truth and justice are solid. Samuel laid again the foundations of the covenant (1 Sam. 12), and Ezra laid again the foundations of the temple (Ezra 3). In spite of all his trials, David lived to make preparations for the building of the temple and the organization of the temple worship. During the checkered history of Judah, godly kings cleansed the land of idolatry and brought the people back to the true worship of the Lord. Christ's messages to the churches in Revelation 2-3 make it clear that local churches need constant examination to see if they're faithful to the Lord, and we need to pray for a constant reviving work of the Spirit.

What God Will Do (vv. 4-7)

When you look around, you see the problems, but when you look up to the Lord by faith, you see the answer to the problems. When the outlook is grim, try the uplook! "In the Lord I put my trust," said David, for he knew that God was on the throne in His holy temple in heaven (Hab. 2:20; Isa. 6) and that He saw everything the enemy was doing. The word "try" or "test" in verse 4 carries the idea of "testing metals by fire," as in Jeremiah 11:20 and 17:10. God's eyes penetrate into our hearts and minds (Heb. 4:12; Rev. 2:23). The Lord tests the righteous to bring out the best in them, but Satan tempts them to bring out the worst. When we trust the Lord in the difficulties of life, our trials work for us and not against us (2 Cor. 4:7-18).

David uses three images to describe the judgment that God has prepared for the wicked. First, he saw fire and brimstone descend on them, such as the Lord sent on Sodom and Gomorrah (v. 6a; Gen. 19:24; see also Isa. 30:33; Rev. 9:17). Then he beheld a terrible storm destroying the enemy, a "scorching wind" such as often blew from the desert (v. 6b). David used the image of the storm in his song about his deliverance from his enemies and King Saul (18:4-19). The third image is that of a poisonous potion in a cup (6c, KJV and NASB). "Drinking the cup" is often a picture of judgment from the Lord (75:8; Isa. 51:17, 22; Jer. 25:15-17; Ezek. 38:22; Rev. 14:10; 16:19; 18:6). On the Lord's hatred of evil and violent people, see 5:5.

What does God have planned for His own people? "The upright will behold His face" (v. 7, NASB; see 17:15 and 1 John 3:1-3.) To "see the face" means to have access to a person, such as "to see the king's face" (2 Sam. 14:24). For God to turn His face away is to reject us, but for Him to look upon us with delight means He is going to bless us (Num. 6:22-27). When Jesus returns, those who have rejected Him will be cast "away from the presence of the Lord and from the glory of His power" (2 Thess. 1:8-10; Matt. 7:21-23), while His own children will be welcomed into His presence (Matt. 25:34).

Psalm 12

On some university campuses, what once was called "Home Economics" is now "The College of Applied Life Studies." In Tucson, Arizona, potholes are no more, because they're now known as "pavement deficiencies." In politics, new taxes are "revenue enhancements," and in military jargon, "retreat" is "backloading of augmentation personnel." If, while you're backloading, you get shot, the bullet hole is "a ballistically induced aperture in the subcutaneous environment."[10] This kind of artificial evasive language is known as "double-speak" and its popularity in almost every area of human life is evidence that language and communication are in serious trouble. Our ability to speak and write words is a precious gift of God, and this psalm deals with the right and wrong use of that gift. (For "Sheminith," see Ps. 6.)

The Righteous—Despairing Words (v. 1)

In Psalm 11, the foundations of society were shaking (v. 3), but here David cried out for help (salvation, deliverance) because the godly remnant of faithful believers was getting smaller and smaller. This wasn't the complaint of a crotchety old man longing for "the good old days." It was the cry of a truly faithful servant of God who wanted to see his nation Israel fulfill her divine purposes on earth. The faithfulness of Israel involved bringing the Savior into the world and blessing all the nations (Gen. 12:1-3). David wasn't alone in his concern. Elijah thought he was the only faithful prophet left (1 Kings 18:22; 19:10, 18), and the prophets Isaiah (Isa. 57:1) and Micah (Mic. 7:1-7) expressed their concern at the absence of righteous leaders. See also Psalm 116:1, Ecclesiastes 10:5-7, and Jeremiah 5:1. When he wrote 1

Timothy, Paul lamented over what "some" were doing in the church (1:3, 6, 19; 4:1; 5:15; 6:10), but in 2 Timothy, that "some" had become "all" (1:15; 4:16). One of the tragedies today is that a new generation of believers doesn't seem to know what it takes to be a godly leader, so they borrow leadership ideas from secular society and all kinds of unequipped and unqualified people to be leaders.

The Wicked—Deceptive words (vv. 2-4)

One mark of a Spirit-filled believer is the ability to detect lies and liars and avoid them (1 John 2:18-29), and David knew that he was living in a society controlled by deception. It wasn't that only a few people were telling lies; deception was a major characteristic of the whole generation. (See 5:9; 28:3; 34:13; 55:21; 141:3.) What would David say if he were alive today and witnessed the propaganda and promotion that make up what we casually call "the media"? He would probably describe today's "communication" as he did centuries ago: empty and useless words ("vanity"), smooth talk ("flattery"), double-talk from double hearts, and boastful talk or "proud words."

Saul used lies to deceive his leaders about David, and Absalom used flattery to poison the minds of the naïve people of Israel against David. Flattery is not communication, it's manipulation (see Prov. 26:28; 28:23). Even in Christian ministry it's possible to use flattery to influence people and exploit them (1 Thess. 2:1-6; Acts 20:28-31). Flattery plays on the ego and especially influences people who want to appear important (Jude 11). You can flatter yourself (36:2), others (5:9; 12:2), and even God (78:34-37). Of course, what the lips speak comes from the heart (Matt. 12:33-37), and that's why David accuses these liars of duplicity, which is a divided heart (literally "a heart and a heart"). This is the opposite of the "perfect heart," total loyalty to God and His truth (86:11; 1 Chron. 12:33, 38; Rom. 16:17-18).

As for "proud words," this describes boastful speech that impresses people by its oratory and vocabulary. "Great swelling words" is the phrase used in 2 Peter 2:18 and Jude 1:16. Daniel (7:20, 25) and John (Rev. 13:2, 5) both tell us that the Antichrist will speak in this way and rule the world. This kind of speech is motivated by pride and is used by people who think they're in control and will never need to answer to anybody, including the Lord. Their lips are their own, and they can speak just as they please.

The Lord—Delivering Words (vv. 5-8)
But God sees the oppression of the weak (Ex. 3:7) and hears the pain in their cries, and He declares that He will arise and judge the liars and deceivers. "I will arise" takes us back to 3:7, 7:6, 9:19, and 10:12, and see Numbers 10:35 and Isaiah 33:11-12. "Safety" in verse 5 ("protect," NIV) comes from the same Hebrew root as "help" in verse 1 and "deliver" in 6:8, and is the basis for the names "Jesus" and "Joshua" ("Jehovah is salvation"). The last phrase in verse 5 should read as in the *New American Standard Bible*: "the safety for which he longs." When God comes to deliver His people, He will "cut off" those who practice flattery and deception (v. 3), which means separation from the covenant community (Gen. 17:14), like the separation of the goats from the sheep (Matt. 25:31-33).

But can the Lord's promises be trusted? Yes! Unlike the worthless words of the deceivers, the Word of the Lord is like precious silver (19:9-10) that is heated seven times in the crucible before it is poured out into the mold. His Word is flawless and can be trusted; His Word is precious and must be valued (119:14, 72, 127, 162). How paradoxical that society today sees the Scriptures as something relatively worthless and yet pays great sums of money to the people who manufacture deception and flattery. No matter how many lies this generation tells, God's Word is safe, for He said, "I am watching over My word to perform it" (Jer. 1:12, NASB). Furthermore, God is able to protect His godly people from the lies of the enemy. God's people are "the generation of the righteous" (14:5), the generation that seeks God (24:6), the generation of His children (73:15), the generation of the upright (112:2). If God's people will saturate themselves with God's Word, they won't be seduced by "this lying generation." When the church adopts the techniques and motives of the world system, the church ceases to glorify the Lord.

The final verse issues a call to action, for "the wicked strut about, and evil is praised throughout the land" (NLT). Vileness ("cheapness") is promoted and exalted in the media: immorality, brutality, murder, lies, drunkenness, nudity, the love of money, the abuse of authority. The things that God condemns are now a means of universal entertainment, and the entertainment industry gives awards to the people who produce these things. People boast about things they ought to be ashamed of (Phil. 3:18-19). Is there a way to restrain and overcome this national decay? Yes! God's people are salt and light (Matt. 5:13-16). If there were more light in the land, there would be less darkness, and if we had more salt, there would be less decay. As God's people worship God, pray, and share the Gospel with the lost, more people will trust Christ and increase the salt and light in the land. We must also share the truth of the Word with the next generation (2 Tim. 2:2) and prepare them for the battles and opportunities to come (78:1-8; 102:18). The church is always one generation short of extinction, so we must be faithful to win the lost and teach the believers, or vileness will conquer the land.

Psalm 13

This psalm was probably written during David's difficult years of exile when King Saul was pursuing him. There were times when he confessed, "There is but a step between me and death" (1 Sam. 20:3). By the grace of God, David turned his sufferings into songs and left those songs behind to encourage us in our trials (2 Cor. 1:2-11). In this brief psalm, David deals with his feelings, his foes, and his faith.

The Inward Struggle—His Feelings (vv. 1-2)

God had promised David the throne of Israel, yet that day of coronation seemed further and further away. Saul was doing evil things, and God wasn't judging him, and yet David was doing good things and felt abandoned by the Lord. David was certainly disturbed by what the enemy was doing, but he was more concerned about what the Lord was *not* doing. "How long?" is a familiar question in Scripture (see 6:3) and is a perfectly good question to ask if your heart is right with God. The saints in heaven even ask it (Rev. 6:10). When we're in trouble and pray for help, but none comes, we tend to feel deserted. David felt that God was ignoring him and that this alienation was final and complete. He also felt that God was hiding His face from him instead of smiling upon him (see 30:7; 44:24; Lam.

5:20). To behold God's face by faith and see His glory was always an encouragement to David (11:7; 17:15; 27:4, 8; 31:16; 34:5; 67:1), but now he felt abandoned.

Feeling like he was left to himself, David tried to devise various ways to overcome the enemy ("wrestle with my thoughts," NIV), but nothing seemed to satisfy him. But faith is living without scheming; it means not leaning on our own experiences and skills and trying to plot our own schedule (Prov. 3:5-6). There were storm clouds in the sky, hiding the sun, but the sun was still shining. It's a dangerous thing to give in to our feelings, because feelings are deceptive and undependable (Jer. 17:9). When Jacob heard the news about Simeon being left hostage in Egypt, he gave up and announced that everything was against him (Gen. 42:36) when actually God was causing everything to work *for* him. We must not deny our feelings and pretend that everything is going well, and there is no sin in asking, "How long?" But at the same time, we must realize how deceptive our feelings are and that God is greater than our hearts (1 John 3:20) and can lift us above the emotional storms of life. David eventually learned to replace the question "How long, O Lord?" with the affirmation, "My times are in your hands" (31:15). This is a lesson that all believers must learn.

The Outward Danger—His Foes (vv. 3-4)

It's good to have peace within you, but you also need protection around you. That's why David prayed to the Lord and made three requests. The first was, "Look on me," a plea for the Lord to fix His eyes on His servant and scrutinize him. David felt that God had hidden His face and he wanted Him to turn His face toward him again. His second request was that the

Lord answer Him and send some kind of encouragement. David felt he had been deserted and that his prayers were accomplishing nothing. "Give light to my eyes" was the third prayer. This involved not only spiritual enlightenment (19:8) but also physical and emotional vitality and strength (Ezra 9:8; 1 Sam. 14:24-30). When the mind and body are weary, how easy it is to be discouraged! Perhaps David was even ill and in danger of death (v. 3; see 7:5). If he died, what would happen to the throne of Israel?

As much as David was concerned about his own needs, he was concerned even more with the glory of God (v. 4). After all, God had chosen David and had commanded Samuel to anoint him king, and if David failed, God's name would be ridiculed. "Don't allow the enemy to gloat over me!" was his prayer. The word "moved" in verse 4 means "to waver, to be agitated, to totter and shake" (see 10:6). If David began to waver, the faithful people of the land would think that God was unable to fulfill His own promises. (See 35:19-21; 38:16-17.)

The Upward Look—His Faith (vv. 5-6)
The little word "but" indicates a transition from fear to faith and from questioning to claiming God's promises. In their false confidence, let the enemy rejoice, but David will rejoice in the Lord his God! David's feelings had been on a roller coaster, but God was still on the throne, and His character had not changed. God's mercy (steadfast love) was all that David needed for it would never fail (see 25:6; Isa. 63:9; Lam. 3:22-23). God's people don't live on explanations; they live on promises, and those promises are as unchanging as the character of God. "According to your faith be it unto you" (Matt. 9:29).

Relying on the Lord leads to rejoicing in the Lord and His salvation (*yeshua*). The word "bountiful" focuses on the goodness of God and His generosity in dealing with His people in grace. (See 103:2; 116:7; 119:17; and 142:7.) The NIV translates it, "The Lord has been good to me." David's circumstances haven't changed, but the Lord has changed him, and that occurred when David stopped looking at his feelings and his foes and by faith started looking to the Lord.

Psalm 14

The psalm deals with the character and conduct of the "practical atheist" and adds to the messages of Psalms 10 and 12. The three psalms present a vivid picture of the ungodly—their proud attitude (10), their deceitful words (12), and now their corrupt deeds (14). All that they are, say, and do comes from their arrogant (and ignorant) belief that "there is no God." Psalm 14 is duplicated in Psalm 53 with two changes: Psalm 53 uses the name "God" (Elohim) instead of "Jehovah" and replaces 14:6 with an addition to verse 5. David contrasted "the workers of iniquity" in Israel with the godly remnant ("the generation of the righteous" vv. 4-5) that sought God and obeyed the terms of His covenant. During the reign of King Saul, the spiritual level of the nation was very low, and many Jews followed the bad example of Israel's first king. But even in the worst of times, God has cared for His faithful remnant and has been their refuge in times of trouble. Note the characteristics of the "practical atheists."

Willful Folly—They Ignore God (vv. 1-3)
Our English word "fool" comes from a

Latin word that means "bellows," suggesting that the fool is a person "full of hot air." In the Hebrew language, there are three basic words for "fool": *kesyl*, the dull, stupid fool; *ewiyl*, the unreasonable and perverted fool; and *nabal*, the brutish person who is like a stubborn animal. *Nabal* is the word used in 14:1, and it was the name of a man who was brutish and refused to help David (1 Sam. 25). People who say "There is no God" are not necessarily lacking normal intelligence; in fact, they may have good minds. However, they lack spiritual wisdom and insight. The *nabal* fool has a moral problem in the heart, not a mental problem in the head. The American evangelist Billy Sunday used to say that sinners can't find God for the same reason criminals can't find policemen—they aren't looking!

Nabal fools are self-righteous and don't need or want God. They want to live their own lives the way they please. Their problem is willful ignorance and not lack of normal intelligence (2 Peter 3:5; Rom. 1:18-28). But this decision causes sad consequences in both their character and their conduct. By leaving God out of their lives, they cause their inner person to become more and more corrupt—the heart (v. 1), the mind (vv. 2, 4), and the will (v. 3). The Hebrew word means "rotten, putrid, decayed." It is used to describe Jeremiah's useless sash (Jer. 13:7). When God looks down to investigate (Gen. 6:5, 11-12; 11:15; 18:21), He sees people who are filthy (v. 3), a word that describes milk that has become rancid. "Gone aside" means they have turned their backs on God (Jer. 2:21) and refuse to fulfill the purpose for which they were created—to glorify God.

This indictment is universal: all people, individually or all together, cannot do anything at all that is good enough to merit heaven—no one, no, not one. Paul quotes from this passage in Romans 3 as part of his proof that the whole world is guilty before God and can be saved only by the grace of God as revealed in Jesus Christ (Rom. 3:9-26). Human depravity doesn't mean that all persons are as wicked as they can be, or that all are equally bad, or that no man or woman can ever do anything good (Luke 11:13). It simply means that all have a fallen nature they cannot change, and that apart from the grace of God, none can be saved from eternal judgment.

Sudden Fear—They Meet God (vv. 4-6)

Someone asked the agnostic British philosopher Bertrand Russell what he would say if, when he died, he suddenly found himself standing before God. Russell replied, "You did not give us sufficient evidence!" If the heavens above us, the earth beneath our feet, the wonders of nature around us, and the life and conscience within us, don't convince us of the existence of a wise and powerful Creator, how much more evidence must the Lord give? An atheistic Russian cosmonaut said he'd looked carefully while in space and didn't see God. Someone commented, "If he'd opened the door of the space capsule, he would have met Him!" The time comes when God and the sinner suddenly meet. See Belshazzar in Daniel 5, the rich farmer in Luke 12:13-21, and the people in Revelation 6:12-17.

Verse 4 gives us two more indictments: these practical atheists take advantage of the weak and the poor, and they will not call upon the Lord. To "eat people like bread" is a biblical metaphor for exploiting the helpless (27:2; 35:25; 53:4; Mic. 3:1-3; Lam. 2:16; and see Isa. 3:12, Jer. 10:25, Amos 2:6-8, and Mic. 2:2 and 7:3). People must never be used as a means to an end or "treated as consumer goods," as Eugene H. Peterson expresses it.[11] Instead of praying to God, the wicked prey on the godly. But then the Lord suddenly appears in judgment, and He identifies Himself with the remnant of faithful believers. We don't know what event David was referring to, but the parallel passage in 53:5 suggests a great military victory that left all the enemy dead, unburied, and therefore humiliated. Some interpret the scene as a metaphor of a court case and connect it with verse 6, "You evildoers frustrate the plans [counsel] of the poor" (NIV). Imagine God suddenly appearing in court and ousting the crooked judge! Whatever the meaning, this much is clear: God is in the generation of the righteous, God is their refuge when the enemy attacks, and God will protect His own people.

Joyless Future—They Have No God (v. 7)

God has promised that the Redeemer will one day come to Zion and deliver His people in mighty power (Isa. 59:16-21; Jer. 31:33-34), and Paul affirmed this at the close of his great discussion of the future redemption of the Jewish nation (Rom. 11:25-32). The word "captivity" in verse 7 doesn't refer to the Babylonian captivity, for Jeremiah made it clear that it would end in seventy years (Jer. 25:8-14). The phrase "bring back the captivity" means "to restore the fortunes, to radically change circumstances from bad to very good." The day will come when Jesus Christ will return, defeat His enemies, cleanse the nation of Israel, and establish His righteous kingdom on this earth (Zech. 10-14). What a time of rejoicing that will be when the prayer "Thy kingdom come" is fulfilled!

But what about the wicked? They have

no future with the Lord because they preferred not to know the Lord or live for Him. They lived according to the desires of their own heart, not to please the Lord and glorify Him. Those who reject Jesus Christ will spend eternity apart from the Lord and will honestly be able to say in hell, "There is no God—here!"

Psalm 15

Psalm 14 informs us that there were two groups in Israel: the "workers of iniquity" and "the generation of the righteous" (vv. 4-5). The former group forsook the law, but the latter group was a believing remnant that kept faith alive in the nation of Israel (Mal. 3:16-18). Today, the church is that "righteous generation," citizens of that heavenly Zion (Heb. 12:19-25), that ought to make a difference in this world (Phil. 2:12-16). Psalms 10 and 12 focus on those who are not acceptable to the Lord while Psalm 15 describes those who are acceptable and are invited to dwell in His tabernacle. David may have written this psalm after his second—and successful—attempt to bring the ark of the covenant to Mt. Zion (2 Sam. 6) where it was housed in a tent.

The rabbis taught that there were 613 commandments for the Jewish people to obey if they wanted to be righteous, but this psalm brings that number down to eleven. Isaiah 33:15-16 gives six requirements, and Micah 6:8 lists three. Habakkuk 2:4 names but one—faith—for faith in Jesus Christ is the only way to have your sins forgiven and be welcomed into the Lord's presence (John 14:6; Rom. 1:7; Gal. 3:11; Heb. 10:38). The psalm says nothing about offering sacrifices, for spiritual Israelites knew that it was their personal faith that brought them salvation (Mark 12:28-34). It's important to note that Psalm 15 is not a *prescription* for being saved but a *description* of how saved people ought to live if they want to please God and fellowship with Him. The list contains both positive and negative qualities, and these qualities must be present in all of life at all times. Believers who would fellowship intimately with God must follow David's example and meet three personal requirements.

Seeking God's Presence (v. 1)

After his men captured Mt. Zion, David made it the site of his residence and of the sanctuary of God, and Jerusalem became "the city of David" (2 Sam. 5:1-16). The tabernacle, the throne, and the "holy hill" belonged together (see 24:3-6; 2:6; 3:4; 43:3). To the believer today, Mt. Zion speaks of the heavenly city where God's people will dwell forever (Heb. 12:19-25). David asked this question because he loved the house of the Lord (26:8; 27:3-5; 65:4) and desired in his heart to know God better and fellowship with Him in a deeper way. The priests could come and go in the house of the Lord, but David, though he was king, had to keep his distance. "Abide" means "to sojourn as a stranger," while "dwell" suggests a permanent residential status, but here the verbs are probably synonymous. Knowing about eastern hospitality, David wanted to enjoy the benefits of being a resident in God's house—enjoying God's fellowship, God's protection, and God's provision. The word "dwell" in the Hebrew is *shakan* and gives us the word *shekineh*, referring to the presence (dwelling) of God's glory in the sanctuary (Ex. 25:8; see also 29:46; 1 Chron. 22:19; Pss. 20:2; 78:69; 150:1). David's great desire was to be with God in heaven and dwell in His house forever (23:6; 61:4), for God is our eternal home (90:1). Believers today can enjoy intimate

fellowship with God through Jesus Christ (John 14:19-31; Heb. 10:19-25).

Obeying God's precepts (vv. 2-5a).

Three basic areas of life are named in verse 2—blameless character, righteous conduct, and truthful conversation—and then these are applied specifically and practically in verses 3-5a. If we are right in these basic virtues, we will "work them out" in every area of life and be obedient to the Lord. Walk, work, and speak are present participles, indicating that the dedicated believer is constantly obeying the Lord and seeking to please Him.

Integrity—blameless character (vv. 2a, 4a, 4b). What we *are* largely determines what we *do* and *say*, so the first emphasis is on godly character. (See Isa. 33:14-16; 58:1-12; Jer. 7:1-7; Ezek. 18:5-9; Hos. 6:6; Mic. 6:6-8; Matt. 5:1-16.) "Blameless" doesn't mean "sinless," for nobody on earth is sinless. Blameless has to do with soundness of character, integrity, complete loyalty to God. Noah was blameless (Gen. 6:9), and the Lord admonished Abraham to be blameless (Gen. 17:1), that is, devoted wholly to the Lord. (See 18:13, 23-25; 101:2, 6; Deut. 18:9-13; Luke 16:13.) People with integrity will honor others who have integrity and who fear the Lord (15:4; 119:63). They will not be deceived by the flatterers (12:2-3) or enticed by the sinful (1:1). When godly people endorse the words and deeds of the ungodly, there is confusion in the church. "Like a muddied fountain and a polluted spring is a righteous man…who compromises his integrity before the wicked" (Prov. 25:26, AMP).

Honesty—righteous conduct (vv. 2b, 5a, 5b). People who "work righteousness" are honest in their own dealings and concerned that justice be done in the land. In the ancient Jewish monarchy, there wasn't much the average citizen could do about crooked judges or extortion (Eccl. 3:16-17; 4:1-3), but in today's democracies, each qualified citizen at least has a vote. Someone defined "politics" as "the conduct of public affairs for private advantage," and too often that is true. In verse 5, David applied the principle of honesty to two areas: asking for exorbitant interest and accepting bribes. Both were "sins in good standing" in the days of the divided kingdom, and the prophets preached against both sins (Isa. 1:23; 5:23; 10:2; Ezek. 22:12; Amos 5:11-12). The Jews were not permitted to charge other Jews interest (Ex. 22:25; 23:7-8; Lev. 25:35-38; Deut. 23:20), and judges were warned not to accept bribes (Ex. 23:8; Deut. 10:17-18; 27:25; 2 Chron. 19:5-7). There can be no justice in a society where money tells the court what is right or wrong.

Sincerity—truthful conversation (vv. 2c, 3-4c). Truth is the cement that holds society together. If people can get away with lies, then every promise, agreement, oath, pledge, and contract is immediately destroyed. The false witness turns a trial into a travesty and causes the innocent to suffer. But we must speak truth in love (Eph. 4:15) and use truth as a tool to build relationships as well as a weapon to fight deception. When truth is in the heart, then the lips will not speak lies, spread gossip (Lev. 19:16), or attack the innocent. People with truthful hearts will keep their vows and promises (Deut. 23:22-24; Eccl. 5:1-5). People of integrity don't have to use oaths to strengthen their words. A simple yes or no carries all the weight that's needed (Matt. 5:33-37). More trouble is caused in families, neighborhoods, offices, and churches by gossip and lies and the people who keep them in circulation than by any other means. The Lord wants truth in our innermost being (51:6), and He wants us to love the truth and protect it.

The Lord is blameless in what He is (1 John 1:6), righteous in what He does (Ezra 9:15), and truthful in what He says (1 Sam. 15:29), and He wants His guests to have the same characteristics.

Trusting God's Promise (v. 5c)
"He who does these things will never be shaken" (NASB). This means that the godly described in this psalm have security and stability in life and don't have to be afraid of earthquakes or eviction notices. "Moved" comes from a Hebrew word that refers to a violent shaking (46:3-4; 82:5; 93:1; 96:10; Isa. 24:18-20). God's promise to the godly is that they are firmly grounded on His covenant promises and need not fear. "He who does the will of God abides forever" (1 John 2:17, NKJV). In these last days, God is shaking things so that the true will remain and the false will be exposed (Heb. 12:18-29). Jesus closed the Sermon on the Mount with a parable about two builders (Matt. 5:24-27) whose structures (lives) were tested by the judgment storm, and only one stood strong. It was the life built by the person who did the will of God. The godly life that our Lord discussed in the Sermon on the Mount parallels the characteristics of the godly person described in Psalm 15,[12] and in both places, the promise is given: "You shall never be moved."

Psalm 16

This is a very personal hymn of joy that focuses on the goodness of the Lord. The personal pronoun "my" is used over a dozen times (my trust, my goodness, my cup, etc.). David's joy (vv. 9, 11) is expressed in words like "delight" (vv. 3, 6), "pleasant" and "pleasure" (vv. 6, 11), and "glad" (v. 9). David finds his delight only in the Lord and confesses that everything good in his life has come from God. This psalm may have been written shortly after the Lord gave His gracious covenant to David and assured him of an enduring throne (2 Sam. 7). That covenant was eventually fulfilled in the Lord Jesus Christ, the Son of David (Luke 1:32-33). The style of David's response to the covenant (2 Sam. 7:18-29) matches that of Psalm 16, a combination of joy, praise to God, humility, and submission to the divine will. This is the first use of Michtam in The Psalms; it is repeated in the inscriptions to 56-60. Students don't agree on the meaning of the word: engraved in gold, to cover, secret treasure, a poem containing pithy sayings. All six of the Michtam psalms end on a happy and triumphant note. This is also a Messianic psalm, for in his message at Pentecost (Acts 2:25-28), Peter said it referred to Jesus, and so did Paul in his sermon in the synagogue at Antioch of Pisidia (Acts 13:35). As he praised God for His grace and goodness, David presented three descriptions of the Lord, and all three may be applied to Jesus Christ today.

The Lord of Life (vv. 1-8)

"Preserve me" ("Keep me safe," NIV) doesn't suggest that David was in trouble or danger, as in Psalms 9 and 13. It simply means that he needed God's constant care and oversight so that he might honor the Lord and enjoy all the good things that only God could give him. God alone is good (Matt. 19:17), and apart from Him, we have nothing good.

A good relationship (vv. 1-2). The Lord is our highest good and greatest treasure (73:25, 28), the giver of every good and perfect gift (James 1:17). To know Him through Jesus Christ is the highest privilege in life. If we have anything that we think is good, and it doesn't come from God, it isn't good. God meets us with "the

blessing of good things" (21:3, NASB), and His goodness follows us until we reach the Father's house (23:6). When Jesus Christ is your Savior (refuge) and Lord, you experience God's goodness even in the midst of trials. Our relationship to ourselves, our circumstances, other people, and the future depends on our relationship to the Lord.

A good companionship (vv. 3-4). We don't live the Christian life alone, because we're part of a great spiritual family and need each other. As in previous psalms, two groups are depicted: the believing remnant ("saints") and the unbelieving worshipers of idols (10:8-10; 11:2-3; 12; 14:5-6). The saints are those who trust God and obey His covenant, those who are set apart for the Lord. They take seriously God's command, "Be holy, for I am holy" (Lev. 19:2; 20:7-8, 26; 21:8). Israel was a kingdom of priests (Ex. 19:6; Deut. 7:6) and a holy nation, just as the church is today (1 Peter 2:9). David called them "the majestic ones" (NASB), a word that carries the meaning of excellence, nobility, and glory. In spite of our faults and failures, believers are God's elite, His nobility on earth. We must all love one another and use our God-given abilities and resources to minister to the family of God (Gal. 6:1-10). Like David, we must not compromise with those who disobey the Lord and worship idols (money, success, fame, etc.) but should seek to lead them to Jesus Christ, the source of all that is good and lasting. Multiplied gods only bring multiplied sorrows. David didn't even want to speak the names of the false gods of those in Israel who forsook the covenant (Ex. 23:13; Josh. 23:7). We are not to be isolationists, for the Lord has left us in this world to be salt and light; but we must be careful not to be defiled by their sins (James 1:27; 4:4; Rom. 12:2). No church is perfect, because no believer is perfect; but let's still give thanks for the people of God and seek to encourage them all we can.

A good stewardship (vv. 5-6). After Israel conquered the Promised Land, each tribe except Levi was assigned a special inheritance (Josh. 13-21). Because they served in the sanctuary and ate of the holy sacrifices, the priests and Levites had the Lord as their special inheritance (Num. 18:20-32; Deut. 10:8-9; 14:27-29; Josh. 13:14, 23), and David saw himself in that privileged position. "The Lord is the portion of my inheritance and my cup" (v. 5, NASB). To possess great wealth but not have the Lord is poverty indeed (Luke 12:13-21), and to enjoy the gifts but ignore the Giver is wickedness indeed. If Jesus is the Lord of our lives, then the possessions we have and the circumstances we are in represent the inheritance He gives us. The measuring lines marked off the inheritance of the tribes, clans and families in Israel, and then each individual lot was marked with a "landmark" that was not to be moved (Deut. 19:14; 27:17; Prov. 15:25; 22:28; 23:10-11). David rejoiced that God had caused the lines of his inheritance to fall in pleasant places, and that he had a "delightful inheritance" (NIV). He wanted to be a good steward of all that the Lord had given him.

A good fellowship (vv. 7-8). David's personal fellowship with the Lord was his greatest joy. This was when God instructed and counseled David and told him what to do and how to do it. David even went to "night school" to learn the will of God. (See 17:3; 42:8; 63:6; 77:2, 6.) "Night" is plural, suggesting "dark nights" or "night after night" learning from God. The word "instruct" carries with it the idea of discipline and chastening, for David learned many lessons when God's loving hand chastened him (Heb. 12:1-12). The Lord at his right hand suggests God as his advocate and defender. (See 73:23; 109:31; 110:5; 121:5; 1 John 2:2; Acts 2:33; 5:31.) With the Lord as his guide and guard, he had nothing to fear; he would not be moved (10:6; 15:5). The future is your friend when Jesus is your Lord.

The Conqueror of Death (vv. 9-10)
To delight in the Lord and His goodness and then lose all these blessings at death would be a great tragedy. "If in this life only we have hope in Christ, we are of all men the most pitiable" (1 Cor. 15:19, NKJV). But in His death and resurrection, Jesus has conquered death, and through faith in Him we have a "living hope" (1 Peter 1:3ff). When David wrote "My body will rest secure" (v. 9, NASB), he was referring to Messiah and not to himself. Using these verses, Peter proved that Jesus had been raised from the dead, for it's obvious that David was dead and his body had decayed in his tomb (Acts 2:22-31). But Jesus did not see corruption! When He arose from the dead on the third day, He had a real and substantial body, but it was a glorified body that could ingest food (Luke 24:36-42) but was also able to appear and disappear (Luke 24:28-31) and pass through locked doors (John 20:19-29). David could face death with a glad heart and soul, and could rest in the grave in hope, knowing that one day, he, too, would have a new glorified body. Paul used this same text to prove the resurrection of Jesus Christ from the dead (Acts 13:26-39). The full light of revelation about death and resurrection had not yet been revealed in Old Testament times, although there are hints in verses like 17:15 and 73:24-26, but through Jesus Christ, God had brought "life and immortality to light through the gospel" (2 Tim. 1:10).

The Joy of Eternity (v. 11)

The noted philosopher and Harvard University professor Alfred North Whitehead once asked a friend, "As for Christian theology, can you imagine anything more appallingly idiotic than the Christian idea of heaven?"[13] But the focal point of heaven is not gates of pearl, streets of gold, or even angels and glorified saints. The central glory and joy of heaven is Jesus Christ (Rev. 4-5). The path of life that He shows us on earth today will end in even greater life when we enter heaven. Then we shall be in His presence and experience fullness of joy and pleasures forevermore. A foolish caricature of heaven shows white-robed saints with halos and harps, resting on little white clouds; but the Bible gives no such description. In our glorified bodies, we shall be like Jesus Christ (Phil. 3:20-21; 1 John 3:1-3), and we shall worship and serve Him forever. The pleasures of heaven will be far beyond any pleasures we have known here on earth, and as we enjoy the Lord and serve Him, we will not be restricted or encumbered by time, physical weakness, or the consequences of sin. So magnificent are the glories of heaven that the apostle John had to ransack human language to find words to describe it (Rev. 21-22).

Is Jesus Christ the Lord of your life? Have you accepted your inheritance and are you making the most of it for His glory? Do you anticipate being with Christ in glory? Is He the joy of your life today; for if He isn't, when will you be prepared to enjoy Him for all eternity?

Psalm 17

This is one of five psalms identified as "prayers" (17, 86, 90, 102, 142). The title is also used in Habakkuk 3:1 and Psalm 72:20. Since most of the psalms contain prayers to the Lord, we wonder why these five were singled out for this special title. Except for 90, written by Moses, they describe the writer in dangerous situations and crying out to God for deliverance. Only 17, 86, and 142 are attributed to David, and they were probably written during the years when Saul pursued him. There are at least a dozen words for prayer in the Hebrew language, and this one (*tepilla*) can also mean "to intervene." Perhaps the title also told the temple musicians what melody to use when using these psalms in public worship. Psalm 17 has definite connections with Psalm 16—"keep me" (16:1/17:8); the night (16:7/17:3); the use of El as the name for God (16:1/17:6); the hand (16:8/17:7, 14); God's presence (16:11; 17:15); maintain or hold up (16:5/17:5). While there are suggestions of danger in Psalm 16 (vv. 1, 8, 10), the atmosphere is much more calm than what we find in 17. In this prayer, David deals with three pressing concerns and makes three major requests to the Lord. Each section opens with David addressing the Lord.

Vindication—"Examine Me" (vv. 1-5)

The psalm begins and ends with "righteousness" (vv. 1 and 15), because David wants God to examine him and vindicate him before his enemies. He saw God as a righteous judge who would give him a fair trial. King Saul and his leaders believed and circulated all kinds of lies about David, but the Lord and David knew the truth. David asked God to hear his plea, examine his life, and declare his integrity by giving him victory over the forces of Saul. Then everybody would know that God was with David, the man He has chosen to be Israel's king. God knew that David's prayer was sincere and that his life, though not sinless, was blameless. He was a man of integrity whose cause was a righteous one. During those years of exile, God had proved David's heart, visited and examined him, and tested him the way gold and silver are tested and refined in the crucible ("tested by fire"). (See 26:2; 66:10; 81:7; 95:9; 139:23-24; also Job 23:10; Rev. 3:18.) No matter what Saul and his men had said about him, David was able to affirm to the Lord that he had not spoken evil of the king. In fact, on at least two occasions, David could have slain Saul, but he refused to lay hands on God's chosen and anointed leader (1 Sam. 24, 26). Saul would have killed David (v. 9, "deadly enemies"), but David obeyed the Word of the Lord and kept himself from violence. Though he was a fugitive in the wilderness, David walked on the paths of the Lord and obeyed God's law.

David's declaration of righteousness was not evidence of pride or hypocrisy but of faithfulness to the Lord in difficult situations. You find similar language in 18:19-28, and see John 18:22-23 and Acts 23:1 and 24:16. David had a good conscience toward God.

Protection—"Keep Me" (vv. 6-12)

The enemy had surrounded him (vv. 9, 11; and see 1 Sam. 23:19-29), and though David was a masterful military tactician, he knew that without the Lord's help, he could not escape. God was not only the righteous judge, but He was also the powerful defender who could shelter David and his men from the enemy. He used the Hebrew name *El* as he addressed the Lord, a name that emphasizes God's great power, for He is "the Mighty God." His request in verse 7 reminds us of the "Song of Moses" in Exodus 15:1-19.

Jehovah is a God of marvels and wonders (Ex. 15:11) and great unfailing love (15:13), and His right hand works for His people (15:12). If God could deliver His people from Egypt, He could deliver David from the hand of Saul. (In Ps. 18, David will celebrate that victory.) David asked for "a marvelous demonstration of God's love" in the defeat of his enemies.

In verse 8, David used two images—the eye and the wings—to remind God that he was precious to Him. The "apple" of the eye is the pupil, the most delicate part of the eye. The Hebrew says "the little man of the eye," for when you look into someone's eyes, you can see yourself. Just as we protect the eye from injury, so David wanted the Lord to protect him. David may have borrowed this image from Deuteronomy 32:10. The phrase "under the shadow of thy wings" sometimes pictures the mother hen protecting her young (Matt. 23:37), but often it refers to the wings of the cherubim in the Holy of Holies of the tabernacle (Ex. 25:18-20). David asked the Lord to make his hiding place into a Holy of Holies, the place of God's throne and God's glory, protected by the angels of God (see 36:7-8; 57:1; 61:4; 63:7; Ruth 2:12). Because of the heavenly intercession of Jesus Christ, God's people today can enter into the Holy of Holies and fellowship with God (Heb. 10:1-25).

The enemy had arrogant mouths and hearts that were "enclosed in fat" (v. 10), that is, they had hearts that were callous from repeated disobedience to the Lord. In Scripture, "fatness" is sometimes associated with a selfish and worldly lifestyle (73:1-9; 119:70; Isa. 6:10). These people were morally and spiritually insensitive to what was right and weren't upset when they did something wrong. Paul called this "a seared conscience" (1 Tim. 4:2), for a heart covered with fat would not be sensitive to the needs of others (1 John 3:17). David's heart was sensitive to God's will; he knew that God wanted him to have "a broken and a contrite heart" (51:17). David was a compassionate shepherd, but Saul was a ravenous beast (v. 12; see 57:3 and 2 Sam. 1:23). Twice Saul threw his spear at David (1 Sam. 18:11; 19:10), on four occasions he sent soldiers to capture him, and Saul went personally to lay hold of him (1 Sam. 19:11-23). Now, like a lion, Saul tracked his prey and waited for the right time to pounce; but the Lord protected David.

Salvation—"Rescue Me" (vv. 13-15)

David now sees the Lord as his gracious Redeemer, rescuing him and his men from the wicked hands of Saul. These verses contrast the "people of this world" to the "people of God" who live for that which is eternal. "Arise, O Jehovah" reminds us of 3:7, 7:6, 9:19 and 10:12, all of which go back to Numbers 10:35. He asks the Lord to confront Saul and his army, cast them down, and use His sword to defeat them. "Cast down" (v. 13) can be translated "make him crouch down like a lion that has been subdued." (See v. 12.) Except for his son Jonathan, Saul and his leaders were not spiritually minded but thought only of the things of this fleeting world (39:5; 49:1; 89:47). As "men of the world," they lived for time, not for eternity, and for their own pleasures, and not for the glory of God. (See Luke 16:8 and 25 and James 5:5.)

Verse 14 is difficult to translate, but the sense seems clear: God was storing up judgment for David's enemies (Matt. 23:32; 1 Thess. 2:16), and their only reward would be in this life, not in the afterlife. They were full, they had many children who lacked nothing, and they would leave their wealth to their descendents. But the consequences of their sins would also be inherited by their descendents (Ex. 34:7; Num. 14:18). "May they have their punishment in full. May their children inherit more of the same, and may the judgment continue to their children's children" (v. 14, NLT). But verse 15 describes David's glorious future: seeing God's face and sharing God's likeness. This is one of the few texts in The Psalms that touches on the future life (see 16:11 and 73:23-26). "Awake" is a metaphor for the resurrection of the human body (2 Kings 4:31; Job 14:12, 14 and 26:19; Dan. 12:2; John 11:11; 1 Thess. 4:13-18). David seems to be saying, "Even when I die, the Lord won't desert me; for I shall be awakened and given a glorified body. I shall see His face, and I shall be satisfied!"

Psalm 18

This psalm of praise and victory was written and sung after the Lord made David king of all Israel and gave him victory over the nations that opposed his rule (2 Sam. 5, 8, 10). Another version of the psalm is found in 2 Samuel 22, and quotations and allusions are found in Psalm 116. No matter how much Saul persecuted David, David did not consider Saul his enemy. "Deliver" is one of the key words in the psalm; it is found in the title as well as in verses 2, 17, 19, 43, and 48 (KJV). It's possible that the new king used this song at a national day of prayer and praise to give thanks to the Lord for His manifold mercies to Israel. The psalm opens (vv. 1-3) and closes (vv. 46-50) with a doxology. David the servant of God (78:70; 89:3, 20, 39; 132:10; 144:10) addressed the Lord in verses 1, 25-29, 35-36, 39-40, 43, and 48, and in the rest of the psalm, he told the people what God had done for him, so the song blends worship and witness. The focus of the psalm is on the Lord and what He graciously did for His servant, but it also tells us what He can do for us today if we will trust and obey.

God Delivers When We Call on Him (vv. 1-18)

When David expressed his love for the Lord, he used a special word that means "to love deeply, to have compassion." It's related to the Hebrew word for "womb" (see Jer. 21:7) and describes the kind of love a mother has for her baby (Isa. 49:15), a father has for his children (103:13), and the Lord has for His chosen people Israel (102:13; Hos. 1:7; Deut. 13:17). It's a deep and fervent love, the kind of love all of us should have for the Lord (31:23). David expressed his love (v. 1), his faith (v. 2), and his hope (v. 3). The seven metaphors he used certainly reflect the life of an outdoorsman and a soldier. "Rock" (vv. 2, 31, 46) is a familiar metaphor for the Lord, speaking of strength and stability, a place of refuge (19:14; 28:1; 31:2-3; 42:9; 62:2, 6-7; 71:3; 78:20; 89:26; 92:15; 94:22; 95:1; 144:1; 1 Sam. 23:25). It goes back to Genesis 49:24 and Deuteronomy 32:4, 15, 18, and 30-31. "Fortress" pictures God as a stronghold, like the city of Jerusalem on Mount Zion (1 Sam. 22:4; 24:22; 2 Sam. 5:17; 23:14). "Shield" speaks of God's protection (3:3; 7:10; 28:7; 33:20; Gen. 15:1; Deut. 33:29), but it also is a symbol of the king (84:9; 89:18). David was Israel's shield, but the Lord was David's shield. "Horn" refers to strength (Deut. 33:17; 1 Sam. 2:1, 10; 1 Kings 22:11) and has Messianic connotations (Luke 1:69). This kind of God is worthy of our prayers and praise! (See 48:1; 96:4; 145:3.)

After expressing his devotion, David described his distress (vv. 4-6) and pictured himself as a man who had been hemmed in on every side, caught in a trap, bound with cords, and thrown into the water to drown. (See 88:16-178; 69:2, 15; 124:4; Job 22:11.) But, when he called, God began to act on his behalf. The great deliverance (vv. 7-19) is depicted as a storm. The Lord had been longsuffering with King Saul, but now His anger arose and began to shake things, like an earthquake and an erupting volcano (vv. 7-8; Ex. 15:8; Deut. 32:22). God came down in a storm, like a warrior in a chariot, carried along swiftly by a cherub. (See Gen. 3:24; Ex. 25:18; 2 Kings 19:15; Ezek. 1, 10). He was accompanied by darkness, rain, wind, hail (a rare thing in the Holy Land), thunder, and lightning (His arrows, v. 14; see 77:17, 144:6). All because David called on the Lord! (v. 6). At just the right time, God reached down and delivered David (vv. 16-19). Like Moses, he was drawn out of the water (Ex. 2:10). The enemy fell in defeat, but David stood firm, supported by the Lord (23:4). He was now king of Israel. Ten years of exile were ended, his life had been spared, and his ministry lay before him.

God Rewards When We Obey (vv. 19-27)

The word "distress" in verse 6 means "to be in a tight place, in a corner, hemmed in," but when the storm was over, David found himself in "a large place" where he could take "large steps" of faith in serving the Lord (v. 36). God enlarged David's trials (25:17) and used them to enlarge David! (4:1). David wasn't perfect, nor are we, but he was "a man after God's own heart" (1 Sam. 13:14, and see 15:28) and a man with a shepherd's heart (78:70-72; 2 Sam. 24:17). God delighted in David the way parents delight in the maturing of their children in character, obedience, and service. David was faithful to the Lord (vv. 20-24; 17:3-5), so the Lord faithfully cared for David (vv. 25-29). David knew

God's law (v. 22) and obeyed it, in spite of the difficult circumstances of his exile. In the spirit of Samuel (1 Sam. 12:3) and Hezekiah (2 Kings 20:3), his affirmation of righteousness was an evidence of humility and honesty, not pride and deception. Note the use of the words righteousness and cleanness (vv. 20, 24), upright (blameless, vv. 23, 25), and pure (v. 26).

David had clean hands (vv. 20, 24) as well as skillful hands (v. 34; 78:72).

The way we relate to the Lord determines how the Lord relates to us (vv. 25-27). David was merciful to Saul, and God was merciful to David (Matt. 5:9). David was loyal ("blameless"), and God was faithful to him and kept His promises to bless him. David wasn't sinless, but he was blameless in his motives. The "pure in heart" (Matt. 5:8) are those whose hearts are wholly dedicated to God. Saul had been devious in his dealings with God, David and the people, but David was honest and straightforward. It's true that early in his exile, he lied to Ahimelech the priest and to Achish, king of Gath (1 Sam. 21), but he soon learned that faith is living without scheming. Read verse 26 in the *New American Standard Bible* or the *New International Version* to see that God meets our "perverseness and crookedness" with His own shrewdness. The word translated "astute" or "shrewd" means "to wrestle," which reminds us of the way God dealt with Jacob (Gen. 32). God's character and covenants never change, but His dealings with us are determined by the condition of our hearts.

God Equips When We Submit to Him (vv. 28-45)

What was God accomplishing during those difficult years of Saul's reign? For one thing, He was disciplining His people for running ahead of Him and making Saul king (Hos. 13:10-11). In His longsuffering, He was also giving Saul opportunities to repent. At the same time, He was equipping David for his years of service. God takes time to prepare His servants: thirteen years for Joseph, forty years for Moses, and forty years for Joshua. The lessons David learned about himself and God during those years of exile helped to make him the man that he was. The images in these verses reveal God developing a great warrior, a compassionate leader, and a godly man.

The image of the lamp (v. 28) speaks of God's grace in keeping David alive during those dangerous years (Job 18:5-6; Prov. 13:9). It also speaks of the perpetuity of his family and dynasty (132:17; 2 Sam. 21:17; 1 Kings 11:36, 15:4; 2 Kings 8:19; 2 Chron. 21:7), culminating in the coming of Jesus Christ to earth (Luke 1:26-33). Because David trusted God (v. 30), God enabled him to run, leap, fight, and defeat the enemy (vv. 29, 32-34, 37-45). He could run through a troop, scale a wall, or leap like a deer up the mountains (see Hab. 3:19). This is not a glorification of war, for God trained him to fight His battles (v. 34) and protect Israel so they could accomplish His purposes on earth. David did not invade other countries just to add territory to his kingdom. Whatever land he gained was the result of his defeating armies that first attacked Israel.

Though David was a man of war, he recognized that it was God's gentleness that made him what he was. The word means "condescension." God condescended to look down and call David (1 Sam. 16), bend down and mold David (v. 35), and reach down and save David (v. 16); and then He lifted him up to the throne (vv. 39-45). This reminds us of what Jesus, the Son of David, did when He "stepped down" to come to earth as a servant and die for our sins (Phil. 2:1-11; see also John 8:1-11 and 13:1-11). Because David was submitted to the Lord, God could trust Him with the authority and glory of the throne. Only those who are under authority should exercise authority.

God is Glorified When We Worship Him (vv. 46-50)

After looking back at God's gracious ministry to him, what else could David do but praise Him? "He must increase, but I must decrease" (John 3:30). David didn't take things into his own hands but allowed the Lord to vindicate him when the time was right (1 Sam. 24:1-7; 26:1-12; Rom. 12:17-21).

Paul quoted verse 49 in Romans 15:9 and applied it to the Jews praising God among the Gentiles. In Romans 15:10-11, the Jews and Gentiles rejoice together—the result of Paul's ministry to the Gentiles—and then Romans 15:12 announces Jesus Christ reigning over both Jews and Gentiles (see Isa. 11:10).

The psalm climaxes with David exalting the Lord for His covenant to him and to his descendants (v. 50; 2 Sam. 7). Little children often use their own names when they ask for something ("Please give Tommy a cookie"), and David used his own name here, just like a little child. (See also 2 Sam. 7:20). David used the word "forever," so he must have realized that it would be through the promised Messiah that the kingdom promises would be fulfilled. "And he shall reign forever and ever" (Rev. 11:15).

Psalm 19

Two quotations help to introduce this psalm. The first is from the German philosopher Immanuel Kant: "Two things

fill the mind with ever new and increasing wonder and awe, the more often and the more seriously reflection concentrates upon them: the starry heaven above me and the moral law within me."[14] The second is from the well-known Christian writer C. S. Lewis: "I take this [Ps. 19] to be the greatest poem in The Psalms and one of the greatest lyrics in the world."[15] The church lectionary assigns this psalm to be read on Christmas Day, when the "Sun of Righteousness" came into the world (Mal. 4:2) and the "Living Word" was laid in the manger (John 1:14). The emphasis in the psalm is on God's revelations of Himself in creation, Scripture, and the human heart.

The Worlds Around Us—God the Creator (vv. 1-6)

David focused on the heavens above him, especially the circuit of the sun; but there are many worlds in God's creation. They include the earth beneath our feet, the plant and animal worlds on earth, in the skies and in the waters, the human world, the world of rocks and crystals, worlds visible to the human eye, and worlds so small we need special equipment to see them. World famous biologist Edward O. Wilson claims there may be as many as 1.6 million species of fungi in the world today, 10,000 species of ants, 300,000 species of flowering plants, between 4,000 and 5,000 species of mammals, and approximately 10,000 species of birds.[16] But these large numbers pale into insignificance when you start examining the heavens, as David did, and begin to calculate distances in light years. David knew none of this modern scientific data, and yet when he pondered the heavens, he was overwhelmed by the glory of the Lord.

The Jewish people were forbidden to worship the objects in the heavens (Ex.

20:4-5; Deut. 4:14-19; 5:8-9), nor were they allowed to practice astrology (Isa. 47:13-14; Jer. 10:1-5). They worshiped the Creator, not the creation (Rom. 1:25). The existence of creation implied the existence of a Creator, and the nature of the creation implied that He was wise enough to plan it and powerful enough to execute His plan and maintain what He had made. So complex a universe demands a Creator who can do anything, who knows everything, and who is present everywhere. But even more, *David knew that God was speaking to the inhabitants of the earth by means of His creation.* Creation is a "wordless book" that everybody can read because it needs no translation. God speaks through creation day after day and night after night; His speech "pours out" silently, abundantly, universally.

In Romans 10:18, Paul quoted verse 4 as part of his explanation of why Israel rejected the Gospel and what this rejection did to the nation. The Jewish people could never say that they had not heard God's message, because Psalm 19:4 says that the whole world has heard. Therefore, both Gentiles and Jews stand guilty before God and need to be saved through faith in Jesus Christ, and we must take the salvation message to them (Rom. 10:1-15). Paul quoted from the Septuagint version of the Old Testament, which uses "sound" (voice) instead of "line," but the sense is the same. Some translators use "influence" instead of "line." God's voice of power in creation prepares the way for His voice of grace in the Gospel. When Paul preached to Gentiles, he started with creation and then moved into the Gospel message (Acts 14:14-18; 17:22-31). Phillips Brooks gave the first instructions about God to Helen Keller, who was blind and deaf, and she replied that she had always

known there was a God but didn't know what His name was. Our task is to tell the world that His name is Jesus (Acts 4:12).

David was an outdoorsman and often watched the sunrise and sunset, and what he saw day after day reminded him of a bridegroom leaving the marriage pavilion to claim his bride,[17] and a vigorous athlete running a race. The first image speaks of glory (the groom was richly attired), love and anticipation, while the second speaks of power and determination.

But in spite of this universal message that pours out day and night to the entire world, most people ignore it and reject God because they want to live as they please (Rom. 1:18-223). The repeated question, "Are people lost who have never heard about Jesus?" has two answers: (1) Yes, they are lost, because God speaks to them all day long, and they refuse to listen; (2) *What are you doing about getting the message to these people?*

The Word Before Us—God the Instructor (vv. 7-11)

The revelation of God in creation is truly wonderful, but it is limited when it comes to manifesting the attributes of God and His purposes for creation. Following the fall of man, creation has been subjected to futility and bondage (Gen. 3:17-19; Rom. 8:20-22), so we need something that reveals more clearly the character of God. That "something" is the inspired Word of God. When he wrote about creation, David used *Elohim* (v. 1), the name that speaks of God's great power; but when he wrote about God's Word, seven times he used the "covenant" name *Jehovah*, for the God of creation is also the God of personal revelation to His people. Israel was a very special nation, chosen by God to receive His law, covenants, and promises (Rom. 9:4). "He declares His words to Jacob, His statutes and his ordinances to Israel. He has not dealt thus with any nation" (147:19-20, NASB). The heavens declare God's glory, but the Scriptures tell us what God did so that we may share in that glory. There is no conflict between what God does in His universe and what He says in His Word. It was by His Word that He created the worlds (33:9), and it is by His Word that He controls the worlds (33:11; 148:8). David recorded six different names for God's Word, six attributes of the Word, and six ministries of the Word in the lives of those who receive it and obey it.

Law of the Lord (v. 7a). This is the Hebrew word *torah*, which means "instruction, direction, teaching." Jewish people call the scrolls of the Law "The Torah," but the word refers to all of God's revelation. It comes from a word that means "to shoot an arrow," for a teacher aims to hit the target and achieve specific goals in the lives of the students. Unlike the textbooks that we write, God's Word is perfect, flawless, and complete. Because human language changes, we require new translations of God's Word; but the Word of God never needs revision or improvement. "Restore" is the same word used in Psalm 23:3 and means "to revive, to give new life." The Word of the Lord not only *has* life (Acts 7:3; Heb. 4:12), but it *imparts* spiritual life to all who receive it (1 Peter 1:23), and it *sustains* life as well (119:25, 37, 40, 88, 107, 149, 156, 159).

Testimony of the Lord (v. 7). The Ten Commandments were known by this name (Ex. 25:21), and they are the basis for God's law. But all of the Scriptures are God's witness to us of who He is, what He has said and done, and what He wants us to be and to do. The witness God bears of Himself in the written Word is sure and reliable. Through the Word, we become wise concerning salvation (2 Tim. 3:15)

and the principles of successful living (Prov. 2; 8:33; 10:8). The "simple" are not mentally deficient people or the naïve people who believe everything, but the childlike people who humbly receive God's truth (Matt. 11:25; Luke 10:21-24).

Statutes of the Lord (v. 8). These are the God's detailed instructions concerning the practical matters of everyday life. For the Old Testament Jew, the statutes related to what they ate, how they dressed, how they kept clean, and so forth. God laid down certain basic laws and commandments, and the statutes applied them to specific situations. The New Testament epistles repeat nine of the Ten Commandments for believers today, omitting the Fourth Commandment, and then give applications of these principles. (See Eph. 4:20-32.) Some of the statutes that legislators have passed are not right and have brought grief, but the statutes of the Lord bring joy.

Commandment of the Lord (v. 8). The word means "that which is appointed." Because the Lord loves us, He commands us what to do and warns us what not to do, and how we respond is a matter of life or death (Deut. 30:15-20). God's commands are pure and lead to a pure life, if we obey from the heart. The Bible is the *Holy* Scriptures (Rom. 1:2; 7:12; 2 Tim. 3:15), and therefore His Word is "very pure" (119:140; Prov. 30:5). We are enlightened and learn God's truth when we obey what He says (John 7:17) and not just when we read it or study it (James 1:22-25). We are strangers on this earth, and the Word of God is the road map to guide us (119:19). Like a traveler on the highway, if we deliberately make a wrong turn, we go on a detour and fail to reach our destination.

Fear of the Lord (v. 9). This is an unusual name for the Scriptures, but it reminds us that we cannot learn the Word of God unless we show reverence and respect for the God of the Word. To teach the Bible is to teach the fear of the Lord (34:11; Deut. 4:9-10), and the mark of a true Bible student is a burning heart, not a big head (Luke 24:32; 1 Cor. 8:1). While some of the fears people have might be distressing and even defiling, the fear of God is clean and maturing. We do not decay or deteriorate as we walk in the fear of the Lord (2 Cor. 4:16-18).

Judgments of the Lord (v. 9). This can be translated "ordinances" or even "verdicts." It refers to the decisions of a judge. Throughout the Bible we see the Lord passing judgment on what people and nations do, and His rewards, rebukes, and punishments help us understand what pleases Him. In the nation of Israel, the ordinances instructed the officers and judges in settling problems between individuals and in meting out punishments to guilty offenders. Believers today are not under the Old Testament law, but how those laws were applied helps us understand the righteousness of God and our need for His grace.

The way we treat the Bible is the way we treat the Lord, so it isn't difficult to determine if we are rightly related to God. Do we *desire His Word* because it's precious to us (12), even more than wealth (v. 10; 119:14, 72, 127, 162) or tasty food (119:103; 1 Peter 2:2)? Do we find satisfaction in "feeding on" God's Word? (See Matt. 4:4; Job 23:12; Jer. 15:16.) Would we skip a meal to spend time meditating on the Scriptures? Do we attend church dinners but not church Bible studies? Furthermore, do we *accept the warnings of the Word and act upon them?* To know the warning and not heed it is sin (James 4:17). Do we *enjoy the blessing of the Lord* because we've obeyed His will? To have an appetite for God's Word is a mark of a healthy Christian whose priorities are straight. The Lord has sent the Holy Spirit to teach us His Word, and if we walk in the Spirit, we will learn and live the truth (John 14:26; 16:12-15; 1 Cor. 2:9-10; 1 John 2:20-29).

The Witness Within Us—God the Redeemer (vv. 12-14)

Unless we have a personal relationship with the Lord so that God is our Father and Jesus is our Redeemer, what we see in creation and what we read in the Bible will not do us much good. The Magi in Matthew 2:1-12 started on their journey by following God's star, a special messenger in the sky to direct them. Then they consulted God's Word and found that the King was to be born in Bethlehem; so they went to Bethlehem and there found and worshiped the Savior.[18] When you study God's creation with a Bible in your hand, you can't help but see Jesus! He is seen in the vine (John 15), the sun (John 8:12; Mal. 4:2), the stars (Num. 24:17), the lambs (John 1:29), the apple trees and lilies (Song 2:3, 16; 6:3), the seed planted in the ground (John 12:23-24), and the bread on the table (John 6:35). The Word in the hand is fine; the Word in the head is better; but the Word in the heart is what transforms us and matures us in Christ (119:11; Col. 3:16-17).

The Word is a light (119:105) and a mirror (James 1:22-25) to help us see ourselves, search our hearts (Heb. 4:12), and recognize and acknowledge our sins. "By the law is the knowledge of sin" (Rom. 3:20; 7:7-14). "Secret sins" are those we don't even see ourselves, "sins of ignorance" we don't realize we've committed. The Old Testament law made provision for their forgiveness (Lev. 4; Num. 15:22-29) because the sinners were guilty even though they were ignorant of what they had done (Lev. 5:17). However, the law provided no atonement for presumptuous sins (Num. 15:30-36; Deut. 17:12-13). When David committed adultery and arranged to have Uriah murdered (2 Sam. 11-12), he sinned insolently with his eyes wide open and therefore could bring no sacrifice (Ps. 51:16-17). When he confessed his sins, God in His grace forgave him (2 Sam. 12:13), but David paid dearly for his transgressions. Unconfessed sins, even if committed ignorantly, can grow within the heart and begin to rule over us, and this can lead to our committing willful disobedience ("great transgression"—there is no article in the Hebrew text).

Creation is God's "wordless book," and the Scriptures are God's holy Word to us, but God wants to hear our words as "sacrifices" that please Him (141:1-2; Hos. 14:2; Heb. 13:15). The word translated "acceptable" refers to the priest's examination of the sacrifices to make sure they were without blemish. If the sacrifice wasn't acceptable to the Lord, the worshiper was not accepted by the Lord (Lev. 1:1-9; 22:17-25; Mal. 1:6-8). The words we speak begin with the thoughts in our heart (Matt. 12:33-37), so it's important that we meditate on God's Word and God's works, the first two themes of Psalm 19. If we delight in God's Word, we will naturally meditate on it and give expression of His truth with our lips, and this will help to keep us from sin (119:9-16, 23-24, 47-48, 77-78, 97-99). The usage here refers to the "kinsman redeemer" (*goel* = "one who has the right to redeem") who could rescue a relative from difficult situations (Lev. 25:25-28; Num. 35:11-34; the book of Ruth; Isa. 43:14). Jesus is our Redeemer (Gal. 3:13; 4:5; Titus 2:14; Heb. 9:12; 1 Peter 1:18), and He became our "kinsman" when He came in sinless human flesh to die for us on the cross. He is both Rock and Redeemer, for He not only paid the price

to set us free, but He also keeps us safe.

Psalm 20

This is a prayer before the battle, and Psalm 21 is the praise after the victory. In verses 1-5, the people pray for their king (we/you); David the king encourages the people in verses 6-8 (I/we/they); and both the king and the people speak in verse 9, where "the king" is Jehovah God, *The King*. The psalm begins and ends with a plea for God to hear them as they pray and to give victory to the army of Israel (vv. 1, 9). The anointed king was the very life and breath of the nation (Lam. 4:20) and the lamp of Israel (2 Sam. 21:17), and the enemy soldiers would make him their special target (1 Kings 22:31). Those who have problems with the military aspects of some of David's psalms should remember that David went to war only when the enemy attacked Israel. He did not invade other nations just to gain territory, and he was fighting the Lord's battles (1 Sam. 17:47; 25:28; 2 Chron. 20:15). The covenant God made with David (2 Sam. 7:11) assured him of victory over his enemies. In this regard, David is a picture of our Lord Jesus Christ, the Commander of the Lord's armies (Josh. 5:14-15), who one day will ride in victory against the armies of this world (Ps. 45:3-7; Rev. 3:14; 17:14; 19:11-21). Just as physicians fight a battle against disease and death, so our Lord wages a war against sin and evil. "Lord Sabaoth His name / From age to age the same / And He must win the battle" (Martin Luther). This psalm describes three essentials for victory as God's people fight against the forces of evil.

A Praying People (vv. 1-5)
Before the army went out to battle, the Jewish law of warfare required the officers

and soldiers first to dedicate themselves to the Lord (Deut. 20:1-4), and this psalm speaks of such a dedication service. "Battles are won the day before," said Marshall Foch, commander of the Allied forces in World War I. The word "may" is used six times in verses 1-5 as the people prayed for their king (see NASB, NIV). Not only were the lives of the king and his army involved, but so also was the glory of the Lord (vv. 5, 7). It was a "day of trouble" (see 50:15; 59:16; 77:2; 86:7; 102:2), but Jehovah is a "very present help in trouble" (Ps. 46:1). In verse 1, the people prayed that God would answer the king's prayers and lift him up above the enemy ("defend"). "The God of Jacob" is a familiar title for the Lord (24:6; 46:7, 11; 75:9; 76:6; 81:1, 4; 84:8; 94:7; 114:7; 132:2, 5; 146:5; and see Isa. 49:26 and 60:16). It suggests that God works on behalf of those who are weak and in special need (see Gen. 35:1-3).

David had brought the ark of the covenant to Mt. Zion (2 Sam. 6), which meant that God was enthroned among His people and would help them (Pss. 80:1 and 99:1, NIV). His holy name was upon the sanctuary (Deut. 14:23; 16:2, 11), and therefore His glory was at stake. Many times David had brought sacrifices to the altar and dedicated himself to the Lord (burnt offerings) and given thanks to Him, and he would have offered sacrifices before coming to lead the army. (See 1 Sam. 7:9ff and 13:9ff.) The Lord did not forget these offerings which were given as memorials to His great name (Lev. 2:1-2, 9, 16; 5:12; and see Acts 10:4). But David had done more than worship God; he had also sought the Lord's will concerning strategy for the battle (see 1 Sam. 23). The people prayed that God would bless those plans, for petitions and plans must go together. The central verse in the psalm is verse 5, a confident affirmation of victory before the battle even started.

Raising the banners and waving them was a sign of victory, and "Jehovah our banner" was one of God's special names (see Ex. 17:15-16). The theme of salvation (victory) is repeated in verses 6 and 9.

A Confident Leader (vv. 6-8)

"Everything rises and falls with leadership," Dr. Lee Roberson often says, and he is right. Now the king speaks and assures his people that he is confident of success because the Lord has chosen him ("anointed") and heard his prayers. The people had prayed "May the Lord hear" (v. 1) and David's reply was, "He will hear" (v. 6). The Lord would not only send help from Zion (v. 2) but also from the very throne of heaven! (v. 6). Just as God's hand had reached down and saved David in the past (18:9-18), so His hand would deliver him from the enemy. In the covenant God made with David, He had promised him success in battle (2 Sam. 7:11), and David claimed this promise by faith.

Was the enemy coming with horses and chariots? There was no need to fear, for Israel's faith was in the Lord. Israel's kings were commanded not to acquire great numbers of horses and chariots (Deut. 17:16), a law that Solomon disobeyed (1 Kings 10:26-27). Note that the law of warfare even mentions horses and chariots (Deut. 20:1-4, and see 32:20 and 2 Sam. 10:18). God had defeated Egypt's best troops (Ex. 14:6ff; 15:4), and He could defeat the enemy attacking David (Ps. 33:16-17; Prov. 21:31; 2 Kings 19:20-23). "If God be for us, who can be against us?" (Rom. 8:31). God's people don't boast in their human resources but in the God who alone can save them in every situation. Only this kind of faith will honor the strong name of the Lord. The enemy will go down in defeat, but Israel will stand upright as victors.

A Sovereign Lord (v. 9)

Translators don't agree as to whether "king" in this verse refers to David or to the Lord, the King of Israel (5:2; 10:16; 48:1-2; 84:3; 95:3; 145:1). The *Prayer Book Version* of the Psalms reads, "Save, Lord, and hear us, O King of heaven, when we call upon thee"; and the *English Revised Version* reads, "Save Lord: Let the King answer us when we call." The *American Standard Version* also reads "King," and so does the *New American Standard Bible*. But whether "king" refers to David or to the Lord, verse 9 affirms that the Lord is sovereign because He hears prayer and is able to answer. I prefer "King," and I can see David, the people, and the troops acknowledging the sovereignty of the great king of Israel. Unless the Lord is King, there can be no victory. "For the Lord is the great God, the great King above all gods" (95:3, NIV). "The Lord Almighty—he is the King of Glory" (24:10, NIV). David plans his strategy (v. 4), but the Lord alone can determine the outcome.

Psalm 21

This is probably the praise hymn David and his people sang after the victories prayed for in Psalm 20 as they celebrated a day of national thanksgiving. They had prayed for specific blessings and God had granted them. The hymn opens and closes with praise for God's strength granted to His king and the army (vv. 1, 13). Answered prayer ought to be acknowledged by fervent praise. Since only Messiah could win the victories prophesied in verses 8-12, the Jewish Targum states that this psalm is about "King Messiah." Of course, David is a type of Jesus Christ.

Looking Back: Celebration for Past Victories (vv. 1-7)

The people and their king address the Lord and thank Him for what He did for them in answer to their prayers. Compare 21:1 with 21:5, 21:2 with 20:4, and 21:5 with 20:1. The word "salvation" in verses 1 and 5 (KJV) means "deliverance, victory." David had prayed that his life be spared (v. 4), and the Lord answered him (v. 2; 20:1, 6). This blessing was part of God's covenant with David (2 Sam. 7:16). The word "prevent" in verse 3 (KJV) means "to see to it beforehand" (69:10; 79:8). The Lord met Joshua before the battle of Jericho (Josh. 5:13-15), and Melchizedek (a type of Jesus Christ) met Abraham after the battle with the kings (Gen. 14); and God went before David and "welcomed" him (NIV) to the battlefield and the victory. That God goes before His obedient people is a great encouragement (48:14; 77:20; John 10:4; Deut. 8:2).

Some students connect the gold crown of verse 3 with Israel's victory over the Ammonites at Rabbah (2 Sam. 12:26-31), but this victory actually belonged to Joab. David didn't join the siege until the very end. The crown is probably symbolic of God's special "blessings of goodness" upon David (v. 5 and see 8:5). To David, the victory God gave was like a second coronation, assuring him that he was indeed God's anointed. Length of days forever (v. 4) and blessings forever (v. 6) remind us of God's covenant with David that was ultimately fulfilled in Christ (2 Sam. 7:6, 13, 16, 29; Luke 1:30-33; and see Pss. 10:16; 45:17; 48:14; and 133:3). It was customary to attribute endless life to kings (Neh. 2:3; Dan. 2:4). While he reigned, David would not be "shaken" by his enemies, because his faith was in the Lord (v. 7; 10:6; 16:8; 55:22; 121:3). This declaration of faith is the central verse of the psalm.

Looking Ahead: Anticipation of Future Victories (vv. 8-12)

The king trusted in the Lord and so did the people, and they affirmed their faith as they addressed these words to the king. The emphasis is now on the future victories God will give David and Israel because they have faith in the living God. (See 20:7.) God's right hand is more than a symbol of power; it actively works for His people and brings defeat to their enemies (89:13; 118:15-16; Deut. 5:15). "Find out" (KJV) means "dispose of." Just as fire devours what it touches, so the Lord will devour David's enemies as a cook burns fuel under the oven (79:5; 89:46; 97:6; Mal. 4:1). The nation of Israel and David's posterity would be preserved (18:50; 2 Sam. 7:16; Gen. 12:1-3), but there would be no future for the enemy. "Fruit" refers to posterity. (See 127:3, 132:11; Deut. 28:4; Hos. 9:16.) God did give David many victories and he greatly extended Israel's borders and brought peace to the kingdom. The nations might get together and plot against him, but David would still win the battle.

Looking Up: Exaltation of the Lord of the Victories (v. 13)

As in 20:9, the psalm concludes with a statement addressed to the Lord and expressing praise for His greatness. David fought battles and won victories, not to exalt himself, but to magnify the Lord, and his people knew this. David showed this same spirit as a youth when he killed the giant Goliath (1 Sam. 17:36, 45-47). Psalm 20 closes with the people and the king asking God to hear their prayers, and Psalm 21 closes with the prayer that God would be "lifted up on high" and exalted. "[T]hose who honor Me, I will honor" (1 Sam. 2:30, NKJV).

Psalm 22

Psalms 22, 23, and 24 form a trilogy on Christ the Shepherd. In 22, the Good Shepherd dies for the sheep (John 10:1-18); in 23, the Great Shepherd lives for the sheep and cares for them (Heb. 13:20-21); and in 24, the Chief Shepherd returns in glory to reward His sheep for their service (1 Peter 5:4). *Aijeleth Shahar* (or *Hash-sha-har*) is interpreted to mean "the doe (or hind) of the morning" or "help at daybreak." It may have been the name of the tune to which this psalm was sung.

David is the author, but we have a difficult time finding an occasion in his life that would call forth this kind of psalm. According to the record, the Lord never deserted him in his hour of need but always provided friends to help him and deliverance from his enemies. The intense suffering described here isn't that of a sick man in bed or a soldier in battle. *It's the description of a criminal being executed!* Numerous quotations from the psalm in the four Gospels, as well as Hebrews 2:10-12, indicate that this is a Messianic psalm. We may not know how this psalm related to the author's personal experience, but we do know that David was a prophet (Acts 2:30), and in this psalm he wrote about the death and resurrection of Jesus Christ. The first part (vv. 1-21) focuses on prayer and suffering and takes us to the cross, while the second part (vv. 22-31) announces the resurrection and expresses praise to the glory of God. An understanding of Messiah's suffering and glory is basic to grasping the message of the Bible (Luke 24:25-27; 1 Peter 1:11). We will try to see both David and the Son of David as we study the psalm.

Prayer in a Time of Suffering
(vv. 1-21)

There were three burdens that moved David to pray for God's help, and they apply to Jesus as well.

He was abandoned by the Lord (vv. 1-5). The opening words of the psalm immediately transport us to Calvary, for Jesus quoted them at the close of a three-hour period of darkness (vv. 1-2; Matt. 27:45-46; Mark 15:34). "I am not alone," Jesus had told His disciples, "because the Father is with me" (John 16:32), and yet He cried out that the Lord had forsaken Him. When He spoke these words, He had been engaged in a mysterious transaction with the Father, dying for the sins of the world (1 John 2:2; 4:14). On the cross, Jesus was "made sin" (2 Cor. 5:21) and made "a curse" (Gal. 3:13) for us. In some inexplicable way He experienced what condemned lost sinners experience "away from the presence of the Lord" (2 Thess. 1:9, NASB; see Matt. 25:41). However, note that both David and Jesus called Him "*my* God," making it clear that they still knew and trusted the Father.

This was not the cry of a complaining servant but the sob of a broken-hearted child asking, "Where is my father when I need him?" As David prayed for help, he wondered why God didn't answer him. After all, He was a God of compassion who was concerned about His people, and He was a holy God who practiced justice. Even more, Israel was God's special covenant nation, and He was "enthroned upon the praises of Israel" (v. 3, NASB; see 80:1; 99:1; Isa. 66:1-2). Only Israel had God's divine law and could worship Him in a way acceptable to Him (John 4:21-24). Many times in the past, the Lord had kept His covenant promises to Israel and fought battles, so why was He distant now? Compassion, justice, and the sacred covenant were strong arguments for God's intervention—but He was silent.

He was despised by the people (vv. 6-11). These words especially apply to our Savior. "I am a worm and not a man" (NASB) is a forgotten "I am" statement that speaks of how little value the leaders of Israel and the Roman officials placed on Jesus of Nazareth. A worm is a creature of the ground, helpless, frail, and unwanted. Isaiah 52:14 predicted that Messiah would be terribly disfigured by His enemies and not even look human. (See also Isa. 49:7, 50:6 and 53:3, and for "reproach," see 69:9 and Rom. 15:3. For the fulfillment of vv. 7-8, see Matt. 27:39 and 43, Mark 15:29, and Luke 23:35-36.) David reminded the Lord that from birth He had cared for him, so why abandon him now? (See 139:13-16.) David had learned to trust in the Lord ("hope," KJV) from infancy, and was not going to relent now. "Trust" is used three times in verses 4-5 and also in verse 8.

He was condemned by the law (vv. 12-21). David looked around and saw his enemies, and so brutal were they that he compared them to animals: bulls (vv. 12, 21), lions (vv. 13, 21; and see 7:2; 10:9; 17:12; 35:17; 57:4; 58:6), and dogs (vv. 16, 20). Bashan was a very fertile area east of the Sea of Galilee and north from the Yarmuk River to Mt. Hermon, now known as the Golan Heights (Jer. 50:19; Deut. 32:14; Ezek. 39:18; Amos 4:1). The wild bulls encircled their prey and then moved in for the kill. The dogs were ravaging savage wild dogs that lived in the garbage dumps and traveled in packs looking for victims. The people involved in arresting and condemning Jesus were only beasts attacking their Creator (2:1-3; Acts 4:23-28). Then David looked within and saw himself (vv. 14-18), and the description is surely that of a man being crucified. He is stripped of his clothing, placed on a cross, and nails are driven through his hands and feet. As he hangs between heaven and earth, his body is dehydrated, intense thirst takes over, and the end of it all is "the dust of death" (v. 15; see Gen. 3:19; Job 7:21; 10:9; 17:16; Eccl. 3:20). Like ebbing water and melting wax, his strength fades away, and he becomes like a brittle piece of broken pottery. (For the application to Jesus, see Matt. 27:35, Mark 14:24, Luke 23:34, and John 19:23-24, 28.) It is remarkable David should describe crucifixion because it was not a Jewish means of capital punishment, and it's unlikely that he ever saw it occur. David the prophetic psalmist (Acts 2:30) saw what would happen to Messiah centuries later.

Finally, David looked up to the Lord and prayed one more time for the strength he needed (vv. 19-21). In verse 1, he mentioned that God was far from helping him, and he repeated this in verse 11, but he asks a third time for the Lord to come near and intervene. "The sword" in verse 20 may refer to the authority of the Roman government (Rom. 13:4), for it was Pilate who authorized Christ's death. "Darling" in verse 20 (KJV) means "my only one," as an only child (Gen. 22:2), and refers to the one and only life that David possessed (see 35:17). Once lost, it could not be regained. We may translate verse 21, "Save me from the lion's mouth, and from the horns of the wild oxen you have delivered me" or "you have heard me." In verse 2, he wrote that God had not answered, but now he almost shouts, "You have answered me!" (See also v. 24.) This is the turning point of the psalm.

Praise in the Time of Victory (vv. 22-31)

We move now from suffering to glory, from prayer to praise (vv. 22, 23, 25, 26). In verses 1-21, Jesus "endured the cross," but

now He enters into "the joy that was set before him" (Heb. 12:2, and see Jude 24). He had prayed to be delivered out of death (Heb. 5:7), and that prayer was answered. Jesus sang a Passover hymn before He went to the cross (Matt. 26:30; Mark 14:26), and according to Hebrews 2:12, the risen Christ praised God in the midst of His people after His resurrection (see Matt. 18:20). Note that in His song, our Lord deals with the expanding outreach of the atoning work He finished on the cross.

The great assembly (vv. 22-25). There is no biblical evidence that Jesus appeared to any unbelievers in the days immediately after His resurrection (1 Cor. 15:1-7). "The great congregation" (assembly) included those who believed in Jesus who became a part of His church when the Spirit came at Pentecost. But the church is made up of believing Jews and Gentiles who form one body in Christ (Eph. 2:11ff), so the song included the seed of Jacob (Israel). The first Christians were Jewish believers, and all Gentiles in the church are, by faith, the children of Abraham (Gal. 3:26-29). God did not despise His Son in whom He is well pleased (v. 24), but accepted His work on the cross and proved it by raising Him from the dead (Rom. 4:24-25).

The glorious kingdom (vv. 26-29). The image here is that of a feast and was a familiar picture to the Jews of the anticipated Messianic kingdom (Isa. 25:6-9; Matt. 8:10-12; Luke 13:29; 14:15). When a Jewish worshiper brought a peace offering to the Lord, he retained part of it to use for a feast for himself, his family, and any friends he wanted to invite (Lev. 3; 7:15ff); and this tradition became a picture of the future glorious kingdom. But believing Gentiles will be also included in this feast (v. 27), and Messiah will reign over all the earth. God promised Abraham that his descendants would bring blessing to the whole world (Gen. 12:1-3). This has been fulfilled in the coming of Christ to die for the world, but when He comes again, it will have a glorious fulfillment in the establishing of His glorious kingdom. Both the prosperous and the poor will submit to Him (v. 29) and find their satisfaction in His grace alone. Orthodox Jews close their religious services by quoting Zechariah 14:9—"And the Lord shall be king over all the earth; in that day there shall be one Lord with one name" (Jewish Publication Society translation).

The generations to come (vv. 30-31). The blessings of the atonement and the kingdom will not be temporary but perpetual, from one generation to another. Three generations are listed here: a seed (see Isa. 53:10), a second generation, and a people that shall be born. This reminds us of 2 Timothy 2:2. But the emphasis isn't on what God's children have done but on the fact that the Lord did it all: "He has done it" (v. 31, NIV). "It is finished" is what Jesus cried from the cross (John 19:30).

Psalm 23

This is the psalm of the Great Shepherd who cares for His sheep and equips them for ministry (Heb. 13:20-21), the "great High Priest" (Heb. 4:14) who "ever lives to make intercession for us" (Heb. 7:25). Certainly this psalm has a message for the sorrowing, but it's unfortunate that it's used primarily at funerals, because Psalm 23 focuses on what Jesus does for us "all the days of [our] life" and not just at death (v. 6). It's also unfortunate that people tend to spiritualize the psalm and fail to see it in its true setting. They see David, a "young shepherd boy," lying on his back in the pasture and pondering the things of God, when he probably wrote this psalm late in his life, possibly during the rebellion of Absalom (2 Sam. 13-19). In it, David deals with some of the difficult things he experienced during his long walk with the Lord. While people of all ages love and quote this psalm, its message is for mature Christians who have fought battles and carried burdens.

Abel, the first martyr, was a shepherd (Gen. 4:2) and so were the patriarchs of Israel. Moses spent forty years caring for his father-in-law's sheep, and David, Israel's greatest king, served his father as a shepherd. The image of God as Israel's shepherd begins in Genesis 48:15 (NIV) and 49:24 and continues throughout Scripture (Pss. 28:9; 80:1; 95:7; 100:3; Isa. 40:11; 49:10; Jer. 31:10; Ezek. 34:11-15; Matt. 10:6; 15:24; Mark 6:34). The promised Messiah was seen as a shepherd (Ezek. 34:16, 23; Mic. 5:4; Zech. 13:7; Matt. 2:6; 26:3; Mark 14:27; John 10). In Psalm 22, David compared the enemy to animals that are clever and strong (22:12-16, 21), but in this psalm, he pictured God's people as lowly sheep. Why? So we would learn about the Shepherd and see how tenderly He cares for us. Sheep are defenseless animals that are prone to get lost, and they need almost constant care. You can't drive sheep, as you do cattle; they must be led. The eastern shepherds know their sheep by name and can call them and they will come (John 10:1-5). The sheep were kept, not for food but for wool, milk, and reproduction. In this psalm, David explains that if we follow the Lord and trust Him, He will meet our every need, no matter what the circumstances may be.

In the Pasture—Adequacy (vv. 1-3)
"The LORD" is Jehovah God, the covenant making God of Israel. The compound

names of Jehovah in the Old Testament reflect the contents of this psalm.

"I shall not want"—Jehovah-Jireh, the Lord will provide" (Gen. 22:14)

"still waters"- Jehovah-Shalom, "the Lord our peace" (Judg. 6:24)

"restores my soul"—Jehovah-Rophe, "the Lord who heals" (Ex. 15:26)

"paths of righteousness"—Jehovah-Tsidkenu, "the Lord our righteousness" (Jer. 33:16)

"you are with me"—Jehovah-Shammah, "the Lord is there" (Ezek. 48:35)

"presence of my enemies"—"Jehovah-Nissi, "the Lord our banner" (Ex. 17:15)

"anoint my head"—Jehovah-M'Kaddesh, "the Lord who sanctifies" (Lev. 20:8)

The verb is a participle and means "is shepherding me." Eastern shepherds guarded their sheep, led them, provided food and water for them, took care of them when they were weary, bruised, cut or sick, rescued them when they strayed, knew their names, assisted in delivering the lambs, and in every way simply loved them. What does this say to pastors today? In the Holy Land, pastures were lush and green following the rainy season but this didn't last all year. There were no fences, the land was rough and dangerous, abounding with wild animals and snakes, and the helpless flock needed constant oversight. Even if he didn't own the sheep, the shepherd treated them as if they were his and had to give an accounting for any that were missing. Our Lord called believers "my sheep" because He died for them (1 Peter 1:18-19) and because the Father gave them to Him (John 17:12). The emphasis in verses 1-3 is that Jesus is ade-

quate for every need the sheep may have as they are in the pasture. Primarily, they need food (grass), water, rest, and a shepherd who knows where to lead them. When God's people follow their Shepherd, they have all that they need and will not lack the necessities of life (37:25; Matt. 6:33; Phil. 4:19). Sheep will not lie down when they are hungry, nor will they drink from fast-flowing streams. Sometimes the shepherd will temporarily dam up a stream so the sheep can quench their thirst. You can read verse 2 "beside the *stilled* water." In heaven, our Shepherd will lead us to fountains of living water (Rev. 7:17).

The word translated "lead" in verse 2 means "to lead gently." You cannot drive sheep. The sheep hear the shepherd's voice and follow him, just as we listen to Christ in His Word and obey Him (John 10:3-5, 16, 27). If a sheep goes astray, the shepherd leaves the flock in charge of his helpers and goes to find the lost animal. (See Matt. 9:36; 18:12-14; and Luke 15:3-7.) The word "paths" in verse 3 means "well-worn paths, ruts." When sheep start to explore an exciting new path, it will lead them into trouble. "Do not be carried about by varied and strange teachings" (Heb. 13:9, NASB). God cares for us because He loves us and wants us to glorify Him ("for his name's sake"). The shepherd cares for the sheep because he loves them and wants to maintain his own good reputation as a faithful shepherd.

In the Valley—Serenity (v. 4)

This is the central verse of the psalm, and the personal pronoun changes from *he* to *you*. David is not speaking *about* the shepherd but speaking *to* the shepherd. In the dark valley, He is not before us but beside us, leading the way and calming our fears. The "vale of deep darkness" represents any difficult experience of life that makes us afraid, and that includes death. Sheep lack good vision and are easily frightened in new circumstances, especially where it's dark; and the presence of the shepherd calms them. The rod was a heavy cudgel with which the shepherd could stun or kill an attacking beast, and the staff was the shepherd's crook, which he used to assist the individual sheep. At evening, he would have the sheep pass under the crook one by one so he could count them and examine them (Lev. 27:32). It gave the flock peace knowing that the shepherd was there and was equipped for any emergency. He is "Immanuel ... God with us" (Matt. 1:23). Jesus is not a hireling who runs away at the sight of danger; he is a true Shepherd who lay down his life for his sheep (John 10:11-15). God's sheep have "peace with God" (Rom. 5:1) and may enjoy "the peace of God" (Phil. 4:4-7) as they trust Him. Through life, as we follow the Shepherd, we will have many and varied experiences, some of which will be very trying, but none of them can take the Lord by surprise. We may trust Him and have peace. The closer we are to our Shepherd, the safer we are and the more His peace will fill our hearts. (See Isa. 40:9-11; 43:1-3; Rev. 1:17-18.)

In the Fold—Certainty (v. 5)
Some students believe there is a change of metaphor here, from the shepherd and his sheep to the host and his guest, but this is not necessarily the case. "Table" doesn't necessarily refer to a piece of furniture used by humans, for the word simply means "something spread out." Flat places in the hilly country were called "tables" and sometimes the shepherd stopped the flock at these "tables" and allowed them to eat and rest as they headed for the fold (see 78:19). After each

difficult day's work, the aim of the shepherd was to bring the flock safely back to the fold where the weary sheep could safely rest for the night. Sometimes at the fold, the shepherd would spread out food in a trough, because sheep lie down and rest after they have eaten. As they slept, they would be protected by a stone wall that surrounded them, and the shepherd himself would sleep across the opening and be the door (John 10:7-9). During the night, thieves and dangerous animals might approach the fold, but there was no way they could reach the sheep. The Lord doesn't always remove the dangers from our lives, but He does help us to overcome them and not be paralyzed by fear. This is what it means to be "more than conquerors" and have peace in the midst of danger (Rom. 8:31-39).

The shepherd would examine the sheep as they entered the fold to be sure none of them was bruised, injured, or sick from eating a poisonous plant. To the hurts, he applied the soothing oil, and for the thirsty, he had his large two-handled cup filled with water. He would also apply the oil to the heads and horns of the sheep to help keep the flies and other insects away. The sheep knew they were safe and they could sleep without fear.

In the Father's House—Eternity (v. 6)
As the shepherd lay each night at the door of the sheepfold, he looked back over the day and gave thanks that the Lord had blessed them with goodness and mercy. As an old man, David looked back over his long life and came to the same conclusion. In spite of his sins and failures, he had been followed by goodness and mercy, which is the Old Testament equivalent of Romans 8:28. "Surely" means "only." As David looked ahead, he knew he would be in heaven—the Father's house—forever.

This isn't a reference to the temple, because the king didn't live in the temple. Furthermore, nobody could live there or anywhere else forever. Jesus used this vocabulary to speak about heaven (John 14:1-6). The things that perplex and disturb us today will all be clear when we get to heaven. We will look back and see "only goodness and mercy." Under the old covenant, the sheep died for the shepherd, but under the new covenant, the Shepherd died for the sheep—*and we shall meet our Shepherd in heaven!* "For the Lamb who is in the midst of the throne will shepherd them and lead them to living fountains of waters. And God will wipe away every tear from their eyes" (Rev. 7:17).

Psalm 24

Most commentators connect this psalm with David's bringing the ark of the covenant into Jerusalem (2 Sam. 6; 1 Chron. 15:1-16:3), and it may well be that David wrote it for that occasion. It appears to be an antiphonal psalm. The people (or a Levitical chorus) opened with verses 1-2, a leader asked the questions in verses 3, 8a, and 10a, and the chorus or the people answered with verses 4-6, 8b and 10b. It was sung in Herod's temple each Sunday, and some connect the psalm with our Lord's entrance into Jerusalem on what we call Palm Sunday. For years, the church has assigned this psalm to be read on Ascension Day, the fortieth day after Easter. Christians see Jesus Christ as "the Lord of Glory," first of all returning to heaven after His passion (Eph. 4:8; Col. 2:15), and then returning in glory to establish His kingdom (Matt. 25:31). This explains the repetition of "Lift up your heads" in verses 7 and 9. The psalm presents a threefold privilege God has given His people.

We Are Stewards Who Enjoy His Goodness in Creation (vv. 1-2)

Of all the heavenly bodies created by the Lord, the earth is the one He has chosen to be His own special sphere of activity. Clarence Benson called the earth "the theater of the universe," for on it the Lord demonstrated His love in what Dorothy Sayers called "the greatest drama ever staged." He chose a planet, a people and a land, and there He sent His Son to live, to minister, to die, and to be raised from the dead, that lost sinners might be saved. The earth is God's, everything on it and in it is God's, and all the people on the earth are God's, made in His image and accountable to Him. The divine name "LORD" is used six times in this psalm. "All the earth is mine" (Ex. 19:5), says the Creator, but in His goodness He has shared it with us. He is "possessor of heaven and earth" (Gen. 14:19, 22), and we are guests on His planet, stewards of all that He gives us to enjoy (1 Tim. 6:17) and to employ. This stewardship is the basis for the way we treat planet earth and protect the treasures God has shared with us. Anything we give to Him, He has first given to us (50:10-12; 1 Chron. 29:14). Paul quoted 24:1 in 1 Corinthians 10:25-26 to remind believers that all food was permitted to them (see also Mark 7:14-23; 1 Tim. 4:3-5). The place of "water" in the creation is seen in 104:5-9; 136:6; Genesis 1:1, 6-7, 9; 49:25; Exodus 20:4; Deuteronomy 33:13.

We Are Worshipers Who Experience His Grace in Redemption (vv. 3-6)

Psalm 15 is a parallel text, and both psalms emphasize the fact that to worship God means going up higher. God's Son sits on the throne in the heavenly Zion (2:6), and the mercy seat on the ark was God's throne in the earthly Zion. The

Levites carrying the ark had to be ceremonially clean, and God's people must be clean if they wish to worship the King and please Him. "Clean hands" speak of righteous conduct (Isa. 1:15-16, 18), and a "pure heart" of godly character and motives (Matt. 5:8). "Vanity" refers to the worship of idols ("worthless things") and "swearing deceitfully" to all kinds of deception, especially false witness in court.

The reward is the gift of salvation, the righteousness of God (Gen. 15:6). However, nobody on God's earth is able to meet these standards. "All have sinned and come short of the glory of God" (Rom. 3:23). Good works or religious character cannot save us. The only way we can enter into God's presence is through the merits of Jesus Christ, which means we must repent of our sins and put our faith in Him. Only Jesus Christ qualifies to enter the Father's presence, and He has gone to heaven to represent His people and intercede for them before the Father's throne. To "seek God's face" means to have an audience with the King (Gen. 44:23; Ex. 10:28; 2 Sam. 14:24, 28, 32), and this is now possible through the work of Christ on the cross (Heb. 10:1-25). God's righteousness is a gift, not a reward for good works (Rom. 3:21-4:9; 5:17; 10:1-10). David compared the generation of God-seeking people to their ancestor Jacob, who saw the face of God and held on by faith until he received a blessing (Gen. 32:24-32). Jacob certainly wasn't a perfect man, but the Lord saved him and even is called "the God of Jacob" (Ps. 46:7, 11).

We are Victors Who Celebrate His Glory in Conquest (vv. 7-10)

Five times in this text God is called "the King of Glory." Jesus is the Chief Shepherd who will one day return in glory and give each faithful servant a crown of glory (1 Peter 5:1-4; and see 1:7, 4:11-14 and 5:10; 1 Cor. 2:8). The gates of Jerusalem opened outward, so what is meant by "be lifted up"? Certainly there would be plenty of headroom for the Levites to carry in the ark, and it wouldn't be required to raise the lintels of the gates. Martin Luther translated it, "Open wide the portals," that is, "Give a hearty welcome to the Lord!" Bringing in the ark may have reminded David of what Moses and the leaders of Israel sang when the ark was carried in the wilderness (Num. 10:33-35; Ps. 68:1-3; 132:8). The administration of an ancient city was transacted at the city gates, so the gates were to those people what the city hall is to citizens in the western world today. David was commanding the whole city to welcome the Lord and give honor to Him. The King of Glory is also "the LORD of Hosts," a title used nearly three hundred times in the Old Testament. "Hosts" means "armies," and this can mean the stars (Isa. 40:26), the angels (Ps. 103:20-21), the nation of Israel (Ex. 12:41), or all believers who belong to the army of Christ (2 Tim. 2:3-4; 2 Cor. 10:3-6; Eph. 6:10ff).

But why were the gates of Jerusalem addressed twice (vv. 7 and 9)? The King of Glory is Jesus Christ. When He entered Jerusalem on Palm Sunday, the whole city didn't receive Him and praise Him. This psalm had been sung that morning at the temple, but it wasn't applied to Jesus of Nazareth. Instead of accepting Him and honoring Him, the leaders rejected Him and sent Him to Golgotha to be crucified. However, in His death and resurrection, Jesus won the battle against Satan and sin, and when He ascended back to heaven and entered the heavenly Zion (Heb. 12:18ff), He was received as the victorious

Lord of Hosts and the King of Glory. However, Jesus will return to the earth and fight a battle against the armies of the world and be victorious (Rev. 19:11ff; Isa. 63:1-3). He will deliver Jerusalem from her enemies (Zech. 12-14) and establish His kingdom on earth. Then His people will receive Him in Jerusalem, the Lord of Hosts, the King of Glory; and "the LORD shall be king over all the earth" (Zech. 14:9). Meanwhile, we can triumph in life through Jesus Christ (2 Cor. 2:14) and be "more than conquerors" through faith in Jesus Christ (Rom. 8:31-39).

As children of God, we belong to three worlds: the world of creation around us, the world of the new creation within us (2 Cor. 5:17), and "the world to come" of the wonderful final creation that will be our home for eternity (Rev. 21-22).

Psalm 25

This psalm pictures life as a difficult journey that we can't successfully make by ourselves. The word "way" is used four times (vv. 4, 8, 9, 12) and "paths" once (v. 10), and we find the psalmist crying out to God for wisdom as he makes decisions (vv. 4-5). He is surrounded by enemies (v. 2) who hate him (v. 19), lay traps for him (v. 15), and want him to fail and be ashamed (vv. 2, 3, 20). The psalmist knows he is a sinner who doesn't deserve God's help (vv. 7, 11, 18), but he relies on the goodness and mercy of the Lord. Psychologist M. Scott Peck writes, "Once we truly know that life is difficult—once we truly understand and accept it—then life is no longer difficult."[19] David knew that the path of life wasn't easy, but he succeeded in the journey because he held to three unwavering assurances.

The Help We Need Comes from God (vv. 1-7)

Other people may lift up their hearts to idols (24:4), which are only manufactured substitutes for God, but David lifted his heart up to the Lord, for He is the only true source of encouragement. In one of the darkest hours of his life, when David had lost everything, he "encouraged himself in the Lord his God" (1 Sam. 30:6). It has well been said, "When the outlook is bleak, try the uplook." He affirmed his faith in the Lord and his desire to glorify His name. He didn't want to fail and bring disgrace to the name of the Lord. So, he waited on the Lord, worshiped, and confidently asked for His help. He desperately needed wisdom to make the right decisions, avoid the traps, and reach the goal.

David not only prayed for God's guidance, he asked for insight to understand the Word; for only there could he learn God's ways and understand his own path. "Lead me in your truth" reminds us that the Word and prayer always go together (1 Sam. 12:23; John 15:7). David is referring to God's covenants with His people, the precepts and promises He gave them to keep them in His will so they could enjoy His blessing (v. 10; Deut. 27-30). David knew the history of Israel, that God had graciously helped them when they cried out to Him, and so he prayed with assurance and faith. But he also prayed with contrition, confessing his sins to the Lord (vv. 7, 11). He had regrets about some of his youthful omissions of obedience or commissions of sin, and he wanted forgiveness. He prayed "for your goodness' sake" (v. 7) and "for your name's sake" (v. 11; see 23:3; 31:3; 79:9; 106:8; 109:21; 143:110). "My help comes from the Lord who made heaven and earth" (121:2, NASB).

Our God Can Be Trusted (vv. 8-14)

At this point, David paused to meditate on the character of the Lord his God. After all, why pray to the Lord if He can't be trusted? But He *can* be trusted! To begin with, He is "good and upright" and what He says and does is always right. If we submit ourselves to Him in meekness, He will teach us His ways, but if we are arrogant, He will be silent. In the New Testament, the word "meek" describes a horse that has been broken, a soothing wind on a hot day, and a healing medicine. Meekness is not weakness; it is power under control. God can be trusted to guide those who obey His Word (v. 10), for a willingness to obey is the first step toward spiritual understanding (John 7:17).

God can be trusted to be merciful and gracious to those who repent (v. 11), but we must walk in the fear of the Lord (v. 12). "He [God] will instruct him in the way chosen for him" (v. 12, NIV). Knowing that the Lord has a plan for our lives, and that this plan is the very best for us, should give us great joy and confidence as we seek His will (16:11; 139:13-16; Eph. 2:10). According to God's covenant arrangement, those who obey will receive His provision and protection, and there will be blessing also for the next generations in the family (Deut. 4:1-14). The word "children" is used nearly forty times in Deuteronomy, reminding us that our descendants can receive blessing from our obedience or sorrow because of our sins. If we love Him, fear Him, and obey His Word, He will draw near to us and share His plans with us. "Secret" in verse 14 means "intimate conversation, plans and purposes," what Jesus spoke about in John 15:15 and what Abraham experienced in Genesis 18:16ff. (See also Jer. 23:18 and 22, Prov. 3:32 and Amos 3:7.) As we "walk with the Lord in the light of His Word," we develop a close fellowship with Him and better understand His ways. Yes, the Lord can be trusted to help us; and when He helps, He does it in mercy and truth ("love and faithfulness," NIV).

Trusting God Brings Us Victory (vv. 15-22)

David once again turns to prayer and mentions to the Lord the special burdens that beset him, the dangerous enemies without, and the distressing emotions within. *But he wouldn't mention them to the Lord if he didn't believe the Lord could help him!* What were the enemies that God helped him to conquer?

Danger (v. 15). The enemy had put snares in the path, but David trusted the Lord to protect him. Satan is a destroyer and a murderer and would trap us all if he could, but if we are in God's will, he can't harm us.

Loneliness (v. 16). Those who have never had to exercise authority and make difficult decisions involving other people sometimes overlook the loneliness of leadership. As we obey the Lord, we sometimes see friends and even family members turn against us, and this is painful. Three of David's sons—Absalom, Amnon, and Adonijah—turned against him, and so did his close friend and counselor Ahithophel.

A broken heart (v. 17). If we sit alone and feel sorry for ourselves, we will never grow in the Lord and accomplish greater things for Him. Enlarged trouble will either make us or break us, turn us into giants or crush us into pygmies. Review 4:1 and 18:19 and 36 to see how God helped David to grow. God can heal a broken heart if we give Him all the pieces and let Him have His way.

Regrets (v. 18). As we have seen from verse 7, David may have had deep regrets because of things he had done in the past, and these regrets were robbing him of peace and joy. Satan is the accuser (Rev. 12:10) and wants to remind us of our sins, even though the Lord has forgiven them and holds them against us no more (Heb. 10:11-18).

Fear (vv. 19-20). We don't know what the situation was, but whatever it was, David feared for his life. Even more, he feared that he would fail and bring disgrace to the name of the God he loved. His enemies were increasing and so was his fear, but he trusted the Lord to take care of both.

Despair (vv. 21-22). "I wait on you" also means "I have hope in you." To lose hope is to surrender the future to the enemy, and that only destroys the meaning of the present. David was a man of integrity (7:8; 26:1, 11; 41:12; 78:72); he was wholehearted in his obedience to the Lord. Whatever lies the enemy was spreading about him, David knew that the Lord saw his heart and approved of his character. The prayer in verse 22 may have been added so the psalm could be used in public worship, but it expresses a basic truth: we are never alone in our trials, for as members of God's believing community, we have encouragement from one another. Our brothers and sisters around the world are also suffering trials (1 Peter 5:9), so we are not alone.

David survived his trials and was able to write Psalm 26:12—"My feet stand on level ground; in the great assembly I will praise the Lord" (NIV). May we follow his example!

Psalm 26

Psalms 26, 27, and 28 reveal David's love for God's sanctuary (26:6-8, 27:4-7, 28:2),

which in David's day was the tabernacle on Mt. Zion. God didn't permit David to build the temple (2 Sam. 7), but He did give him the plans for the temple and helped him accumulate from the spoils of battle great wealth to provide material for constructing the temple (1 Chron. 22, 28-29). But not all who gathered to worship at the sanctuary were sincere in their walk or their worship, and some of them were openly disobedient and spread lies about the king. It was this situation that led to the writing of this psalm. In it, David makes three requests of the Lord.

Vindicate Me (v. 1)

The enemies who were slandering David are described in verses 4-5 and 9-10. They were deceitful, hypocritical, and wicked evildoers, sinners who schemed to rob others and even accepted bribes (Ex. 25:8; Amos 5:12), murdering those who stood in their way. David the king was a godly man, but not every judge and official in the government was walking with the Lord. Perhaps all of this occurred at the time when Absalom was trying to seize the throne by spreading lies about his father (see 2 Sam. 14-15). David would see these deceitful men at the tabernacle altar, bringing their offerings, and it deeply grieved him. (See 119:28, 115, 136, 150, 158.) Throughout the history of both Israel and the church, there was a "congregation of evildoers" (v. 5; 50:16-21) along with the congregation of true worshipers (v. 12), the tares among the wheat (Matt. 13:24-30, 36-41), and wolves in sheep's clothing (Matt. 7:15, Acts 20:26-31).

"Vindicate" means "give me justice, defend my reputation" (see 7:8; 35:24; 43:1). David was a man of integrity (7:8; 25:21; 41:12; 78:72), a fact that was affirmed by the Lord Himself (1 Kings 9:4-5). The people attacking him were "dissemblers" (v. 4, KJV) or "hypocrites," play-actors who wore masks to cover up their evil character. Integrity means wholeness of character, an undivided mind and heart, completely devoted to the Lord. Without wavering, David stood for what was right, but double-minded people are unstable in all their ways (James 1:8). His life revealed a balance of faith ("I have trusted") and works ("I have walked"), as commanded in James 2:14-26. When your character and conduct are attacked, it isn't wrong to vindicate yourself, as Paul did (2 Cor. 10-12), or to ask the Lord to vindicate you. We aren't just defending ourselves; we're defending the name of the Lord whom we serve. Our vindication is "for his name's sake" (23:3; 25:11).

Examine Me (vv. 2-8)

As with David's words in 18:20-24, this is not an expression of self-righteousness (see Luke 18:9-14), but rather the honest testimony of a real man of God. The words translated "examine" and "try" refer to the testing of metals to determine their true value and also to remove the dross (12:6; 17:3). "Heart and mind" is "kidneys and heart" in the original, the kidneys being the seat of the emotions and the heart the place of moral decision. (See 139:23, Phil. 4:7 and Rev. 2:23.) David's life was motivated and controlled by God's love and truth (faithfulness; see 6:4; 25:5-7, 10; 40:10; 57:3; Ex. 34:6). The Lord was faithful to His covenant and David was faithful to the Lord. Though David occasionally fell, as we all do, the habitual bent of his life was toward the Lord and His Word. He refused to have fellowship with the hypocrites in the congregation, the "men of vanity, nothing-ness" who pretended to worship the Lord and keep His covenant. This doesn't imply that he was isolated from the real

world (1 Cor. 5:10), but rather that he didn't allow it to defile him (1:1-2; 2 Cor. 6:14-7:1). While the assembly of the wicked needs our witness, it's with the congregation of the righteous that we share our worship (35:18; 40:9-10; 89:5; 107:32; 149:1). David was balanced: he hated sin but he loved the things of God (vv. 5, 8). In walking (vv. 1, 3, 11), standing (v. 12), and sitting (v. 4), he kept himself from evil (see 1:1).

The wicked came to the sanctuary to hide their sins; they made it a "den of thieves," the place where criminals run and hide (Matt. 21:13; Jer. 7:1). But David went to the sanctuary to worship God and bear witness to His grace and mercy. His hands were clean (24:4), his sacrifice was acceptable (see Isa. 1:10-17), and his voice was clear as he praised the Lord. Cleansing comes from the blood of Christ (1 John 1:7, 9) and the water of the Word (Eph. 5:26-27; John 15:3). In order to serve God acceptably, the priests were required to wash their hands and feet at the laver (Ex. 30:17-21). Nowhere in the law of Moses do we find instructions about pro-cessions and praise around the altar, but neither were they forbidden. David was an enthusiastic worshiper of the Lord (see 43:4; 2 Sam. 6:12-23) and enjoyed his times of worship. (On washing hands to prove innocence, see Deut. 21:1-9.) The king brought sacrifices of thanksgiving (Lev. 3:1-17; 7:11-38) because he loved the Lord and the Lord's house (27:4-6; 42:4; 122:1-4, 9; 1 Chron. 29:3). He glorified God at the place where God's glory dwelt (Ex. 40:35). David is a good example for us to follow in our own worship.

Redeem Me (vv. 9-12)

David couldn't stop the hypocrites from joining the worshiping congregation, but he could help from becoming like them;

so he asked the Lord to deliver him from that sin. "Don't sweep me away with the wicked!" The sheep and goats and the wheat and tare may be mixed today, but there is coming a day when God will separate them; on that day, the wicked will perish (1:4-6; Matt. 7:21-23; 25:31-46). The godly must constantly beware of the evil influences of the world and especially of those who profess to love God but are using "religion" as a cover up for their sins. To remain faithful, we must also ask God to be merciful to us and help us to maintain our integrity. Once we begin to waver (v. 1, NASB), it becomes easier to stumble and fall. "Therefore let him who thinks he stands take heed lest he fall" (1 Cor. 10:12, NKJV). David was standing on level ground (see 27:11; 143:10; Isa. 40:4). He would not waver.

Psalm 27

According to the title of this psalm as recorded in the Septuagint, David wrote it "before he was anointed." This means it was probably written when he was exiled from home and being hunted by King Saul and his men. The psalm does reveal that David was in great danger from violent evildoers (v. 2) who were lying about him (v. 12) and wanting to kill him (vv. 2 and 12), and Saul and his men qualified. But in spite of this difficult and dangerous situation, David was confident (v. 3), courageous (v. 14), and unafraid (v. 1). In this psalm, David teaches us that when we know the Lord and trust Him, He helps us overcome the fears that can paralyze our lives.

Fear of Circumstances (vv. 1-6)
David didn't close his eyes to the circumstances around him; rather, he looked by faith to the Lord and examined his circumstances from heaven's point of view (Heb. 12:1-3). The Lord was everything he needed just as He is everything we need today. He is our light, so we need not fear because of darkness; He is our strength (or stronghold; see 18:2; 31:3-2), so we need not fear because of our weakness; and He is our salvation, so the victory is sure. This is the first time in Scripture that light is used as a metaphor for God (see John 1:4, 9; 8:12; 1 John 1:3; Rev. 21:23), although in many texts He is associated with the light (4:6; 18:28; 43:3; 84:11; Isa. 10:17; 60:1, 20; Mic. 7:8). David didn't know if the enemy would make a sudden attack, like a beast devouring its prey (v. 2; see 1 Sam. 17:43-47), or settle down for a long siege (v. 3a), or at a propitious time declare war and attack (v. 3b). No matter what the tactics might be, the enemy didn't frighten David. "If God be for us, who can be against us?" (Rom. 8:31).

The secret of David's public confidence was his private obedience: he took time to fellowship with the Lord and get directions from Him. David knew that the most important part of his life was the part that only God could see, and this was one priority he would not negotiate.[20] David was living in the wilderness of Judea, away from the sanctuary of the Lord, but he was still able to enter into fellowship with his God. God's house was but a tent (vv. 5-6), for the temple had not yet been built, but it was still referred to as "God's temple" (see 1 Sam. 1:9; 33). The imagery in verses 4-6 is the Old Testament equivalent of "abiding in Christ" (John 15:1-8). In the ancient Near East, when a visitor entered his host's tent, the host was personally responsible for his protection and provision, and the flimsy tent became a fortress. The word "beauty" in verse 4 means not only the glory of God's character but also the richness of His goodness and favor to His people (16:11; 90:17; 135:3). David took time to meditate and to contemplate the wonders of God's grace. He came away from his times of worship feeling the rock under his feet and seeing above and beyond the enemy to the victory God had prepared. No wonder he vowed to God that, when he returned to Jerusalem, he would bring thank offerings to Him and joyfully worship Him.

Fear of Failure (vv. 7-10)
David's confidence in the Lord didn't prevent him from being concerned about himself, for he knew he was a sinner and a man of clay. It's one thing to behold the Lord in the sanctuary and quite something else to see the enemy approaching on the battlefield. What if there was something wrong in David's life and the Lord abandoned him in the midst of the battle? When David cried out, God answered him in his heart and said, "Seek my face." (See 24:6; 105:4; Deut. 4:29; 1 Chron. 16:11; 2 Chron. 7:14; Hos. 5:15.) When the Lord's face "shines upon us" (Num. 6:22-27), it means He is pleased with us and will help us; when His face is turned from us, He is displeased (69:16-18; 143:7), and we must search our hearts and confess our sins. David's parents never abandoned him (see 1 Sam. 21:3-4). His statement was a familiar proverb. God cares for us as a father and mother care for their children (Isa. 49:15; 63:16); and though it's unlikely that parents would abandon their children, it's certain that God never forsakes His own (Heb. 13: 5-6).

Fear of the Future (vv. 11-14)
Did David write these words after he had won the battle? As a wise soldier, he realized that one victory did not guarantee that the enemy would stop attacking.

Perhaps the enemy had retreated and David was now concerned about their return. "Let us be as watchful after the victory as before the battle," said the godly Scottish preacher Andrew Bonar, and wise counsel it is. He asked the Lord for guidance (see 25:4-5), for a level path without traps in it, and for victory over the liars who were slandering his good name. His statement in verse 13 is incomplete: "If I had not believed in the goodness of the Lord in the land of the living"—then what? Where would I be? David believed that God's goodness followed him (23:6) and also anticipated him (21:3), that God stored up goodness to use when it was needed (31:19). God's goodness never ran out (52:1), for David could go into God's house (presence) and receive all he needed (65:4). The key was *faith in God.*

Instead of rushing ahead, David calmly waited on the Lord, for faith and patience always go together (Isa. 28:16; Heb. 6:12; 10:36). Perhaps in verse 14 he was addressing his soldiers, for the men would need courage and strength for the next battle and for the journey that lay before them. This admonition reminds us of the words of Moses to Joshua (Deut. 31:7, 23), God's words to Joshua (Josh. 1:6-7, 9), and the Jewish leaders' encouragement of Joshua (Josh. 1:18). Stuart Hamblin wrote in one of his familiar songs, "I know not what the future holds / but I know who holds the future." If Jesus is your Savior and Lord, then the future is your friend, and you have nothing to fear.

Psalm 28

Once again, David found himself in difficulty and cried out to the Lord for help. We don't know what caused the problem, but it involved wicked people and workers of iniquity, and deceptive people who pretended to be David's friends but were working for his ruin. The period leading up to Absalom's rebellion would fit this description, but would David pray for his own son's destruction when he asked to have Absalom spared (vv. 4-5; 2 Sam. 18:5)? Regardless of the background, this psalm teaches us some important lessons about prayer and patience.

The Problem of Unanswered Prayer (vv. 1-5)

David had prayed fervently about his dangerous situation, but the Lord hadn't answered him. (See 13:1; 35:22; 39:12; 40:17; 69:3; 83:1; 109:1; 119:82.) It has often been said that "God's delays are not God's denials," and David was learning that important lesson. In verse 1, he "called" on the Lord, and in verse 2, he "cried out" to Him in desperation, but the Lord didn't answer. The unchanging Rock had changed! (19:14; 31:2-3; 62:2). Was the Lord silent because He could no longer hear and speak? David lifted his hands in worship as he prayed toward the sanctuary of God (63:4; 141:2; Ex. 17:19; 1 Kings 8:44ff; Lam. 2:19; 3:41; 1 Tim. 2:8), but the Lord apparently didn't see him. But Jehovah is the "living God" who sees His people, hears their cries, and speaks His Word to them! (115:1-8). David felt like a dead man whose body was in the tomb and whose soul was in sheol, the realm of the departed (22:20; 30:9; 88:4; 143:7). He also felt like a criminal who was being dragged away with the wicked to be executed (vv. 3-5). They were hypocrites, but he was speaking the truth. They had no regard for the words and works of the Lord, but David was a servant of God who worshiped Him faithfully. According to God's covenant

with Israel, David's idolatrous enemies should have been judged and condemned, but the Lord was doing nothing. How could God treat His anointed king like a criminal? But we should remind ourselves that the Father allowed His own Son to be unjustly treated like a common criminal (Isa. 53:7-8, 12; Luke 22:37). David's prayer was not an expression of personal revenge but a call for God to fulfill His covenant and bring righteousness and peace into the land. "Let them reap what they have sown," was his request.

The Joy of Unbounded Praise (vv. 6-7)

Suddenly, the scene changes and David is singing instead of sobbing! The reason is given in verse 7, "My heart trusts in Him, and I am helped" (NASB). Faith in Jehovah made all the difference. The hands of the enemy were busy doing evil (v. 4), but when David believed God and lifted up his hands in prayer (v .2), then God's hands went to work and met the need (v. 5). Faith moves the hands of God, and God's hands control the universe.

David blessed the Lord for his deliverance and wasn't ashamed to confess it. His testimony was clear: "God heard me and God helped me! I trusted Him and now I praise Him!" David now had the strength to obey God's will, no matter what the enemy might do. He also had the Lord as his shield (3:3; 7:10; 18:2, 30; 33:20; 84:11; Gen.15:1; Deut. 33:29). David had God's power and God's protection. How wonderful that David turned a painful experience into a song of praise to the Lord and that he left behind a witness that has encouraged other believers for centuries.

The Promise of Undeserved Blessing (vv. 8-9)

David closed his song by encouraging his people with what he had learned from the

Lord. Not only had God saved His anointed king, but He would also save His people Israel. "God save the king" included "God save the people," so they must trust Him. David saw the nation as God's inheritance (33:12; 78:62, 71; 79:1; 94:14; Deut. 4:20; 9:26, 29; 32:11; Mic. 7:14, 18), God's flock, and God's family. The word "feed" in verse 9 (KJV) means "to shepherd." (see Ps. 23), and "lift up" means "to carry like a child." Of course, the faithful shepherd sometimes has to carry the lambs, so the two images merge (Isa. 40:11). Though he was Israel's king, David always saw himself as a shepherd (2 Sam. 24:17). Indeed, the nation of Israel is God's inheritance, for He has invested in them the spiritual treasures that the bankrupt world needs (Rom. 9:1-5). "Salvation is of the Jews" (John 4:22). God has not forsaken His people.

Psalm 29

David was an outdoorsman who appreciated nature and celebrated the power of Jehovah the Creator. Jewish worshipers today use this psalm in the synagogue as a part of their celebration of Pentecost. When you read Acts 2 and discover the sound of wind, tongues of fire, and the "thunder" of God's voice through His Word, you can see that God's church today can also use Psalm 29 to celebrate Pentecost. Israel's neighbors believed that Baal, the storm god, controlled rain and fertility, but this psalm says otherwise. It magnifies the sovereignty of God and the power of God in His creation, both of which bring glory to God. The word "glory" is used four times in the psalm (1-3, 9), for David saw in the storm God's glory revealed in three different places.

God's Glory in the Heavenly Temple (vv. 1-2)

Heaven is a place of worship (see Rev. 4-5), and here the command is given for the angels ("mighty ones, sons of the Mighty") to ascribe (attribute; 96:7-9) to God glory and strength, because these divine attributes magnify His name. The psalm begins and ends mentioning God's "strength" (v. 11), and verses 4-9 demonstrate that strength in the description of the storm. Angels are called "sons of God" in Job 1:6, 2:1 and 38:7; and see Psalm 89:6. The Jewish priests and Levites had to dress properly as they served at the sanctuary (Ex. 28:1ff), and even God's angels must come before Him in proper "attire," what is called "holy array" (NASB) and "the splendor of his holiness" (NIV). (See 27:4 and 96:9.) True holiness is a beautiful thing to behold, and certainly the greatest demonstration was in the life of Jesus Christ when He ministered on earth. Sin is ugly, no matter what we may call it, but true holiness is beautiful and brings glory to God.

God's Glory in the Earthly Tempest (vv. 3-9)

This is an inspired and dramatic description of a thunderstorm that started somewhere over the Mediterranean Sea (v. 3) and moved eastward to the Lebanon mountain range in the northern part of the land of Israel (v. 5). The storm continued moving eastward overland to Mount Hermon (v. 6; Sirion, Deut. 3:8-9), where it turned south and traveled about two hundred miles down to Kadesh in the wilderness (v. 8), and there it dispersed. It was accompanied by loud thunder ("the voice of the Lord"—see 18:13-14 and Job 37:1-5; 40:9) and also by lightning (v. 7). Seven times you find the phrase "the voice of the Lord" (see Rev. 10:3-4), and it was "the God of glory" who was thundering and revealing His majesty. He is also "the King of Glory" (24:7).

The Lebanon range was about ten thousand feet above sea level, and the Canaanites believed it was the home of their gods. It was famous for its cedar forests (72:16; 1 Kings 4:33), but the thunder of God broke even those stalwart trees (v. 5). In fact, the thunder made the trees and the mountains skip like calves! (v. 6; see 114:1ff). In Scripture, the cedar tree is sometimes a symbol of a nation or a kingdom, including David's dynasty (Ezek. 17:1-3), Assyria (Ezek. 31:3), and even Israel (Num. 24:6). The prophet Isaiah saw the fall of the proud cedars as a picture of the defeat of the nations in the day of the Lord (Isa. 2:10-17). Note that it was the thunder—the voice of God—that broke the trees, and not the wind or the lightning. The voice of God is powerful and can shake the wilderness like an earthquake (v. 8). So frightened were the animals that the hinds went into premature labor and delivered their calves. Imagine being born in a thunderstorm! During this demonstration of God's great power, the angels were watching with amazement and shouting, "Glory!" The angels learned about God's grace, wisdom, and power by watching the Son of God when He served on earth (1 Tim. 3:16). They also learned during the week of creation (Job 38:7), and they are learning today as they behold the church on earth (Eph. 3:10; 1 Peter 1:12). According to verse 9, after the angels watched the storm described in this psalm, they cried, "Glory!"

God's Glory on the Heavenly Throne (vv. 10-11)
Seeing the rain and the mounting streams of water, hearing the thunder and watching the lightning, David began to meditate

on the flood that occurred in the days of Noah (Gen. 6-9). "The Lord sat as King at the flood" (v. 10, NASB); He was in charge, not Baal. He sent the rain, He opened the fountains of the deep, He stopped the rain, He waited for the water to drain off and the land to dry, and then He brought Noah and his family out of the ark. As he watched the storm move down to Kadesh, David rejoiced that the God who created the universe was also in control of the forces of nature, and there was nothing to fear. Eighteen times in these eleven verses, He is called "Lord," and that means He is Lord of heaven and earth, Lord of all.

The Lord is King today and will sit as King forever! He can give strength to His people and see them through the storms of life. After the thunder, lightning, wind, and rain comes the calm after the storm when "the Lord blesses His people with peace" (v. 11, NIV; and see 107:29 and 148:8.) Noah saw the rainbow of the covenant after the storm (Gen. 9:8-17), the apostle John saw it before the storm (Rev. 4:3), and Ezekiel saw the rainbow in the midst of the storm (Ezek. 1:26-28). We always have God's promise to encourage us.

Psalm 30

The psalm opens and closes on a note of thanksgiving (vv. 1, 12; and see 4 and 11).

The emphasis is on praise to the Lord for rescuing David from a dangerous and difficult situation that included sickness (v. 2), being near death (vv. 3, 9), God's anger (v. 5), weeping (vv. 5, 11), and emotional turmoil (v. 7). But the trial also involved the nation, for David addressed them in verses 4-5. Apparently this was a national crisis that David had helped to precipitate because he disobeyed the will of God. It came at a time when he was enjoying ease and security and was proud of himself and his kingdom (vv. 6-7). According to the superscription, David wrote this psalm for "the dedication of the house." The word "house" can be translated "palace," referring to David's house, or "temple," referring to the Lord's house. If it's the first, then perhaps 2 Samuel 5 describes the historical setting, when David captured Mt. Zion and made Jerusalem his capital city. (Note "my mountain" in Ps. 30:7.) All Israel had crowned David king, he had won great victories over the Philistines, and he had built had himself a palace. He knew that his kingdom was established and exalted by the Lord (5:12). This context has all the ingredients necessary to make David proud and thus invite the chastening of the Lord.

However, if "house" refers to the temple of the Lord, then we must look to 1 Chronicles 21:1-22:1 and 2 Samuel 24 for the context. This is the record of the national plague David caused when he arrogantly numbered the people and 70,000 people died. This caused David great distress (2 Sam. 24:10, 14), and he put on sackcloth and begged God for mercy for the people (1 Chron. 21:16; see Ps. 30:11). David purchased a plot of ground from Ornan and dedicated it to be the site for the temple (1 Chron. 22:1), and he began to use the plot as his own personal place of worship. This second explanation seems to cover the facts better. In either case, the message of the psalm is clear: the Lord forgave David and gave him the blessing of a new beginning. "The victorious Christian life," wrote the noted Scottish preacher George Morrison, "is a series of new beginnings." That definition beautifully fits this psalm.

A New Victory—From Death to Life (vv. 1-3)

David experienced three problems: the sinking mire beneath him that would take him down to the pit, the enemies around him who wanted him to die, and the distress within him that was like a painful sickness—and the Lord delivered him from all three! Because of his disobedience, David was in the depths, and the Lord had to lift him up. (See 18:4-6; 69:1-2, 14-15; 71:20; 88:6; 130:1-3; Lam. 3:55; and Jonah 2:2.) The "grave" or the "pit" refers to sheol, the realm of the departed spirits. (The Greek equivalent is hades.) But instead of allowing David to go down, God lifted him out and brought him up. God had done this for David before (18:16).

David's foes would have been glad to see him die (13:4; 25:2; 41:11), but the Lord saved David's life and silenced their taunts. The "healing" mentioned in verse 2 may not have involved actual physical sickness, because the word is also used to describe not only forgiveness and spiritual restoration (41:4; Isa. 6:10; 53:5; Hos. 6:1 and 7:1) but also deliverance from mental and emotional distress (Jer. 8:21-22; 14:19; Lam. 2:13). It was David's pride that had brought the plague to the land, and he felt the pain of this deeply, so much so that he thought his convicted conscience and broken heart would kill him. But God heard his pleas and brought him from death to life.

A New Day—From Night to Morning (vv. 4-5)

The psalm is not only David's personal expression of praise and thanksgiving, but it was also used by the congregation in worship; and here David addressed them. "Oh, magnify the Lord with me, and let us exalt his name together" (34:3).

Personal worship that doesn't enrich our corporate worship may become selfish and lead to more pride! The contrasts in verse 5 are the motivation for David's praise: from God's anger to God's favor; from chastening for only a moment to a lifetime of His grace (Isa. 54:7-8); from a night of weeping to a morning of joy. For David, this was the dawning of a new day after a painful time of suffering in darkness. Each morning, God's mercies are new (Lam. 3:22-23), and God's special help often arrives in the morning. "God will help her when morning dawns" (46:5; NASB; and see 59:16; 143:8). The resurrection of Jesus Christ brought the dawning of a new day for all who trust in Him (Matt. 28:1). Weeping comes as a guest, but God's gracious favor is with us for a lifetime. (See 2 Cor. 4.) As Jesus explained to His disciples, God doesn't *replace* sorrow with joy; He *transforms* sorrow into joy (John 16:20-22). The same baby that causes the mother pain also brings the mother joy.

A New Heart—From Pride to Humility (vv. 6-10)

This is where the story really began, for it was David's pride that made it necessary for the Lord to chasten him. "Prosperity" means "careless ease, a carefree self-assurance because things are going so well." This is frequently the attitude of the unconverted (10:6; 73:12; Luke 12:16-21), but it is a constant temptation to believers also (read Deut. 8). One reason the Lord permits trials is that we might not get comfortable in our faith and stop growing. "I was at ease," said Job, "but He shattered me, and He has grasped me by the neck and shaken me to pieces: He has also set me up as His target" (Job 16:12, NASB). Prosperity with-

out humility can lead to adversity. David's mountain (kingdom, as in Jer. 51:25) seemed strong, but the Lord showed David how weak he was.

When God's face is shining upon us (Num. 6:23-27), then we enjoy His rich blessings; but when we rebel, He may hide His face, and this causes trouble (see 10:11; 13:1; 27:9; 88:14; Deut. 31:17-18; 32:20). The Hebrew word translated "troubled" describes "intense agony, terror, anguish." It's used in 1 Samuel 28:21 to describe King Saul's feelings in the house of the witch. Knowing he had sinned, David kept crying out to the Lord for mercy and even debated with Him. "Am I more useful to you in the grave than I am alive on earth? Can the dead praise you and serve you?" (See 88:7-12; 115:17; Isa. 38:18-19.) David was a great king with a strong kingdom, but he was only dust, one short breath away from the grave. He humbled himself and confessed his sin, and the Lord mercifully forgave him and restored him.

A New Song—From Mourning to Rejoicing (vv. 11-12)

Seven times in the psalm David wrote "You have" (vv. 1-3, 7, 11), bearing witness to the strong and gracious hand of the Lord working on his behalf. Even God's chastening of David was an expression of His love (Heb. 12:1-11). Once David knew he was forgiven and accepted, he moved from the funeral to the feast. He took off the sackcloth of sadness and put on the garments of gladness. In Scripture, a dramatic alteration of one's life was often marked by a change of clothing (Gen. 35:2; 41:14; 45:22; Ex.19:10, 14; 2 Sam. 12:20; Luke 15:22). "My glory" means "my heart, my soul." David was singing to the Lord from the depths of his being. He realized that he would be singing praises to God forever (v. 12), so he wanted to start getting ready now! Every difficult experience of life—and David had many of them—is an opportunity to have a "pity party" or attend a rehearsal for singing in the choirs of heaven! We have a lifetime of grace (v. 5) to prepare us for an eternity of glory.

Psalm 31

The emphasis is on trusting ("taking refuge") in the Lord, no matter how difficult the circumstances might be (vv. 1, 6, 14, 19). David was surrounded by subversive whispering campaigns and wicked conspiracies (vv. 8, 13, 15, 18, 20), and everything seemed against him. Even his best friends and neighbors didn't want to be seen with him (vv. 11-13), and there was "fear on every side" (v. 13). The reference to "a besieged city" in verse 21 (NIV, NASB) has led some students to connect this volatile situation with David's experience at Keilah (1 Sam. 23:1-15) or perhaps at Ziklag (1 Sam. 30). However, it appears that what is described in the psalm best fits what happened during the rebellion led by Absalom (2 Sam. 15-18). Over many months, Absalom led a subversive campaign against his father, and even Ahithophel, David's wisest counselor, deserted the king and followed Absalom. "They took counsel together against me" (v. 13) reminds us of the conference recorded in 2 Samuel 17. If we take the phrase "besieged city" literally, it could refer to Jerusalem. After fleeing Jerusalem, David had made Mahanaim his headquarters (2 Sam. 17:24, 27), but it was never under siege. Perhaps the phrase should be taken metaphorically: "God showed me marvelous kindness as

if I were in a besieged city." If so, then it would parallel verse 20 which pictures God hiding His faithful ones in the Holy of Holies, which certainly isn't to be taken literally. Out of this harrowing experience, David learned some valuable lessons and recorded them in this psalm. They can be summarized in three statements.

When Others Do Evil, Trust God for His Strength (vv. 1-8)

The first three verses are quoted in 71:1-3, an untitled psalm probably written by David. He affirms his trust in the Lord and asks Him to deliver him and defend him on the basis of divine righteousness. "Shall not the Judge of all the earth do right?" (Gen. 18:25). How can the righteous Lord permit wicked people to prosper and overthrow His anointed king? Such a thing would make David ashamed, a statement he repeats in verse 17. As he often did, he begged God to act speedily (69:17; 70:1, 5; 71:12; 141:1; 143:7) and be to him a rock and a fortress (see 18:1-3). Along with God's protection, David needed God's direction so he would avoid the traps the enemy had set for him. "You are my strength" was his affirmation of faith (v. 4), for his own strength had failed (v. 10).

His prayer of commitment in verse 5 was quoted by our Lord from the cross (Luke 23:46, and see Acts 7:59). Peter also borrowed the idea (1 Peter 4:19) and used the word "commit," which means "to deposit in trust, as money in a bank." The hand of the enemy was against David (vv. 8, 15), but he knew he was safe in God's hand (see John 10:27-30). The God of truth would keep His promises. His enemies were idolaters; they weren't trusting in the living God but in "lying vanities, worthless idols." Note the repeated "but I trust" (vv. 6, 14). The word means to depend on, to lean on. Jonah quoted verse 6 in his prayer from the great fish (Jonah 2:8). In His mercy, God had delivered David from many dangerous places, and David knew he could depend on Him again, and this brought him joy. As in the past, God would deliver him from a "tight place" and enable him to stand in a "spacious place" (v. 8; see 18:19, 36, and 4:1). He would grow because of his trials and his faith in the Lord.

When Others Cause Pain, Ask God for His Mercy (vv. 9-18)

David had prayed, "You are my strength" (v. 4), but now he said, "You are my God" (v. 14) and asked Him for the mercy he desperately needed (v. 16). When you consider the vocabulary he used to describe his plight, you can well understand his need for mercy. He was filled with grief; he was sighing; his physical strength was failing; and his very bones were weakening. His soul and inner being were pained because of the troubles others were causing. He must have examined his heart and discovered sin there, so he confessed it to the Lord. Along with his physical and emotional anguish was the way people were treating him (vv. 11-13). His enemies were spreading malicious lies about him and people believed them. Of course, these lies spread rapidly, and David's close friends and neighbors heard and believed them. Even casual acquaintances avoided him when they saw him coming, for who wants to be seen speaking to an evil man? He became like a dead man who had been forgotten and like a useless piece of pottery that had been thrown away. It didn't take long for "the strife of tongues" (v. 20) to poison the nation and prepare the way for Absalom to take over.

The phrase "fear [terror] on every side" (v. 13) is used six times by the prophet Jeremiah (6:25; 20:3, 10; 46:5; 49:29; Lam. 2:22). In David's day, the dis-ruption of the government and the exile of the king brought great fear to the people, and all sorts of rumors spread throughout the land. David's answer to this confusion? "My times are in your hands" (v. 15, NIV). He had committed himself into God's hands (v. 5), and now he committed his circumstances into God's hands. "My times" refers, not to some special schedule, but to all the events and circumstances that surrounded David (see 1 Chron. 29:30). We would say, "All the affairs and details of my life are in the Lord's hands." This is the Old Testament version of Romans 8:28. David trusted God to bring light into the darkness and truth into the sea of lies that was overwhelming the people. Instead of the king being ashamed, his enemies would be ashamed when the Lord exposed their wickedness and defeated them.

When Others See the Victory, Give God the Glory (vv. 19-24)

The face of the Lord did smile upon David (Num. 6:22-27), and though he was severely chastened by the Lord, he was not abandoned. David knew that the Lord had laid up a supply of goodness and kindness for him (see 21:3), and that His mercies would never fail. Throughout the tragedy of the insurrection, God had protected David from danger, and he was as safe as if he had hidden in the Holy of Holies. As for the plots of the enemy and the lies they spread about the king, the Lord also took care of them and revealed the truth to the people. God's great goodness and marvelous lovingkindness were all that David needed to weather the storm and survive to lead his people.

However, at one point, David may have been ready to give up: "In my alarm I said, 'I am cut off from your sight!'" (v.

22, and see 30:6). It wasn't the enemy that frightened him but the thought of being abandoned by the God he trusted and served. He did what all of us must do when we sense that God is no longer near: he cried out to the Lord for His mercy, and the Lord answered. When the terrible experience of the rebellion was over, David spoke to the people (vv. 23-24) and gave God the glory for delivering him. David had written about his faith in the Lord (vv. 1, 6, 14, 19), but now he encourages his people to love the Lord and put their hope in him. Faith, hope, and love always go together (1 Cor. 13:13). The courage and strength we need in the trials of life are available from the Lord if we will put our faith in Him. Let's be sure that we give Him the glory.

Psalm 32

This is the second of the seven penitential psalms (see Ps. 6). David wrote it after confessing to God his sins of adultery, murder, and deception (see 51; 2 Sam. 11-12). In 51:13, he vowed to share what he had learned from this costly experience, and this psalm is a part of the fulfillment of that promise. This is the first "Maschil" psalm (see 42, 44, 45, 52-55, 74, 78, 88, 89, 142). The word had been interpreted many ways: "a skillful song, a song of instruction, a contemplative poem." The word means "instruction" and is translated that way in verse 8. However, Maschil may be a musical direction, the meaning of which is still unknown. This psalm is used by our Jewish friends at the close of the annual Day of Atonement; on the church calendar, it's assigned to be read on Ash Wednesday. Paul quoted verses 1-2 in Romans 4:7-8 as part of his argument for salvation by grace alone,

apart from the works of the law. In this psalm, David shared four basic facts about sin and forgiveness that need to be understood by every believer.

The Blessing of Acceptance (vv. 1-2)

Instead of starting with a catalog of his sins, David launched into the psalm with a song of praise for everybody in the assembly to hear. The first beatitude in the Psalms pronounces blessing on the obedient (1:1), but this second beatitude pronounces blessing on the disobedient who have been forgiven. (For other beatitudes, see 34:8; 40:4; 65:4; 84:5, 12; 94:12; 112:1.) Chronologically, his experience of forgiveness came long after he had committed his sins and covered them up for almost a year (vv. 3-5). But having now entered into the freedom of forgiveness, David couldn't wait to shout about it. If we have acceptance with God, it matters not what else may happen to us.

Transgression is "crossing over the line" and rebelling against God. David knew the Ten Commandments and that adultery, murder, and deceit were forbidden. *Sin* means "to miss the mark" and not live up to the standards God has set. *Iniquity* means "twisted" and describes what happens to the inner character of the sinner. *Guile* means "deception." David tried to cover his sins and pretend nothing had happened, but the Lord chastened him until he confessed he had sinned. This vocabulary will reappear in verse 5. *Forgive* means to remove a burden; it's pictured by the "scapegoat" in the Day of Atonement service, for symbolically the goat "carried" the sins of the people into the wilderness (Lev. 16:20-22; Ps. 103:12; John 1:29). Like Adam and Eve (Gen. 3:8), David tried to "cover" his sins, but his schemes didn't work. They never do (Prov. 28:13), but when God covers the sins we confess to Him, they are hidden from sight and never seen again. (See Isa. 38:17, 43:25, 44:22; Jer. 31:34; Mic. 2:18-19; 1 John 1:7-9.) On the Day of Atonement, the blood of the sacrifice was sprinkled on the mercy seat by the high priest, and that covered the sins the people had committed. *Impute* is a bookkeeping term that means "to put on the account, to add to the record." When we confess our sins, God cancels the debt and it's no longer on the books. As the children say, "It doesn't count any more." Why? Because Jesus paid the debt on the cross, and His blood cleanses the record and the heart of the offender. The forgiveness of the Lord is certainly something to sing about! It's unfortunate that too many of God's children take it for granted.

The Folly of Impenitence (vv. 3-4)
Now David tells his own story and honestly admits what a fool he had been to hide his sins for almost a year. Charles Spurgeon said, "God does not permit His children to sin successfully." John Donne wrote, "Sin is a serpent, and he that covers sin does but keep it warm, that it may sting the more fiercely, and disperse the venom and malignity thereof the more effectually." The Lord chastened David for almost a year and made him miserable until he stopped lying, humbled himself before God, and confessed his sins. Chastening isn't a judge punishing a criminal; it's a loving Father dealing with His disobedient children to bring them willingly to the place of surrender. According to Hebrews 12:1-13, God's chastening is proof that He loves us and that we are genuinely His children.

What happened to David during those difficult months? For one thing, he became a physical wreck. He was probably about fifty when he disobeyed the Lord, but he began to feel and look like a sick old man. Usually robust and ready for action, David now had constant pain in his body (see 51:8) and was groaning ("roaring," KJV) because of it. The hand of God was heavy upon him, and instead of feeling fresh and full of vigor, he was dried up like a plant during a drought (see 38:2 and 39:10). Did he have a fever that dehydrated him? Whatever it was, he was miserable, for he had a defiled conscience, a worried mind ("When will I be found out?"), and a sick body. But it was worth the pain, for the experience brought him back to the Lord.

The Way of Deliverance (vv. 5-7)
The Lord sent the prophet Nathan to David to confront him with his sins and bring him God's word of forgiveness (2 Sam. 12). David's confession "I have sinned against the Lord"[21] was answered with, "The Lord also has put away your sin" (2 Sam. 12:13, NKJV). The king didn't have to do penance or go on probation; all he had to do was sincerely confess his sins, and the Lord forgave him (1 John 1:9). The burden of transgression had been carried away, the debt was canceled, the twisted was made straight, and the Lord didn't put David's sins on the record. Instead of imputing our sins, the Lord puts the righteousness of Christ on our account, and we are accepted in Him (see Rom. 4:3ff; 5:13; 2 Cor. 5:19-21; Gal. 3:6). David offered no excuses; he admitted that he had sinned and was guilty before God. Guilt is to the conscience what pain is to the body: it tells us that something is wrong and must be made right, or things will get worse. The promise is for everybody ("godly" = chosen ones, God's people; 4:3), and we must confess our sins immediately, when we find them out and while God may be

found (69:14; Isa. 55:9; Prov. 1:24-33). The waters of chastening will only get deeper and the storm increase, so don't tempt the Lord!

But God's forgiveness isn't a negative thing; the Lord adds positive blessings to help us on the road to recovery. David exchanged hiding his sins for a hiding place in the Lord. God removed his troubles and put a wall of protection around him. Did David deserve these blessings? Of course not—nor do we! But this is the grace of God as found in Jesus Christ our Lord. "God's kiss of forgiveness sucks the poison from the wound," wrote Alexander Maclaren, and that says it all. This doesn't mean that David didn't suffer because of the consequences of his sins. God in His grace forgives us, but God in His government says, "You shall reap what you have sown." Bathsheba conceived and gave birth to a son, but the baby died. David's son Amnon raped his half-sister Tamar (2 Sam. 13) and was slain by David's son Absalom. Then Absalom tried to seize the throne and was slain by Joab (2 Sam. 14-18). While David was dying, his son Adonijah tried to take the scepter from Solomon (1 Kings 1), and Adonijah was slain. However, David faced these calamities with God's help and lived to assemble what was needed for the temple so that Solomon (Bathsheba's second son) could build it.

After David was forgiven and restored, he went to the sanctuary to worship the Lord (2 Sam. 12:15-23), and there with the other worshipers, he was surrounded by "songs [shouts] of deliverance," that is, praise to God for His mercies. That's exactly what David needed to hear!

The Joy of Obedience (vv. 8-11)

God speaks to David in verses 8-9, assuring him that the joy of salvation would be restored to him (51:12) if he obeyed the Lord and walked in His way. David's wrong thinking got him into serious trouble, but the Lord would instruct him, guide him, and keep His loving eye on him (see 33:18; 34:15). David's faith (vv. 5-6) must now issue in obedience, for faith and works must go together. God doesn't forgive us so that we can go back and sin! "But there is forgiveness with You, that You may be feared" (130:4).

When he gazed at Bathsheba, lusted after her, and then committed adultery, and when he plotted to kill her husband, David saw himself acting like a free man; *but God saw him acting like an animal!* We are made in God's image, but when we choose to knowingly rebel against God's law, we descend into what the older translations call acting "brutish" (see 92:6; 94:8; Jer. 10:8, 14, 21) and modern translations "senseless." Like the horse, David rushed ahead impetuously, and like the mule, he was stubborn and tried to cover his sins. The only way to control animals is to break them and harness them, but God didn't want to do that to His beloved servant David. Instead, He would teach him His Word and keep His eye upon him, surrounding him with mercy (see 23:6).

When he joined the assembly at the sanctuary of God (vv. 1-2), David began his song with the joyful announcement that God had forgiven him. Now he closed the psalm by exhorting the other worshipers to join him in celebrating the joy of the Lord. "Be glad! Rejoice! Shout for joy!" Years later, his son Solomon would write, "He who covers his sins will not prosper, but whoever confesses and forsakes them will have mercy" (Prov. 28:13, NKJV).

Psalm 33

The verbs in this psalm are plural, which means it involved the worshiping community at the sanctuary. The leader called them to worship (vv. 1-3), the choir led the assembly in praising the Lord, and all closed with the affirmation of faith in verses 20-22. It's likely that their praise was occasioned by the nation's victory over an enemy (vv. 10-11, 16-19). Except for the prayer in verse 22, the entire psalm is devoted only to praise and forms a helpful "primer on praise."

Who Should Worship the Lord? (v. 1)

This verse parallels 32:11 and reminds us that only those who are righteous by faith and obedient in their walk ("upright") can sincerely worship the Lord (Ps. 15; Gen. 15:1-6). It's a fitting and proper thing for those who have experienced the grace of God and his forgiveness (32:1-3) to praise the Lord (147:1). He is the Creator and cares for us. He is the Lord of all and watches over us. "We are his people, and the sheep of his pasture" (100:3). He has redeemed us and we belong to Him. No wonder the worship leader exhorted the people to rejoice, praise, play instruments, and sing to the Lord. A sinner who has been saved by God's grace ought to have no problem praising the Lord.

How They Should Worship the Lord (vv. 2-4)

Both voices and instruments were used in public worship at the sanctuary (see 1 Chron. 25). According to verse 3, the voices were to be enthusiastic ("shout for joy") in the Spirit but not demonstrative in the flesh, and joyful in the Lord but not jovial and jolly. The instruments should be played with skill and the players give their very best to the Lord. The "new song" may mean new in time or new in expression. The term is used nine times in Scripture (40:3; 96:1; 98:1; 144:9; 149:1; Isa. 42:10; Rev. 5:9 and 14:3). The Spirit of God can make an old song new to us as we grow in our knowledge of God and His Word, or as we have new experiences, and He can also open our hearts to a song completely new to us. (Some people don't like to learn new songs.) Our growth in our appreciation of "psalms and hymns and spiritual songs" (Eph. 5:19) is one indication of our development in the Christian life. Of greatest importance is that the worship be Scriptural (v. 4a; and see Col. 3:16). A choir has no more right to sing a lie than a preacher has to preach a lie, and not all "religious songs" are doctrinally correct. When God works, He obeys His own Word; so any worship that is contrary to God's Word will not please the Lord.

Why They Should Worship the Lord (vv. 5-19)

The mention of God's Word in verse 4 reminds us that by knowing the Word of God, we get better acquainted with the God of the Word. Creation reveals His existence, power, wisdom, and majesty, but the revelation in Scripture tells us about His mercy and grace and His wonderful plan of salvation. He is a faithful God, a God of truth, righteousness, justice, and goodness. God's throne is built on righteousness and justice (89:14; 97:2; Isa. 9:7; 32:1, 17). To eyes of faith, the earth is full of His goodness (v. 5), His glory (Isa. 6:3; Num. 14:21-22), and His praise (Hab. 3:3), and one day will be filled with the knowledge of the Lord (Hab. 2:14). The beauty of God's character should elicit from His people songs of praise and thanksgiving. Unless our worship focuses on the character of God, we have ignored the Person who ought to be the center of true worship.

We also worship the Creator and praise Him for His wonderful works (vv. 6-9). Out of nothing, He created everything by the power of His Word (vv. 6, 9; 119:89-91; 147:15, 18; 148:5; Gen. 1:1-2:1; Heb. 11:3). The Word that created the universe is also holding it together (Heb. 1:3; 2 Peter 3:5-7). "The breath of his mouth" may refer to the Holy Spirit of God (Gen. 1:1-2), for "breath" and "spirit" are the same word in Hebrew. "Host" includes the stars and planets (Gen. 2:11), and verse 7 takes us back to Genesis 1:9-10. When you see the heavens above and the earth and seas below, you must marvel at the handiwork of God and stand in awe at the power of His Word. As we worship the Lord, we must praise the Creator and the provisions He has made for us to live on this planet. We must also resolve to be good stewards and not abuse and waste His wonderful gifts.

In our praise, we must thank God for the wisdom of His counsel (vv. 10-11). People with authority make decisions that affect the destinies of nations, and when God isn't permitted to rule, then He overrules; for His will shall be accomplished. He can turn the policies and plans of nation into nothingness (Isa. 8:10; 19:3). The will of God for His children comes from the heart of God and is an expression of His love for them, so there is no cause for us to be alarmed or afraid (Jer. 29:11). What a privilege it is for Israel to be the people of God and the Lord's treasured inheritance (v. 12; 28:9; 74:2; 78:62, 71; Deut. 4:20; 32:9). May the church never lose the wonder of being the people of God! (1 John 3:1-3).

We worship the Lord because of the assurance of His divine care (vv. 13-19). Not only does He keep His eye on His individual saints (32:8; 34:15; 1 Peter 3:12), but He watches "all the sons of men" and "all their works." He knows what the saints are doing and what the sinners are doing to the saints! The word translated "look" in verse 14 means "to gaze intently." As God watches, He sees not only the actions of the body but the "thoughts and intents of the heart" (Heb. 4:12). He made the human heart, He understands it better than we do (Jer. 17:9), and He knows our motives (11:4; 34:15; 2 Chron. 16:9). The king's heart is just like the heart of any other man, and no nation can win a war just because it has a big army and a large supply of weapons and ammunition. At The Exodus, God looked down at the great Egyptian army and destroyed it (Ex. 14:24ff). God delivers His people from danger and death, and He keeps them alive when times are difficult. He cares for us (1 Peter 5:6-7).

What Should Happen Because They Worship the Lord (vv. 20-22)

These words may have been expressed by the congregation and choir as the song came to an end, a confession of faith in the living God. Because they had worshiped the Lord, they had peace in their hearts and could quietly wait for Him to work. Their hope had been strengthened, and they looked expectantly for Him to accomplish His purposes in them, through them, and for them. They had confidence in the Lord that He would send help when they needed it (see 30:10; 40:17; 46:1; 54:4; 63:7; 70:5; 115:9-11; 146:5). On "shield," see 3:3, and note that "help" and "shield" often go together (28:7; 115:9-11; Deut. 33:29). God protects us, not to pamper us but to prepare us to go back into the battle. He is a "refuge and strength" who hides us long enough to help us.

Worship should not only strengthen our inner peace and power, increase our hope, and give us greater confidence in the Lord, but it should also increase our joy. The psalm begins and ends with the theme of joy. Along with that blessing, we find our faith strengthened as we behold the beauty and glory of the Lord in our worship. "Let your unfailing love surround us" is the closing prayer (NLT), so we have the three great Christian virtues brought together: faith (v. 21), hope, and love (v. 22). It isn't enough to leave the place of worship simply "feeling good," because feelings are temporary and sometimes deceptive. If we find ourselves loving God and His people more, having greater faith and hope in the Lord, and going forth into the battle of life with greater confidence and joy, then our worship has accomplished what God wanted it to accomplish.

Psalm 34

Like Psalm 25, this is an acrostic psalm with the Hebrew letter *waw* omitted and an extra *pe* added at the beginning of verse 22. The title connects the psalm with David's dangerous experience with the Philistines in Gath, as recorded in 1 Samuel 21:10-22:1, after which he fled to the cave of Adullum. The emphasis on fearing the Lord (vv. 7, 9, 11) and trusting His goodness (vv. 8, 10, 12) would fit into this historical context. The Philistine king is called Achish in 1 Samuel, but the dynastic title of Philistine kings was Abimelech, as in the title of the psalm. Egyptian rulers were called Pharaoh and the Amalekite kings called Agag. Verse 8 is quoted in 1 Peter 2:3 and verses 12-16 in I Peter 3:10-12. Out of his experience in Gath, David shared in this psalm four

instructions for his own followers (1 Sam. 22:1-2), as well as for us today, to help us keep out of tight situations and live a life that pleases God.

Bless the Lord (vv. 1-3)

David was delighted to be out of enemy territory (where he probably shouldn't have gone to begin with) and back in the wilderness with his men. Note the verbs: bless, boast, magnify, exalt. The name "Lord" is used sixteen times in the psalm. If initially, David was speaking to his own men, then he was calling them to interrupt warfare and focus on worship. "In prayer, we act like men [people]," wrote Puritan preacher Thomas Watson, "in praise we act like angels." David gave thanks to the Lord by magnifying Him and exalting His name. See what He did for David: He answered prayer (vv. 4, 15), provided his needs (vv. 9-10), delivered him from trouble (v. 17), and protected him from danger (v. 7). David didn't boast about his own cleverness or skill; he boasted about the Lord, who He is and what He does. David saw God's people as nothing in themselves, for they were only the humble and the poor (vv. 2, 6); but they had everything because they belonged to the Lord. They feared the Lord (vv. 7, 9), were set-apart ("saints") as His righteous ones (vv. 10, 15, 19, 21), and were the servants of the Lord God (v. 22). Knowing who we are in Christ and who the Lord is ought to make us want to bless the Lord.

Seek the Lord (vv. 4-8)

David gave a threefold witness of what the Lord does for His own: He saves (vv. 4-8), He keeps (v. 7), and He satisfies (v. 8). He sought the Lord and was saved from the fears ("terrors"; see 31:13) within him, and he cried to the Lord and was delivered from the troubles around him. To seek the Lord is the same as to look to the Lord; and when we look to Him by faith, He looks to us and "shines upon us" (4:6; Num. 6:22-27). If we walk in unbelief, our faces will be ashamed; if we walk by faith, our faces will be aglow (Ex. 34:29; Matt. 17:2; Acts 6:15; 2 Cor. 3:18). The word "radiant" in verse 5 describes the joyful countenance of a mother who is welcoming her children home (Isa. 60:4-5). After the Lord saves us, He keeps us and sends His angels to protect us (v. 7; 35:5-6; Gen. 48:16; Ex. 14:19). The Angel of the Lord is Jesus Christ, the second Person of the Trinity (Josh. 5:13-15), the Lord of the hosts of the angels, who made pre-incarnation visits to His people during Old Testament times. When David envisioned a camp of angels around him, he may have been recalling Jacob's experience at Mahanaim ("the two camps"; Gen. 32:1-2). The angels are servants of the saints today and minister to us in ways we will never know about until we get to heaven (Heb. 1:14).

Those who seek the Lord discover that He not only saves and keeps but that He also satisfies (v. 8). "Taste" doesn't suggest a sip or a nibble; it implies feeding on the Lord through His Word and experiencing all He has for us (1 Peter 2:3; see Heb. 2:9 and 6:3). It means knowing Him better and enjoying Him more. It was a great blessing for David to be delivered from Gath, and it was a greater blessing for him to be protected by the Lord after he fled, but the greatest blessing was drawing nearer to God and enjoying His presence, not just His gifts. David found God's Word sweet (119:103), and he rejoiced in the goodness of the Lord. "Good" is an important word in this psalm (vv. 8, 10, 12, 14).

Fear the Lord (vv. 9-16)

Those who fear the Lord (vv. 7, 9, 11) need fear nothing else, for this is the fear that drives out all fear (112:1). When we fear the Lord, He provides all that we need when we need it. Verse 9 is the Old Testament equivalent of Matthew 6:33. "No good thing does he withhold from those who walk uprightly" (84:11, NASB). God promises to give us what is good for us and to cause all things to work together for good (Rom. 8:28). If we don't receive what we think we need, it means it isn't good for us and we don't need it at this time. At this point, David may have gathered the children and youths around him to teach them the secret of real living. Peter quoted verses 12-14 in 1 Peter 3:10-12, and his instructions are wise and workable.

Desire what is good (v. 12). To "love life" means to desire a full life, the abundance life Christ came to give (John 10:10). This kind of life has little to do with possessions, status, or fame, but it has a lot to do with character, faith, and a desire to honor the Lord. They seek the Lord and want nothing less than His will for their lives. Solomon had wealth, knowledge, fame, and power, yet he wrote, "Therefore, I hated life ..." (Eccl. 2:17-20). To cultivate a heart that desires what is good, a heart that delights in the Lord (37:4), is the first step toward the life that overflows with the blessing of the Lord.

Speak what is true (v. 13). If we can control the tongue, we can control the body (James 3:1-12); "whoever guards his mouth and tongue keeps his soul from troubles" (Prov. 21:23, NKJV). To speak the truth in love (Eph. 4:15) and to speak nothing evil is not easy in today's competitive and corrupt society, but it can be done. Note David's prayer in 141:3-4.

Pursue what is right (v. 14). This means abandoning sin once and for all, doing good as God gives strength and opportunity, and being a peacemaker and not a troublemaker. Christians don't seek "peace at any price," for peace depends on purity (James 3:13-18; Isa. 32:17), but they do make every effort not to make enemies (Matt. 5:9; Rom. 14:19; Heb. 12:14-21). Sometimes our best efforts seem to be in vain, but at least we obeyed the Lord (Matt. 5:21-26; 18:15-35). "Pursue" means that we have to work at it, with the help of the Lord.

Expect what is best (vv. 15-16). We must live by faith, trusting the Lord to guide us, care for us, and help us do the right thing. We need not fear because His eyes are upon us (32:8) and His ears are attentive to our prayers. God's face is against those who would do evil to us. This promise is illustrated in Acts 12, when Peter was in prison awaiting execution, the church was praying, and King Herod seemed to be having his way. God saw Peter's plight, He heard the prayers of the saints, and He delivered Peter but destroyed Herod.

Trust the Lord (vv. 17-22)

Nowhere in this psalm does David suggest that the life of faith and obedience will exempt the child of God from trouble (see vv. 4, 6, 17, 19). He does promise that, if we trust Him and call on Him, the Lord can see us through our troubles and make them a blessing to us and through us to others. (See 28:7, Isa. 41:10, Heb. 13:6.) He is also able to help us with our feelings (v. 18). The assurance is that God is near us when our hearts are broken and our spirits are crushed, *whether we feel like it or not.* This is not a promise with conditions attached to it; *it is a fact.* (See 69:20; 119:151; 147:3; Isa. 50:8 and 61:1; Luke 4:18.)

The Lord will take care of our physical safety (vv. 19-20) until our work is fin-

ished. The word "keep" means "to exercise great care over," as when Adam cared for the garden (Gen. 2:15) or Jacob cared for his sheep (Gen. 30:31). The apostle John quoted verse 20 in John 19:36 and applied it to Jesus, the Lamb of God (Ex. 12:46; Num. 9:12). The Lord is able to keep our enemies in check, and their own evil deeds will destroy them, for sin is its own executioner (v. 21; see 7:14-16; 9:16; 10:2; Prov. 5:22; Rom. 12:17-21). "Desolate" in verses 21-21 (KJV) means "condemned." The wicked are condemned, but the righteous face no condemnation because they trust the Lord (Rom. 8:1, 33-34). God redeemed David, just as He had redeemed Israel from Egypt, and He is able to redeem us from our troubles.

Psalm 35

Once again, David was being hounded by Saul and slandered by Saul's men, many of whom had been David's friends. David was championing the right cause, for he was God's chosen king, while Saul was trying to destroy him so that one of his own sons would become king. Instead of managing the affairs of the kingdom, Saul was driven by his paranoia to pursue David and seek to kill him, and his zeal was fueled by the lies of his officers. (For the background, see 1 Sam. 19:5; 20:1; 23:25; 24:9-15; 25:29; 26:18-19.) This is classified as an imprecatory psalm (see Ps. 5 for discussion). David made three requests of God, and eventually He granted all of them.

Protect Me (vv. 1-10)

David merged two images in verse 1—the law court ("plead my cause"; see 43:1; 74:22; Jer. 2:9; Mic. 6:1) and the battlefield. Saul chose the battlefield, but David turned to the Lord and asked Him to be Advocate and Judge in the dispute. "The Lord is a man of war" (24:8; 45:3-5; Ex. 15:3; Josh. 5:13-15), so if Saul wanted a fight, God would accept the challenge (see 18:25-27). A soldier himself, David envisioned the Lord dressed in armor and wielding his weapons. The buckler was a large shield that covered most of the body. The enemy hated David (v. 19), lied about him (v. 11), persecuted him (v. 2), and wanted to hurt him and kill him (vv. 4, 26), so the conflict was a matter of life and death; *but there was no just cause for this opposition.* (See vv. 7, 19; 38:19; 69:4; 109:3; 119:78, 86, 161.)

David asked the Lord to block the way and stand between him and Saul and his army (v. 3), just as He had done at The Exodus (Ex. 14:19ff). Then he asked that the angel of the Lord (34:7) confuse the enemy, turn them around, and chase them (v. 4). This would lead to their disgrace, defeat, and eventual destruction (v. 8). In verse 26, he repeated the prayer of verse 4. David frequently mentioned that he was a man with a price on his head (37:32; 38:12; 40:14; 54:3; 63:9; 70:2), so it's no wonder he asked the Lord for a special word of assurance (v. 3; 27:1-3). Confronted by God's heavenly army, Saul and his men were like the chaff: weightless, worthless, defenseless, and harmless. (See 1:4; 83:13; Isa. 17:13; 29:5; Dan. 2:35; Matt. 3:12). They would try to run on the slippery mountain trails and in the darkness fall to their death or fall into one of their own traps (vv. 7-8). These traps were probably pits with nets over them, covered with branches and leaves. Saul treated David like an animal, but it was Saul and his army that were the animals (vv. 15, 17, 25).

In this psalm, David followed each of his three requests with a song of praise to the Lord (vv. 9-10, 17-18 and 27-28), showing that his great desire was to magnify Him. David's joy was in God's salvation, for which only God could receive the glory. His whole being ("all my bones"; see 51:8) would give thanks and praise to the Lord. "Who is like you?" (v. 10) reminds us of Israel's triumph song after The Exodus (Ex. 15:11). David knew that God had chosen him to be king of Israel and that his greatest task would be to unite and strengthen the kingdom and lead the people back to God. Israel had an important work to do in the world and David's leadership was essential.

Reward Me (vv. 11-18)
David stated the evidence that proved he was innocent. The enemy depended on lies, false ("malicious") witnesses who accused him of being a traitor. (See 27:12; Deut. 19:15-21; 1 Sam. 24:10.) Quite the contrary, it was Saul and his officers who were the traitors, for they returned evil for the good David did to them. On two occasions, David could have killed Saul, but instead, David returned good for evil (1 Sam. 24, 26; and see 38:20; 109:5; Jer. 18:18-23). Saul even admitted that David was the better man (1 Sam. 24:17). It pained David deeply that the men he had served with in Saul's army had betrayed him (see 41:9; 55:12-14). He had prayed for them when they were in need, but his prayers returned to him unanswered. David received a blessing because he prayed, but God couldn't send a blessing to such evil people. The only "return" David got from his prayers was evil for good, so he asked the Lord to send him good to compensate for their evil. Those who criticize David for his imprecatory prayer in verses 4-8 should remember that first he prayed for their help and healing. Saul's men "tore David apart" with their wicked words (v. 15).

Like court jesters, at their meals they made him the butt of their vicious jokes (v. 16, and see 69:12). (On the question "How long?" see 6:3.) David knew that God would eventually reward him for his faithfulness, but he didn't know when. His first praise to God (vv. 9-10) was personal, but the second expression of praise (v. 18) is in the congregation with the saints.

Vindicate Me (vv. 19-28)

The trial was about to end and the enemy was confident of victory. "Aha, aha, our eyes have seen it" [David's defeat, v. 21, NASB]. In his imagination, David saw Saul's men winking at each other arrogantly (Prov. 6:13; 10:10), as if to say, "He's done for!" They would never accept a truce or even talk about peace, but this was God's way of judging Saul for his sins and eliminating him from the political equation in Israel. After Saul's death, David had seven years of trouble with Saul's son (2 Sam. 1-4), but the Lord eventually solved that problem. David prayed that God would vindicate him, because David's cause was God's cause, and the Lord's reputation was at stake (v. 24). In verse 26, he repeated his request from verse 4 and asked that the enemy be shamefully defeated. David's desire was that the Lord be magnified in His own way and His own time.

In contrast to the shame of the enemy in their defeat are the joyful shouts of the righteous in David's victory. Unlike Elijah, who felt he was fighting all alone (1 Kings 19:10-18), David knew that many people in Israel supported him, those who were living "quietly in the land" (v. 20). Even in the darkest days of Israel's history, there has always been a faithful remnant that stayed true to the Lord and prayed for His will to be done. David closed the psalm with a song of

confidence and joy, witnessing to God's righteousness and power. The word translated "prosperity" (v. 27, KJV) is the familiar Hebrew word "shalom—peace," which means much more than a mere cessation of hostilities. It carries the idea of well being in every aspect of life, including peace with God, with others, with yourself, and with the circumstances of your life.

David's experience reminds us of Jesus Christ, the Son of David, who was also hated without a cause (John 15:25) and falsely accused and attacked by those for whom He had shown nothing but kindness and live. God delivered David from his enemies, but the Father "spared not his own son" (Rom. 8:32) but willingly gave Him to die for the sins of the world.

Psalm 36

The psalm is attributed to David "the servant of the Lord" (see 18, title; 35:27; Deut. 34:5; Josh. 24:29; Dan. 6:20; James 1:1; Titus 1:1). David pondered the reality of evil in God's world (vv. 1-4), he praised God's character (vv. 5-9), and then he prayed that God would protect him from evil and eventually judge the wicked. He solved the perplexing problem of evil in the world by being a worshiper, not a philosopher, and by taking personal responsibility to obey God and serve Him. If there were more salt and light in this world, there would be less decay and darkness in society.

Revelation: The Corruption of the Human Heart (vv. 1-4)

In Scripture, an oracle is usually an authoritative pronouncement from the Lord; but here it is sin that is speaking an oracle deep in the heart of the sinner. In

Psalm 10, the sinner talks to himself, but here sin speaks to the sinner. Sin deceives us (Rom. 7:11) and flatters us (10:3; Deut. 29:18-19), giving us the false assurance that our rebellion will go unpunished (Gen. 3:1-5). "Listen to your heart!" the world tells us, forgetting that "The heart is more deceitful than all else and is desperately sick; who can understand it?" (Jer.17:9, NASB).

Of course, the sinner's self-confident arrogance brings tragic consequences, starting with *an absence of the fear of God* (v. 1). This is not the word for the reverential respect of God that all believers should cultivate, but rather the word that means the dread of God and of His judgment. Paul quotes this verse in Romans 3:8, along with others Old Testament statements that reveal the wickedness of the human heart. When we don't fear God, we flatter ourselves, and that flattery gives us more confidence to sin. We don't really see ourselves as the Lord sees us, and we are blind to our own sins and what they can do to us. (On the fear of the Lord, see 34:9; 55:19; 64:4; 111:10; 119:120; Josh. 24:14; Prov. 1:7.) This kind of person doesn't hate sin (v. 2) or despise it or reject it (v. 4) but finds delight in doing it.

When they lose the fear of God, they start to lose everything else that is important to good character and conduct. Out of a sinful heart come sinful words and sinful deeds (v. 3; Matt. 12:34-35). Instead of acting wisely, they set themselves and are determined to do evil. They don't meditate on God's truth while in bed (1:2; 16:7; 42:8; 63:6) but devise evil schemes. They can't relax and go to sleep until they've hatched a new plot (Mic. 2:1). The corrupt heart has produced a defiled conscience, a confused mind, and a perverted will.

Adoration: The Character of God's Heart (vv. 5-9)

David did a wise thing when he stopped contemplating the sinners and started focusing on the glories of the Lord. Knowing the character of God is essential to a balanced Christian life, and these five verses are a concise systematic theology. *Mercy* (vv. 5, 7, 10) is translated "lovingkindness" in the *New American Standard Bible* and "love" in the *New International Version*. Some translations use "covenant love" or "steadfast love." Mercy and faithfulness are often joined (57:3; 61:7; 85:10; 86:15), as are righteousness and justice (33:5; 89:14; 97:2). God's mercy and faithfulness are as limitless as the skies, His righteousness as firm as the mountains, and His judgments (justice) as inexhaustible and mysterious as the ocean depths (see Rom. 11:33-36). Yet He takes care of people and animals on the earth! What a gracious and generous God! His mercy is priceless, for it took the death of His Son to accomplish salvation for a lost world (1 Peter 1:18-19).

The "refuge" in verse 7 is probably the Holy of Holies in the sanctuary of the Lord, for he mentions God's house in verse 8. If so, then the "wings" are those of the cherubim on the mercy seat of the ark (Ex. 37:9). (See 57:1; 61:4; 63:7; Ruth 2:12; Heb. 10:19-25.) God's "shadow" offers us better protection than the world's armies! In 90:1 and 4, the image is that of the mother hen protecting her young with her outspread wings. (See Matt. 23:37 and Luke 13:34.) The priests received portions of some sacrifices for their own use and would feast in the sanctuary (Lev. 6:14-23; 7:11-38; Deut. 18:1-5; 1 Sam. 2:12-17). But David sees all of God's people enjoying a feast in God's house where there is an abundance of food and water (63:1-5; 65:4). The image of the Lord's satisfying river is found often in

Scripture: 46:4; Isaiah 8:5-8; Jeremiah 2:13-19; Ezekiel 47; John 4:1-15 and 7:37-39; Revelation 22:1. The word "pleasures" (delights) in verse 8 comes from the same Hebrew root as "Eden" in Genesis 2 and 3, and it means "delight." Man sinned and was cast out of Eden, but through faith in Christ, we have access into God's presence and can delight in His blessings. The river in verse 8 reminds us of the rivers in Eden (Gen. 2:8-14). Life and light go together (v. 9; 49:19; 56:13; John 1:4; 8:12), and the Lord is the source of both. The wicked feed on flattery (v. 2), but the righteous feed on the Lord's rich blessings.

Expectation: The Confidence of the Believer's Heart (vv. 10-12)

What a privilege it is to be God's children! We are resting safely under His wings, feasting joyfully at His table, drinking abundantly from His river, and walking confidently in His light! In response to these blessings David prayed that the Lord would continue His blessings on His people (v. 10) and one day judge the wicked (vv. 11-12). God will continue to bless us if we love Him, get to know Him better, and walk in obedience to His will. David knew that the enemy was subtle and that he dared not become overconfident, so he prayed for the Lord's protection from their hands and feet. He didn't want to be knocked down and trampled upon and forced to leave his own land. By faith, David looked ahead and saw the enemies of the Lord completely defeated, and on this confidence, he continued to serve the Lord.

Psalm 37

David had written about the wicked in Psalm 36 (see vv. 1 and 11), and he will pick up the theme again in Psalm 39. He wrote Psalm 37 in his mature years (v. 25), and in it he discussed the age-old problem of why the righteous suffer while the wicked seem to prosper. Perhaps this psalm was part of David's preparation of Solomon for the throne (1 Kings 2:3; see Prov. 23:17-18, 24:19-20). Honest atheists and agnostics don't have to wrestle with this problem because their philosophy of relativism forbids them to use words like good, bad, righteous, and wicked. However, those who believe in God sometimes wonder why He allows the wicked to succeed while the righteous suffer. The word "wicked" is found fourteen times in the psalm (KJV). The theological foundation for the psalm is the covenant God made with Israel, recorded in Leviticus 26 and Deuteronomy 27-30. God owned the land, and if the nation obeyed Him, they could live in the land and enjoy its blessings. But if Israel disobeyed the Lord, He would first chasten them *in the land* (invasion, drought, famine), but if they continued to rebel, He would then take them *out of the land* (captivity). (See Deut. 11 and 33:28, and Lev. 26:3-10.) But it seemed that the wicked were prospering and that God wasn't doing anything about it (see Jer. 12). The righteous could fret over the problem (vv. 1, 7-8), leave the land (v. 3), or go on being faithful, trusting the Lord to keep His Word (vv. 3, 5, 7, 34, 39). Like any mature believer who had been through his own share of suffering, David took the long view of the situation and evaluated the immediate and the transient in terms of the ultimate and the eternal. He encouraged Solomon and the people to believe God's promises and wait on Him. In the psalm, he gave four encouraging assurances to believers who question how God is running His world. (See also Pss. 49 and 73.)

The Lord Can Be Trusted (vv. 1-11)

David gave one negative instruction—"Don't fret" (vv. 1, 7, 8)—and four positive instructions: trust in the Lord (v. 3), delight in the Lord (v. 4), commit yourself to the Lord (vv. 5-6), and rest in the Lord (v. 7).

Fret not (vv. 1-2). The word translated "fret" means "to burn, to get heated up." David's message was, "Cool down and keep cool!" When we see evil in the world, we ought to feel a holy anger at sin (Eph. 4:26), but to envy the wicked only leads to fretting, and fretting leads to anger (v. 8). His argument is that the wicked are temporary and will one day be gone (see vv. 9, 22, 28, 34, 38). They are like grass that either fades away or is cut down and burned. In the east, vegetation is abundant during and immediately after the rainy seasons, but it quickly vanishes when the moisture is gone. (See 90:5-6; 102:11; 103:15-16; Isa. 40:6-8; James 1:10-11; 1 Peter 1:24.)

Trust in the Lord (v. 3). A fretful heart is not a trusting heart, because it lacks joy and peace (Rom. 15:13). Faith and works go together, so we should also do good as we wait on the Lord (34:14; Luke 6:35; Gal. 6:10). Some of God's people were tempted to leave the land (see Ruth 1; 1 Sam. 26:19), which was tantamount to saying that God wasn't faithful and couldn't be trusted. But David urged them to stay in the land and trust God for what they needed (v. 27). Each tribe, clan, and family in Israel had its assigned inheritance which was not to pass into other hands, and the Lord promised to care for the land of the faithful (vv. 9, 11, 22, 29, 34). The promise in verse 3 is variously translated: "enjoy safe pastures" (NIV), "feed on His faithfulness" (NASB margin; NKJV), "enjoy security" (RSV). If we are faithful to God, He will be faithful to us. Trusting the Lord is a key theme in this psalm (vv. 4, 5, 7, 34, 39).

Delight in the Lord (v. 4). The word translated "delight" comes from a root that means "to be brought up in luxury, to be pampered." It speaks of the abundance of the blessings we have in the Lord Himself, totally apart from what He gives us. To enjoy the blessings and ignore the Blesser is to practice idolatry. In Jesus Christ, we have all God's treasures, and we need no other. If we truly delight in the Lord, then the chief desire of our heart will be to know Him better so we can delight in Him even more, and the Lord will satisfy that desire! This is not a promise for people who want "things," but for those who want more of God in their lives.

Commit your way to the Lord (vv. 5-6). The verb means "to roll off your burden" (1 Peter 5:7). God doesn't take our burdens so that we can become irresponsible, but so we can serve Him better. Sometimes less care means we become careless, and that leads to failure. One of the things He will "bring to pass" is the vindication of His servants who have been slandered by God's enemies (v. 6, NIV; see vv. 28, 32-33).

Rest in the Lord (vv. 7-11). The verb means "be silent, be still." It describes calm surrender to the Lord (62:5). Creative silence is a rare commodity today, even in church worship services. People cannot tolerate silence. A silent radio or TV screen invites listeners and viewers to switch to another station or channel. But unless we learn to wait silently before God, we will never experience His peace. For us to get upset because of the evil schemes of the ungodly is to doubt the goodness and justice of God (vv. 7, 12, 32). "Meekness" does not mean "weakness." It means force under the control of faith. Moses was meek (Num. 12:3), but he was a man of great power. Jesus quoted verse 11 (Matt. 5:5) but expanded it to include "the earth." "Inherit the land" (vv. 9, 11, 22, 29) refers to the security of future generations in the Land of Promise, according to God's covenant (Gen. 12:1-3; 13:14-18; 15:7-17), for God had a great work for His righteous remnant to do in that land, culminating in the coming of Messiah. Eventually, the wicked will be cut off (vv. 9, 22, 28, 34, 38), which in Israel usually meant exclusion from the covenant community (Ex. 12:15; 30:33, 38; 31:14; Lev. 7:20-21), but it could mean execution (Gen. 9:11; Lev. 20:17; Num. 15:30-31).

The Lord Understands Your Situation (vv. 12-20)
Since God can be trusted, we should not fret, and since God understands our situation, we should not fear. The wicked plot against the poor and needy (v. 12, and see 7, 32) and act like wild beasts about to devour them ("slay" in v. 14 means "to butcher an animal"), but the Lord laughs at the wicked (see 2:4) for He knows their judgment is coming. He also knows that their own weapons will turn against them (v. 15; 7:15ff; 9:15ff). God upholds the righteous (vv. 16-17) and sees to it they have what they need (Prov. 15:16; 16:8). Just as Jesus met a great need with a few loaves and fishes, so the Lord can "make a little go a long way." "Know" in verse 18 refers to much more than intellectual understanding—"God knows what's going on"—but indicates that He is involved and caring for us daily (see 1:6; 31:7, 15). "Give us this day our daily bread" (Matt. 6:11).

There is in verse 18 the suggestion of something beyond the needs of this life. The emphasis in Psalm 34 is on Israel's national life in the land, and the ancient Jew saw his "immortality" in his posterity, but occasionally in The Psalms you catch a glimpse of the eternal. (See 16:11, 17:15 and the "forever" statements in 37:18 and 27-29.) The wicked will perish like smoke at the altar (102:3; Hos. 13:3; the *New International Version* reads "like the beauty of the fields," an image used in v. 2). If the punishment of the wicked involves more than suffering and death in this life, will not the blessing of the righteous go beyond this life as well?

The Lord Blesses His People (vv. 21-31)
He blesses them first of all with *provision of their daily needs* (vv. 21-22). The wicked may succeed for a time, but eventually they have to borrow in order to survive; while the godly have what they need and can lend to others (Deut. 15:6; 28:12, 44). This isn't a promise for every believer at all times in all places, for many believers have died in poverty and hunger. Like the statements in the book of Proverbs, it's a generalization that proves true in so many cases that we can safely apply it to life. God not only gives provision, but He also gives *protection* (vv. 23-24). "Ordered" means "secured, established" (119:133), and even if believers stumble, God will pick them up and get them going again. He can keep us from stumbling (Jude 24), and He can restore us if we do stumble. Why? Because the Father delights in His children and wants them to learn to walk.

Along with the blessing of provision and protection is the blessing of the Lord's *presence with His people* (vv. 25-26). As an elder saint, David bore witness to God's faithfulness to him and his descendants. Not only did God meet every need, but He gave enough so that David could share it with others (Luke 6:38). As we pray for daily bread (Matt. 6:11), the Lord answers. God also blesses His people by enabling them to live *obedient lives* (vv. 27-29), which means righteousness in character and justice in conduct. God's blessing on the godly continues in the lives of their children, but the descendants of the wicked are cut off. Alas, the sins of ungodly fathers influence their children to disobey God, and the Lord has to punish them as well. Finally, God blesses the righteous with *His Word* (vv. 30-31). God's Word in the heart is the secret of a holy life (1:1-3; 40:8; 119:9-16; Deut. 6:6).

The Lord Judges the Wicked (vv. 32-40)
Three images illustrate God's judgment of those who reject Him and rebel against His law: the court trial (vv. 32-34), the tree (vv. 35-36), and the rescue (vv. 37-40). The wicked watched the godly and tried to find some reason for accusing them. In spite of David's integrity and Solomon's great wisdom, the judicial system in Israel was far from efficient, and it was easy for the rich to oppress the poor and take what little they possessed (Amos 2:4-8; 4:1-3). But the Lord is the highest judge, and He knows how to deliver the righteous from lying witnesses and judges who have been bribed.

The godly are pictured by the fruitful tree (1:3) and the ungodly by a luxurious ("overbearing and towering") shrub or tree, planted in its native soil where its roots can go down deep (vv. 35-36). Not only did the tree die and fall, but there was no evidence left behind that there had ever been a tree there at all! So God will do to the wicked, who appear to be successful and permanent but are destined for judgment. God not only judges the wicked but He also rescues the righteous from their clutches (vv. 37-40). The key question isn't what people look like or what they possess, but what is their final end? (See Prov. 5:4; 14:12-13; 16:25;

24:20). "There is a future for the man of peace ... but the future of the wicked will be cut off" (vv. 37-38, NIV). Some see this as referring to posterity, and that may be included, but certainly it describes the final destiny of the righteous and the wicked. The Lord delivers the righteous from eternal judgment, but He also delivers them from the attacks and accusations of the wicked in this world today. Why? "Because they trust in him" (v. 40). Fretting and fear cannot stand before faith in the living God.

Psalm 38

This is the third of the penitential psalms and, as you would expect, it has things in common with its predecessors (6, 32). Compare 6:1 with 38:1; 32:3 with 38:3, 8, 13-14; and 32:5 with 38:18. The description here of David's physical condition is similar to the one in 32, so perhaps both psalms (along with 51) came out of the same sad situation. David's sins (vv. 3, 4, 18) had brought God's chastening to his life and David was a very sick man. Not all affliction comes from disobedience (John 9:1-3), but physical troubles can be a consequence of sin (John 5:14). David doesn't question the legitimacy of his suffering, for he admitted his sins (v. 18), but he wonders why his suffering is so severe. Like the prophet Habakkuk, David wanted God to remember to be merciful (Hab. 3:2). The title "to bring to remembrance" (KJV) is found also at Psalm 70. The *New American Standard Bible* reads "for a memorial" and the *New International Version* "a petition." For God to "remember" someone means that He begins to act on their behalf and meet some need (Gen. 8:1; 19:29; 30:22; 1 Sam. 1:19). David wanted God to remember him and grant forgiveness and healing. When God's people suffer the consequences of sin and feel the chastening hand of God, they must choose one of three responses.

We Can Focus on Ourselves and Experience Sin's Painfulness (vv. 1-8)

Pain hurts, and David wasn't ashamed to write about it, using a number of vivid images to convey to the Lord and to us the severity of his suffering. Like a loving Father, the Lord first rebuked David and then chastened him, both of which are evidences of His love (Prov. 3:11-12; Heb. 12:1-11). If we don't listen to the words of His heart, we will have to feel the weight of His hand (32:4; 39:10-11). Alexander Maclaren compared "hot displeasure" to "hot bubbling lava" about to erupt. God was also shooting "arrows" at David, hurling down one affliction after another with great force (see Job 6:4; 7:20; 16:12; "mark" means "target"). He was drowning in a sea of suffering (v. 4; see 42:7; 69:2, 14; 88:16; 124:4; 130:1-2), and the whole experience became a burden too heavy for him to carry.

In great detail, David described his "loathsome disease" (v. 7, KJV). This was not one isolated sickness but a collection of physical disorders that produced "searing pain" (NIV), fever, and inflammation. He had festering wounds (v. 5) that smelled foul and looked ugly, his heart wasn't functioning properly, and his eyes were getting dim (v. 10). There was no health in his body (vv. 3, 7); one minute he was burning with fever, the next minute he was numb with cold (vv. 7-8). His body was feeble and twisted with pain, and he walked about all day like a man at a funeral (vv. 6, 8). At times, his pain was so severe, he cried out like a wild beast (v. 8). All this happened because he had been foolish and had

sinned against the Lord (v. 5; 107:17). We are free to disobey the Lord, *but we are not free to change the consequences.*

We Can Focus on Others and Experience Sin's Loneliness (vv. 9-14)

David opened the psalm with "LORD—Jehovah," and now he addressed God once more, this time as "Lord—Adonai—Master." He will use both names in verses 15 and 21-22. For a brief moment, he took his eyes off his own sufferings and looked to the Lord, knowing that God saw his heart and knew all his longings. God knows what we want, but He also knows what we need. Then why pray? Because God has commanded us to pray, and "you do not have because you do not ask" (James 4:2, NKJV). Furthermore, as we pray, God works in our hearts to give us a clearer understanding of ourselves and of His will for us. Prayer isn't a theological concept to analyze and explain; it's a privilege to cherish and a blessing to claim.

David's focus now was on the people around him, and he felt abandoned and lonely. The people who should have encouraged and comforted him—his loved ones and friends—kept their distance, along with his enemies, who wanted him to die. David expected his enemies to plot against him (v. 12), gloat over his fall (v. 16), hate him, slander him, and return evil for the good he did to them (vv. 19-20), but he didn't think his friends and relatives would turn against him. (See 31:11-12; 41:9; 69:8; 88:8, 18; Job 19:13-19.) "Sore" in verse 11 means "a stroke, a blow" and is sometimes translated "a plague," the word used to describe leprosy. David's family and closest friends were treating him like a leper and keeping their distance. They didn't want to be contaminated! But before we criticize them, have we been obeying Galatians 6:1-2 and 2 Corinthians 2:5-11?

As he grieved over his sins and over the unconcern of his loved ones, David realized that his enemies were plotting to get him out of the way (v. 12). They talked about his ruin and destruction, and he heard what they were saying; but he did not reply to their threats or their false accusations. He knew he had sinned, so why put up a feeble defense? But he also knew that his accusers were sinning and really had no cause for deposing him. But suppose he did win his defense and then fall again (v. 16)? His enemies would then have a stronger case against him. So, the wisest course was to remain silent. That being the case, he kept quiet and turned the matter over to the Lord. He followed the instructions he had given in Psalm 37.

We Can Focus on the Lord and Experience Sin's Forgiveness (vv. 15-22)

For the third time, David addressed the Lord, but this time he got down to business and dealt with his sins. He hoped in (waited for) the Lord, knowing that God would hear his prayers. He wasn't praying only for his own deliverance just so he could be comfortable; he wanted God to work so the enemy couldn't use him as an excuse for sinning (vv. 16, 19-20; 25:2; 35:19). When they slandered David's name, they also slandered the Lord (see 2 Sam. 12:14), and David wanted to honor the Lord. He felt like he was about to die (v. 17), and he confessed his sins to the Lord in true repentance and faith.

What did David mean when he described his enemies as "lively" (v. 19)? He was contrasting his own condition with their condition: he was weak, they were strong; he was about to die, they were very much alive; he was sick, they were "vigorous" (NASB, NIV). Confident that the Lord

had forgiven him, he closed his prayer with three requests. *Be with me* (v. 21) is answered by Deuteronomy 4:31 and 31:6, 8, and Hebrews 13:5. *Be near me* (v. 21) finds its answer in 16:8, 34:18 and James 4:8. *Be for me and help me* (v. 22) leads us to 28:7, Isaiah 41:10 and Romans 8:33-39. These three requests cover just about everything!

Psalm 39

Both 38 and 39 record David attempting to remain silent in a time of trial, lest he say something that would offend believers or give ammunition to unbelievers (38:13-14; 39:1-3, 9; see 73:15). (For other parallels, see 38:15-16/39:7-8; 38:1-3, 11/39:10-11.) In this psalm, David doesn't seem to be gravely ill, but he has been visited by some "stroke" from the Lord because of his sins (vv. 9-11). Also, the old problem of the prosperity of the wicked is in the picture (v. 1). It appears that the wicked ("the foolish" v. 8) were blaspheming God and maligning David in his affliction, and the king was greatly concerned lest he bring reproach on the name of the Lord. There is a dirge-like quality to the psalm, and we marvel that David gave the hymn to the chief musician to use in public worship. Jeduthun was one of three musicians David put in charge of the worship at the sanctuary; the others were Heman and Asaph (see 1 Chron. 16:37-43; 2 Chron. 5:12; 35:15). Jeduthun is mentioned in the titles to Psalms 62 and 77. Recorded in this psalm are four progressive stages in David's overcoming his difficult experience.

He Was Silent—A Burning Heart (vv. 1-3)

Seeing the prosperity of the wicked and hearing their blasphemous words so angered David that he wanted to retaliate and say something to defend God, but he deemed it best to keep quiet. But this restraint only made his heart burn with intense pain (see 32:3 and Jer. 20:9) until finally he had to speak out. The two Emmaeus disciples had "burning hearts" because of the way the Lord had expounded the Word to them, and Ezekiel had anguish in his spirit because of the difficult calling God had given him. David didn't even say good things; he just kept quiet as long as he could. There is "a time to keep silence, and a time to speak" (Eccl. 3:7), and wise is the person who knows the difference. David didn't argue with God (v. 9) or with those who reproached him, but he did pray to the Lord.

He Was Despondent—A Burdened Heart (vv. 4-6)

When we find ourselves burying our true feelings and creating physical and emotional pain for ourselves, then it's time to talk to the Lord and seek His help. David knew that life was short and that the days would pass swiftly; he also knew that he was frail and that one day would die. He began to measure his days (90:12; 119:84) and saw that they were but a handbreadth (four fingers) and his age nothing in God's sight. (See 90:1-11.) "Verily, every man at his best state [in his vigor] is altogether vanity" (v. 5) sounds like a statement from Ecclesiastes by David's son Solomon, and he repeated the thought in verse 11. The Hebrew word translated "vanity" means "a breath, emptiness" (see 62:9; 144:4; Job 14:2; Eccl. 6:12). One of my Hebrew professors described "vanity" as "what's left after you break a soap bubble." In verse 6, he compared life to an "empty show," with shadow people bustling about, trying to get rich. Busy for what? Wealthy for what? Years later,

Solomon raised the same questions (Eccl. 2:18-19), and Jesus emphasized the same truth in Luke 12:16-21. If you measure the length of life, you may become despondent, but if you look around you and measure the depth of life, you are appalled. Life is swift, life is short, and for most people, life is futile. In modern vocabulary, people are living for the image and not the reality.

He Was Confident—A Believing Heart (v. 7)

This is the central verse in the psalm and the turning point in David's experience. "If life is short and goes past so swiftly," asks David, "what am I waiting for? If the world is nothing but a shadow image, let me give myself to the Lord, who is the foundation of all that is real and lasting." Today we would say, "The reality is of Christ" (Col. 2:17, NIV). The main concern is not *how long we live* but *how* we live. Life is measured, not by how rich we are in material wealth, but whether we have values that last. Are we living with eternity's values in view? "He who does the will of God abides forever" (1 John 2:17, NKJV). In turning by faith to the Lord, David moved from hopelessness to hope and from paralysis to action. The next verses describe what he did to bring about change.

He Was Repentant—A Broken Heart (vv. 8-13)

We begin with David the sinner and listen to his prayer for forgiveness (vv. 8-9). Like every truly convicted sinner, his mouth had been stopped (Rom. 3:19), and he admitted his guilt before God (see 1 Sam. 3:18; Lam. 1:21). We don't know the particular sins that had brought this stroke from the Lord, and we don't have to know. We do know that God listens to the cry of the brokenhearted (51:17) and forgives when we confess (1 John 1:9). David was especially concerned that he not give occasion to "the foolish" to ridicule his faith (14:1; 69:7; 74:22; 79:4).

Next, David the sufferer pleaded with God to remove the stroke and heal his body (vv. 10-11; see 32:4; 38:2). He used three images to get his point across: a plague or sickness, draining away his life; the blow of God's hand, like a loving parent disciplining a child; the rebuke of His Word, that cut deeply into David's heart. C. S. Lewis was correct when he wrote in *The Problem of Pain,* "God whispers to us in our pleasures, speaks in our conscience, but shouts in our pains: it is His megaphone to arouse a deaf world."[22] The human body ages, decays, and dies; and the material wealth we gather gradually loses its value, like a moth silently destroying a garment. Jim Elliot's oft-quoted statement certainly applies here: "He is no fool who gives what he cannot keep to gain that which he cannot lose."[23] Vanity of vanity, all is vanity—unless we put our faith and hope in God.

Finally, David the sojourner prays for God's direction as he makes his pilgrim way through life with its joys and sorrows. The world is a "vain show" (v. 6)—John Bunyan called it "Vanity Fair"—and God's people are aliens and strangers here (119:19; Gen. 23:4; Lev. 25:23; 1 Chron. 29:15; Heb. 11:13; 1 Peter 1:1; 2:11). We are not strangers to God, for He knows us and we know Him, but we are strangers with God as His welcomed guests (90:1; 23:6). He hears our prayers and cries, and He sees our tears. "In the world you will have tribulation," Jesus told His disciples, "but be of good cheer, I have overcome the world" (John 16:33, NKJV). His closing prayer was that God would turn away His frowning face and

give him strength to return to life with its duties and burdens, and then one day enable him to pass into eternity. The phrase "no more" doesn't suggest annihilation or the absence of an afterlife, but that David would "no more" be on his earthly pilgrimage. "I will dwell in the house of the Lord forever" (23:6).

Psalm 40

Hebrews 10:5-9 quotes 40:6-8 and applies the passage to Christ, which makes this a Messianic psalm. Some see the birth of Christ in verse 7, His sinless life in verse 8, and His sacrificial death in verse 6. However, it was first of all a psalm about David and his needs and how the Lord met them, but the historical setting is obscure. David may have written it during his difficult exile years or perhaps during the early years of his reign. It's unusual for a psalm to have a prayer for mercy following praise and dedication. However, if verses 1-5 picture his deliverance during the dangerous exile years, and verses 6-10 describe his dedication as the new king, then verses 11-17 could be a record of his prayer for personal forgiveness (v. 12; see 38:3-5 and 39:8-9) and victory over his enemies following his coronation. It does seem that verse 16 is a royal prayer for God's blessing on the nation. You find verses 13-17 repeated in modified form in Psalm 70. From whatever experiences led to the writing of this psalm, David learned some valuable lessons and gave us three important instructions to follow in the difficult times of life.

Praise God for All He Has Done (vv. 1-5)

No matter what our trouble or trial, it's always good to look back and recall the goodness of the Lord. David remembered how long he had waited before the Lord delivered him from his enemies and from Saul, but the day came when God inclined His ear (31:3), heard his cries, and lifted him up from the pit. If David learned anything from his exile years, it was that ultimate success depends on faith in the Lord and patience during His providential working (5:3; 33:20; 37:34; 38:15; Heb. 6:12). We are not to take the description of the pit literally (slime, mud, mire), but figuratively, as a picture of those difficult years David endured. "The pit" is also a term for sheol, the realm of the dead, and David's life was certainly in danger. A quaint country preacher used verses 2-3 for a sermon text, and his "points" were: God brought him up, God stood him up, and God tuned him up! David had a new beginning with a new song of praise in his mouth (18:49; 22:22; 33:3). God helped David because he trusted the Lord, did not show respect to the arrogant who opposed God, and remained true to the God of Israel. "Lies" in verse 4 refers to idols. Unlike David, King Saul was a proud man who trusted in himself and made himself more important than God. In looking back on those years as an exile and a hunted man, David saw the greatness of God's works (wonders) and the wisdom of His plans (v. 5). This is his version of Romans 8:28.

Give God All That He Asks (vv. 6-10)
David has moved from the pit to the rock, and now he goes to the sanctuary of God. After all God had done for David, how could the king express to the Lord his appreciation for His mercies? He could bring sacrifices to the altar, but that wasn't God's first desire. This doesn't mean that such sacrifices were wrong, or that God didn't want His people to offer

them, but that God wanted their hearts first of all. Throughout the Old Testament, the Lord made it clear that He could not accept sacrifices unless the worshiper showed sincere devotion, dedication, and obedience. No doubt David heard how Saul learned that important lesson—too late (1 Sam. 15:22). (See 50:8-15; 51:16-17; Prov. 21:3; Isa. 1:11-17; Jer. 7:22-23; Hos. 6:6; Mic. 6:6-8; Mark 12:32-33.)

In verse 6, *sacrifice* means any animal whose blood was offered at the altar, followed by a communal meal. *Offering* refers to the meal offering that could accompany the sacrifices, and the *burnt offering* symbolized total dedication to the Lord. The *sin offering* was given to cover specific offenses and bring reconciliation between the offender and God. All of these were fulfilled in Jesus Christ whose sacrifice on the cross satisfied the justice of God once and for all, for time and eternity (Lev. 1-7; Heb. 10:1-17). The "open ears" refer to his readiness to hear and obey God's will (1 Sam. 9:15; 20:2; Isa. 48:8; 50:4-5; Matt. 3:9, 43; Acts 7:51, 57). This is not a reference to the servant in Exodus 21:1-6. The passage is paraphrased in Hebrews 10:5-10 as "a body you have prepared for me," i.e., the body in which Messiah served the Father here on earth. An open ear means a yielded will and a surrendered body. When the heart delights in God's law, the will has no problem obeying (119:11; Deut. 6:6; 11:18; Prov. 3:3, 7:3; Jer. 31:33). "Lo, I come" means "Here I am, ready to obey" (see 1 Sam. 3:4, 6, 8; Isa. 6:8). The scroll may be a reference to Deuteronomy 17:14-20, and see 2 Kings 11:12 and 22:13. The Old Testament predicts the coming of the Messiah (Luke 24:27).

David was enthusiastic about telling others what the Lord had done for him, and he is a good example for us to follow (22:25; 26:12; 35:18; 111:1; 149:1). Among the worshipers at the sanctuary, the king gave glory to the Lord. This reminds us of our Lord's resurrection praises (22:31; Heb. 2:12).

Trust God for All That Remains (vv. 11-17)

When the worship service was ended and David had returned to his royal duties, he discovered that there were new battles to fight and fresh problems to solve, so he turned again to the Lord for help. Worship is not an escape from life but the opportunity to honor God and be equipped to face life and live for His glory. David had his own personal problems to deal with (vv. 11-13), for he had a sensitive conscience and knew that he was a sinful man. He also had enemies who wanted to dethrone him (vv. 14-15) and so he prayed for victory. (See 25:4, 21-27.) Most of all, David wanted the Lord to be magnified and His people to be blessed as they served Him (vv. 16-17). David couldn't see what lay ahead (v. 12; 31:9; 38:10), but God knew the future and had everything under control. As he often did (7:1, 5; 22:19; 38:22; 71:12), David prayed for speedy deliverance. "I am—You are" (v. 17) says it all. The great I AM is adequate for every need.

Psalm 41

Sickness (vv. 8,10) and sin (v. 4) again unite to put David into distress and danger as his enemies plot against him and wait for him to die. These factors seem to place this psalm in the time of Absalom's rebellion. David's illness prevented him from leading the nation as he wanted to (2 Sam 15:1-6), and Absalom took advantage of this to promote himself as king. If the "dear friend" of verse 9 is David's counselor Ahithophel, then the matter of the historical setting is settled (2 Sam. 16:15ff). Jesus quoted verse 9 in the upper room when referring to Judas (John 13:38), so the psalm has Messianic overtones. When we find ourselves in difficulty, we may use this psalm to take an inventory of our spiritual condition by asking and answering four questions.

Integrity: How Do We Treat Others (vv. 1-4)?

Before we can claim God's promises, we must examine our own hearts to see if we have sincerely met the conditions the Lord had laid down. David no doubt based his prayer on the stipulations given in the covenant (Lev. 26:1-13; Deut. 7:13-16; 28:1-14). He knew that he had no right to claim mercy from the Lord if he himself had not shown mercy to others. But David had fully obeyed the Lord's rules and had shown mercy to King Saul, to Saul's grandson Mephibosheth, and to the needy in the land. (See Matt. 5:7 and Luke 6:37-38.) "Poor" refers to the helpless, the miserable people whose lot was difficult and who depended on the help of others. To "consider" these pitiable people meant being attentive to their needs and assisting them. It also meant not judging and blaming them, as Job's friends blamed him and the disciples blamed the blind man (John 9:1-4). We have every reason to believe that David sought to care for the poor and needy in his kingdom and therefore was praying with integrity. In verse 1, he referred to himself in the third person, a true mark of his humility before the Lord.

He listed in verses 2-3 the blessings God would send because he confessed his sins and asked God to be merciful to him (v. 4). God would protect him from his enemies and prolong his life in the land. That in itself would bear witness to his enemies that David was a man favored by God. God would also heal him of his sickness and raise him up from the sickbed. "Make all his bed" (v. 3, KJV) simply means "heal him and raise him up." This would be the gracious and merciful act of the Lord, undeserved by David but lovingly granted by Jehovah. "If I regard wickedness in my heart, the Lord will not hear" (66:18, NASB), so it's important that we confess our sins to the Lord. If we haven't been merciful to others, how can our heart be right to ask Him for mercy?

Treachery: How Do Others Treat Us (vv. 5-9)?

It wasn't enough that David was sick in bed, but he also had to deal with treachery among his own family and friends, including men like Ahithophel, his official counselor, who sided with Absalom. Ahithophel was Bathsheba's grandfather (2 Sam. 11:3 and 23:34) and hated David for what he did to her and to her husband Uriah. These false friends visited the king and lied to him ("We hope you'll get well soon"), but they really wanted David to die and even plotted against him. But if Absalom became king, that would be the end of the Davidic dynasty, for Absalom had no son (2 Sam. 18:18). God promised David that his descendants would sit on the throne of Israel forever (2 Sam. 7:11-16), a promise ultimately fulfilled in Jesus Christ (Luke 1:31-33). David was gifted at reading people (2 Sam. 14:17-20) and knew the truth.

Jesus used verse 9 when referring to the traitor Judas (John 13:18-19; and see 55:12-14; 69:25; 109:8; Matt. 26:63; Mark 14:18; Luke 22:21; Acts 1:16-20). Note that our Lord didn't quote the phrase "whom I trusted" from verse 9, for He knew that Judas had no saving faith (John 6:70-71). This psalm opens with a statement about

the poor, and Judas tried to identify himself with the poor (John 12:4-6; 13:26-30). David's enemies wanted the king's name to perish, but it was Judas who destroyed a good name—"Judah," which means "praise." We call our sons David but we would never call a son Judas. (See 2 Sam. 16:15-17:23 for Ahithophel's part in the rebellion.) The phrase "lifted up his heel" pictures a deceptive and underhanded attack, but see Joshua 10:4 and Romans 16:20.

Mercy: How Does God Treat Us (vv. 10-12)?

God in His mercy doesn't give us what we do deserve, and God in His grace gives us what we don't deserve, and He does this because of Jesus Christ His Son who died for us on the cross. David prayed for mercy, because he knew he had sinned (v. 4). He also affirmed his integrity (v. 12), for he had walked before the Lord in humility and submission (7:8; 18:19-25; 25:21; 78:72). When confronted with his sins, he confessed them and sought the face of the Lord (2 Sam. 12:13ff). David wanted mercy for himself but not for his enemies, except for his son Absalom (2 Sam. 18:5). Why? Because his enemies (especially Absalom) had committed treason against the Lord's chosen and anointed king. This was not a personal vendetta on David's part, but a concern for the future of the nation of Israel and the dynasty of David. As ruler of the land, David wielded the sword of justice (Rom. 13:1-4), and nations today punish treason with death.

More than anything else, David wanted to please God (v. 11; 18:19; 22:8; 35:27; 2 Sam. 15:26). He had confidence that the Lord would heal him, restore him to the throne, and deal with those who opposed him. Even more, he was certain that one day he would be in the presence of the Lord and serve in His holy courts in heaven forever (v. 12; 16:11; 17:15; 21:6; 101:7; 2 Sam. 7:16).

Glory: How Do We Treat God (v. 13)?

This verse was probably added later by an editor to mark the end of book one of the Psalms. Each of the first four books ends with a similar doxology (72:18-20; 89:52; 106:48), and Book Five ends with a praise psalm (150). But the verse reminds us that the main thing in our lives must be the eternal praise and glory of the Lord. "Hallowed be thy name" is the first request in the Disciple's Prayer (Matt. 6:9), and it governs all the other requests. God answers prayer, not to make His people more comfortable, but to bring glory to His name. The Lord still had more work for David to do, particularly the preparation for the building of the temple, and His glory would one day move into that holy sanctuary (1 Kings 8:1-11).

Can we honestly say "Amen and amen!" to the prayer in verse 13?

BOOK II

Psalms 42 and 43

The repeated refrain (42:5, 11; 43:5) and the general theme of these two psalms would indicate that the two psalms were no doubt originally one, but nobody seems to know why they were separated. Korah was a grandson of Kohath and was killed for rebelling against the Lord (Num. 16). However, his sons escaped judgment (Num. 16:11) and became worship leaders in the sanctuary (1 Chron. 9:19ff; 26:1-19). They are also named in the titles to 44-49, 84 and 87-88, and see the introduction to Psalm 39. Some associate these psalms with Absalom's rebellion, but the geography in verse 6 seems to put the stetting too far north for that, since David camped over the Jordan at Mahanaim. The author was evidently a Levite exiled among Gentiles (43:1) who oppressed him and questioned his faith (42:3, 10; 43:2). He was a worship leader who had led groups of pilgrims to Jerusalem for the assigned festivals (84:7; Ex. 23:14-17; 34:18-26; Deut. 16:1-17). It was time for such a journey but he wasn't able to go, and this grieved his heart because he felt that the Lord had forgotten him (42:9; 43:2). In the psalm, he uses *El* or *Elohim* twenty times and *Jehovah* only once (42:8). The psalms are intensely personal, containing over fifty personal pronouns; and the writer fluctuated between faith and despair as he wrestled with the Lord. He questions the Lord eleven times as he wonders why God doesn't do something for him. We see him passing through three stages before he comes to victory and peace.

Longing for God (42:1-5)

During a drought, the writer saw a female deer (hind) panting and struggling to reach water to quench her thirst (Joel 1:20), and this reminded him that he thirsted for the Lord and wanted to go on pilgrimage to Jerusalem. The living God was the God of his life (v. 8; see 84:2), and he could not live without Him. Note that the essentials for physical life are mentioned here: air (panting), water (v. 2), and food (v. 3), but without worship (v. 4), life to him was meaningless. Hunger and thirst are familiar images of the quest for fellowship with God and the satisfaction it brings (36:8-9; 63:1; Matt. 5:6; John 4:10-14; 7:37-39; Rev. 21:6; 22:17). Day and night (vv. 3, 8) he felt the pain caused by separation from God's sanctuary and by the constant ridicule of the people around him. He "fed" on his grief (not a wise thing to do) as his tears became his bread. His weeping was as regular as his eating had been.

"Where is your God?" (vv. 3, 10) was a standard question the Gentile idolaters asked the Jews (79:10; 115:2; Joel 2:17; Mic. 7:10; see Matt. 27:43). However, the question indicates that the writer must have been a devout believer who wasn't ashamed of his faith; otherwise, his tormentors wouldn't have questioned him. He remembered better days when he used to lead processions of pilgrims to Jerusalem to celebrate the feasts. Memory can be either a blessed medicine for the troubled heart or it can open new wounds and keep the pain fresh. The writer poured out his soul in prayer (v. 4; 62:8; 104 title), pleading for the Lord to set him free and take him back to Jerusalem. But then he confronted himself (v. 5) and admonished himself not to be downcast but to hope in the Lord and wait on Him. The repetition of this admonition (v. 11; 43:5) suggests that the writer was having his "ups and downs" as he struggled with his circumstances and himself. He would find his consolation and peace only in the Lord, and not in nature (vv. 1, 6-7), memories (v. 4), or nursing grief (v. 3). His hopes had been shattered, his prayers were unanswered, his enemies were vocal, and his feelings were more than he could handle, *but God was still on the throne.* God's presence was with him and he would yet have the joy of worshiping God in Jerusalem. That was God's promise in His covenant (Deut. 30).

Remembering God (42:6-11)

The emotional and spiritual landscape changes from drought to a storm, with the writer feeling like he was drowning in sorrow and pain (vv. 6-7). The Jordan River has its source in the Hermon range, and the rains and melting snow would turn the rivulets into cascades of water and dangerous cataracts, a picture of intense suffering (69:1-2; 88:7; Jonah 2:4). "Mizar" means "littleness," and certainly the writer felt very small in the midst of that storm. But he made a wise decision when he decided to remember God and not "the good old days" (v. 6). The cascades, cataracts, and waves were *His* and the psalmist had nothing to fear. This reminds us of the night Jesus walked on the water and frightened His disciples, yet He was in full command of the situation (Matt. 14:22-33). God was in command (v. 8; see 33:9; 44:4; 71:3; 91:11), a new day would dawn, and the situation would look different. Like David's storm experience recorded in Psalm 29, see God on His throne and anticipate the glory and peace after the storm. Believers today remember that the waves of God's wrath went over Jesus on the cross when He experienced His Calvary "baptism" (Matt. 20:22; Luke 12:50). Meanwhile, God can give us "songs in the night" as we wait for the dawning of a new day (77:4-6; Job 35:10; Matt. 26:30; Acts 16:25).

In verse 8, the writer used *Jehovah* instead of *Elohim,* and this was a turning point in his difficult experience. Jehovah is the God of the covenant, the faithful God who cares for His people. He is the God who showers His people with lovingkindness, gives them promises they can claim when they pray, and hears them when they praise and worship. The writer didn't have to go to Jerusalem to worship; he could worship God right where he was! The hand of God was with him in the daytime and the song of the Lord in the long hours of the night. Everything might be changing, but the Lord was still his Rock—stable, strong, and unchanging. (See 18:2, 31, 46; Ex. 33:22; Deut. 32:4; 1 Sam. 2:2.)

Trusting God (43:1-5)

The landscape changes a third time as the dawn announces the morning and reminds the psalmist of God's light and truth (v. 3). The Lord had led Israel from Egypt to the Promised Land by a pillar of cloud by day and a pillar of fire by night, and so His light and truth (faithfulness) would bring him back to Jerusalem. The innocent exile would be vindicated before his accusers and be rescued from an ungodly nation. His strength was in the Lord alone, the Rock of his salvation (42:9), and soon his despair would be replaced by joy. As they trust in the Lord, God's people must remember that His goodness and mercy follow them (23:6), and His light and truth lead them (43:3; see 27:1; 26:3; 30:9; 40:10). God's "holy hill" is Mt. Zion, where God's sanctuary was located, the dwelling place of God.

But the writer wasn't exulting simply in freedom from his enemies and a return to his native home, but in the privilege of visiting God's altar, offering his sacrifices, and praising the Lord. He has made great progress since he watched the hind seeking for water. The "living God" (42:2) became "the God of my life" (42:8), and now He is "God my exceeding joy ... God, my God (43:8, NASB). His focus is no longer on himself, his disappointments, or his circumstances, but on the Lord his God, and that makes all the difference. The refrain in 43:5 must not be read with the same dejected voice as 42:5 and 11, for faith in Jehovah has changed everything. The *New American Standard Bible* and the *New King James Version* translate verse 5, "Hope in God, for I shall yet praise Him, the help of my countenance, and my

God." The word "help" can be translated "health." When by faith we see the face of God smiling upon us (Num. 6:22-27), our own countenance brightens up and becomes spiritually healthy. We know God is for us, that God will set us free and guide us to His holy city, where we shall worship Him and sing His praises. "Weeping may endure for a night, but joy comes in the morning" (30:5, NKJV).

Psalm 44

The Jewish people sang praises to God after their great victories (Ex. 15; Judg, 5), but this psalm was sung after a humiliating defeat (vv. 9-14, 22). The parallels between Psalms 44 and 60 suggest that Edom and the Arameans were the enemies involved (44:3/60:5; 44:5/60:12; 44:9, 23/60:1, 10). (See 2 Sam. 8 and 10; 1 Chron. 18.) Although Israel finally won great victories over their enemies, there must have been some defeats along the way that greatly disturbed the people. After all, Jehovah was their King (v. 4) and had enabled Israel to conquer the land; so why would He desert His people as they sought to protect their inheritance? Perhaps this psalm was used at a national "day of prayer" with a worship leader speaking the "I/my" verses and the people the "we/our" verses. The four stanzas that make up this psalm reveal four different attitudes on the part of the people.

Boasting in God: "You Have Helped Us" (vv. 1-8)

Reviewing Israel's history since the exodus from Egypt, the writer glorified God for all He did to defeat the Canaanite nations and enable Israel to claim their inheritance (v. 8). The Jewish parents were faithful to obey God and tell their children and grandchildren what the Lord had done (see 78:3; Ex. 12:26-27; 13:8, 14; Deut. 6:1ff; 32:7; Josh. 4:6, 21). God had rooted out the godless nations, planted Israel in the land, and enabled the nation to take root and grow (80:8-11; Ex. 15:17; Isa. 5). All of this was done, not because Israel deserved it, but because of God's love and grace (Deut. 4:34-37; 7:7-9, 19; 8:17; 9:4-6; 26:8-9). God's power gave the victory and His countenance smiled upon His people (4:6; 31:16; 80:3, 7, 19). The psalmist affirmed that Jehovah was still their King (v. 4; 10:16; 29:10; 47:6; 74:12) and could easily command (decree) victories for His people. The nation wanted no glory for itself; they wanted the Lord to receive all the glory.

Forsaken by God: "You Are Not Helping Us" (vv. 9-16)

But the people were perplexed. If God gave them the land in His grace, and enabled them to defeat their enemies, why was He now forsaking them and allowing the idolatrous nations to win the victories? For many years, the Lord had been the "invisible warrior" who went before the Jewish armies and led them to victory (Josh. 5:13-15; 6:6; Num. 10:35; 2 Sam. 11:11), but now He seemed to have forsaken His people and abandoned His covenant. Israel was God's precious flock (74:1; 77:20; 80:1; 100:3; Num. 27:17; Ezek. 34), but He was permitting them to be slaughtered by the enemy and treated as worthless (Judg. 2:14; 3:8; 4:2, 9). Those prisoners of war that weren't slain were sold as slaves and scattered among the neighboring pagan nations. These nations rejoiced that Israel had been humiliated by defeat, and they taunted and ridiculed the Jews. It was a dark day for the people of God, and they could not understand what the Lord was accomplishing. (See 42:10; 74:10, 18, 22; 79:4, 12.) Dishonor and disgrace brought the people to the place of submission and intercession.

Faithful to God: "You Should Help Us" (vv. 17-22)

Whenever there was trouble in Israel, the first explanation was usually, "Somebody has sinned." Certainly this was true when Israel was defeated at Ai (Josh. 7), when there was a three-year famine in David's time (2 Sam. 21), and when David numbered the people (2 Sam. 24). But as far as the psalmist knew, there was no sin to be confessed because the people were faithful to the Lord. God could search their minds and hearts and not find any breach of the covenant. They were faithful to God, they had not turned to the idols for help, and now they were giving their lives to protect the land that He had so graciously given them.

Paul quoted verse 11 in Romans 8:36 as part of his magnificent argument that nothing could separate God's people from His love, *not even defeat after a record of victories!* The principle is the same for both God's old covenant people and His new covenant people: those who give their lives in His cause are conquerors, not victims, and God can be glorified even in seeming defeat. When the five young men gave their lives in Ecuador to help reach the Auca Indians, many people asked, "Why this waste?" But what looked like terrible defeat turned out to be glorious victory as many young people around the world felt the call of God and surrendered to serve Him. Israel's defeat didn't mean that God loved them less; it meant that He was permitting this to happen so that He could carry out a purpose known only to Him. Like the martyrdom of Stephen (Acts 6:9-8:3), Israel's defeat gave their enemies further opportunity to come to know the Lord. Saul of Tarsus was greatly moved by Stephen's death (Acts 22:17-21), and this undoubtedly helped to prepare him for his meeting with Christ on the Damascus Road. No matter how their lives may end, God's servants never die like beasts, for "Precious in the sight of the Lord is the death of His saints" (116:15, NKJV).

Trusting in God: "You Will Help Us" (vv. 23-26)

In verse 23, the writer used the name "Adonai" (Lord) when speaking to God. This is the name that declares that He is Owner and Master of all, including the nations of the world. It is sometimes translated "Sovereign LORD" (Adonai Jehovah; 2 Sam. 7:18-20, NIV). He is "Lord [Adonai] of all the earth" (97:5), and the earth should tremble "at the presence of the Lord [Adonai]" (114:7). The psalmist came to the place where he knew he could trust God to handle the defeats of life and ultimately turn them into victories. Yes, it seemed like God was asleep, and the nation had to awaken Him (7:6; 78:65), but "He who keeps Israel shall neither slumber nor sleep" (121:4, NKJV). The people of Israel had come to the place that Job reached when he said, "Though he slay me, yet will I trust him" (Job 13:15).

We can't always explain the so-called "tragedies" of life, especially those that happen to God's people, but Romans 8:28 is still in the Bible. The prophet Isaiah gives us wise counsel in 50:10—"Who is among you that fears the Lord and obeys the voice of His servant, that walks in darkness and has no light? Let him trust in the name of the Lord and rely on his God" (NASB). We may look like sheep for the slaughter, but in God's sight we are "more than conquerors through him that loved us" (Rom. 8:37).

Psalm 45

"A song of loves" identifies this as a marriage song, and "Shoshannim" (lilies) identifies the tune to which it was to be sung (see 60, 69, 80). The wedding was obviously that of a king (vv. 1, 11, 14; and note the mention of throne, scepter and majesty), and some have identified him with Solomon, who married an Egyptian princess (1 Kings 3:1; 9:24). Of all David's sons, only Solomon was anointed king (v. 7). Solomon was noted for his wealth in gold (vv. 9, 13; 1 Kings 9:28), and he had a close association with the great city of Tyre (v. 12; 1 Kings 9:10-14). But it's clear that one "greater than Solomon" (Matt. 12:42) is present in this beautiful psalm, and that one is Jesus Christ, the King of kings. If this were merely a secular love song, why would it be given to the chief musician to be used in the worship of the Lord at His sanctuary? That would be blasphemy. Solomon was not a warrior (vv. 3-5), and certainly an inspired writer would not address Solomon as "God" (v. 6). Hebrews 1:8-9 marks it as a Messianic psalm, so whatever may have been the historical use of this psalm, the ultimate message is about Jesus Christ and His bride, the church (Eph. 5:23ff; Rev. 19:6-21; 22:17). The writer presents four pictures of our Lord and in so doing also described His bride.

The Gracious Son of Man (vv. 1-2)

This is a song for the heart from the heart of an inspired and excited writer. His heart was "bubbling over" with his theme, for it is the greatest theme in the universe: the glories of the Son of God. Jesus endured the cross "for the joy that was set before him" (Heb. 12:2), which was the joy of presenting His bride to the Father in glory (Judg. 24; John 17:24). It is the work of the Holy Spirit to glorify Jesus Christ in this world (John 16:14), and He inspired this writer to do just that. The King described in this psalm is both God (v. 6) and man (v. 2), and that can only be Jesus.

The writer began with the beauty of the King (v. 2), "fairer than the children of men," literally, "beautified with beauty." King Saul was known as a handsome man (1 Sam. 9:2; 10:23) and so was David (1 Sam. 16:12), but none surpasses Jesus. When He ministered on earth, our Lord had no special physical beauty (Isa. 53:2), and when His persecutors were through with Him, He didn't even look human (Isa. 52:14). But today, Jesus Christ is the center of heaven's glory and the focus of heaven's worship (Rev. 4—5). We love Jesus even though we have never seen Him, but one day we shall behold the King in His beauty (Isa. 33:17), and we shall be like Him (1 John 3:1-3). The writer also marveled at His gracious speech, but so did the people who heard Him preach and teach on earth (Luke 4:18, 22, 32; John 7:46; see Mark 1:22; 6:2; 11:18). Visitors from distant lands came to hear Solomon's wisdom (1 Kings 4:29-34), but the Father has hidden all the treasures of divine wisdom in Jesus Christ (Col. 2:3). Solomon died, and except for what he wrote in Scripture, his wisdom died with him, but Jesus is blessed forever (v. 2), has a throne forever (v. 6), and His name will be praised forever (v. 17). In the Bible, "forever" can mean "as long as you live" (Ex. 21:6), but here it means "for eternity." He is "King forever" (29:10).

The Victorious Warrior (vv. 3-5)
We live in a day when the militant side of the Christian faith is criticized and even eliminated, an attitude that is both unbiblical and dangerous. Since Genesis 3:15, God has been at war with Satan and sin,

for the Lamb of God is also "the Lion of the tribe of Judah" (Rev. 5:5). Jesus suffered and died on the cross, not only to save sinners but also to defeat Satan (Col. 2:13-15), and one day He will return as a warrior and defeat His enemies and establish His righteous kingdom (Rev. 19:11ff). Indeed, His right hand will accomplish "awesome things." The church of Jesus Christ doesn't use human weapons to accomplish His will (John 18:10-11, 36-37) but instead uses the sword of the Spirit, the Word of God (Heb. 4:12; Eph. 6:17; see Rev. 1:16 and 19:15). Jesus is fighting on behalf of "truth and meekness and righteousness" (v. 4, NASB), and it's difficult to believe that anyone would want to oppose that kind of war. As God's people share His love, serve others, and declare the Word, they are "waging peace" and seeking to reconcile men and women with God (2 Cor. 5:14-21). The Father has promised to give His Son the nations of the earth for His inheritance (2:8-9), and He will keep that promise.

The Righteous King (vv. 6-7a)
Those who deny the deity of Christ refuse to accept the translation "Thy throne, O God," because they want to make the psalm only Jewish history and not Messianic prophecy. However, "Thy throne, O God" is the plain sense of the text and is supported by Hebrews 1:8-9 and Luke 1:30-33. "He shall reign forever and ever" (Rev. 11:15). While it is true that Scripture uses *elohim* to refer to human rulers (82:6-7; Ex. 21:6; John 10:35), that is not the meaning here. The writer clearly affirmed the eternal reign of the eternal Son of God. His reign would also be righteous and all evil would be removed. Jesus Christ is reigning now in heaven, seated at the right hand of the Father (110:1-2; Matt. 26:64; Acts 2:33, 5:31, 7:55-56; Rom.

8:34; Eph. 1:20; Col. 3:1; Heb. 1:3). He is the King-Priest "after the order of Melchizedek" (Heb. 7-9). One day, His people will reign with Him and share His glory (Rev. 5:10; 20:6).

The Glorious Bridegroom (vv. 7b-17)

These verses describe the royal wedding, beginning with *the preparation of the Bridegroom (vv. 7b-9)*. The anointing in verse 7b is not His anointing as King but as the honored guest at the wedding feast. It is the "oil of gladness" representing the eternal joy that belongs to the happy bride and Bridegroom (Isa. 61:3). The soldiers gambled for our Lord's garments when He hung on the cross (John 19:23-24), but at the wedding feast, His garments will be fragrant and glorious. To have ivory inlay on the walls of your house was the height of prosperity (Amos 3:15; 1 Kings 22:39), but the King's palace is made of ivory. As the King prepares to meet the bride, the musicians play beautiful music. In ancient times, a Jewish bridegroom went to the bride's house to claim her and then took her to his own home, and Jesus will do that when He returns to claim His church (1 Thess. 4:13-18). The "king's daughters" (v. 9) are princesses who accompany the bride; we would call them bridesmaids. In verse 14 they are called "virgin companions" (NIV), so they must not be confused with harem women, who certainly would not be in a wedding procession.

Next comes *the preparation of the bride (vv. 10-13)*. Today, the church of Jesus Christ is spotted by the world and looking old and wrinkled because of inner decay, but one day it shall be a glorious bride, spotless, blameless, and without spot or wrinkle (Eph. 5:27). Though criticized today, the church in that day will be beautiful and bring great glory to Christ (Eph. 1:6-12, 18). As the queen waits within her palace chamber (v. 13), she is dressed in the finest garments, embroidered with the finest gold (1 Kings 9:28), and she is given counsel as she enters this new relationship. She must forget the past, submit to her Husband the King, and seek only to please Him. What a word for the church in the world today—"forgetting those things which are behind" (Phil. 3:13). Our Lord loves us and sees beauty in His bride, and we must acknowledge that He is Lord and worship Him, showing respect and homage to Him (1 Peter 3:6; Gen. 18:12). It would be idolatry to worship a human king, but this is the King of Glory (24:7-10). "The daughter of Tyre" means "the people of Tyre," just as "the daughter of Zion" means "the inhabitants of Jerusalem" (Matt. 21:5; Isa. 4:4). Tyre was a powerful and wealthy city in David's day, and its king was the first foreign ruler to recognize the kingship of David (2 Sam. 5:11). There will come a time when the kings of the earth will bring their wealth and glory into the city of the great King (Rev. 21:24-26).

In the next stage of the wedding, *the bride is brought to the King (vv. 14-15)*, and her companions are with her. It is a time of beauty and joy as the wedding party enters the banquet hall in the palace and shares in the wedding feast. (See Rev. 19:1-10.) As the King and His queen leave, the writer pronounces *a benediction (vv. 16-17)*, speaking especially to the King. (The pronouns are masculine.) We may paraphrase it: "No matter how great your ancestors were, your descendants will be even greater. They will be princes in all the earth, not just government officers in the kingdom. You will reign forever and ever and your name will never be forgotten. The people will praise you forever." Words like these spoken at an ancient eastern wedding would be considered polite exaggeration, but when applied to Jesus Christ, they aren't strong enough! He is bringing many children to glory (Heb. 2:10, 13), and His family will share His glory and His reign.

Hallelujah, what a Savior!

Psalm 46

Most people recognize this psalm as the basis for Martin Luther's hymn "A Mighty Fortress Is Our God." The historical background is probably God's deliverance of Jerusalem from the Assyrians in the time of King Hezekiah (2 Kings 18-19; 2 Chron. 32; Isa. 36-37). It would be helpful for you to read these accounts before examining the psalm. King Hezekiah was a poet and may have written not only this psalm but also 47 and 48, which probably came out of the same historical context and celebrate God's victory over the enemy. The personal pronouns in 46 are plural (our, we, us), so this is a song for communal encouragement and worship. "Alamoth" means "young women" and is a musical direction we can't define. No female choir was used in the sanctuary liturgy, although 68:25 indicates that the women did participate (see Ex. 15:20-21). The emphasis in this psalm is on the presence of the Lord with His people (vv. 1, 5, 7, 11) and the difference it makes when we trust Him in the changes and difficulties of life. The psalm focuses on the Lord and what He is to His trusting people.

God Is Our Tower of Strength (vv. 1-3)
The word translated "refuge" in verse 1 means "a shelter, a rock of refuge," while the word in verses 7 and 11 means "a

stronghold, a high tower, a fortress." Both words declare that God is a dependable refuge for His people when everything around them seems to be falling apart. See 61:3; 62:7-8; 142:5. But He doesn't protect us in order to pamper us. He shelters us so He can strengthen us to go back to life with its duties and dangers (29:11; 68:35; Isa. 40:31). Both concepts are found in 71:7. In times of crisis, the Jewish leaders were too prone to turn to Egypt for help (Isa. 30:1-2) when they should have turned to the Lord and trusted Him. He is an "ever-present help," but He cannot work for us unless we trust Him (Matt. 13:58).

The word "trouble" describes people in tight places, in a corner and unable to get out; and when that occurs, the admonition is, "Don't be afraid!" When the Assyrian officials threatened Jerusalem, Isaiah told the king, "Do not be afraid because of the words that you have heard" (2 Kings 19:7, NASB). The earth may change, the mountains may be hurled violently into the sea, there may come earthquakes and tidal waves, but all things are in the control of our sovereign Lord. The "waters" in verse 3 may also symbolize the unrest of the nations, mentioned in verse 6 (Dan. 7:2-3; Luke 21:25; Rev. 13:1; 17:15). Circumstances may change, but God's covenant with His people will never change (Isa. 54:10). He is our high tower and our refuge in the uncertainties of life.

God Is Our River of Joy (vv. 4-7)
The scene shifts into the city of Jerusalem where the people are confined because of the Assyrian army camped around them. Water was a precious commodity in Palestine and especially in Jerusalem, one of the few ancient cities not built on a river. Wisely, Hezekiah had built an

underground water system that connected the Spring of Gihon in Kidron with the Pool of Siloam within the city, so water was available (2 Kings 20:20; 2 Chron. 32:30). But the psalmist knew that God was their river and provided them with the water of life (36:8; 65:9; 87:7; and see John 7:37-39). In the days of King Ahaz, Isaiah compared an Assyrian invasion to an overflowing river, but he reminded the Jews that their God was like a quiet river (Shiloah) and would bring them peace (Isa. 8:1-10). God's people have always depended on the hidden spiritual resources that come from God alone. Whenever Israel turned to a pagan nation for help, they ended up in worse trouble.

Jerusalem was indeed the holy city, set apart by God, and His sanctuary was there, but these things were no guarantee of victory (Jer. 7:1-8). The king and the people needed to turn to the Lord in confession and faith, and He would hear and save them, and this is what they did. God did help Jerusalem when the morning dawned (v. 5 "right early," KJV), for the angel of the Lord killed 185,000 Assyrian soldiers and sent Sennacherib home (Isa. 37:36).

Indeed, Jehovah is God Most High! (v. 4). All He had to do was speak the word (v. 6), and the enemy was defeated. He is the "Lord of Hosts—the Lord of the armies of heaven and earth." This name for God is found first in Scripture when Hannah asked God to give her a son (1 Sam. 1:11). The Commander of the armies of the Lord is always with us (Josh. 5:13-15), for He is "Immanuel, God with us" (Matt. 1:23; Isa. 7:14; 8:8). No matter what the circumstances, we may drink at the river of His joy and blessing and find the peace and strength we need.

God Is Our God! He Will Be Glorified! (vv. 8-11)

The third scene is on the fields surrounding Jerusalem where the Assyrian soldiers lay dead, their weapons and equipment scattered and broken. There had been no battle, but the angel of the Lord left this evidence behind to encourage the faith of the people. "Come and see the amazing things (desolations) the Lord has made!" The Lord defeated and disarmed His enemies and destroyed their weapons, and they could attack no more.

"Be still" literally means "Take your hands off! Relax!" We like to be "hands-on" people and manage our own lives, but God is God, and we are but His servants. *Because Hezekiah and his leaders allowed God to be God, He delivered them from their enemies.* That was the way King Hezekiah had prayed: "Now therefore, O Lord our God, I pray, save us from his hand, that all the kingdoms of the earth may know You are the Lord God, You alone" (2 Kings 19:19, NKJV). The Lord calls Himself "the God of Jacob," and we remember how often Jacob got into trouble because he got his hands on circumstances and tried to play God. There is a time to obey God and act, but until then, we had better take our hands off and allow Him to work in His own time and His own way. If we seize His promises by faith with both hands, we won't be able to meddle!

God allows us to get into "tight places" so our faith will grow and He will be exalted. (See 22:27; 64:9; 86:9; 102:15.) The theme of the next psalm is the exaltation of God in all the earth (47:9), and it's likely Hezekiah wrote it. People boast of the great things they have done and never give God credit for anything, not even the strength and breath He gives them freely. But that will change. "The lofty looks of man shall be humbled, the haughtiness of men shall be bowed down, and the Lord alone shall be exalted in that day" (Isa. 2:11, NKJV).

Psalm 47

The promise of 46:10 is fulfilled in 47, "I will be exalted among the nations, I will be exalted in the earth" (NASB). Five times the people are commanded to "sing praises" to the Lord who "reigns over the nations" (v. 8, NASB). If this psalm was written to celebrate the defeat of Sennacherib (see 46), then it describes the people of Israel proclaiming to the surrounding Gentile nations the glorious victory of their God, a victory won without their having to fight a battle! The psalm is used in the synagogues on Rosh Hashana, the Jewish New Year's Day, and in the church, it is used on Ascension Day (see v. 5, 68:18 and Eph. 4:8-10). This also makes it a Messianic psalm, with an emphasis on the coming kingdom. As the people of Israel praise their God to the Gentiles around them, they make three affirmations about Him.

Our God Is an Awesome King (vv. 1-4)
We have moved from "Be still" (46:10) to shouting, clapping, and the blowing of trumpets. Jewish worship was enthusiastic, but they also knew how to be quiet before the Lord and wait upon Him (Lam. 2:10; Hab. 2:4; Zeph. 1:7; Zech. 2:13). Since the theme of the psalm is the kingship of the Lord, they worshiped Him the way they welcomed a new king (1 Sam. 10:24; 2 Kings 11:12-13, 20). "The shout of a king is among them" (Num. 23:21). The early church patterned its worship after the synagogue and emphasized prayer, the reading and expounding of Scripture, and the singing of psalms, hymns, and spiritual songs. When the Jewish people clapped their hands and shouted, it was

to the Lord in response to His marvelous works. They did not do it to praise the people who participated in the worship service.

To know God is to know One who is awesome in all that He is, says, and does (65:8; 76:7, 12). Jerusalem's deliverance from Sennacherib proved once more that the God of Israel was greater than all gods and deserved all the praise His people could bring to Him. He gave them victory over the nations in Canaan and gave them the land for their inheritance (135:4; Ex. 15:17; 19:5; Deut. 4:21, 37-38; 32:8). Since God chose the Jews in His love and gave them their land in His grace, what right did the Assyrians have to try to take it from them? (See 2 Chron. 20:10-12.) The land of Israel is very special to the Lord and He watches over it (Deut. 8:7-20; 11:10-12).

Our God Is a Triumphant King (v. 5)
God fills heaven and earth, but when He acts on earth on behalf of His people, the Scriptures sometimes describe Him as "coming down." He came down to visit the tower of Babel and judged the people building it (Gen. 11:5), and He also came down to investigate the wicked city of Sodom and destroyed it (Gen. 18:21). The night 185,000 Assyrian soldiers were slain by the angel, God came down and brought judgment (Isa. 37:28-29, 36) and then "went up" in great glory to His holy throne (v. 8). David gave a similar description of victory in 68:18, a verse Paul quoted in Ephesians 4:8-10, applying it to the ascension of Jesus Christ. From the human viewpoint, the crucifixion of Jesus Christ was a great defeat and tragedy, but not from God's viewpoint. In His sacrifice on the cross, Jesus won the victory over the world and the devil (John 12:31-32; Col. 2:15) and satisfied the claims of God's holy law so that sinners

could believe and be saved. What a victory! He then ascended to heaven, far above every enemy (Eph. 1:19-22), where He sits at the right hand of the Majesty on high (Heb. 1:3).

Our God Is King of Kings (vv. 6-9)

A remarkable thing occurs: the rulers and peoples of the Gentile nations join Israel in praising the Lord Jehovah! He is not simply the God and King of Israel, but He is the "king of all the earth." It was God's plan when He called Abraham that Israel would be a blessing to all the earth (Gen. 12:1-3; John 12:32; Gal. 3:7-9), for "salvation is of the Jews" (John 4:22). Throughout their history, Israel has been persecuted by many nations of the world, yet it is Israel that has blessed the world. Israel brought us the knowledge of the one true and living God, they gave us the Scriptures, and they gave us Jesus Christ, the Savior of the world. Today, Jews and Gentiles in the church are praising God together (Eph. 2:11ff), and one day in the glorious kingdom, Jews and Gentiles will glorify and praise Him (67:1-7; 72:8-11; Rom. 15:8-13).

The psalmist saw God's defeat of the Assyrians as a sign of His defeat of all the nations and the establishment of His glorious kingdom. The prophets announced that the Gentiles would turn to the Lord and share the kingdom with Israel (Isa. 2:1-5; 11:1-10; Mic. 4:1-5), and the psalmist looked down the ages and saw this fulfilled. The Gentile leaders, representing their people, will come and give their allegiance and their praise to Jesus Christ, "[a]nd the Lord shall be king over all the earth" (Zech. 14:9). Paul alludes to verse 7 in 1 Cor. 14:15 when he admonishes us to "sing with the understanding." The word "shields" can refer to kings since they are the protectors of the people (89:18). The kings of the earth belong to the Lord because He is the King of Kings (Rev. 19:16). The image of God sitting upon His holy throne is used often in the book of Revelation (4:2, 9-10; 5:1, 7, 13; 6:16; 7:10, 15; 19:4; 21:5).

For God's people, everyday is Ascension Day as we praise and worship the exalted and ascended Lord.

Psalm 48

This is the third of the psalms celebrating Jehovah's victory in delivering Jerusalem from the Assyrians (see 46 and 47). The emphasis is on the Lord and Mount Zion. Other psalms about Zion are 76, 84, 87, 122, and 132. Believers today are citizens of the Zion that is above (Gal. 4:21-31; Heb. 12:18-24; Phil. 3:20) and rejoice that the Lord cares for us even as He cared for His ancient people Israel. The various speakers in this psalm deal with four important topics.

God and Their City (vv. 1-3)

In this first section, the people of Jerusalem speak about their city with pride and gratitude. David took Mount Zion from the Jebusites (2 Sam. 5:6-9; 2 Chron. 11:4-7) and made Jerusalem the capital of his kingdom. Ideally situated 2500 feet above sea level, the city was almost impregnable. Not far away was the juncture of the north-south and east-west trade routes, important for the economy and for communications. David brought the ark of the covenant to Jerusalem, and this made Zion a "holy mountain," for the Lord dwelt there (2:6; 3:4; 15:11 43:3; 99:9). Jerusalem thus became "the city of God" (vv. 1, 8) and the "city of the Great King" (v. 2; 47:2; see Matt. 5:35). The greatness belongs to the

Lord and not to the city (47:9), for in His grace, the Lord chose Zion (78:68; 132:13). The Jews saw Jerusalem as a beautiful city (50:2), a safe fortress, and "the joy of all the earth" (but see Lam. 2:15). Spiritually speaking, the city has brought joy to all the earth because outside its walls Jesus died for the sins of the world, and from Jerusalem first sounded out the Gospel of Jesus Christ. One day in the future, Jerusalem will be the center of Christ's glorious kingdom (Isa. 2:2ff and 60:1ff). Zaphron (NIV) refers to the north, a mountain in northern Syria where the god Baal was supposed to dwell. (See Ex. 14:1 and 9 and Num. 33:7.) The safety of Jerusalem was not in her location or her walls (vv. 14-15) but in her God; for He was their fortress (v. 3; see 46:1, 7). It was in the defeat of Sennacherib's army that God "made himself known as a stronghold" (v. 3, NASB).

God and Their Enemies (vv. 4-7)

The citizens had been speaking *about* the Lord, but now they speak *to* the Lord about what He did to the Assyrians. Sennacherib and his huge army, plus the vassal kings of his empire (v. 4; Isa. 10:8), surrounded Jerusalem and hoped to capture it, but godly King Hezekiah, with the help of Isaiah the prophet (Isa. 14:24-27), turned to the Lord for help, and He came to their rescue (Isa. 36-37). The Lord fought for Israel just as He had fought against the Egyptians (Ex. 14:25). God sent His angel to the Assyrian camp and he killed 185,000 men. The judgment came suddenly, like the pain of a woman in labor, and the destruction was like that of a storm shattering a fleet of ships (Ezek. 27:26). Note the shattered weapons in 46:8-9. The overconfident Assyrians and their allies found themselves defeated and disgraced and had to go home.

God and Their Worship (vv. 8-11)

The speakers in this section appear to be a group of pilgrims going to Jerusalem after the great victory. They had heard about Assyria's defeat, but now they could see with their own eyes the great things that the Lord had done for His people. (It's likely that Ps. 126 also fits into this event.) The pilgrims immediately went to the temple to worship the Lord, to meditate on His faithfulness, and joyfully praise Him. Worship is the proper human response to divine mercies. Note how the fame of the Lord spread from the city itself (v. 11a) to the towns of Judah that Sennacherib had plundered (v. 11b; Isa. 36:1) and then to the ends of the earth (v. 10). So may it be with the message of the Gospel! (Acts 1:8). When the Lord Jesus Christ returns to defeat His enemies and establish His kingdom, His glory and dominion will be from sea to sea (Zech. 9:9-10), and the city of Jerusalem will be named "The Lord our Righteousness" (Jer. 23:6; 33:16).

God and Their Future (vv. 12-14)

After the worship was completed, perhaps one of the sons of Korah (see title) became "tour guide" for the pilgrims and led them around the city. He showed them the towers and the outer walls (ramparts), but he was careful to remind them that the city's protection was the Lord Jehovah and not stone and mortar. The Assyrian officers had counted the towers (Isa. 33:18) and calculated how to capture the city, but they hadn't taken the Lord into consideration. The guide told the visiting Israelites that it was their responsibility to teach the coming generation about the Lord, lest the nation abandon the God of Abraham and Isaac and Jacob. The greatest danger a nation faces is not the invading enemy on the outside but the eroding enemy on the inside—a people gradually turning away from the faith of their fathers. Each generation must pass along to the next generation who the Lord is, what He has done, and what they must do in response to His goodness and faithfulness (71:18; 78:4, 6; 79:13; 109:13; 145:4; 2 Tim. 2:2). God's plan is to make Jerusalem a joy to many generations (Isa. 60:15). To trust and obey a Lord who is "our God" and "our Guide" is to have a future that is secured and blessed.

Psalm 49

The psalmist had a message for everybody in the world, the important people and the nobodies, the rich and the poor (vv. 1-2). The word "world" is the translation of an unusual Hebrew word that means "the total human scene, the whole sphere of passing life," not unlike "world" in 1 John 2:15-17. The writer spoke from his heart (v. 3; see 45:1) the wisdom and understanding that the Lord gave him, and he dealt with an enigma that only the Lord could explain (v. 4). The enigma was life itself and its puzzling relationship to the distribution of wealth and the power that wealth brings. How should believers respond when they see the rich get richer? Should they be afraid that the wealthy will abuse the poor? Should they be impressed by the wealth that others possess and seek to imitate them? The writer gives us three reminders to help us keep our perspective in a world obsessed with wealth and the power it brings.

Wealth Cannot Prevent Death (vv. 5-12)
It isn't a sin to be wealthy if we acknowledge God as the Giver and use what He gives to help others and glorify His name

(1 Tim. 6:7-19; Matt. 6:33). But an increase in wealth often leads to an increase in evil. It's good to have things that money can buy, if we don't lose the things money can't buy. It's sad when people start to confuse prices with values. Jesus concluded a sermon on riches by saying, "For what is highly esteemed among men is an abomination in the sight of God" (Luke 16:15, NKJV). The psalmist feared that the wealthy in the land would start to take advantage of poorer people. It was easy for the rich to bribe judges and rob the poor of their rights. (See James 2:1-9; 5:1-6; Amos 4:1-3; 5:10-15.)

Those who boast of their wealth have a false sense of security, because their wealth can't protect them from "the last enemy"—death (1 Cor. 15:26). Jesus had this truth in mind when He spoke about the rich farmer in Luke 12:13-21. If a relative was poor, a Jew could redeem him by paying his debts (Lev. 25:23ff), but if a relative was dying, no amount of money could come to the rescue—and to whom would you give the money? A murderer could not be redeemed (Num. 35:31), even if you could calculate the worth of a human life. So, money can't rescue you on this side of the grave, nor can it rescue you on the other side of the grave, because you can't take your money with you (vv. 10-12 and 17; Eccl. 2:18, 21; 7:2; 9:5). Whether you are rich or poor, wise or foolish, you leave everything behind. Many wealthy people think they will go on forever and enjoy their houses and lands, only to discover that death is a great leveler. After death, the rich and the poor stand equal before God. The rich may call their lands after their own names, but the names engraved in stone will outlast the owners. The phrase "he is like the beasts that perish" (v. 12, KJV and see Eccl. 3:10, 19, and 7:2) doesn't suggest that humans are on the same level as brute beasts, but only that both face ultimate death and decay.

Wealth Will Not Determine Your Destiny (vv. 13-15)

When Jesus told His disciples that it was hard for a rich person to enter the kingdom of heaven, they were astonished; for most Jews believed that the possession of wealth was a mark of God's blessing (Matt. 19:23-30). If wealthy people have a hard time getting into the kingdom, what hope is there for the rest of us? But people with wealth tend to trust themselves and their money and to believe the nice things people say about them (v. 13). The writer pictured wealthy lost people as dumb sheep being led to the slaughterhouse by Death, the shepherd, who would devour them. (See Luke 16:14, 19-31.)

For the believer, death is only a valley of temporary shadows, and Jesus is the Shepherd (23:4). There is coming a "morning" when the dead in Christ will be raised and share the glory of the Lord (1 Thess. 4:13-18; see Ps. 16:10-11; Isa. 26:19; Dan. 12:3). We can't ransom someone who is about to die (vv. 7-8), but the Lord has already ransomed us from sin and the power of the grave (v. 15; 1 Cor. 15:20ff). When we die, God will receive us to Himself (73:24; 2 Cor. 5:1-8; Gen. 5:24), and when Jesus returns, He will raise our bodies from the grave. Decision for Christ, not the possession of great wealth, determines our eternal destiny.

Wealth Must Not Increase Your Desires (vv. 16-20)

Don't be impressed and "over-awed" (NIV) when you see others getting wealthy and buying bigger houses and cars. All their wealth will be left behind when they die and ultimately lose its value. They won't be able to praise themselves, nor will they be able to hear others praise them. We take nothing with us when we die (Job 1:21; Eccl. 5:14; 1 Tim. 6:7). If we have been faithful stewards of what God has given us, we possess eternal riches that will never fade (Matt. 6:19-34). We can't take wealth with us, but we can send it ahead.

The statement in verse 12 is repeated in verse 20 with the addition of the phrase "without understanding." The writer penned this psalm so we would have understanding! We need to understand that wealth cannot prevent death or determine our destiny, and that we must not become covetous when we see others prospering in this world. It isn't a sin to have wealth, provided we earned it honestly, spend it wisely, and invest it faithfully in that which pleases the Lord.

Psalm 50

Every seventh year, during the Feast of Tabernacles, the priests were obligated to read the law to the people and explain its meaning (Deut. 31:9-18; Neh. 8), and this psalm may have been written for such an occasion. The emphasis is on the consistent godly living that should result from true spiritual worship. Asaph was one of David's worship leaders (see Ps. 39 introduction and 1 Chron. 15:17ff and 16:4ff). A group of eleven psalms attributed to Asaph is found in 73-83. God the Judge summons the court (vv. 1-6) and confronts two offenders: the formalist, to whom worship is a ritual to follow (vv. 7-15), and the hypocrite, to whom worship is a disguise to cover sin (vv. 16-21). The psalm closes with a call to all worshipers to be faithful to God (vv. 22-23).

The Holy Judge (vv. 1-6)

Human judges are called "The Honorable," but this Judge is called "The Mighty One" (El), "God" (Elohim), "the LORD" (Jehovah), "the Most High" (Elyon, v. 14), and "God" (Eloah). He is Judge (vv. 4, 6), Prosecutor, and Jury—and He knows all about those who are on trial! He calls heaven and earth to witness the proceedings (vv. 1, 4, 6; see Deut. 4:26, 32; 31:28; 32:1; Isa. 1:2; Mic. 1:2 and 6:1-2). When a judge enters a courtroom, everybody stands respectfully; but God's entrance into this assembly is accompanied by the shining of His glory (80:1; 94:2) and a fiery tempest, not unlike the scene at Mount Sinai when He gave His law (Ex. 19:18; 24:17; Deut. 4:11-12; 33:2; Heb. 12:18, 29). When we forget the transcendence of God, we find it easier to sin. The ark was with the people on Mount Zion ("Immanual, God with us"), but the nation must not forget Mount Sinai where their God revealed His holiness and greatness. The psalmist praised Zion for its beauty (v. 2; 48:2; Lam. 2:15), but he also wants us to remember "the beauty of holiness" (27:4; 90:17; 110:3).

God is Judge (vv. 4, 6; 7:11; 9:8; 11:4-7; 75:2; 96:10, 13; 98:9), and judgment begins with His own people (1 Peter 4:17). They are "godly ones," that is, a people set apart exclusively for the Lord because of the holy covenant (vv. 5, 16; Ex. 19:1-9; 24:4-8; Amos 2:3). Some of His people had sinned, and He had been longsuffering with them and silent about the matter (vv. 3, 21). They have interpreted His silence as consent (Eccl. 8:11; Isa. 42:14; 57:11), but now the time had come for the Holy God to speak. The purpose of this "trial" was not to judge and condemn the sinners but to expose their sins and give them opportunity to repent and return to the Lord.

The Heartless Worshipers (vv. 7-15)

"Hear, O my people" has a majestic ring to it (Deut. 4:1; 5:6; 6:3-4; 9:1; 20:3; 27:9). The Lord speaks first to those who are indeed His people, but their hearts are not in their worship. Their devotion is faithful but only routine. Like the church at Ephesus, they had "left their first love" (Rev. 2:4) and were worshiping the Lord out of habit and not from the heart. Outwardly, they were doing what the Lord commanded and honoring the daily sacrifices (Ex. 29:38-42), but inwardly they lacked love and fellowship with God. They forgot that God wanted their hearts before He wanted their sacrifices (Isa. 1:11-15; Jer. 7:21-23; Hos. 6:6; 8:13; Amos 5:21-26; Mic. 6:6-8; Mark 12:28-34).

The sacrifices that the Lord commanded were indeed important to the spiritual life of the nation, but they did no good to the worshipers unless there was faith in the heart and a desire to honor the Lord. The animals they brought belonged to Him long before the worshipers ever saw them! The world and everything in it belongs to Him (v. 12; 24:1; 89:11; Acts 17:24-25; 1 Cor. 10:26), and there is nothing we can give to God. Some of the pagan religions of that day taught that their gods and goddesses "ate" the animals that people sacrificed, but this was not a part of the Hebrew religion (Deut. 32:37-40). What the Lord wanted from His people was thanksgiving from their hearts, obedience to His Word, prayer, and a desire to honor Him in everything (vv. 14-15). But the Lord doesn't want ritualism or formalism. He wants our worship to come from the heart.

The Hypocritical Sinners (vv. 16-21)

This message was addressed to "the wicked," the Israelites in the covenant community who were reciting the creed with their lips but deliberately disobeying God's law. After breaking God's law, they would go to the sanctuary and act very religious so they could cover up their sins. They helped to make the sanctuary a "den of thieves"—the place where thieves go to hide after they have committed their wicked deeds (Jer. 7:11; Matt. 21:13). They had no respect for God's Word (v. 17) and not only consented to the sins of others but participated in them and enjoyed doing so (vv. 18-20). To "hate instruction" means to reject an ordered way of life patterned after God's Word, to reject a responsible life. The Lord specifically named stealing (the 8th commandment, Ex. 20:15), adultery (the 7th commandment, Ex. 20:14) and deceitful speech and slander (the 9th commandment, Ex. 20:16). These are not "old covenant sins," for believers today who live under the new covenant can be just as guilty of committing them.

Once again, the silence of God is mentioned (v. 21; see v. 3). God is longsuffering with sinners, but these wicked people interpreted God's silence as His approval. (See Isa. 42:14; 57:11; 64:12; 65:6; Mal. 2:17; 3:14-14.) Their thinking was so confused that they ended up creating a god in their own image (v. 21). God was in the hands of ignorant sinners! They had forgotten God (Rom. 1:22-28) and didn't want Him to interfere with their lifestyle. They had a false confidence that they could sin and get away with it.

The Honest Worshiper (vv. 22-23)
In the two closing verses, the writer succinctly summarized the characteristics of the kind of worshiper God is seeking (John 4:23-24). The true worshiper has a proper fear of the Lord and seeks only to honor Him in his worship. He obeys God's will ("orders his way aright," NASB)

and is able to experience ("see") the salvation of the Lord. When you combine these characteristics with verses 14-15—gratitude to God, obedience, prayer, and a desire to glorify God—you have a description of worshipers who bring joy to the heart of God.

Psalm 51

Duse uring his lifetime, King David did what had pleased the Lord, "except in the case of Uriah the Hittite" (I Kings 15:5, NASB). This is the fourth of the Penitential Psalms (see 6) and is David's prayer of confession after Nathan the prophet confronted him with his sins (see 32; 2 Sam. 11-12). This is also the first of fifteen consecutive psalms in Book II attributed to David. In his prayer, David expressed three major requests.

"Cleanse Me" (vv. 1-7)
What dirt is to the body, sin is to the inner person, so it was right for David to feel defiled because of what he had done. By committing adultery and murder, he had crossed over the line God had drawn in His law ("transgression"); he had missed the mark God had set for him ("sin") and had yielded to his twisted sinful nature ("iniquity"). He had willfully rebelled against God, and no atonement was provided in the law for such deliberate sins (Lev. 20:10; Num. 35:31-32). David could appeal only to God's mercy, grace, and love (v. 1; Ex. 34:6-7; 2 Sam. 12:22). "Blot out" refers to a debt that must be paid (130:3; Isa. 43:25), and "cleanse" refers to defilement caused by touching something unclean (Lev. 11:32) or from disease (Lev. 13:1-3). "Wash" (vv. 2, 7) refers to the cleansing of dirty clothing (Isa. 1:18; 64:6).

In the Jewish society of that day, to wash and change clothes marked a new beginning in life (Gen. 35:2; 41:14; 45:22; Ex. 19:10, 14), and David made such a new start (2 Sam. 12:20).

David had certainly sinned against Bathsheba and Uriah, but his greatest responsibility was to the Lord who had given the law to His people (2 Sam. 12:13; Ex. 20:13-14). Godly Jews saw all sins primarily as offenses against the Lord (Gen. 39:9). David openly acknowledged his sins and vindicated the Lord (v. 4; 1 John 1:9-10). Paul quoted verse 4 in Romans 3:4 as part of his argument that the whole world is guilty before God. He also confessed that he was not only a sinner by choice but also by nature (v. 5; 1 John 1:8). His statement doesn't suggest that sex in marriage is sinful, or that his inherited fallen nature was an excuse for disobedience, but only that he was no better than any other man in the nation. (See Gen. 6:5; 8:21; Jer. 17:9; Matt. 15:19; Rom. 1:19ff.) The sinfulness of humans doesn't mean that people can't do anything good (Luke 11:13) but that their "goodness" can't earn them entrance into God's family (Eph. 2:8-10; Titus 3:3-7).

David knew the truth of God's Word and loved it (19:7-11), but he had deliberately lied to himself ("I can get away with this") and to the people, and he tried to lie to God. For nearly a year he attempted to cover up his sins, but God does not allow His children to sin successfully. Now he asked God for truth and wisdom in his innermost being (v. 6).

"Hyssop" (v. 7) was a shrub with hairy stems that could be dipped into liquid, and the priests used hyssop to sprinkle blood or water on people needing ceremonial cleansing (Lev. 14:4, 6; Num. 19:6, 18; see Ex. 12:22). Today's believers find their cleansing in the work Jesus accomplished on the cross (1 John 1:5-10; Heb. 10:19-25).

"Restore Me" (vv. 8-12)

David's sins had affected his whole person: his eyes (v. 3), mind (v. 6), ears and bones (v. 8; see 32:3-4; 35:9-10; 38:8), heart and spirit (v. 10), hands (v. 14), and lips (vv. 13-15). Such is the high cost of committing sin. David knew this, so he asked for more than cleansing, as important as that is; he wanted his entire being to be restored so he could serve the Lord acceptably. He wanted the joy of the Lord within him (see v. 12) and the face of the Lord smiling upon him (10:1; 44:24; 88:14; 104:29). "Joy and gladness" is a Hebrew phrase meaning "deep joy." David asked the Lord to create a new heart within him and to give him a steadfast spirit that would not vacillate. Verse 10 is the central verse of the psalm and it expresses the heart of David's concern. David knew that the inner person—the heart—was the source of his trouble as well as the seat of his joy and blessing, and he was incapable of changing his own heart. Only God could work the miracle (Jer. 24:7; Ezek. 11:19; 36:25-27).

The Lord gave the Holy Spirit to David when Samuel anointed him (1 Sam. 16:13), and David didn't want to lose the blessing and help of the Spirit, as had happened to Saul when he sinned (1 Sam. 16:1, 14; see 2 Sam. 7:15). Today the Spirit abides with believers forever (John 14:15-18), but God's children can lose His effective ministry by grieving the Spirit (Eph. 4:30-32), lying to Him (Acts 5:1-3), and quenching Him by deliberate disobedience (1 Thess. 5:19). The phrase "willing spirit" in verse 12 refers to David's own spirit, as in verse 10. A "willing spirit" is one that is not in bondage but is free and yielded to the Spirit of God, who ministers to and through our own spirit (Rom. 8:14-17). It isn't enough simply to confess sin and experience God's cleansing; we must also let Him renew us within so that we will conquer sin and not succumb to temptation. The Lord did forgive David but permitted him to suffer the tragic consequences of his sins (2 Sam. 12:13-14).

"Use Me" (vv. 13-19)

David was God's servant, and he wanted to regain his ministry and lead his people. He especially wanted to make careful preparations for the building of the temple. It's interesting that Solomon, the child eventually born to Bathsheba, was chosen to be David's successor and the one to supervise the temple construction. "But where sin abounded, grace abounded much more" (Rom. 5:20, NKJV). David wanted to witness to the lost and wandering and bring them back to the Lord (v. 13), and he wanted to sing the Lord's praises (vv. 14-15). "Bloodguiltiness" refers to Uriah's blood on David's hands, for it was David who ordered his death (2 Sam. 11:6ff; see Ezek. 3:18-20; 18:13; Acts 20:26).

David was wealthy enough to bring many sacrifices to the Lord, but he knew that this would not please the Lord (50:8-15; see 1 Sam. 15:22) and that their blood could not wash away his sins. David wasn't denying the importance or the validity of the Jewish sacrificial system; he was affirming the importance of a repentant heart and a spirit yielded to the Lord (Isa. 57:15). God could not receive broken animals as sacrifices (Mal. 1:6-8), but He would receive a broken heart!

Some students believe that verses 18-19 were added later to adapt this very personal psalm for corporate worship, but there's no reason why David could not have written these words. As king, he was certainly burdened for the welfare of Jerusalem and the kingdom, and he knew that his sins had weakened Israel's position among the nations (2 Sam. 12:14). David must have begun building and repairing the walls, otherwise Solomon couldn't have completed the work early in his reign (1 Kings 3:1). David destroyed much good when he sinned, but he also did much good during his lifetime and served the Lord faithfully.

Psalm 52

When David wrote this psalm, he was angry and rightly so. (For the reason, see 1 Sam. 21:1-9 and 22:6-23.) Doeg was one of many men around Saul who catered to his whims and inflated his ego in order to gain power and wealth. He typifies all who promote themselves at the expense of truth and justice. Doeg was an Edomite, which means he was descended from Esau, the enemy of Jacob (Gen. 27-28; Heb. 12:16-17). The battle between the flesh and the Spirit still goes on. However, it's possible that David was also writing about Saul, who certainly fits the description given of the proud powerful tyrant. There has always been a certain amount of evil in high places, and God's people must learn to handle it in a godly manner. David paints for us three contrasting scenes.

The Sinners Are Boasting (vv. 1-4)

The phrase "mighty man" is the equivalent of our "big shot" and was spoken derisively. Doeg and Saul were mighty in their own eyes but insignificant in God's eyes; David was insignificant in their eyes but important to God. David depended on the mercy of the Lord (vv. 1, 8) while Saul and his men depended on themselves and their own resources. With tongues like honed razors, they issued orders and told lies without considering the consequences (see 5:9; 55:21; 57:4; 59:7; 64:3). Even when they told the truth—as Doeg did about David—they did it with evil intent because they were possessed by a malignant spirit. Their words devoured people and destroyed them (see 35:25). It isn't difficult to find people like Doeg and Saul in our twenty-first century world.

The Saints Are Laughing (vv. 5–7)

Verse 5 is the central verse of the psalm and marks the turning point in David's experience as he contemplated the wickedness of the human heart. He was confident that God would one day judge Saul, Doeg, and all who follow their evil philosophy of life. Note the powerful verbs: "break you down ... snatch you up ... tear you away ... uproot you ... ." (NASB). (See Job 18 for a similar description.) The righteous would only *see* but not experience this devastation (91:8), and they would stand in awe of the holy wrath of God (40:3). Then they would laugh in derision at the humiliating fall of these pompous leaders (2:4). What Saul and Doeg did to the priestly community at Nob (1 Sam. 22:6ff), the Lord would do to them, for sinners ultimately fall into the pits they dig for others (9:15; Prov. 26:24-28; 29:6).

The Faithful Are Serving (vv. 8-9)

The contrast is clear: the wicked are like uprooted trees, but the godly are like flourishing olive trees that are fruitful and beautiful. Saul and Doeg would perish, rejected by the Lord, but David and his dynasty would be safe in the house of the Lord! It's possible that the tabernacle at Nob had olive trees growing around it and David would have seen them. The olive tree lives for many years and keeps bearing fruit (1:3; 92:12-15; see Jer. 17:7-8,

and note 37:35-36), and certainly David was a blessing to the nation while he lived and long after he died—and he is a blessing to us today. He trusted God's lovingkindness and the Lord did not fail him, and he never failed to give God the glory. The phrase "wait on thy name" (v. 9, KJV) means to hope and depend on the character of God as expressed in His great name. The psalm ends with David vowing to praise the Lord in the congregation as soon as God established him in his kingdom. The private victories God gives us should be announced publicly for the encouragement of God's people. Meanwhile, though evil may seem to triumph, we must continue to obey and serve the Lord and not get discouraged. The "last laugh" belongs to the Lord's people.

Psalm 53

This is Psalm 14 with some minor revisions and the addition of the last two lines in verse 5. One of the sanctuary musicians revised the original psalm to fit a new occasion, perhaps the defeat of the Assyrian army in the days of King Hezekiah (v. 5; Isa. 37). It's a good thing to adapt older songs to celebrate new experiences with the Lord. The major change is the use of Elohim ("God") instead of Jehovah, the God of the covenant. The psalm still exposes and refutes the foolish unbelief of those who reject God. The boasting of the Assyrians is a good example.

Verse 5b describes the scattered corpses of a defeated army after God's great victory. For a body to remain unburied was a great disgrace in the ancient Near East, even an executed criminal was supposed to have a decent burial (Deut. 21:23; see 2 Kings 23:14; Ezek. 6:5). The Lord despised the arrogance of the Assyrians and put them to open shame. So will He do to the armies of the world that oppose Him (Rev. 19:11-21).

Psalm 54

The Ziphites lived about fifteen miles southeast of Hebron (see 1 Sam. 23:13-24 for the background). Twice they betrayed David to Saul (see 1 Sam. 26:1) and both times the Lord delivered him. This psalm reveals three stages in David's experience as he turned to God for help.

The Starting Point—Danger from the Enemy (vv. 1-3)

David's life was in danger (v. 3; see 1 Sam. 23:15), and he called on God to save him and vindicate his cause (1 Sam. 24:15). David was the rightful king of Israel, and the future of the nation and the dynasty lay with him. This included the promise of Messiah, who would come from David's line (2 Sam. 7). "By your name" means "on the basis of your character," especially His strength (v. 1) and faithfulness (v. 5). David promised to praise God's name after the great victory (v. 6). He used three different names of God in this brief psalm: Elohim (vv. 1, 2, 3, 4), Adonai (Lord, v. 4), and Jehovah (LORD, v. 6). "Hear my prayer" (v. 2) is a favorite approach with David (4:1; 39:12; 143:1).

"Strangers" (v. 3) doesn't suggest that his enemies were Gentiles, for the Ziphites belonged to the tribe of Judah, David's own tribe. The word is used in Job 19:13 to describe Job's family and friends, and David used it in a similar way in 69:8. It can describe anybody who has turned his or her back on someone, which the Ziphites certainly did to David, their king. Why did they do it? Because

they disregarded the Lord and His will for the nation of Israel. Unlike David (16:8), they did not set God before them (see 10:4-5; 36:1; 86:14).

The Turning Point—Confidence in the Lord (v. 4)

This is the central verse of the psalm, and it records the turning point in David's experience. The word translated "help" or "helper" is related to "Ebenezer" in 1 Samuel 7:12, "Thus far the Lord has helped us" (NASB) and is a word David often used in his prayers (10:14; 30:10; 33:20; 79:9; 86:17; 115:9-11). It's worth noting that Jonathan visited David about this time, and the Lord used him to encourage His servant (1 Sam. 23:16-18). The Lord doesn't always send angels to encourage us; sometimes He uses other believers to minister to us (see Acts 9:26-28; 11:19-26). Every Christian ought to be a Barnabas, a "son of encouragement."

The Finishing Point—Praise to the Lord (vv. 5-7)

Twice David had opportunity to slay Saul but refrained from doing so, for He knew that God would one day deal with the rebellious king (see 1 Sam. 26:8-11). "He will pay back evil to my enemies" (v. 5, AMP). (See 7:15-16, 35:7-8, Prov. 26:27, 28:10, 29:6.) David was away from the sanctuary, but he lifted his voice in praise to God, and his words were like a freewill offering to the Lord (Heb. 13:15). In verses 1-6, David spoke directly to the Lord, but in verse 7, he spoke to those around him and gave witness to the blessing of the Lord. His words revealed his faith, for he spoke of his deliverance as already completed as he looked calmly at his enemies (22:17; 59:10; 92:11; 118:7). David had more suffering and peril to experience before he would ascend the throne, but he was confident that the Lord would see him through—and He did!

Psalm 55

It's likely that this psalm was written early in Absalom's rebellion (2 Sam. 15-17), when David was still in Jerusalem (vv. 9-11) and the revolt was gathering momentum. If so, then the "friend" of verses 12-14 and 20-21 had to be David's counselor Ahithophel who had sided with Absalom. Many commentators claim that the king and his officers didn't know about Ahithophel's treachery until after David had fled the city (2 Sam. 15:31), but this isn't clearly stated in Scripture. David was a man with keen discernment, and it is difficult to believe that his closest advisor's treachery was hidden from him. If this psalm was David's prayer while still in Jerusalem, then his prayer in 2 Samuel 15:31 is simply a repetition of verse 9. The psalm reveals four possible approaches to handling the painful problems and battles of life.

We Can Look Within at Our Feelings (vv. 1-5)
David opened with a plea to the Lord that He would not hide His face from his supplications. "Don't ignore my prayer!" (See 10:1; 13:1; 27:9; 44:24; 69:17; 143:7.) David knew that his own negligence as a father had turned Absalom against his father, the Lord, and the nation. He also knew that the revolt was part of the discipline that Nathan the prophet promised because of David's adultery and the murder of Uriah (2 Sam. 12:9-12). What David heard and saw in the city distressed him greatly (vv. 2, 17), and he realized that his

own life was in danger. The opposition was bringing trouble upon him the way soldiers fling stones at the enemy or roll down rocks upon them (v. 3). But David's concern was for the safety of his people and the future of the Lord's promises to his own dynasty (2 Sam. 7). He felt like everything was falling apart and there was no hope. It's natural to look at our feelings and express our fears, but that isn't the way to solve the problems.

We Can Look Beyond for a Safe Refuge (vv. 6-8)
When we find ourselves in the midst of trouble, our first thought is, "How can I get out of this?" But the dedicated believer needs to ask, "*What* can I get out of this?" David had learned some strategic lessons while hiding in the wilderness from Saul, but in his later years, he had some more important lessons to learn. The human heart longs for a safe and peaceful refuge, far from the problems and burdens of life. Elijah fled from the place of ministry and hid in a cave (1 Kings 19). Jeremiah longed for a quiet lodge where he might get away from the wicked people around him (Jer. 9:2-6), but when given the opportunity to leave Judah, like a true shepherd, he remained with the people (Jer. 40:1-6). Doves can fly long distances and they seek for safe refuges in the high rocks (Jer. 48:28). But we don't need wings like a dove so we can fly away from the storm. We need wings like an eagle so we can fly *above* the storm (Isa. 40:30-31). More than once David had prayed that the Lord would "hide him," and He answered his prayers (17:8; 27:5; 64:2). David did flee Jerusalem (2 Sam. 15:14ff) and lodged in the wilderness across the Jordan River at Mahanaim.

We Can Look Around at the Circumstances (vv. 9-15; 20-21)

David wasn't living in denial; he knew what was going on around him, and he directed operations in a masterful manner, worthy of his reputation. But he also prayed that God would bring confusion to Absalom's ranks (v. 9; 2 Sam. 15:31), and that's just what happened. The Lord used Hushai to influence Absalom to reject Ahithophel's counsel, and this led to the defeat of Absalom's forces (2 Sam. 16:15-17:31).

While still in Jerusalem, David witnessed violence and strife as people took sides and many followed Absalom (2 Sam. 15:10-14). "They" in verse 10 refers to violence and strife, which are personified as walking the walls along with mischief (malice) and sorrow (abuse). Among the rebels, David singled out one person who broke his heart, and that was Ahithophel, "a man like myself." As David's counselor, Ahithophel was not equal to the king in rank or authority, but he was very close to David. They had worshiped the Lord together, but now Ahithophel was counseling David's son to rebel against his father! In verses 20-21, David again mentioned Ahithophel, his violation of the covenant of friendship with David, and his deceptive persuasive speech. (See 5:9; 7:4; 12:2; 28:3; 41:9; Prov. 5:3) But God used Hushai to overrule Ahithophel's plans so that Absalom was defeated and David spared (2 Sam. 17). The picture in verse 15 reminds us of God's judgment on Korah, Dathan and Abiram because of their rebellion against Moses (Num. 16:28-33). David was God's anointed king, and the Lord protected him.

We Can Look up to God and Trust Him (vv. 16-19, 22-23)

While it's normal for us to hope for a quick way of escape, and important for us to understand our feelings and circumstances, it's far more important to look up to God and ask for His help. David could no longer lead an army into battle, but he was able to pray that God would defeat the rebel forces, and God answered his prayers. David used Jehovah, the covenant name of God, when he said, "The LORD will save me" (v. 16, NASB). The Jews did have stated hours of prayer (Dan. 6:10; Acts 3:1), but "evening, morning, and at noon" (v. 17) means that David was praying all day long! He no doubt also prayed at night (v. 10). David was certain that the Lord would hear him and rescue him because He was enthroned in heaven and in complete control. David's throne was in danger, but God's throne was secure (9:7-8; 29:10; 74:12).

During his difficult years of preparation, David had experienced many changes, and this taught him to trust the God who never changes (Mal. 3:6; James 1:17). Absalom and his friends had lived in luxury and ease and knew very little about the challenge of changing circumstances, so they had no faith in God or fear of God. A prosperous life is an easy life until you find yourself in the midst of the storm, and then you discover how ill-prepared you are; for what life does to us depends on what life finds in us.

The pronouns "you" and "your" in verse 22 are singular, but who is speaking and to whom? Did God speak to David through Nathan or another prophet and then David speak to the person reading the psalm? That's probably the correct answer. This promise is repeated in 1 Peter 5:7. The word translated "burden" ("cares," NIV) means "that which he has given you," reminding us that even the burdens of life come from the loving heart and hand of God (Ps. 33:11; Rom. 8:28). When David's lot was a happy one, it came from the Lord (16:5-6), and when he experienced times of pain and sorrow, the Lord was still in control.

He closed the psalm by speaking to the Lord and affirming his faith (7:1; 10:1), confident that God would judge his enemies. Was he anticipating the suicide of Ahithophel (2 Sam. 17:23)?

We must remind ourselves that our Lord Jesus Christ also had a traitor who hanged himself (Matt. 27:1-10), that Jesus also crossed the Kidron Valley (2 Sam. 15:23; John 18:1), and that He wept on the Mount of Olives (2 Sam. 15:30; Luke 22:39-44; Heb. 5:7). Rejected by His own people, today He is enthroned in heaven and will one day return to Jerusalem to establish His kingdom (Zech. 14:4ff).

Psalm 56

In an hour of deep despair and doubt, David left Judah and fled to Gath, the Philistine city identified with the giant Goliath whom David had slain (1 Sam. 17). David was alone and didn't get a very good reception. (The second time he went to Gath, he was accompanied by his men and was accepted. See 1 Sam. 27–30.) This psalm reveals that his life was in great danger, and history tells us that he had to pretend to be insane in order to escape (1 Sam. 21:10-22:1). Psalm 34 also came out of this experience in Gath. The musical inscription is translated variously: "the silent dove among those far away," "the silent dove among the strangers," "the dove on the distant oaks (or terebinths)." Some connect this inscription with 55:6-8 and see David as the dove (innocence), silent under attack while far from home. In the midst of peril and fear (vv. 3, 4, 11), David lifted three requests to the Lord, and the Lord answered.

Deliver Me from Death (vv. 1-4)

"All day long" David was harassed by the Philistines, who remembered that Israel sang his praises as a great military leader. They pursued him like hungry panting animals, and David cried out for mercy (see 51:1, 57:1). The record in 1 Samuel doesn't record any physical attacks on David, but he heard a great deal of slander and his life was in danger. David manifested both fear and faith as he cried out to God (Matt. 8:26; 14:30; Mark 5:6). The refrain in verses 3-4 is repeated in verses 10-11 as David affirms that God alone gives him the power to praise Him and trust Him. "So then faith comes by hearing, and hearing by the Word of God" (Rom. 10:17, NKJV). Faith and praise cannot be "manufactured"; they must be received as God's gift. "Mortal man" is "mere man, man who is flesh." This phrase is quoted in 118:6 and Hebrews 13:6. What Scripture says about fallen human nature is negative (John 6:63; Rom. 7:18; Phil. 3:3).

Deliver Me from Stumbling (vv. 5-11)

David literally had to "watch his step" in Gath, not only in what he did but also what he said, because he was a man under suspicion and was being watched. He had a target on his back and only the Lord could protect him. David chose Gath because he thought it was the last place Saul would expect to find him, but when he made that choice, he was walking by sight and not by faith. Faith is living without scheming. David prayed that God would judge Israel's enemies.

In verses 8-9, David reminded the Lord of the sufferings he had endured in exile, and then suggested that these sufferings qualified him to have his prayers answered and his enemies defeated. That would assure David that God is behind his cause (Rom. 8:31-39). God knew about

David's wanderings and numbered them (121:8), and He had preserved his tears as well (see 2 Kings 20;1-6). God listed his tears on His scroll (v. 8, NIV), or put them in His bottle or wineskin (KJV, NASB). Archaeologists have unearthed small "tear bottles" in which mourners collected their tears and then deposited the bottle at the gravesite. The point is simply that God is aware of what we feel and how we suffer, and His records are accurate (69:28; 87:6; 130:3; 139:16; Ex. 32:32; Neh. 13:14; Ezek. 13:9; Dan. 7:10; Mal. 3:16; Rev. 20:12; 21:27). David repeated the refrain in verses 10-11, but he used the covenant name "Jehovah" this time.

Deliver Me so I Can Praise You (vv. 12-13)

David's greatest desire was to glorify the Lord, and this is why he wrote this psalm. He had vowed to serve the Lord and he meant to keep his vow. He had also vowed to present thank offerings to the Lord when his days of wandering were ended. Part of the thank offering was retained by the worshiper so he could enjoy a fellowship meal with his family and friends, and David looked forward to that blessing.

According to verse 13, God answered David's prayers. He delivered him from death; He kept him from stumbling; and He enabled him to walk in a godly way and praise the Lord. "Light of the living" can also be translated "light of life," as the phrase used by Jesus in John 8:12. As we follow the Lord Jesus today, we enjoy fullness of life and the glorious light of His presence. We walk in the light.

Psalm 57

After his deliverance from Gath, recorded in 56, David fled for protection to the cave of Adullam (1 Sam. 22:1ff), and later he would move to a cave in Engedi (1 Sam. 24; see Ps. 142). Better to be in the will of God in a cave than out of His will in a king's palace. The melody "Destroy not" was also assigned to 58, 59, and 75. This psalm covers one day in David's life as a fugitive, for verse 4 records his lying down and verse 8 his waking up to greet the dawn. God quieted his heart and gave him the sleep he needed (see 4:8 and 5:3). Note the repetition of *mercy* and *refuge* (v. 1), *sends* (v. 3), *steadfast* (v. 7) and *awake* (v. 8), and refrain in verses 5 and 11. From his difficult experience in Gath, David shares with us some responsibilities (and privileges) believers have every day.

Each Day Is a Day of Prayer (vv. 1-5)

As in 56:1, he began with a cry for mercy, for David depended on the grace of God to see him through his trials. His worship and prayer turned the cave into a Holy of Holies where he could hide under the wings of the cherubim on the mercy seat of the ark (Ex. 25:17-20, and note the verb "overshadowing"). This image is found frequently in Scripture and must not be confused with the wings of the bird as in 91:4, Deuteronomy 32:11, Matthew 23:37, and Luke 13:34. (See 17:8; 36:7-8; 61:4; Ruth 2:12.) David wanted the wings of a dove to fly away (55:6), when what he needed was the wings of the cherubim in "the secret place of the Most High" where he could safely hide (Heb. 10:19-25). David had taken refuge in the Lord many times in the past, and he knew the Lord was faithful. The word "calamities" means "a destructive storm that could engulf me."

Saul and his men were like panting animals pursuing their prey (vv. 3-4; see 7:2; 10:9; 17:12; 57:4; Dan. 6; 1 Peter 5:8), but God would protect David with His love and faithfulness. If David lay down in the cave to sleep, perhaps Saul's men would find him. But David's God is "God Most High" (7:17; 57:2; 78:56) and "possessor of heaven and earth" (Gen. 14:19), and He would fulfill His great purposes for David (138:8). David included a song of praise in his evening prayer (v. 5) and lay down and went to sleep. David didn't pray only at bedtime, as too many people do, but all day long; however, he closed the day with a special time of worship and commitment.

Each Day Is a Day of Praise (vv. 6-11)

In verses 1-5, the order is prayer (v. 1), witness (vv. 2-3), and a description of the enemy (v. 4), followed by the refrain, but in this section the order is the enemy (v. 6), witness to the Lord (vv. 7-8), and praise (vv. 9-11), with praise as the emphasis. David now compared his enemies to hunters who dug pits and set traps for their prey, an image frequently used in biblical poetry (7:15; 9:15ff; 35:7). However, David trusts God and has good reason to sing and praise the Lord. A steadfast heart is one that is fixed on the Lord's promises and not wavering between doubt and faith (51:10; 108:1; 112:7; 119:5). This same word is used to describe the constancy of the heavenly bodies (8:3; 74:16). Note that verses 7-11 are found also in 108:1-5. David praised the Lord all day long, but he opened the day with special praise and even anticipated the sunrise. Instead of the dawn awakening him, his voice awakened the dawn. (See 30:5; Lam. 3:22-23.)

David wanted his victory in the Lord to be a witness to the other nations, for as king, he knew that Israel was to be a light to the Gentiles. His psalms bear witness today of the great things God did for him. In verse 3, God sent His mercy and truth *down* from heaven, but in verse 10, mercy

and truth *reach up* to the clouds! There is plenty for everybody!

Each Day Is a Day of Exalting the Lord (vv. 5, 11)

This refrain calls upon the Lord to manifest His greatness in such a way that people had to say, "This is the Lord's doing; it is marvelous in our eyes" (118:23, KJV). In his other psalm from Gath, David called on people to exalt the Lord (34:3; and see 18:46; 21:13; 30:1; 35:27; 40:16; 99:5, 9; 107:32; 145:1; 108:5; Matt. 5:16). If we are praying, trusting, and praising the Lord, we should have no problem exalting His name in all that we say, do, and suffer. We're commanded to do everything to the glory of God (1 Cor. 10:31), and if "everything" includes hiding in caves, then may the Lord be magnified! The elements of prayer, praise, and a desire for God to be magnified will transform any cave into a Holy of Holies to the glory of God.

Psalm 58

During David's exile years, Saul led the nation down a path of political and spiritual ruin as he disobeyed God's law and opposed God's anointed king. Saul was surrounded by a group of fawning flatterers who fed his ego and catered to his foolish whims (1 Sam. 22:6ff), and he put into places of authority people who used their offices for personal gain and not for the national good. They wanted to get as much as they could before the kingdom collapsed. David himself had been treated illegally, and it's likely that many of his men lost all they had because they followed David (1 Sam. 22:1-2). This psalm was probably written late in David's exile, or very early in his reign in Hebron, and may have grown out of his pondering the mess he had inherited from his father-in-law. (See 82 for a parallel psalm by Asaph.) The prophets often preached against the lawlessness of the leaders in Israel (Isa. 1:23-28; 5:22-25; 10:1-4; Amos 5:7-13; Mic. 3:1-4, 9-12; 7:1-6). Certainly nations, corporations, and even churches today need to take this kind of leadership crisis seriously. This is an imprecatory psalm (see 6).

Accusation—Lawlessness Practiced (vv. 1-5)

David addressed the lawless leaders and asked them if their words were just, their decisions legal, their sentences fair, and their silences honest. Were they upholding the law and defending the righteous or twisting the law and benefiting the wicked? He knew the answer, and so do we. When they should have spoken, they were silent, and when they spoke, they ignored God's law. The problem? They had evil hearts, for they were born in sin just like the rest of us (51:5; Gen. 8:21). However, they made no effort to seek God's help in controlling that sinful nature but gave in to its evil impulses. It's because humans are sinners that God established government and law, for without law, society would be in chaos. It's from the heart that evil words come out of our mouth and evil deeds are done by our hands.

These unjust judges were liars. Their words were like venom that poisoned society instead of like medicine that brought health (Prov. 12:18; 15:4). David compared them to snakes (vv. 4-5) and lions (v. 6), both of which are images of the devil (Gen. 3; 2 Cor. 11:3; 1 Peter 5:8). Like the cobra, they obeyed the charmer only when they got something out of it, but they had a mind of their own. Snakes have no visible ears or internal eardrums, but they do have small bones in the head

that conduct sound vibrations. The cobra responds more to the movements of the charmer than to the tune he plays.

Condemnation—Lawlessness Punished (vv. 6-8)

Seeing innocent people suffer because of unjust judges made David angry, and rightly so. There is a righteous anger that ought to show itself whenever innocent people are condemned or helpless people are abused. David didn't do any of the things he mentioned but instead asked the Lord to do them. He knew that vengeance belongs to the Lord (Deut. 32:35; Heb. 10:30; Rom. 12:19). A lion without teeth is severely limited in his attacks; water that has soaked into the ground has lost the power to destroy (2 Sam. 14:14); and arrows without points won't penetrate the body. The snail doesn't actually "melt away" while moving along the rock, but the trail of slime left behind makes it look that way. The stillborn child is dead and can't function at all. "Let these unjust leaders be gone!" said David.

Vindication—Righteousness Praised (vv. 9-11)

David added a sixth image to describe their ultimate judgment, which would happen suddenly and without warning. A desperate traveler in the wilderness could cook a meal over a fire of thorns, but the fire might suddenly go out because the fuel burned quickly—or a whirlwind might come up and scatter fuel, fire, and cooking pots. To use a modern colloquial expression, these godless leaders are only "a flash in the pan." There is coming a day of judgment and they will not escape (118:12; 2 Sam. 23:6).

David's second picture comes from the battlefield and is even more vivid (v. 10).

When victorious soldiers walked around the field and picked up the spoils of battle, their feet were stained by the blood of their enemies. Walking in cream and oil was a picture of wealth (Job 29:6), and walking in blood was a picture of great victory (see 68:23; Isa. 63:1-6; Rev. 14:17-20). The fact that the righteous rejoice at this is no more sinful than that prisoners of war rejoice at their release from a death camp or that downtrodden citizens are set free from a cruel dictator. After all, heaven rejoices at the fall of Babylon (Rev. 18:20-19:6). God vindicates Himself, His law, and His people, and He does it justly. So effective is His judgment that outsiders will say, "Surely there is a God who judges on earth" (v. 11, NASB).

Psalm 59

King Saul's fear and hatred of David became so compulsive that he finally gave orders to kill his son-in-law, and twice Saul tried to do it himself (1 Sam. 19:1-10). Then he plotted to have David murdered in his bed at home (1 Sam. 19:11-18), but his wife helped David escape by letting him out a window (see Acts 9:23-25). Before this attempt, Saul sent out search parties to spy on David (vv. 6, 14), and David wrote this psalm to ask God for the help he needed. The focus of the psalm is on God—the Deliverer (vv. 1-9) and the Judge (vv. 10-17). Note David's repeated "statement of faith" in verses 9 and 17. David waited and watched for God to work, and then he sang praises to the Lord for His mercies.

God the Deliverer (vv. 1-9)
God's people can always turn to the Lord in times of danger and testing because *He hears our prayers* (vv. 1-2). "Defend me"

means "set me on high," for David saw the Lord as his fortress and high tower (18:2; 20:1; 46:7, 11; 91:14). However, David's prayer wasn't a substitute for action, for "faith without works is dead" (James 2:26). Michel's warning and immediate action saved his life, and her use of the "dummy" in the bed helped to buy time for her husband to get to Samuel in Ramah. But it was the Lord who answered prayer and orchestrated the escape. The Lord also *knows our hearts* (vv. 3-4) and recognized that David was innocent of the charges Saul's men were making against him (7:1-5; see 1 Sam. 20:1 and 24:11). David was not a traitor, but Saul had to have some excuse for hunting him down. David addressed the Lord as if He had been sleeping (vv. 4-5; see 7:6 and 44:23). In times of great danger, we sometimes feel that God needs to start acting on our behalf and doing it very soon!

The Lord *sees and hears our enemies* (vv. 5-7) and knows what they are saying and doing. David addressed Him as Jehovah (the God of the covenant), the Lord of Hosts (armies), and the God of Israel. David was Israel's anointed king and a son of the covenant God made with His people, so he had every right to seek God's help. Jehovah is the Lord of the Armies (Lord Sabaoth) and can defeat anyone who challenges His will. Since Saul and his men were the immediate problem, to whom was David referring when he spoke of "the nations" (vv. 5 and 8)? The nations around Israel were usually poised and ready to attack their old foe, and Saul's mismanagement of the kingdom would make such a move even easier. He was so obsessed with destroying David that he neglected his duties as king and made the nation vulnerable. But David was God's anointed king, and Saul's attacks were exactly what the

Gentile nations would do if they could. Unlike Saul, David understood the unique position of Israel among the nations and sought to maintain it (Gen. 12:1-3; Num. 23:9; 24:8-9).

David's graphic description of Saul's men (vv. 6-7 and 12-15) reveals how much he held them in disdain. They were nothing but prowling, snarling dogs, frothing at the mouth, spewing out evil words, and rummaging in the garbage dumps of the city. The Jews usually referred to *the Gentiles* as dogs! Finally, as our great Deliverer, the Lord *defends our cause* (vv. 8-9). The "dogs" were prowling and growling, but the Lord was laughing (see 2:4 and 37:13). The spies were watching David, but David was "on watch" looking for the Lord to act (vv. 9, 17; see 121:3-5, 7-8). God was his strength and fortress (46:1), and he had no reason to be afraid.

God the Judge (vv. 10-17)

God would not only take care of David, but He would also confront David's enemies and deal with them. If David's requests seem brutal and not in the spirit of Christ, keep in mind that Israel's future and the future of David's chosen dynasty were both at stake. This was not a personal crusade on David's part, for he asked God to fight the enemy for him (Rom. 12:17-21).

When it comes to facing and fighting the enemy, *the Lord goes before us* (v. 10). The mercy (lovingkindness) of the Lord would go before David and prepare the way for victory, just as when David killed the giant Goliath. The Lord also *fights for us* (vv. 11-13a) by scattering the enemy, causing them to wander and bringing their attack to a halt. The Lord is our Shield who can protect us in any battle (3:3; 18:2; Gen. 15:1; Deut. 33:29), but we must make a distinction here. David was

willing that God destroy the Gentile nations and thus reveal His great power (v. 13), for God's victories bear witness to those who don't know Him. However, he asked God not to kill Saul and his men with some sudden judgment, but to allow their own sins to catch up with them and consume them gradually. This would be a strong witness and a warning to the people of Israel and teach them lessons they could learn no other way. God's victories *glorify His great name* (v. 13b) and magnify the name of the Lord to the ends of the earth (Ex. 9:16; Deut. 28:9-10; Josh. 4:23-24; 1 Sam. 17:46; 1 Kings 8:42-43). Finally, the Lord *gives us a song* (vv. 16-17) *and even before the victory,* we praise Him for who He is and what He does! The night of danger is never enjoyable, but we have His "mercy in the morning" (v. 16, KJV) because His love and compassion are "new every morning" (Lam. 3:22-23).

Psalm 60

According to the superscription, this psalm is a part of the history recorded in 2 Samuel 8:1-14 and 10:6-18 and 1 Chronicles 18:1-13 and 19:6-19, when David was winning battles and getting a name for himself (2 Sam. 8:13). While he was up north fighting the Arameans (Syrians), the Edomites attacked Israel from the south, doing a great deal of damage. David dispatched Joab with part of the army, and Joab and Abishai (1 Chron. 18:12) defeated Edom in the Valley of Salt, south of the Dead Sea. David must have written the psalm shortly after hearing the bad news of the invasion by Edom, but the psalm manifests a spirit of trust and confidence that the Lord would give Israel the victory, and He did. The musical direction means "Lily of the testimony [covenant]." (See 45, 69 and 80.)

Abandonment—A Troubled People (vv. 1-5)

The plural pronouns indicate that David was speaking to the Lord for the Israelites who felt themselves abandoned by God. The initial victory of Edom hit Israel like water bursting through a broken dam (v. 1; 2 Sam. 5:20) or an earthquake shaking the entire country (v. 2). The people acted like they were drunk on wine, staggering in bewilderment from place to place (v. 3; 75:8; Isa. 51:17, 22). David interpreted Israel's defeat as a sign that God had rejected His people (44:9-16; 89:38-45). However, being a man of faith, he didn't give up but rallied the people around the Lord's banner (v. 4; 20:5). Israel's God is "Jehovah Nissi—the Lord our Banner" (Ex. 17:15). David knew that Israel was God's own people, His beloved people ("David" means "beloved") who feared Him, and that God had covenanted to give them success against their enemies (2 Sam. 7:9-11). In David's heart, faith was conquering fear.

Encouragement—A Triumphant Message (vv. 6-8)

How David received this message from the Lord isn't explained to us, but he was quick to believe it and pass it along to the people. The message describes Jehovah as a Warrior who defeated the nations in Canaan and divided the land among His people (vv. 6-7; see Ex.15:3, 13-18; Josh. 18:10). Shechem was the chief city in Ephraim, and with Succoth, was located west of the Jordan River, while Gilead and Manasseh (the half tribe) were east of the Jordan River. The patriarch Jacob was connected with both Succoth and Shechem (Gen. 33:17-18). Ephraim was a strong tribe, called to defend Israel ("helmet"); and Judah was chosen to be the royal tribe, bearing the scepter (Gen.

49:10). The Lord didn't give the land to His people so they might lose it to their enemies! The Lord spoke with disdain of the enemies who attacked Israel, for both Edom and Moab were known for their arrogance (Isa. 16:6-14; Obad.; and see Ex. 15:14-15 and Num. 20:14-21). In God's eyes, Moab was nothing but a basin used for washing dirty feet, and Edom was a servant who cleaned dirty shoes! (David was related to the Moabites. See Ruth 4:13-22.) As for Israel's perpetual enemies, the Philistines, over them God would "raise the shout of victory" (v. 8, AMP). David claimed these promises by faith, sent part of the army led by Joab and Abishai to the south to fight Moab, and later David joined them for a great victory. Fighting on two fronts isn't easy, but God gave the victory.

Enablement—A Trustworthy Lord (vv. 9-12).

David earnestly prayed that the Lord would honor His Word and give His beloved people victory over their enemies, and the Lord answered. David made it clear that he wasn't looking back at the defeat (vv. 9-10). He was the kind of leader who looked to the future and trusted the Lord. The "fortified city" was probably Petra (or Sela), the capital of Edom. David didn't interpret one setback as the sign of total defeat. He was making a great name for himself by his many victories, so perhaps he needed this one defeat to humble him and drive him closer to the Lord. David didn't trust in himself or in his capable officers or his valiant soldiers (v. 11). He trusted fully in the Lord, and the Lord honored his faith. The enemy would be completely defeated—trampled into the dirt—and Israel would triumph. Israel rallied to the "banner of God's truth" (v. 4), and the

Lord gave them victory (1 John 5:4). "Edom will be conquered; Seir [Edom], his enemy, will be conquered, but Israel will grow strong" (Num. 24:18, NIV).

Psalm 61

David could have written this psalm during any of the many times he was in danger, but perhaps the best context is the rebellion under Absalom (2 Sam. 15-18). David prayed about a foe (v. 3), protection for his life (v. 6), and the security of his throne (v. 7, where "abide" means "be enthroned"). The psalm opens with David crying out in distress but closes with him singing praises to God.

"Hear Me"—A Cry to the Lord (vv. 1-4)
There was an urgency in David's cry because he was overwhelmed by what was happening and fainting under the pressure. (See Ps. 142.) He was obviously not at "the ends of the earth," but he felt that way, for he was away from home and away from the sanctuary of God. He was describing "spiritual geography" and his need to know the presence of God in what was going on. The image of the Lord as "rock" is a familiar one in David's writings (18:2, 31, 46; 62:2, 6, 7; etc.). David was unable to "climb" higher by himself; he needed the Lord to help him and sustain him (see 62:2, 6, 7). We are never so far away that we can't pray to God, or, as in the case of Jonah, so far down (Jonah 2). David looked back at his life and was encouraged to remember that God had never failed him in any crisis (v. 3), and He would not fail him now. To David, God's home was the tabernacle, the place where His glory dwelt; and David longed to be back in Jerusalem to worship and adore his Lord (v. 4). "Wings" probably

refers to the cherubim on the mercy seat that covered the ark of the covenant in the Holy of Holies (36:7-8; 57:1; 63:2, 7). David was not a priest, so he couldn't enter the Holy of Holies, but he could abide in the Lord and find refuge in Him (46:1; 90:1). God's "wings" provided safety right where David was, so he didn't need his own "wings" to fly away (55:6-8). "Forever" in verse 4 carries the meaning of "all my life" (1 Sam. 1:22).

"You Have Heard Me"—Confidence in the Lord (vv. 5-8)
When David became king, he made some promises to the Lord and to the people, and he intended to keep those promises. All during his wilderness exile, while hiding from Saul, David obeyed the Lord (18:19-27), and he sought to be a shepherd to the nation. Why would the Lord care for David all those years, give him his throne, and then allow him to be replaced by his wicked son? His throne was his heritage from the Lord (16:5-6), just as the land of Israel was the heritage (possession) of God's people (37:9, 11, 22, 29, 34).

His requests in verses 6-7 relate to God's gracious covenant with David (2 Sam. 7). The Lord promised David a throne forever and a dynasty forever (89:36), and this has been fulfilled in Jesus Christ (Luke 1:30-37; Acts 2:22-36). David's concern was not for his own name or family but for the future of Israel and God's great plan of redemption. His own throne was in jeopardy at that time, but he had confidence that God would keep His promises. "May he sit enthroned forever" (v. 7, AMP) meant "May King David live out his full life," protected by God's mercy and truth, but to believers today it means, "May Jesus Christ reign forever!" The throne of glory is secure, for God has set His King on His holy hill of

Zion! (2:6). In view of this, let's follow David's example and trust the Lord, call on Him, obey Him "day after day," and sing His praises.

Psalm 62

This psalm may have come out of David's time of trial when his son Absalom sought the throne (vv. 3-4), but it also may have been written while David was ruling over Judah in Hebron (2 Sam. 1-4). Those were difficult years as the forces of Saul tried to continue his dynasty and dethrone God's anointed king. (For "Jeduthun," see Ps. 39, and note how the two psalms parallel each other in a number of ways.) In this psalm, David shows remarkable faith as he rests in God alone (vv. 1, 2, 5, 6) and trusts Him to defeat the enemy and restore peace to the land. Three powerful truths emerge from his experience.

God Alone Saves Us (vv. 1-4)
The word translated "only" or "alone" in verses 1, 2, 4, 5, and 6, and "surely" in verse 9 (all KJV) is a Hebrew adverb that is also translated "indeed, verily, but" and is even ignored completely. David wants us to know that his faith isn't in God plus something else, but in God alone. Yes, God uses means to accomplish His work, and the same God who ordains the end also ordains the means, but our faith is in Him and not in the means. David didn't argue with the enemy or try to tell God what to do; he simply prayed, trusted and waited, knowing that God would give him the kingdom in His good time. The images of God as "rock" and "fortress" remind us of Psalm 18:1-2. A humble man, David saw himself as a bowing stone wall about to collapse and a tottering fence ready to fall down (see 1 Sam.

24:14 and 26:20). But God was his strong tower! The enemy could threaten him, lie about him, and even assault him, and he would not lose the peace God put in his heart. To wait in silence before the Lord is not idleness or inactivity. It is calm worship and faith, resting in His greatness and submitted to His will. It is preparation for the time when God gives the orders to act (18:30-45).

God Alone Encourages Us (vv. 5-8)
David has moved from "I shall not be greatly shaken" (v. 2, NASB) to "I shall not be shaken" (v. 6, NASB). The greater the realization that God was his fortress, the greater the calmness in his heart. He was not depending on himself or his own resources but on the Lord God Almighty. His throne, his reputation, and his very life depended only on the faithfulness of the Lord. In verse 8, David exhorted the people with him to see God as their refuge, to trust Him always, and to pour out their hearts in prayer (42:4; 142:2). David depended on the prayers of others and, like Paul, wasn't afraid to say, "Pray for us" (1 Thess. 5:25; 2 Thess. 3:1). Times of waiting can be difficult if we don't depend wholly on the Lord. God's delays are not God's denials, but our impatience can be used by the devil to lead us on dangerous and destructive detours.

God Alone Rewards Us (vv. 9-12)
When David looked to the Lord, he saw himself as a weak tottering fence and wall (v. 3). Now, when he looked at the enemy, he saw them as—nothing! No matter how high socially or how powerful economically, all men are but vanity ("a breath"—102:3; James 4:14; Job 7:7). Put them on the scales and nothing will register, because they weigh nothing (Job 6:2; Isa. 40:15; Dan. 5:27). David's enemies had acquired

their power and wealth by oppressing and abusing others, and David warned his own people not to adopt their philosophy of life. How tragic when God's people today put their trust in their wealth, positions, and human abilities and not in the God who alone can give blessing.

The phrase "once ... twice" in verse 11 is a Hebrew way of saying "many times, repeatedly" (Amos 1:3, 6, 9, 11, 13; Job 33:14). David had often heard these words and the lesson they carried was written on his heart: God is powerful and God is merciful. God's strength and lovingkindness are sufficient for every crisis of life, for we are in the hands of a God whose omnipotent love can never fail. "Let us fall now into the hand of the Lord, for his mercies are great" (2 Sam. 24:14). God did vindicate David and give him his throne, and he reigned with great distinction. No matter what people may say about us or do to us, God keeps the books and one day will give sinners and saints the rewards they deserve. "And each one will receive his own reward according to his own labor" (2 Cor. 3:8).

Psalm 63

The superscription informs us that David was in "the wilderness of Judah" when he wrote this psalm, suggesting that it was probably during Absalom's rebellion (2 Sam. 15:23). However, he didn't look back in regret at the mistakes he had made as a father, nor did he look around in fear or complaint at the discomforts and dangers of the wilderness. Instead, he looked up to the Lord and reaffirmed his faith and love. In an hour when David might have been discouraged, he was excited about God, and in a place where there was no sanctuary or priestly ministry, David

reached out by faith and received new strength from the Lord. Note the progressive experiences he had as he sought for the Lord's guidance and help at a difficult time in his life.

Desiring God (vv. 1-2)

To be able to say "my God" by faith transformed David's wilderness experience into a worship experience. There in the desert, he was hungry and thirsty, but his deepest desires were spiritual, not physical. With his whole being, body and soul, he yearned for God's satisfying presence (v. 5; 42:1-2). Just as we have physical senses that are satisfied by God's creation, so we have spiritual senses (Heb. 5:14) that can be satisfied only by Christ. He is the bread of life (John 6), and He gives us the water of life by His Spirit (John 4:1-14; 7:37-39; Rev. 22:17). Those who hunger and thirst for spiritual food and drink shall be filled (Matt. 5:6). David could say with Jesus, "I have food to eat of which you do not know" (John 4:32, NKJV).

How did David acquire this wonderful spiritual appetite? By worshiping God at the sanctuary (v. 2; see 27:4; 84:1-2). He had erected the tent on Mt. Zion and returned the ark to its rightful place, and he had found great delight in going there and contemplating God (36:8-9; 46:4). Because he didn't belong to the tribe of Levi, David couldn't enter the sanctuary proper, but from his study of the Books of Moses, he knew the design and the assigned rituals, and he understood their deeper meaning. *It is our regular worship that prepares us for the crisis experiences of life.* What life does to us depends on what life finds in us, and David had in him a deep love for the Lord and a desire to please Him. Because David had seen God's power and glory in His house, he was able to see it in the wilderness as well!

Praising God (vv. 3-5)

David didn't depend on the tabernacle or its furnishings—in fact, he sent the ark back to Jerusalem (2 Sam. 15:24-29)—but on the living God whose character and works were declared in those furnishings. Unlike the superstitious people of Judah in Jeremiah's day (Jer. 3:16; 7:1-16), David looked beyond material objects and saw spiritual realities. He had no priest or altar there, but he could lift his hands like the priests and bless the Lord and His people (Num. 6:22-27). His uplifted hands, though holding no sacrifice, signified his prayers and the love of his uplifted heart (see 28:2; 141:2; 1 Tim. 2:8). By faith he was under the wings of the cherubim in the Holy of Holies, protected from his foes (v. 7; 36:7). There in the wilderness, he had no sacrificial meal to enjoy, but his soul feasted on spiritual delicacies that even the priests were not permitted to eat (v. 5; Lev. 3:16-17). "Marrow and fatness" typify the very finest of food (81:16; 147:14; Deut. 32:14; Isa. 25:6). Instead of complaining, as we are prone to do when things go wrong, David sang praises to the Lord.

Remembering God (vv. 6-8)

David's heart was at peace, and he was able to go to bed and calmly worship the Lord and meditate on Him (3:5-6; 42:8). The phrase "earnestly seek" in verse 1 can mean "early will I seek," so we see David at both morning and evening. The phrase "remember God" means to recall what He has said and done in the past and apply it to our present situation (42:6; 77:1-11; 105:1-5; 119:55). It was because Israel forgot what God did that they rebelled and disobeyed Him (78:40-43; 106:6ff). Our God is I AM, not "I was," and He must always be recognized in our present situation. The Jews had three night watches, from sunset to ten o'clock, from ten to two o'clock, and from two to sunrise, so whenever David awakened during the night, he immediately remembered the Lord. (Or it could mean he was awake all night, but not tossing and turning.) His bed was under the wings of the cherubim and he felt secure as he meditated on the Lord (16:7; 119:148; Deut. 6:4-9).

But David wasn't passive in his devotion, for he continued to cling to the Lord and rest in the safety of His right hand (17:7; 18:35; 41:12). Faith without works is dead. Believers are safe in the hands of the Father and the Son (John 10:27-29), but that doesn't give us license to do foolish things that would endanger us. "My soul cleaves after you" is a literal translation of verse 8, including both submissive faith in God and active pursuit of God. Jesus described this experience in John 14:21-27.

Rejoicing in God (vv. 9-11).

Some people criticize David for wanting his enemies destroyed and their bodies left for the scavengers to devour. But they should remember that these rebels were the enemies of God and God's purposes for Israel, and that those purposes included the coming of Messiah into the world. (See at Ps. 55.) David didn't execute the enemy himself but asked God to deal with them, and He did (2 Sam. 18:6-8). David only wanted the God of truth to triumph over the liars (31:5; 40:11; 43:3; 45:4). David didn't rejoice in the destruction of his enemies; he rejoiced in the God of Israel. Furthermore, he encouraged all the people to praise God with him. Often David's personal praise became communal praise as he publicly glorified the Lord for His mercies, and so it should be with us today.

Psalm 64

"The first quality for a commander-in-chief is a cool head to receive a correct impression of things," said Napoleon I. "He should not allow himself to be confused by either good or bad news." David was probably serving in Saul's court when he wrote this psalm (1 Sam. 18-20). He knew that Saul was his enemy and wanted to kill him and that most of Saul's officers were in a conspiracy against him. Though he was the anointed king, David had no authority to oppose Saul, and eventually he had to flee and hide in the wilderness. People give us all kinds of trouble, but our battle is not against flesh and blood, but against Satan and his hosts (Eph. 6:10ff). This psalm instructs us what to do in the battles of life.

Seek the Lord's Protection (vv. 1-2)

Frequently David addressed the Lord by saying, "Hear my voice" or "Hear me when I call," not because God wasn't paying attention but because David was in earnest (4:1; 5:3; 27:7; 28:2; 39:12; 54:2; 55:17; 61:1; 64:1; 140:6; 143:1). The word translated "prayer" (v. 1, KJV) also means "complaint" or "trouble" (see 142:2). David didn't ask God to change the circumstances but to fortify his own heart and deliver him from fear. The fear of the Lord mobilizes us, but the fear of man paralyzes us. As a young courtier, loved by the people but envied and hated by the king, David face two problems: the secret conspiracy of Saul and his officers, and the open "tumult" (v. 2, NASB) of those who wanted to please Saul by oppressing David. "Insurrection" in verse 2 (KJV) doesn't suggest Absalom's rebellion, but rather what is described in 2:1-2 and 31:13. Lies about David were being passed from person to person and

David knew he wasn't safe in Saul's court. Both his life and his reputation were being attacked, and only the Lord could rescue him.

Ask for the Lord's Wisdom (vv. 3-6)

David knew exactly what the enemy was saying and doing, and we need to know the strategy of Satan when he attacks us (2 Cor. 2:11). As a lion, he comes to devour (1 Peter 5:8), and as a serpent, he comes to deceive (2 Cor. 11:1-4), and one of his chief weapons is accusation (Rev. 12:10; Zech. 3). David compared his enemies' tongues to swords (55:21; 57:4; 59:7) and their words to poisoned arrows (57:4; Prov. 25:18; 26:18-19; Jer. 9:8). But they also set traps for him, confident that nobody knew what they were doing, not even the Lord (10:11, 13; 12:4; 59:7). (For some of Saul's traps and how the Lord frustrated them, see 1 Sam. 18-19.) David knew that the human heart is "deep" ("cunning," NIV; see Jer. 17:9) and that there are always new dangers to avoid, so he constantly sought the Lord's wisdom as he made decisions. James 1:5 is a great promise to claim!

Trust the Lord for Victory (vv. 7-8)

By depending on the Lord and obeying His directions, David was confident that God would defeat his enemies. "Be strong in the Lord, and in the power of his might" (Eph. 6:10). David's enemies shot arrows at him suddenly (vv. 3-4), so the Lord suddenly shot arrows at them (v. 7). They tried to trip him and trap him (v. 5), so the Lord caused David's enemies to stumble and fall (v. 8, AMP). God would use their own sword-like tongues to fight against them, and they would end up in shame and disgrace (v. 8). The very weapons that the enemy uses against us, the Lord uses to defeat them.

Give Glory to the Lord (vv. 9-10)

As the nation watched the defeat of David's enemies and his exaltation as king, it all brought great glory to the Lord. Some people stood and shook their heads in disbelief (v. 8a). Dr. Bob Cook used to say, "If you can explain what's going on, the Lord didn't do it." Faith expects to see God do the impossible! The nation had a new fear of the Lord as they saw sin judged and their godly king vindicated (59:9-13). The people praised the Lord for what He had done, and as they worshiped, they meditated on His character and His purposes. It isn't enough to know the works of the Lord; we must also seek to understand His way and learn how to please Him (103:6-7). David's great concern was that the Lord be glorified, and that was why God blessed Him. Rejoice!

Psalm 65

This is the first of four psalms (65-68) that focus on praising the Lord for His manifold blessings in nature and for His gracious dealings with His people. He is the God of creation and the God of the covenant. The psalm acknowledges our total dependence on the Lord to provide both our spiritual and material needs. The phrase "crown the year" (v. 11) suggests a harvest festival in October, the first month of Israel's civil year. (The religious calendar opened with Passover; Ex. 12:2.) Perhaps verse 3 suggests the annual Day of Atonement that ushered in the Feast of Tabernacles, a harvest festival (Lev. 17; 23:26-44). The early rains usually began in late October, softening the hard soil and enabling the farmers to plow the ground and sow their seed (vv. 9-13). Perhaps God had disciplined His people by sending drought and famine (Lev. 26:3-6;

Deut. 11:8-17) and allowing other nations to threaten Israel (v. 7). This discipline brought them to repentance and they anticipated the promised rains and a blessed harvest from the Lord. David's unusual experience involving the Gibeonites might have been the occasion (2 Sam. 21:1-14). Whatever the historical setting, the psalm helps us to worship our great God and glorify Him for who He is and what He does for us.

He Is the Savior of Sinners (vv. 1-4)

The opening phrase is literally, "To you praise is silence," which doesn't convey very much. The *New American Standard Bible* combines both: "There will be silence before Thee, and praise in Zion, O God." The Hebrew word for "silence" is very similar to the word for "fitting, proper," so some translate it, "Praise is fitting for you," that is, "It is fitting that your people praise you." But silence is also a part of worship, and we must learn to wait quietly before the Lord (62:1). Israel has no sanctuary today, but one day the temple will be rebuilt (Ezek. 40-48; Dan. 9:20-27), and the Gentile nations will come and worship the true and living God (v. 2; Isa. 2:1-3; 56:7; Mic. 4:1-5; Mark 11:17).

Before we approach the Lord, we must confess our sins and trust Him for forgiveness (1 John 1:9, and see Ps. 15 and Isa. 6). The priests were chosen by God to serve in the sanctuary (Num. 16:5), but God wanted all of His "chosen people" to live like priests (Ex. 19:3-8; Deut. 7:6-11; Ps. 33:12). Believers today are "a kingdom of priests" (1 Peter 2:9-10; Rev. 1:5-6), chosen by the Lord, offering Him their praise and worship. What the Jewish worshipers had in their sanctuary, believers today have in Jesus Christ, and we find our complete satisfaction in Him. We have all these blessings only because of the grace of God, for He chose us (John 15:16).

He Is the Ruler of All Nations (vv. 5-8)

We move now from the people of Israel to all the nations of the world, and from God's grace to the Jews to God's government of the Gentiles. God performed "awesome deeds" for Israel (47:2-4; 66:1-7; 68:35; 89:5-10), and these gave witness to the pagan nations around them that Jehovah alone is the true and living God and the Lord of all nations (Rom. 9:17; Josh. 2:1-14; Acts 14:15-17; 17:26-28; Amos 1-2 and 9:7). He chose Israel to be a light to the Gentiles (Isa. 42:6; 49:6), and this was ultimately fulfilled in the coming of Christ to the world (Luke 2:32; Acts 13:47). Day and night, God's creation witnesses to the nations and they are without excuse (19:1-6; Rom. 1:18-25; 10:14-18). Jesus Christ is the only hope of the world. The "roaring seas" are a symbol of the nations in tumult and confusion (v. 7; Isa. 17:12-13; 60:5; Dan. 7:2-3; Rev. 13:1; 17:15). From the east to the west (sunrise to sunset), His name will be reverenced. What a missionary text! The nations of the earth need to know the Gospel of Jesus Christ so they can sings songs of joy to the Lord.

He Is the Provider of All We Need (vv. 9-13)

The psalm opened in the tiny land of Israel (God's grace) and moved from there to the nations of the earth (God's government). Now the entire universe comes into the picture, for the Creator of the universe provides the sunshine and rain in their times and seasons so that people can plow the earth, plant seeds, and eventually harvest food. (See Gen. 1, 8:20-9:17.) The emphasis is on God's goodness and generosity to His people. The rains come in abundance; the rivers and streams overflow; the harvest is plenteous; the grain wagons are full; and the grain spills into the wagon ruts. Why? Because God covenanted to care for the land of Israel and visit it with His blessing, if His people honored and obeyed Him (Deut. 11:8-15; Lev. 26:3-5).

This blessing was promised all during the year and year after year, even during the Sabbatical years when the people didn't cultivate the land (Lev. 25:1-22). According to verses 12-13, the "pastures of the wilderness" (uncultivated land) would produce vegetation and the hills would be clothed with beauty. The meadows would feed the flocks and herds, and the valleys would produce the grain. All of them would unite as one voiceless choir shouting for joy to the God of the universe, the Creator of every good and perfect gift. We can't read these verses without expressing appreciation and adoration to our God for His goodness and vowing not to waste food (John 6:12) or waste the precious land and resources He has given us. One day God will destroy them that destroy the earth (Rev. 11:18), who fail to see that we are stewards of His precious gifts.

Psalm 66

At the close of the previous psalm, you hear nature praising the Lord, and this psalm exhorts all mankind to join creation in celebrating God's greatness. It appears that Israel had gone through severe trials (vv. 8-12) and yet won a great victory with the Lord's help. Some students believe this event was the Lord's miraculous defeat of Assyria (Isa. 36-37) and that the individual speaking in verses 13-20 was King Hezekiah, whose prayer the Lord answered (37:14-20). The exhortation to praise the Lord begins with the Gentile nations (vv. 1-7), moves to Israel (vv. 8-12), and concludes with the individual believer (vv. 13-20).

A Global Invitation: "All Nations, Praise the Lord!" (vv. 1-7)

The psalmist invited all the Gentile nations to praise God for *what He had done for Israel!* Why? Because through Israel, the Lord brought truth and salvation to the Gentiles. "Salvation is of the Jews" (John 4:22). This is a missionary psalm showing the importance of taking the good news of Jesus Christ into all the world. God's purpose is that all the nations shall praise Him (98:4; 100:1; Rom. 15:9-12), but they can't do that until they trust Him (Rom. 10:1fl). It's tragic that the nations today attack and persecute Israel instead of thanking God for her spiritual contribution to them. But the nations don't know the Lord, and Israel has been blinded and hardened by her unbelief (Rom. 11:25ff). When Israel sees her Messiah and trusts Him, then the world situation will change (Zech. 13-14), and all the nations will worship the Lord. One day there shall be universal praise lifted for Jesus Christ (Phil. 2:10-11; Rev. 11:15-18).

The nations are invited to "come and see what the Lord has done," and the writer reviews some of the miraculous history of Israel: the Exodus from Egypt, the crossing of the Jordan, and the defeat of the nations in Canaan (vv. 5-7; see Ex. 15:18). The Exodus was the "birthday" of the Jewish nation and has always been Israel's main exhibition of the glorious power of the Lord (77:14-20; 78:12ff; 106:7-12; 114; 136:13; Isa. 63:10-14). What the resurrection of Jesus Christ is to believers today, the Exodus was to Israel (Eph. 1:15-23). The Jews remember the Exodus at Passover, and the church remembers the death and resurrection of Christ at the Lord's Supper. "God's work is never antiquated," wrote Alexander Maclaren. "It is all a revelation of eternal activities. What He has been, He is. What He did, He does. Therefore faith may feed on all the records of old time and expect the repetition of all that they contain." (*Expositor's Bible* [Eerdmans, six vol. edition], vol. 3, p. 170).

A National Proclamation: "Israel, Praise the Lord!" (vv. 8-12)

If any nation has reason to praise the Lord, it is Israel; for He rescued them from slavery, guided them through the wilderness, took them into their land, and enabled them to defeat their enemies and claim their inheritance. He gave them His law, His sanctuary, and His priests and prophets, and He blessed them with all they needed. When they disobeyed, He disciplined them. Like a careful craftsman, He put them through the furnace and removed the impurities. (See 17:3; 26:2; Jer. 9:7; Mal. 3:2-3; 1 Peter 1:6-7; 4:12.) When they turned to the Lord, He transformed their sufferings into blessings and enlarged them (v. 12; see 4:1; 18:19, 36; 25:17). So it has been with the church. When the Lord has permitted persecution, this has invariably led to growth and blessing. We can go through fire and water and be the better for it (Isa. 43:2).

A Personal Affirmation: "Praise God with Me!" (vv. 13-20)

The change from "we/our" to "I/my" is significant, for corporate worship is the ministry of many individuals, and God sees each heart. During his times of trial, the psalmist had made vows to God, and now he hastened to fulfill them. He brought many burnt offerings to the altar, the very best he had, and they symbolized his total dedication to the Lord. We today obey Romans 12:1-2 and present ourselves as living sacrifices. When the Lord does something wonderful for us, we ought to share this with other believers and help to strengthen their faith. The entire Bible is a record of God's gracious dealings with His people, and while our words are not inspired, our witness can bring glory to the Lord. Prayer and praise go together (v. 17).

The verb "regard" (v. 18) means "to recognize and to cherish, to be unwilling to confess and forsake known sins." It means approving that which God condemns. When we recognize sin in our hearts, we must immediately judge it, confess it, and forsake it (1 John 1:5-10); otherwise, the Lord can't work on our behalf (Isa. 59:1-2). To cover sin is to invite trouble and discipline (Prov. 28:13; Josh. 7).

Psalm 67

Except for verses 1 and 6, each verse in this brief psalm mentions "all nations" or "all peoples," and in that respect fits in with Psalms 65 and 66. It's a psalm of praise to God for all His blessings, as well as a prayer to God that His blessings will flow out to the Gentiles, especially His salvation. This was part of God's covenant with Abraham (Gen. 12:1-3). A blessing is a gift from God that glorifies His name, helps His people, and through them reaches out to help others who will glorify His name. God blesses us that we might be a blessing to others. The psalm describes the stages in this sequence.

Israel Blesses the Nations (vv. 1-2)
This prayer asks God to bless Israel so that His ways (laws) and His salvation

might be known ("experienced personally") throughout the world. It's adapted from the High Priestly prayer in Numbers 6:24-26, with the psalmist using Elohim instead of Jehovah. (Other references to this prayer are 4:6; 29:11; 31:16; 80:3, 7, 19.) The glory of God was an important part of Israel's heritage (Rom. 9:1-5), for God's glory led Israel through the wilderness and rested over the tabernacle wherever the nation camped. To have the light of God's countenance smile upon them was the height of Israel's blessing, and to lose that glory meant judgment (1 Sam. 4, especially vv. 21-22). The prophet Ezekiel watched the glory depart before the temple was destroyed (Ezek. 8:4; 9:3; 10:4, 18; 11:22-23). God's people today have God's glory within (1 Cor. 6:19-20; 2 Cor. 4:6), and in our good works, godly character, and loving ministry we should reveal that glory to the world (Matt. 5:16; Phil. 2:14-16). In the same manner, Israel was to be a light and a blessing to the nations (Isa. 42:6; 49:6-7; Acts 13:47). Israel gave us the knowledge of the true and living God, the Word of God and the Son of God, Jesus Christ, the Savior of the world.

The Nations Praise the Lord (vv. 3-5)
These three verses form the heart of the psalm and focus on the Gentile nations worshiping and praising the God of Israel. Today, the nations have conspired to dethrone the Lord, and they want nothing of "his ways" (2:1-3), but the day will come when all the nations will come to the mountain of the Lord and worship the God of Jacob (Isa. 2:1-5). The *New International Version* translates these verses as a prayer, "May the peoples praise you ... ." When will this occur? When Jesus Christ establishes His kingdom, judges the peoples with justice, and

guides ("shepherds"—Mic. 5:2; Matt. 2:6) the nations in the ways of the Lord. The prayer in these verses is the Old Testament equivalent of "Thy kingdom come" in the Lord's Prayer (Matt. 6:9-13). Because there is no king in Israel today, the nations of the world are doing as they please (Judg. 17:6; 18:11; 19:1; 21:25), but that will all change when the kingdoms of the world belong to Jesus Christ (Rev. 11:15).

The Lord Sends the Harvest (vv. 6-7)
What does the harvest have to do with the conversion of the nations of the world? The phrase "Then the land shall yield her increase" (v. 6) is a quotation from Leviticus 26:4, and Leviticus 26 is a summary of God's covenant with Israel. (See also Deut. 28-30.) God made it clear that His blessing on the land depended on Israel's obedience to His law (Lev. 26:1-13). The blessings He would send Israel would be a witness to the pagan nations that Jehovah alone is the true and living God, and this would give the Jews opportunity to share the Word with them (Deut. 28:1-14). But if Israel disobeyed the Lord, He would withhold the rain and their fields would yield no harvest (Lev. 26:14-39), and this would put Israel to shame before the Gentile nations (Jer. 33:1-9; Joel 2:17-19; Deut. 9:26-29). Why would "all the ends of the earth" fear a God who didn't provide food for His own people? The application to the church today is obvious: as we obey the Lord, pray and trust Him, He provides what we need, and the unsaved around us see that He cares for us. This gives us opportunity to tell them about Jesus. While verse 6 speaks of a literal harvest, it also reminds us of the "spiritual harvest" that comes as we witness for the Lord (John 4:34-38).

God blesses the nations through His people Israel and through His church, and all the nations should trust Him, obey Him, and fear Him.

Psalm 68

Read the "Song of Deborah" (Judg. 5) as preparation for studying this psalm, and compare the parallels: Ps. 68:4/Judg. 5:3, 7-8/4-5, 12/30, 13/16, 18/12, and 27/14, 18. The emphasis is on God's mighty acts on behalf of Israel resulting in His decision to dwell on Mount Zion. Several names of God are used, including Elohim (23 times), Jehovah, Jah (short for Jehovah, as in hallelujah, Elijah, etc.), Adonai (6 times), and Shaddai. The psalm is Messianic; Paul quotes verse 18 in Ephesians 4:8 and applies it to the ascension of Christ. The use of "temple" in verse 29 doesn't prohibit Davidic authorship since the word *hekal* was applied to the tabernacle as well (1 Sam. 1:9; 3:3; and see Pss. 5:7; 41:4; 18:6; 27:4; 65:4). The psalm is a jubilant hymn of praise to Jehovah in which the nation of Israel gives four expressions of triumph through their God.

Our God Is Coming to Us (vv. 1-6)
Verse 1 is a quotation from Numbers 10:33-35, Israel's "marching cry" whenever they set out on their journeys. The quotation is fitting because the psalm pictures the Lord "on the march" on behalf of His people. He fights their battles, leads them into the land of their inheritance, and takes up residence in the sanctuary on Mt. Zion. The enemies of Israel are blown away like smoke (37:20) and melted like wax (97:5), while the righteous (Israel) rejoice at God's works and sing His praises. The phrase "extol him

who rides upon the heavens" or "upon the clouds" (v. 4, KJV, NIV) should probably read "cast up a highway for him who rides through the deserts" (AMP). It's the picture of an oriental monarch and his entourage approaching a town, and the citizens clearing away the obstacles on the road (Isa. 40:3; 57:14; 62:10; Matt. 3:1-3). The coming of the King encourages the helpless people, especially the orphans and widows, the lonely, and those imprisoned unjustly (vv. 5-6; see Deut. 10:18-19; 27:17-19; Luke 4:16-19). But the rebels had better be careful! They might be cast out of the Promised Land that flows with milk and honey!

Our God Is Marching Before Us
(vv. 7-18)
David reviewed the triumphant march of Israel, beginning with their exodus from Egypt and the journey to Sinai (vv. 7-8). (See Ex. 12-19, especially 19:9 and 16.) The rain can be taken literally, but it might also refer to the manna that came down six days a week (Ps. 78:24, 27; Ex. 16:4; Deut. 11:10-12). Then Israel entered the land and conquered it (vv. 9-14) because the Lord spoke the Word of victory (v. 11; see 33:11). He had promised Israel they would take the land, and they did (Ex. 23:20-33; Deut. 11:22-32). As at the Exodus (Ex. 15:20-21), it was the women who sang the praises of the Lord. (See also v. 25, Judg. 5 and 1 Sam. 18:6-7.) Students have long been puzzled by verses 13-14 and don't always agree on either their translations or their interpretations. There appears to be a reference to the "Song of Deborah" in Judges 5:15-18 where she shamed Reuben for staying home and not fighting the enemy, but praised Benjamin, Zebulun, and Naphtali for joining in the battle. These three tribes are commended in 68:27, but we don't know of any tribes

that failed to participate in the conquering of Canaan. The *New Living Translation* interprets verses 12-14: "Enemy kings and their armies flee, while the women of Israel divide the plunder. Though they lived among the sheepfolds, now they are covered with silver and gold, as a dove is covered by its wings. The Almighty scattered the enemy kings like a blowing snowstorm on Mount Zalmon." Israel is compared to a turtledove in 74:19.

But God conquered Canaan, not only to give His people a home but also to secure a "home" for Himself. He chose Mount Zion, though it was much smaller and less imposing than Mount Hermon, which is over 9,000 feet high, perhaps the highest mountain in Palestine. David pictured the other mountains showing jealousy because they weren't selected. God made a temporary visit to His people when He came down on Mount Sinai (Ex. 23:16), but Zion was to be His permanent dwelling place (132:13-14; 1 Kings 8:12-13). The "chariots of God" make up His heavenly army, for He is the Lord of Hosts (46:7, 11; 2 Kings 2:11; 6:17; Dan. 7:10; Matt. 26:53). To "ascend on high" means to win the victory and return in triumph (47:1-6). Some think this refers to a time when the ark was "in the field" with the army and then brought back to the sanctuary on Zion (2 Sam. 11:11; 12:26-31). Paul quoted verse 18 in Ephesians 4:8 when referring to the ascension of Christ (see also Acts 2:30-36; Col. 2:15). A king ascending the throne both receives and gives gifts, and even those who reject him will honor him outwardly.

Our God Is Dwelling with Us
(vv. 19-27)
David saw the Lord's presence on Zion as a blessing first of all to those who were burdened and in danger. Jehovah our

King bears our burdens and defeats our enemies. Certainly David saw the Lord win great victories for Israel so that the borders of the kingdom were greatly enlarged. "Hairy crowns" (v. 21) signifies the virile enemy warriors who trusted in their youth and strength. The enemy may flee, but the Lord will chase them down and bring them back from the tops of the mountains and the depths of the sea, from the east (Bashan) and the west (the sea). (See Amos 9:1-3.) The picture in verse 23 isn't a pretty one, but "dogs licking blood" was a common phrase for the most complete kind of judgment and humiliation (58:10; 1 Kings 21:17-24; 2 Kings 9:30-37).

The King now receives the homage of His people who gladly say, "My God, My King." (vv. 24-27). Both men and women, lay people and priests, join in praising the Lord. Zion was situated at the border of Judah and Benjamin; David came from Judah and King Saul from Benjamin. As the youngest of the sons of Jacob, and perhaps as the tribe of Israel's first king, Benjamin leads the procession along with the leaders of Judah (representing the southern tribes), and the leaders of Zebulun and Naphtali (the northern tribes). Israel is a united people, praising the Lord. "Fountain of Israel" (v. 26) refers to the Lord (NASB, and see 36:9) or the patriarchs, especially Jacob (AMP).

Our God Receives Universal Tribute (vv. 28-35)

This closing section has prophetic overtones as it describes the Gentile nations submitting to Jehovah, the God of Israel, and bringing Him their worship (Isa. 2:1-4; Rev. 21:24). Until the Lord reigns in Jerusalem, there can be no peace on earth (Isa. 9:6-7; 11:1-9). God will defeat Israel's old enemy Egypt, along with her allies

(see Ezek. 29), and they will send envoys to Jerusalem with tribute. The Gentile nations will join Israel in singing praises to the Lord and extolling His majesty and power. Perhaps the sanctuary of verse 35 is the one described in Ezekiel 40-48. It certainly is awesome!

Psalm 69

This is a Messianic psalm, an imprecatory psalm, and after 22 and 110, the most frequently quoted psalm in the New Testament. It is attributed to David and has definite affinities with 35, 40, and 109, which are also Davidic psalms. But what about verses 35-36? When during David's reign did the cities of Judah need to be rebuilt and the people brought back home? When were the drunkards singing about him in the gates (v. 12) and his enemies about to destroy him (vv. 4, 18-19)? Selected data from the psalm fits the times of both Jeremiah and Hezekiah, but it is difficult to fit everything into the times of David. Perhaps David's original psalm ended at verse 29 and the Holy Spirit directed the prophet Jeremiah to add verses 30-36 after the fall of Judah and Jerusalem to the Babylonians. The collection of psalms was a "living heritage" and some of the psalms were adapted to new occasions. Whatever the answer, when you read the psalm, you find the author confronting the Lord with three important concerns.

Deliverance: "Save Me!" (vv. 1-18)

He begins by asking for deliverance for *his own sake (vv. 1-5)* and describes his dangerous situation with the metaphor of a drowning man. (See 18:4-6; 30:1; 32:6; 42:7; 88:7, 17; 130:1-2.) His cries to God show how desperate the situation was:

"Save me" (v. 1); "deliver me" (v. 14); "hear [answer] me" (vv. 16-17); "redeem [rescue] me" (v. 18); "set me up on high [protect me]" (v. 29). He had prayed to the Lord, but the Lord had not yet answered (v. 3), and he wanted an answer now! (v. 17). Though he was not sinless (v. 5), he was innocent of the charges his enemies were making, and yet he was being treated as though he were guilty (v. 4). This reminds us of our Savior, who was sinless yet treated like a transgressor (Isa. 53:5-6, 9, 12). (See also 35:11-19; 38:19; 109:3; 119:78, 86, 161.) Jesus quoted verse 4 in the upper room discourse (John 15:25). Referring to verses 1-2, Amy Carmichael wrote, "Our waters are shallow because His were deep." How true!

His second reason for praying for deliverance was *for the Lord's sake (vv. 6-12)*, because those who lied about David were blaspheming the name of the Lord. David did not want God's people to suffer shame because of him (v. 6; see 25:3; 38:15-16). The word "reproach" (scorn, insults) is used six times in the psalm (vv. 7, 9, 10, 19, 20). He was scorned because he stood up for the Lord (v. 7) and because he was zealous for God's house (v. 9). He even alienated his own family (v. 8; see John 7:5; Mark 3:31-35), and the insults that people threw at the Lord also fell on him (v. 9; John 2:17; Rom. 15:3; and see Isa. 56:7 and Jer. 7:11). When they blasphemed God, they blasphemed David, and their attacks against David were attacks against God, and David felt them. David had a great zeal for God's house and received the plans for the temple from the Lord and gathered the materials for its construction. It takes no special gift to discover Jesus in this psalm and to see the way people treated Him when He was ministering on earth.

His third argument for deliverance is based on *the character of God (vv. 13-18)*. What the Lord said to Moses in Exodus 34:5-9 is reflected here. In verses 14 and 15, David repeats the metaphor from verses 1-2, but he sees hope in God's lovingkindness and compassion, for the Lord is merciful and gracious. His truth endures and He will always keep His promises.

Vindication: "Judge My Enemies!" (vv. 19-29)

David told the Lord that his foes had dishonored and insulted him to the point that he was physically ill (vv. 19-21). When he looked for sympathy, none was to be found (Matt. 26:37), and his food and drink were unfit for human consumption (v. 21; Matt. 27:34, 48; Mark 15:23, 36; Luke 23:36; John 19:29). Then David prayed that the Lord would judge his enemies and give them what they deserved (vv. 22-29). (For a discussion of this type of prayer, see the comments on Ps. 5.) The enemy had put gall and vinegar on David's table, so he prayed that their tables would turn into traps. This meant that judgment would catch them unprepared in their careless hours of feasting (1 Thess. 5:3). It could also apply to the feasts associated with the sacrifices. While rejoicing after worship, they would experience God's judgment. In Romans 11:9-10, Paul applied verses 22-23 to Israel whose religious complacency ("We just sacrificed to the Lord!") only led to spiritual blindness. In verses 22-25, David prayed that some of the basic blessings of life would be taken away from his enemies—eating, seeing, walking, and having descendants—and then that life itself would be snatched from them! (vv. 27-28). In Acts 1:20, Peter applied verse 25 to Judas.

David asked in verse 28 that his enemies be slain, blotted out of the book of the living. Even more, he didn't want them identified with the righteous after they died, which meant they were destined for eternal judgment. While this kind of prayer is hardly an example for God's people today (Matt. 6:12; Luke 23:34), we can understand David's hatred of their sins and his desire to protect Israel and its mission in the world.

Praise: "Be Glorified, O Lord!" (vv. 30-36)

Perhaps this is a promise David made to the Lord, and no doubt he fulfilled it. He wanted the Lord to be glorified in his worship (vv. 30-31), his witness to the needy (vv. 32-33), in all of creation (v. 34), and in all of Israel (vv. 35-36). He asked the Lord to protect and provide for the poor whom the sinners were abusing and exploiting. He saw a day coming when the land would be united and healed and the cities populated again. "Pray for the peace of Jerusalem" (122:6). "Even so, come, Lord Jesus!" (Rev. 22:21).

Psalm 70

With a few minor changes, this is a duplicate of 40:13-16.

Psalm 71

The psalm is anonymous, written by a believer who had enemies and needed the Lord's help and protection (vv. 4, 10, 13, 24). He was probably past middle age and was greatly concerned about the burdens of old age (vv. 9, 18). He wanted to end well. From birth he had been sustained by the Lord (v. 6), and in his youth he had

been taught by the Lord (v. 17). He may have been one of the many temple musicians assigned to praise God in the sanctuary day and night (vv. 22-24; 134:1). Whoever he was, he made four affirmations about the Lord and the help He gives to those who call on him and trust him.

"The Lord Helps Me Now" (vv. 1-4)

The first three verses are adapted from 31:1-3, a perfectly legitimate practice among psalmists. This writer borrowed from 22, 31, 35, and 40, to name just a few of his sources. On verse 1, see 7:1, 11:1, 16:1, 22:5, 25:2 and 20, and 31:17. (On the image of the rock, see 18:2.) If the author was indeed a temple musician, his mind and heart would have been filled with the psalms that he had sung in the sanctuary day after day. He asked the Lord to protect and deliver him so that he might remain true to the faith and not be ashamed (1 John 2:28). During the decadent years of the kingdom of Judah, some of the rulers promoted worshiping idols along with the worship of Jehovah and pressured the Levites to compromise. The writer didn't want to run away and hide from life but receive the strength needed to face life with its challenges. The Lord was his habitation (90:1) and his help. "Righteousness" is mentioned five times in the psalm (vv. 2, 15, 16, 19, 24) and refers not only to one of God's attributes but also to His faithfulness in keeping His word. A righteous God is active in helping His people in their times of need. He issues the command and the deed is done (v. 3; 33:9; 44:4; 68:28). His people can always come to Him (v. 3; Heb. 10:19-25), always praise Him (vv. 6, 8, 15, 24), and always hope in Him (v. 14). He never fails. Perhaps verse 4 describes evil people who exploited the poor and helpless, which could include the Levites, who had no inheritance in

Israel but lived by the gifts of God's people (Deut. 10:8-9; Num. 18:20-24). They served from age twenty-five to age fifty (Num. 8:23-26), so perhaps our psalmist was approaching retirement age and was concerned about his future.

"The Lord Helped Me in the Past" (vv. 5-13)

When you are discouraged and worried, look back and count your blessings. Remind yourself of the faithfulness of the Lord. Like Samuel erect your own "Ebenezer" and say, "Thus far the Lord has helped us" (1 Sam. 7:12, NASB). From conception to birth, and from birth to young manhood, the Lord had been with the psalmist, and He was not about to abandon him now or in his old age (22:9-10; 37:25; 92:14; 139:13-16). Hope doesn't end with retirement! (vv. 5, 15). (See 1 Tim. 1:1; Col. 1:27; Heb. 6:18-19; 1 Peter 1:3.)

The word "portent" means a sign or wonder, a special display of God's power, such as the plagues of Egypt. Sometimes the Lord selected special people to be signs to the nation (Isa. 8:18; Zech. 3:8), and sometimes those portents were messengers of warning (Deut. 28:45-48). Paul saw himself and the other apostles as "portents" to honor the Lord and shame the worldly believers (1 Cor. 4:8-13). The writer of this psalm must have been a high profile person because people knew him well and saw the things that happened to him. Apparently he had endured many troubles during his life but didn't falter or deny the Lord. His entire life was a wonder, a testimony to others of the goodness and faithfulness of the Lord (vv. 20-2 1). His enemies were sure the Lord would forsake him, but he was sure the Lord would *never* forsake him (Heb. 13:5). His enemies tried to bring reproach on him, but he trusted the Lord to uphold him and to turn their reproach back upon them.

"The Lord Will Help Me in the Future" (vv. 14-21)

The psalmist looked to the future and moved from "You are my hope" (v. 8) to "I will hope continually" (v. 14; see 36:5; 47:10). The future is secure when Jesus is your Lord. The word translated "hope" in verse 14 means a long and patient waiting in spite of delays and disappointments. If we trust God, then the trials of life will work for us and not against us and will lead to glory (2 Cor. 4:16-18; Rom. 5:1-5). We admire the psalmist's "But as for me" in verse 14 (NIV, NASB) because it reveals his courage and commitment. Others may drift with the crowd and deny the Lord, but he would continue to be faithful and bear witness of God's mercies. He couldn't begin to measure or count the Lord's righteous acts or "deeds of salvation" (v. 15 AMP), but he would never stop praising the Lord, especially in old age. Why? Because he wanted to tell the next generation what the Lord could do for them (v. 18; see 48:13; 78:4, 6; 79:13; 102:18; 145:4; 2 Tim. 2:2).

He was even certain that death would not separate him from his God (vv. 19-21). Some believe that the phrase "depths of the earth" is a metaphor for the troubles he had experienced ("buried under trouble"), but his trials were pictured in verses 1-2 as floods of water. Also, some texts read "us" instead of "me," which could refer to the future "resurrection" and restoration of the nation of Israel (80:3, 19; 85:4; Ezek. 37). Perhaps both personal (16:8-11; 17:15; 49:15) and national resurrection are involved. No matter what his enemies had said about him, the day would come when God would honor him and reward him.

**"The Lord Be Praised for His Help!"
(vv. 22-24)**

The writer was a poet, a singer, and an instrumentalist, and he used all his gifts to praise the Lord. The divine name "Holy One of Israel" is used thirty times in Isaiah but only three times in the Psalms (71:22; 78:41; 89:18). The name connects with the emphasis in the psalm on God's righteousness. "Shall not the judge of all the earth do right?" (Gen. 18:25). The psalmist sang and shouted all day long (vv. 24, 8), not just during the stated services at the temple. He opened the psalm with a request that he would never be put to shame and confusion, and now he closed the psalm with the assurance that *his enemies* would be put to shame and confusion! He had looked back at a life of trials and blessings from the Lord; he had looked around at his enemies; he had looked ahead at old age and its problems; and he had even looked down into the depths of the earth (v. 20). But it was when he looked up and realized that God's righteousness "reaches to the heavens" (v. 19, NASB; see 36:5; 57:10; 108:4) that he grew in confidence and left his worries with the Lord. This is a good example for us to follow.

Psalm 72

Solomon is connected with this psalm and 127. If the inscription is translated "of Solomon," then he was the author and wrote of himself in the third person. This would make it a prayer for God's help as he sought to rule over the people of Israel. But if the inscription is translated "for Solomon," David may have been the author (v. 20), and the psalm would be a prayer for the people to use to ask God's blessing upon their new king. If Solomon did write the psalm, then it had to be in the early years of his reign, for in his later years, he turned from the Lord (1 Kings 11; Prov. 14:34). But beyond both David and Solomon is the Son of David and the one "greater than Solomon" (Matt. 12:42), Jesus Christ, the Messiah of Israel. The psalm is quoted nowhere in the New Testament as referring to Jesus, but certainly it describes the elements that will make up the promised kingdom when Jesus returns.

A Righteous King (vv. 1-7)

The Lord was King over His people, and the man on the throne in Jerusalem was His representative, obligated to lead the people according to the law of God (Deut. 17:14-20). He had to be impartial in his dealings (Ex. 23:3, 6; Deut. 1:17; Isa. 16:5) and make sure that his throne was founded on righteousness and justice (89:14; 92:2). When the Lord asked Solomon what coronation gift he wanted, the inexperienced young man asked for wisdom, and God granted His request (1 Kings 3:1-15). One of his first judgmental decisions revealed this wisdom (1 Kings 3:16-28). Note that righteousness is mentioned four times in verses 1-3 and 7, and see Proverbs 16:12. Messiah will one day reign in righteousness and execute justice throughout the world (Isa. 9:7 and 11:4-5; Jer. 23:5-6; Zech. 9:9). In the whole land of Israel, from the mountains to the hills, Solomon's reign would bring peace and prosperity, for both of these blessings depend on righteousness (Isa. 32:17). It is because Jesus fulfilled God's righteousness in His life and death that sinners can be forgiven and have peace with God (Rom. 5:1-8), and He is our "King of righteousness" and "King of peace" (Heb. 7:1-3). Solomon's name is related to the Hebrew word *shalom* which means "peace, prosperity, well-being." The king's ministry to the poor and afflicted reminds us of the ministry of Jesus (vv. 2, 4, 12-14; Matt. 9:35-38). Early in his reign, Solomon had that kind of concern, but in his later life, his values changed, and he burdened the people with heavy taxes (1 Kings 12:1-16; 4:7; 5:13-15).

"Long live the king!" is the burden of verses 5 and 15, as long as the sun and moon endure (89:29, 36-37; 1 Sam. 10:24; 1 Kings 1:31, 34, 39; Dan. 2:4). God promised David an endless dynasty (2 Sam. 7:16, 19,26), and this was fulfilled in Jesus, the Son of David (Luke 1:31-33). The image of the rain (vv. 6-7) reminds us that a righteous king would encourage righteousness in the people, and a righteous people would receive God's promised blessings, according to His covenant (Lev. 26:1-13; Deut. 11:11-17; 28:8-14). David used a similar metaphor in 2 Samuel 23:34. Godly leaders are like the refreshing rain that makes the land fruitful and beautiful, so that even the newly mown fields will produce a second crop. They are also like lamps that light the way (2 Sam. 21:17), shields that protect (84:9; 89:16), and the very breath of life that sustains us (Lam. 4:20). Alas, very few of the kings who reigned after David were models of godliness.

A Universal Dominion (vv. 8-11)

God promised Abraham that he would give his descendants all the land from the River of Egypt in the south to the Euphrates in the north (Gen. 15:18), and He reaffirmed this promise through Moses (Ex. 23:31). Both David and Solomon ruled over great kingdoms (1 Kings 4:21, 24; 1 Chron. 9:26), but neither of them ruled "from the river [Euphrates] to the ends of the earth" (v. 8). This privilege is reserved for Jesus Christ (2:8; Zech. 9:9-10; Mic. 4:1-5; Luke 1:33). David gained the kingdom through conquest, and left it to his son who strengthened it by means of treaties. His marriages to the daughters of neighboring kings were guarantees that these nations would cooperate with Solomon's foreign policy. Even Sheba and the nomadic tribes in Arabia would pay tribute to Solomon, and so would Seba in Upper Egypt; and kings as far away as Tarshish in Spain would submit to him. (See 1 Kings 4:21, 34; 10:14-15, 24-25; 2 Chron. 9:23-24.) But there is only one King of kings, and that is Jesus Christ, the Son of God (Isa. 2:1-4; Dan. 7:13-14; Rev. 17:14; 19:16). There can be no peace on earth until the Prince of Peace is reigning, and the nations have submitted to Him.

A Compassionate Reign (vv. 12-14).

The king of Israel was looked upon as God's shepherd who lovingly cared for God's flock (78:70-72; 100:3; Ezek. 34). Any citizen had access to the king to get help in solving legal problems, and the king was to make certain that the local judges were being fair and honest in their decisions. Solomon didn't reach this ideal even though he had a vast bureaucracy, but unfortunately his officers didn't always aid the people (Eccl. 4:1). The picture here is surely that of our Savior who had such great compassion for the needy and met their needs (Matt. 9:3 6). Not only does He hold their blood (life) precious to Him (v. 14; 116:15), but He shed His own precious blood for the salvation of the world (1 Peter 1:19). The word "redeem" ("rescue," NASB, NIV) is used for the "kinsman redeemer" illustrated by Boaz in the book of Ruth.

A Prosperous Nation (vv. 15-17)

God's covenant with Israel assured them of prosperity so long as the rulers and the people obeyed His commandments. The Lord also assured David that he would always have an heir to his throne if he and his descendants obeyed God's will (2 Sam. 7:11-12, 16). Because of the promise of the coming Savior, it was important that the Davidic dynasty continue. But in the case of Jesus, He reigns "according to the power of an endless life" (Heb. 7:16). He is the life (John 14:6) and He is alive forever (Rev. 1:18). He is King forever!

Israel's prosperity would be not only political (the king), but also economic (gold), spiritual (prayer), and commercial (thriving crops). In fulfillment of His covenant with Abraham (Gen. 12:1-3), God would bless all the nations through Israel, as He has done in sending Jesus Christ (Gal. 3). The prophets wrote of this glorious kingdom and their prophecies will be fulfilled (Isa. 35 and 60–62; Ezek. 40–48; Amos 9:11-15; Mic. 4; Zech. 10 and 14). There will be abundant grain even on top of the hills in the most unproductive land. The grain fields will look like the forests of the cedars in Lebanon (1 Kings 4:33).

The closing benediction (vv. 18-19) is not a part of the psalm proper but forms the conclusion to Book II of the book of Psalms (see 41:13; 89:52; 106:48). A fitting conclusion it is, for it focuses on the glory of the Lord. Solomon's kingdom had its share of glory, but the glory did not last. When Jesus reigns on earth, the glory of God will be revealed as never before (Num. 14:21; Isa. 6:3; 11:9; 40:5; Hab. 2:14).

Isaac Watts used Psalm 72 as the basis for his great hymn "Jesus Shall Reign." Read it—or sing it—and never stop praying, "Thy kingdom come!"

BOOK III
Psalm 73

Asaph, Heman, and Ethan (Jeduthun) were Levites who served as musicians and worship leaders at the sanctuary during David's reign (1 Chron. 15:16-19; 16:4-7, 37-42; 2 Chron. 5:12-14; 29:13; 35:15). Apparently they established "guilds" for their sons and other musicians so they might carry on the worship traditions. Twelve psalms are attributed to Asaph (50, 73-83). This one deals with the age-old problem of why the righteous suffer while the ungodly seem to prosper (37; 49; Job 21; Jer. 12; Hab. 1:13ff). Asaph could not lead the people in divine worship if he had questions about the ways of the Lord, but he found in that worship the answer to his problems. Note five stages in his experience.

The Believer: Standing on What He Knows (v.1)

The French mystic Madame Guyon wrote, "In the commencement of the spiritual life, our hardest task is to bear with our neighbor; in its progress, with ourselves; and in the end, with God." Asaph's problems were with God. Asaph affirmed "God is," so he was not an atheist or an agnostic, and he was certain that the God he worshiped was good. Furthermore, he knew that the Lord had made a covenant with Israel that promised blessings if the people obeyed Him (Lev. 26; Deut. 28-30). The phrase "a clean [pure] heart" means, not sinlessness, but total commitment to the Lord, the opposite of verse 27. (See 24:4 and Matt. 5:8.) But it was these foundational beliefs he stated that created the problem for him, because unbelievers don't face problems of this sort. If the Lord was good and kept His covenant promises, why were His people suffering and the godless prospering? This first verse marked both the beginning and the end of his meditations. He came full circle. Note that he used "surely" or "truly" in verses 1, 13, and 18, and that "heart" is used six times in the psalm (vv. 1, 7, 13, 21, 26). When pondering the mysteries of life, hold on to what you know for sure, and never doubt in the darkness what God has taught you in the light.

The Doubter: Slipping from Where He Is Standing (vv. 2-3)

The Hebrew word translated "but" in verses 2 and 28, and "nevertheless" (yet) in verse 28, indicates a sharp contrast. In verse 2, the more he measured his situation against that of the ungodly, the more he began to slip from his firm foundation. There is a difference between doubt and unbelief. Doubt comes from a struggling mind, while unbelief comes from a stubborn will that refuses surrender to God (v. 7). The unbelieving person *will not believe*, while the doubting person struggles to believe but cannot. "Prosperity" in verse 3 is the familiar Hebrew word *shalom*. It's an act of disobedience to envy the wicked (37:1; Prov. 3:31; 23:17; 24:1, 19).

The Wrestler: Struggling with What He Sees and Feels (vv. 4-14)

From Asaph's viewpoint, the ungodly "had it made." They were healthy (vv. 4-5) and had no struggles in either life or death (Job 21:13,23). They were proud of their wealth and stations in life, and they wore that pride like jewelry. They used violence to get their wealth and wore that violence like rich garments. Like an overflowing river, their hard hearts and evil minds produced endless ideas for getting richer, and

they frequently spoke words of opposition against the Lord in heaven. The words of the arrogant would "strut through the land" and take possession of whatever they wanted. But the greatest tragedy is that many of God's people don't seem to know any better but follow their bad example and enjoy their friendship! (v. 10). These ungodly men are sinning, but their foolish followers are "drinking it all up." (For drinking as a metaphor for sinning, see Job 15:16; 34:7; Prov. 4:17; 19:28; Rev. 14:8.) To encourage their hard hearts and quiet their evil consciences, the wicked affirmed that God didn't know what they were doing (Ps. 10).

Based on the evidence he could see around him, Asaph came to the wrong conclusion that he has wasted his time and energy maintaining clean hands and a pure heart (vv. 13 and 1, and see 24:4 and 26:6). If he had ever read the book of Job, then he had missed its message, for we don't serve God because of what we get out of it but because *He is worthy of our worship and service regardless of what He allows to come to our lives.* Satan has a commercial view of the life of faith and encourages us to serve God for what we get out of it (Job 1-2), and Asaph almost bought into that philosophy. (See also Dan. 3:16-18.)

The Worshiper: Seeing the Bigger Picture (vv. 15-22)

Before going public with his philosophy and resigning his office, Asaph paused to consider the consequences. How would the younger believers in the land respond if one of the three sanctuary worship leaders turned his back on Jehovah, the covenants, and the faith? To abandon the faith would mean undermining all that he had taught and sung at the sanctuary! The more he pondered the problem, the more his heart was pained (see vv. 21-22), So he decided to go to the sanctuary and spend time with the Lord in worship. There he would be with other people, hear the Word and the songs of praise, and be a part of the worshiping community. After all, Jehovah isn't a problem to wrestle with but a gracious Person to love and worship—especially when you are perplexed by what he is doing. God is awesome in His sanctuary (68:35, NIV), and when we commune with Him, we see the things of this world in their right perspective.

Asaph did get a new perspective on the problem when he considered, not the circumstances around him but the destiny before him. He realized that what he saw in the lives of the prosperous, ungodly people was not a true picture but only pretense: "you will despise them as fantasies" (v. 20, NIV). In New Testament language, "the world is passing away, and the lust of it ..." (1 John 2:17, NKJV). Although God can and does give success and wealth to dedicated believers, worldly success and prosperity belong to the transient dream world of unbelievers, a dream that one day will become a nightmare. (See Luke 12:16-21.) Asaph was humbled before the Lord and regained his spiritual balance.

The Conqueror: Rejoicing over God's Goodness (vv. 23-28)

The psalm opened with "Truly God is good to Israel," but Asaph wasn't sure what the word "good" really meant. (See Matt. 19:16-17.) Is the "good life" one of wealth and authority, pomp and pleasure? Surely not! The contrast is striking between Asaph's picture of the godless life in verses 4-12 and the godly life in verses 23-28. The ungodly impress each other and attract admirers, but they don't

have God's presence with them. The Lord upholds the righteous but casts down the wicked (v. 18). The righteous are guided by God's truth (v. 24) but the ungodly are deluded by their own fantasies. The destiny of the true believers is glory (v. 24), but the destiny of the unbelievers is destruction (vv. 19, 27). "Those who are far from You shall perish" (AMP). The ungodly have everything they want except God, and the godly have in God all that they want or need. He is their portion forever (see 16:2). The possessions of the ungodly are but idols that take the place of the Lord, and idolatry is harlotry (Ex. 34:15-16; 1 Chron. 5:25). Even death cannot separate God's people from His blessing, for the spirit goes to heaven to be with the Lord, and the body waits in the earth for resurrection (vv. 25-26; 2 Cor. 5:1-8; 1 Thess. 4:13-18).

When the worship service ended and Asaph had gotten his feet firmly grounded on the faith, he left the sanctuary and told everybody what he had learned. He had drawn near to God, he had trusted God, and now he was ready to declare God's works. "Yet in all these things we are more than conquerors through Him who loved us" (Rom. 8:37, NKJV).

Psalm 74

Psalm 73 deals with a personal crisis of faith, but Psalm 74 moves to the national scene and focuses on the destruction of the temple in Jerusalem by the Babylonians in 587-86 B.C. The author is obviously not the Asaph of David's day but a namesake among his descendants. Psalm 79 is a companion psalm, and you will find parallel passages in the book of Lamentations (4/2:6-7; 7/2:2; 9/2:6, 9) and Jeremiah (6-7/10:25; 1, 13/23:1). Even though the prophets had warned that judgment was coming (2 Chron. 36:15-21), the fall of Jerusalem and the destruction of the temple were catastrophic events that shook the people's faith. As he surveyed the situation, Asaph moved from despair to confidence and in the end affirmed that all was not lost.

The Sanctuary: "The Lord Has Rejected Us!" (vv. 1-11)

This was a logical conclusion anyone would draw from beholding what the Babylonians did to the city and the temple (Lam. 5:20-22). But the Lord had promised not to abandon His people (Deut. 4:29-31; 26:18-19), for they were His precious flock (77:20; 78:52; 79:13; 100:3; Num. 27:17), and He was the Shepherd of Israel (80:1). Israel was the tribe of His inheritance, and the future of the Messianic promise depended on their survival. (*The Authorized Version* reads "rod" in v. 2, and the word can also be translated "scepter." Num. 17 shows the connection between rods and tribes.) He had redeemed them from Egypt and made them His inheritance (Ex. 19:5; 34:9; Deut. 32:9), and He had come to dwell with them on Mt. Zion. The word "remember" (v. 2) doesn't mean "call to mind," because it's impossible for God to forget anything. It means "to go to work on behalf of someone." *Why did God permit a pagan nation to defeat the Jews and destroy their holy city and sacred temple, and why was He doing nothing about it?*

The people of Judah thought that the presence of the temple was their guarantee of security no matter how they lived, but the prophet Jeremiah refuted that lie (Jer. 7). Jeremiah even used the phrase "everlasting (perpetual) ruins" (v. 3; Jer. 25:9) and warned that the temple would be destroyed and the nation taken into captivity. Many times in the past, God had intervened to save Israel, but now He seemed to be doing nothing. Asaph prayed, "Lift up your feet! Take your hand out of your garment! Get up and plead our cause!" (vv. 1, 11, 22). Do something!

Shouting their battle cries, the Babylonian soldiers brought their pagan ensigns into the holy precincts of the temple and began to chop at the gold-covered panels of the walls (see 1 Kings 6:18-22). The sanctuary was where God had met with His people (Ex. 29:42), yet He didn't come when they needed Him. The word "synagogues" in verse 8 (KJV) means "meeting places," for there were no synagogues until after the Jews returned to their land following the captivity. There was only one temple and one altar for sacrifices, but there must have been other places where the people met to be taught the Scriptures and to pray. Babylon was determined to show its power over the God of Israel. God's messengers had already warned the leaders and the people that judgment was coming, but they refused to listen. Therefore, the Lord didn't raise up any new prophets (Lam. 2:9). As far as the captivity was concerned, the question "How long?" (vv. 9-10) was answered by Jeremiah (25; 29:10). As far as the length of Babylon's destroying and disgracing Israel's capital city and temple, there was no answer. The people felt that they were cast off forever (v. 1), desolate forever (v. 3), humiliated forever (v. 10), and forgotten forever (v. 19). If we had been there, perhaps we might have felt the same way.

The Throne: "The Lord Reigns!" (vv. 12-17)

Verse 12 is the central verse of the psalm and the turning point in Asaph's experience. He lifted his eyes by faith from the burning ruins to the holy throne of God in the heavens and received a new perspective on the situation. (The Asaph who wrote 73 had a similar experience. See 73:17.) No matter how discouraging his situation was, Asaph knew that God was still on the throne and had not abdicated His authority to the Babylonians. Jeremiah came to the same conclusion (Lam. 5:19) "'Thou/You" is the important pronoun in this paragraph. God brings "salvations" (plural) on the earth (v. 12; see 44:4), so Asaph reviewed the "salvation works" of God in the past. The Lord orchestrated Israel's exodus and the defeat of the "monster" Egypt (vv. 13-14; Ex. 12-15). He provided water in the wilderness (15a; Ex. 17; Num. 20) and opened the Jordan River so Israel could enter Canaan (15b; Josh. 3-4). Asaph even reached back to creation (v. 16; compare 136:7-9; Gen. 1–2) and the assignment of territory to the nations (v. 17a; Gen. 10–11; Acts 17:26). What a mighty God! What a mighty King! When the outlook is bleak, try the uplook.

The Covenant: "The Lord Remembers Us!" (vv. 18-23)

Since righteousness and justice are the foundation of His throne (89:14), it was logical for Asaph to move in his thoughts from God's throne to God's covenant with Israel (Lev. 26; Deut. 28-30). Asaph knew the terms of the covenant: if Israel obeyed the Lord, He would bless them; if they disobeyed, He would chasten them; if they confessed their sins, He would forgive them. If the Babylonians were mocking the Lord as they destroyed the city and temple, the Jews had mocked the prophets that God sent to them to turn them from their idolatry (2 Chron. 36:16). Israel had not honored God's name but had turned His temple into a den of thieves (Jer. 7:11).

Asaph saw the nation as a defenseless dove that had no way of escape. Had the kings and leaders listened to their prophets and led the nation back to the Lord, all this carnage and destruction would have been averted. *But the Lord was paying attention to His covenant!* That was why He was chastening His people. Asaph was concerned about the glory of God's name and the survival of God's people. It was God's cause that was uppermost in His mind. The prophet Jeremiah had preached about the dependability of God's covenant (Jer. 33:19-26), and Asaph was asking God to fulfill His purposes for the nation.

The nation had been ravaged, the city of Jerusalem had been wrecked, and the temple had been destroyed and burned—*but the essentials had not been touched by the enemy!* The nation still had Jehovah God as their God, His Word and His covenant had not been changed, and Jehovah was at work in the world! God is at work in our world today, and we need not despair.

Psalm 75

This psalm by Asaph may be read as the "digest" of a worship service called to thank the Lord for what He had done for His people. Because of the warning against boasting (vv. 4-7), some students associate the psalm with King Hezekiah and Jerusalem's deliverance from the Assyrian invaders (Isa. 36-3 7). They also associate 76, 77, and 78 with that great event. Sennacherib's officers certainly boasted about their achievements, but when the right time came, God destroyed the Assyrian army encamped around Mt. Zion. The tune "Destroy Not" is used with 57, 58, and 59. Now let's go to the worship service.

We Begin with an Invocation of Praise (v. 1)

True worship centers on the Lord and not on us, our personal problems, or our "felt needs." We praise God for who He is—His glorious attributes—and for His wonderful works (see 44:1-8; 77:12; 107:8, 15). God's name is a synonym for God's person and presence (Deut. 4:7; Isa. 30:27). He is indeed "a very present help in trouble" (46:1), and when God's people call on the Lord, they know He will hear them. We thank the Lord for all He has done and we tell others about His wonderful works. Though God wants us to bring our burdens to Him and seek His help, worship begins with getting our eyes of faith off the circumstances of life and focusing them on the Lord God Almighty.

We Hear the Lord's Message (vv. 2-5)

If we expect the Lord to receive our words of praise, we must pay attention to His Word of truth as it is read, sung, and preached. The message delivered here was twofold: a word of encouragement for believers (vv. 2-3) and a word of warning to the godless (vv. 4-5). As we see the wicked prosper in their evil deeds, we often ask God "How long?" (See 10:6; 74:9-10; 79:5; 89:46; 94:3-4; and Rev. 6:9-11.) God assured His people that He had already chosen the appointed time for judgment and that His people could wait in confidence and peace because He had everything under control. The Lord has His times and seasons (102:13; Acts 1:7), and He is never late to an appointment. It may seem to us that the foundations of society are being destroyed (11:3; 82:5), and the "pillars" of morality are falling down, but the Lord knows what He is doing (46:6; 1 Sam. 2:8). Jesus Christ is on the throne and holds everything together (Col. 1:17; Heb. 1:3).

But there is also a message for the godless (vv. 4-5), and it warns them not to be arrogant and deliberately disobey the will of God. Before it lowers its head and attacks, a horned beast proudly lifts its head high and challenges its opponent, and the ungodly were following this example. The Hebrew word translated "lift up" is used five times in this psalm (vv. 4, 5, 6, 7, 10), and in verses 4-5, it is associated with arrogance that leads to trouble. A "stiff neck" and proud speech are marks of an insolent and rebellious person, not one who is bowed down in submission to the Lord (Deut. 31:27; 2 Kings 17:14; 2 Chron. 36:13; Jer. 7:26).

We Apply God's Message Personally (vv. 6-8)

How easy it is to hear God's message, leave the meeting, and then forget to obey what we heard! The blessing doesn't come in the hearing but in the *doing* of God's Word (James 1:22-25). The word translated "lifted up" or "exalted" in verses 6, 7, and 19 has to do with God delivering His people from trouble and setting them free. ("Promotion" in v. 6, KJV has nothing to do with getting a better job or being highly publicized.) The arrogant were lifting themselves up only to be cast down by God, but the humble wait on the Lord and He lifts them up (1 Peter 5:6). A Jew could search in any direction—east, west, or the desert (south, Egypt)—and he would never find anybody who can do what only God can do. Why is north omitted? To look in that direction would mean seeking help from the enemies, Assyria and Babylon! (See Jer. 1:13-16; 4:6; 6:22-26.) The Lord delivered Joseph and made him second ruler of Egypt. He delivered David and made him king of Israel. He delivered Daniel and made him third ruler of the kingdom. (See 1 Sam. 2:7-8 and Luke 1:52-53.)

The cup (v. 8) is a familiar image of judgment (Job. 21:20; Isa. 51:17, 22; Jer. 25:15ff; Rev. 16:19; 18:6). The Jews usually drank wine diluted with water, but this cup contained wine mixed with strong spices, what they called a "mixed drink." (Prov. 23:30). If the believers went home from the worship service trusting the Lord to deliver them and judge their enemies, the ungodly should have gone home concerned about future judgment. The Lord Jesus Christ drank the cup for us (Matt. 26:36-46), but those who refuse to trust Him will drink the cup of judgment to the very dregs.

We Close with Praise and the Fear of the Lord (vv. 9-10)

"As for me" (v. 9, NASB) indicates decision on the part of the psalmist. Asaph had participated in the sanctuary worship and helped lead the music, but he, too, had to make a decision to obey the Lord and tell others about Him. Witness and praise go together. "The God of Jacob" is a frequent title for Jehovah in The Psalms (20:1; 24:6; 46:7; 81:1, 4; 84:8; 94:7; 114:7; 132:2, 5; 146:5). It's easy for us to identify with Jacob, who was not always a great man of faith, and yet God deigns to be called by Jacob's name! What an encouragement to us! The fact that God will one day judge the wicked ought to motivate us to share the gospel with them, and the fact that God's people ("the righteous") will be exalted ought to humble us and give us faith and courage in the difficult hours of life.

Psalm 76

The background of this psalm is probably God's judgment of the Assyrian army as recorded in Isaiah 37-38 and 2 Kings 18-19. Other "Zion" psalms include 46, 48, 87, 126, 132, and 137. But the emphasis in this psalm is on the God who accomplished the victory and not on the miracle itself. God's mighty works reveal the greatness of His character and His power (75:1). Sennacherib's officers boasted of their king and his conquests, but their dead idols were no match for the true and living God (115:1-18). Asaph shares four basic truths about Jehovah God.

God Wants Us to Know Him (vv. 1-3)

When the northern kingdom of Israel was taken by the Assyrians in 722 B.C., many godly people moved into Judah where a descendant of David was on the throne and true priests ministered in God's appointed temple (2 Chron. 11:13-17; 15:9). Asaph named both Israel and Judah, for though the kingdoms had been divided politically, there was still only one covenant people in the sight of the Lord. God's name was great in Judah and Jerusalem (47:1-2; 48:1, 10; 77:13), but it needed to be magnified among the neighboring nations, for that was Israel's calling (v. 11; Gen. 12:1-3; Isa. 49:6). "You who are far away, hear what I have done; and you who are near, acknowledge My might" (Isa. 33:13, NASB).

Jehovah had chosen Judah to be the ruling tribe (Isa. 49:10) and Jerusalem to be the site of His holy sanctuary (Ezra 7:19; Zech. 3:2). When the Assyrian army camped near Jerusalem and threatened to attack, the angel of the Lord visited the camp and killed 185,000 soldiers. All their abandoned implements of war were but silent monuments to the power of the God of Israel.

"Salvation is of the Jews" (John 4:22), and if we are to know the true and living God, we must read the Bible, a Jewish book, and trust the Lord Jesus Christ, the Son of God who came through the Jewish nation and died for the sins of the world. The true and living God is the God of Abraham, Isaac, and Jacob, and the God and Father of our Lord Jesus Christ (2 Cor. 1:3; Eph. 1:3; 1 Peter 1:3).

God Wants Us to Trust Him (vv. 4-6)

When you read in 2 Kings and Isaiah the account of Assyria's invasion of Judah, you see how difficult Hezekiah's situation was and how much faith he needed to trust God for victory. But the God of glory, more resplendent than the brightest light and more majestic than the mountains, wiped out the Assyrian soldiers as they slept. Instead of Assyria plundering Jerusalem, Jerusalem plundered Assyria, and the Assyrian lion was defeated by the Lion of Judah (Isa. 14:24-27; Nah. 2:11-13). The God of Jacob (v. 6; see 75:9) not only put an end to those soldiers and their chariot horses, but He took the weapons (v. 3) and put the fear of the Lord into their leaders (v. 12). Why? Because King Hezekiah, the prophet Isaiah, and the elders of Judah in Jerusalem all listened to God's Word and put their faith in the Lord. "For I will defend this city to save it for My own sake and for My servant David's sake" (Isa. 37:35, NASB). "So faith comes from hearing, and hearing by the word of Christ" (Rom. 10:17, NASB).

God Wants Us to Fear Him (vv. 7-9)

The fear of the Lord is a major theme in this psalm (vv. 7, 8, 11, 12). It means, of course, the reverential awe, the respect and veneration that belong to God alone. God's people love Him and rejoice in Him, but they also "[w]orship the Lord with reverence, and rejoice with trembling" (2:11, NASB). "No one can know the true grace of God," wrote A. W. Tozer,

"who has not first known the fear of God" (*The Root of the Righteous*, p. 38). The Lord had been longsuffering toward Sennacherib's officers as they blasphemed His name and threatened His people, but then He revealed His wrath, and the siege was over that never really started. The question asked in verse 7 is also asked in 130:3 and Revelation 6:17, and it is answered in Ezra 9:15. We rejoice that "God is love" (1 John 4:8, 16), but we must remember that "our God is a consuming fire" (Heb. 12:29).

From His throne in heaven, the Lord announced the verdict and the trial was over (v. 8). There could be no appeal because God's court is the very highest and His judgment leaves the defendants speechless (Rom. 3:19). "The earth feared, and was still" (v. 8, NASB). According to verses 9 and 10, God's judgments accomplish at least three purposes: they bring glory to God as they reveal His justice and holiness; they punish the wicked for their evil deeds; and they bring salvation to those who trust the Lord. (See 72:4.)

God Wants Us to Obey Him (vv. 10-12)

Compared to the wrath of God, the wrath of man is nothing. The more men rage against Him, the more God is glorified! The longer Pharaoh refused to submit to God, the more Egypt was destroyed and the more God was glorified (Ex. 9:16; Rom. 9:14-18). Scholars have wrestled with the translation of the second line of verse 10, and some translations append a note stating that "the meaning is uncertain" or "the Hebrew is obscure." The idea expressed seems to be that the Lord isn't agitated about man's wrath but wears it like a sword (or a garment) and will use it against His enemies at the right time.

Instead of resisting the Lord—a losing battle—we should be grateful to Him for rescuing us (v. 9) and saving us from our sins. Asaph spoke to the Jewish believers and told them to keep the promises they made to the Lord when Jerusalem was in danger. How easy it is to make vows and not keep them! (Eccl. 5:1-6). The Lord's great victory should also have witnessed to the neighboring nations and motivated them to go to Jerusalem with gifts to worship Him. (See 2 Chron. 32:23.) The psalm begins at Jerusalem and its environs (vv. 1-6), then moves to the entire land of Israel (vv. 7-9), and now it reaches the whole earth (v. 12). There will be a day when the rulers of the earth will bow to Jesus Christ and worship Him as King of Kings (Isa. 2:1-4; 11:1ff; Rev. 19:11-16).

Psalm 77

This appears to be a companion psalm to 74, which also lamented the destruction of Jerusalem and the captivity of Israel. Both deal with the Lord's apparent rejection of His people (74:1; 77:7), and both look for renewed hope back to the Exodus (74:12-15; 77:16-19). When Jerusalem fell, many Jews were slain and many were taken captive to Babylon. Asaph may have been in Jeremiah's "circle" and left behind to minister to the suffering remnant (Jer. 30-40). But Asaph himself was suffering as he lay in bed at night (vv. 2, 6) and wrestled with the meaning of the terrible events he had witnessed. In this psalm, he described how he moved from disappointment and despair to confidence that the Lord would care for His people.

The Darkness of Despair (vv. 1-9)
Unable to sleep, Asaph began by *praying* (vv. 1-2), then moved into *remembering* (vv. 3-6), and finally found himself *questioning*

(vv. 7-9). In times of crisis and pain, prayer is the believer's natural response, and Asaph reached out his hands in the darkness and cried out to the Lord. He was God's servant and had led the people in worship in the temple, yet he found no comfort for his own heart. When he remembered the Lord and pondered the matter (v. 3; see 6, 11-12), he only groaned, for it seemed that the Lord had failed His people. But had He? Wasn't the Lord being faithful to His covenant and chastening Israel for their sins? Their very chastening was proof of His love (Prov. 3:11-12). Asaph remembered the former years when Israel enjoyed God's blessing, and he also recalled the songs he had sung at the temple, even when on duty at night (134; see 42:8; 92:2; Job 35:10). He had lifted his hands in the sanctuary and received the Lord's blessing, but now he lifted his hands and received nothing.

It isn't a sin to question God, for both David and Jesus asked the Lord the same question (22:1; Matt. 27:46), but it is a sin to demand an immediate answer or to suggest that God needs our counsel (Rom. 11:33-36). Asaph asked six questions, all of which dealt with the very character and attributes of God.

Has He rejected us? No! He is faithful to His Word (Lam. 3:31-33).

Will He ever again show favor to Israel? Yes! (Ps. 30:5. Isa. 60:10)

Has His unfailing love vanished forever? No! (Jer. 31:3)

Have His promises failed? No! (1 Kings 8:56)

Has He forgotten to be gracious? No! (Isa. 49:14-18)

Is He so angry, He has shut up His compassions? No! (Lam. 3:22-24)

It has well been said that we should never doubt in the darkness what God had told us in the light, but Asaph was about to do so. No matter what His hand is doing in our lives, His heart has not changed. He still loves us and always will.

The Dawn of Decision (vv. 10-12)

During the crisis experiences of life, there comes a time when we must get ourselves by the nape of the neck and shake ourselves out of pity into reality, and that's what Asaph did. The repeated "I will" indicates that he had come to the place of decision and determination. "It is my grief, that the right hand of the Most High has changed" (v. 10, NASB). That would be grief indeed if the character of God had altered! "God has deserted His people, and this is a burden I must bear!" He was wrong, of course, because the Lord doesn't change (102:26; Num. 23:19; 1 Sam. 15:29). But he was right in that, by an act of will, he abandoned his former posture of doubt and determined to see the matter through, come what may. He decided to meditate on what God had done for Israel in the past and to learn from His deeds what He was intending for His people.

The Day of Deliverance (vv. 13-20)

The pronouns suddenly change from "I" and "my" to "Thee" and "Thou," referring to the Lord. When we look at our circumstances, we focus on ourselves and see no hope, but when we look by faith to the Lord, our circumstances may not change *but we do*. Asaph didn't completely solve his problems, but he did move out of the shadows of doubt into the sunshine of communion with the Lord and confidence in Him.

First, he *looked up* by faith and rejoiced in the greatness of God (vv. 13-15). He realized that God's ways are always holy, that He is a great God, and that His purposes are always right. See Exodus 15:11, 13, 14, and 16. Then Asaph *looked back* to Israel's exodus from Egypt (Ex. 12-15) for proof of the grace and power of the Lord. Would God have bared His mighty arm to redeem Israel only for their destruction? No! These are the descendants of Jacob whose twelve sons founded the twelve tribes of Israel. These are the brethren of Joseph, whom God sent to Egypt to preserve the nation. Why preserve them if He planned to destroy them? The Exodus account says nothing about a storm, although it does mention a strong wind (Ex. 14:21). Some think that verses 17-18 refer to creation rather than to the Exodus, and creation does magnify God's power and glory (but see Gen. 2:5-6).

As believers, we look back to Calvary, where the Lamb of God gave His life for us. If God the Father did not spare His own Son for us, will He not give us everything else that we need (Rom. 8:32)? There is a wonderful future for the people of God!

Finally, Asaph realized afresh that the Lord was the Shepherd of Israel (v. 20; see 74:1; 78:52, 70-72; 79:13; 80:1). Just as He called Moses and Aaron (Num. 33:1) and David (78:70-72) to lead His flock, so He would appoint other shepherds in the years to come. One day, the Good Shepherd would come and give His life for the sheep (John 10). Asaph had some struggles during this difficult period in his life, but in the end, he knew he could trust the Lord to work out everything for good, and like an obedient sheep, he submitted to the Shepherd. That is what we must do.

Psalm 78

This is a history psalm; see 105, 106, 114, 135, and 136. The German philosopher

Hegel said that the one thing we learn from history is that we don't learn from history. If you study the Bible and church history, you discover that God's people make that same mistake. As Asaph reviewed the history of his people, he saw a sad record of forgetfulness, faithlessness, foolishness, and failure, and he sought to understand what it all meant. These things were written for the profit of believers today (1 Cor. 10:11-12), so we had better heed what Asaph says. As A. T. Pierson said, "History is His story."

The psalm concludes with the coronation of David, but the mention of the temple in verse 69 indicates that David's reign had ended. "Ephraim" in verse 9 probably refers, not to the tribe, but to the Northern Kingdom (Israel) that had split from Judah and Benjamin when Rehoboam became king (1 Kings 12). The leaders of Israel abandoned the faith of their fathers and established a religion of their own making, while the people of Judah sought to be faithful to the Lord. In this psalm, Asaph warned the people of Judah not to imitate their faithless ancestors or their idolatrous neighbors and disobey the Lord. He admonished them to know the Scriptures and teach them to their children. Judah had the temple on Mt. Zion, the covenants, the priesthood, and the Davidic dynasty, and all this could be lost in one generation (see Judg. 2). Since Israel is a covenant nation, she has the responsibility of obeying and honoring the Lord, and this psalm presents three responsibilities God expected His people to fulfill.

Protecting the Future (vv. 1-8)

Where would we be today if over the centuries the remnant of Jewish spiritual leaders had not preserved the Scriptures for us! Until the New Testament was completed near the end of the first century, the only Bible the early church had was the Old Testament. It was God's law that each generation of Jewish people pass on God's Word to the next generation (71:18; 79:13; 102:18; 145:4; see Ex. 10:2; 12:26-27; 13:8, 14; Deut. 4:9; 6:6-9, 20-25), and this law applies to His church today (2 Tim. 2:2). In telling the "praises of the Lord"—His deeds worthy of praise—Asaph helped his readers understand an enigma in their history. (See Matt. 13:35.) He explained why God rejected the tribe of Ephraim and chose the tribe of Judah and David to be king, and why He abandoned the tabernacle at Shiloh and had a temple built on Mt. Zion. Future generations needed to understand this so they would obey the Lord and do His will. Asaph did not want the people to imitate the "exodus generation" that died in the wilderness, or the third generation in Canaan that turned to idols, or the ten tribes that forsook the Lord and established a new kingdom and a false religion. The nation had been stubborn and rebellious (vv. 8, 37; Deut. 21:18) and had suffered because of their disobedience. On the positive side, Asaph wanted the future generations to trust God, to learn from the past, and to obey God's Word (v. 8). Only then could they be sure of the blessing of the Lord. That principle still applies today.

Understanding the Past (vv. 9-64)

Asaph reviewed the past, beginning with the apostasy of Ephraim (vv. 9-11) and continuing with Israel's sins in the wilderness (vv. 12-39) and in Canaan (vv. 54-64). One of the causes of their rebellion was that they forgot God's victory over the gods of Egypt and His deliverance of Israel from bondage (vv. 12-13, 40-53). They also did not take to heart His care for them during their wilderness journey. "Those who cannot remember the past are condemned to repeat it" (George Santayana).

The apostasy of Ephraim (vv. 9-11). This passage refers to the Northern Kingdom of Israel. When the ten tribes broke away from Judah and Benjamin, they informally adopted the name of their strongest and largest tribe, Ephraim. Joseph's sons, Manasseh and Ephraim, were adopted and blessed by Jacob, who made Ephraim the firstborn (Gen. 48:8-20; see Deut. 33:13-17). This added to the tribe's prestige. Moses' successor, Joshua came from Ephraim (Num. 13:8) and so did Jeroboam, the founding king of Israel/Ephraim (1 Kings 11:26; 12:16ff). Proud and militant, the tribe created problems for both Joshua (Josh. 17:14-18) and Gideon (Judg. 8:1-3). The tabernacle was in Shiloh, which was located in Ephraim, and this also added to the honor of the tribe. Like a warrior fleeing from the battlefield, Israel turned back from following the Lord, disobeyed Him, and forgot what He had done for them. For the image of the "bow," see also verse 57 and Hosea 7:16. By opening this long historical section with a description of the apostasy of the Northern Kingdom, Asaph was warning Judah not to follow their example.

The nation's sins in the wilderness (vv. 12-39). Asaph now returned to the account of the sins of the whole nation, before the political division after Solomon's death. The Jews forgot what the Lord did for them in Egypt when He sent the plagues to Egypt and delivered the Jewish people at the Exodus. The people saw one miracle after another as the Lord exposed the futility of the Egyptian gods and goddesses (Ex. 12:12; Num. 33:4), but the memory soon faded. (Asaph

will again mention the Egyptian experience in vv. 40-53.) God led the nation both day and night and miraculously provided water for all the people. In verses 15-16, he combined the water miracles of Exodus 17:1-7 and Numbers 20:1-13. But the people would not trust the Lord but tempted Him by asking for food, "a table in the wilderness" (vv. 17-31). He sent manna, the "bread of heaven," as well as fowl to eat (Ex. 16; Num. 11), but He judged them for their insolence and fleshly appetite. Sometimes God's greatest judgment is to give us what we want. (See vv. 21, 31, 49-50, 58-59, 62.) "He brought their days to an end in futility" (v. 33, NASB; 90:7-12) at Kadesh Barnea when they refused to enter the land (Num. 13-14). They wandered for the next thirty-eight years until the people twenty years and older all died (Num. 14:28-38). From time to time, God's discipline did bring them to their knees in temporary repentance, but their confessions were insincere flattery (v. 36) and they soon rebelled again. In His mercy, God forgave them and held back His wrath, but they were a generation that grieved His heart.

The forgotten lessons of Egypt (vv. 40-53). The people did not remember the demonstrations of God's power in sending the plagues to Egypt (Ex. 7-12; Num. 14:32-35) and in opening the Red Sea to set the nation free (Ex. 12-15). Asaph listed six of the ten plagues but did not mention the gnats (Ex. 8:16-19), the killing of the livestock (Ex. 9:1-7), the boils (Ex. 9:8-12), and the three days of darkness before the death of the firstborn (Ex. 10:21-29). After this great display of divine power, the people should have been able to trust the Lord in any situation, knowing that He was in control, but they grieved Him, provoked Him, and tempted Him to display His anger against them! Human nature has not changed. Spurgeon said that we are too prone to engrave our trials in the marble and write our blessings in the sand. They opposed the Holy One of Israel (v. 41; 71:22; 89:18), and He disciplined them time after time.

The sins in Canaan (vv. 54-64). After caring for the nation in the wilderness for thirty-eight years, the Lord brought them again to Kadesh Barnea (Deut. 1:1-2). There he reviewed their history and taught them God's Law as he prepared the new generation to enter the land and conquer the enemy. Often in his farewell speech (which we call Deuteronony— "second law"), Moses exhorted them to remember and not forget what the Lord had said to them and done for them. They were a new generation, making a new beginning with a new leader (Joshua) and a new opportunity to trust God. Under Joshua's able leadership, they conquered the land and claimed their inheritance, and for two generations obeyed the Lord. But the third generation repeated the sins of their ancestors and forgot what the Lord had said and done (vv. 56-57; Josh. 2:7-10). The "faulty bow" image shows up again in Hosea 7:16. Instead of destroying the altars and idols, the Jewish people mingled with the people of the land and learned their evil ways, and God had to discipline His people by turning them over to their enemies (v. 59). The book of Judges records how seven different nations invaded the nation of Israel and how God raised up judges to deliver Israel when the people repented and turned to Him for help. During the days of Eli the high priest, the Lord severely punished the people and even allowed His ark to be taken captive by the Philistines (1 Sam. 1-7). This meant the end of the tabernacle at Shiloh. It was at Nob in Benjamin for a time (1 Sam. 21:22;

2 Sam. 6:1-2) and also at Gibeon in Benjamin (1 Kings 3:4). When David brought the ark to Mt. Zion (v. 68; 2 Sam. 6), he erected a tent there for the ark and there the ark remained until it was moved into the temple during the reign of Solomon (1 Kings 8:3-9).

It has well been said that a change in circumstances does not overcome a flaw in character, and the history of the Jewish nation illustrates the truth of that statement. Whether living in Egypt, journeying in the wilderness, or dwelling in their own land, the people of Israel were prone to want their own way and rebel against the Lord. When chastened, they feigned repentance, experienced God's help, and were forgiven, but before long, they were back in trouble again. But is any people or individual free from this malady? At least the Jewish writers who gave us the Bible were honest to record their sins as well as their achievements! The church today can learn from both (1 Cor. 10).

Appreciating the Present (vv. 65-72)

The statement in verse 65 is metaphorical, for the Lord neither gets drunk nor goes to sleep. During the time of Samuel and Saul, with the help of young David, Israel beat back her enemies, but it was when David ascended the throne that the nation achieved its greatest victories and experienced the greatest expansion of its boundaries. This is one reason why God rejected the tribe of Ephraim and chose the tribe of Judah, and why He abandoned the tabernacle at Shiloh in Ephraim and chose Mt. Zion for the site of the temple. Jacob had prophesied that the king would come from Judah (Gen. 49:10), and King Saul was from Benjamin. When the Lord directed David to capture Mt. Zion and make Jerusalem his capital city, it was an act of His love (47:4; 87:2). If Asaph wrote this psalm after the division of the kingdom, then he was reminding the people of Judah that they were privileged indeed to have Jerusalem, Mt. Zion, and a king from the line of David, *from which line the Messiah would come!* (See Luke 1:30-33, 66-79; Matt. 2:6.) If they appreciated these privileges, they would not follow the bad example of the Northern Kingdom and sin against the Lord by turning to idols.

Kings were called "shepherds" (Jer. 23:1-6; Ezek. 34) because God's chosen people were the sheep of His pasture (v. 52; 77:20; 100:3), and no one was better qualified than David to hold that title (2 Sam. 5:1-3). He loved his "sheep" (2 Sam. 24:17) and often risked his life for them on the battlefield. His hands were skillful, whether holding a sword, a harp, a pen, or a scepter, and, unlike his predecessor Saul, his heart was wholly devoted to the Lord. (On "integrity," see 7:8; 25:21; 26:1, 11; 41:12.) Integrity and skill need each other, for no amount of ability can compensate for a sinful heart, and no amount of devotion to God can overcome lack of ability.

Psalm 79

God gave His people victory over Egypt (77) and helped them march through the wilderness and then conquer Canaan (78). He also gave them King David who defeated their enemies and expanded their kingdom. But now God's people are captive, the city and temple are ruined, and the heathen nations are triumphant. (See also 74 for parallels: 79:1/74:3, 7; 79:2/74:19; 79:5/74:10; 79:12/74:10, 18, 22.) We see Asaph playing four different roles as he contemplates the defeat of Judah by the Babylonians. Each division of the psalm opens with an address to

Jehovah: "O God" (v. 1); O Lord" (v. 5); "O God our Savior" (v. 9); and "O Lord" (v. 12).

The Mourner: Beholding God's Judgment (vv. 1-4)

Babylon was the leading nation in the conquest of Judah, but the neighboring nations (Ammon, Moab, Edom) were delighted to see the Jews defeated (vv. 4, 12; see 44:13; 80:6; 137:7; Ezek. 25). The land was God's inheritance (Ex. 15:17), and He shared it with the people of Israel who were His inheritance (28:9; 33:12; Deut. 4:20). They could live in the land and enjoy its blessings as long as they obeyed the covenant (Lev. 26; Deut. 28-30), but repeated rebellion would only bring painful discipline to them, including expulsion from the land (Lev. 26:33-39; Deut. 28:64-68). They would be defeated before their enemies (v. 1; Deut. 28:25) and the dead bodies left unburied, a terrible disgrace for a Jew (v. 2; Deut. 28:26; Lev. 26:30; and see Jer. 7:33; 8:2; 9:22). Her cities would be destroyed (v. 1; Deut. 28:52) and Israel would be reproached by her neighbors (vv. 4, 12; Deut. 28:37). Note how Asaph identified the Lord with the situation: "your inheritance ... your holy temple ... your servants ... your name."

The Sufferer: Feeling God's Anger (vv. 5-8)

The question "How long?" is found often in Scripture (see 6:3). God is not jealous *of* anyone or anything, for He is wholly self-sufficient and needs nothing, but He is jealous *over* His land and His people. (See 78:58; Ex. 20:5; Deut. 4:24; 6:15-16; 29:20.) He is jealous for His name (Ezek. 39:25), His land (Joel 2:18), and His inheritance (Zech. 1:14). Asaph doesn't deny that he and the people deserve chastening (v. 9), but if the Jews are guilty, then how much guiltier the heathen nations are that have attacked the Jews! He asked God to pour out His anger on the invaders because of what they have done to the land, the city, and the temple (vv. 6-7).

As the kingdom of Judah declined, their kings and leaders became less and less devoted to the Lord. There were a few godly kings, such as Asa, Josiah, Joash, and Hezekiah, but foreign alliances, idolatry, and unbelief combined to weaken the kingdom and ripen it for judgment. The sins of the fathers accumulated until God could hold back His wrath no longer (Gen. 15:16; Matt. 23:32-33; 1 Thess. 2:13-16). We are guilty before God for only our own sins (Deut. 24:16; Jer. 31:29-30; Ezek. 18), but we may suffer because of the sins of our ancestors (Ex. 20:5; 34:7; 2 Kings 17:7ff; 23:26-27; 24:3-4; Lam. 5:7; Dan. 9:4-14).

The Intercessor: Pleading for God's Help (vv. 9-11)

His concern was for the glory of God's name (vv. 9, 12), and he felt that a miraculous deliverance for Judah would accomplish that, but no deliverance came. Asaph was quick to confess his own sins and the sins of his contemporaries, for it was not only their ancestors who had disobeyed the Lord (v. 8). (See 25:11, 31:3, 65:3, and 78:38.) In ancient days, a nation's victory was proof that its gods were stronger than the gods of the enemy, so the Babylonians taunted the Jews and asked, "Where is your God?" (See 42:3, 10; 115:2.) Moses used this same argument when he pled with God to forgive the nation (Ex. 32:12; Num. 14:13).

Asaph was also concerned about the justice of God. Twice he mentioned the pouring out of blood (vv. 3, 10), the slaughter of people, for the blood was very sacred to the Jews (Lev. 17). The

shedding of animal blood at the altar at least covered the sins of the worshipers, but to what purpose was the shedding of so much human blood? In verse 11, he prayed on the basis of the Lord's great compassion, perhaps remembering Jehovah's words to Moses (Ex. 33:12-23, and see Deut. 32:36). God had felt the burdens of the Jews when He called Moses to lead them out of Egypt (Ex. 2:24-25, 6:1-9), so surely He would have pity on the prisoners and those ready to die. The cross of Jesus Christ is for us today the only evidence we need that God loves us (Rom. 5:8).

The Worshiper: Promising to Praise God (vv. 12-13)

How could any person witness what Babylon did to the Jews and not cry out to God for retribution? (See 55 for a discussion of the imprecatory prayers in the Psalms.) God had chosen Babylon to chasten Judah for her sins, but the Babylonians had rejoiced at the privilege and had gone too far in their cruelty (Jer. 50:11-16; 51:24). Asaph's burden was that Babylon had reproached the Lord and not just punished His people, and he asked God to pay them back in like measure (see Isa. 65:6; Jer. 32:18; Luke 6:38). God's covenant with Israel often uses the phrase "seven times" (Lev. 26:18, 21, 24, 28; Deut. 28:7, 25). The prophet Jeremiah promised that God would judge Babylon for her sins (Jer. 50-51), and if Asaph knew of these prophecies, then he was simply praying for God to accomplish His will on earth.

The people of Judah were but sheep (vv. 74:1; 77:20; 78:72; 95:7; 100:3), but they had been ruthlessly slaughtered by their enemies, and God's name had been slandered. God had called His people to praise Him and to bear witness to the heathen nations (Isa. 43:21), and this is what

Asaph promised to do if God would only deliver the people. There were sons of Asaph who left Babylon for Judah when the captivity ended, so Asaph's promise to the Lord was fulfilled (Ezra 2:41; 3:10; Neh. 7:44; 11:17, 22; 12:35-36).

Psalm 80

This is Asaph's prayer to God on behalf of the Northern Kingdom ("Israel," "Samaria") after it was taken captive by Assyria in 722-21 B.C. While "Joseph" can refer to the whole nation (77:15; 80:4-5), the mention in verse 2 of Ephraim and Manasseh (Joseph's sons) and Benjamin (Joseph's brother) suggests that the Northern Kingdom is meant. These are the children and grandchildren of Rachel, Jacob's favorite wife. Samaria, the capital of the Northern Kingdom, was located in Ephraim. The temple was still standing in Jerusalem (v. 1), and the fall of Samaria should have been a warning to Judah not to disobey the Lord. That Asaph would pray for Samaria and ask God for restoration and reunion for the whole nation indicates that some of the old rivalries were ending and that some of the people of Judah were concerned over "the ruin of Joseph" (Amos 6:6). It's unfortunate that it sometimes takes dissension, division, and destruction to bring brothers closer together. Joseph and his brothers are a case in point. The refrain "Restore us" (vv. 3, 7, 19) marks out the three requests Asaph made to the Lord for both kingdoms.

"Save Your Flock" (vv. 1-3)
Both in the Old Testament and the New, the flock is a familiar image of the people of God (23:1; 28:9, NASB, NIV; 74:1; 77:20; 78:52; 79:13; John 10; 1 Peter 5:1-4; Heb.

13:20-21). The request here is that the Lord might lead His people through this crisis as He led them safely through the wilderness. He led the way by the ark (the throne of God; Num. 10:33; 99:1; 1 Sam. 4:4 and 6:2) and the cloud (the shining forth of the glory of God; Num. 14:14; see 50:2, 94:1, Deut. 33:2). After the ark came the people of Judah, Issachar, and Zebulun. Next were the Levites from Gershom and Marari carrying the tabernacle structure, followed by Reuben, Simeon, and Gad. Then came the Levites from Kohath carrying the tabernacle furnishings, followed by Ephraim, Manasseh, and Benjamin, with Dan, Asher, and Naphtali bringing up the rear (see Num. 10). Asaph asked the Lord to "stir up His might" (7:6; 78:65) and bring salvation to His people. This reminds us of the words of Moses whenever the camp set out, "Rise up, O Lord! May your enemies be scattered" (Num. 10:35, NIV). The "shining of His face" of the refrain reminds us of the priestly benediction (Num. 6:22-27), and see 4:6; 31:16; 67:1; and 119:135. When God hides His face, there is trouble (13:1; 27:9; 30:7; 44:24; 69:17; 88:14. "Turn us again" (KJV) means "restore us to our former state of blessing and fellowship with the Lord." (See 85:4; 126:1,4; Lam. 5:21.)

"Pity Your People" (vv. 4-7)
The shepherd image blends in with the image of Israel as God's people: "We are his people and the sheep of his pasture" (100:3). But the Lord was now angry with His people, and His anger smoldered like a fire about to erupt and consume them. (See 74:1 and 79:5; Deut. 29:20; Isa. 65:5.) He was even angry at their prayers, or "in spite of" their prayers. [For "How long?" see 6:3. See also Lam. 3:8 and 44, and recall that God told Jeremiah not to pray

for His wayward people (Jer. 7:16; 11:14; 14:11; and see 1 John 5:16).] During Israel's wilderness wanderings, God provided bread from heaven and water from the rock (Ex. 16-17; Num. 20), but now His people had only tears as both their food and drink. (See 42:3; 102:9; Isa. 30:20.) To make matters worse, the neighboring peoples were laughing at God's people (44:13-16; 79:4). Again we read the plaintive refrain (v. 7), but note that the "O God" of verse 3 now becomes "O God of hosts" ("God Almighty," NIV). Jehovah is the Lord of the armies of heaven and earth, but His people no longer marched in victory.

"Revive Your Vine" (vv. 8-19)

The image now changes to that of Israel the vine (Isa. 5:1-7; Jer. 2:21; 6:9; Ezek. 15:1-2; 17:6-8; 19:10-14; Hos. 10:1; 14:7; Matt. 20:1-16; Mark 12:1-9; Luke 20:9-16). Jesus used this image to describe Himself and His followers (John 15), and in Revelation 14:17-20, John wrote of "the vine of the earth," the corrupt Gentile nations in the end times. The Lord transplanted Israel from Egypt to Canaan, uprooted the nations in Canaan, and planted His people in the land of their inheritance. As long as the people obeyed the Lord, the vine grew and covered more and more of the land. The boundaries of the nation reached from the hill country in the south to the mighty cedars of Lebanon in the north, from the Mediterranean Sea on the west to the Euphrates on the east—and beyond (72:8; Ex. 23:21; Deut. 11:24; 2 Sam. 8:6; 1 Kings 4:24).

But the luxurious vine disobeyed the Lord, produced "worthless fruit" (Isa. 5:2), and felt the chastening hand of the Lord. He withdrew His protection and permitted the enemy to enter the land and ruin the vineyard. Asaph prayed that

the Lord might forgive and once again bless His people. The word "branch" in verse 15 (KJV) is translated "son" in the *New American Stamdard Bible* and the *New International Version*, perhaps a reference to Jacob's words about Joseph in Genesis 49:22. Israel was called God's "son" (Ex. 4:22-23; see Hos. 11:1, which is a Messianic reference in Matt. 2:15), and Benjamin means "son of my right hand." While there may be Messianic overtones in verses 15 and 17 (see 110:1, 5), the main idea is that Israel is God's own people, His vine, and His chosen son. He planted the nation in Canaan, and He alone can protect and deliver them. He had treated the people like a favored son, just as Jacob had laid his right hand of blessing on Ephraim rather than the firstborn Manasseh (Gen. 48:12-20). They did not deserve His blessing, but in His grace He bestowed it. It is also possible that verse 17 refers to Israel's king and expresses hope in the Davidic dynasty.

The final refrain introduces a third name for God, borrowed from verse 4: "O LORD God of hosts [Almighty, NIV]." LORD is the name "Jehovah," which is the covenant name of God. The psalmist appealed to the covenant and asked God to be faithful to forgive His people as they called upon Him and confessed their sins (Lev. 26:40-45; Deut. 30:1-10). This is the Old Testament version of 1 John 1:9. Spiritually speaking, the roots of Israel are still strong (Rom. 11:1ff, especially vv. 16-24), and one day the vine and olive tree will be restored, and Asaph's prayer will be answered.

Psalm 81

The psalmist called the people together to worship the Lord, but then the Lord's messenger received a special message from God and delivered it to the people. The occasion was a stated feast on the Jewish calendar, but we are not told which feast it was. Passover is suggested by verses 5-7 and 10, but the mention of the new moon and the full moon (v. 3, NASB) suggests Trumpets and Tabernacles. The Jewish religious year begins in the month of Nisan (our March-April), during which the Feast of Passover is celebrated (Ex. 12). The civil year begins with Tishri (our September-October), the seventh month in the religious year, during which the Jews celebrate the Feast of Trumpets (first day, "Rosh Hashanna"), the Day of Atonement (tenth day, "Yom Kippur"), and the Feast of Tabernacles (days fifteen to twenty-two). (See Lev. 23:23-44 and Num. 29.) The first day would be new moon and the fifteenth day the full moon. The trumpets mentioned here are not the silver trumpets (Num. 10) but the "shofar," the ram's horn, as was used at Jericho (Josh. 6). This argues for the occasion being the Feast of Tabernacles, although perhaps Asaph conflated Passover and Tabernacles, for they go together. Passover celebrated the deliverance from Egypt and Tabernacles the Lord's care of His people during their wilderness years. Tabernacles was also a joyful harvest festival. The psalm reminds us of three different aspects of true worship.

Praising God's Name (vv. 1-5)

The leader called together the people (v. 1), the musicians (v. 2), and the priests to blow the trumpets (v. 3). In the Old Testament Law, you find stated times of worship (the weekly Sabbath, the annual feasts, etc.) as well as spontaneous times of worship (at the defeat of the enemy, for example). Both are essential to balanced worship, and both should focus on the goodness of the Lord. If all worship were personal and spontaneous, there would be diversity but no unity; but if all worship only followed a schedule, there would be uniformity and no diversity. Both voices and instruments were used in worship. The nation is called "Jacob, Israel, and Joseph" (vv. 4-5). Jacob and his wives built the family, and Joseph preserved them alive in Egypt. God gave Jacob the name "Israel," which means "he strives with God and prevails" (Gen. 32:22-32).

Hearing God's Word (vv. 6-10).

The last clause of verse 5 could be translated, "We heard a voice we had not known" (NIV margin), referring to the message God sent in verses 6-10. At some point in the festal celebration, a priest received God's message and declared it to the people. The emphasis in this psalm is on hearing the Word of God (vv. 6, 11, 13; see 95:7-11 and Heb. 3). Every seventh year at the Feast of Tabernacles, the priests read the book of Deuteronomy to the people, and perhaps this was one of those special sabbatical years. (See Deut. 31:9-13, and note the emphasis in Deuteronomy on "hearing God" [Deut. 4:1, 6, 10; 5:1; 6:3-4; 9:1].) It is delightful to sing praises to God and to pray, but if we want Him to listen to us, we must listen to Him.

Frequently the Lord reminded His people of their miraculous deliverance from Egypt (v. 6), the power of God that accomplished it, and the love of God that motivated it. He also reminded them of the covenant they accepted at Sinai (v. 7a; see Deut. 5:2-3). The people hearing this message were not at Sinai, but the decision of their ancestors was binding on them and their descendants. God's message also mentioned their failure to trust Him at Meribah (Ex. 17; Num. 20). At the

Feast of Tabernacles, the priests poured out water in the temple to commemorate these events (John 7:37-39). The Lord emphasized that He would not tolerate His people worshiping idols (vv. 8-9; Ex. 20:1-4; Deut. 4:15-20). What could the false gods of the neighboring nations give to them? "Open your mouth wide and I will fill it" (v. 10, NASB).

Obeying God's Will (vv. 11-16)

Worship and service go together (Matt. 4:10; Deut. 6:13), and this means we must obey what the Lord commands. But the nation did not obey God's Word, and He had to destroy all the people twenty years and older (Num. 14:26ff). But this attitude of spiritual "deafness" and willful disobedience persisted even after Israel entered the Promised Land, as recorded in the book of Judges. (See 78:10, 17, 32, 40, 56.) The greatest judgment God can send is to let people have their own way (see Rom. 1:24, 26, 28).

Had His people obeyed Him, the Lord would have kept the promises in His covenant and blessed them with protection and provision (Deut. 28:15ff; Lev. 26:17-20; 27-31). When we disobey the Lord, not only do we feel the pain of His chastening, but we also miss out on the blessings He so desires to give us. The Lord gave Israel water out of the rock, but He was prepared to give them honey out of the rock (Deut. 32:13). He sent manna from heaven, but He would have given them the finest of wheat. The word "if" (v. 13) is small, but it carries big consequences (Deut. 5:29; 32:29; Isa. 48:18; Matt. 23:37).

> Of all sad words of tongue or pen,
> The saddest are these: "It might have been."
> John Greenleaf Whittier

Psalm 82

In the previous psalm, Asaph described the Lord judging His people during one of their feast days, but in this psalm it is the judges of the people that He indicts. (See also 50 and 75.) The psalmist speaks in verse 1 and announces that the Judge will speak, and in verse 8, Asaph prays that God will bring justice to the whole earth. Between these statements, the Lord Himself speaks to the judges.

The Judge (v. 1)

Since God is the Lawgiver, He is also the Judge (Isa. 33:22), and the Judge of all the earth does what is right (Gen. 18:25). He presides over the congregation of Israel and over the judges of the nation. The Lord is not sitting at a bench, patiently listening to the presentation of the case, because God is Judge and jury and needs nobody to tell Him the facts. He knows what people are doing on the earth and will execute judgment righteously (11:4-7). In His court, there is no "defense" or "appeal." He is omniscient and His verdict is final. It is an awesome occasion: He is standing and about to announce His decision (Isa. 3:13-15).

The "gods" (vv. 1, 6) are not the false gods of the heathen, for such nonexistent gods are not Jehovah's judicial representatives on earth. Nor are these "gods" the holy angels, for angels cannot die (v. 7). These "gods" (elohim) are people who have been given the awesome responsibility of representing the Lord on earth and interpreting and applying His Law (Ex. 18:13-17; 21:6; Deut. 16:18-20; 17:2-13; 19:15-20; 21:2). Jesus made this clear in His quotation of verse 6 in John 10:34-36. It is a great responsibility to represent the Lord on earth (Lev. 19:15; Deut. 1:17; 16:19) and seek to execute justice by applying the law correctly. Civil servants are "ministers of the Lord" and will answer to Him for what they have done (Rom. 13).

The Judges (vv. 2-7)

"And what does the Lord require of you but to do justice, to love kindness, and to walk humbly with your God?" (Mic. 6:8, NASB). These judges did not do justly (v. 2) or love mercy (vv. 3-4), and they walked in defiance of God's will (v. 5). The pronoun "you" in verse 2 is plural, for the Lord is addressing all the guilty judges. They championed the causes of the guilty because they were bribed, and they failed to care for the orphans and widows. (See Ex. 22:21-24; Deut. 10:17-18; Isa. 1:17; 10:1-2; Jer. 5:28; 22:3, 16; Amos 2:7; 4:1; 5:11-12; 8:6; Ezek. 16:49; 18:12; 22:29.) Judges are to uphold the Law and not show partiality (Lev. 19:15; Deut. 16:19; Isa. 3:13-15; Mic. 3:1-4), a principle that also applies in the local church (1 Tim. 5:21). Even during the glorious days of Solomon's kingdom, the state officers were abusing people and disobeying the Law (Eccl. 5:8)—yet Solomon had asked for an understanding heart (1 Kings 3:9).

Does verse 5 describe the evil judges or the abused people? If the judges, then it is a terrible indictment against people who are supposed to know the Law and walk in its light (Isa. 8:20; 59:1-15; Rom. 1:21-22). But it's possible that the pronoun "they" in verse 5 refers back to the weak and needy people described in verse 4. The priests and Levites did not always do their jobs well, and the common people did not know the Law well enough to defend themselves. "My people are destroyed for lack of knowledge" (Hos. 4:6). When the Law of God is ignored or disobeyed, this shakes and threatens the very foundations of society (11:3; 89:14;

97:2), for God's moral Law is the standard by which man's laws must be judged.

The Judgment (vv. 6-8)

Though these people held high offices and were called "elohim—gods" (Ex. 21:6), they were only humans and would be judged for their sins. Privilege brings responsibility, and responsibility brings accountability. Jesus quoted verse 6 (John 10:34-36) to defend His own claim to be the Son of God. For, if the Lord called "gods" the imperfect human judges chosen by men, how much more should Jesus Christ be called "the Son of God," He who was set apart by the Father and sent to earth! In spite of their titles and offices, these judges would die like any other human and pay the price for their sins. When God the Judge ceased to speak, then Asaph added his prayer that God would bring justice to all the earth and not just to Israel (v. 8; 9:7-8). When the Lord comes to judge the earth, no one will escape and His sentence will be just. Asaph's prayer echoes the church's prayer, "Thy kingdom come, Thy will be done on earth as it is in heaven" (Matt. 6:10).

Psalm 83

This is the last of the psalms identified with Asaph (50, 73-83). It describes a coalition of ten Gentile nations that attempted to wipe Israel off the face of the earth. Some students connect this psalm with Jehoshaphat's great victory over a smaller coalition (2 Chron. 20), although it's possible that the historian did not list all the nations involved. Second Chronicles 20:11 parallels 83:12, and 20:29 parallels 83:16 and 18, but these similarities are not proof that the psalmist wrote about the same event. Israel has been the object of hatred and opposition since their years in Egypt, but God has kept His promises and preserved them (Gen. 12:1-3). Pharaoh, Haman (The book of Esther), Hitler, and every other would-be destroyer of the Jews has ultimately been humiliated and defeated. This reminds us that the church of Jesus Christ is likewise hated and attacked by the world (John 15:18-19; 17:14), and like the Jews in Asaph's day, our defense is in prayer and faith in God's promises (Acts 4:23-31). Commenting on this psalm, Alexander Maclaren wrote, "The world is up in arms against God's people, and what weapon has Israel? Nothing but prayer." But is there any better weapon? As he saw the enemy armies surrounding Israel,

Asaph lifted three heartfelt requests to the Lord

"Lord, See What Is Happening!" (vv. 1-8)

Two names of God open the psalm—Elohim and El, and two names close it—Jehovah and El Elyon (God Most High). The last name reminds us of Abraham's victory over the kings and his meeting with Melchizedek (Gen. 14:18-20). Asaph was troubled because the Lord had said nothing through His prophets and done nothing through His providential workings to stop the huge confederacy from advancing. Literally he prayed, "Let there be no rest to you" (see 28:1-2; 35:21-22; 39:12; 109:11; Isa. 62:6). These were God's enemies, attacking God's people, and threatening God's "protected ones" (see 27:5 and 31:21), so it was time for God to take notice and act!

The invaders were many, they were united, and they proudly lifted their heads as they defied the Lord God of Israel (see 2:1-3). They had secretly plotted together but were now "roaring like

the sea" (v. 2 "tumult"; see 46:3). Their purpose was to destroy God's people and take possession of the land (v. 12). It appears that Moab and Ammon, the incestuous sons of Lot (Gen. 19), were the leaders of the coalition, encouraged by Assyria, which was not yet a world power (v. 8). Moab and Ammon would come from the east, along with the Ishmaelites, and Edom would come from the southeast along with their neighbor Gebal. Ishmael was the enemy and rival of Isaac (Gen. 21:1-21). The Hagerites lived northeast of Israel and the Amalekites lived southwest. The people of Philistia and Phoenicia (Tyre) were west of Israel. The enemy came against Israel from every direction and had the people surrounded!

"Lord, Do What Is Necessary!" (vv. 9-15)

Even if Jehoshaphat's situation was not the same as that described by Asaph, his prayer would have fit the occasion: "O our God, will You not judge them? For we have no power against this great multitude that is coming against us; nor do we know what to do, but our eyes are upon you" (2 Chron. 20:12, NKJV). Asaph remembered some of Jehovah's great victories in Israel's past history, especially Gideon's victory over the Midianites (vv. 9a, 11; Judg. 6-8) and the victory of Deborah and Barak against Sisera and Jabin (vv. 9b-10; Judg. 4-5). Endor is not mentioned in Judges 4-5, but it was a city near Taanach (Judg. 5:19), which was near Endor (Josh. 17:11). The phrase "as dung for the ground" (v. 10, NASB) describes the unburied bodies of enemy soldiers rotting on the ground. The enemy was defeated and disgraced. Oreb and Zeeb were commanders (princes) of the Midianite army, and Zeba and Zalmunna were Midianite kings (Judg. 7:25-8:21). The victory of Gideon ("the day of Midian") stood out in Jewish history as an example of God's power (Isa. 9:4; 10:26; Hab. 3:7). Asaph closed his prayer by asking God to send such a victory to Israel that the enemy soldiers would flee in panic and look like tumbleweeds and chaff blowing before the wind. Like a forest burning on the mountainside, their armies would be consumed. The image of God's judgment as a storm is found in 18:7-15, 50:3 and 68:4. If Asaph's prayer seems vindictive, remember that he was asking God to protect His special people who had a special work to see on earth. (See 55 for more on the "imprecatory psalms.")

"Glorify Your Name!" (vv. 16-18)

Before asking for their destruction, Asaph prayed that the enemy would be "ashamed and dismayed" and would turn to the true and living God. This is what happened in Jehoshaphat's day: "And the fear of God was on all the kingdoms of those countries when they heard that the Lord had fought against the enemies of Israel" (2 Chron. 20:29). King Hezekiah prayed a similar prayer for the invading Assyrians (Isa. 37:14-20). The armies of the ten nations depended on many gods to give them success, but the God of Abraham, Isaac, and Jacob defeated the armies and their gods! "Hallowed be Thy name" is the first request in the Lord's Prayer (Matt. 6:9) and must be the motive that governs all of our praying. The Most High God is sovereign over all the earth!

Psalm 84

The phrase "appears before God in Zion" (v. 7, NASB) suggests that this psalm was penned by a Jewish man who could not go to Jerusalem to celebrate one of the three annual feasts (Ex. 23:17; 34:23). For forty years after their exodus from Egypt, the Jews were a wandering people, but even after they had moved into the Promised Land, the three feasts reminded them that they were still pilgrims on this earth (1 Chron. 29:15), as are God's people today (1 Peter 1:1; 2:11). A vagabond has no home; a fugitive is running from home; a stranger is away from home; a pilgrim is heading home. The psalmist's inability to attend the feast did not rob him of the blessings of fellowship with the Lord. All who are true pilgrims can make the same three affirmations that he made.

My Delight Is in the Lord (vv. 1-4)

In his opening statement, the psalmist said two things: "The temple is beautiful" and "The temple is beloved by all who love the Lord." It was the dwelling place of the Lord, His house (vv. 4, 10), the place where His glory dwelt (26:8). Although God doesn't live today in man-made buildings (Acts 7:47-50), we still show special reverence toward edifices dedicated to Him. We can worship God anytime and anywhere, but special places and stated rituals are important in structuring our worship experience. The important thing is that we have a heart devoted to the Lord, a spiritual "appetite" that cries out for nourishing fellowship with the Lord (42:1-4; Matt. 5:6). The psalmist cried out for God with his entire being. He envied the birds that were permitted to nest in the temple courts, near the altar, as well as the priests and Levites who lived and worked in the sacred precincts (v. 4). How easy it is for us to take for granted the privilege of worshiping "the living God" (see 115:1-8), a privilege purchased for us on the cross.

My Strength Is in the Lord (vv. 5-8)

Though he had to remain at home, the psalmist's heart was set on pilgrimage, and the very map to Jerusalem was written on that heart. His love for God and His house helped him make right decisions in life so that he did not go astray. A geographic site named "the Valley of Baca" is nowhere identified in Scripture. "Baca" is a Hebrew word meaning "balsam tree," and the sap of this tree oozes like tears. The "Valley of Baca" is a name for any difficult and painful place in life, where everything seems hopeless and you feel helpless, like "the pit of despair." The people who love God expect to pass *through* this valley and not remain there. They get a blessing from the experience, and they leave a blessing behind. Like Abraham and Isaac, they "dig a well" (Gen. 21:22-34; 26:17-33), and like Samuel and Elijah, they pray down the rain (1 Sam. 12:16-25; 1 Kings 18). It's wonderful to *receive* a blessing, but it's even greater to *be* a blessing and transform a desert into a garden. True pilgrims "go from strength to strength" (Deut. 33:25; Isa. 40:28-31; Phil. 4:13) and trust God to enable them to walk a step at a time and work a day at a time. They are people of prayer who keep in communion with the Lord, no matter what their circumstances may be. "Blessed are those whose strength is in you" (v. 5, NIV).

My Trust Is in the Lord (vv. 9-12)

From pleading "Hear my prayer" (v. 8), the psalmist then lifted his petitions to the Lord, beginning with a prayer for the king (v. 9). A "shield" is a symbol of both the Lord (3:3; 7:10; 18:2, 30; Gen. 15:1) and Israel's anointed king (89:18; see 2 Sam. 1:21). But why pray for the king? Because the future of the Messianic promise rested with the line of King David (2 Sam. 7),

and the psalmist wanted the Messiah to come. Believers today should pray faithfully for those in authority (1 Tim. 2:1-4).

When you walk by faith, you put the Lord and His will first, and you keep your priorities straight (v. 10). This is the Old Testament version of Matthew 6:33 and Philippians 1:21. According to the inscription, this psalm is associated with "the Sons of Korah," who were Levites assigned to guard the threshold of the sanctuary (1 Chron. 9:19), an important and honorable office. Their ancestor rebelled against God and Moses and was slain by the Lord (Num. 16; note "tents of wickedness" in 84:10 and Num. 16:26). Korah's children were not killed because of their father's sins (Num. 26:11) but continued to serve at the sanctuary. The psalmist didn't aspire to a high office ("gatekeeper" in 1 Chron. 9:19 is not the same word as "doorkeeper" in 84:10) but was willing to "sit at the threshold" of the temple, just to be close to the Lord.

To men and women of faith, the Lord is all they need. He is to them what the sun is to our universe—the source of life and light (27:1; Isa. 10:17; 60:19-20; Mal. 4:2). Without the sun, life would vanish from the earth, and without God, we would have neither physical life (Acts 17:24-28) nor spiritual life (John 1:1-14). God is our provision and our protection ("shield"; see references at vv. 8-9). He is the giving God, and He gives grace and glory—grace for the journey and glory at the end of the journey (see Rom. 5:1-2; 1 Peter 5:10). If we walk by faith, then whatever begins with grace will ultimately end with glory. God does not give us everything we want, but He bestows upon us all that is good for us, all that we need. (See 1:1-3.)

Although times of solitude and spiritual retreat can be very beneficial to us spiritually, believers today have constant open access into the presence of God because of the shed blood of Jesus Christ and His constant intercession for us in heaven (Heb. 7:25; 10:19-25). Do we delight in the Lord and seek Him? Do we depend on His strength? Do we walk and work by faith? Are we among those who walk uprightly (v. 11)?

Psalm 85

This psalm was probably written after the Jewish people returned to their land following their seventy years of captivity in Babylon (Jer. 29). Note the emphasis on *the land* (vv. 1, 9 and 12) and on God's anger against His people (vv. 3-5). God gave them favor with their captors, raised up leaders like Zerubbabel the governor, Joshua the high priest, and Ezra the scribe, and protected the Jewish remnant as they traveled to their war-ravaged land. When you read Ezra 6 and the prophets Haggai, Zechariah, and Malachi, you learn that life was very difficult for them in the land. They did not always obey the Lord or show kindness to each other, but they did make a new start. The Scottish preacher George H. Morrison said, "The victorious Christian life is a series of new beginnings," and he is right. It is a sin to disobey God and fall, but it is also a sin to stay fallen. We must always make a new beginning, and this psalm gives us some instructions that we can follow after times of failure and chastening.

Give Thanks to the Lord (vv. 1-3)
It should have been no surprise to the people of Judah that the Babylonians would invade their land, destroy their city and temple, and take them captive. After all, they knew the terms of the covenant (Lev. 26; Deut. 28-30), and time after time, the Lord had sent His prophets

to warn them, but they would not listen (2 Chron. 36:15-21). Jeremiah had told the people that their captivity would last seventy years and then the Lord would restore a remnant to the land (Jer. 29). God protected the people as they made the long journey home. He forgave their sins and gave them a new beginning, and for this they thanked the Lord (Isa. 40:1-2). The Hebrew word *shuv* basically means "to turn or return," and it is used in verse 1 ("brought back"), verses 3, 4, and 8 ("turn"), and verse 6 ("again"). When we turn back to God, repent, and confess our sins, He turns back to us and restores us.

Ask Him for Renewed Life (vv. 4-7)
It is one thing for the nation collectively to have a new birth of freedom, but there must also be changes in individuals. The praise begun in verses 1-3 (possibly by a choir) now becomes prayer from the hearts of the people. Note that the word *us* is used six times, for it is the people who are praying, not the choir or worship leader. "Turn (restore) us" is the burden of their prayer. It has well been said that a change in geography will never overcome a flaw in character. The return of the people to the land was no guarantee that all of them had returned to the Lord. Not only were they concerned that God's chastening would end in their own lives, but they did not want it to be passed on to their children and grandchildren. The word "revive" simply means "to live again, to be renewed in life." (We must not confuse this with the modern meaning—"special meetings for winning the lost.") Establishing the nation, rebuilding the temple, and restoring the liturgy would not guarantee God's blessing on His people. They desperately needed His life at work within them. While in Babylon, had they heard or read Ezekiel's

message about the dry bones (Ezek. 37), and did they long for the wind of the Spirit to blow upon their own lives and homes? New life is not something that we manufacture ourselves; new life can come only from the Holy Spirit of God. God gave a special message about this to Haggai (Hag. 2:1-9) and also to Zechariah (Zech. 4:6).

Listen for God's Message to You (vv. 8-13)

"I will hear" suggests that the worship leader or a prophet stepped forward and said, in effect, "Now it is time to be silent before God and listen for His message to us for this hour." God and His people were now reconciled and He was speaking peace to them (Jer. 29:11). "Saints" means "people who are set apart for God." Alas, Israel had a long record of "turning to folly"! According to the book of Judges, seven different nations were sent by God to chastise Israel; they repented, but they always lapsed back into idolatry again. After Solomon died, his son Rehoboam was a fool not to listen to the wise men of the land, and this led to a division of the kingdom. Jeroboam, ruler of the northern kingdom, manufactured his own religion and led the nation astray. How foolish! The task of God's people is to fear God and glorify Him (v. 9). The word "dwell" is the Hebrew word *shechinah*, and we speak of God's glory dwelling in the tabernacle (Ex. 40:34) and the temple (2 Chron. 7:1-3). Before the temple was destroyed, Ezekiel saw God's glory leave the structure (Ezek. 9:3; 10:1-4, 18-19; 11:22-23). When the Jewish remnant rebuilt the temple, the prophet Haggai promised that God's glory would return in an even greater way (Hag. 2:6-9).

In verses 10-13, the Lord announced future blessings that He would send if His

people continued to walk with Him. Righteousness and peace—attributes of God—are personified and would "kiss" each other, for the warfare would be over. (See Isa. 32:17; Rom. 3:21-31 and 5:1-3.) Surely there is a glimpse here of the person and work of Jesus Christ, for only in Him can mercy and truth become friends, for if you tell the truth, you may not receive mercy! But the blessing changes the people, for truth springs up from the earth! God's people are faithful and walk in the truth. The psalmist described a world of holiness and harmony, a picture of the coming kingdom over which Christ shall reign. And what a harvest there will be, not only of food necessary for survival (Hag. 1:3-11) but of heaven-sent blessings that will bring joy to the land. As people walk through the land, God's righteousness will go before them and their way will be prepared. God's will shall be done on earth just as it is now done in heaven.

"Even so, come, Lord Jesus!" (Rev. 22:20).

Psalm 86

In the midst of a group of four psalms attributed to the Sons of Korah you find one psalm by David, the only Davidic psalm in the entire third book of Psalms. When David wrote it, he was facing some formidable enemies whom we cannot identify (v. 14), at a time when he was "poor and needy" (v. 1) and calling for God's help. The remarkable thing about the psalm is that it is a mosaic of quotations from other parts of the Old Testament, especially 25-28, 40 and 54-57, and Exodus 34. Since David wrote these psalms, he had every right to quote from them and adapt them to his present needs. At a time of danger, when he felt inadequate to face the battle, David found three encouragements in the Lord, and so may we today.

God's Covenant Is Secure (vv. 1-7)

His statement "I am holy [godly, devoted]" was not an egotistical statement but rather the declaration that David was a son of the covenant and belonged wholly to the Lord. It is the translation of the Hebrew word *hesed* (4:3; 12:1) and is the equivalent of "saints" in the New Testament, "those set apart by and for the Lord." The word is related to *hasid*, which means "mercy, kindness, steadfast love" (vv. 5, 13, 15). As he began his prayer, David pleaded for help on the basis of his covenant relationship with the Lord, just as believers today pray in the name of Jesus and on the basis of His covenant of grace (Luke 22:20; 1 Cor. 11:25; Heb. 10:14-25).

The psalm has many connections with the Davidic covenant (2 Sam. 7). We get the impression that David had the covenant text before him and selected verses from his psalm to parallel what the Lord had said to him and he had said to the Lord. David is called "servant" (7:5, 8, 19, 20, 25, 26, 29; 86:2, 4, 16), and both texts refer to the great things God had done (7:21; 86:10). The uniqueness of the Lord is another shared theme (7:22; 86:8) as well as Jehovah's supremacy over all the supposed "gods" (7:23; 86:8). In both, God's great name is magnified (7:26; 86:9, 11, 12). In his psalm, David used three basic names for God: Jehovah (vv. 1, 6, 11, 17), Adonai (vv. 3, 4, 5, 8, 9, 12, 15), and Elohim (vv. 2, 10, 12, 14). On the basis of God's covenant promises, David could "argue" with the Lord and plead his case. In verses 1-7, the word "for" usually signals one of David's persuasive reasons why the Lord should

help him. In verse 5, he changes from "for I" to "for you" (vv. 5, 7, 10), climaxing in verse 10 with "For you are great." There are at least fourteen personal requests in the psalm, which suggests to us that effective praying is specific. David "cried [called]" and the Lord answered (vv. 3, 5, 7).

(For some of the citations and parallels in the Old Testament, see: **v. 1**—17:6; 31:2; 35:10; 37:14; 40:17; 70:5; **v. 2**—25:20; **v. 3**—57:1-2; **v. 5**—Ex. 34:6ff; **v. 6**—28:2; 55:1-2; **v. 7**- 17:6; 77:2; **v. 8**—35:10; 71:19; 89:6; Ex. 8:10; 9:14; 15:11; **v. 10**—72:18; 77:13-14; **v. 11**—27:11; **vv. 12-13**—50:15, 23; 56:13; 57:9-10; **v. 16**—25:16.)

God's Character Is Unchanging (vv. 8-13)

"There is none like you!" (v. 8) is the confession of a man who truly knows God and remembered Israel's confession at the Exodus (Ex. 15:11). During ten years of exile in the wilderness of Judea, David had learned much about God's character and the way He worked in the lives of His people. God is great in who He is and what He does, and the false gods of all the nations are nothing. In spite of his present troubles, David the prophet (Acts 2:30) saw the day coming when all the nations would enter the Messianic kingdom (v. 9; see Rev. 15:3-4). God made the nations and assigns their boundaries and determines their destinies (Acts 17:22-28; Isa. 2:1-4; 9:6-7; 11:1-16). In verses 11-13, David focused on his own walk with the Lord. After he was delivered from danger, he wanted to walk so as to please and honor the Lord. "Unite my heart" means "I want to have an undivided heart, wholly fixed on the Lord." A perfect heart is a sincere heart that loves God alone and is true to Him (James 1:8; 4:8; Deut. 6:4-5; 10:12). He promised to praise

God forever for delivering him from the grave (sheol), a hint here of future resurrection. (See 49:15 and 73:23-24.)

God's Glory Shall Prevail (vv. 14-17)
David's enemies were proud of themselves and their abilities, violent, and totally ignorant of and indifferent to the God of Israel. But David looked away from them to the Lord who had saved and guided him all his life. (His confession in v. 15 is based on Ex. 34:6ff; and see v. 5; 103:8-13; 116:5; 145:8; Neh. 9:17; and Jonah 4:2.) The apostle Paul tells us that knowing these attributes of God ought to lead people to repentance (Rom. 2:4). "The son of your handmaid" (v. 16) means "your devoted servant" (116:16; Ruth 2:13, 3:9; 1 Sam. 1:11, 12, 18). Children born to servants were considered especially faithful since they were brought up in the master's household (Gen. 14:14). Since David was the Lord's faithful servant, it was his Master's duty to protect and deliver him (143:11-12). But David wanted that deliverance to bring glory to the Lord and to demonstrate to the nations that Jehovah alone was God. It wasn't just warfare, it was witness, a "sign" of the goodness of the Lord to David. It was his way of praying, "Hallowed be Thy name" (Matt. 6:9). When our requests are in God's will and glorify His name, we can be sure He will answer.

Psalm 87

This is another psalm that extols the glory of Mount Zion (see 46-48, 76, 125, 129, 137). The writer was not indulging in arrogant nationalism but only seeking to glorify the God of Israel and the blessings He bestows. The psalm must be read on two levels. It is a prophecy of the future kingdom, when all nations will come to Jerusalem to worship (86:9; Isa. 2:1-5), and it is also a picture of the heavenly Zion where the children of God have their spiritual citizenship (Luke 10:20; Gal. 4:21-31; Phil. 3:20-21; Heb. 12:18-24). God promised that Abraham would have an earthly family, like the sands of the sea, which is Israel, and a heavenly family, like the stars of the heaven, which is the church (Gen. 13:16; 15:4-5). The psalm was probably written in the time of King Hezekiah, after the Assyrian army had been defeated and Babylon was on the rise (Isa. 36-39). Following this great victory, the neighboring nations, usually hostile to the Jews, honored Hezekiah and brought gifts to him as well as sacrifices to the Lord (2 Chron. 32:23). The psalmist shares three wonderful truths about the city of Jerusalem.

The City Is Built by God (vv. 1-3)
After the battle of the kings (Gen. 14:18), Abraham met Melchizedek, the king-priest of Salem (Jerusalem, "city of peace"; see 76:2), and Hebrews 7 informs us that Melchizedek is a type of Jesus Christ, our Priest-King in heaven. David chose Jerusalem for his capital city (2 Sam. 5:6-10), and the Lord validated that choice by putting His temple there. The nation of Israel was to be separate from the other nations both politically (Num. 23:9) and geographically. That is why God called Jerusalem "my city" (Isa. 45:13) and "the holy city" (Isa. 48:2; 52:1) and Zion "my holy mountain" (Isa. 11:9; 56:7; 57:13). It is "the city of the great King, the joy of all the earth" (48:2). It is "His foundation" from which He has built His great work of redemption (Isa. 14:32.). "Salvation is of the Jews," said Jesus (John 4:22), and were it not for Israel, the world would not have the knowledge of the true and living God,

the inspired Scriptures, or the Savior. Jesus died and rose again outside the walls of Jerusalem, the Holy Spirit descended on the church meeting in Jerusalem on Pentecost, and it was from Jerusalem that the early Jewish believers scattered to carry the Gospel to the nations.

The phrase "the gates of Zion" refers to the city itself, a city God loves above all cities in the Holy Land. (See Deut. 7:6-9; 2 Chron. 6:5-6; Isa. 60:11-12; Zech. 1:14.) In Jerusalem was not only the temple of the true God, but also the throne of David, and it would be the Davidic line that would give us the Savior, Jesus Christ. In the end times, Jerusalem will be a center of controversy and conflict, but the Lord will rescue His beloved city (Zech. 12:1-13:1). But the prophets have written some "glorious things" about the future Jerusalem, and the apostles have written even more glorious things about the heavenly Jerusalem!

The City Is Inhabited by His Children (vv. 4-6)

The Lord is described as a king taking a royal census and registering individual names ("this one ... that one ..."), but the remarkable thing is that these people are Gentiles and that God is making them His own children and citizens of His holy city! Even more, the nations named are the avowed enemies of the Jews! The emphasis in all three verses is on *birth*, indicating that the people who enter the future glorious kingdom will experience a "new birth" and belong to the family of God. Like Paul, they will be citizens by birth (Acts 22:25-29) and not by purchase. The phrase "those that know me" indicates more than an intellectual appreciation of the Lord. It describes a personal relationship with Him, like that of husband and wife (Gen. 4:1; 19:8; 1 Sam. 2:12; 3:7).

"Rahab" refers to Egypt (89:10; Isa. 51:9), Israel's enemy in the south, and the word means "arrogant, boisterous." Egypt enslaved the Jews and yet will share with them citizenship in the city of God and membership in the family of God! (Isa. 19:18-25). Israel's northern enemy, Babylon, would one day destroy Jerusalem and ravage the kingdom of Judah, and the Jews would vow to pay her back (137:1, 8-9), but she, too, will be part of the glorious kingdom! Philistia and Tyre on the west were always a threat to Israel, but they will be included. Ethiopia is "Cush," a nation in Africa. Of course, of all these nations, only Egypt is still on the map, but the message is clear: when the Lord establishes His glorious kingdom, and Messiah reigns from Jerusalem, Israel's enemies will be transformed into fellow citizens. Through the preaching of the Gospel today, this miracle is happening in His church (Eph. 2:11-22; Gal. 3:26-29). The Old Testament prophets promised that believers from all the nations of the earth would be included in Messiah's reign (Isa. 2:1-5; Mic. 4:1-5; Zech. 8:23; 14:16-20), and so did the psalmists (22:27; 46:10; 47:9; 57:5, 11; 98:2-3; 99:2-3). "For the earth will be filled with the knowledge of the glory of the Lord, as the waters cover the sea" (Hab. 2:14, NKJV).

The City Enjoys His Abundant Blessings (v. 7)

As citizens of Zion and the children of God, the Jews and Gentiles not only live together but they sing together and play musical instruments as they rejoice in God's blessings. Jerusalem is one of the few ancient cities that was not built near a great river, and it was always a problem to supply enough water, especially during a siege. To help solve this problem, King

Hezekiah had ordered an underground water system constructed (2 Kings 20:20; 2 Chron. 32:30). The word translated "fountains" or "springs" refers to "living water" and not water brought up from a well. A fountain or spring symbolizes the source of something, as Jacob is the "fountain" from which the nation came (Deut. 33:28). All blessings, especially spiritual blessings, will flow from the Lord who reigns in the City of David, just as today we draw upon the wealth found only in our exalted Lord (Rom. 2:4; 9:23; 11:33; Eph. 1:3; 2:4-10; 3:8; Phil. 4:19; Col. 1:27). The image of a river of living water is found also in 36:8-9; 46:4; 89:6; Ezekiel 47; John 7:37-39; and Revelation 22:1-2.

Psalm 88

Heman, the son of Joel, was a temple musician during the reign of David (1 Chron. 6:33, 37; 15:17; 16:41-42; 2 Chron. 35:15) and is the most likely candidate for the authorship of this psalm. Second choice is Heman, the son of Mahol, one of the wise men during the reign of King Solomon (1 Kings 4:31). The Hebrew words *mahalath* and *leannoth* mean "sickness" and "for singing" or "for humbling." The first word probably refers to a sad melody to accompany this somber song, and the second might identify the purpose of the psalm, to bring us low before the Lord. This is the last "sons of Korah" psalm in the psalms and is perhaps the most plaintive song in the entire book. In the Hebrew text, the psalm ends with the word *hoshek*, "darkness," and there is no closing note of triumph as in other psalms that begin with pain and perplexity. The psalm speaks of darkness (vv. 1, 6, 12, 18), life in the depths (vv. 3-4, 6), the immanence of death (vv. 5, 10-11),

feelings of drowning (vv. 7, 16-17), loneliness (vv. 5, 8, 14, 18), and imprisonment (v. 8). Heman was a servant of God who was suffering intensely and did not understand why, yet he persisted in praying to God and did not abandon his faith. Not all of life's scripts have happy endings, but that does not mean that the Lord has forsaken us. From Heman's experience, as recorded in this psalm, we can discover four instructions to follow when life falls apart and our prayers seemingly are not answered.

Come to the Lord by Faith (vv. 1-2)

Heman's life had not been an easy one (v. 15) and now it had grown even more difficult, and he felt that death was very near (vv. 3, 10-11). But he did not give up! He still trusted in God, whom he addressed as "LORD—Jehovah" four times in this prayer (vv. 1, 9, 13, 14). "Jehovah" is the name of the Lord that emphasizes His covenant relationship with His people, and Heman was a son of that covenant. Heman also addressed Him as "God—Elohim," the name that expresses His power. The phrase "God of my salvation" indicates that Heman had trusted the Lord to save him, and the fact that he prayed as he did indicates that his faith was still active. Three times we are told that he cried to the Lord, and three different words are used: verse 1—"a cry for help in great distress"; verse 2—"a loud shout"; verse 13—"a cry of anguish." He was fervent in his praying. He believed in a God who could hear his prayers and do wonders (vv. 10, 12), a God who loved him and was faithful to His people (v. 11). All of this is evidence of faith in Heman's heart, even though he spoke as though he was ready to give up. He prayed day and night (vv. 1, 9) and trusted that no obstacle would come between his prayers and the Lord (v. 2; 18:6; 22:24; 35:13; 66:20; 79:11). No matter how we feel and no matter how impossible our circumstances, we can always come to the Lord with our burdens.

Tell the Lord How You Feel (vv. 3-9)

There is no place for hypocrisy in personal prayer. One of the first steps toward revival is to be completely transparent when we pray and not tell the Lord anything that is not true or that we do not really mean. Heman confessed that he was "full of troubles" and felt like a "living dead man." He was without strength and felt forsaken by the Lord. Old Testament believers did not have the full light of revelation concerning death and the afterlife, so we must not be shocked at his description of sheol, the world of the dead. The Lord does not forget His people when they die, nor does He cease to care, for "to be absent from the body" means to be "present with the Lord" (2 Cor. 5:6-8). (See 25:7; 74:2; and 106:4.)

But Heman also told the Lord that *He* was responsible for his servant's troubles! God's hand put him into the pit (sheol, the grave), and God's anger was flowing over him like breakers from the sea (see 42:8). Whatever sickness he had was caused by the Lord and made him so repulsive that his friends avoided him (see 31:1). He was without health, without light, and without friends—and he felt like he was without God! He was a prisoner and there was no way to escape. Like Job, Heman wanted to know why all this suffering had come to him.

Defend Your Cause Before the Lord (vv. 10-14).

The saintly Scottish minister Samuel Rutherford (A.D. 1600-1661), who suffered much for his faith, wrote, "It is faith's work to claim and challenge lovingkindnesses out of all the roughest strokes of God." He also said, "Why should I tremble at the plough of my Lord, that maketh deep furrows in my soul? I know He is no idle husbandman; He purposeth a crop." Hamen's argument is simply that his death will rob God of a great opportunity to demonstrate His power and glory. Of what service could Hamen be to the Lord in sheol?

The spirits of the dead will not arise in the world of the dead and do the Lord's bidding (see Isa. 14:9-11), but Heman could serve the Lord in the land of the living. (See 30:8-10; 115:17.) Before he went to the sanctuary to assist in the worship, Heman prayed to the Lord for healing and strength, and at the close of a busy day, he prayed again. During his daily ministry, he heard the priestly benediction: "The Lord bless you, and keep you; the Lord make His face to shine upon you and be gracious to you; the Lord lift up His countenance on you, and give you peace" (Num. 6:24-26, NASB)—but the blessing did not come to him! He felt rejected and knew that God's face was turned away from Him. But he kept on praying!

Wait for the Lord's Answer (vv. 15-18)

We do not know what this affliction was that came to him early in life, but it is painful to think that he suffered all his life long and all day long (vv. 15, 17). He could not even look back to a time in his life when he enjoyed good health. The billows that almost drown him (v. 7) now became fiery waves of torment (v. 16) as God's "burning anger" went over him (see 42:7). The flood was rising and he felt he was about to drown (see 130:1), and there was nobody near enough to rescue him. He was alone!

The darkness was his friend because it hid him from the eyes of those who observed his sufferings and may have said (as did Job's friends), "He must have sinned greatly for the Lord to afflict him so much!"

But he continued to pray and to look to God for help! "Though he slay me, yet will I trust him" (Job 13:5). "I would have despaired unless I had believed that I would see the goodness of the Lord in the land of the living. Wait for the Lord; be strong, and let your heart take courage; yes, wait for the Lord" (Ps. 27:13-14, NASB). The Lord always has the last word, and it will not be "darkness." We should never doubt in the darkness what God has taught us in the light.

Psalm 89

If the author is the wise man Ethan of Solomon's reign (1 Kings 4:31), then verses 39-45 describe the invasion of Shishak and the Egyptian army recorded in 1 Chronicles 12, which occurred during the reign of Solomon's son Rehoboam. But this invasion did not mean the end of the Davidic dynasty, which is the major theme of this psalm. However, the invasion and captivity of Judah by the Babylonians did mean the end of the Davidic dynasty, so this psalm could have been written after that crisis by an unknown "Ethan." Young King Jehoiachin had already been taken captive to Babylon and Zedekiah, his uncle, named king in his place (2 Kings 24), and Jeremiah had announced that none of Jehoiachin's sons would ever sit on David's throne (Jer. 22:24-29). What, then, becomes of God's covenant that promised David a throne forever (vv. 3, 28, 34, 39, and see 2 Sam. 7)? Does Jehovah no

longer keep His promises? The faithfulness of the Lord is the major theme of this psalm (vv. 1, 2, 5, 8, 14, 33, 49). Of course, God's great promises to David have their ultimate fulfillment in Jesus Christ, the Son of David (Luke 1:26-38, 68-79). The psalm gives us four assurances about the faithfulness of the Lord.

God Is Faithful in His Character—Praise Him (vv. 1-18)

The psalm opens on a joyful note of worship with praise to God from the psalmist (vv. 1-4), in heaven (vv. 5-8), and on earth (vv. 9-13), and especially from the people of Israel (vv. 14-18), who rejoice in the Lord all day long (v. 16). The psalmist sings (v. 1), the angels praise (v. 5), and even the mountains sing for joy (v. 12). Ethan praised the faithfulness of God's character (vv. 1-2) and His covenant (vv. 3-4), about which he has much to say (vv. 3, 28, 34, 39). Because he wanted to instruct and encourage the coming generations (see 78:1-8), Ethan wrote down his praise and his prayer. God had sworn to David that his dynasty and throne would continue forever (vv. 28-29, 35-36, 49; 2 Sam. 7:13), but future generations of Jews would live without any king, let alone a king from David's line. Ethan wanted them to know that God's mercy (lovingkindness, NASB; love, NIV) was being built up (v. 2) even though the city and temple had been torn down and the crown and throne of David had been cast down (vv. 39, 44). God was still on His throne (v. 14), and David's line ("seed") was secured forever in Jesus Christ, the Son of God (vv. 4, 29, 36-37; see Heb. 1:8; 5:6; 7:28; 10:12; 13:8, 21; Rev. 11:15). The "sure mercies (lovingkindnesses, v. 1) of David" will never fail (Isa. 55:3; Acts 13:34). God had not forsaken His servant David (vv. 3, 20, 39; 2 Sam. 7:5, 8, 20, 21, 25-29).

Heaven is a place of worship, and the angels praise the Lord for His glorious attributes (vv. 5-8; see Rev. 4 and 5), for there is no god like Him (Ex. 15:11). But the earth joins the hymn and even the mighty waves of the sea obey Him and praise Him. The tumultuous sea is an image of the nations (93:3; Isa. 17:12-13; Rev. 13:1; 17:15), so Ethan mentioned God's victory over Egypt (Rahab, 87:4; Isa. 51:9). The "scattering" of God's enemies (v. 10) reminds us of Numbers 10:35. Hermon is an imposing mountain to the far north, near Damascus, and Tabor is a much smaller mount about fifty miles southwest of Hermon. Ethan heard the mountains singing praises to God, just as Isaiah did centuries before (Isa. 55:12).

If any people on earth have a right to praise God, it is the nation of Israel, God's chosen people. They had a holy land, given to them by God, a royal dynasty chosen by God, and the light of the holy law that guided their steps in the ways of the Lord. They had a holy priesthood to serve them and bless them (v. 15; see Num. 6:24-26), men who would blow the trumpets to signal the special holy days and feasts ("the joyful sound"; see 81:1). In verse 18, "our shield" (NASB, NIV) refers to their king (84:9), now in captivity. In many Jewish synagogues today, verses 15-18 are recited on their New Year's Day after the blowing of the shofar.

God Is Faithful to His Covenant— Trust Him (vv. 19-29)

From verse 19 to verse 37, it is the Lord who speaks and reminds us of what He did for David. The question in the mind of the writer was probably, "If you did so much for David, why then did you break your covenant and reject us?" What was the vision and to whom was it given? God gave Samuel the message that David would succeed Saul (1 Sam. 13:13-15 and 16:1-13), and He gave Nathan the message that David would not build the temple but would have a "throne forever" and a "house" (family) built by the Lord (2 Sam. 7:1-17). The Lord may have led Ethan to rehearse this important information because the generations living after the exile needed to know it. Israel had a tremendously important ministry to fulfill in bringing the Messiah into the world, and He would come through the family of David. (Be sure to refer to 2 Sam. 7:1-17, for vv. 19-29 are a summary of the promises the Lord made to David.)

In a sovereign act of grace, the Lord *elected* David to be king of Israel (vv. 19-20). Their first king, Saul of Benjamin, was never supposed to establish a dynasty because he was not from the royal tribe of Judah (Gen. 49:10). David had proved himself before the Lord even before he stepped out on the stage of history and killed Goliath (1 Sam. 17:32-37). He had been faithful over a few things, and now the Lord would promote him to greater things (see Matt. 25:21). The Lord who elected David also *equipped* him to fight battles, lead the army, and build the kingdom (vv. 21-23). Even as a youth, he was known for his military prowess. The Lord *exalted* David, because David was a humble man who would not promote himself (vv. 24-27). Indeed, God helped David to expand the borders of the kingdom so that it reached from the Mediterranean Sea on the west to the Tigris and Euphrates Rivers on the east (see Ex. 23:31). It was David's close relationship to the Lord and his desire to exalt the Lord alone that made him a success (v. 26). David was the eighth son in Jesse's family (1 Sam. 16:13), but God made him His firstborn, the honored son that received the greatest inheritance. David's greater Son, Jesus Christ, was also called "the firstborn" (Rom. 8:29; Col. 1:15, 18; Heb. 1:6; Rev. 1:5). If David was "the highest of the kings of the earth" (v. 27, NASB), then he was "King of kings" like our Savior (see Rev. 17:14 and 19:16). Finally, the Lord *established* David and promised him a throne and a dynasty forever (v. 4; 2 Sam. 7:13, 16, 24-26, 29, 31), a promise fulfilled in Jesus Christ.

God Is Faithful in His Chastening (vv. 39-45)

Again, Ethan faced the question: "If God did so much for David, why did his throne and crown fall in defeat and disgrace?" The answer: because the terms of His covenant declare that the same Lord who blesses the obedient will also chasten the disobedient. The principle applied not only to David's successors on the throne (vv. 30-37; 2 Sam. 7:12-15) but also to the nation of Israel collectively (Deut. 28). "For whom the Lord loves He corrects, just as a father the son in whom he delights" (Prov. 3:12, NKJV; Heb. 12:3-11). Because of their disobedience and self-will, many of the kings of Judah were chastened by the Lord, but the Lord never broke His promise to David. The "witness" in verse 37 is probably the Lord Himself in heaven (see NASB), but the constancy of the heavenly bodies is also a witness to the faithfulness of the Lord's promises (Gen. 8:20-22; Jer. 31:35-36; 33:19-26).

Ethan told the Lord what He had done to Judah's anointed king, the descendant of David. The Lord was angry with the kings because of their sins, especially idolatry (v. 38), so He permitted the Babylonians to come and ravage the land, destroy Jerusalem, and burn the temple (vv. 40-41). To Ethan, the Lord was actually aiding the enemy! (vv. 42-43). But the glory had once more departed from the temple (v. 44; see 1 Sam. 4:21-22; Ezek. 8:1-4; 9:3; 10:4, 18; 11:22-23) because the leaders had turned their backs on the Lord and turned to idols. It appears that verse 45 applied especially to King Jehoiachin, who was but eighteen years old when he became king and reigned for three months and ten days (2 Kings 24:8). He became a captive in Babylon for thirty-seven years.

God's Faithfulness Will Never Cease—Wait for Him (vv. 46-52)

Ethan looks ahead (vv. 46-48) and asks the painful question, "How long, O Lord?" (See 6:3 for other references.) Surely he knew the prophecy of Jeremiah that the people would be in exile for seventy years and then permitted to return to their land (Jer. 25:1-14; 29:4-14), but when you are in the midst of the storm, you long for God to deliver you as soon as possible. To Ethan, it all seemed so futile. Life is short, all people will die, and God's people had to spend their days in exile. Then Ethan looked back (v. 49) and asked what had happened to the great lovingkindnesses the Lord had shown to David. But God's love had not changed; it was Judah's love for the Lord that had waned. Like any good parent, God shows His love to His children either by blessing their obedience or chastening them for their disobedience, but in either situation, He is manifesting His love.

Finally, Ethan looked around and felt keenly the reproaches of the enemy (vv. 50-51). The king of Judah was now a common prisoner in a foreign city! No doubt Jehoiachin was paraded shamelessly in Babylon as living proof that the gods of Babylon were greater than Judah's God.

How the Babylonians must have enjoyed following the parade and taunting the captive Jews, especially the anointed king!

Verse 52 is not a part of the original psalm but forms the conclusion of Book III of The Psalms (see 41:13 and 72:18-19). But it expresses a great truth: no matter how much we suffer because of the sins of others, and no matter how perplexed we may be at the providential workings of the Lord, we should still be able to say by faith, "Praise the Lord! Hallelujah!" And our fellow sufferers ought to respond with, "Amen and amen! So be it!"

That's the way of trust—faith in the faithfulness of the Lord.

BOOK IV
Psalm 90

This is the oldest psalm in The Psalms and it was written by Moses, the man of God (Josh. 14:6; Ezra 3:2). It deals with themes that began with the fall of our first parents and will continue to be important and puzzling until the return of our Savior: eternal God and frail humans, a holy God and sinful man, life and death, and the meaning of life in a confused and difficult world. It's possible that Moses wrote this psalm after Israel's failure of faith at Kadesh Barnea (Num. 13-14), when the nation was condemned to journey in the wilderness for forty years until the older generation had died. That tragedy was followed by the death of Moses' sister Miriam (Num. 20:1) and his brother Aaron (Num. 20:22-29), and between those two deaths, Moses disobeyed the Lord and struck the rock

(Num. 20:2-13). How did Moses manage to become a "man of God" after forty years in pagan Egypt that ended in failure, forty years in Midian as a humble shepherd, and forty more leading a funeral march through the wilderness? Life was not easy for Moses, but he triumphed, and in this psalm he shared his insights so that we, too, might have strength for the journey and end well.

We Are Travelers and God Is Our Home (vv. 1-2)

"For we are aliens and pilgrims before you, as were our fathers" said King David (1 Chron. 29:12, NKJV). For all mortals, life is a pilgrimage from birth to death, and for believers, it is a journey from earth to heaven, but the road is not an easy one. Jacob called the 130 years of his pilgrimage "few and evil" (Gen. 47:9), and he was a pilgrim to the very end, for he died leaning on the top of his staff (Heb. 11:21). For eighty years, Moses had lived a somewhat settled life, first in Egypt and then in Midian, but after that he spent forty years in the wilderness, leading a nation of complaining former slaves who didn't always want or appreciate his leadership. Numbers 33 names forty-two different places Israel camped during their journey, *but no matter where Moses lived, God was always his home.* He "lived in the Lord." He knew how to "abide in the Lord" and find strength, comfort, encouragement, and help for each day's demands. Moses pitched a special tent outside the camp where he went to meet the Lord (Ex. 33:7-11). This is the Old Testament equivalent of the New Testament admonition, "Abide in me" (see John 15:1-11). We must all make the Lord "our dwelling" (91:9).

Moses addressed God as "Elohim," the God of power and the God of creation. He described God "giving birth" to the mountains (v. 2; Job 15:7; 38:8, 28-29) and forming the world. To people in the ancient world, mountains symbolized that which was lasting and dependable, and to the Jews, mountains spoke of the everlasting God of Israel (93:1-2). There were six generations from Abraham to Moses—Abraham, Isaac, Jacob, Levi, Kohath, Amram, and Moses—and the same God had guided and blessed them! Those of us who have godly ancestors certainly have a rich heritage and ought to be thankful. In the midst of a changing world, living as we do in a "frail tent" (2 Cor. 5:1-4), it is good to hear Moses say, "The eternal God is your refuge and dwelling place, and underneath are the everlasting arms" (Deut. 33:27, AMP).

We Are Learners and Life Is Our School (vv. 3-12)

Moses was "educated in all the learning of the Egyptians" (Acts 7:22, NASB), but the lessons he learned walking with God were far more important. In the school of life (v. 12), we need to learn two important lessons: life is brief and passes swiftly (vv. 4-6), so make the most of it; and life is difficult and at times seems futile (vv. 7-11), but this is the only way to mature. Were there no sin in the world, there would be no suffering and death; but people *made of dust* defy the God of the universe and try to repeal the inexorable law of sin and death, "For dust you are, and to dust you shall return" (Gen. 3:19, NKJV). While we all thank God for modern science and the ministry of skilled medical personnel, we cannot successfully deny the reality of death or delay it when our time comes. The school of life is preparation for an eternity with God, and without Him, we cannot learn our lessons, pass our tests, and make

progress from kindergarten to graduate school!

The older we get, the better we understand that life is brief and moves past very swiftly. God dwells in eternity (Isa. 57:15) and is not limited by time. He can cram many years of experience and work into one person's lifetime or make the centuries flash past like the days of the week (2 Peter 3:8). Compared with eternity, even a long life is like yesterday when it is past or like the changing of the guards while we are sleeping (a "watch" was four hours). Only God is eternal, and we humans are like objects suddenly swept away by a flash flood (Matt. 7:24-27) or grass that comes and goes. In the east, the grass often grows on very thin soil and has no deep roots (Matt. 13:20-21). A field will be lush and green in the morning but become withered before nightfall because of the hot sun. (See 37:1-2; 92:7; 103:15; Isa. 40:6-7; and 1 Peter 1:24.) God is the one whose command "turns us back" (v. 3; see 104:29; 146:4; Job 34:15; Ecc. 3:20), and we need to fear and honor Him and use our lives for His glory. In the school of life, those students learn the most who realize that the dismissal bell rings when they least expect it!

In verses 7-11, Moses reflected on Israel's sad experience at Kedesh Barnea (Num. 13-14), when the nation refused to obey God and enter the Promised Land. This foolish decision led to four decades of trials and testings in the wilderness while the older generation died off, except for Joshua and Caleb. God is "slow to anger" (Ex. 34:6), but the repeated complaints and rebellions of His people tested even His longsuffering. (See Ex. 32:10; Num. 11:11, 33; 12:9; 25:3; 32:10, 13; Deut. 4:24-25; 6:15; 9:7, 18-19.) God saw what Israel did and God knew what Israel *intended to do!* No secrets are hidden from

Him. The twenty-year-olds would be close to sixty when the nation returned to Kadesh Barnea, and Moses saw eighty years as the limit for humans. He died at 120 and Joshua at 110, but King David was only 70 when he died. Sin takes its toll on the human race, and we no longer see lifespans recorded like those in Genesis 5. We don't like to think about the wrath of God, but every obituary in the newspaper is a reminder that "the wages of sin is death" (Rom. 6:23). We finish our years "like a sigh" (v. 9, NASB) and marvel that it all went by so fast! So, now is the time to ask God for wisdom to become better students and stewards of our time and opportunities (v. 12; Deut. 32:29). We number our years, not our days, but all of us have to live a day at a time, and we do not know how many days we have left. A successful life is composed of successful days that honor the Lord.

We Are Believers and the Future Is Our Friend (vv. 13-17)

Yes, life is a difficult school, and God disciplines us if we fail to learn our lessons and submit to His will, but there is more to the story. In spite of the "black border" around this psalm, the emphasis is on *life* and not death. The past and present experiences of life prepare us for the future, and all of life prepares us for eternity. When you contrast verses 13-17 with verses 7-12, you can see the difference. This closing prayer emphasizes God's compassion and unfailing love, His desire to give us joy and satisfaction, even in the midst of life's troubles, and His ability to make life count for eternity. When Jesus Christ is your Savior and Lord, the future is your friend.

"Return" (v. 13) carries the idea of "turn again—turn from your anger and show us the light of your countenance"

(Ex. 32:12; Num. 6:23-26; Deut. 32:36). "How long?" is a question frequently asked; see 6:3. In verse 14, Moses may have been referring to the manna that fell each morning, six days a week, and met the physical needs of the people (Ex. 16:1-21). It was a picture of Jesus Christ, the bread of life. The manna sustained life for the Jewish people for nearly forty years, but Jesus gives life to the whole world for all eternity! When we begin the day with the Lord and feed on His Word (Deut. 8:3; Matt. 4:4), then we walk with Him throughout the day and enjoy His blessing. The nourishment of the Word enables us to be faithful pilgrims and successful learners.

There are compensations in life that we may not appreciate until we enter eternity. Moses prayed that God would give him and his people as much joy in the future as the sorrow they had experienced in the past. Paul may have had this in mind when he wrote Romans 8:18 and 2 Corinthians 1:5 and 4:16-18—except that God promises His children far more blessing than the burdens they carried! The glory to come far exceeds the suffering that we bear today. Moses lost his temper and could not enter Canaan (Num. 20:2-13), but he did get to the Promised Land with Jesus and share God's glory with Elijah and three of the disciples (Matt. 17:1-8).

Whatever the Lord doesn't compensate for here on earth will be compensated in heaven (1 Peter 5:10), and this includes our works for Him. At times, Moses must have felt that his work was futile, temporary, and not worth doing. Many times the people broke his heart and grieved his spirit. He sacrificed to serve them and they rarely appreciated him. But no work done for the Lord will ever go unrewarded, and those who do the will of

God abide forever (1 John 2:17). Even a cup of cold water given in Jesus' name will receive its reward (Matt. 10:42; 25:31-46). The favor of the Lord does not desert us in our old age, in times of affliction, or when we come to die, and the blessings of our work and witness will go on. In verse 13, Moses addressed God as Jehovah, the God of the covenant who will never break His promises, and that is the God we love, worship, and serve.

Life is brief, so Moses prayed, "Teach us." Life is difficult, and he prayed, "Satisfy us." His work at times seemed futile, so he prayed, "Establish the work of our hands." God answered those prayers for Moses, and He will answer them for us. The future is your friend when Jesus is your Savior and Lord.

Psalm 91

Psalm 90 focuses on dealing with the difficulties of life, but the emphasis in this psalm is on the dangers of life. The anonymous author (though some think Moses wrote it) warns about hidden traps, deadly plagues, terrors at night and arrows by day, stumbling over rocks, and facing lions and snakes! However, in view of terrorist attacks, snipers, reckless drivers, exotic new diseases, and Saturday night handgun specials, the contemporary scene may be as dangerous as the one described in the psalm. The saints who abide in Christ (vv. 1, 9) cannot avoid confronting unknown perils, but they can escape the evil consequences. Moses, David, and Paul, and a host of other servants of God, faced great danger in accomplishing God's will, and the Lord saw them through. However, Hebrews 11:36 cautions us that "others" were tortured and martyred, yet their faith was just as real. But generally speaking, walking with the Lord does help us to detect and avoid a great deal of trouble, and it is better to suffer in the will of God than to invite trouble by disobeying God's will (1 Peter 2:18-25). The psalmist described the elements involved in living the life of confidence and victory.

Faith in God—the Hidden Life (vv. 1-4)
The most important part of a believer's life is the part that only God sees, the "hidden life" of communion and worship that is symbolized by the Holy of Holies in the Jewish sanctuary (Ex. 25:18-22; Heb. 10:19-25). God is our refuge and strength (46:1). He hides us that He might help us and then send us back to serve Him in the struggles of life. (See 27:5; 31:19-20; 32:7; 73:27-28; 94:22; 142:5; Deut. 32:37.) The author of the psalm had two "addresses": his tent (v. 10) and his Lord (vv. 1, 9). The safest place in the world is a shadow, if it is the shadow of the Almighty. Through Jesus Christ we find safety and satisfaction under the wings of the cherubim in the Holy of Holies (36:7-8; 57:1; 61:4; 63:2, 6-7). Jesus pictured salvation by describing chicks hiding under the wings of the mother hen (Matt. 23:37; Luke 13:38), and the psalmist pictured communion as believers resting under the wings of the cherubim in the tabernacle.

The names of God used in these verses encourage us to trust Him. He is *the Most High* (Elyon; vv. 1, 9), a name found first in Genesis 14:18-20. He is higher than the kings of the earth and the false gods of the nations. He is also *the Almighty* (Shaddai), the all-sufficient God who is adequate for every situation. (See Gen. 17:1; 28:3; 35:11.) He is LORD (vv. 2, 9, 14), Jehovah, the covenant-making God who is faithful to His promises. He is *God* (Elohim, v. 2), the powerful God whose greatness and glory surpass anything we can imagine. *This is the God who invites us to fellowship with Him in the Holy of Holies!* This hidden life of worship and communion makes possible the public life of obedience and service. This God shelters us beneath the wings of the cherubim, but He also gives us the spiritual armor we need (v. 4; Eph. 6:10-18). His truth and faithfulness protect us as we claim His promises and obey Him. The shield is the large shield that covers the whole person. (See Gen. 15:1; Deut. 33:29; 2 Sam. 22:3.) Some translations give "bulwark" or "rampart" instead of "buckler." The Hebrew word means "to go around" and would describe a mound of earth around a fortress. But the message is clear: those who abide in the Lord are safe when they are doing His will. God's servants are immortal until their work is done (Rom. 8:28-39).

Peace from God—the Protected Life (vv. 5-13)

When we practice "the hidden life," we are not alone for God is with us and compensates for our inadequacies. This paragraph emphasizes that we need not be afraid because the Lord and His angels watch over us. In the ancient Near East, travel was dangerous, unless you were protected by armed guards. (It is not much different in some large cities today.) "Terror by night" could mean simply "the fear of the dark" and of what can happen in the darkness. Contaminated water and food, plus an absence of sound health measures, made it easy to contract diseases by day or by night, although "the destruction that lays waste at noon" (v. 6, NASB) could refer to the effects of the burning rays of the sun.

Verses 7 and 8 read like the description of a battle and may have a direct relationship to the covenant promises God made with Israel (Lev. 26:8; Deut. 32:30). With their own eyes, Israel saw the grief of the Egyptians over their firstborn who died on Passover night (Ex. 12:29-30), and they also saw the Egyptian army dead on the shore of the Red Sea (Ex. 14:26-31), yet no harm came to the people of Israel. God's angel went before them to prepare the way and to lead the way (Ex. 23:20). Satan quoted part of verses 11-12 when he tempted Jesus in the wilderness (Matt. 4:6), and the Lord responded with Deuteronomy 6:16. If the Father had commanded Jesus to jump from the temple pinnacle, then the angels would have cared for Jesus, but to jump without the Father's command would have been presumption, not faith, and that would be tempting the Father. In Scripture, the lion and serpent (cobra) are images of Satan (1 Peter 5:8; Gen. 3; 2 Cor. 11:3; Rev. 12:9; 20:2; and see Luke 10:19 and Rom. 16:20). In the ancient Near East, both were dangerous enemies, especially for travelers walking along the narrow paths.

Love for God—the Satisfied Life (vv. 14-16)

The Lord spoke and announced what He would do for those of His people who truly loved Him and acknowledged Him with obedient lives. The word translated "love" is not the usual word but one that means "to cling to, to cleave, to be passionate." It is used in Deuteronomy 7:7 and 10:15 for the love Jehovah has for His people Israel. (See John 14:21-24.) Among His blessings will be deliverance and protection ("set him on high"), answered prayer, companionship in times of trouble, honor, satisfaction, and a long life (see 21:4; Ex. 20:12; Deut. 30:20). The salvation mentioned at the end of the psalm may mean help and deliverance during life, as in 50:23, or the joy of beholding the glory of God after a long and satisfied life. To the Jewish people, living a long life and seeing one's children, grandchildren, and great-grandchildren, was the ultimate of blessing in this life. Like Abraham, they wanted to die in a good old age and "full of years" (Gen. 25:8), which means "a fulfilled life." It's one thing for doctors to add years to our life, but God adds life to our years and makes that life worthwhile.

Psalm 92

The major theme is the sovereign rule of God, as stated in verse 8, which is the central verse of the psalm. It proclaims that God is most high (KJV), He is on high (NASB), and He is exalted forever (NIV). The covenant name Jehovah (LORD) is used seven times; Elyon (Most High) is found in verse 1 and Elohim in verse 13. The inscription relates the psalm to the Sabbath Day worship at the sanctuary. During the week, a lamb was sacrificed each morning and another in the evening, but on the Sabbath Day, those sacrifices were doubled (Ex. 29:38-46; Num. 28:1-10). Because our God reigns supremely, and always will, we can be the people of God that He wants us to be. The psalm describes the characteristics of believers who trust a sovereign God.

A Worshiping People (vv. 1-5)
A part of Israel's covenant relationship with the Lord was their honoring of the weekly Sabbath. It was a special sign between Israel and the Lord (Ex. 20:8-11; 31:12-17; Neh. 9:13-15) and reminded them that God had delivered them from Egypt (Deut. 5:12-15). But the Sabbath also reminded them of God the Creator (Gen. 2:1-3; Ex. 20:8-11), and seven times in Genesis 1 we are told that what God

made was "good." The psalmist added an eighth "good thing"—it is "good to give thanks [praise] unto the Lord." Believers today can praise the Lord for His generous creation gifts, His salvation through the blood of the Lamb, and His gracious covenant with us because of what Jesus did on the cross. Worship ought to be the natural outflow of a heart that loves the Lord and appreciates who He is and what he has done for His people.

Whether we use voices alone or voices accompanied by instruments, we can express our praises to God and focus on His wonderful attributes. We can worship all day long, from morning to evening. We can begin the day assured of His love and end the day looking back on His faithfulness. We can look around and marvel at His works, including His providential care and leading in our own lives, and we can look into His Word and probe the depths of His great thoughts (Rom. 11:33-36). Whether we are stirred by the creation around us or the Scriptures before us, we have every reason to worship and praise God, for He is reigning above us! The prayer of 90:15-16 is answered in verse 4.

An Overcoming People (vv. 6-11)
The psalmist shifts our attention to the enemies of the Lord who make life difficult for God's people. *The Authorized Version* calls them "brutish," which means "beastly, lacking values and discernment, savage, living only to satisfy the appetite." Other translations use "stupid, senseless, rude, uncultivated." The fool in Psalm 14 would qualify, and see also 49:10-12, 20, and 94:8-11. These people are like grass; they have no deep roots and their luxuriant growth passes quickly (90:5-6). God's faithful people, however, are like palm trees and cedars

(v. 12). The "horn" is a symbol of power (v. 10), and God gives His people power to overcome their foes (75:4-5, 10; 89:17, 24; 1 Sam. 2:1, 10; Luke 1:69). Oil was used to anoint special people—kings, priests, and prophets—but the anonymous psalmist rejoiced because the Lord had anointed *him* with fresh oil. He may also have been speaking for all Israel and praising God for a special victory He had given them. God wants His people to be overcomers (Rom. 12:21; 1 John 2:13-14; 4:4; 5:4-5; Rev. 2:7, 11, 17, 26; 3:5, 12, 21; 21:7), and this comes when first we are worshipers.

A Flourishing People (vv. 12-15)

The senseless brutish crowd is like grass (v. 7), but the righteous are like trees (see 1:3; 52:8; Prov. 11:30; Isa. 1:30; 61:3; Jer. 11:16; 17:8). The wicked may look like sturdy trees, but they don't last (37:35-36; 52:5). The word "flourish" in verse 7 means "to be conspicuous, to shine," while the word in verses 12-13 means "to be vigorous, to flourish richly." The stately date palm and cedar were highly valued by people in the Near East, the palm for its fruit and the cedar for its wood. Both were appreciated for their beauty, and both trees can survive for many years. Not all godly people live long; some, like Robert Murray M'Cheyne and David Brainerd, die very young. But generally speaking, those who obey God avoid a great deal of the danger and disease that can cause an early death. The promise in 91:16 is still true, and so is the picture in 92:13-14. To stay "fresh and green" in old age and not spend one's life complaining and demanding is a mark of God's special blessing. (See Ps. 71 for a description of an older saint who is fresh, fruitful and flourishing.) We change as we grow older, but the Lord never changes. He is our Rock

(32:4, 15, 18, 30-31), and what He wills for us is perfect, so we will not complain.

Psalm 93

Psalms 93 and 95-100 emphasize the sovereign rule of Jehovah, the King of Israel, in the affairs of the nations. (Ps. 94 focuses on God the Judge, which is an important aspect of His righteous rule.) Psalm 93 was perhaps written by one of the Levites who returned to Judah with the Jewish remnant after the Babylonian captivity. The Medes and Persians defeated Babylon in 539 B.C., and the next year Cyrus, the new king, gave the Jews permission to return to their own land, rebuild their temple, and restore their nation. It was an especially difficult time for the Jewish remnant (see Ezra and Haggai) and their work was interrupted, attacked, and neglected. The leaders and the people needed encouragement to continue the work, and this encouragement could come only from the Lord. This brief hymn magnifies the Lord by presenting three divine assurances.

God Reigns Supremely (vv. 1-2)

It was God who allowed Nebuchadnezzar to attack and conquer the kingdom of Judah and to destroy the temple and the holy city. The Lord used Daniel in Babylon to teach this basic truth to Nebuchadnezzar (Dan. 1-4; see especially Dan. 4:17, 25, 32), but Nebuchadnezzar's successor Belshazzar learned it when it was too late (Dan. 5). The Medes and Persians attacked Babylon and killed Belshazzar the very night he was boasting of his kingdom and blaspheming the Lord. "Jehovah is king!" (See 92:8; 96:10; 97:1; 99:1; Ex. 15:18; Deut. 33:5.) He is enthroned in heaven, robed in the majestic robes of glory, and armed with all the power He needs to humble puny rulers. His eternal throne is majestic, strong and firmly established (65:6; 104:1), and the world He created is also firmly fixed (24:2; 78:69; 119:90). No matter what happens to human rulers on earth, the throne in heaven is safe and secure.

God Is Greater Than Our Circumstances (vv. 3-4)

The raging seas and the pounding waves are often used as symbols of the rise and fall of the nations and the great noise that rulers make as they try to impress people. (See 46:1-3, 6; 60:5; 65:6-7; 74:13-14; Isa. 17:12-13; 51:15; 60:5; Jer. 31:5; 51:42; Dan. 7:1-3; Luke 21:25; Rev. 13:1; 17:15.) God used the Euphrates River to illustrate the Assyrians (Isa. 8:7-8), and He connected Egypt with the Nile River (Jer. 46:7-8). No matter how stormy the nations on earth may become, God is still on His throne and is not frustrated by the foolish words and deeds of "great leaders" who are only made of clay. Do not focus on the threats around you; focus on the throne above you (see 29; Isa. 6; Rev. 4-5).

God Always Keeps His Word (v. 5)

When the tempest is around us, we look by faith to the throne of grace above us and the Word of God before us. The truth about what is going on in this world is not in the newspapers but in the Scriptures. The false prophets among the Jews in Babylon gave a message different from that of Jeremiah, the true prophet of the Lord (Jer. 29), but it was the messages of God's servants that finally proved true. "Your testimonies are very sure" (v. 5, NKJV). (See Jer. 25:12; 27:22; 29:10; 2 Chron. 36:22-23; Ezra 1:1; and Isa. 44:28-45:3.) False prophets, false teachers, and

scoffers abound (2 Peter 2-3), but God's promises will all be fulfilled in their time, and God's children live by promises, not explanations. Satan has attacked God's Word since he lied to Eve in Genesis 3, but the Word still stands. "The counsel of the Lord stands forever, the plans of His heart to all generations" (33:11, NKJV).

Led by Zerubbabel the governor, Joshua the high priest, and the prophets Haggai and Zechariah, the Jewish remnant trusted God, labored, sacrificed, and completed the temple. We don't read that the glory of the Lord moved into the second temple, as it did the tabernacle (Ex. 40) and the first temple (1 Kings 8:10-11), but the Lord was with His people just the same and accomplishing His purposes. It is a holy people that makes the temple holy, and "the beauty of holiness" (29:2) is the greatest adornment for any structure dedicated to the Lord.

Psalm 94

Along with 10, 14, 73, and 92, the writer deals with the seeming triumph of the wicked and the unjust treatment of the helpless. But it is not foreign conquerors who were guilty, but the leaders of the nation cooperating with the local judges. Even the king was abusing the people by issuing unjust edicts (v. 20). Perhaps the psalm came out of the sufferings of the godly during the reign of wicked King Manasseh (2 Kings 21), whom the Lord blamed for the destruction of Jerusalem (2 Kings 24:1-4). But why is this psalm included in the section that magnifies the kingship of the Lord (93-100)? Because few problems cause God's people to question His rule more than, "Why do the helpless and the godly suffer and the wicked get away with their crimes?"

When it comes to dealing with the injustices in society, the psalm teaches us that the righteous have four responsibilities.

Praying to the Lord for Justice (vv. 1-7)
God's requirement for His people is that they "do justly ... love mercy, and ... walk humbly with [their] God" (Mic. 6:8), for the Lord loves justice (33:5; 37:28) and hears the prayers of those who have been treated unjustly (Ex. 22:26-27; Deut. 24:14-15; James 5:1-4). The word "vengeance" is often misinterpreted to mean "revenge" or "being vindictive," as though God were having a temper tantrum, but "to avenge" means to uphold the law and give justice to those who have been wronged. Since the Lord is omniscient, He is able to judge motives as well as actions and deal with situations and people justly (Lev. 19:18; Deut. 32:35, 41; Rom. 12:17-21; Heb. 10:30-31). He is the Judge of all the earth (58:11; 82:8) and always does what is right (Gen. 18:25). "Shine forth," means "show yourself, reveal your power and glory" (50:2; 80:1; Deut. 33:2; Hab. 3:1-5).

We want the Lord to act immediately (v. 3; see 6:3), but He is gracious and long-suffering (Ex. 34:6-7) and we must walk by faith (Luke 18:1-8). The proud and arrogant "belch out" evil words and commit evil deeds (10:2-11), and the godly can do nothing to stop them. Orphans, widows, and aliens in the land were under the special care of the Lord (68:5-6; 146:9; Ex. 22:20-24; Deut. 10:18-19; 14:28-29; 24:17-18; 26:12-13; 27:19; Isa. 1:17; 7:6; 22:3). The helpless are God's covenant people and He is Jehovah—the LORD—a name used nine times in the psalm (vv. 1, 3, 5, 11, 14, 17, 18, 22, 23). The wicked convince themselves that God does not see their evil deeds (v. 7; 10:11; 59:7), but He does!

Warning the Wicked of Their Danger (vv. 8-11)
After praying to the Lord, we must confront the wicked with the truth, as the Lord gives us opportunity. In verses 8-11, the psalmist speaks to the offenders and calls them "senseless people," the word "brutish" that we have met before (49:10; 92:6, KJV; and see 2 Peter 2:12 and Jude 10). These people were behaving like animals and not like humans made in the image of God. They had such a low view of God (v. 7) that they were unable to think logically. If God made the eye and ear, is He unable to see and hear? Is the creature greater than the Creator? If God is able to rule the nations by His providential decrees (Acts 17:24-28), is He unable to deal with a band of wicked officials who are breaking His law and exploiting His people? The Lord gave Israel His law and taught them what it meant, so is He not intelligent enough to apply that law? The word translated "thoughts" in verse 11 means "inventions, schemes, plans." The subversive plans and plots of these evil leaders cannot be hidden from the Lord, nor will they go unpunished. Paul quoted this verse in 1 Corinthians 3:20 to warn church leaders in Corinth not to try to guide the church using the world's wisdom, but to rely only on the wisdom of God found in Scripture—the gold, silver, and precious stones (3:12-15; Prov. 2:1-4; 3:13-15; 8:10-11, 18l-19).

Accepting God's Discipline (vv. 12-15)
The words "chasten" or "discipline" (v. 12) mean "teaching and instruction from God's law" (Deut. 8:5; Prov. 3:11-12). The psalmist recognized the fact that the difficulties of life could help him mature in his faith. If God immediately rescued His people from their personal difficulties, they would become "spoiled brats" and

never grow in faith or character. "For whom the Lord loves He chastens" (Heb. 12:6). God uses personal difficulties to teach us new truths from His Word (Ps. 119:50; 75; 92-95). There is coming a time of judgment ("days of adversity"), but the Lord will spare His people from it. The longer the wicked persist in their sins, the deeper is the pit they are digging for themselves and the stronger the net that will trap them (9:15-16). God cannot reject His people who are bound to Him in His covenant (37:28-29; Deut. 32:9; Isa. 49:14-18; Jer. 10:16). The psalmist believed in the justice of God, the future judgment of the wicked, and the promise of a righteous kingdom for the upright in heart.

Working with God for Justice (vv. 16-23)

Even in Solomon's day, people who were abused and exploited had no redress and found no one to execute justice on their behalf (Eccl. 4:1), so it must have been much worse in the days of Manasseh, just before the fall of Jerusalem. The question in verse 16 is rhetorical and the writer answered it himself in verse 17—"the LORD." The psalmist was experiencing the devious plots of the evil leaders and cried out to God for help. He knew that the judges were twisting the law to exploit the poor (v. 20), and he was slipping into a deep and dangerous situation. His heart was anxious within him, but the Lord held him up, pulled Him out, and gave him peace within. He was grateful for other believers who stood with him and prayed with him, for "my God" in verse 22 became "our God" in verse 24. He trusted the Lord to bring about the judgment that the evil leaders deserved. Like Asaph in Psalm 73, he had been slipping in his faith and walk, but God showed him that the wicked were in slippery

places and heading rapidly toward judgment (73:2-3, 18, 27-28).

In evil days, we give thanks that we have the Lord as our refuge and fortress. But we hide in Him, not that we may escape responsibility, but that we might be equipped to go forth and fight the enemy. As the salt of the earth and the light of the world (Matt. 5:13-16), God's people should do all they can to encourage justice in this world. As Edmund Burke said, "It is necessary only for the good man to do nothing for evil to triumph." But in the end, it is the Lord who knows the hearts of people and who will judge justly.

Psalm 95

The annual Feast of Tabernacles was a joyful event as the people looked back on their ancestors' wilderness wanderings, looked around at the bountiful harvest, and looked up to give thanks to the Lord (Lev. 23:33-44). It has been conjectured that this psalm was written for this feast after the exiles returned to Judah from Babylon.[24] Certainly verses 8-11 would remind them of those wilderness years, but they are quoted in Hebrews 3:7-4:13 and applied to believers today. The church must take heed to what happened to Israel (see 1 Cor. 10:1-13). While 95 calls on Israel to worship, 96 calls all the nations of the earth to worship the God of Israel (96:1, 3, 7, 10, 13). As the psalmist calls God's people to celebrate the Lord, he gives us three admonitions to obey.

Come and Praise the Lord (vv. 1-5)

He tells us *how* we should praise Him (vv. 1-2) and *why* we should praise Him (vv. 3-5). This is communal praise, not individual, although both are important. Our praise should be joyful and enthusiastic—he even commands us to shout (v. 1, NASB)—and wholly focused on the Lord. The verb "come" in verse 2 means "to go to meet God face-to-face, to be in His presence." Believers today do this through Jesus Christ (Heb. 10:19-25). We should be thankful in our praise as we extol the Lord for His great mercies. (On God the Rock, see 18:2.)

Why should we praise Him? Because He is great and above the false gods of this world (v. 3; 81:8; 92:8; 93:4; 96:4; Ex. 18:11). After His ascension to heaven, Jesus Christ was enthroned "far above all" (Acts 2:33; Eph. 1:19-23; Phil. 2:9-11; Col. 1:15-18), and nothing can separate us from His love (Rom. 8:37-39). He is our "great God and Savior" (Titus 2:13) and we should delight in praising him. But our God is also the Creator of the universe and controls all things (vv. 4-5). The depths of the sea and the earth, and the heights of the mountains all belong to Him, and He knows what is going on in the waters as well as on the earth. The pagan nations had gods and goddesses for different parts of creation—the seas, the land, the mountain peaks, the sun, moon and stars, the storms, the crops—but our God is King over all. No wonder we praise Him!

Bow Down and Worship the Lord (vv. 6-7a)

Praise means looking up, but worship means bowing down. Alas, some people who enjoy lifting their hands and shouting do not enjoy bowing their knees and submitting. True worship is much deeper than communal praise, for worship involves realizing the awesomeness of God and experiencing the fear of the Lord and a deeper love for Him. Too often Christian "praise" is nothing but religious entertainment and it never moves into spiritual enrichment in the presence of the Lord. Our singing must give way to silence as we bow before the Lord. He alone is Jehovah, the LORD, the covenant-making and covenant-keeping God. He is our Maker and our Shepherd. (See 23 and John 10.) Jubilation has its place only if it becomes adoration and we are prostrate before the Lord in total submission, "lost in wonder, love, and praise." What a remarkable miracle of grace that we sinners should be called "His people." He made us, He saved us, and He cares for us! Why should we hesitate to fall before Him in total surrender?

Hear and Obey the Lord (vv. 7b-11)

The Word of God is a vital part of Christian worship, especially in this age when inventing clever new worship forms is a common practice and novelty is replacing theology. Hearing and heeding God's Word must be central if our worship, private or corporate, is to be truly Christian. It isn't enough for God to hear my voice; I must hear His voice as the Word of God is read, preached, and taught. The Scriptures written centuries ago have authority today, and we have no right to ignore them, change them, or disobey them. We are to respond to God's Word *now*, when we hear it, and not just later in the week when we review our sermon notes or listen to the message on cassette tape. How tragic when worshipers go home with full notebooks and empty hearts! (See Heb. 3:7-4:13 where this passage is applied to the church today, warning us not to harden our hearts against the Lord.) *The way we treat the Word of God is the way we treat the God of the Word.* Jesus admonishes us to take heed *that* we hear (Matt. 13:9), take heed *what* we hear (Mark 4:24), and take heed *how* we hear (Luke 8:18).

The writer reached back and cited two tragic events in the history of Israel—the nation's complaining at Rephidim (Ex. 17:1-7) and their unbelief and disobedience at Kadesh Barnea (Num. 13-14). The Jews had seen God's wonderful works in Egypt, especially His defeat of the Egyptian army when He opened and closed the Red Sea—but they refused to trust Him for their daily needs. No sooner were they liberated from Egypt than they complained that they were hungry, so He sent them the manna, the bread of heaven (Ex. 16). When they arrived at Rephidim, the people complained again because they were thirsty (Ex. 17:1-7). Instead of trusting God, they blamed God and His servant Moses. God graciously gave them water out of the rock, but Moses commemorated the event with two new names for the site: Meribah means "strife, quarreling, contention" and Massah means "testing." (See also Num. 20:1-13.) Instead of trusting God, the people had contended with God and had even tempted Him by their arrogant attitude and words. He could have sent immediate judgment, and they dared Him to act.

Israel spent a year and two months at Sinai (Num. 10:11) and then departed for Kadesh Barnea, the gateway into Canaan (Num. 13-14). Here they refused to trust the Lord and obey His orders to enter the land and claim their inheritance. In spite of all they had seen Him do, the Israelites hardened their hearts and refused to do God's will. God judged His people at Kadesh Barnea and consigned them to thirty-eight years in the wilderness while the older generation died off. It was the world's longest funeral march. "They shall not enter into My rest" (v. 11; Num. 14:26-38). The writer of Hebrews used this event to warn Christians not to harden their hearts and thereby fail to claim what God had for them to do, to receive, and to enjoy. God has a perfect plan for each of His children (Eph. 2:10), and we claim that inheritance by faith in God's Word, the kind of faith that leads to obedience.

In Moses' day, God's "rest" was the land of Canaan, where the Jews would do no more wandering (Ex. 33:14; Deut. 12:9-10; Josh. 1:13, 15). But Hebrews 4 broadens the meaning of "rest" to include the salvation rest and inheritance we have in Christ (Matt. 11:28-30; Eph. 1:3, 11, 15-23) and the future eternal "Sabbath rest" in glory (Heb. 4:9; Rev. 14:13). Hebrews 1-4 is God's admonition to the church today to live by faith, and "faith comes by hearing, and hearing by the word of God" (Rom. 10:17, NKJV). Because the Jews refused to hear His Word but hardened their hearts instead, God was disgusted with His people, and all the people twenty years old and older died during that wilderness journey. We harden our hearts when we see what God can do but refuse to trust Him so He can do it for us. We fail to cultivate a godly heart that fears and honors the Lord. It is a grievous sin to ask for the gifts (food, water, etc.) but ignore the Giver, and the consequences are painful.

Psalm 96

This psalm is found in another version in 1 Chronicles 16:23-33. The psalm in Chronicles is a combination of quotations from 96, 105 (1-15 = 16:8-22), and 106 (1, 47-48 = 16:35-36). The Jewish worship leaders, led by God's Spirit, felt free to excerpt and combine portions of existing psalms to construct songs for special occasions. Some students believe Psalm 96 was used in the dedication of the second temple when the Jews returned to

Judah from their exile in Babylon. As you read the psalm, you can see how it would apply to the weak Jewish remnant surrounded by strong Gentile nations. The psalm also looks ahead to the kingdom age when Messiah shall reign and the Gentile nations will worship the God of Israel. The psalmist gives four commands to God's people and backs up each command with a reason for their obedience.

Sing! The News Is Good! (vv. 1-3)

Three times we are commanded to sing to the Lord, and this parallels the three times in verses 7-8 that the psalmist commands us to "give" ("ascribe," NASB, NIV) glory to Him. (For "a new song," see 33:3.) A new experience of God's blessing, a new truth discovered in the Word, a new beginning after a crisis, a new open door for service— all of these can make an old song new or give us a new song from the Lord. This call to worship is not extended to Israel alone but also to the Gentile nations (see also vv. 3, 7, 9, 11, 13). One day when Jesus reigns on earth, all nations will come to Jerusalem to worship Him (Isa. 2:1-4). It will be a time when the glory of God will be revealed to all peoples (vv. 3, 7-8; Gen. 12:1-3; 22:18; Isa. 60:1-3). In the Greek translation of the Old Testament, "show forth" (v. 2; "proclaim," NASB, NIV) is the word used in the New Testament for "preaching the good news" and gives us the English word "evangelize." The good news of the victory of Jesus Christ gives us something to sing about, for He is the only Savior and will save all who trust Him (John 14:6; John 4:22; Acts 4:12; Rom. 10:1-15).

Praise! Our God Is Great! (vv. 4-6)

The gods of the nations were "no-gods," for the word translated "idols" in verse 5 means "things that are nothing, things that are weak and worthless." "We know that an idol is nothing in the world" (1 Cor. 8:4, NKJV). It was Jehovah who created the universe, and His great glory rested in His sanctuary in Jerusalem (Ex. 40:34-38; 1 Kings 8:10-11; Rom. 9:4). The presence of this glory brought the divine splendor, majesty, and strength to the people. The ark of the covenant in the Holy of Holies was the throne of God, and He ruled over His people. (See 21:5; 45:3; 104:1.) Both in His sanctuary in heaven and His sanctuary on earth, God was enthroned in glory and power. How we ought to praise Him!

Worship! The Lord Is Worthy! (vv. 7-9)

When praising the Lord, the Jews lifted their hands and voices and looked up, but in their worship, they reverently bowed down. (See 29:1-2.) The invitation went out to all nations to come to God's sanctuary, bring a sacrifice, and worship Him. (See 65:4; 84:2, 10; 92:13; 100:4; 116:19; 135:2.) "Fear before him" (v. 9) is translated "tremble before him" in the NIV and NASB (see 29:9; 97:4; 114:7). Just as the Jewish priests had to dress in the garments required by the Lord (Ex. 28), so God's people must worship with "clean hands and a pure heart" (24:4) and experience cleansing from the Lord before they worship Him (Heb. 10:19-25). The only beauty that God accepts is "the beauty of holiness," the righteousness of Christ imputed to us by faith (Rom. 4) and the righteousness we live as we obey Him in the power of the Spirit (Rom. 8:1-4). We approach God only through Christ's righteousness, but we please God when we are obedient children.

Rejoice! The King Is Coming! (vv. 10-13)

"The Lord reigns" (v. 10; see 93:1) can also be translated, "The Lord has become

King" (see Rev. 11:17), referring to the day Jesus will sit on David's throne and rule over the nations (Luke 1:26-33; Rev. 19:11-16). Only then will there be true justice on the earth (Isa. 9:6-7; 32:1, 16; 42:1-4). Today, creation is in bondage to corruption and futility because of Adam's sin, but when the children of God are fully redeemed at Christ's return, creation will also be set free (Rom. 8:18-23). No wonder the psalmist described the joy of heaven and earth, the seas and the dry land, and even the trees of the earth as they welcome their Creator, and then there will be justice on the earth (7:6-8; 9:7-8; 98:7-9; Isa. 55:12). "The whole creation is on tiptoe to see the wonderful sight of the sons of God coming into their own" (Rom. 8:19, PHILLIPS). Rejoice!

Psalm 97

The psalmist picked up the theme in 96:13 and described the King coming to judge His enemies and reward His people. In 95, the emphasis was on God's people, and 96 focused our attention on the nations of the world. This psalm combines both themes and tells us that Jehovah is "the Lord Most High" in heaven (v. 9, NASB) who has all things under His control. Believers today see Jesus as God's exalted King (see Acts 2:32-33; 5:31; Eph. 1:17-23; Phil. 2:5-11; Heb. 1:3; 1 Peter 3:22; Rev. 3:21).

The Lord Is Exalted on His Throne (vv. 1-2)
No matter what the circumstances around us or the feelings within us, "the Lord reigns" (93:1; 96:10; 99:1; 117:1), and He reigns over all the earth (vv. 1, 4, 5, 9; 96:1, 9, 11, 13; 98:3, 4, 9). His sovereign authority reaches beyond the land of Israel to the farthest islands and coastlands, places

that the Jews had never visited. God's desire was that Israel be a light to the Gentiles (Gen. 12:1-3; Isa. 42:6; 49:6) to show them the truth of the one true and living God, just as the church today is to be a light to the world by sharing the gospel message (Luke 2:32; Acts 13:47). Knowing that "the Lord God omnipotent reigns" (Rev. 19:6) ought to bring joy to our hearts and our worship (vv. 1, 8, 11, 12; see 96:11). Though His throne is surrounded by clouds and darkness, and we do not fully understand the mysteries of His providence, we know that His throne rests on righteousness and justice and that "the Judge of all the earth [will] do right" (Gen. 18:25). The psalm begins with darkness (v. 1) but ends with light for the righteous (v. 11).

The Lord Is Exalted over His Enemies (vv. 3-6)
The picture is that of a storm sweeping across the land and destroying everything in its path (see 18:9-12; 29; Hab. 3:3-15). The image of the storm takes us back to the exodus of Israel from Egypt (68:7-8; 77:15-20) as well as Israel's meeting with God at Sinai (Ex. 19:9, 16-19; 20:21; 24:15-16; Deut. 4:11; 5:22; Heb. 12:18-21). The storm also speaks of the future "day of the Lord" when God will judge the nations of the world (Isa. 2:10-21; 8:22; Joel 2:2; Amos 5:16-20; Zeph. 1:7-18). The fire and lightning remind us that God is a consuming fire (Deut. 4:24; 32:22; Heb. 12:29). His judgments bring Him glory and manifest His holiness to a godless world. The name "Lord of all the earth" (v. 5) is found in only four other places in the Old Testament: on the lips of Joshua before Israel crossed the Jordan River (Josh. 3:11, 13), and from the prophets Micah (4:13) and Zechariah (4:14; 6:5). (See also 50:12.) From the beginning of

Israel's national history, the people knew that Jehovah was not a "tribal god" like the false gods of the neighboring nations, but the Lord of all the earth (Ex. 19:5; Deut. 10:14. Jesus used this title when speaking to His Father [Luke 10:21]).

The Lord Is Exalted over the False Gods (vv. 7-9)

In the ancient Near East, when one nation conquered another, people interpreted the victory to mean that the gods of the conquering nation were greater than those of the defeated nation. But the Jews were taught that Jehovah was the God of all the earth and that the idols were nothing (see 95:3; 96:5). God allowed Babylon to defeat the Jews because the Jews had greatly sinned against the Lord, not because Babylon's gods were stronger than Jehovah. The defeat of Babylon by the Medes and Persians was the work of the Lord and not of their false gods, for the prophets predicted this event would occur (Isa. 45-47; Jer. 50-51; Dan. 2:36-38; 7:1-5). Israel's release from captivity was proof that Jehovah was in control (Jer. 25:1-14; 29:1-14). God's victories over the idolatrous nations put the idols and their worshipers to shame (v. 7; see Isa. 45:15-17). No wonder the people of Israel rejoiced, for God's victories were evidence that He alone is "Most High over all the earth" (v. 8, NASB; 83:18). People may not bow down before ugly man-made idols today, but there are certainly plenty of false gods for them to worship—money, power, possessions, sex, pleasures, recognition—for whatever people serve and sacrifice for, that is what they worship (Matt. 4:10).

The Lord Is Exalted among His People (vv. 10-12)

God's people are those who love Him and do not turn to idols for help (91:14; 1 Cor.

8:1-3). But if we love Him who is holy, we will hate that which is unholy (34:14; 36:4; 37:27; 119:104; Prov. 8:13; Rom. 12:9). In this paragraph, God's people are called "saints" or "godly ones," "the righteous," "the upright in heart," and all of these names speak of a life devoted to God. We should love Him, obey him ("hate evil"), rejoice in Him, and give thanks to Him for all His mercies. After all, He protects His people, delivers them, gives them light for their path, and puts gladness into their hearts. What more could they want?

The image in verse 11 is that of the sower; the Lord plants light like seeds so that His people will not always walk in darkness, and what He plants will eventually bear fruit. "Sowing" is a frequent metaphor in Scripture for the deeds of both God and people (112:4; Prov. 11:18; Hos. 8:7; 10:12; James 3:18). The psalm begins with a universal revelation of God's glory (vv. 2-6), with dramatic flashes of lightning, but it ends with His light quietly shining on the paths of His people. Some see the image as that of the dawn, with the morning light diffused along the ground as though the Lord were planting it like seed. But God also sows joy with that light, for when we walk in the light, we also have joy in the Lord (16:11; Isa. 60:1-5). God's people have their dark days when life is difficult, but there are always seeds of light and joy to accompany us along the way. Is there any reason why we should not be rejoicing *now*?

Psalm 98

From this psalm Isaac Watts found the inspiration for his popular hymn "Joy to the World," often classified as a Christmas carol but more accurately identified as a "kingdom hymn." Watts described

Christ's *second* advent and not His first, the Messianic kingdom and not the manger. The parallels to 96 are obvious but the psalms are not identical. This psalm was written to praise the Lord for a great victory over Israel's enemies ("salvation," vv. 1-3), perhaps the victory of the Medes and Persians over Babylon (Dan. 5) that led to the return of the Jewish exiles to their land (Ezra 1). Some of the vocabulary in the psalm reflects the language of Isaiah the prophet, who in chapters 40-66 of his book wrote about the "exodus" of the Jews from Babylon (44:23; 49:13; 51:3; 52:9-10; 59:16; 63:5). But the psalm also speaks of a future judgment (vv. 7-9). The psalmist saw in the destruction of ancient Babylon a picture of God's judgment of end-time Babylon (Rev. 17-18).

A Marvelous Salvation (vv. 1-3)

The focus in this section is on the Jewish people and the wonderful new demonstration of God's power they had seen. It was so great it demanded a new song from His people (see 33:3; 96:1). The picture of God as warrior disturbs those who seem to forget that a holy God cannot compromise with sin. (See 68:1-10; 77:16-19; and Ex. 15:1-2.) The cross declares not only that God loves sinners (Rom. 5:8), but also that God hates and opposes sin (Matt. 12:22-30; Col. 2:15). Since God is a spirit (John 4:24), He does not have a body, so the references to His hand and arm are metaphorical (17:7; 18:35; 20:6; 44:3; 60:5; 77:10; Ex. 15:6, 11-12; Isa. 52:10; 59:16; 63:5). What God did for Israel was a witness to the Gentile nations and a vivid demonstration of His faithfulness to His covenant and His love for His chosen people. But surely the writer was looking beyond a mere local victory, for he wrote about the witness of this event to the nations (v. 2), the earth (vv. 3, 4, 9), and the

world (vv. 7, 9). It appears that the psalm points ahead to the return of Jesus Christ. (See Isa. 52:1-10.)

A Joyous Celebration (vv. 4-6)

The command went out to all nations of the earth to shout joyfully in praise to the Lord for what He had done for Israel, and the emphasis is on the King (v. 6). Again we are reminded of what the prophet Isaiah wrote concerning the Jewish "exodus" from Babylon (Isa. 14:7; 44:23; 49:13; 52:9; 54:1; 55:12). But the shout was only the beginning, for singing and the playing of instruments followed. Loud music played and sung with enthusiasm was characteristics of Jewish worship (2 Chron. 5:11-14; Ezra 3:10-13; Neh. 12:27-43).

A Glorious Expectation (vv. 7-9)

The psalmist has written of the Lord as Deliverer and King, and now he presents Him as the Judge who will one day come and deal with the world as He once dealt with the kingdom of Babylon. He had seen Israel delivered from bondage (vv. 1-3) and he had heard the nations of the world praising the Lord (vv. 4-6). Now he heard all creation eagerly anticipating the Lord's return, for the second advent of Jesus sets creation free from the bondage of sin caused by Adam's fall (Rom. 8:18-25). The lapping of the waves of the sea on the shore sounds to him like a prayer to the Lord and the flowing of the river like applause in response to the announcement, "The King is coming!" The play of the wind on the mountains sounded like a song of praise. (See Isa. 55:12.) All nature combined to sing, "Even so come, Lord Jesus" (Rev. 22:20). There will come a day when all wrongs will be righted and all sins will be judged, and the Judge will bring justice and equity to the earth.

Psalm 99

This is the sixth of the "royal psalms" (93, 95-100), all of which magnify the sovereign rule of Jehovah the King. Like 93 and 97, it opens with "The Lord reigns," and it emphasizes that Jehovah is exalted above all the nations (v. 2) and not just Israel. The psalmist describes the throne of the Lord and encourages the people to exalt the Lord as they worship Him (vv. 5, 9).

An Awesome Throne (vv. 1-3)

Jehovah sits upon the throne in heaven (9:11; 110:2; 146:10), but in the psalmist's day, He was also enthroned on the mercy seat in the Holy of Holies of the sanctuary on Mount Zion (see 80:1; 1 Sam. 4:4; 2 Sam. 6:2; 2 Kings 19:15 [Isa. 37:16]; 1 Chron. 13:6). It was there that God's glory rested, and from there God spoke to Moses and ruled the nation of Israel (Num. 7:89). God chose the Jews to be His vehicle for telling the Gentile nations about the true and living God, and God chose Mount Zion to be His dwelling place. The prophet Isaiah saw the heavenly throne (Isa. 6) and so did the prophet Ezekiel (Ezek. 1). The name LORD is used seven times in this psalm, for God made His covenant with Israel alone and they were His special people. "Salvation is of the Jews" (John 4:22). When the Gentiles beheld what God did for Israel, they should have trembled with awe and put their trust in Him (96:9; 114:7). God's throne is awesome because He is holy (Lev. 11:44-45; 1 Peter 1:15-16). "The Holy One of Israel" is a name found thirty times in the book of Isaiah. The word "holy" means "separate, set apart, totally different." God's nature is "wholly other," yet He was willing to dwell with His people and meet their needs. (Note the repetition of "he is holy" [vv. 3, 5, 9], and see Isa. 6:3.)

A Just Throne (vv. 4-5)

The Lord ruled His people of Israel through the kings in the Davidic dynasty (Deut. 17:14-20). The Lord is perfectly righteous in His character and just in His actions, and He wanted the throne of Israel to be just. A leader who loves justice will have the strength to obey God's Word and will seek to please Him. Romans 13 teaches us that civil authorities are the ministers of God, not just the employees of the government. In Scripture, the "footstool" (v. 5) could be the ark of the covenant (1 Chron. 28:2), the sanctuary of God (132:7; Isa. 60:13; Ezek. 43:7), the city of Jerusalem (Lam. 2:1), or even planet earth (Isa. 66:1; Matt. 5:35). Solomon's throne had a footstool of gold (2 Chron. 9:18), and visitors would kneel there in homage before him. The sanctuary on Mount Zion was God's chosen dwelling place, and the ark in the sanctuary was His appointed throne, so when the Jewish pilgrims came to Jerusalem, they were worshiping at His footstool. Note that verse 5 is the central verse of the psalm and emphasizes the three major themes of the psalm: God's holiness and our privilege and responsibility to worship Him and exalt Him (see vv. 3 and 9).

A Gracious Throne (vv. 6-9)

You could not approach the throne of the king of Persia unless he held out his scepter and gave you permission (Est. 4:10-11), but access to God's throne is available to His children through Jesus Christ (Heb. 10:19-25). Under the old covenant, God provided priests who ministered at the altar and were mediators between His needy people and their Lord, but today Jesus Christ is the Mediator (1 Tim. 2:5) who constantly intercedes for us (Rom. 8:34; Heb. 7:25). To the lost sinner, God's throne is a throne of judgment, but

Psalms

to the believer, it is a throne of grace (Heb. 4:14-16), and we can come to Him with our worship and praise as well as our burdens and needs.

Often Moses, Aaron, and Samuel had to intercede for the disobedient people of Israel, and the Lord heard them and answered (Ex. 17:1; 32-33; Num. 14:11-38; 16:48; 1 Sam. 7, 12). God named Moses and Samuel as great men of prayer (Jer. 15:1). God's gracious ministry to His old covenant people is still available to His new covenant family: He speaks to us from His Word (Ex. 33:9; Num. 12:5-6; 1 Sam. 3:3), hears our prayers and answers, disciplines us when we sin, and forgives us when we confess (1 John 1:9). How many times the Lord forgave Israel and gave them another opportunity to serve Him! (103:13-18). The throne and the altar were not far apart in the sanctuary (see Isa. 6:1-7).

How should we respond to this kind of a God who sits on this kind of a throne? We must worship Him (vv. 5, 9), praise and exalt Him (vv. 3, 5, 9), and remember that He is holy (vv. 3, 5, 9). We must pray to Him and seek to glorify His name by our obedience and service. The next psalm describes all of this and climaxes the "royal psalm" series.

Psalm 100

For centuries, Christian congregations have sung William Kethe's paraphrase of this psalm, wedded to the beloved tune "Old Hundredth." First published in 1561, the words summarize the message of the psalm and help the worshipers give thanks to the Lord. Sometimes the traditional "Doxology" ("Praise God from whom all blessings flow") by Thomas Ken is sung as the last verse. The

psalm is a fitting climax to the collection of "royal psalms" (93, 95-100) and sums up their emphasis on God's sovereign rule, His goodness to His people, the responsibility of all nations to acknowledge Him, and the importance of God's people exalting and worshiping Him. (See 95:1-2, 6-7.)

We are admonished in Ephesians 5:18 to be filled with the Spirit of God, and the evidence of this fullness is that we are joyful (5:19), thankful (5:20), and submissive (5:21-6:9). In Colossians 3:16-25, we are instructed to be filled with the Word of God, and when we are, we will be joyful (3:16), thankful (3:17), and submissive (3:20-25). These three characteristics of the believer controlled by God's Spirit and God's Word—and they go together—are presented in this wonderful psalm of thanksgiving.

Joyful (vv. 1-2)

We can easily understand the people of Israel shouting joyfully in praise to their great God (vv. 3, 5), but the psalmist calls for all the nations of the earth to praise Him. This is a recurring theme in the "royal psalms" (97:1, 6; 98:2-4, 7; 99:1-2), for it was Israel's responsibility to introduce the Gentiles to the true and living God. The church has been commissioned to take the good news into all the world (Matt. 28:18-20; Mark 16:15), and it will be a glorious day when God's people gather at His throne from "all nations, tribes, peoples and tongues" (Rev. 7:9). But our shouting ought to lead to serving Him, for He is the only true God (Deut. 6:13; 10:12; Josh. 24:15-24). Worship leads to service, and true service is worship. If we sing in the Spirit and with understanding, our songs are received in heaven as sacrifices to the Lord (Heb. 13:15).

Submissive (v. 3)

The verb "know" means "to know by experience." It also carries the meaning of "acknowledge." What we have experienced in our hearts we openly confess to others and bear witness of our glorious God. (See 1 Kings 18:39.) The phrase "made us" means much more than "He created us," for He also created the nations that do not know Him. It means "Jehovah constituted us as a nation, His chosen people." (See 95:6-7; 149:2; Deut. 32:6, 15; Isa. 29:23; 60:21.) The phrase "not we ourselves" can also be translated "and we are his." This connects with the next statement, "We are his people ..." (see Isa. 43:1). The image of God's people as a flock of sheep is frequently found in Scripture (74:1; 77:20; 78:52; 79:13; 80:1; 95:7; Gen. 48:15; 49:24; Num. 27:17; Isa. 40:11; John 10; 21:16-17; Heb. 13:20-21; 1 Peter 2:25; 5:1-4). This verse is a simple statement of faith: Jehovah is God, Creator, Redeemer and Shepherd, and we are submitted to Him. If the sheep do not submit to their shepherd, they will stray into danger.

Thankful (vv. 4-5)

The procession of worshipers has now reached the gates of the sanctuary, and they burst out in songs of praise. Why? Because of the Lord's goodness, mercy (lovingkindness), and faithfulness. (See parallels in 106:1, 107:1, 118:1, and 136:1-3; and see also 1 Chron. 16:34 and 2 Chron. 5:13.) "O, taste and see that the Lord is good" (37:8), and He gives that which is good (85:12; Rom. 8:28). The word "truth" is a form of the Hebrew word *amen* and refers to God's faithfulness and reliability. It is the same word used in Exodus 17:12 to describe Moses's hands "staying steady," and in Genesis 15:6 it is translated "believed" ("relied on," literally

"said amen to the Lord"). (See Deut. 7:9 and 32:4.) From generation to generation, the Lord can be trusted (90:1; Ex. 34:5-7). It is significant that the fathers' and mothers' worship today will have an important influence on their children tomorrow.

If we are controlled by the Holy Spirit of God and the holy Word of God, we will reveal it in the way we worship God. Instead of imitating the world, we will be led by the Word and the Spirit to be joyful in the Lord, submissive to the Lord, and thankful to the Lord, and the world will see the difference. Finally, note that a spirit of thanksgiving helps us overcome some of the "sins in good standing" that too often invade our lives: complaining (v. 1), idolatry (v. 2), pride (v. 3), and ingratitude (v. 4). It was when our first parents became "unthankful" that the human race began that terrible descent into sin and judgment (Rom. 1:18-32; note v. 21). Instead of being thankful for what they had, Adam and Eve believed Satan's lie that the Lord was holding out on them (Gen. 3:1—"every tree"), and this led to their sin. A thankful spirit is a triumphant spirit.

Psalm 101

When David became king, first in Hebron and then at Jerusalem, he inherited a divided land and a discouraged people whose spiritual life was at low ebb. Asaph described the situation in 78:56-72 and named David as God's answer to Israel's problems. Everything rises and falls with leadership, but many of King Saul's officers were fawning flattering "toadies" who were unable to work with a man like David. Once David was established on the throne in Jerusalem, he had a consuming desire to bring the ark of God back to the sanctuary so that God's throne might near his throne. His question in verse 2, "When will you come to me?" reflects this desire. The ark had been in the house of Abinidab for many years (1 Sam. 6:1-7:2) and then in the house of Obed-Edom after David's aborted attempt to relocate it (2 Sam. 6:1-11). This psalm of dedication was probably written early in his reign in Jerusalem. We could accurately call this psalm "Leadership 101" because in it David spells out the essentials for successful leadership in the work of God.

Devotion to God (vv. 1-2)

The king of Israel was God's representative on earth and was expected to rule the way God commanded. (Deut. 17:14-20, and see 2 Kings 23:1-3.) The emphasis here is on the heart, for the heart of leadership is the leader's devotion to the Lord. This devotion results in a life lived blamelessly to the glory of the Lord. David was determined to be that kind of leader, and he opened the psalm with "I will" and repeated this promise eight more times. He made it clear that there must be no separation between the leader's personal life and his or her official life, the private and the public. David wanted his reign to be characterized by lovingkindness (mercy) and justice, for this is the way God rules the world (89:14; Isa. 16:5).

"Blameless" does not mean "sinless," for David was a sinner like the rest of us. However, unlike David, we have not seen the account of our sins written down for all the world to read! "Blameless" is another word for integrity, cultivating wholeness of heart and singleness of mind, instead of a double heart and a double mind (15:2; 18:23, 25; 26:1, 11; 78:70-72; 86:11; Gen. 6:9; 17:1). Believers

today should have integrity whether we are leaders or not (119:1; Matt. 5:8; Eph. 1:4; Phil. 1:10; 2:15). Faith is living without scheming, and the way of faith is "the blameless way" (v. 2, NASB). David vowed to live a godly life in his "house" (palace) and have an administration characterized by mercy, justice, and integrity.

Discernment (vv. 3-5)

David moved from the heart of the leader to the hearts of the sinners (vv. 4-5) and turned the emphasis to the leader's eyes and what he saw (vv. 3, 5, 6, 7 ["tarry in my sight," KJV]). The heart and the eyes work together, for what the heart loves, the eyes will seek and find (Eccl. 2:10; Jer. 22:17). This section parallels Psalm 15 where David described the ideal worshiper whom God welcomes to His dwelling. David did not want anyone in his official family who was not walking with the Lord. "I will set no worthless thing before my eyes" (v. 3a, NASB) means more than beholding vile things "the lust of the eyes" (1 John 2:16). It also means setting worthless goals and seeking to reach them. Leaders must set the best goals, guided by God's will, for outlook determines outcome. The spiritual leader not only sets the best goals but he or she also uses the best methods for achieving those goals (v. 3b). "Faithless" people are apostates, people who have abandoned God's way for their own way and the world's way. David had his eyes on the faithful, not the faithless (v. 6). A "perverse heart" is a twisted heart, one that does not conform to God's will (Prov. 3:32; 6:16-19; 11:20), and a twisted heart produces a deceitful tongue (v. 7; Matt. 12:34-35; see Prov. 17:20). The word translated "proud" in verse 5 means "wide, expanded" and describes people who are inflated with their own importance. It is important that leaders cultivate humility and lead by being servants, not dictators.

Decision (vv. 6-8)

We have moved from the leader's heart to the leader's eyes, and now we look at the leader's will. The repeated "I will" statements in the psalm give evidence of David's determination to serve God and God's people successfully and be a man of decision. He would not make excuses and he would not delay making decisions. But some of those decisions would be difficult to make and perhaps more difficult to implement. He wanted associates who were not defiled by sin, whose walk was blameless, and who would treat people with fairness. He knew that no king could build a lasting government on lies (31:5; 43:3; 57:10). Deception is the devil's tool, and Satan goes to work whenever a lie moves in (2 Cor. 11:1-3). Eastern kings often administered justice in the mornings at the city gate (2 Sam. 15:1-2; Jer. 21:12), so David promised to hear these cases patiently, consider them carefully, and render judgment wisely. He vowed to God that he would punish offenders according to God's law, silencing the liars and expelling the evildoers. Jerusalem was known as "the city of God," (46:4; 48:1) "the city of the great King," (48:2) and the city God loved the most (87:1-3), and David did not want to blemish that reputation.

Was David successful in maintaining the high standard of this declaration? No, not completely; but what leader besides Jesus Christ has ever maintained an unblemished record? David failed in his own family. His sin with Bathsheba set a bad example for his sons and daughters (2 Sam. 11-12), and David failed to discipline Amnon and Absalom for their sins (2 Sam. 13-15). He had problems with his generals

Joab and Abishai, and his trusted counselor Ahithophel betrayed him. But David reigned for forty years, during which time he expanded the borders of the kingdom, defeated Israel's enemies, gathered the wealth used to build the temple, wrote the psalms, and established the dynasty that eventually brought Jesus Christ into the world. Like us, he had his weaknesses and failings, but over all, he sought to honor the Lord and be a good leader. Jerusalem is known as "the city of David" and Jesus as "the Son of David." Could any compliment be higher than that?

Psalm 102

This is both a penitential psalm (see 6) and a Messianic psalm (vv. 25-27 = Heb. 1:10-12). The anonymous author probably wrote it long after the destruction of Jerusalem (vv. 8, 14, 16), about the time he thought Jeremiah's prophecy of the seventy-year captivity was about to be fulfilled (v. 13; Jer. 25:11-12; 29:10; see Dan. 9:2). According to the title, the psalmist was afflicted and faint (61:2; 77:3; 142:3; 143:4) and burdened to present his complaint ("lament," NIV) to the Lord. He was groaning in distress (vv. 2, 5) and weeping over the ruins of Jerusalem (v. 9). His opening prayer in verses 1-2 draws from a number of other psalms, giving us an example of what it means to pray the Word of God. (See 18:16; 27:9; 31:2; 37:20; 59:16; 69:17; 88:2.) As believers face and deal with the painful crises that come to us, if we are to overcome and glorify God, we must keep three assurances before us.

The Changing Circumstances of Life (vv. 1-11)

The longer we live, the more evidence we see that *things will change.* The Greek philosopher Heraclitus wrote, "There is nothing permanent except change," a statement that John F. Kennedy paraphrased as, "Everything changes but change itself." There are the normal changes of life, from birth to maturity to death, but there are also providential changes that God sends for our good and His glory. Many Jewish leaders in the days of Jeremiah the prophet thought that God would never allow Judah to be captured and Jerusalem and the temple destroyed (Jer. 7), but the Babylonian army did all three. They also took prisoners to Babylon and left only the poorest of the people to care for the land. Because of their rebellion against the law of God, Israel was left without a king, priesthood, temple, or sacrifice. Instead of the Lord's face shining upon them with blessing (Num. 6:25), His face was turned away from them in judgment (27:9; 59:17; Gen. 43:3, 5; Deut. 31:17-18).

Whether we are suffering because of our sins, or because we stand up for the Lord, or simply because we need to be better equipped for service, these changes are not pleasant. The psalmist recorded his personal plight in a series of vivid pictures. With his days as flimsy and temporary as drifting smoke, and his frame burning with fever (31:10; 32:3; 42:10), he was like a man in a furnace. His heart was like the cut and withered grass (vv. 4, 9; 90:4-5; Job 19:20; Lam. 4:8), paining him so much that he forgot to eat. When he did eat, the food tasted like ashes and his drink like tears (v. 9; 42:3; 80:5; Lam. 3:16). Therefore, he became a living skeleton that could only groan because of his wretched situation (v. 5). He compared himself to the unclean birds (Lev. 11:17-18) that lived solitary lives amid the ruins of the city. He was awake all night, a lonely man, like a sparrow bereft of his mate and chirping his lament on the roof. The enemy officers showed no sympathy but used his name in their curses (v. 8). It was as though God's hand picked him up and threw him on the trash heap, like a piece of discarded junk (v. 10; 51:11; 71:9; 147;17; Isa. 22:17-18). Like the evening shadows as the sun goes down, his life kept changing, *but his days had no substance.* Then the darkness fell and the long hard night lay before him. (See Deut. 28:66-67.)

One of the first steps toward personal peace and victory is to accept the fact that there will be changes in life, and how we respond will determine what these changes do to us and for us. The psalmist responded by turning to the Lord for help.

The Unchanged Covenant of God (vv. 12-22)

"But you, O Lord" marked a change in the psalmist's outlook as he turned from himself and his problems to behold by faith the Lord enthroned in heaven (see 93:2; 97:2; 99:1; 113:5; Lam. 5:19). The throne of David was gone and would not be claimed until the Son of David came to earth (Luke 1:30-33), but the throne of God in heaven was secure. Judah and Jerusalem were experiencing shame, but God's "memorial name" of great renown would not change. One day the nations would respect that name (v. 15) and praise that name in a new Jerusalem (v. 21). From generation to generation, His people had known and revered that name and the Lord had not failed them, but they failed the Lord. He had made a wonderful covenant with His people (Lev. 25-26; Deut. 28-30) and had not changed it. If His people obeyed His law, He would bless them, but if they disobeyed and turned to idols, He would chasten them. Either way, He would show His love and faithfulness.

The writer was confident that God would arise and rescue Zion, for it was time for His promises to be fulfilled (Jer. 25:11-12; 29:10). Even more, The Lord loved Zion more than the Jewish people did, and they revered her very dust and stones! (see 46:4; 48; 69:35-36; 87:1-5; 132:13; 137). Even more, the restoration of Zion means the glory of the Lord (vv. 15-16, 21-22), and this involves the salvation of the Gentile nations. When the Jewish exiles were released from captivity in Babylon and allowed to return to Judah, this was a witness to the surrounding nations that Jehovah was on the throne and guiding in the destiny of His people. And what about the future generations in Israel? The Lord made His covenant with them as well, and He will fulfill it (vv. 18, 28). God's compassion, God's covenant, God's glory, and God's people are all a part of the future of Jerusalem! As Alexander Maclaren wrote, "Zion cannot die while Zion's God lives." Surely the Lord will keep His promises and His glory will return to Zion (Ezek. 40-48). He hears the prayers of His people and one day will answer them. Israel and the Gentile nations will assemble and worship the Lord together (vv. 21-22; Isa. 2:1-4).

The Changeless Character of God (vv. 23-28)

The psalmist was afraid he would die in mid-life and never see the restoration of Judah, Jerusalem, and the temple. (See Isa. 38:10.) The eternal God would remain forever, but frail humans have only a brief time on earth (90:1-12). This passage (vv. 25-27) is quoted in Hebrews 1:10-12 and applied to Jesus Christ, which reminds us that it is in Him that these promises will be fulfilled. He is God and He is the same from generation to generation (Heb. 13:5-8). Leaders come and go, cities and buildings appear and vanish, but the Lord is the same and never abdicates His throne. God's eternality reminds us of our own frailty and the transitory nature of our lives, but it also reminds us that His promises and purposes will be fulfilled. The psalmist closed his prayer by remembering the future generations, for though he did not see his prayer answered in his day, he knew that the answer would come. May we today be concerned about God's work on earth and the future generations who will serve Him after we are gone! May the future not weep because we have not been faithful!

Psalm 103

The four psalms that close Book Four of the book of Psalms (90-106) emphasize praise to the Lord for several reasons: His benefits to His people (103), His care of His creation (104), His wonderful acts on behalf of Israel (105), His longsuffering with His people's rebellion (106). There are no requests in this psalm; it is only praise to the Lord. In studying this psalm, we must remember that God's blessings on Israel depended on their obedience to His covenant (vv. 17-18), and believers today must also be obedient to God's will if they would enjoy God's best (2 Cor. 6:14-7:1). The psalm also admonishes us not to *forget* the blessings after we have received them and enjoyed them. "In everything give thanks; for this is the will of God in Christ Jesus for you" (1 Thess. 5:18, NKJV).David started with individual and personal praise (vv. 1-6), then moved to national praise (6-19), and concluded with universal praise (vv. 20-22).

Personal Praise to the Lord (vv. 1-6)

To "bless the Lord" means to delight His heart by expressing love and gratitude for all He is and all He does. Parents are pleased when their children simply thank them and love them, without asking for anything. True praise comes from a grateful heart that sincerely wants to glorify and please the Lord. "All that is within me" means that all of our inner being is focused on the Lord—heart, soul, mind, and strength (Mark 12:28-31). It also means that we are prepared to obey His will after our praise has ended. The word "all" is found at least nine times in the psalm (1-3, 6, 19, 21-22), for the psalm is a call for total commitment to God. We give thanks to the Lord before we receive our food, and this is right, but the Jewish people were also to give thanks *after* they had eaten and to remember that the Lord had given them their food (Deut. 8:7-20). My immigrant Swedish relatives used to follow this practice. At least fourteen times in the book of Deuteronomy, Moses admonished the people to remember the Lord and what He did for them, and nine times he cautioned them not to forget. (See Deut. 32:18.) It was when the third generation of Jews came on the scene and forgot the Lord that the nation began to decay (Judg. 2:7-3:7).

David listed six special blessings from the hand of the Lord (vv. 3-5): forgiveness, healing, redemption, love, satisfaction, and renewal. The word translated "forgives" is used in Scripture only of God's forgiveness of sinners (see vv. 10-12). The word for "iniquity" pictures sin as something twisted and distorted. Those who have trusted Christ have experienced God's forgiveness (Eph. 1:7; Col. 1:14 and 2:13). When you read 32 and 51, you learn that David knew something about God's gracious forgiveness (and see vv. 10-12).

God is able to heal every disease (Matt. 9:35), but He is not obligated to do so. Paul was not able to heal two of his friends (Phil. 2:25-30; 2 Tim. 4:20), and David's own baby son died in spite of his fasting and praying (2 Sam. 12:15-23). The believer's body will not be completely delivered from weakness and disease until it is redeemed and glorified at the return of Jesus Christ (Rom. 8:18-23). In Scripture, sickness is sometimes used as a picture of sin and healing as a picture of salvation (41:4; 147:3; Isa. 53:10; Luke 5:18-32; 1 Peter 2:23-24).

The word "redeem" (v. 4) would remind the Jewish people of their deliverance from the bondage of Egypt at the Exodus (Ex. 12-15). The statement describes God rescuing someone about to fall into a pit, and "the pit" is a symbol of sheol (6:5; 16:10; 28:1), the world of the dead. David himself was often very near to death, so perhaps he had premature death in mind. David also knew something about crowns, but no crown he ever wore compared with God's lovingkindness and compassion (tender mercies). These attributes also appear in verses 8, 11, 13, and 17. Believers should "reign in life through the One, Jesus Christ" (Rom. 5:17, NKJV; and see Rev. 1:1:6). We are seated with Christ in the heavenlies (Eph. 2:1-7), and He helps us to "reign in life."

There is no satisfaction in this world, but we have satisfaction in Christ who is the Bread of Life (John 6:33-40) and the Good Shepherd who leads us into green pastures (23:2). (See 107:9 and 145:16.) The word translated "mouth" is a bit of a puzzle since it is usually translated "ornaments" or "jewelry," words that hardly fit this context. Some students interpret the word to mean "duration" or "years" (see NASB). No matter how old we become, God can satisfy the needs of our lives and the spiritual desires of our hearts. The legend about the physical renewal of the eagle is not what David had in mind in verse 5. Like most birds, eagles do molt and have what seems to be a new lease on life. But the picture here is that of the believer being strengthened by the Lord even in old age and able to "soar" like the eagle (Isa. 40:31). (See 71:17-18; 92:14; 2 Cor. 4:16-18.)

National Praise to the Lord (vv. 6-18)
The nation of Israel was certainly blessed of the Lord and therefore obligated to express their praise and thanksgiving to Him. Jehovah was their righteous Deliverer (v. 6), not only when He rescued them from Egypt, but all during their history. He gave David many great victories on the battlefield. The Lord also gave His people guidance (v. 7), leading them by His glory cloud, His Word, and His prophets. The people know God's acts, *what* He was doing, but Moses knew God's ways, *why* He was doing it. Moses was intimate with the Lord and understood His will. Jehovah was also the merciful and compassionate Savior who forgave His people when they sinned. In verses 8-12, we have a summary of what Moses learned about God while on Sinai (see Ex. 33:12-13; 34:5-9; and see Num. 14:18). Being a holy God, He did get angry at sin, and the Israelites were prone to rebel against Him, but in His compassion, He forgave them. This was possible because one day His Son would die for those sins on a cross. (See 86:15; Isa. 57:6.) The picture in verses 8-12 is that of a courtroom in which God is both judge and prosecuting attorney. He has all the evidence He needs to condemn us, but He doe not prolong the trial. When the judge is your Father, and when Jesus has died for your sins, there is full and free forgiveness available to all who will ask for it. If God gave us the punishment we deserved, we would be without hope (Ezra 9:13). The punishment that we deserve was given to Jesus (Isa. 53:4-6).

David looked up to the heavens and said that God's love reached that high and higher. David remembered the ceremony on the annual Day of Atonement (Lev. 16) when the goat was released in the wilderness, symbolically bearing Israel's sins far away (see John 1:29). (For other descriptions of God's forgiveness of sin, see Isa. 1:18; 38:17; 43:25; Jer. 31:34.) But we must remember that it is not God's love or pity that saves us, but God's grace (Eph. 2:8-10), for grace is love that has paid a price. Were it not for the death of Christ on the cross, there could be no forgiveness of our sins. Yes, God is like a tender Father, but His pity is not a shallow sentimental feeling. A holy God demands that His law be satisfied, and only His perfect Son could provide that satisfaction (Rom. 3:19-31). Is the human race worth saving? We are only grass that grows up and then fades away and dies (vv. 15-16; see 37:2, 10, 36; 40:6-8; 90:6-8). But the Lord knows our "formation" (frame) because He formed us from the dust (Gen. 2:7) and even kept watch on us in the womb (139:13-16). He is eternal God and wants to share His eternal home with us. What grace! He promised His people that He would bless them and their descendants if they feared Him and kept His precepts. (See Deut. 6:1-15.) Believers today have already been blessed "with every spiritual blessing … in Christ" (Eph. 1:4), and as we trust Him and obey His will, He meets our every need.

Universal Praise to the Lord (vv. 19-22)
When we worship the Lord God, we worship the King of the universe. The "Lord

of Hosts" is sovereign over all things He has created, including the stars and planets (33:6; Isa. 40:26) and the angels (91:11; 2 Kings 6:17-20), who are servants to the saints (Heb. 1:14). As a youth, David confronted the giant Goliath with, "I come to you in the name of the Lord of hosts, the God of the armies of Israel" (1 Sam. 17:45, NKJV). The apostle John heard the vast choir of all creation praise the Lord (Rev. 5:13), and one day, we shall join in that anthem. But the final shout of praise in the psalm comes, not from the angels, but from David the psalmist: "Bless the Lord, O my soul." After all, redeemed men and women have more to praise the Lord for than do all the angels in heaven and all the galaxies in the universe.

Nobody in hell blesses the Lord, but every creature in heaven does nothing else but bless the Lord. We who are in this world can enjoy "heaven on earth" as we join them in expressing thanksgiving and blessing to our great God. "Bless the Lord, O my soul!"

Psalm 104

This is a magnificent hymn celebrating the glory of the Creator and the incredible greatness of His creation. Paul may have had this psalm in mind when he spoke to the Athenian philosophers (Acts 17:22-34, especially vv. 24-28), for it presents a God who created and now sustains a beautiful and bountiful world that reflects His glory (v. 31). The writer of the psalm certainly had Genesis 1 in mind when he wrote, even though he did not follow all six days of creation in detail, nor did he include the creation of man and woman (see vv. 14, 23). He began with light (v. 2; Gen. 1:1-5) and continued with the separation of the upper and lower waters (vv. 2-4; Gen. 1:6-8) and the separation of land and water (vv. 5-9; Gen. 1:9-10). The provision of vegetation is mentioned (vv. 14-17; Gen. 1:11-13), as well as the placing of the sun and moon (vv. 19-23; Gen. 1:14-19), and the creation of land and sea creatures (vv. 24-25; Gen. 1:20-28). The psalm declares that our God is very great (v. 1), very wise (v. 24), and very generous (v. 27). In spite of the fact that creation is in bondage to sin since the fall of man (Rom. 8:18-23), we still live in an amazing universe run by divinely ordained laws that are so remarkable we can send people to the moon and bring them back! Whether the scientist uses the telescope, the microscope, or the x-ray, he beholds the wonders of God's creation.

The Greatness of Our God (vv. 1-9)

The psalm opens with the description of a King so great (95:3; Hab. 3:4) that He wears light for a robe (93:1; Isa. 59:17; 1 John 1:5; 1 Tim. 6:16) and has a palace in heaven above the waters (Gen. 1:7). He uses the clouds for His chariot and the winds to move them (18:7-15; 68:4; 77:16-19). His servants (the angels, 148:8; Heb. 1:7) serve as quickly and invisibly as the wind and possess awesome power like flames of fire. This King is so great that creating the heavens was as easy as putting up a tent (19:4; Isa. 40:22). Though He hung the earth on nothing (Job 26:7), it remains firmly fixed as if resting on a foundation that cannot be moved (Job 38:6). When He made the earth, it was "wearing" deep waters like a garment (Gen. 1:2, 6-10), but one command from the King and those waters "were frightened away." They settled where they belonged on the planet and dared not go beyond the established boundaries (Job 38:8-11; Jer. 5:22). In all this creative activity, the Lord has revealed Himself in His power and glory. "The heavens are telling of the glory of God; and their expanse is declaring the work of His hands" (19:1, NASB). Day and night, the visible things of creation shout aloud to the inhabitants of the earth that there is a God, that He is powerful and wise, and that all people are accountable to Him (Rom. 1:18-32). Are the people paying attention?

The Generosity of Our God
(vv. 10-23, 27-30)

God did not wind up the clock of creation and then let it run down, for the tenses of the verbs indicate that God is constantly at work, meeting the needs of His creatures. Note the emphasis on water, both the springs (v. 10) and the rain (v. 13), for water is a precious commodity in the Near East. The "mountains" (v. 13) refer to the upland regions where the grain grows (76:16; Deut. 11:10-12). God supplies not only water for vegetation but also food for the birds and animals (vv. 14, 21, 27-28), and the plants and animals provide food for the people. God uses the cooperation of the farmers and herdsmen to provide this food (v. 14; Gen. 2:8-15; Ex. 20:9), but ultimately He is the giver. Wine, oil, and bread were basics in the life of the people in biblical days. The wine was diluted with water and drunkenness was not acceptable (Judg. 9:13 and Eccl. 10:19). Wine, oil, and water are symbols of the Holy Spirit (Eph. 5:18; John 7:37-39; Zech. 4:1-7;), and bread speaks of the nourishing Word of God (Matt. 4:4). God has written spiritual truths into the very world of nature.

But without the days, nights, and seasons, there could not be fruitfulness on earth, and therefore he praises God for the sun and moon (see Gen. 1:14-19). The Hebrew religious calendar was built around the seasons (Lev. 23), and there were special monthly celebrations as well (Ex. 12:2; Num. 10:10; 28:14; 1 Chron. 23:31). Without the cycle of day and night and of the seasons, life would come to a halt. "To everything there is a season, a time for every purpose under heaven" (Eccl. 3:1, NKJV). All of creation looks expectantly to the Lord to provide what it needs (vv. 27-30), and He does so generously. However, people made in the image of God think they can "make it" alone. Yet God provides the very breath in our nostrils, and when He turns it off, we die (Gen. 2:7; Eccl. 12:7). On the first day of creation, the Holy Spirit brooded over the waters (Gen. 1:1-2), and that same Spirit gives new life to creation when the winter season ends (v. 30). The Spirit also provides life and power to the church, God's "new creation." Mankind has learned to control a great deal of nature, but the issues of life and death are still in the hands of God. How generous He is to a world that ignores Him, rebels against Him, and rarely gives thanks for His generous gifts! (Ponder Job 34:14-15; Acts 17:25-28; Col. 1:17.)

The Wisdom of Our God (vv. 24-35)

Whether we study invisible microscopic life, visible plant and animal life, human life, or the myriad of things that have no life, the diversity in creation is amazing. God could have made a drab colorless world, one season everywhere, only one variety of each plant and animal, cookie-cutter humans, no musical sounds, and a few minimal kinds of food—but He did not, and how grateful we are! Only a wise God could have planned so many different things, and only a powerful God could have brought them into being. "The earth is full of thy riches" (v. 24, KJV). The word translated "riches" means "possessions, property," reminding us that God made it all, God owns it all, and God has the right to tell us how to use it all. God wants us to enjoy His creation (1 Tim. 6:17) and employ it wisely. When we exploit our wonderful world, we sin and forget that we are stewards, not owners, and that one day we must give an account of how we have used these precious and irreplaceable gifts. The sea monsters (whales? Gen. 1:21) frolic and play in the ocean and God enjoys them! But God does not enjoy seeing us ruin His handiwork just to make money. Creation is glad for what the Lord has done (v. 26), mankind ought to be glad (v. 15). God's people especially should be glad (v. 34)—and the Lord Himself rejoices over His works! (v. 31).

Knowing all this about God and His creation, we have some serious responsibilities to fulfill, and the first is *glorifying the Lord (vv. 31-32).* Beginning with our own bodies and minds, our abilities and possessions, we must gratefully accept all He has graciously given us and use it to glorify Him, not to please ourselves (Rom. 12:1-2; 1 Cor. 4:7). Second, *we must praise the Lord, the Creator.* What a marvelous gift is His creation! We need to get back to singing the great hymns and paraphrases of the psalms that exalt God the Creator. The more we thank God, the less we will exploit His gifts. Third, *we should think about His creation and rejoice in it (v. 34).* The study of natural science is but "thinking God's thoughts after Him." If earth and sky are declaring the glory of God (19:1), we who have been saved by His grace ought to be glorifying Him even more! Finally, *we must pray for Christ's return (v. 35),* for only then will the curse of sin be lifted from creation (Rom. 8:18-25). We must share the gospel with sinners so that they might be able to sing with us, "This is my Father's world."

Psalm 105

Psalm 104 magnifies the God of creation and 106 the God who chastens His people and forgives them, but this psalm focuses on the God of the covenant (vv. 8-10) who works out His divine purposes in human history. "Make known his deeds" (vv. 1-2, 5) is the major thrust, referring, of course, to God's mighty acts on behalf of Israel. (See also 78, and note that 105:1-15 is adapted in 1 Chron. 16:8-22.) The psalm does not go beyond the conquest of Canaan (v. 44) or mention the Davidic dynasty, which suggests that it may have been written after the Babylonian exile, possibly by one of the Levites who returned to Judah with the Jewish remnant. The psalmist saw the hand of God in the events of Jewish history, and this was the kind of encouragement the struggling remnant needed. He reminded them that they were God's chosen people and that God worked according to His schedule. Beginning with Egypt, the Lord had already revealed His power over the Gentile nations, and He will always keep His promises. Remembering these truths can bring God's people encouragement at any time in history! (v. 5).

The Patriarchs—God's Gracious Election (vv. 1-15)

As in 32:1-2, the joyful praise recorded in verses 1-5 is the worshipers' response to the wonderful truths stated in the psalm. The name "Jehovah—LORD" is used five times (vv. 1, 3, 4, 7, 19) and is the covenant name of God, the "holy name" that Israel was to call on (v. 1) and glory in (v. 3) as they worshiped. Israel was a chosen people; Jehovah had made no covenant with any other nation (147:20; Rom. 9:1-5). There are ten commandments in verses 1-5 ("seek" is found twice), climaxing with "remember" (v. 5). Their thanksgiving, praying, and singing were a witness to the nations around them and a testimony to the power and glory of the Lord. An obedient Israel was to be God's "exhibit A" to the nations so that they would want to know the true and living God of the Jewish people.

In His sovereign grace, the Lord chose Abraham (vv. 6, 9, 42) and made His covenant with him (Gen. 12:1-5; 15:9-21; Acts 7:1-8), a covenant that would apply to all of Abraham's physical descendants as well as to believers today as Abraham's spiritual children (Luke 1:68-79; Gal. 3:1-9, 29). One of the covenant promises was the gift of the land of Canaan to the people of Israel (vv. 11, 42-44), and this promise was repeated to Abraham's son Isaac (Gen. 26:1-6) and to his grandson Jacob (Gen. 28:13-17). We see here the electing grace of God, for He chose Isaac, not Ishmael, and Jacob, not Esau (Rom. 9:6-18). This covenant will endure forever (vv. 8-11; Deut. 7:9). Again, this was an act of grace on the part of the Lord, for none of the patriarchs had any claim to upon God nor did He owe them anything. They were homeless nomads—pilgrims and strangers (Heb. 11:8-16)—who depended on the Lord to protect and guide them (Gen. 34:30; Deut. 7:6-11; 26:5). Even when they erred, the Lord protected them and even reproved kings on their behalf (Gen. 12:10ff; 20; 26; 32-33). God is sovereign, and though He does not turn men and women into robots, He does rule and overrule when they disobey. His will shall be done and His plans shall be fulfilled (vv. 8-11; 19; 42; 33:11).

Joseph—God's Wise Preparation (vv. 16-25)

According to verse 6, the Jewish people are the descendants of Abraham, who believed God and received the covenant,

and also the sons of Jacob, whose sons built the nation of Israel. In Joseph's dreams, God had promised him that his brothers would bow before him one day, but He did not explain how this would occur. Envy and a family quarrel took Joseph to Egypt where he prepared the way for his relatives and kept them alive during the famine (Gen. 45:55-57; 50:20). But before he became the second ruler of Egypt, Joseph experienced great suffering in prison, for in God's economy, suffering precedes glory (1 Peter 5:10), and being a servant precedes being a ruler (Matt. 25:21). But the Word that God gave Joseph came true, and Jacob and his family moved from Canaan to Egypt (Gen. 46, the land of Ham; vv. 23, 27; 78:51; 106:22; Gen. 10:6). It was there that God in His grace turned Jacob's family of seventy persons into a nation so large and powerful that it threatened the security of Egypt. No matter how dark the day, God always sends His servant ahead to prepare the way. God permitted the Egyptians to persecute His people, for suffering is one of the secrets of fruitfulness. God did not force the Egyptians to hate the Jews nor did He force Pharaoh to harden his heart. The Lord arranged the circumstances so that Pharaoh and his officers could either obey or disobey His Word, and their repeated disobedience hardened their hearts more. The record in Exodus reports that Pharaoh hardened his heart (Ex. 7:13-14, 22; 8:15, 19, 32; 9:7, 34-35; 13:15) but also that God hardened it (4:21; 7:3; 9:12; 10:1, 20, 27; 11:10; 14:4, 8, 17). God sent the plagues, but Pharaoh would not obey. The same sun that melts the ice will harden the clay.

Moses—God's Awesome Judgments (vv. 26-41)

Again, God had His servants prepared to take Israel through another crisis. The ten plagues were both a demonstration of the power of the God of Israel and a condemnation of the gods of Egypt (Ex. 12:12; 18:11; Num. 33:4). Egypt worshiped the sun, so God sent three days of darkness. The Nile River was a god, so God turned the water to blood. The Egyptians worshiped over eighty different gods and goddesses, all of whom were helpless to deliver the land from the onslaught of the plagues, the judgments that God pronounced (v. 5). Jehovah proved that they were false gods who could do nothing.

The psalmist began his list with the plague of darkness (v. 28), which was actually the ninth plague. After mentioning this plague, the writer stayed with the original sequence: water turned to blood, and the invasions of frogs, flies, and gnats. He omits the fifth and six plagues—the death of the livestock and the boils—and moves on to the hail, locusts, and the death of the firstborn on Passover night. What a demonstration of the awesome power of Jehovah! This led to the triumphant exodus of the Jewish people from Egypt, like a victorious army carrying the spoils of battle (v. 37; Ex. 3:21-22; 11:1-3; 12:36-37; Gen. 15:14). This wealth was payment for the slave labor that the Jews had provided for many years. God went before His people, led them by a cloud (78:14; Ex. 13:21-22; 14:19-20), opened the sea for them to pass through, and then closed the waters and drowned the Egyptian army. It was "a night of solemn observance to the Lord" (Ex. 12:42, NKJV).

But the Lord did not abandon His people after He delivered them, for He had brought them out that He might bring them into the Promised Land (Deut. 4:37-38). He led them in the wilderness, sheltered them from the sun, fed them bread (manna) and meat, and provided water to drink. (See Ex. 16 and 17 and Num. 20.) "The Lord is my shepherd; I shall not want" (23:1). Remembering God's deliverance and His care of His people would give courage to the Jewish remnant as they returned to Judah to reestablish the nation. God remembers His covenant (v. 8), and God's people must remember the Lord and what He has done.

All Believers—God's Dependable Promise (vv. 42-45)

The psalmist moved immediately from the Exodus to the conquest of Canaan. He wrote nothing about Israel's failures at Sinai (the golden calf), in the wilderness (repeated complaining), and at Kadesh Barnea (refusing to enter the land). After all, the purpose of the psalm was to magnify God's great works, not to expose man's great failures. God kept the promise He made to Abraham and gave his descendants the land, helping Joshua and his army defeat the enemy on every side. The people of Israel claimed their inheritance, including the wealth they took from the former inhabitants, another payment for their service in Egypt. "Not a word failed of any good thing which the Lord had spoken to the house of Israel. All came to pass" (Josh. 21:45, and see 23:14; 1 Kings 8:56; Neh. 9:8).

God's people live on promises, not explanations, and it is "through faith and patience" that we see these promises fulfilled (Heb. 6:12). But God's keeping His promise meant much more for Israel than victory over the enemy and the acquisition of riches. *It meant accepting the responsibility of obeying the God who had been so faithful to them.* Before his death, Joshua reminded the people what the Lord had done for them and admonished them to serve the Lord and not turn to idols (Josh. 24:1-28). When we consider all that the

Lord has done for us, we find we have the same obligation.

Psalm 106

After reading this psalm, we might be tempted to say, "Those Israelites were certainly a sorry band of sinners!" Instead, we ought to be commending the psalmist for telling the truth about his own people. Most historians present their nations in the best possible light and blame other nations rather than their own, but our anonymous psalmist told the truth. "History will bear me out," said Sir Winston Churchill, "particularly as I shall write that history myself." But the writer is also to be commended for identifying himself with his struggling people and saying "*We* have sinned" and "Save *us*" (vv. 6 and 47, italics mine). We noted that 105 said nothing about Israel's failings, but that deficiency is remedied by 106. However, the purpose of the psalm is not to condemn Israel but to extol the Lord for His longsuffering and mercy toward His people. In order to glorify God, the writer had to place God's mercies against the dark background of Israel's repeated disobedience. The psalm was probably written after the Babylonian captivity, when the Jewish people were scattered and a remnant had returned to the land to rebuild the temple and restore the nation (vv. 44-47). After expressing his praise to the Lord (vv. 1-6), the writer pointed out nine serious offenses the nation had committed. He began with the Exodus and closed with the Babylonian captivity, and at the heart of the list he placed Israel's rebellion at Kadesh Barnea. He did not arrange these selected events in order of their occurrence, for his purpose was to teach us theology and not chronology.

Joyful Faith (vv. 1-6)
The psalm begins on a high note of worship and praise. Before he looked back on the failures of his people, or looked around at the ruins of the kingdom, the psalmist looked up and gave thanks to God for His goodness and mercy (vv. 1-3). Jehovah had been merciful in all that He had done, and the writer accepted God's will as just and right. Then the psalmist turned from praise to prayer and asked God to include him in the blessings of the promised restoration of the nation (vv. 4-5). The prophets had promised that the captivity would end and the people would return and rebuild, and he believed those promises. But his prayer was not selfish, for he wanted the whole nation to prosper, to rejoice in the Lord, and to give praise to His name. His prayer climaxed with penitence as he confessed his sins and the sins of his people (v. 6). "We have sinned with our fathers" is better than "Our fathers sinned." (See Neh. 1:6, Dan. 9:5, 8, 11, and 15; and Lam. 5:16.) The psalmist claimed the promise that King Solomon asked God to honor when he dedicated the temple (1 Kings 8:46-53). As we study this psalm, it may be like witnessing an autopsy, but we will benefit from it if, like the psalmist, we keep our eyes on the Lord of glory and see His kindness and faithfulness to His sinful people.

Triumphant Beginnings (vv. 7-12)
The reference here is to Israel's fear and unbelief at the Exodus, when they were caught between the Egyptian army behind them and the Red Sea before them (Ex. 14:10-31). They had witnessed the mighty power of God as He had devastated Egypt with plagues, but Israel did not believe that the Lord could successfully deliver them from the Egyptians.

They were looking back instead of looking up and were walking by sight and not by faith. They preferred the security of slavery to the challenges of liberty. "Let us go back to Egypt!" was frequently their response when they found themselves in a situation that demanded faith. In that desperate hour, they did not remember God's kindness or His promises, and they panicked. But God led them through the sea on dry land and utterly destroyed the enemy army that tried to follow them. "Then they believed His words; they sang His praise" (v. 12, NASB; see Ex. 15). This one miracle should have assured them for all the trials to come, but they did not take it to heart or understand God's ways (78:42-51; 95:10; 103:7). For Moses, this was an experience of faith that glorified God, but for the people, it was just another spectacular event. They were spectators at a performance, not participants in a miracle. But are God's people any different today?

Dangerous Decline (vv. 13-23)

The seeds of unbelief buried in the hearts of the Jewish people took root and bore bitter fruit in the years to come. As George Morrison wrote, "The Lord took Israel out of Egypt in one night, but it took Him forty years to take Egypt out of Israel." The people were slow to remember God's past deeds but quick to rush ahead and ignore His desires. However, they did not hesitate to make known their own desires, for they craved water (Ex. 15:22-27), food (Ex. 16), and meat (Num. 11:4-15, 31-35). "What shall we eat? What shall we drink?" (See Matt. 6:25ff.) God provided daily manna ("angels' food"—78:12), water at an oasis and then from the rock (Ex. 17), and enough fowl to give meat to the whole nation. People who grumble and complain are people not walking by

faith in the promises of God (Phil. 2:14-15). We must resist the temptation to yield to our fleshly cravings (1 Cor. 10:1-13).

The rebellion of Korah (Num. 16-17) followed soon after Israel's apostasy at Kadesh Barnea when the nation refused to enter the Promised Land. Korah enlisted his 250 fellow rebels because of this crisis; all he had to do was blame Moses and claim that the nation needed new leadership. (Political candidates have been doing this ever since.) Korah was a Levite in the family of Kohath whose privilege it was to carry the tabernacle furnishings. But Kohath was not satisfied with that task; he wanted to function at the altar as a priest (Num. 14:8-10). Pride and selfish ambition have always brought trouble to God's people (Phil. 2:1-11; James 4:1-10). These rebels were opposing the will of God, for it was the Lord who chose Moses and Aaron to lead the nation, and so the Lord destroyed Korah and his followers. Respect for God's leaders is important to the success of the Lord's work (Heb. 13:7, 17).

The first failure involved the lusts of the flesh and the second involved the pride of life (see 1 John 2:15-17). The third failure, the worship of the golden calf (Ex. 32; Deut. 9:8-29), involved the lust of the eyes. For forty days, Moses had been on Sinai with the Lord, and the Jewish people were nervous without their leader. (When he was with them, they opposed him and criticized him!) In spite of what the Lord had taught them at Sinai, they wanted a god they could see (Deut. 4:12-19). Aaron collected gold jewelry and molded a calf for the people to see and worship, and Moses had to intercede with the Lord to turn away His wrath. They rejected the eternal God ("their Glory"—Rom. 1:26) for a man-made piece of gold that could not see, hear, speak, or act! Once again, Israel forgot what the Lord had done for them. The phrase "stood in the breach" (v. 23) describes a soldier standing at a break in the city walls and preventing the enemy from entering. What a picture of intercessory prayer! (Ezek. 22:30).

Tragic Failure (vv. 24-27)
Israel had been out of Egypt about two years when the Lord brought them to Kadesh Barnea on the border of the Promised Land (Num. 13-14). Instead of trusting God to give them the land, the people asked Moses to appoint a committee to survey the land. (God had already done this for them—Ezek. 20:6). But Israel did not need more facts; they needed more faith. It was a "pleasant [beautiful] land" (v. 24; Jer. 3:19; 12:10) and a "good land" (Deut. 8:7-9), but ten of the twelve spies reported that Canaan was a dangerous land filled with giants, high-walled cities, and formidable armies. The people reverted to their usual crisis mode of weeping, complaining, and planning to return to Egypt (Num. 14:1-10). The Lord announced that the generation twenty years and older would all die in the wilderness during the next thirty-eight years, and then He sent a plague that killed the ten unbelieving spies. What should have been a triumphant victory march became a tragic funeral march. That is what happens when we want our own way and refuse to trust the Lord and obey Him.

Costly Disobedience (vv. 28-33)
These two events occurred toward the end of Israel's march through the wilderness, and both of them illustrate the high cost of willful disobedience to the Lord. The failure at Baal Peor is described in Numbers 25, but read Numbers 22-24 to get the background. The king of Moab hired the

prophet Baalam to curse the nation of Israel, but God turned his curses into blessings (Deut. 23:5; Neh. 13:2; see 109:28). But Baalam knew how to trap Israel: he suggested that the king act like a good neighbor and invite the Jewish tribal leaders to share a feast with the Moabites. This would be a religious feast, of course, which meant eating meat dedicated to demons and dead people and cohabiting with cult prostitutes. Once more, the people of God yielded to their fleshly desires and tasted the wrath of God, and 24,000 people died (Num. 25:9). The plague would have claimed more lives, but Phinehas, the son of the high priest, killed a Jewish man and his Moabite partner as they arrogantly sinned in the camp of Israel. "The wages of sin is death" (Rom. 6:23). (On v. 30, see Gen. 15:6 and Rom. 4.)

The second demonstration of carnality was seen in Moses, not a sin of the flesh but of the spirit: he became proud and angry and took for himself the glory that belonged only to the Lord (Num. 20:1-13). Provoked by the people, the "pride of life" possessed Moses and he lost his temper and spoke rash words that offended the Lord (78:40; Isa. 63:10; 1 John 2:15-17). This sin cost Moses the privilege of leading the people into the Promised Land (Deut. 3:23-29). "Meribah" means "quarreling" (see Ex. 17:1-7).

Repeated Rebellion (vv. 34-46)
God in His grace took His people into Canaan and gave them victory over the nations living there. The twelve tribes claimed their inheritance and settled down to enjoy the land and serve the Lord. They were faithful all during the leadership of Joshua and the elders that he selected and trained, but when the third generation came along, they compromised and began to serve the false

gods of their defeated enemies (Judg. 2:7-23). The people knew the terms of the covenant that Moses had given them (Lev. 26; Deut. 28-30), but they disobeyed it. Instead of destroying the godless society of the nations in Canaan as God commanded (Num. 33:50-56; Deut. 7:12-26; 20:16-18), the Israelites gradually compromised with them and then imitated them, including the inhumane practices that defiled the land God gave them (Lev. 18:24-28; Num. 35:30-34; Deut. 21:22-23; Jer. 3:1-10). They had been "married" to Jehovah at Sinai, but now they prostituted themselves to idols and grieved the Lord, inviting His chastening. The Lord brought six nations against Israel and for over one hundred years punished His people right in their own land. When they cried out to Him for mercy, He heard them and raised up judges to deliver them from their enemies; but then the nation lapsed into idolatry again, and the cycle was repeated. In His mercy, the Lord heard their cries and forgave them (Judg. 3:9, 15; 4:3; 6:6-7; 10:10; Lev. 26:40-42), but this could not go on forever.

Final Discipline (v. 47)

In His covenant, the Lord warned that if Israel continued to resist and disobey, even after experiencing His chastening, He would take them out of their land and scatter them (Lev. 26:27-39; Deut. 28:48-68). First, the kingdom was divided between the ten tribes of Israel (the northern kingdom) and the two tribes of Benjamin and Judah (the southern kingdom). In 722 B.C., the Assyrians captured Israel and absorbed the ten tribes into their own empire. In 606-586 B.C., the Babylonians invaded Judah, destroyed Jerusalem and the temple, and took the best of the people captive to Babylon. The Jewish people were rooted out of their own "beautiful land" and scattered among the nations. The Medes and Persians conquered Babylon in 539 B.C. and the next year Cyrus decreed that the Jews could return to their land. However, the Davidic dynasty was not restored in their kingdom. The psalmist closed with a prayer that the scattered children of Abraham, Isaac, and Jacob would one day be gathered together so that they might worship Jehovah and give glory to His name.

The last verse, written by an ancient editor, brings to a close the Fourth Book of the Psalms.

BOOK V
Psalm 107

The emphasis in 105 is on Israel's exodus from Egypt and in 106 on God's longsuffering care of His people. This psalm focuses on the Lord's redemption of the nation from captivity in Babylon (vv. 2-3). While the circumstances described in the psalm could be experienced by almost anyone, they especially apply to what Israel had to endure while in captivity. The word "redeemed" is often used in Isaiah to describe this great deliverance (Isa. 35:9; 43:1; 44:22-23; 48:20; 62:12). Note the words describing their plight: adversity (v. 2), trouble and distress (vv. 6, 13, 19, 28), misery (vv. 10, 26, 39), labor (v. 12), affliction (vv. 17, 41), destruction (v. 20), oppression (v. 39), and sorrow (v. 39). The psalmist begins by urging us to give thanks to the Lord for His goodness and mercy (lovingkindness), and he closes by exhorting us to be wise and learn from the mistakes of other people (v. 47). The people described in this psalm needed God's help, either because of their own folly or because of circumstances beyond their control, and they called on the Lord and He delivered them. Five specific situations are described involving people who lose something valuable.

When You Lose Your Way (vv. 4-9)

It was a long way from Babylon to Judah and the dangers were many, but the Lord brought His people safely home (Ezra 1-2; Isa. 41:14-20; 43:1-21). In their need, they cried out to Him (vv. 6, 13, 19, 28) and He brought them out, led them through the wilderness, and brought them to their own land where they found cities to live in. During their journey, He provided food and drink for them (see Luke 1:53; Jer. 31:25). Surely they would want to give thanks to Him for all that He did for them (vv. 8, 15, 21, 31).

When You Lose Your Freedom (vv. 10-16)

These people were in prison (vv. 10, 14, 17) because they had rebelled against the Lord, a good description of the Jewish people exiled in Babylon (2 Chron. 36:15-23). They violated their covenant with the Lord, and He had to discipline them (Lev. 26:33; Deut. 28:47-48). God used Cyrus, a pagan king, to set His people free (Isa. 45:1-7, and note 45:2 and 107:16). Anyone who rejects God's message of life in Christ is imprisoned in sin, and only Jesus can set him or her free (Luke 1:79; 4:18ff).

When You Lose Your Health (vv. 17-22)

Again we meet rebellious fools who deliberately disobeyed God's law and suffered for their folly. The "gates of death" (v. 18) led into sheol, the land of the dead (9:13; Job 17:16; 38:17; Isa. 38:10). The Lord heard their cries and stopped them at the very gates and permitted them to live. They did not deserve this blessing, but such is the mercy of the Lord. In Scripture, sickness is often used as a picture of sin and its painful consequences, but not all sickness is the result of sin (John 9:1-3; 2 Cor. 12:7-10). Because the Lord healed these repentant rebels, they should praise Him, sing to Him, and bring thank offerings to Him. In verse 20, the Word of God is compared to medicine that God sends for their healing. This reminds us of the three people Jesus healed *from a distance*: the centurion's servant (Matt. 8:5-13), the demonized girl (Matt. 15:21-28), and the nobleman's son (John 4:46-54).

When You Lose Your Hope (vv. 23-32)

Being away from home and living as captives in Babylon was to the exiles like being on a boat in a terrible storm (see Isa. 54:11). The Jews were not a seafaring people like the Phoenicians, but Solomon did carry on a lucrative trading business (1 Kings 9:26-27). In the previous two pictures (vv. 10-22), the people were in trouble because they sinned against the Lord, but these sailors didn't cause the storm that almost drowned them. This is one of the most powerful descriptions of a storm at sea to be found anywhere in literature. The crew had used every device they knew to save the ship, but to no avail, so they called on the Lord for His help. Not only did He still the storm (see Luke 8:22-25), but He guided them to the right port (John 6:21). This wonderful deliverance should motivate the sailors to give thanks to the Lord personally, to exalt Him in the sanctuary worship, and to bear witness to the leaders of the people. The thanksgiving continues to expand! There are no hopeless situations in God's sight, for He can do the impossible. Nobody but the crew and the Lord saw the miracle, so it was up to the grateful crew to spread the word and give glory to the Lord.

When You Lose Your Home (vv. 33-43)
The approach changes and the focus of attention is not on the people in trouble but on the Lord. He can turn the garden into a desert and the desert into a garden (Isa. 35; 41:18; Deut. 28:1-5). God can judge the land because of the wickedness of the people who live there (v. 34; see Gen. 19:24-28), and He can also heal the land and bless it because of the faith and obedience of the people. This is a part of His covenant relationship with Israel (Deut. 28:15, 22-24, 58-59, 62-63). If necessary, the Lord can summon foreign armies like Babylon to invade the land and use them to chasten the leaders (vv. 39-40; Job 12:21, 24). However, His purpose is not to destroy but to cleanse, and He will restore the blessing to the land and the people (vv. 41-42). This closing paragraph (vv. 39-42) reminds us of Mary's song in Luke 1:46-55.

And what should we learn from these five pictures that depict God's power and mercy in action? To be wise and heed the Word of God (v. 43; Hos. 14:9). Yes, God shows His love and mercy to the disobedient who repent and call on His name, but our Father would rather share that love with *obedient* children who would enjoy it more (2 Cor. 6:14-7:1).

Psalm 108

The worship leader took the first five verses from 57:7-11 and the last eight from 60:5-12 and made a new psalm. (For commentary, see those psalms.) God's truth is adaptable to new situations and old songs become "new songs" when new challenges are matched with changeless theology. The writer opened with praise to the Lord (vv. 1-5) and then reminded Him of His promises to conquer Israel's enemies and give them the land (vv. 6-9). He closed with prayer for God's help and an expression of confidence in the power of the Lord (vv. 10-13). Praise, prayer, and promises form a combination found often in the psalms, a pattern that we ought to imitate in our own daily lives.

Psalm 109

This is the last of the "imprecatory psalms," and some consider it to be the most vehement. (See Ps. 5.) The psalm is ascribed to David (Acts 1:20), but it must have been written before he took the throne, for no king would be obligated to put up with this kind of treatment from an officer (v. 8) in his own court. The man was outwardly religious (v. 7) but hated David (vv. 3, 5) and falsely accused him (vv. 1-2, 4; see Ex. 23:6-8; Deut, 19:15-21) and cursed him (vv. 17-19). David's attempts to return good for evil failed (vv. 4-5), and the man showed him no mercy (v. 16). This unknown opponent may have been King Saul himself, whose life David spared on at least two occasions, or perhaps one of Saul's important officers who wanted to please his master. Had we been in this situation with David, we might have prayed as he did! There was terrible injustice in the land, and only God could remove Saul and put the rightful king on the throne. David did not avenge himself but put the matter in the hands of the Lord (Rom. 12:17-21). The psalm is built around three major requests.

Lord, Do Something! (vv. 1-5)
The silence of God indicated that the Lord was not answering prayer and working

on David's behalf (28:1; 35:22-24; 50:3; 83:1). Often we cry out to Him but nothing seems to happen. David reminded the Lord that he did not pray only when he needed help, for he praised the Lord often and thanked Him for His mercies ("God of my praise"; see v. 30; 22:25; Deut. 10:21; Jer. 17:14). In fact, in the Hebrew text, "O God of my praise" opens the psalm. God was silent but the enemy was vocal, speaking hateful lying words and accusing David of crimes he had never committed. The word translated "adversaries" or "accusers" (vv. 4, 6, 20, 29) gives us the English word "Satan," one of the names of the Devil (see 38:20; 71:13; Job 1-2; Zech. 3). Satan is the accuser (Rev. 12:10) and the adversary of believers (1 Peter 5:8), and he uses people to accomplish this work. Like our Savior who was falsely accused, David was innocent of the charges (v. 3; 35:7, 19-20; 69:4; Jer. 18:18; 20:10). God's people return good for evil, most people return good for good and evil for evil, but Satan's crowd returns evil for good (v. 5; 35:12; 38:20; Jer. 18:20). David responded to God's silence and to the enemy's attacks by praying to the Lord. His faith did not waver.

Lord, Judge the Enemy! (vv. 6-20)

Some students try to take the barbs out of David's prayer by making verses 6-20 the words of the enemy about David, but the approach will not work. Does verse 18 apply to David? And what about verse 20? Years later, the prophet Jeremiah prayed a similar prayer against the enemies that wanted to kill him (Jer. 18:18-23), and the Lord did not rebuke him. It has also been suggested that the tenses of the verbs should read as futures and not as requests: "His days will be few ... His children will be beggars," and so on. Knowing God's covenant, David was predicting what would happen because of the sins his enemy had committed. (See Lev. 26:14-39.)

David was willing for the court to solve the problem, for that is the image found in verses 6-7. Note that the pronouns shift from *they* and *them* to *he, him* and *his*. David focused his prayer on the leader of the evil band that was attacking him, and he asked God to appoint a judge or prosecuting attorney as wicked as the defendant himself! After all, the way we judge others is the way we ourselves will be judged (Matt. 7:1-2). Or perhaps he wanted Satan himself to be there (Zech. 3:1ff). David expected the Lord to stand at his right hand to defend him (v. 31; 16:8). Our Savior is enthroned at the right hand of God and intercedes for us (110:1; Acts 2:25, 34; Rom. 8:34).

David prayed that God's judgment would be thorough and would include the family of his enemy (vv. 9-13). Certainly he knew what the law said about this (Deut. 24:16), so the family must have participated in the father's sins. Every Jewish man wanted many descendants so that his name would be perpetuated, along with much wealth and a long life, but David prayed that none of these blessings would come to his enemy. Even more, he asked that his enemy's parents' sins would never be forgiven. (This must have been a very wicked family.) This would mean perpetual judgment on the family until it died out (Ex. 20:5; 34:7; Lev. 26:39). Peter quoted verses 8 and 69:25 in Acts 1:20 when the church elected a new apostle to replace Judas. In verses 16-20, David focused on his enemy's sins of omission: he did not show kindness to the poor and he did not seek to be a blessing to others (see Ex. 22:22-24; Deut. 10:18; 14:29; 16:11-14; 24:17-21). All of this would come right back on his own head and penetrate his very being, for sinners hurt themselves far more than they hurt their victims.

Lord, Help Me! (vv. 21-31)

As a faithful son of the covenant, David had a right to ask God for the help he needed. His desire was that God might be glorified by showing mercy to His servant (vv. 21, 27). He wanted God to do some wonderful thing that only He could do, and this would tell his enemies that Jehovah was fighting David's battles. "Magnify your mercy!" was David's cry (vv. 21, 26). He wanted the Lord to be mindful of his needs, for he was "poor and needy" (vv. 22-25; 70:5; 86:1). He had a broken heart and he felt as if his life was fading away like the shadows of evening. As the sun sets, the shadows grow longer and longer and then vanish. Like a locust hanging on clothing, his grip on life was feeble and he could be shaken off at any minute. Imagine the future king of Israel comparing himself to a fragile insect! David asked the Lord to send him a blessing every time his enemy cursed him and to bring shame to the enemy but joy to His servant. Finally, David promised to praise the Lord and give glory to Him when all these trials were ended, and he did. After David had been made king over all Israel, he brought the ark of the covenant to Jerusalem and sought to honor the Lord (2 Sam. 5-6). God did help David, in His own time and His own way, and so He will do for us.

Psalm 110

Jesus and Peter both stated that David wrote this psalm (Matt. 22:43; Mark 12:36; Luke 20:42; Acts 2:33-35), and, since David was a prophet, he wrote it about the Messiah (Acts 2:30; 2 Sam. 23:2). He certainly did not write about any of his own descendants, for no Jewish king was ever a priest, let alone a priest forever (v. 4; 2 Chron. 26:16-23). Also, no Jewish king ever conquered all the rulers of the whole earth (v. 6). The psalm is quoted or alluded to in the New Testament more than any other psalm, verse 1 at least twenty-five times and verse 4 another five times. Ten of these quotations or allusions are in the book of Hebrews alone. Jesus used verse 1 to prove His deity and silence the Pharisees (Matt. 22:41-46) and also to answer the high priest during His trial (Matt. 26:64). The psalm presents two pictures of Messiah from the past—His exaltation as King (vv. 1-3) and His consecration as Priest (v. 4)—and a third picture from the future, His victory over the enemies of God (vv. 5-7).

Exaltation: Jesus is King (vv. 1-3)

"Jehovah says to my *Adonai*" is the way the psalm opens, and since David was the highest ruler in the kingdom, his *Adonai* had to be the Lord Himself. It was this fact that Jesus presented to the Pharisees (Matt. 22:41-46), asking them how David's Lord could also be David's son (Messiah). The only answer is *by incarnation*: the eternal Son of God had to come to earth as a human born into the family of David (Luke 1:26-38). As eternal God, Jesus is the "root [originator] of David" and as man He is "the offspring of David" (Rev. 22:16; 5:5). Had the Pharisees honestly faced this truth, they would have had to confess that Jesus is indeed the Son of God come in the flesh, but they refused to do so.

To sit at a ruler's right hand was a great honor (1 Kings 2:19; Matt. 20:21). When Jesus ascended to heaven, the Father honored Him by placing Him at His own right hand, a statement repeated frequently in the New Testament. (See Acts 2:33-34; 5:31; Rom. 8:34; Eph. 1:20; Col. 3:1; Heb. 1:3, 13; 8:1; 10:12; 12:2; 1 Peter 3:22). Jesus is "far above all" (Eph. 1:21; 4:10; Col. 2:10; see Phil. 2:9-11). When the Son was exalted and enthroned at His ascension, the Father made three promises to him, that He would defeat His enemies (v. 1), extend His kingdom (v. 2), and give Him a victorious army (v. 3). Note that in verses 1-3, the key phrase is "I will," the Father speaking to the Son, but in verses 5-7, the key phrase is "he will," the psalmist speaking about the Son. To use the enemy soldiers as footstools meant to defeat and humiliate them (Josh. 10:24; see 1 Cor. 15:24-25 and Eph. 1:22), and this victory is described in verses 5-7. See also the Messianic promises in Psalm 2. Both David and Solomon extended the borders of the kingdom of Israel, but when Messiah establishes His kingdom, with Jerusalem as the center (2:6), the whole earth will share in the glory and the blessing (72:1-11; Isa. 2:1-4; Mic. 4:1-3). Today, the Lord has enemies who oppose Him, but He is sovereign and rules from His throne even though they refuse to submit. When our Lord was here on earth, the powerful ministry of the apostles brought defeat to the devil (Luke. 10:17-20), and today His church has victory through Him as we pray, share the Word, and depend on the Spirit.

The third promise is that Messiah would have a great army assist Him in the final battle against the enemies of the Lord (v. 3). This army is remarkable in three ways: it is made up of willing volunteers; they are dressed in holy garments like priests (Rev. 19:14); and they are a great multitude, like the dew that falls in the early morning (2 Sam. 23:4). Just as the dawn gives birth to the sparkling dew, so the Lord will "give birth" to this vast holy army. You expect *kings* to be warriors—David is a good example—but you don't expect *priests* to be warriors. However, Benaiah was a priest (1 Chron. 27:5) who was also a soldier. He was one of David's mighty men (2 Sam. 23:20-23), became captain over the king's bodyguard (1 Chron. 18:17), and eventually was made general over King Solomon's army (1 Kings 2:35). Imagine a huge army of men like Benaiah! The book of Revelation indicates that there will be great battles fought in the end times (see 14:14-20; 16:12-16; 19:11-21; 20:7-10) and that Jesus Christ will defeat the enemy.

Consecration: The King Is a Priest (v. 4)
This central verse of the psalm announces that Messiah will also be a priest, something unheard of in Old Testament history. This verse is important to the message of the book of Hebrews (Heb. 5:6, 10; 6:20; 7:17, 21; see Rom. 8:34) because the present high priestly ministry of Christ in heaven is described in that book. If Jesus were on earth, He could not minister as a priest because He was from the tribe of Judah and not from Levi. But because His priesthood is after the order of Melchizedek, who was both a king and priest (Gen. 14:18-24), He can minister in heaven today. Melchizedek was not an appearance of Jesus Christ on earth; he is only a type of Jesus in His present priestly ministry. (See Heb. 5:1-11; 7-8; Zech. 6:12.) No Aaronic priest was "a priest forever" because each high priest died and was replaced by his eldest son. Being a mere human, Melchizedek died, *but there is no record of either his birth or death in the Scriptures.* This makes him a type of Jesus Christ, the eternal Son of God and the High Priest forever. In Jesus Christ, David has a throne forever (2 Sam. 7:13, 16, 25, 29; Luke 1:30-33) and a priest forever, and

all who have trusted Christ share in those blessings. Jesus Christ is our glorified King-Priest in heaven, interceding for us (Rom. 8:34). His throne is a throne of grace to which we may come at any time to find the help we need (Heb. 4:14-16).

Vindication: The King-Priest Is a Conqueror (vv. 5-7)

All of the "royal psalms" contain predictions about battles and victories for God's King (2:7-9, 12; 18:16-19, 31-34, 37-42; 20:1-2, 7-8; 21:8-12; 45:3-5; 61:3; 72:8-9; 89:22-23; 132:18). Today is the Lord's "day of salvation" (2 Cor. 6:1-2) when He is calling sinners to be reconciled to God (2 Cor. 5:18-21). But there will come a day of wrath, "the day of the Lord," when Jesus the Lamb of God will begin to "roar" as the Lion of the tribe of Judah (Rev. 5:5-6), and judgment will fall on the world. This is the victory the Father promised in verse 1 and also in 2:5, 9. The psalmist describes stacks of corpses on the battlefield with nobody to bury them. Even allowing for poetic license, the picture is not a pretty one—but consider what John (the apostle of love) wrote in Revelation 14:17-20 and 19:11-19 (and see Isa. 66:24). The word in verse 6 translated "heads" (KJV) or "chief men, rulers" (NASB, NIV) is singular in the Hebrew. It could be a collective noun or it may refer to the last great world ruler, the Antichrist or Beast (Rev. 13:1-10) whom Jesus Christ will destroy at His coming (2 Thess. 2:1-2; Rev. 19:17-21).

The image in verse 7 is difficult to decipher. The NIV margin reads, "The One who grants succession will set him in authority," meaning that Christ will win the victory and receive the promised throne. But it is necessary to alter the Hebrew text to get this meaning. The picture is obviously not to be taken literally, for a King riding out of heaven on a horse doesn't need a drink of water to keep going. The warrior David, who knew something about battles, is saying, "Nothing will detain Him, detour Him, or discourage Him as He attacks the enemy. Like every good soldier, He will linger only long enough to get a sip of water, and then He will raise His head and continue the chase." We remember that before His crucifixion, Jesus refused to receive the narcotic drink, but tasted death to the full on the cross (Matt. 27:34). Gideon and his men also come to mind (Judg. 7:4-7), for their fitness for the battle was tested by the way they drank at the river.

Jesus Christ is exalted and enthroned in heaven! One day He will come and conquer the devil and his armies and establish His kingdom on earth! Hallelujah, what a Savior!

Psalm 111

Life was not easy for the Jewish remnant that returned to Jerusalem after their exile in Babylon. Their neighbors were often hostile, the Persian officials were not always cooperative, and the economic situation was difficult. Ezra the scribe and the prophet Haggai describe some of these problems in their books and point out that the Jewish people were not always faithful to the Lord or generous to each other. This was why God withheld His blessing. This psalm may have been written by one of the Levites to remind the people to put the Lord first and trust Him to meet every need. The next psalm describes the blessings God will give to those who truly fear Him and do His will. Both psalms are acrostics with each line beginning with a successive letter of the Hebrew alphabet. Other acrostic psalms are 9, 10, 24, 34, 37, 119, and 145. This was a special style of writing and perhaps the arrangement helped the people to memorize God's Word. The writer gives us four instructions to follow if we would enjoy the help and blessing of the Lord in the difficult situations of life.

Begin with Worship and Praise (v. 1)

Psalms 111 and 112, along with 115-117, are "hallelujah" psalms that either begin or end with "Praise the Lord!" If we cannot rejoice in our circumstances, we can always rejoice in the Lord (Phil. 4:4). This opening verse is actually a vow; the writer is determined to praise God no matter what happens. Sometimes we simply need to get ourselves by the nape of the neck and decide to do what is right no matter how we feel! But he does not stay at home and worship in private, as important as that is; he goes to the sanctuary and joins in with others, for we encourage one another as we praise God together. The "company [assembly, council] of the upright" is a smaller group of the psalmist's friends who, like him, are a part of the larger "congregation." All of us have people in church who are very special to us, and as long as we do not form an exclusive clique, there is nothing wrong with worshiping God with your close friends. The "growth group" movement in the church today has proven very helpful, especially in larger congregations. But the important thing is that we are wholehearted in our worship, giving God our very best.

Remember God's Great Works (vv. 2-6)

God's people do not live in the past, but they know how to use the past to give them encouragement in the present and hope for the future. The celebrating of special days and weeks as commanded in Leviticus 23 was one way the Lord helped His people recall His great deeds on their behalf. But even more, His works reveal His attributes, for like Him they are great (v. 2), glorious, majestic and righteous (v. 3), wonderful, gracious and compassionate (v. 4), powerful (v. 6), faithful, just and trustworthy (v. 7), and holy and awesome (v. 9). Who could not trust a God with that kind of character!

In reviewing the kinds of works God did, the psalmist also reminded us of what some of those works were. He provided food for His people after they left Egypt and gave them His covenant at Sinai (v. 5). He helped them conquer the nations in Canaan (v. 6; Deut. 4:35-40) and delivered them from bondage in Babylon (v. 9). As A. T. Pierson used to say, "History is His story," and we should read it with that in mind. We should delight in pondering the record of God's works and learn more about the Lord from our study, but we should also review how He has worked in our own lives. The word "remembered" in verse 4 is "memorial." We may read it, "He has caused His wonders to be a memorial." In fact, Israel itself is a memorial to the power and grace of God. As Abraham went from place to place, he left behind altars and wells as memorials that God had brought him that way, and the Jewish nation left "memorial stones" after they entered Canaan (Josh. 4:1-7) and during their passage through the land. Jewish parents were commanded to teach their children the meaning of the special days and the memorial stones (Ex. 13:3-10; Deut. 6:4-9; Josh. 4:4-7). There are no "sacred places" where God dwells in some unique way, but there are special places where God can bring edifying memories to mind that will help us remember His greatness and grace.

Rely on God's Word (vv. 7-9)

From the works of God it was an easy transition to the Word of God, for it is God's Word that brought all things into being and that keeps things together (33:6-11). God gave His law to His people so that they might enjoy His blessings. His righteousness is forever (v. 3), but so are His covenants (vv. 5, 9) and His precepts (v. 8). God's Word is trustworthy and we can rely on it. His precepts are given in love and His promises never fail. As for the covenant He made with Israel, He has been faithful to keep it even when Israel was not faithful to obey it. If we obey His Word, He is faithful to bless; if we disobey, He is just to chasten us in love. As the people of God, we bear His name and want to glorify His name in all that we say and do. "Reverend is his name," says the KJV (v. 9), meaning "His name should be revered and held in honor." The word "reverend" is usually applied to the clergy, but there is no biblical basis for this. Both the NIV and NASB use "awesome." To the Jewish people, God's name was so awesome that they would not speak the name "Jehovah" but substituted "Adonai" lest they would inadvertently blaspheme His holy name. Would that God's people today had such reverence for the name of the Lord!

Obey His Will (v. 10)

The awesomeness of God's name leads to the importance of fearing the Lord and obeying His will. The fear of the Lord is a topic mentioned frequently in Scripture, especially in the book of Proverbs. It is not the slavish fear of a criminal before a judge but the loving and reverential fear of a child for his or her parents. *If we want to understand God's works and God's Word, we must maintain this reverential fear of the Lord, for this attitude is the basis for receiving*

spiritual wisdom and understanding. (See Job 28:28; Prov. 1:7 and 9:10.) The word "beginning" means "the principal part," and without this we are unprepared to learn God's truth. But fearing the Lord leads to obeying the Lord, and obedience is important to spiritual understanding (John 7:17). How all of this works out in our practical daily life is explained in the next psalm.

Psalm 112

In the previous psalm, the writer extolled the Lord for His great and marvelous works, and he ended by admonishing us to fear the Lord and obey His precepts (111:10). The blessings of obeying that admonition are described in 112 (note v. 1). Like 111, this psalm is an acrostic, and you will find the vocabulary of 112 similar to that of 111. Both psalms use delight (111:2; 112:1), righteousness (111:3; 112:3-4, 6, 9), established (111:8; 112:8), grace and compassion (111:4; 112:4), and just (111:7; 112:5). Both psalms must be read in light of God's covenant with Israel in which He promises to bless them if they fear Him and obey His Word (Lev. 26:1-13; Deut. 28:1-14). Nothing is said about the wife and mother in this home, but surely a man of such godly character would have a wife like the one described in Proverbs 31. We must not conclude that, on the basis of this psalm, all believers today can claim health, wealth, success, and happiness if they faithfully obey the Lord, for this promise is not found in the new covenant. For that matter, the believer described in this psalm had times of darkness (v. 4), occasionally received bad news (v. 7), had his enemies (vv. 8, 10), and had to consider the justice of his decisions (v. 5). We who live under the new covenant have in Jesus

Christ every spiritual blessing that we will ever need (Eph. 1:3; 2 Peter 1:3-4), and we have the promise that our God will meet our needs (Phil. 4:19). The attributes of God given in 111 become the character qualities of the godly believer in 112, for becoming more and more like Jesus Christ is the greatest reward of a faithful life of obedience (Rom. 8:29; 2 Cor. 3:18). We want more than the blessing; we want to be like the One who gives the blessing. The psalmist describes the faithful believer in various relationships of life.

Our Relationship to the Lord (v. 1)

The psalmist wrote about fear of bad news (v. 7) and fear of the enemy (v. 8), but the first and most important fear is the fear of the Lord. This verse takes us back to 111:10, for if we fear God, we need fear nothing else. Solomon came to the same conclusion: "Fear God and keep His commandments, for this is the whole duty of man" (Eccl. 12:13, NKJV). Of itself, fear is not an evil thing. We teach children to fear danger when they cross the street, use sharp objects, or are approached by strangers, but those are rational fears that energize us and protect us. The psalmist is writing about fears that can paralyze us and make life miserable. To overcome these fears, we cultivate a right relationship with the Lord: we fear Him, learn His will from His Word, and obey what He commands. Learning His will and doing it is not a burdensome thing, because we delight in His Word (1:2; 119:16, 35, 47-48, 70, 97, 143). Fear and delight can live together in the same heart because they are tied together by love (2:11; 119:19-20; 1 John 4:16-19). Because we love the Lord, His commands are not burdensome to us (1 John 5:3).

The person described in this psalm praises the Lord in worship, stands in awe of the Lord, delights in fellowship with the Lord, and seeks to obey the Lord. This kind of life brings blessing to the entire family (34:8-14; 37:25; 127:3-5; 128:3). If our life doesn't make an impact at home, among people we know and love, it is not going to make much of a difference out in the marketplace where people blaspheme the name of the Lord. The person also is a blessing to "the generation of the upright" (v. 2), the people of God who frequent the sanctuary (33:1; 37:37; 111:1; 140:13). The Scriptures know nothing of an isolated believer who ignores other believers. We all need each other, and our united worship and witness can accomplish more than anything we can do by ourselves. Once again, we must not use verse 1 as a "charm" to ward off the troubles of life, for Job had the qualities listed in verse 1 (Job 1:8) and still suffered greatly. This kind of godly character does not protect us from pain and trials but it does enable us to use those trials to glorify the Lord and to grow in grace (1 Peter 3:13-17; 4:12-19; 5:10).

Our Relationship to Material Wealth (vv. 3-5, 9)

Under the old covenant, material wealth was one of the evidences of the Lord's blessing on His people as they moved into the Promised Land (Deut. 7:12ff; 28:1-14). This explains why the apostles were shocked when Jesus said that it was difficult for rich people to enter God's kingdom (Matt. 19:16-30). If rich people could not be saved, then who could? To Job's three friends, the fact that Job had lost everything was proof that God was punishing him for his sins. It was faulty logic, but they held to it tenaciously. The person described in this psalm was righteous before the Lord (vv. 3, 4, 6, 9) and did not acquire his wealth in some unlawful manner. He was generous in his use of the wealth the Lord gave him, sharing it with the poor and lending it freely without interest (Deut. 23:19-20). He was certainly not miserly or covetous, and he was obedient to the Lord's admonition to care for the poor and needy (Ex. 23:11; Lev. 25:35-38; Deut. 15:7, 11). When he quoted verse 9 in 2 Corinthians 9:9, the apostle Paul used him as an example for believers today to follow. (See also Prov. 11:24.) The word "horn" in verse 9 is an image of power and dignity (75:5; 132:17; Luke 1:69). Because of this man's generosity, the Lord allowed him to be lifted up in the eyes of his peers. As you see this man's faith in the Lord and love for those in need, you cannot help but think of the promise in Matthew 6:33.

Our Relationship to Circumstances (vv. 6-8)

A believing heart is a steadfast heart, one that is not easily shaken by bad news or difficult circumstances. The person described was confident that the Lord could handle any problem that might come to him. A double-minded person has no stability (119:113; James 1:8; 4:8) and therefore, no ability to face the demands of life. (See 57:7; 108:1; and Isa. 26:3.) Believers with a confident heart and a clear conscience have nothing to fear when they receive bad news because they know the Lord is in control. If there is darkness around them, they wait for the Lord to send the light (v. 4). This is what encouraged Joseph during thirteen years of waiting and suffering in Egypt. "Wait on the Lord; be of good courage, and He shall strengthen your heart; wait, I say, on the Lord" (27:14, NKJV).

Our Relationship to the Wicked (v. 10)

God rewards the delight of the righteous (v. 1) but ignores the desires of the wicked (v. 10; see 35:16; 37:12). Those who walk with the Lord and live godly lives are opposed and hated by the wicked, because the good works of the godly are like lights that reveal the evil in the world (Matt. 5:14-16; Eph. 5:1-14). The fact that the wicked oppose the godly is a good sign that the godly are living as they should. The witness of one dedicated life is a witness in the darkness of this world. Having seen and heard the witness of the godly, the wicked will have no excuse when they face the Lord (John 15:22).

Psalm 113

It was traditional for the Jewish people to sing 113-114 before they ate their Passover meal, and they closed the meal by singing 115-118 (Matt. 26:30; Mark 14:26). These psalms were also sung in celebration of Pentecost, Tabernacles, the new moon festivals, and the Feast of Dedication. Because of the emphasis in 114, this small collection of psalms was called "The Egyptian Hallel." The psalm opens and closes with "hallelujah" ("praise Jehovah") and gives us three wonderful reasons for praising the Lord.

God's Name Is the Greatest (vv. 1-3)

Four times you find the word "praise" (vv. 1, 3), but who are the "servants" that the writer admonished to sing God's praises? Perhaps the temple choir in the newly restored temple, for this is a post-exilic psalm, but most likely he addressed the entire nation of Israel, which is often called "God's servant" (34:22; 69:36; 136:22; Isa. 41:8-9; 54:17). They had the privilege and responsibility of sharing the true and living God with their Gentile neighbors (Isa. 42:6), and Paul applied that verse to his own ministry and the ministry of the church (Acts 13:47; 26:26; and see Luke 2:32). The word "name" is used three times in these verses and refers to the character of God and the revelation of who He is and what He does. God has a "good name" and that name should be magnified among those who have never trusted Him. To "glorify God" means to make God look good to those who ignore Him, oppose Him, or do not know Him. This kind of praise pays no attention to time ("forever more") or space (from east to west). The prophet Malachi foresaw the day when the Gentiles would honor the name of the Lord (Mal. 1:11). God's name is attached to His covenant with Israel (Deut. 28:1-14, note v. 10), and both His name and His covenant can be trusted.

God's Throne Is the Highest (vv. 4-6)

Earthly kings are concerned about the splendor and prominence of their thrones (2 Kings 25:27-30), but the Lord's throne is exalted above the nations and even above the heavens (57:5, 11; 99:2). Jesus Christ, the King of Kings (Rev. 19:16), is today exalted "far above all" (Eph. 4:10; Phil. 2:9-11). The question in verses 5-6 remind us of Exodus 15:11 (and see 35:10; Deut. 3:24; Isa. 40:18 and 25; and Mic. 7:18). It is not our Lord's transcendence that captivates the psalmist but His willingness to "stoop down" and pay attention to mere mortals who do not always honor Him. Most ancient kings were inaccessible to their people, but our God sees us and knows our every need (138:6; Isa. 57:15). For the believer, God's throne is not only a throne of glory and authority, but it is also a throne of grace, a topic the psalmist explained in the next three verses.

God's Love Is the Kindest (vv. 7-9)

The Lord in His grace not only sees us but He cares for us and helps us. He "stoops down" and condescends to work on our behalf (138:6-8). The picture in verses 7-8 comes from verses 7 and 8 of the song of Hannah (1 Sam. 2:2:1-10), part of which was borrowed by Mary in her song of praise to God (Luke 1:46-55). Hannah was a barren wife to whom God gave a son, Samuel the judge and prophet. The history of Israel contains the stories of several barren women to whom God gave sons. It begins with Abraham's wife Sarah who gave birth to Isaac (Gen. 17:15-19), and then Isaac's wife Rebekah became the mother of Jacob, who fathered the twelve tribes of Israel (Gen. 25:19-23). Jacob's favorite wife Rachel gave birth to Joseph (Gen. 29:31; 30:22-24), the man who protected the sons of Israel in Egypt. Hannah gave birth to Samuel (1 Sam. 1:1-2:11), and Elizabeth gave birth to John the Baptist (Luke 1:13-15), the forerunner of Jesus Christ.

The ash heap was the gathering place of the outcasts of the city, the unwanted poor, and the diseased (Job 2:8). The sun would warm the ashes during the day and the ashes would keep the people warm at night. It was the one place that people avoided going near, but our God visits rejected people and changes their lives! If this is a post-exilic psalm, as many believe it is, this truth must have been a great encouragement to the Jewish remnant struggling to rebuild their nation and their lives. The love of God and the grace of God made our God stoop to our level, especially when He sent Jesus Christ to become one of us and die for us on the cross (Phil. 2:1-11). In John 8:6 and 8 and 13:1-11, Jesus stooped to forgive a sinful woman and to wash His disciples' feet. But His greatest demonstration of grace was when He died for us on the cross. He condescended to become like us that we might become like Him (1 Cor. 1:26-29; Eph. 2:1-10). There can be no greater love (John 15:13). Only Jesus Christ can lift sinners out of the ash heap and put them on the throne! (Eph. 2:1-10). One day the Lord will visit "barren Israel" and bless the nation with many children (Isa. 54:1-3; 66:8-11). No matter how dark the day or impossible the circumstances, our God is able to do the impossible (Eph. 3:19-20).

Psalm 114

In beautiful poetic language, this psalm describes Israel's exodus from Egypt, God's provision for their wilderness journey, their entrance into the Promised Land, and their conquest of their enemies. The psalmist used striking poetic metaphors to teach history and theology, and this approach reaches the imagination and stirs the heart. When Jewish families sing this psalm at Passover, it must be very meaningful to them. But the psalm is about God and reveals His gracious relationship to His own people.

God Is for Us (v. 1)
The Exodus is mentioned frequently in the psalms (74:13; 77:17-20; 78:12-16, 52-53; 106:9-12; 136:10-15) because Israel's deliverance from Egypt was their "national birthday." The people were now set free to serve God and accomplish the important tasks He had assigned to them: bearing witness of the true and living God, writing the Scriptures, and bringing the Savior into the world. In terms of "biblical geography," Egypt represents the world and the bondage of the sinner to its evil forces (Eph. 2:1-3). It was the blood of the lamb applied to the doors that protected the Jewish firstborn from death, just as the blood of Christ, God's Lamb, saves us from sin and death. God's power in opening the Red Sea liberated Israel and separated them from their cruel taskmasters. This is a picture of the resurrection of Christ and the believer's participation in it (Eph. 2:4-10; Col. 3:1ff). In the centuries that followed, each annual celebration of Passover reminded the Jewish people that Jehovah was their God and that He was for them. "If God be for us, who can be against us?" (Rom. 8:31). The prophet Isaiah saw the Jewish exiles' deliverance from Babylonian captivity as a "second exodus" (Isa. 43:14-21). What an encouragement it was to that struggling Jewish remnant to know that Jehovah God was for them!

God Is with Us (v. 2a)
The Lord not only separated Israel *from* Egypt, but He also separated Israel *unto* Himself. They were His people, His treasure and His inheritance. "Judah" and "Israel" refer to the whole nation and not to the two kingdoms that formed after the death of Solomon. After the tribes conquered the land of Canaan, the sanctuary of God was placed in Judah (Ex. 15:17) and that was where Solomon built the temple. The nations around Israel had their temples, but they were empty. God's glorious presence dwelt in the tabernacle (Ex. 40) and later in the temple (1 Kings 8:1-11). Today, God does not dwell in man-made houses (Acts 7:48-50), but He does dwell with His people, for our bodies are His temples and the church is His sanctuary (1 Cor. 3:16-17; 6:19-20; 2 Cor. 6:14-18; Eph. 2:19-22). Jesus is "Immanuel, God with us" (Matt. 1:23; 28:19-20). What a privilege it is to be in the family of God!

God Is over Us (v. 2b)

Not only was God's sanctuary in Judah but so was His throne (Ex. 19:6). David and his descendants were God's chosen rulers, but they represented the Lord God and had to obey His law. God made a covenant with David in which He promised him a throne forever and an heir forever on that throne (2 Sam. 7). David's throne is gone (Hos. 3:4-5), but that covenant is fulfilled in Jesus Christ (Luke 1:30-33, 68-73). One day He will sit on David's throne and rule over His kingdom. Had the people of Israel obeyed the Lord and allowed Him to exercise dominion over them, they would have been a great witness to the Gentile nations around them. Instead, they followed the ways of these nations and worshiped false gods instead of the true and living God.

God Is before Us (vv. 3-8)

Most of the psalm is devoted to describing the miracles God performed for Israel as they left Egypt and headed for Canaan. The key thought is that God went before His people, and everything in nature trembled at His presence and obeyed His will (v. 7). The Red Sea opened and Israel marched through on dry land. Forty years later, the Jordan River opened and the people of Israel marched into the Promised Land. During their long march, God gave them bread and meat to eat and water to drink. Two different Hebrew words are used for "rock" in verse 8; the first refers to Exodus 17:1-7 and the second ("flint cliff") refers to Numbers 20:1-13, one at the beginning of their journey and the other near the end. It is likely that the mountains and hills mentioned in verses 4 and 6 were in Canaan, and the picture is that of God removing all obstacles from before Joshua and the victorious Jewish army. God goes before His people and takes them through the hopeless places (Red Sea, Jordan River) and the hard places (mountains, hills), and He even provides water out of rocks! (He can also provide honey, see 81:16. Sweetness out of hardness!)

The Lord is not mentioned by name until verse 7, and then the psalmist calls upon the whole world to tremble at His presence! The Exodus may have been past history, but the presence of the God of Jacob is a present reality to those who trust Christ and allow Him to lead (John 10:4). Remember that the Jews used this psalm in those difficult post-exilic days when the work was hard and the dangers were many. This vivid picture of God going before His people must have helped them grow in their faith and trust Him for their needs. It can also help us today. "If God be for us—and with us—and over us—and before us—who can be against us?"

Psalm 115

The Lord had given His people a great victory, and they wanted to acknowledge it before their pagan neighbors and give God the glory. If their neighbors had visited the returned exiles and seen their rebuilt temple, they would have asked, "Where is your god?" There were no idols in the temple or in the city. (See Acts 17:16 for contrast.) The question gave the Jews the opportunity to contrast the false gods of their neighbors with the true and living God of Israel. This psalm was written as a litany, with the leader opening in verse 1. The people then responded in verses 2-8, the choir in verses 9-11, and the people again in verses. 12-13. The priests or the choir spoke in verses 14-15, and the people closed the litany in verses 16-18. The psalm may have been used at the dedication of the second temple (Ezra 6:16). It not only tells where the God of Israel is but what kind of a God He is.

The Reigning God (vv. 1-3)

Where is the God of Israel? In heaven on His glorious throne, reigning as the sovereign God of the universe! His throne is founded on mercy and truth (love and faithfulness), which reminds us of His covenant with Israel. Because He loved them, He chose them (Deut. 7:7-11) and gave them His covenant, which He faithfully kept. All of God's people can shout, "Alleluia! For the Lord God omnipotent reigns!" (Rev. 19:6, NKJV).

The Living God (vv. 4-8)

Idolatry had always been Israel's most habitual and costly sin (Judg. 2:11-3:6), and even though their prophets ridiculed these man-made gods (1 Kings 18:27; Isa. 44:9-20; Jer. 10:1-16) and the Lord chastened Israel often, the people persisted in breaking God's laws. Israel did not seem to learn its lesson until Babylon carried the people away captive after destroying Jerusalem and the temple. In the great city of Babylon, two or three generations of Jews saw idolatry firsthand and the kind of society it produced. This cured them. They needed to remember that they were the servants of the living God (42:2; 84:2; Deut. 5:26; Josh. 3:10; 1 Sam. 17:26, 36; 2 Kings 19:4, 16), and the church today also needs to keep this truth in mind (Acts 14:15; 1 Thess. 1:9; 1 Tim. 3:15; 4:10; 6:17).

God is a Spirit and does not have a body (John 4:24), so when writers in Scripture speak about His eyes, ears, hands, and feet and so on, they are using what theologians call "anthropomorphisms" (*anthropo* = human; *morphos* = form, shape). This is a literary device which uses human characteristics to describe divine attributes. God uses the known to teach us the unknown and the unknowable. This section is repeated in 135:15-18. Because the dead idols lacked the attributes of the living God, they were unable to do either good or evil, yet the people worshiped them!

No mouths—They cannot speak to their people, make covenants, give promises, guidance, or encouragement. Our God speaks to us!

No eyes—They offer their followers no protection or oversight. Our God's eyes are upon us (32:8; 1 Peter 3:12) and we can trust Him.

No ears—No matter how much the idolaters pray, their gods cannot hear them! Remember Elijah on Mt. Carmel (1 Kings 18:20ff). Our God's eyes are upon us and His ears open to our cries (34:15).

No noses—This speaks of God receiving our worship (Gen. 8:21) and being pleased with what we bring Him. (See John 12:1-8; Eph. 5:2; Phil. 4:18.)

No hands—The workers whose hands made the idols have more power than the idols they call "gods." Our God is able to work for us as we seek to serve Him. His fingers made the universe (8:3) and His arm brought salvation (Isa. 53:1). (See also Isa. 41:10 and 46:1-7.)

No feet—The people had to carry their idols (Isa. 46:1-7; Jer. 10: 1-10), but our God carries us and walks with us. (See Isa. 41:10, 13.)

But the greatest tragedy is not what the idols cannot do but what they *can do* to the people who worship them. *We become like the God we worship.* As we worship the true and living God, He transforms our ears to hear His truth and the cries of those in need. He gives us eyes to see His Word and His world and the path He wants us to walk. Our "spiritual senses" develop and we become more mature in Jesus Christ (Heb. 5:10-14). But those who worship false gods lose the use of their spiritual senses and become blind to the light and deaf to God's voice.

The Giving God (vv. 9-15)

"Trust the Lord and He will give His blessing" is the theme of this section, and how the discouraged remnant needed that assurance! They needed His blessing on their crops, and they wanted their number to increase (v. 14). Of course, the Lord had stated this in His covenant with Israel (Lev. 26:1-13; Deut. 28:1-14), and all they needed was His reminder. In verses 11 and 13, "those who fear God" were not the Gentile "God fearers" that we meet in the New Testament (Acts 13:16, 26; 16:14; 17:17; 18:7), but the devoted Jewish believers in the nation of Israel (22:23; 111:10). You find similar threefold lists in 118:1-4 and 135:19-21. Both Ezra 6:21 and Nehemiah 10:28 indicate that the returned remnant was not too hospitable to the "strangers" in the land. God had been Abraham's "help and shield" (Gen. 15:1), and He will also protect us and provide for us (3:3; 28:7; 33:20; Deut. 33:29). Because Jehovah God is the "Maker of heaven and earth" (v. 15; 121:2; 124:8; 134:3; 146:6; Isa. 40:12-26; Jer. 10:11), we should worship Him and not what He has created *or what we manufacture ourselves.*

The God Who Deserves Our Praise (vv. 16-18)

The word "bless" is used five times in verses 12-15, and we cannot live without His blessing, but it is also good for us to bless the Lord (v. 18). To "bless the Lord" means to ascribe all glory and praise to Him, to delight His heart with our joyful and willing thanksgiving and obedience. (See 16:7; 26:12; 34:1; 100:4; 103:1; 134:2.) He made the earth and gave it to men and women to meet their needs and give them work to do, cooperating with Him in the development of His abundant resources (Gen. 2:8-25). The people who worship dead idols are also dead, but we are alive in Jesus Christ and ought to extol the Lord! After all, if we expect to praise Him forevermore, we had better start now and be ready when we see Him!

Psalm 116

At a time when the psalmist was "at rest" (v. 7), unscrupulous men whom he had trusted lied about him (v. 11) and created trouble for him. In fact, their deception almost cost him his life (vv. 3-4), but he called on the Lord and was saved from death (vv. 1-2). The psalm is very personal, with "I," "my," and "me" used over thirty times. In expressing his praise to the Lord, the writer borrowed from other psalms, especially 18, 27, 31, and 56, and it appears that he knew the texts of King Hezekiah's prayer (Isa. 37) and his psalm of thanksgiving (Isa. 38). As the psalmist reflected on his life-threatening experience, he discovered several reasons why the Lord God delivers people from danger and death.

God Answers His Children's Prayers (vv. 1-4)

The writer could not trust in himself for deliverance (v. 3), nor could he trust the people around him, some of whom were liars (v. 11), but he knew he could trust in the Lord and call on Him for help (vv. 2,

13, 17). To "incline" one's ear is to pay attention and concentrate on what is being said (113:5-6; 17:6). Only a God as great as Jehovah can hear the voices of millions of His children who are praying to Him at the same time. The writer was in deep trouble and sorrow, like a man drowning who is so entangled in a net that death seems inevitable (vv. 3, 8, 15; see 18:4-6). The name of the Lord represents all that God is and does, and to call on His name is to trust Him to work on our behalf. (See vv. 4, 13, 17.) Like Peter sinking in the sea during the storm, he prayed, "Lord, save me!" (Matt. 14:29-31) and the Lord rescued him. When through no fault of our own we find ourselves in great danger, we can call on the Lord for His help. Peter referred to verse 3 in his sermon at Pentecost (Acts 2:24, "loosed the pains of death") and applied it to the resurrection of Jesus Christ.

God Is Merciful and Gracious (vv. 5-11)

God's name represents God's character, and He is gracious, righteous, compassionate, and powerful. The Lord loved the psalmist and saved him, and the psalmist then loved Him even more (vv. 1, 5; see 1 John 4:19). Note the phrase "our God" in verse 5, which indicates that the writer was giving his testimony to a group of people, probably at the sanctuary (vv. 14, 18-19). "Simplehearted" does not refer to ignorant or superstitious people but to childlike believers with sincerity and integrity, people who dare to believe that God means what He says.

But the Lord did even more than deliver him from death. He also "dealt bountifully" with him (v. 7), and some of this "bounty" is described in verses 8-9. God wiped away his tears, He held him up and prevented him from stumbling

(Jude 24), and He walked with him to protect him from his enemies. And He did all of this in spite of the ambivalence of the psalmist's faith, one minute dismayed at the lies of so-called friends, the next minute affirming his faith in the Lord (vv. 10-11). In the pressure of danger and pain, we often say things we really do not mean, but the Lord sees our hearts and knows what we really believe. The psalmist held to his faith even though he said what he did, and the Lord ignored what he said with his lips and responded to what he was saying in his heart. Paul quoted verse 10 in 2 Corinthians 4:13.

God Holds His Children Precious (vv. 12-15)

After he had been delivered, the psalmist wanted to express his gratitude to the Lord, and he did so in four ways. First, he brought a thank offering to the Lord at the sanctuary (v. 17; Lev. 3; 7:11-21). Second, part of this sacrifice, the priest would pour out a portion of wine on the altar as a symbol of the worshiper's life poured out to serve the Lord. This was indeed a "cup of salvation" for the psalmist whose life could have been destroyed by the enemy. Third, the priest kept back part of the offering for a feast held after the sacrifice, and there the worshiper shared his food and his joy with his family and friends. At that feast, the psalmist called on the Lord and publicly thanked Him for His mercies. Fourth, following the ceremony and feast, the psalmist began to keep the promises he had made to the Lord during his time of great suffering and danger (vv. 14, 18). We must not consider these vows to be "holy bribes" given in payment for God's help, for the psalmist surely knew that God's will cannot be influenced by man's gifts. (See Job 41:11, quoted in Rom. 11:35.) "Or who has first given to Him and it shall be repaid to him?" (NKJV).

God's Son is precious to the Father and to all believers (1 Peter 2:4-7), and the Father loves us so much that He gave Jesus Christ to die on the cross in our place (Rom. 5:8). If our Father loves us that much, then He must be concerned not only with how we live but also how and when we die. For believers, death is not an accident but an appointment (Ps. 139:16, and see 39:4-6 and 92:12). If the Father pays attention to the death of every sparrow, surely He will be concerned about the death of His saints (Matt. 10:29-31; John 11:1-16). Just as the blood of Christ is precious (1 Peter 1:19), so our blood is precious to God (72:12-14). *God's servants are immortal until their work on earth is done.* They can be foolish and hasten the day of their death, but they cannot go beyond their appointed time. That is in God's hands (48:14; Job 14:5, NIV; Luke 2:26).

God Is Faithful to His Covenant (vv. 16-19)

The phrase "I am your servant" is equivalent to "I am a son of the covenant." His father and mother had brought him to the priest eight days after his birth, and there he received the sign of the covenant and the name his parents had selected for him (Lev. 12:3; Luke 1:57-63; 2:21). If he kept the covenant and obeyed the Lord, he had the right to come to the Lord with his needs and ask Him for help. Believers today belong to God's new covenant family in Christ, but this does not guarantee protection from pain and trials. However, it does mean that God is in control and will work all things for our good and His glory, even our death (Rom. 8:28; John 21:17-19; 2 Peter 1:12-15). Even our Lord lived on a divine timetable and they could

not crucify Him until the chosen hour had come (John 2:4; 7:30; 8:20; 12:23; 13:1; 17:1). May the Lord help us to end well and be faithful to Him (2 Tim. 4:6-8).

Psalm 117

An anonymous writer composed the shortest psalm and in three brief sentences encompassed the whole world. The psalm is an invitation to people everywhere to turn to the Lord and join with believers everywhere in praising Him. A proper understanding of this psalm will help us appreciate at least four privileges that belong to God's people.

Worshiping God (v. 1a)

The psalm opens and closes with "praise the Lord," for praising the Lord ought to be a mark of every believer today as it was of the new Christians in the early church (Acts 2:47). The first "praise" translates the familiar Hebrew word *hallel* which gives us "hallelujah—praise the Lord." The second "praise" is *shavah*, which means "to boast, to extol and laud." When we praise the Lord, we not only tell Him of His greatness, but we also "brag on Him" to those who hear our songs. Worship and praise are the highest occupations to which we can dedicate our voices, the activities that will occupy us for all eternity!

Sharing the Gospel (v. 1b)

The word translated "nations" is often translated "Gentiles," that is, all people who are not of Semitic origin. The Hebrew word translated "peoples" refers to the diverse nationalities in the world (Rev. 7:9). You find the phrases "all the earth" and "all peoples" frequently in the book of Psalms (47:1; 66:1; 96:1; 98:4, 7; 100:1). The

Jewish people were supposed to be *separated* from the Gentiles but not *isolated* from them, for God called Abraham to found a nation that would bring blessing to all the earth (Gen. 12:1-3; Rom. 4:17-18; Gal. 3:8). However, Israel failed and became guilty of imitating the Gentiles instead of illuminating the Gentiles with the light of God's truth (Isa. 42:6; 49:6). "Salvation is of the Jews" (John 4:22; Luke 2:32), for God chose the Jewish people to give the world the knowledge of the true God, the Scriptures, and the Savior.

The church today needs to carry the light of the Gospel to the whole world (Acts 13:47). Paul quoted this verse in Romans 15:11 as part of his explanation of the relationship of the church to Israel. The apostles and other early Jewish Christians praised the Lord *among* both Jews and Gentiles (Rom. 15:9) as recorded in the book of Acts. Through this expanding witness, many Gentiles trusted Christ and praised God *with* the Jewish believers (Rom. 15:10), for believing Jews and Gentiles were one body in Christ (Eph. 2:11-22).

If we are a worshiping people, praising the Lord, then we will be a witnessing people, telling others how wonderful He is. Like the lepers outside the gates of Samaria, believers today must confess, "We are not doing right. This is a day of good news, but we are keeping silent" (2 Kings 7:9, NASB). May we imitate the apostles who said, "For we cannot but speak the things which we have seen and heard" (Acts 4:20, NKJV).

Depending on God's Great Love (v. 2a)

Have we forgotten that "it is of the Lord's mercies that we are not consumed" (Lam. 3:22)? We have been saved by grace, not by our good works (Eph. 2:8-9), and were it not for God's merciful lovingkindness, we would still be in darkness and death. How unfortunate that some of the Jewish leaders became proud of being God's chosen people and began to look down upon others. They even called the Gentiles "dogs." But God's people today are guilty of the same sin. "His lovingkindness is great toward us" (v. 2a, NASB) so we have nothing to boast about. "Not of works, lest anyone should boast" (Eph. 2:9). If we are humble before the Lord, He can use us to reach others, but if we are proud, He will reject us. "God resists the proud, but gives grace to the humble" (1 Peter 5:5). We are saved by grace and we live by grace, depending wholly on the Lord's generosity in Jesus Christ. A proud church is a weak church. To enjoy the praise of men is to lose the blessing of God.

Resting on Divine Assurance (v. 2b)

Yes, God's people are saved by faith and live by faith, but our faith would mean nothing were it not for His faithfulness that "endures forever." The word translated "truth" or "faithfulness" means in Hebrew "to be firm, to be unshakable." God's character cannot change and His promises will not change, so why are we fretting about the feelings within us and the circumstances around us? Why do we hesitate to obey Him when He abounds in faithfulness (Ex. 34:6)? If God calls us to do something, He is faithful to help us do it (1 Thess. 5:24). To rely on our faith is to put faith in faith, but to rely on God's faithfulness is to put faith in the Lord. Our assurance is in the Word of God and the God of the Word.

Psalm 118

Sandwiched between the shortest psalm and the longest, this is the last song in the

Egyptian Hallel. The background is probably the dedication of the restored walls and gates of Jerusalem during the Feast of Tabernacles in 444 B.C., in the time of Ezra and Nehemiah. The Jews in the city were surrounded by enemies who first ridiculed them and then threatened to attack them and stop the work (vv. 10-14; Neh. 2:19-20; 4:1-9; 6:1-9). The rebuilding project took fifty-two days, and the report of this remarkable accomplishment astounded the nations (vv. 15-16, 23-24; Neh. 6:15-16). The psalm mentions gates (vv. 19-20) and building (vv. 22) and certainly expresses the joy the people experienced as they beheld what the Lord had done. The repeated phrases in verses 2-4, 10-12, and 15-16 suggest that the psalm was written for public worship. The pronouns "I" and "me" in verses 5-21 refer to the nation of Israel and not to the psalmist. But the psalm speaks to all believers in every age and gives them four practical instructions.

Give Thanks to the Lord at All Times (vv. 1-4)

The psalm is bracketed by thanksgiving (vv. 1-4, 28-29), for this is one of the purposes of the "hallelujah" psalms, and we have met the threefold address before (115:9-11). The human situation may change many times, but God's merciful lovingkindness endures forever. The nation of Israel certainly ought to praise God for all the blessings and privileges God has bestowed on her (Rom. 9:1-5). The house of Aaron ought to thank God for the great privilege of serving in the sanctuary and at the altar. "Those who fear the Lord" would include all of God's faithful people, Jews and Gentiles—"the upright in heart"—who faithfully obeyed His Word and feared His name. God's people today have every spiritual blessing in Jesus Christ (Eph. 1:3) and certainly ought to praise His name.

Trust the Lord in Every Crisis (vv. 5-14)

"The Lord" is mentioned in every verse in this paragraph because He was the one who protected Israel from their enemies and enabled the people to complete the work in difficult times. In 537 B.C., Israel had been set free from captivity (v. 5), and about 50,000 Jews returned to Jerusalem under the leadership of Zerubbabel the governor and Joshua the high priest. (See Ezra 3-6.) The Jews laid the foundation of the temple in 536 B.C., but local officials interfered and the work stopped from 536 to 520 B.C. The nations around the city did not want a restored Jewish state in the neighborhood, so they opposed both the rebuilding of the temple and the fortifying of the city. The work was resumed in 520 B.C. and the temple was completed and dedicated in 515 B.C. The people learned to trust, not in kings and princes, but in the Lord alone (vv. 8-9). They also learned that, though the enemy might attack them like bees, the Lord would give them victory (vv. 10-12). This was also true when Nehemiah came to Jerusalem in 444 B.C. and directed the work of rebuilding the walls and restoring the gates. Knowing that the nation of Israel was God's chosen instrument for bringing blessing to the world, Satan opposed the work and sought to destroy both the people and their city, but faith and courage carried Israel through to victory (vv. 5-7; Heb. 13:6). The statement in verse 14 is significant. The Jews sang it when they were delivered from Egypt (Ex. 15:2) and when God enabled them to rebuild their temple and the city walls (118:14). They will sing it in the future when Messiah redeems them and establishes His kingdom (Isa. 12:2, see context).

Just as "all nations" attacked Israel in the past, they will do so again in the future (Isa. 29:2-7; Zech. 12:9; 14:1-5; Joel 3:1-2), and the Lord will again rescue them. God's people must learn to trust Him in every crisis of life.

[Note: For what it is worth, vv. 8 and 9 are the central verses of the Bible. Of course, the verse divisions of the Bible are not inspired.]

Glorify the Lord after Every Victory (vv. 15-21)

When the wall was dedicated, the joyful shouts of the people were heard afar off (Neh. 12:47), and the psalmist mentions this (vv. 15-16). The "tents of the righteous" are the homes of the people of Israel as well as their temporary dwellings during the Feast of Tabernacles (Lev. 23:33-44). The people were careful to give the Lord all the glory for what Israel had done in the restoring of the city. Israel has been sorely chastened, but Israel will not die (vv. 17-18). A festive procession came to the gates of the city (see Ps. 24), or perhaps to the temple courts (see v. 27), for the celebration would involve sacrifices offered at the temple. One of the best ways to "seal" God's blessing to our hearts and make sure He gets the glory is to publicly praise Him—and keep on praising Him!

See the Lord in Every Experience (vv. 22—29)

Under Zerubbabel and Ezra, the Jewish people had been rebuilding the temple, and under the leadership of Nehemiah, they had rebuilt the walls of Jerusalem and restored the gates. During these activities, did they find among the ruins a large stone that they rejected, only to discover it was the most important stone of all? The Gentile nations had despised and rejected Israel (Neh. 2:18-20; 4:1ff), but God had spared them to finish the work He gave them to do.

In Scripture, the stone is a familiar image of the Lord God (18:2, 31, 46; Gen. 49:24; Deut. 32:4, 15, 18, 30-31; 2 Sam. 22:2-3, 32, 47; Isa. 17:10; 26:4; 30:29; 33:6). It particularly points to the Messiah (Isa. 8:14; 28:16; Dan. 2:34-35, 45; Matt. 21:42-44; Mark 12:10; Luke 20:17-18; Acts 4:11; Rom. 9:32-33; 1 Cor. 10:4; 1 Peter 2:6-8). Peter made it clear that the Jewish leaders ("builders") had rejected their Messiah, the Stone (Acts 4:11), and He became to them a stone of stumbling (Isa. 28:16; Rom. 9:32-33). But in His death, resurrection, and ascension, Jesus Christ has become the chief cornerstone of the church, God's temple, binding Jews and Gentiles together in one sanctuary (Eph. 2:19-22). One day Jesus will return as the Stone of judgment and crush the arrogant kingdoms of this world (Dan. 2:34, 44-45). Every Christian believer can use verses 22-24 to praise the Lord for the salvation provided in Jesus Christ. "Save now" (v. 25) is the word "hosanna" which the people shouted when Jesus rode into Jerusalem (Matt. 21:9; Mark 11:9-10), and note the words, "Blessed is he who comes in the name of the Lord."

The blood of a sacrifice was applied to the horns of the altar (v. 27; Lev. 4:7), but there is no evidence that the sacrifices were tied to the altar before they were slain. The altar was considered so holy that it was not likely it would be used for tethering animals. The *New International Version* marginal reading suggests that the bound sacrifices were brought *up to the altar* where the priests cut the animals' throats, caught the blood, and offered both the animals and the blood on the altar to the Lord. Of course, each sacrifice was a picture of the death of Jesus Christ, the Savior of the world. On each of the seven days of the Feast of Tabernacles, the priests led a procession once around the altar and then offered one burnt offering, but on the eighth day, the procession marched seven times around the altar and seven sacrifices were offered.

Jesus Christ is seen in this psalm—His triumphal entry (vv. 25-26), His rejection (v. 27), His death and resurrection (v. 17), and His exaltation as God's chosen Stone (vv. 22-23). Perhaps verse 24 hints at the Lord's Day, the day of resurrection, as "the new day" of the new creation made possible by His atoning work. It is important that we see Jesus Christ in every experience of life, for then these experiences will help us grow in grace and become more like the Savior.

Psalm 119

The emphasis in this, the longest psalm, is on the vital ministry of the Word of God in the inner spiritual life of God's children. It describes how the Word enables us to grow in holiness and handle the persecutions and pressures that always accompany an obedient walk of faith. The psalm is an acrostic with eight lines in each section, and the successive sections follow the letters of the Hebrew alphabet. Each of the eight lines of 1-8 begins with the Hebrew letter *aleph*, the lines in 9-16 begin with *beth*, in 17-24 with *gimel*, and so on. The unknown author used eight different words for the Scriptures: law (*torah*), testimony, precept, statute, commandment, judgment (in the sense of "a rule for living"), word (of God), and promise. All eight are found in 33-40, 41-48, 57-64, 73-80, 81-88, and 129-136. Students disagree on this, but it appears that every verse contains a *direct* mention

of God's Word except seven: verses 3, 37, 84, 90, 121, 122, and 132. If you count "ways" as a synonym for God's Word, then you can eliminate verses 3 and 37. (The NIV has "your word" in v. 37, but most Hebrew texts read "your ways.") The writer may have been meditating on Psalm 19 where David listed six names for the Scriptures, five of which are found in 119—law, testimony, precept, commandment, and judgment. Some of the vocabulary of 19 is also found in 119, including perfect or blameless (13/119:1, 80); pure (8/119:9, 140); righteous and righteousness (9; 119:7, 40, 62, 75, 106, etc.); and meditate or meditation (14/119:21, 51, 69, 78, 85, 122). Both compare the Word of God to gold (10/119:72, 127) and honey (10/119:103), and in both there is an emphasis on keeping or obeying God's Word (11/119:4, 5, 8, 9, 17, 34, 44, 55, 57, 60, 63, 67, 88, 101, 106, 134, 136, 146, 158, 167, 168).

The Writer and His Times

Since we do not know who wrote the psalm, we cannot know for certain when it was written, but our ignorance need not hinder us from learning from this magnificent psalm. Some attribute the psalm to Moses, which is unlikely, and others to a priest or Levite who served in the second temple after the Babylonian captivity. Whoever the author was, he is a good example for us to follow, for he had an intense hunger for holiness and a passionate desire to understand God's Word in a deeper way. In all but fourteen verses, he addresses his words to the Lord personally, so this psalm is basically a combination of worship, prayer, praise, and admonition. The writer must have been a "high profile" person because he mentioned the opposition of rulers (vv. 23, 161; "princes" in KJV and NASB), a word that can refer to Gentile rulers or local Jewish tribal leaders (Neh. 3), and he also spoke to kings (v. 46). In the psalm, there are no references to a sanctuary, to sacrifices, or to a priestly ministry. The cast of characters includes the Lord God, a remnant of godly people in the nation (vv. 63, 74, 79, 120, etc.), the psalmist, and the ungodly people who despised him (v. 141), persecuted him (vv. 84-85, 98, 107, 109, 115, 121-122, etc.), and wanted to destroy him (v. 95). The psalmist referred to them as "the proud" or "the arrogant" (vv. 21, 51, 69, 78, 85, 122). They were people who were born into the covenant but did not value the spiritual riches of that relationship. They disdained the law and openly disobeyed it. The writer was reproached by them (vv. 22-23, 39, 42) and suffered greatly from their false accusations (vv. 50-51, 61, 67, 69-71, 75, 78).

Whether right or wrong, I have often thought that the prophet Jeremiah might have been the author of Psalm 119 and that he wrote it to teach and encourage his young disciples (v. 9) after the destruction of the temple. Many of the statements in the psalm could be applied to Jeremiah. He spoke with kings, five of them in fact (Jer. 1:2), and bore reproach because he faithfully served the Lord (Jer. 15:15; 20:8). He was surrounded by critics and enemies who did not seek God's law (Jer. 11:19) but wanted to get rid of the prophet (Jer. 18:23). Jeremiah was definitely the prophet of "God's Word in the heart" (Jer. 31:31-34), and this is an emphasis in 119 (vv. 11, 32, 39, 80, 111). The writer wept over the plight of his people (vv. 28, NASB, 136; Jer. 9:1, 18; 13:17; 14:17; Lam. 1:16; 2:18; 3:48). However, in the midst of catastrophe and danger, Jeremiah rejoiced in God's Word and nourished himself in it (v. 111; Jer. 15:16). In both vocabulary and message, this psalm is rooted in the book of Deuteronomy ("second law"), which is Moses's second declaration of the law. However, unlike Exodus, Deuteronomy emphasizes love and obedience from the heart, not just a "ritual" following of God's rules. Jeremiah was a priest as well as a prophet and had a working knowledge of Deuteronomy.

The Theme

The basic theme of Psalm 119 is the practical use of the Word of God in the life of the believer. When you consider that the writer probably did not have a complete Old Testament, let alone a complete Bible, this emphasis is both remarkable and important. Christian believers today own complete Bibles, yet how many of them say that they love God's Word and get up at night or early in the morning to read it and meditate on it (vv. 55, 62, 147-148)? How many Christian believers ignore the Old Testament Scriptures or read the Old Testament in a careless and cursory manner? Yet here was a man who rejoiced in the Old Testament Scriptures—which was the only Word of God he had—and considered God's Word his food (v. 103) and his greatest wealth! (vv. 14, 72, 127, 162). His love for the Word of God puts today's believers to shame. If the psalmist with his limited knowledge and resources could live a godly and victorious life feeding on the Old Testament, how much more ought Christians today live for the Lord. After all, we have the entire Bible before us and two millennia of church history behind us!

When the psalmist used the word "law" (*torah*), or any of the seven other words for the Scriptures, he was referring to much more than the Ten Commandments and the ceremonial instructions that have now been fulfilled in Christ. He was referring to the entire revelation of

God as found in the Old Testament Scriptures. Until the books in our New Testament were written and distributed in the first century, *the Old Testament Scriptures were the only Word of God possessed by the early church!* Yet with the Old Testament and the help of the Holy Spirit, the first Christians were able to minister and win the lost in a dynamic way. Peter used Psalms 69:25 and 109:8 to receive guidance in choosing a new disciple (Acts 1:15-26). He quoted Joel 2:28-32 at Pentecost to explain the advent of the Holy Spirit and Psalms 16:8-11 and 110:1 to prove the resurrection of Jesus Christ (Acts 2:14-39). In his defense before the council (Acts 7), Stephen opened with Genesis 12:1 and closed with Isaiah 66:1-2, and between those two referred to Exodus, Deuteronomy, and Amos. Philip led a man to faith in Christ by using only Isaiah 53 (Acts 8:26-40). Paul found in Isaiah 49:6 a mandate to continue ministering to the Gentiles (Acts 13:47), and James concluded the Jerusalem conference by quoting Amos 9:11-15 (Acts 15:13-21). Paul even quoted an Old Testament verse about oxen to encourage churches to support their spiritual leaders (Deut. 25:4; 1 Cor. 9:9; 1 Tim. 5:18). (Hab. 2:4 is quoted as a key verse in Rom. 1:17, Gal. 3:11, and Heb. 10:37-38). In their theology, decisions, and ministry, the first Christians depended on guidance from the Old Testament Scriptures.

Many believers today stand guilty of ignoring the Old Testament, except for reading "favorite psalms," and therefore many are ignorant of what God's law teaches. "The law is a yoke," they exclaim, and point to Acts 15:10 and Galatians 5:1, but the psalmist found freedom through the law (vv. 45, 133). "To pay attention to the law is to move into the shadows!" they argue, referring to Colossians 2:16-17 and Hebrews 10:1, but the writer of Psalm 119 found the law to be his light (vv. 105, 130). "By the law is the knowledge of sin" (Rom. 3:20), but the psalmist used the law to get victory over sin (vv. 9-11). "The law kills!" (Rom. 7:9-11), but the law brought the psalmist new life when he was down in the dust (see NASB vv. 25, 40, 88, 107, 149, etc.). "Law and grace are in opposition!" many declare, but the psalmist testified that law and grace worked together in his life (vv. 29 and 58). God used Moses to liberate the people from Egypt, but then God gave Moses the law to give to Israel at Sinai. The German philosopher Goethe wrote, "Whatever liberates our spirit without giving us self-control is disastrous." Law and grace are not enemies, for law sets the standard and grace enables us to meet it (Rom. 8:1-3).

The writer of Psalm 119 *delighted* in God's law (vv. 16, 24, 35, 47, 70, 77, 92, 43; and see 1:1 and 19:8 and 10), and this joy was echoed by Paul (Rom. 7:22). Paul did not annul God's law and set it aside; rather, he said that the law was "holy, just and good" and even "spiritual" (Rom. 7:12-14). Though we are carnal (fleshly), there is a lawful use of the law in our inner person. The law of God is spiritual and can be used by the Spirit to minister to our spirit. To be sure, nobody is saved or sanctified by striving to obey the law. But for the dedicated Christian believer, there is a deeper meaning to the law, a writing of the Word upon our hearts (Deut. 4:9, 29, 39; 6:5; 10:12; etc.), because of the new covenant in Jesus Christ (Jer. 31:31-34; Heb. 8:8-12; 10:16-17; 2 Cor. 3).

To unsaved sinners, the law is *an enemy* because it announces their condemnation and cannot save them. To legalistic believers, the law is *a master* that robs them of their freedom. But to spiritually minded believers, the law is *a servant* that helps them see the character of God and the work of Christ. The Old Testament believer who wrote Psalm 119 was not satisfied with having the law in his home, his head, or his hand; he wanted the law in his heart where it could help him love what was holy and do what was right (v. 11). It was this approach that Jesus took in the Sermon on the Mount. The attributes of God as revealed in the Old Testament parallel the characteristics of the Word of God as seen in Psalm 119. Both are gracious (vv. 29, 58; 86:15), true and the truth (vv. 30, 43, 160; Ex. 34:6), righteous (vv. 106, 123, 137-138, 143, 151), good (vv. 39, 68), trustworthy (vv. 9, 73, 86, 90, 138), eternal (vv. 89, 152, 160; Deut. 33:27), and light (v. 107; 27:1). The way we treat the Word of God is the way we treat the God of the Word.

The Word of God performs many wonderful ministries in the life of the devoted believer. It keeps us clean (v. 9), gives us joy (vv. 14, 111, 162), guides us (vv. 24, 33-35, 105), and establishes our values (vv. 11, 37, 72, 103, 127, 148, 162). The Word helps us to pray effectively (v. 58) and gives us hope (v. 49) and peace (v. 165) and freedom (vv. 45, 133). Loving the Word will bring the best friends into our life (vv. 63, 74, 79), help us find and fulfill God's purposes (v. 73), and strengthen us to witness (vv. 41-43). When we think we are "down and out," the Word will revive us and get us back on our feet (vv. 25, 37, 40, 88, 107, 149, 154, 156, 159). If we delight in His Word, learn it, treasure it within, and obey what it says, the Lord will work in us and through us to accomplish great things for His glory! As you read and study Psalm 119, you will see the writer in a variety of experiences, but His devotion to the Lord and His Word will not change. Circumstances may change, but God and His Word remain the same.

Aleph (vv. 1-8)—Blessed and Blameless

The opening word of the psalm— "blessed"—is repeated in verse 2 but found nowhere else this psalm. How can we receive God's blessing? By being blameless before the Lord, obedient to His law, and wholehearted in our relationship to Him. But some of the words that follow—law, precepts, statutes, decrees, commands—have a way of frightening us and almost paralyzing us with despair. When we think of law, we usually think of "cursing" and not "blessing" (see Deut. 27:1-28:68; Josh 9:30-35), but we must remember that Jesus bore the curse of the law for us on the cross (Gal. 3:10-13). The law is not a weapon in the hands of an angry judge but a tool in the hands of a loving Father, used by the Spirit to make us more like Jesus Christ. The Word enables us to know God better and draw closer to Him. "Blameless" does not mean sinless but wholehearted devotion to the Lord, sincerity, and integrity. Only Jesus Christ was totally blameless in His relationship to God and His law, but because believers are "in Christ," we are "holy and without blame before Him" (Eph. 1:4)). His love is in our hearts (Rom. 5:5) and His Spirit enables us (Gal. 5:16-26), so His law is not a heavy yoke that crushes us, for "His commandments are not burdensome" (1 John 5:3, NKJV).

Seeking God means much more than reading the Bible or even studying the Bible. It means hearing God's voice in His Word, loving Him more, and wanting to delight His heart and please Him. It means wholehearted surrender to him (vv. 2, 10, 34, 58, 69, 145) and an unwillingness to permit any rival love to enter. All of the psalms make it clear that this kind of life is not without its dangers and disappointments, for we often fail. The writer of this psalm found himself in the dust and had to cry out for "reviving" (vv. 25, 37, 40, 50, 88, 93, 107, 149, 154, 156, 159). Once he had done that, he confessed his sins, got up and started walking with God again. *The victorious Christian life is a series of new beginnings.* As we cultivate an appetite for the Word (vv. 10, 20, 40, 81, 131) and feed upon it, we give the Spirit something to work with in our hearts, and He enables us to walk in God's paths. If we feel ashamed when we read the Word (v. 6; see v. 80), then we have to stop and find out why and then confess it to the Lord. If we are ashamed because of our disobedience, then we cannot witness to others (v. 46) and we will be ashamed of our hope (v. 116). Better to be ashamed now and confess it than to be ashamed when we meet the Lord (1 John 2:28).

Praise is good preparation for learning about God and His Word (v. 7). It is so important that he repeated it in verses 12 and 171. Our ways (v. 5) may not yet be God's ways (v. 3), but as we press on by faith, He will help us and not forsake us (v. 8; Heb. 13:5). Jacob was far from being a spiritual man when he ran away from home, but the Lord promised not to forsake him, and Jacob believed that promise and became a godly man (Gen. 28:10-22). God even deigns to be called "the God of Jacob."

Beth (vv. 9-16)—Take Time to Be Holy

The writer closed the first section determined to keep the law of the Lord (v. 8), a promise he repeated in verse 145. He began this section like a true Jewish teacher by asking a question of the young men he was instructing: "How can we fulfill this promise?" He also promised to meditate on the Word (vv. 15, 48, 78), to delight in the Word and not forget it (vv. 16, 47, 93), and to run in the way of the Lord (v. 32). But he knew that it is easier to make promises than to keep them, a lesson Paul learned when he tried in his own strength to obey God's law (Rom. 7:14-25). Paul learned, as we must also learn, that the indwelling Holy Spirit enables the child of God to fulfill God's righteousness in daily life (Rom. 8:1-11). We must live according to God's Word, which means cultivating a heart for God. Paul called this "seeking the things that are above" (Col. 3:1).

We need a heart that seeks God, for if our heart is seeking God, our feet will not stray from God (v. 10; Prov. 4:23). Such a heart will see Him in all of life, learn more about Him, fellowship with Him, and glorify Him in all that is said and done. Again, the Holy Spirit enables us to do this as we yield to Him. But we must also spend time in the Word and treasure it in our hearts (v. 11; Job 23:12; Prov. 2:1; 7:1). It is not our promises to the Lord but His promises to us that will give us victory over sin. We also need a thankful heart and a teachable spirit that will enable us to learn from the Lord (vv. 12, 108, 171). A. W. Tozer used to warn against being "man taught" instead of "God taught" (v. 102). The Lord has given teachers to His church and we should heed them. But unless the truth we hear moves from the head (and the notebook) into the heart, written there by the Spirit (2 Cor. 3:1-3), and then to the will, we have not really learned the Word or been blessed by it. The blessing comes, not in hearing the Word but in doing it (James 1:22-25). We should also speak with others about the Word (v. 13) and seek to enrich them with spiritual treasures. The heart is a treasury from which we draw spiritual wealth to encourage and help ourselves and others (Matt. 12:35; 13:51-52). The Scriptures as riches is a repeated theme in 119 (vv. 14, 72, 127, 162; see 19:10). To treasure any possession above the Word of God is idolatry and leads to trouble. Consider Lot (Gen. 13, 18-19), Achan (Josh. 6-7), King Saul (1 Sam. 15), and Ananias and Sapphira (Acts 5). On the positive side, consider Abraham (Gen. 14:18-24), Moses (Heb. 11:24-27), Mary of Bethany (Mark 14:3-9), and Paul (Phil. 3:1-11).

Whatever delights will capture our attention and we will think about it and meditate on it. This is true of God's Word. In this psalm, delighting in the Word, loving the Word, and meditating on the Word are found together (vv. 15-16, 23-24, 47-48, 77-78, 97-99), and they should be found together in our hearts and lives. We must take time to be holy.

Gimel (vv. 17-24)—We Need God's Word!

If ever we feel we can ignore our daily time with God in His Word, then this is the Scripture to read. We need the Word because we are *servants* (vv. 17, 23, 38, 49, 65, 76, 84, 122, 124, 125, 135, 140, 176), and in His Word, our Master gives us directions for the work He wants us to do. Eli the priest was wrong in many things, but he was right when he taught young Samuel to pray, "Speak, Lord, for your servant is listening" (1 Sam. 3:9, NASB). As God's faithful servant, the anonymous writer of this psalm is ranked along with Moses, Joshua, David, Daniel, James, Paul, and Timothy, all of whom carried that title. But each child of God can serve the Lord and bear that same title (113:1; 134:1; 2 Tim. 2:24; 1 Peter 2:16). Everything in creation serves the Lord (v. 91), and we who are His redeemed people

ought to join them. He always deals bountifully with His servants and provides for them adequately (13:6; 116:7; 142:7; Luke 22:35; Phil 4:19).

Not only are we servants, but we are also *students* (v. 18), and our basic manual is the Word of God. However, unless God opens our eyes, we will never see the wonderful things hidden in its pages (Eph. 1:17-18). God's Word is wonderful (v. 129), His works are wonderful (107:8, 15, 21, 24, 31), and His love is wonderful (31:21, NIV), and we must meditate on the wonder of His Person, His truth, and His mighty works. The eyes have an appetite (vv. 82, 123; 1 John 2:16) and we must be careful where we focus them (v. 37). Eyes that feast on the vanities of this world will never see the wonders in God's Word.

Like the patriarchs of old, we are also *strangers* in this world (vv. 19-20; 39:12; 105:12, 23; Gen. 23:4; Ex. 2:22; Lev. 25:23; Heb. 11:8-9, 13-16; 1 Peter 1:1; 2:11), and we need the Lord's guidance as we walk the pilgrim path. The laws for driving in Great Britain are different from the laws in the United States and it is dangerous to confuse the two. God's people are being led on the narrow road that leads to life, while the people of the world are on the broad road that leads to judgment (Matt. 7:13-14). Just as the cloud and fiery pillar led Israel in their wilderness journey (Num. 9:15-23), so the Scriptures lead us (v. 105). The psalmist felt a crushing burden to read and ponder God's ordinances, and unlike many travelers today, he was not afraid to ask the Lord for directions. If we take time to meditate on the Word and seek the Lord, He will show us the path of life (16:11).

Because we serve a different Master, obey a different set of laws, and have our citizenship in a different country (Phil. 3:20), we are different from the lost people whom Jesus called "the children of this world" (Luke 16:8). We will not conform to the world (Rom. 12:2), and the world opposes and persecutes us because of this. Therefore, we are *sufferers* who bear reproach for Jesus Christ (vv. 21-14; Matt. 13:20-21; Heb. 13:13). The psalmist called these persecutors "the arrogant [proud]" (v. 21) and described them as disobeying God's law (vv. 126, 158), ignoring it (v. 139), wandering from it (vv. 21, 118), and forsaking it (v. 53). Because they reject God's Word, they reject God's people and mock them (v. 51), lie about them (v. 69), try to trap them (v. 85), and oppress them without cause (vv. 78; 122). These are the "willful sins" that David wrote about in 19:14. This opposition was in high places among the rulers (vv. 23, 161), which would mean the nobles and officers of the land. The psalmist wanted God to remove the reproach they had put on him like a garment (v. 22; see 35:26; 109:29; 132:18), but the psalmist's suffering gave him opportunity to bear witness to nobles and kings (v. 46; and see Matt. 10:18; Acts 9:15; Phil. 1:12-18; 4:22). The writer needed wisdom to know how to handle these difficult situations and he found counsel in God's Word (v. 24). Instead of listening to the enemy's slander, he meditated on God's truth. That is a good way to keep your mind clean and confident (Phil. 4:4-7).

Daleth (vv. 25-32)—Down but Not Out
The previous section ended with the psalmist delighting in God's Word, and this one opens with him down in the dust! The enemy attacks us the hardest when we are enjoying the blessings of God, and we must expect it. When things are going well and we "feel good," it is dangerous to relax and lay aside the armor (Eph. 6:10-18). "We must be as watchful after the victory as before the battle," said Andrew Bonar, and he was right. When

he found himself down, the psalmist knew what to do—he prayed!

"Revive me" (v. 25; see 143:11). His enemies were slandering his name (v. 23), restricting him (v. 61), lying about him (v. 69), causing him to suffer (v. 83) and be despised (v. 141), and even threatening his life (v. 109), so it is no wonder that he felt like an insect in the dust. But when we seem to be at our worst, the Lord comes along with the very best and gives us the grace that we need (2 Cor. 1:3-11; 12:1-10). The *New International Version* translates the Hebrew word "preserve my life," but much more is involved in this request. It involves saving his life, of course, but also invigorating him and breathing new life within him. He prayed this prayer often (vv. 25, 37, 40, 50, 88, 93, 107, 149, 154, 156, 159), and the Lord answered him each time.

"Teach me" (vv. 26-27). Too often we ask, "How can I get out of this trouble?" when we should be asking, "*What* can I get out of this experience?" In times of trouble, we need God's wisdom lest we waste our suffering (James 1:2-8). The psalmist knew there were still lessons to learn in the school of life and he did not want to miss them. He talked to the Lord about what was happening to him, and the Lord answered by giving him wisdom and strength. By faith, he expected to see God's wonders displayed in the midst of his battles.

"Strengthen me" (vv. 28-30). Throughout the psalm, the writer makes it clear that he is suffering because of his commitment to God and His Word (vv. 28, 50, 67, 71, 75, 83, 92, 107, 143, 153). He was actually risking his life to obey the Lord (v. 109). Yet he did not rage against his enemies and seek to destroy them; rather, he wept over them and turned them over to God (vv. 115, 136). All he

wanted was strength to keep on living for the Lord and magnifying His Word. He discovered that God's grace was indeed all that he needed (2 Cor. 12:9). He would walk in the way of God's truth and avoid the enemy's way of deception (vv. 29-30, 104, 128). When we find ourselves pressured by the enemy, our first response is usually to pray that God will change them, when perhaps our best response would be that God would change us and enable us to overcome.

"Defend me" (vv. 31-32). The writer did not want to bring shame to the name of the Lord (vv. 31, 46, 78, 80), so he turned the situation over to Him by faith. If we think up clever schemes to defend ourselves and slander others, then the Lord will not be able to defend us (Rom. 12:17-21). As we hold to His Word and trust His promises, the Lord is able to work in His way and in His time. Faith delivers us from the confinement of the enemy's plots and sets us free to enjoy a larger place. He has gone from biting the dust (v. 25) to running freely in the way of the Lord! (See vv. 45, 96; 4:1 and 18:36.)

He (vv. 33-40)—Ending Well

Paul (2 Tim. 4:6-8) and Jesus (John 17:4) both ended well, to the glory of God, but not every believer achieves that coveted goal. A good beginning ought to lead to a good ending, but that is not always the case. Lot, Samson, King Saul, Ahithophel, and Demas all made good beginnings, but their lives ended in tragedy. The psalmist wanted to end well (v. 33), but ending well is the consequence of living well. What are the essentials for a consistent life that ends well?

Learning (vv. 33-34). We must pray for spiritual enlightenment so we may learn God's Word and the way of His Word. It is not enough to read the Bible, outline the

books, get answers to questions, and be able to discuss theology. We must come to understand the character of God and the workings of His providence (27:11; 86:11; 103:7). Just as children come to understand the character of their parents and what pleases them, so we must get to know God better and discern His desires. We have a complete revelation of the Lord and His will in the Scriptures, but we need inner illumination to discover what it means to our own lives. Our prayer "Teach me" must be balanced with "Give me understanding," and both must lead to obedience.

Obeying (v. 35). What we learn with our mind and apprehend with our heart must motivate the will to do what God commands. But our obedience cannot be that of a slave obeying a master in order to avoid discipline. It must be the obedience of a grateful child who delights to please his or her parents. "Doing the will of God from the heart" (Eph. 6:6). This was the way Jesus obeyed His Father: "I delight to do Your will, O my God, and Your law is within my heart" (Ps. 40:8). "I always do those things that please Him" (John 8:29). If we want to know God's truth, we must be willing to obey God's will (John 7:17).

Delighting (vv. 36-37). These verses warn us that our hearts and minds ("eyes") must be focused on the truth of God and not material wealth and the vanities of the world (vv. 51, 157). Outlook determines outcome. Abraham looked for the heavenly city and ended well; Lot looked at Sodom and ended badly (Gen. 13; Heb. 11:8-16). What the heart loves and desires, the eyes will see (101:2-6; Num. 15:37-41; Jer. 22:17). To have one eye on the world and the other on the Word is to be double-minded, and God does not bless double-minded people (James 1:5-8).

Fearing (vv. 38-39). The fear of the Lord is the fear that conquers every fear. The fear of man is the fear that leads to bondage and defeat (Prov. 29:25). The psalmist was not afraid of his enemies; he was afraid of disgracing the Lord and bringing dishonor to His great name. The psalmist claimed the promises of God and trusted God to deal with his enemies; for we live on promises, not explanations. Our faith is tested by the promises of God and our faithfulness is tested by the precepts of God, and both are important. (For more on God's promises, see vv. 41, 50, 58, 76, 82, 116, 123, 140, 148, 154, 162, and 170.) It is not our promises to Him (v. 57) but His promises to us that really count.

Longing (v. 40). To have a deep longing for God's truth is the mark of a maturing believer. His soul was "consumed with longing" and he even "fainted with longing" (vv. 20-21, NIV), so much so that he even "panted" for God's commands (v. 131). He longed for the day when God's salvation would be revealed (v. 174; Rom. 8:18-23). Meanwhile, his longing was satisfied by the living Word of God, which is the believer's honey (v. 103), bread (Matt. 4:4), milk, and solid food (1 Cor. 3:1-3; Heb. 5:12-14; 1 Peter 2:1-3).

Vau (vv. 41-48)—Walking and Talking
We hear several voices in this section, and it begins with *God speaking to us (v. 41).* He does this, of course, as we read His Word and meditate on it. He speaks in love and in mercy, and even the warnings come from His compassionate heart. The Word of God is the expression of the love of God to us (33:11) and it should result in love from our hearts to the Lord, to His people, and to the lost. God's Word shares God's promises, and promises always imply future hope. Scripture is "the word of his promise" (1 Kings 8:56), and all His promises have their realization in Jesus Christ (2 Cor. 1:20). The Scriptures are also "the word of this salvation" (Acts 13:26), for the Word declares that Jesus is the only Savior and we can trust in Him. What a wonder that God has spoken to us! (Heb. 1:1-2). Are we listening?

But while God is speaking, *the enemy is also speaking* (v. 42). We have learned that the writer of this psalm was oppressed by enemies who lied about him, slandered his name, and even threatened his life. Our main weapon against these attacks is "the sword of the Spirit, which is the word of God" (Eph. 6:17), for only God's truth can silence the devil's lies (Matt. 4:1-11). We need God's truth in our hearts, not only to keep us from sin, but also to equip us to answer those who oppose us or ask us why we believe as we do (1 Peter 3:15).

God's people speak to the Lord (v. 43). Like Nehemiah, we can send up "telegraph prayers" to the Lord right in the midst of our work and our battles (Neh. 2:5; 4:4; 5:19; 6:9, 14; 13:14, 22, 31). When we are confronted by the enemy, the Lord will not give us words we have never pondered from the Scriptures, but His Spirit can remind us of what we have read and learned (John 14:25-26). The writer connected God's Word with his mouth, because the word "meditate" in the Hebrew means "to mutter." The ancient Jews spoke the Word audibly as they meditated and prayed (Josh. 1:8).

Our lives speak for the Lord (vv. 44-45) if our "walk" agrees with our "talk." The best defense of the faith is a transformed life that is compassionate toward others. Our obedience to the Lord and our loving ministry to others (Matt. 5:13-16) demonstrates the reality of our faith far better than anything else. Because we know and obey "the word of truth" (v. 43), we are able to enjoy freedom from the bondage of sin (v. 45), for it is the truth that makes us free (John 8:32; James 1:25; 2:12).

Finally, *God's people speak to others (vv. 46-48).* If we truly love God and His Word, we will not be ashamed to share the Word even with important people like kings (vv. 6, 80; Rom. 1:16; Phil. 1:20; 2 Tim. 1:12; 2:15; 1 Peter 4:16). When we delight in the Word, love it, and obey it, sharing the message with others comes naturally. To witness means to tell others what we have seen and heard concerning Jesus Christ (Acts 4:20) and what He has done for us. A satisfied Christian is an awesome witness whose testimony God can use to convict and convert others. We do not worship the Bible but we do honor God's Word and lift our hands to the Lord in praise and thanksgiving for His gift. In many churches, the entire congregation stands when the Scriptures are brought in and publicly read. (See 28:2, 63:4, 134:2 and 141:2.)

The basic Christian virtues (1 Cor. 13:13) are seen in those who live by God's Word: faith (v. 42), hope (v. 43), and love (vv. 41, 47, and 48). Love is mentioned three times because "the greatest of these is love." (On loving God and His Word, see vv. 97, 113, 119, 127, 140, 159, 163, 165, 167; 1 Tim. 1:5.)

Zayin (vv. 49-56)—The Ministry of Memory

If the psalmist was a priest or a Levite, and he probably was, then he was required to be an expert on the book of Deuteronomy. Deuteronomy means "second law." The book records Moses's "farewell speech" that he gave to prepare the new generation of Israelites for the conquest of Canaan. After forty years of wandering, the nation would stop being nomads and would become settlers, but new generations would come along and be prone to forget the lessons of the past. In Deuteronomy, you find the word "remember" fifteen times and the word "forget" fourteen times. Some things in the past we must forget (Phil. 3:12-14), but some things we must never forget. "He who does not remember the past is condemned to repeat it" (George Santayana).

God remembers His people (vv. 49-51). When applied to the Lord, the word "remember" means "to pay attention to, to work on behalf of." Being omniscient, God cannot forget anything, but He can decide not to "remember it against us" (Isa. 43:25; Jer. 31:34; Heb. 8:12; 10:17). That is the negative side; the positive side is that He "remembers" to do us good and give us His blessing. He remembered Noah and delivered him (Gen. 8:1); He remembered Abraham and delivered Lot (Gen. 19:29); He remembered Rachel and Hannah and enabled them to conceive (Gen. 30:22; 1 Sam. 1:19). Remembering is not recalling, for God never forgets; it is relating to His people in a special way. The psalmist prayed that God would use the Word to work on his behalf. The writer had hope because of the promises God had given to him, and he prayed that those promises would be fulfilled. When Daniel found in the prophecy of Jeremiah the promise of Israel's deliverance from captivity, he immediately began to pray for the promise to be fulfilled (Dan. 9). True faith not only believes the promises but also prays for God to work. In his believing and praying, the writer found encouragement ("comfort" comes from the Latin meaning "with strength"), and he did not abandon his faith or run away from his problems. He was revived with new life!

His people remember God's Word (vv. 52-54). How could this spiritual leader know the "ancient laws" that God gave

Moses centuries before? The nation had preserved the Word (Deut. 31:24-29) and taught it to each new generation (Deut. 4:1-14), and this is the obligation of the church today (2 Tim. 2:2). Unless the Word of God is honored, taught, and obeyed in a church, that congregation is one generation short of extinction. The psalmist was indignant at what the worldly people ("the arrogant") were doing as they abandoned Israel's spiritual heritage (vv. 53, 104, 128, 163), and he wept over their evil deeds (v. 136). Anger alone can be very destructive, but anger plus love produces anguish, and anguish can lead to constructive action. His response was to turn God's statutes into songs and to use the Word to praise the Lord (v. 54; Eph. 5:19; Col. 3:16). He did not consider God's law a burden to bear; he saw the Word as a blessing to share— and he sang it! Praise that is not based on the truth of Scripture is unacceptable to the Lord. We are on a difficult pilgrimage from earth to heaven, and we need God's songs to encourage us and to help us witness to others along the way (Acts 16:22-34). We are strangers on the earth, and the Bible is our guidebook to this world (vv. 19, 64) and to ourselves (v. 64).

His people remember His name (vv. 55-56). The name of God—Jehovah, Yahweh—is full of meaning and power. To translate it only as "I AM" is to miss much of the dynamic that it contains (Ex. 6:1-3). We might paraphrase it, "I am present, I am actively present, and I can do what I choose when I choose to do it." God's name Yahweh speaks not only of His existence and His eternality, but also of His sovereignty, His power, and the dynamic working out of His will in this world. The ancient Jewish people so revered His name that they feared to use it and substituted Adonai, lest they sin

against their God. In the book of Psalms alone, there are more than one hundred references to the name of the Lord. We are to love His name (5:11), sing praises to His name (7:17; 9:2; 18:49), and glorify His name (29:2). It is through His great name that we triumph over our enemies (44:5; 54:1; 118:10-12), so we should always call on His name for help (116:4, 13, 17). To remember His name is to encourage our hearts to trust Him, obey Him, and not be afraid. "And those who know Your name will put their trust in You, for You, LORD [Yahweh], have not forsaken those who seek you" (9:10, NKJV).

To remember God's name is to ask Him to remember us and work on our behalf. We must do this when we are in the darkness and afraid (v. 55), or when we are lonely and discouraged (42:6). "The name of the LORD is a strong tower; the righteous run to it and are safe" (Prov. 18:10). If you want to know how strong His name is, study the names of God in the Old Testament and the "I AM" statements of Jesus in the Gospel of John. But be sure to imitate the psalmist and make it your practice to trust and honor His name in every aspect of life (v. 56, NIV), not just during emergencies.

Heth (vv. 57-64)—God Is All We Need
Whenever the people of Israel failed God and turned to idols for help, it was evidence that they did not really believe Jehovah was adequate to meet their needs. In the time of Elijah, Israel tried to remedy the drought by turning to Baal, the Canaanite storm god, but it was the Lord who sent the rain in answer to the prophet's prayer. When the enemy threatened to invade their land, the leaders of Israel often ran to Egypt for help, as though Jehovah was unconcerned and unable to deliver them. The psalmist in

this section makes it clear that the Lord God Almighty is all we need.

God is our portion (vv. 57-58). This is real estate language and refers to the apportioning of the land of Canaan to the tribes of Israel (78:55; Josh. 13-21). The priests and Levites were not given an inheritance in the land because the Lord was their inheritance and their portion (Num. 18:20-24; Deut. 10:8-9; 12:12). Jeremiah, the priest called to be a prophet, called the Lord "the Portion of Jacob" (Jer. 10:16; 51:19; Lam. 3:24), and David used the same image in Psalm 16:5-6. The "lines" in 16:6 refer to the property lines of one's land, the inheritance given by God. Believers today have a rich spiritual inheritance in the Lord Jesus Christ, for God's fullness is in Him and we are "complete in him" (Col. 2:9-10). He is our life (Col. 3:4) and our "all in all" (Col. 3:11). Because we are in Him, we have "all things that pertain to life and godliness" (2 Peter 1:3). Our riches in Christ are revealed in the Word, which is our "spiritual bankbook," and His wealth can never diminish. The psalmist had made promises to obey the Lord (vv. 8, 15-16, 32-34, 47, 106, 115), but that is not how we get our wealth from the Lord. What He provides for us is a gracious gift, not a loan, and we are not required to promise to repay Him (Rom. 11:33-36). Accept the inheritance He has given you, rejoice in it, and trust Him to supply every need.

God is our Master (vv. 59-61). The land inherited by the Israelites actually belonged to the Lord (Lev. 25:23) and He cared for it (Deut. 11:8-17). If the people obeyed the terms of the covenant, God would bless the people and their labors in the land, but if they turned to idols, He would chasten them, first in the land and then in other lands. Loving obedience was the condition for God's blessing,

even as it is today. Our mind belongs to Him ("I considered my ways") and our feet belong to Him ("turned my steps"). Our time belongs to Him and we must not delay obeying His will (v. 60). In ancient days, no servant could say "No," no servant could linger or postpone doing the master's will, and no servant could give excuses or say "I forgot." The servant's responsibility is to hear the master's orders, remember them, and obey them immediately.

God is our greatest joy (vv. 61-64). It should be the Christian's greatest joy to know God, love Him, hear His voice, and obey His will. Praying to Him and praising Him should be more refreshing to us than sleep. Being with His people should satisfy our hearts, and we should see the love and glory of God in all of creation. Whether we are lying on our bed at midnight, meditating on His Word (vv. 55, 62, 147-148), fellowshipping with God's people, or taking a walk in God's glorious creation, we love God, listen to Him, and thank Him. "All who fear you" is a fine description (vv. 63, 74, 79, 120), for the fear of God ought to mark the people of God. In spite of the disobedience of mankind and the ravages of sin that destroy God's creation, the earth is still full of God's lovingkindness, and though we are pilgrims and strangers on this earth, God is our home (90:1) and we have nothing to fear.

Teth (vv. 65-72)—God Is Good, All the Time

The emphasis in this psalm is on what is good in the life of the believer. The Hebrew word *tob* is used six times in these eight verses and can be translated good, pleasant, beneficial, precious, delightful, and right. God does what is good because God *is* good and because what He does is "according to his word" and His Word is good (v. 39). Neither His character nor His Word will ever change, so, "God is good all the time."

God does what is good (v. 65-66). The phrase "according to" is used frequently in Psalm 119 to relate a request or a fact to the Word of God. God acts according to the precepts, promises, and principles revealed in His Word, and we should pray and act accordingly. To ask God for something that is not according to His will and His Word is to ask ignorantly and selfishly (James 4:3), and if He gives the request to us, *we will be sorry and wish we had not prayed.* This happened to Israel when they asked God for flesh to eat (106:15; Num. 11:31-35). Therefore, we should pray the prayer of verse 66, for the better we know God's Word, the better we can pray in God's will and obey God's will.

God overrules evil and from it brings good (vv. 67-71). The psalmist had disobeyed the Word and gone astray. His sin was probably not a flagrant act of rebellion but of ignorance (Lev. 5:17-19; Num. 15:28), and God in His love sent affliction to discipline him (Heb. 12:1-11). At the time, this discipline was not pleasant, but it brought God's servant back to the place of obedience, so it was worth it (vv. 71, 75). However, there are times when we are *obedient* and we still experience suffering, but God uses that suffering to mature us and teach us His Word. Spurgeon said that the promises of God shine the brightest in the furnace of affliction. There are times when suffering comes from the enemies of God, whose hearts are insensible ("covered with fat"; 17:10; 73:7), but the Lord can even use godless opposition for our good and His glory (Rom. 8:28; 1 Peter 1:6-9 and 4:12-19). The most evil act ever performed on this earth was the crucifixion of the Lord of Glory on a cross, yet God used that to bring His salvation to the world.

God uses the Word to show us good (v. 72). The word "better" ("precious," NIV) is *tob* in the Hebrew. This is the second time in the psalm that the writer has compared God's truth to treasure (v. 14), and he will use this image again in verses 127 and 162. David used it in 19:10. The person of faith does not live by the priorities and values of the world (Heb. 11:24-27) but puts the will of God ahead of everything else. When we find the good treasures of truth in the precious Word of God, we rejoice in the goodness of the Lord and have no desire to wallow in the things of this world. No matter what our situation may be, we can affirm from our hearts, "God is good—all the time!"

Yodh (vv. 73-80)—Read the Instructions

Led by God's Spirit, the author wrote this long psalm to convince us to make knowing and obeying the Word of God the most important activities in our lives. In the previous section, he reminded us how necessary God's Word is when we are experiencing difficulties, but it does not stop there. We need God's Word for all of life. He mentioned several ministries of the Word that are necessary in the life of the faithful child of God.

We learn about ourselves (v. 73). When you purchase a new appliance, you take time to read the owner's manual. The Bible is the owner's manual for God's people. It is the only book that tells the truth about where we came from, why we are here, what we must do to succeed in life, and where we are going. God made us (139:13-18) and knows us better than we know ourselves, and He shares this knowledge in His Word. As we read, we "see ourselves" in the people and circumstances described in the pages of the Bible. We do not see "past history" but present reality! Unbelievers have no idea what the world and its people are really like, for the "real world" and the "real people" are presented in the pages of the Bible. The Bible is a mirror in which we see ourselves—and do something about what we see (James 1:22-27).

We become a blessing to others (vv. 74, 79). When we hope in God's Word, we have joy in life, and this helps us to encourage others. "Be kind, for everyone you meet is fighting a battle" (Ian Maclaren). Are people happy to see us arrive or are they happier when we leave? When our friends and acquaintances have burdens, do they turn to us for help, or do we add to their burdens? We are commanded to bear our own burdens courageously and to help others bear their burdens (Gal. 6:2, 5).

We receive God's best in our afflictions (vv. 75-78, 80). Life is difficult and we must accept from the hand of God both the pleasant experiences and the unpleasant (Job 2:1-10; Phil. 4:10-13). In the dark hours of life, the Word is a light that shows us the way (v. 105), and we do not go stumbling down the wrong paths. We have the love of God to comfort us and the promises of God to encourage us. We may not delight in our circumstances, but we pray that God will use them to spread the Gospel and glorify His name (Phil. 1:12-16). The enemy attacks us, but we turn to the Word and find the help that we need. Our determination in Christ is that we shall not be ashamed. God's decrees are perfect and they come from His loving heart (33:11), so we have nothing to fear.

When all else fails, read the instructions.

Kaph (vv. 81-88)—Faith and Patience

The focus is on the responses of the believer while he waited for the Lord to judge his enemies and deliver him from persecution and danger. His oppressors were also the enemies of the Lord and of Israel, so his concern was more than personal. Satan has been seeking to exterminate the Jews (v. 87) since the time the nation was in Egypt, and he will continue until the end-times (Rev. 12). The Christian life is a battleground, not a playground and we must expect tribulation (John 16:33).

Fainting but hoping (vv. 81-83). His inner person was exhausted from longing for God to work. His eyes were strained from watching for some evidence of His presence (Lam. 2:11). He felt like a dried-up wineskin that had been thrown aside as useless. However, he never gave up hope, for no matter how dark the hour, the future is our friend because Jesus is our Lord. "It is always too soon to quit" (V. Raymond Edman).

Questioning but waiting (vv. 84-85). "How long?" he asked in verse 84, and "When" in verses 82 and 84. These questions have often been asked by suffering saints (see on 6:3), even by the martyrs in heaven (Rev. 6:9-11), because they are the natural response of people who are suffering. (See Jer. 12:3-4; 15:15; and 20:11-12.) It is difficult for most people to wait for the things they can see—a traffic jam to end, a checkout line to speed up, an important letter or e-mail to arrive—and it is even more difficult to wait for our unseen Lord to work out His will. It is through "faith and patience" that we inherit what God has appointed for us (Heb. 6:12; see Rom. 15:4). Our trials will produce patience if we trust in the Lord (James 1:3-4). The enemy may be digging pits, but the Lord will see to it that they fall into them first (9:15; Prov. 26:27).

Trusting and reviving (vv. 86-88). Is the enemy spreading lies about you? God's

Word is dependable and can be trusted (vv. 128, 142, 151, 160). Do you feel like your defeat is very near? Rest on His promises and rely on His love. When the Father allows His children to go into the furnace of affliction, He keeps His eye on the clock and His hand on the thermostat. He knows how long and how much. To walk by faith will bring unrest and weakness, but to meditate on the Word will bring peace and power. Once again, the psalmist prayed for new life (see v. 25) and the Lord revived him. "Your Father in heaven loves you too much to harm you, and He is too wise to make a mistake" (Robert T. Ketcham).

Lamedh (vv. 89-96)—Change and the Changeless

The familiar hymn "Abide with Me" says, "Change and decay in all around I see." If that was true in 1847 when Henry Lyte wrote those words, how much truer it is today! To younger people, change is a treat, but to older folks, change is a threat. We like to relax in our comfort zone and resist the dramatic changes going on around us and within us. But if we do, we fail to grow spiritually and we miss the opportunities God gives us to reach others with the Gospel. The psalmist made some wonderful affirmations, which if heeded, will anchor us to the eternal and enable us to be used of God during these turbulent times.

God's Word is settled (v. 89). Ever since Satan asked Eve, "Indeed, has God said …?" (Gen. 3:1), the enemy has been attacking the Word of God. Atheists, agnostics, philosophers, scientists, and garden-variety sinners of all kinds have ignored the Bible, laughed at it, and tried to do away with it, but it still stands. Though born in eternity, God's Word is rooted in history and speaks to every generation that will listen. The Word is "founded forever" (v. 152) and will endure forever (v. 162). (See Matt. 24:34-35.) Build your life on the Word of God and you will weather all the changes of life!

God is faithful (v. 90a). Pause and read Psalm 90 and see what Moses had to say about the eternal God and the changes of life. From generation to generation, He is God, and we can commit ourselves, our children, our grandchildren, and our great-grandchildren to His care. Abraham, Isaac, and Jacob were three decidedly different kinds of men, but God was the "God of Abraham and of Isaac and of Jacob."

God's creation is established (vv. 90b-91). Until that last day when God's fire purifies all things and He ushers in a new heaven and earth (2 Peter 3; Rev. 21-22), this present creation will stand. The laws that He built into creation will also stand, whether scientists understand them or not. People may abuse and waste the earth and its resources, but God's creation will continue to serve the Creator. Everything in creation serves the Lord except human beings made in the image of God. What a tragedy! This is still our Father's world and we can trust Him to manage it wisely.

God's peace is available (vv. 92-95). We do not go to the Bible to escape the realities of life but to be strengthened to face life and serve God effectively. We may not be able to delight in what is going on in the world, but we can delight in what God says in His Word. The Word equips us to deal with the changes of life and the crises that come. The verb "sought out" in verse 94 means "to consult, to inquire, to beat a path, to read repeatedly. Here is a believer who beat a path to the Bible, read it over and over, studied it, and when he had to make a decision, consulted it carefully. Philosophies change, political expedients fail, promises and contracts are broken, but the Word of God still stands.

God wants us to get out of our rut (v. 96). So much truth is buried in this verse, you could meditate on it for hours. Whatever mankind does will never reach perfection, because our human work comes from our limited mind, strength, and ability. Perhaps the psalmist was reading the book of Ecclesiastes, for the limitations of human achievement is one of the themes of that book. "Vanity of vanities, all is vanity!" In contrast to the limits of mankind, God's Word and works have no limits. His commandment (singular—it is one united Book)—is limitless, boundless, immeasurable. Though Jesus lived, taught, and died in the little land of Palestine, His life and ministry have reached a whole world. Mary gave her sacrificial offering to Jesus in a home in Bethany, but what she did has blessed generations of people around the world (Mark 14:1-9).

Why should God's people stay in a rut when the Word of God is so boundless and there are no limits to what He can do! We may not like all the changes going on in the world, but we need not be frustrated and afraid. Although the news coverage was not as good, the situation was not much different in the days of the apostles, and they turned the world upside down! God is on the throne; He holds the world in His hands; His promises can never fail; so, let's get moving!

Mem (vv. 97-104)—Beyond Bible Study

Never have there been so many tools available for serious Bible study, and we are grateful for them. However, the Word of God is unlike any other book: we must be on good terms with the Author if we are to learn from what He has written. Our relationship to the Lord is determined by our relationship to His will, and that is determined by how we relate to His Word. Too many believers have only academic head knowledge of the Word, but they do not know how to put this knowledge into practice in the decisions of daily life. What we all need is a heart knowledge of the Word, and this means being taught by God (v. 102). Here are the conditions we must meet.

We must love His Word and meditate on it (vv. 97-100). We enjoy thinking about people and activities that we love, and meditation means loving the Lord by pondering His Word and allowing its truths to penetrate our hearts. (See vv. 48, 113, 127, 159, 165, 167; and 1:2.) This does not mean that we abandon our daily responsibilities or that we constantly quote Bible verses to ourselves and ignore our work. Rather, it means that our minds and hearts are so yielded to the Spirit that He can remind us of the Word when we need it and give us fresh understanding in the new challenges we face. There are many ways to learn truth. We can learn from our enemies in the encounters of life (v. 98), from our teachers in the explanations of life from books and lessons (v. 99), and from the older saints who have had the experiences of life and know the principles that work (v. 100). Joshua learned from serving with Moses, from the battles that he fought, and from the experiences, good and bad, that came to his life. But the most important thing he did was to meditate on the Word (Josh. 1:1-9), because his meditation helped him to test what he had learned in the other three "classrooms" and to put it all together into one balanced whole. God shares His truth with babes (Luke 10:21) and those who are humble enough to receive it (1 Cor. 1:18-2:8).

We must obey His Word (vv. 101-102). A true student of the Word is not a person with a big head, full of all sorts of knowledge, but one who has an obedient heart and loves to do God's will. While God's truth is food for our souls, it is not a "buffet" from which we select only the things we like. If the Bible tells us something is wrong, we stay off that path. If God tells us something is right, we do not abandon it. "Obedience is the organ of spiritual knowledge" (F. W. Robertson; John 7:17).

We must enjoy His Word (vv. 103-104). Honey would be the sweetest thing the psalmist could taste. However, the Word contains both sweetness and bitterness, and we must learn to receive both (19:10; 104:34; Prov. 16:24; Ezek. 2:9-3:15; Rev. 10). Samson got into trouble because of eating defiled honey from the carcass of a lion (Judg. 14:1-18). He was a Nazarite and was never to touch a dead body (Num. 6), so he defiled both himself and his parents, for Jewish people had to avoid dead animals (Num. 5:2; 9:10). God's Word is pure, not defiled, and gives us the sweetness and energy we need to obey His commands. The unsaved person finds the Bible boring, but the devoted child of God feeds on the Scriptures and enjoys the sweet taste of truth. This is what it means to go beyond Bible study.

Nun (vv. 105-112)—We Will Be Faithful

It has well been said that the greatest ability is dependability, and this especially applies to the Christian life. We want God to be faithful to us, so is it wrong for God to expect us to be faithful to Him? Faithfulness is an evidence of faith, and faith comes from hearing and receiving the Word of God (Rom. 10:17; 2 Thess.

2:13). The psalmist described several areas of faithfulness in the life of the believer.

Faithful feet (v. 105). Two familiar biblical images combine in this verse: life is a path (vv. 32, 35, 101, 128; 16:11; 23:3; 25:4) and God's Word is the light that helps us follow the right path (v. 130; 18:28; 19:8; 36:9; 43:3; Prov. 6:23; 2 Peter 1:19). The ancient world did not have lights such as we have today; the people carried little clay dishes containing oil, and the light illuminated the path only one step ahead. We do not see the whole route at one time, for we walk by faith when we follow the Word. Each act of obedience shows us the next step, and eventually we arrive at the appointed destination. We are told that this is "an enlightened age," but we live in a dark world (John 1:5; 3:19; 8:12; 12:46; Col. 1:13; 1 Peter 2:9) and only God's light can guide us aright. Obedience to the Word keeps us walking in the light (1 John 1:5-10).

Faithful words (vv. 106-108). Making vows constantly to the Lord will not lift us to the highest levels of Christian living (Rom. 7:14-8:4), but when we do make promises to the Lord or to our friends, we should keep them (Matt. 5:33-37; Num. 30:2; Deut. 23:21; Eccl. 5:1-7). The Holy Spirit can help us fulfill new resolutions if we depend on His power. What we say when we are praying (v. 107) should also be truthful. To talk to God piously without being willing to obey Him in the matters we are praying about is to bring hypocrisy into our fellowship with God. After we have prayed, are we available to be a part of the answer (Eph. 3:20-21)? Perhaps the highest use of speech is in the worship of the Lord (v. 108), and we must see our words as sacrifices offered to the Lord (Hos. 14:1-2; Heb. 13:15). Do we sing to Him from the heart (Eph. 5:19)? Do we mean the words that we pray, sing, and read aloud from the litany? If worship is the highest use of words, then to be careless in worship is to commit a great sin.

A faithful memory (vv. 109-110). The Old Testament believer did not have a pocket Bible that he could consult at will, for the Scriptures were written on large scrolls and deposited with the priests. This meant that the people had to listen carefully to the public reading of the Word and remember what they heard, an art that has almost vanished today. One of the ministries of the Holy Spirit is to bring God's Word to our remembrance when we need it (John 14:25-26; 16:12-15), but we cannot remember what we have never heard and learned (v. 11; Heb. 5:12-14). The psalmist was taking risks, just as we all do as we walk through the mine fields of this world, but he knew the Word would direct him.

A faithful heart (vv. 111-112). What a precious treasure is the Word of God! (vv. 14, 72, 127, 162; 61:5). It is like a deep mine, filled with gold, silver, and precious gems, and we must take time to "dig" for these treasures (Prov. 2:1-9; 3:13-15; 8:10-11; 1 Cor. 3:9-23). A mere surface reading of Scripture will not put spiritual treasure into our hearts. Mining treasure is hard work, but it is joyful work when we "mine" the Bible, as the Spirit guides us into truth. Then, the Spirit helps us to "mint" the treasure so we can invest it in our lives (obedience) and in the lives of others (witness). Sometimes God takes us through the furnace of suffering so we can better receive the treasure into our own lives (1 Peter 1:6-12). The Word needs no purifying (v. 140; 12:6; 19:8), but we need to be cleansed so we can appreciate God's truth and appropriate it. Once your heart is set on obeying the Word, the life is on the right course (Matt. 6:33; Prov. 4:20-27).

Samekh (vv. 113-120)—Dealing with the Enemy

If the life of faith consisted only of meditating on the Word and loving God, life would be easy, but people of faith have enemies, and life in this world is not easy. "Through many tribulations we enter the kingdom of God" (Acts 14:22, NKJV). Like the ten faithless men who spied out Canaan, if we look only at the enemy and ourselves, we will be discouraged and want to quit. But if like Caleb and Joshua, we look to the Lord, we can conquer the enemy (Num. 13:27-33). Four assurances in these verses help us face the enemy with courage and win the battle.

God protects His people (vv. 113-115). The "double-minded" were the people who were undecided and therefore uncommitted to the Lord (1 Kings 18:21; James 1:8; 4:8). Today, we would call them "half-hearted." There is nothing strange about believers experiencing both love toward God and His Word and hatred toward those who reject the Lord (vv. 104, 128, 163; 101:3; Amos 5:55; Mic. 3:2). "Hate evil, you who love the Lord" (97:10, NASB). If we love the Word, we will hate lies and oppose liars. The psalmist knew that his shelter and shield was the Lord alone, and he trusted in Him. He is not hiding in the Lord from fear of facing the enemy, because he addresses the enemy in verse 115. Only in the Lord could he find the help he needed. The Lord protects us that He might equip us to face the enemy and fight the battle (3:3; 27:5; 28:7; 31:20; 32:7; 33:20; 46:1-2; 61:4; 84:11; 91:1). The psalmist had his heart set on the Lord (v. 112), so there was no need to reconsider the matter. It was settled!

God upholds the obedient (vv. 116-117). The NASB and NIV each use "sustain" in verse 116 and "uphold" in 117, but the words are almost synonyms. "Sustain" pictures the believer leaning on the Lord for support and rest, while "uphold" mean that plus the idea of giving aid and refreshment. (For the first, see 3:6 and 37:17 and 24, and for the second, see Gen. 18:15.) When we feel like falling down and just giving up, the Lord comes to our aid in ways we could never fully understand.

God rejects the wicked (vv. 118-119). God's people in the Old Testament fought their enemies with swords and slings, but God's people today use the sword of the Spirit (Eph. 6:17; Heb. 4:12). It is a conflict between truth and lies, and God's truth must prevail. The writer described the enemy as sheep that had gone astray (vv. 10, 21, 176) and as cheap dross that must be discarded (Prov. 25:4; 26:23; Isa. 1:22, 25). God in His judgments purifies the saints but reveals the wickedness of the sinners, the way the refiner's furnace reveals the dross (Jer. 6:28-30; Ezek. 22:18-19; Mal. 3:2-3). "Their deceitfulness is useless" (v. 118, NASB) means that the thoughts and plans of the wicked are based on lies, but they are only deceiving themselves because their plans will fail.

God alone should be feared (v. 120). On the fear of God, see the comments on verse 63. The fear of the Lord is the fear that conquers every fear. "The Lord is my helper; I will not fear. What can man do to me?" (Heb. 13:6, NKJV; Ps. 118:6). The psalmist did not approach God as a criminal about to be slain but as a son showing loving respect to the father. God honors those who fear Him (15:4) and blesses them (115:13). If we fear the Lord, we depart from evil (v. 115; Prov. 3:7). This takes us back to verse 113: if we are single-minded, we will fear only the Lord and trust Him. "[T]he battle is not yours, but God's" (2 Chron. 20:15).

Ayin (vv. 121-128)—Blessed Assurance

For the first time, the word "oppressors" and "oppress" appear in this psalm (vv. 121-122, and see 134). The word describes the abuse of power and authority, taking advantage of the underprivileged by either violence or deceit. The word includes the ideas of accusation and slander. The Jews were commanded not to oppress one another (Lev. 25:14, 17; Deut. 24:5-22), and this included the strangers in the land (Ex. 22:2; 23:9). Often, God's people suffer oppression while the guilty go free. When that happens, we need to remember the Lord and what He does for us.

The Lord is the Rewarder (v. 121). The psalmist was not boasting but affirming to the Lord that he was not guilty of anything that deserved punishment. He was a man of integrity who had a clear conscience; he had treated others justly and had practiced God's holy laws diligently. That in itself was a blessing, but God's people long to see justice reigning on the earth. When God rewards His people, it is a witness to sinners that their day of judgment is certain (58:10-11). "Therefore do not cast away your confidence, which has great reward" (Heb. 10:35, NKJV; Isa. 40:10; Rev. 22:12).

The Lord is our Surety (v. 122). The *King James Version* and *New American Standard Bible* are superior here to "ensure" in the *New International Version*. A person became surety when he or she pledged to pay another person's debt or fulfill a promise. When Jacob refused to allow Benjamin to go to Egypt for food with his brothers, it was Judah who willingly became surety for his youngest brother (Gen. 43:1-10; 44:18-34). Judah's passionate speech before his brother in Egypt assured Joseph that Judah had truly experienced a change of heart and that it was safe to reveal his identity to the men. To become surety for a friend's debts is forbidden in Scripture, lest you end up with a burden greater than you can handle (Prov. 11:15; 17:18; 22:26-27). But the Son of God became surety for those who have trusted Him! (Heb. 7:22). No matter how many promises we might make to the Lord, we can never fulfill them. But in His death on the cross, Jesus has paid the debt for us, and in His ministry of intercession at the throne in heaven, He is our living Surety. As long as He lives, our salvation is secure, and He lives "by the power of an endless life" (Heb. 7:16). So, no matter what people do to us and no matter how we feel, our Surety is secure and we remain in the family of God. Jesus has taken the responsibility for our salvation, and He will never fail.

The Lord is our Master (vv. 123-125). Whenever people attack us, they also attack the Lord, for we belong to Him. When Saul of Tarsus persecuted Christians on earth, He also persecuted their Lord in heaven (Acts 9:1-5). God cares for His servants. He does not always prevent us from being oppressed, but He always has a good reason for permitting it to happen. He is a loving Master who teaches us His will and gives us the discernment we need to handle the problems of life. Even more, He gives us promises that we can claim and thereby find the strength and wisdom we need. God's servants do not live by explanations; they live by promises.

The Lord is the Final Judge (vv. 126-128). In our impatience, we sometimes want God to work immediately and set everything right, but His ways and times are not always the same as ours. Faith and patience go together (Heb. 6:12), and God's delays are not God's denials. The day will come when the truth will be revealed and sin will be judged; meanwhile, instead of complaining about what we have paid or lost, let us rejoice in the wealth that we have in God's Word, wealth that can never be taken from us. All of God's precepts concerning all things are always right, so we can depend on the Scriptures and have the guidance that we need. If we love the Word, we will hate the wrong paths of sinners and stay away from them. We do not even put *one foot* on the path of the wicked! (Prov. 1:13).

Pe (vv. 129-136)—A Chain Reaction

This section begins with the wonder of God's Word and ends with the weeping of the writer because the arrogant disobey the Word. Just as love and hate (vv. 127-128) and joy and affliction can exist in the same heart (vv. 111, 107), so can awe and anguish. In fact, when we begin to see the beauty and wonder of the Scriptures, we also begin to understand the ugliness of sin and the cheapness of what the world has to offer. This section describes a "spiritual chain reaction" in the life of the psalmist, one that can occur in our lives if we ponder the wonder of God's Word.

Wonder leads to obedience (v. 129). People obey God's Word for different reasons, some because of fear of punishment, others to secure blessings, and still others because they love God and want to please Him. The psalmist stood in awe at the wonder of God's Word—its harmony, beauty, perfection, practicality, power, and revelations. The longer I read and study the Bible, the more wonderful it becomes, and a God who wrote a book that wonderful deserves my obedience. To obey the Word is to become part of that wonder, to experience power and spiritual transformation in our lives.

Obedience leads to understanding (v. 130). The light of the Word comes into our hearts and minds and brings spiritual insight and understanding (2 Cor. 4:1-6). The word "entrance" (KJV) is translated "unfolding" in the *New American Standard Bible* and the *New International Version*; it means "disclosure" and "opening up" as in Luke 24:32 and 35. When Spirit-led teachers and preachers "open up" the Word, then the light of God's truth shines forth and brings about spiritual transformation (v. 135; 2 Cor. 3:18).

Understanding leads to deeper desire (v. 131). As a suffocating person pants for air or a thirsty person for water, so the child of God pants for the Word of God, and nothing else will satisfy. "I have treasured the words of His mouth more than my necessary food" (Job 23:12, NASB). When we lose our desire for God's Word, then we are vulnerable to the substitutes the world has to offer (Isa. 55:1-2).

Desire leads to love for God (v. 132). Just as children long to share the love of their parents, so the child of God experiences God's love through the Word (John 14:21-24). To love God's name is to love God, for His name reveals all that He is. The psalmist is here claiming the covenant promises that the Lord gave to the nation of Israel (69:36). Had Israel loved the Lord and kept the terms of the covenant, God would have blessed them and exhibited to them His power and mercy.

God's love leads to guidance and freedom (vv. 133-134). When we experience the love of God in our hearts, we keep His commandments (John 14:15), and obedience to His commandments sets us free from the slavery of sin (Rom. 6). The word "dominion" means "autocratic rule," but sin is not supposed to have dominion over us (Rom. 6:12-16). But there is more: we

are also set free from the oppression of people and the enslavement it can bring (v. 134). When you are the servant of Jesus Christ, you are free from slavery to people. "You were bought with a price; do not become slaves of men" (1 Cor. 7:23, NASB).

Freedom in Christ brings us God's blessing (vv. 135-136). When God hides His face from His people, He is disciplining them (13:1; 80:3-7), but the shining of His face upon them is a sign of His blessing (4:6; 67:1; Num. 6:25). To seek His face is to seek His blessing (v. 58). As we walk with the Lord in freedom, we walk in the light and have nothing to hide. But enjoying His freedom and blessing does not eliminate the burden we carry because of the wickedness in the world (v. 136). A broken heart and a blessed heart can exist in the same person at the same time. Jeremiah wept over the sins of a nation about to be destroyed (Jer. 9:1, 18; 13:17; Lam. 1:16), and Jesus wept over Jerusalem because they had rejected Him (Luke 19:41-44). The apostle Paul wept over lost souls (Rom. 9:1-3) as well as over professed believers in the church who were living for the world and the flesh (Phil. 3:17-21). If our enjoyment of God's Word and God's gracious blessings has truly reached our hearts, then we ought to have a burden for the lost and want to try to reach them for Christ.

Tsadhe (vv. 137-144)—In God We Trust

The Spirit of God uses the Word of God to implant faith in our hearts (Rom. 10:17), and the more we live in God's Word, the stronger our faith will become. Some people have no faith (Mark 4:40), others have little faith (Matt. 8:26; 14:31), and a few have great faith (Matt. 8:10; 15:28). Like a mustard seed, faith has life in it, and if the seed is planted and cultivated, it will grow and bear fruit (Matt. 17:20). The message in this section of the psalm is that you can depend on the Word of God, so—have faith!

God's Word is trustworthy no matter what people do (vv. 137-139). The psalmist had worn himself out trying to convince people to trust God's Word (see 69:9; John 2:12), but they ignored both him and the Scriptures. He must have felt that his ministry had failed, but he had been faithful even as the Word is faithful. God and His Word are righteous and what He says is right. His Word is fully trustworthy. Though intellectual giants may attack it and even ridicule it, the Word stands and will be here long after they are dead and their books have been forgotten. People may sin and die, but God's righteousness and righteous Word remains (vv. 137, 138, 142, 144).

God's Word is trustworthy no matter what people say (vv. 140-141). Over many centuries, the Scriptures have been thoroughly tested in the fires of persecution and criticism, the way a goldsmith tests precious metals (12:6-7; 18:30), and the Word has been found pure. One of the joys of the Christian life is to find new promises in the Word, test them in daily life, and find them trustworthy. The enemy wants to forget the Word (v. 139), but we remember the Word and depend on it. The world may look upon God's people as "small and despised," but when you stand on God's promises, you are a giant.

God's Word is trustworthy regardless of how you feel (vv. 142-143). You may experience trouble and distress, as did the psalmist, and still find delight in God's truth. Our feelings change but God's Word never changes. God's Word is not only true, but it is truth (v. 142, NASB; John 17:17). The Word of God is truth, the Son of God is truth (John 14:6), and the Spirit

of God is truth (1 John 5:6). The Spirit of truth wrote the Word of truth, and that Word reveals the Son of God. When your feelings deceive you into concluding that it is not worth it to serve the Lord, immediately turn to the Scriptures and delight in your Lord.

God's Word is trustworthy no matter how long you live (v. 144). When we read the Word to ourselves, we see words in ink on paper. When we read the Word aloud, we hear puffs of sound that quickly disappear. Paper and ink and puffs of sound may not seem very lasting, but the Word of God is eternal and fixed forever (vv. 89, 160). To build your life on God's Word means to participate in eternity (Matt. 7:24-29; 1 John 2:17). It is not the length of life but the depth of life that counts, and depth comes from laying hold of God's Word and obeying it. Jesus spent only thirty-three years on this earth, and His public ministry lasted only three years, yet He accomplished a work that is eternal.

Qoph (vv. 145-152)—A Primer on Prayer

The writer prayed throughout this entire psalm, but in these verses he concentrated on prayer and cried out to God day and night. From his experience, we receive some basic instructions about successful prayer.

Pray wholeheartedly (vv. 145-146). We must seek God with our whole heart (vv. 2, 10, 58) and obey Him with our whole heart (vv. 34, 69). "In prayer, it is better to have a heart without words than words without a heart" (John Bunyan). In the Old Testament sanctuary, the golden altar of incense represented intercessory prayer (Ex. 30:1-10). The special incense was burned on the altar, and the fragrant smoke rising heavenward pictured prayer going up to the Lord (141:1-2; Rev.

8:3-4). The devotion of the heart is what "ignites" our prayers and enables us to present our requests to the Lord. The phrase "and I will keep" may be translated "that I may keep." The psalmist was not bargaining with God ("Answer my prayers and I will obey you") but dedicating himself to God to obey Him no matter how He answers his prayers. Before we can pray as we ought, we must pray for ourselves that God will give us a heart ignited by the fire of the Spirit.

Pray without ceasing according to the Word (vv. 147-148). Two important elements of successful prayer are involved here. The first is that we constantly cultivate an attitude of prayer and remain in communion with the Lord. At morning and during the watches of the night (sunset to 10 P.M., 10-2, 2 until dawn), the psalmist prayed to the Lord. Jesus called this "abiding" (John 15:1-11). To "pray without ceasing" (1 Thess. 5:17) does not mean to walk around muttering prayers. It means to "keep the receiver off the hook" so that nothing comes between the Father and us.

The second element in successful prayer is the Word of God, for apart from God's Word, we cannot know God's will. Each verse in this section mentions the Scriptures and the writer's devotion to God's Word. We must balance the Word and prayer in our devotional life and ministry, for all Bible and no prayer means light without heat, but all prayer and no Bible could result in zeal without knowledge. Samuel emphasized both the Word and prayer in 1 Samuel 12:23 and so did Jesus in John 15:7. The spiritual leaders in the early church gave themselves to prayer and the Word (Acts 6:4). When we meditate on the Word, the Father speaks to us, and when we pray, we speak to the Father. We need both instruction and intercession if we are to be balanced children of God.

Pray as an act of love (v. 149). This verse combines both love and law, for if we love the Lord, we will keep His commandments. Too often we think of prayer as an emergency measure, rushing into God's presence and crying for help. But what would you think of children who spoke to their parents only when they needed something? Prayer is more than asking; prayer is loving. If we love the Word of God, we must also love the God of the Word and express that love to Him. To tell Him we love Him only because we want to receive something is to practice prayer on a juvenile level. When we share our love with the Lord, we receive new life from Him.

Pray with your eyes open (vv. 150-152). As he prayed, the psalmist saw his enemies drawing near, so he asked for God to draw near to help him. The familiar phrase "watch and pray" goes back to when Nehemiah was leading the people in rebuilding the walls of Jerusalem and restoring the gates. The enemy did not want the holy city to be rebuilt, so they used fear, deceit, and every kind of ruse to hinder the work. What was Nehemiah's defense? "Nevertheless we made our prayer to our God, and because of them [the enemy] we set a watch against them day and night" (Neh. 4:9, NKJV). Jesus (Matt. 26:41; Mark 13:33), Paul (Col. 4:2), and Peter (1 Peter 4:7) commanded God's people to "watch and pray," to be on guard and pray with intelligence and alertness. We are soldiers in a battle and we dare not go to sleep while on duty.

Resh (vv. 153-160)—Strength for the Journey
Have you noticed that the writer became more urgent as he drew near the end of

the psalm? The Hebrew alphabet was about to end, but his trials would continue, and he needed the help of the Lord. The last three stanzas all speak of persecution and trials, yet the writer still trusted the Lord. The Christian life is like the land of Canaan, "a land of hills and valleys" (Deut. 11:11), and we cannot have mountaintops without also having valleys. The key phrase in this stanza is "revive me" (vv. 154, 156, 159), which means "give me life, lift me up and keep me going." He had prayed this prayer before (vv. 25, 37, 40, 88, 107, and 149), and the Lord had answered. The psalmist not only prayed but also gave reasons why the Lord should answer.

Revive me, for you are my Redeemer (vv. 153-155). "Look upon [consider] my affliction" is a request for the Lord to "see to" his needs. Abraham used this word when he answered his son's question in Genesis 22:8—"The Lord will see to it," in other words, provide the sacrifice. Our wonderful Lord not only "sees" the need but can "see to" providing what is needed. "The eyes of the Lord are on the righteous, and His ears are open to their cry" (34:15; 1 Peter 3:12). The word "redeem" speaks of the kinsman redeemer who could rescue a family member in need, as Boaz rescued Ruth. (See Lev. 25:23-34.) In His incarnation, Jesus entered the human family and became our kinsman, and in the crucifixion, He paid the price to redeem us from sin, death, and hell. "Plead [defend] my cause" ties in with Jesus as our Kinsman Redeemer and also as our Surety (v. 122), Mediator, and Advocate, who represents us before the throne of God (1 John 2:1-2). In our affliction, it is comforting to know that the Son of God intercedes for us, hears our prayers, and meets our needs.

Revive me, for you are merciful (vv. 156-158). If we prayed on the basis of our own merit, God could never answer, but we come to the Father in the name of the Son (John 14:14; 15:16) and with the help of the Spirit (Eph. 2:18; Rom. 8:26-27). God in His grace gives us what we do not deserve, and in His mercy He does not give us what we do deserve. His throne is a throne of grace where grace and mercy are abundantly available to us (Heb. 4:16). The psalmist was still disgusted with the way the unbelievers lived (v. 158; see 53, 136), but their bad example did not change his own convictions.

Revive me, for your Word can be trusted (vv. 159-160). "The sum of your word is truth" (v. 160, NASB) and this means all of it can be trusted. The totality of God's written revelation is not just true—it is truth. To love the Word is to obey it, and to obey it is to receive life from it. The Bible is not a magic book that conveys divine life to anyone who picks it up and reads it. God's living Word communicates His life and power to those who read it, meditate on it, and obey it because they love God and His Word. When Jesus raised the dead, it was through speaking the Word (Luke 7:11-17; 8:40-56; John 11:38-44; see John 5:24), and His Word gives us life today when we find ourselves in the dust (v. 25).

Shin (vv. 161-168)—Blessed Are the Balanced

During our time of study in Psalm 119, we have noticed that the writer practiced a balanced life of faith, and this quality is seen especially in this stanza.

Respect and rejoicing (vv. 161-162). The princes began their campaign against him by speaking against him (v. 23), but now they were persecuting him in a direct way. But the psalmist was not afraid of his persecutors; he stood in awe of God's Word. Once again we learn that when we fear God, we need not fear anyone else. He respected the Word and rejoiced in the Word at the same time, for the joy of the Lord and the greatness of the Lord are friends, not enemies. The princes wanted to rob him, but he found great wealth in the Word of God (see vv. 14, 72). The promises of God in the Bible are better than money in the bank, because they will never lose their value, and nobody can take them from us.

Love and hate (v. 163). "You who love the Lord, hate evil" (97:10). He loved God's law but hated every false way (vv. 97, 104, 127-128). He loved God's law but hated double-minded people (v. 113). Here he declared that he loved God's law but hated falsehood. Whoever loves and practices a lie will not enter the heavenly city and will be banished from God's presence forever (Rev. 21:17; 22:15).

Praise and poise (vv. 164-165). The devoted Jewish worshiper would praise God and pray three times a day (55:17; Dan. 6:10-11), but the psalmist went beyond that and worshiped seven times a day. The phrase means "often, many times, beyond what is expected." The legalist would set a goal and be proud that he reached it; the Spirit-filled believer sets no goal but goes beyond any goal he might have set. Just as prayer can bring peace to our hearts (Phil. 4:4-7), so praise can bring peace as well. Focusing on the Lord, asking for nothing, and totally lost in our praise of Him, has a way of making the problems look much smaller and the future much brighter. But praise also helps us to have poise in our Christian walk and to not stumble (Jude 24) or cause others to stumble (1 Cor. 8:13; Rom. 14:13). The singing saint is a stable saint, walking on a level path even when the enemy digs pits and sets up obstacles.

Walking and waiting (vv. 166-168). Like the psalmist, we are waiting for "the salvation of the Lord," when the Lord shall come and set His creation and His people free (Rom. 8:18-25; 13:11; Heb. 9:28; 1 Peter 1:9). This is the "blessed hope" that every believer anticipates and longs for (Titus 2:13). But as we wait and hope, we must walk and work, for we want to be found faithful when Jesus comes (Matt. 24:45-51). When we love His Word, we will also love His appearing (2 Tim. 4:6-8) and live like those who are ready to meet their Lord (1 John 2:28).

Tav (vv. 169-176)—Hear My Prayer!

Except for 174, each of the verses is a prayer to the Lord, and the focus is on His wonderful ability to meet our needs as we trust Him. The word "your" ["Thy"] is often repeated and helps us understand the requests the psalmist was making.

I need your Word (vv. 169-72). We never outgrow our need for God's Word, no matter how long we have been walking with Him. There is always something new to learn and we often see new applications of old truths. Believers who boast that they "know the Bible from cover to cover" are only revealing how little they know about God's Word, for we shall spend eternity learning from His Word. The psalmist asked for understanding and deliverance, for he knew that the truth would set him free (John 8:32). After learning the statutes of God, he began to praise the Lord, for study and worship belong together. After Paul discussed the wonderful decrees of the Lord (Rom. 9-11), he broke out in worship and praise (Rom. 11:33-36).

I need your hand (v. 173). We all know that "God is spirit" (John 4:24) and therefore does not have a body with hands, feet, and so forth. In order to reveal Himself to us, He uses the familiar to explain the unfamiliar, and therefore the Bible describes Him in human terms. The hand of the Lord is mentioned only here in the psalm, but it is found many times in the book of Psalms. The idols of the heathen have hands that do not move or feel (115:7), but God's hand is active on the behalf of His people. We are the sheep of His hand (95:7), an image that Jesus used in John 10:28-29.

I need your salvation (v. 174). In his case, "salvation" meant deliverance from his enemies who were threatening him, but "salvation" can mean freedom from worry, the healing of a sickness, the provision of funds to pay a bill, or deliverance from Satanic oppression. As we saw in verse 166, our ultimate salvation is the return of Jesus Christ to deliver all creation from the bondage of sin.

I need your help (v. 175). The writer prayed "Help me!" in verse 86, but God's people are always crying for help. "My heart trusted in Him, and I am helped" (28:7, NKJV). God's hand can help us (v. 173), but so can God's judgments. "Judgments" is a synonym for the Word of God, but it can also refer to the working of God's providence in this world (105:7; Rom. 11:33). Of course, the two go together, because God always obeys His own Word when He works in this world. God helps us as He arranges the affairs of this world and of our lives, for there are no accidents in the life of the believer—only appointments. Our Father watches over us and accomplishes His will (23:3; John 10:4; Rom. 8:28).

I am your servant (v. 176). He did not say that he had greatly sinned against the Lord or that he was rebelling against God's will. At this point, he felt his own weakness and ignorance and expressed it in terms that were meaningful to him. In verse 110 he affirmed that he had not strayed away, but now he realized the danger of feeling overconfident (1 Cor. 10:12). During the spiritual journey recorded in this psalm, the psalmist had experienced his ups and downs, but he had always stayed himself on the Word of God, and he did this to the very end. He opened the psalm with a benediction (v. 1), but he closed it with a warning, and both are important to the balanced Christian life. God gives us promises and assurances so we will not despair, but He gives us warnings that we might not presume. He was still the servant of God and not the servant of sin, and he still remembered God's Word, so he would not stray for long. The Good Shepherd would find him and lead him back to the fold. He would anoint his wounds with healing oil and give him a long refreshing drink of water (23:5).

The Pilgrim Psalms (Pss. 120-134)

Each of these fifteen psalms is called "A Song of Degrees." The Hebrew word translated "degrees"[25] or "ascents" comes from a root that means "to go up," as ascending a stairway. Ten of the psalms are anonymous, four are attributed to David (122, 124, 131, 133) and one to Solomon (127). These psalms were selected to form a "hymnal" to be used by the people who went to Jerusalem for the three annual feasts (Ex. 23:14–19)—Passover in spring, Pentecost in early summer, and Tabernacles in the autumn. The pilgrims sang these songs together as they journeyed in family groups to Jerusalem (Luke 2:41-52), and this helped to focus their minds on what the Lord had done for their nation. The sanctuary is mentioned in 122:1 and 9; 132:7-8; and 134:1-2, and Mount Zion and Jerusalem are mentioned in 122:2-3, 6; 125:1-2; 126:1; 128:5; 129:5;

132:13; 133:3; and 134:3. Three special themes are repeated: (1) the afflictions that Israel experienced at the hands of the other nations, (2) the gracious way God cared for and protected His chosen people, and (3) the blessing of being in Jerusalem. Israel had suffered contempt and scorn (123:3-4), near extinction (124:1-5; 130:1), traps (124:6-7), bondage (126:1, 4), and affliction (129:1-3), yet she is still here!

Under the leadership of Moses, the Israelites were a nomadic people for forty years. But after they settled in Canaan, the Lord required them to go to Jerusalem three times a year. This reminded them that, spiritually speaking, they were still a pilgrim people and needed to depend on the Lord. "For we are aliens and pilgrims before you," said David (1 Chron. 29:15; and see Pss. 84:5-7 and 119:19 and 54.) Too many believers today want to be "settlers," not pilgrims and strangers (Heb. 11:8-10, 13-16; 1 Peter 1:1; 2:11). We are happy to settle down in our comfort zones and live as though Jesus never died, Jesus is not coming again, and our lives will never end. We are guilty of what Eugene Peterson calls "the tourist mindset," content to make occasional brief visits with the Lord that are leisurely and entertaining, all the while conforming to this world and enjoying it. (See *A Long Obedience in the Same Direction*, IVP, p. 12.) Our citizenship is in heaven (Luke 10:20; Phil. 3:20; Heb. 12:22-24), and that should make a difference in our lives on earth. We need to "feel temporary" as we make this pilgrim journey called life.

Psalm 120

The psalm begins with distress (v. 1), concludes with war (v. 7), and in between deals with deception and slander. It hardly seems a fit hymn for a group of pilgrims to sing as they made their way to the sanctuary of God. However, it appears that the author of this psalm was in the same situation as the writer of Psalm 42: circumstances prevented him from attending the feast, so he had to stay home among people who made life difficult for him (see 42:3, 9-10). The singing of this psalm would remind the pilgrims that they were indeed privileged to be able to go to Jerusalem and that others would have liked to go with them. It also reminded the travelers that when they returned home, they needed to carry some of the blessing to those who stayed behind and to help make life easier for them. The psalm reminds believers today that worship is a privilege and the blessings we receive must be shared. When we find ourselves experiencing distress and disappointment, we have three responsibilities to fulfill if our burdens are to become blessings.

We Must Pray (vv. 1-2)

The opening phrase can be translated "I cried" or "I cry," because the past and the present are combined in the tense of the verb. (Compare NASB and NIV.)The writer had prayed in a previous time of trouble, and the Lord had answered him, so now he had confidence to pray again. Instead of complaining about his situation, he shared it with the Lord and, in this psalm, shared it with us. His problem was that people were lying about him and slandering his name. (See 5:9, 12:1-8; 26:24; 31:18; 52:3ff; Prov. 10:18 and 26:24.) It's possible that he was involved in some kind of litigation and the opposition had bribed false witnesses to testify against him. He did not dare go to Jerusalem for fear his enemies would take advantage of his absence and do even more damage.

We Must Trust God (vv. 3-4)

It is not likely that the psalmist was actually addressing his enemies, but this is the message God gave him in answer to his prayers. The writer did not need to attack the enemy, because the Lord would do it for him. *Arrows* and *fire* are images of their evil lying words, images that occur frequently in Scripture (55:21; 57:4; 59:7; 64:3-4; Prov. 16:27; 25:18; 26:18-19; Jer. 9:3, 8; James 3:6). The writer was confident that God would punish the enemy with their own weapons, but the consequences would be far worse. The arrows would be sharpened and shot at them by a mighty warrior, probably a reference to the Lord God Himself (24:8; Isa. 9:6, "Mighty God"). The broom tree is a desert shrub that affords shade (1 Kings 19:4), and its roots can be made into excellent charcoal. There is so much godless speech in our world today that believers must be careful what they hear and how it affects them. We must not only turn away our eyes from beholding vanity (119:37) but also turn away our ears from hearing foolishness. "Take heed what you hear" (Mark 4:24). When we are slandered and lied about, we must leave the matter with the Lord and trust Him to work.

We Must Patiently Endure (vv. 5-7)

In the ancient Near East, Meshech was located in Asia Minor, to the northwest of Israel, and Kedar was a nomadic nation in northern Arabia, southeast of Israel. Meshach was a Gentile nation (Gen. 10:2) and the people of Kedar were descended from Ishmael, Abraham's son by Hagar (Gen. 16; 25:13, 18). Both peoples were at great distance from Israel and were considered enemies of the Jews. The writer was not actually dwelling with these people, because he could not live in two places at once, especially places thousands of miles apart. Rather, he was dwelling with Jewish people *who were behaving like people who lived outside the covenant blessings of God.* Any Jew who feared God and respected the Ten Commandments would not bear false witness against another Jew or seek to slander his or her name. It would be difficult to dwell with these foreign peoples, but it would be even more difficult to dwell with Jewish people who acted like foreigners.

Believers today must not only live with unbelievers but also with professed believers who live like unbelievers. Paul sometimes shamed the believers to whom he wrote by comparing them to the Gentiles, meaning "the outsiders, the unsaved" (1 Cor. 5:1, 12-13; Eph. 4:17; Col. 4:5; 1 Thess. 4:12; 1 Tim. 3:7). The psalmist was a peacemaker and tried to encourage his godless Jewish neighbors to be peaceable, but they were more intent on making war. His loving words only made them more and more angry. After over fifty years of ministry, I am convinced that most of the problems in families and churches are caused by professed Christians who do not have a real and vital relationship to Jesus Christ. They are not humble peacemakers but arrogant troublemakers. Until God changes them or they decide to go elsewhere, the dedicated believers must be patient and prayerful. This is the way Joseph dealt with his brothers in Canaan and his false accusers in Egypt. It is also the way David dealt with King Saul and Jesus dealt with His enemies (1 Peter 2:18-25).

Psalm 121

This may have been used as an antiphonal psalm that the pilgrims sang as they journeyed to Jerusalem to celebrate a feast. The leader of the company opened with verses 1-2, which are in the first person, and different people or groups answered him with verses 3-4 and so on, which are in the second person. The theme is God's protection over His people; the word "keeps" (watches over) is used six times. Safety is something about which the pilgrims would be especially concerned as they journeyed on the roads through the hill country. A pilgrim could stumble and hurt himself, or someone might suffer sunstroke, or a chilly night of camping out might give somebody a bad cold. There was always the possibility of robbers swooping down. But the message of the psalm applies to God's pilgrims today and gives us the assurances we need as we journey in this life.

"My Father's Creation Is Before Me" (vv. 1-2)

The opening line can be translated "I lift up my eyes" (NIV) instead of "I will lift" (KJV, NASB). If Jehovah created the heavens and the earth, then He is a God of power, wisdom, and glory, and we have nothing to fear. Satan and his demonic army may be at work opposing the saints, but this is still our Father's world. The apostate Jews worshiped other gods at the shrines ("high places") in the hills (2 Kings 16:4; Jer. 3:23; 13:27; 17:2; Hos. 4:11-13), but the faithful people of God looked above the hills to the great God who created all things. When the travelers caught sight of Jerusalem, situated on the mountains (87:1; 125:1-2; 133:3), they knew that God dwelt there in His sanctuary and provided the help they needed (3:4; 20:2; 46:1; 124:8; 134:3; 1 Kings 8:29-53). Everything in the heavens and on the earth bears witness to the great Creator who is also our heavenly Father, so why

should we fear? (See 33:3; 89:11-13; 96:4-5; 104:2-9; 115:15; 124:8; 134:3; 136:4-9.)

"My Father's Eyes Are upon Me" (vv. 3-4)

The word translated "moved" means "to slip and slide, to stagger, to be shaken." How easy it would be to sprain an ankle or even fall and break a bone while walking on uneven rocky paths. The Lord is concerned about our feet and our walk. (See 31:8; 56:13; 66:9; 125:1; 1 Sam. 2:9; Prov. 2:8; 3:21, 23, 25-26.) "Keep" means "to guard and protect" and is used six times in the psalm (vv. 3, 4, 5, 7 [two times] and 8). It is first used in the Bible in Genesis 2:15 where the Lord put Adam in the garden "to keep it." This means to guard and protect it and take good care of it. Even while we sleep, God watches over us because He does not go to sleep. (See 1 Kings 18:41.) The Lord promised to keep Jacob, who became the father of the twelve tribes of Israel (Gen. 28:15; 48:15-16), and He protects Jacob's descendants as well (Deut. 32:10). "The eyes of the Lord are on the righteous, and His ears are open to their cry" (34:15, NKJV; 1 Peter 3:12). "I will instruct you and teach you in the way which you should go; I will counsel you with my eye upon you" (Ps. 32:8, NASB).

"My Father's Presence Is Beside Me" (vv. 5-6)

Our Keeper is not only on the throne looking down on us, but He is at our side to shield us from all harm. This does not mean that obedient believers never find themselves in difficulty or danger, or that they will never feel physical and emotional pain. The things that God permits to happen to us in His will may hurt us *but they will not harm us.* David had many experiences that brought heartache and even threatened his life, but the Lord enabled him to turn those seeming tragedies into beautiful psalms that encourage us today. The Lord at our right hand provides the "shade" that we need (17:8; 36:7; 57:1; 63:7; 91:1; Isa. 25:4; 49:2; 51:16).

In writing about the sun and the moon, the psalmist was saying several things. To begin with, in that part of the world, the burning sun is menacing (2 Kings 4:18-19; Jonah 4:8), but at night, the sudden drop in temperature is both uncomfortable and unhealthy, if you lack warm covering. Day and night, our Father is with us to shelter us from that which could harm us. The Jewish people followed a lunar calendar (81:3), so the writer was also referring to days (the sun) and months (the moon). From day to day, from month to month, from season to season (Gen. 1:16-18), from year to year, our Father is with us in the many challenges and changes of life. The psalmist did not believe the superstition that the phases of the moon affected the minds and bodies of people. The English word "lunatic" comes from the Latin word *luna*, which means "moon"; and the word "epileptic" comes from a Greek word that means "moon-struck" (see Matt. 4:24 and 17:15). Whether by day or by night, in heat or cold, whatever the changes might be, the Father's presence provides all that we need. We need not be afraid of sudden attacks that can come in the day or the night, for "the shadow of the Almighty" covers us (see Ps. 91).

"My Father's Care Is Around Me" (vv. 7-8)

We need not fear life or death, today or tomorrow, time or eternity, for we are in the loving care of the Father. "All evil" means anything that could harm us, but in His grace, He turns into good the things we think are evil. Joseph had to endure the slander and hatred of his brothers, thirteen years of separation from his father, the false accusations of his employer's wife, and years in prison, all because of his brothers' sins. But in the end, Joseph was able to say, "[Y]ou meant evil against me; but God meant it for good" (Gen. 50:20, NKJV)—and Paul said the same thing in Romans 8:28!

The phrase "going out and coming in" refers to the daily activities of life (Deut. 28:6; 1 Sam. 29:6; 2 Sam. 3:25). Yes, the Father is concerned about our tasks and our schedules and even the so-called "minor details" that we too often take for granted. Orthodox Jews take Deuteronomy 6:9 and 11:20 literally and affix small metal boxes containing Scripture portions to the right-hand doorpost of the house, and they touch the box reverently each time they go in and out of the house. These boxes are called *mezuzas*; the word means "doorpost." Some Jewish people also attach *mezuzas* to the right-hand doorposts of individual rooms in the house. What a delight it is to know that, as we go in and out of the house, to and fro in the city, and even fly from city to city and country to country, the Father is with us and cares for our every need. "Casting all your care upon Him, for He cares for you" (1 Peter 5:7, NKJV). And His loving care will go on forever! (v. 8). "You will guide me with Your counsel, and afterward receive me to glory …. My flesh and my heart fail; but God is the strength of my heart and my portion forever" (73:23, 26, NKJV).

"Who can mind the journey when the road leads Home?"

Psalm 122

Three of the "Pilgrim Psalms" are assigned to David. This one focuses on

Jerusalem (vv. 2, 3, 6) and the house of God (vv. 1 and 9). Psalm 124 describes God's protection of Israel from her enemies, and 131 speaks of David's submission to the Lord. Some deny David's authorship of 122 and move the psalm to the times of Ezra and Nehemiah, but such a move seems contrary to what the psalm says. David's dynasty did not exist in the post-exilic days (v. 5), nor was Jerusalem the well-built city in post-exilic times that it was even during the reign of David (v. 3; 2 Sam. 5:9, 11). The phrase "house of God" was used for the tabernacle (1 Sam 1:7, 24; 2 Sam. 12:20), so it could certainly be used for the tent David pitched for the ark in Jerusalem (2 Sam. 6). The psalm speaks of a united people, which was true in David's time, but the kingdom was divided after Solomon's death (1 Kings 12:25-33) and the tribes were hardly a strong united nation during the post-exilic days. The fact that King Jeroboam set up his own religion after the kingdom divided is evidence that the tribes must have been going up to Jerusalem annually during the reigns of David and Solomon. In the days of the monarchy, the throne and the temple were separated, but today, the Lord Jesus Christ is both King and Priest (110; Heb. 7-9), and God's people are citizens of "Jerusalem which is above" (Gal. 4:25-26; Phil. 3:20; Heb. 12:22-29). One day there will be a new Jerusalem, a holy city prepared by God for His people (Rev. 3:12; 21:1-10).

Believers today need not make long pilgrimages to "holy places" in order to worship God, for the Lord does not dwell in man-made buildings (Acts 7:48-50). Nor do we need the kind of "religious entertainment" that draws people to some meetings. The key thing is the heart. From David's words in this psalm, we can easily discern the kind of heart believers need if we are to please God in our worship.

A Heart for God (vv. 1-2)
"Let us go" sounds tame, like an invitation to a tea. "We will go" is the better translation. Whether this was an invitation to someone living far from Jerusalem, or to David living in Jerusalem, the statement expressed determination and dedication. After the tent had been set up and the ark placed in it, no doubt David frequently went there to worship God, for David's love for God's house was well-known (27:4; 65:4; 2 Sam. 7:1-3). He rejoiced at an opportunity to go with other worshipers to praise the Lord. Nothing is said here about a pilgrimage, although this psalm is placed among the "Songs of Ascent." David lived in Jerusalem and had to go but a short distance to reach the tent and the ark. Though he lived in the holy city, David did not take this privilege for granted, for he had a heart for God and for God's house. David was a man after God's own heart (1 Sam. 13:14). The pilgrim coming from a distance would not complain about the journey, for his heart was set on the Lord. Love makes burdens lighter and distances shorter. Note that Jerusalem is mentioned not only in verses 2, 3, and 6, but also in 125:1; 126:1; 128:5; 129:5;, 132:13; and 133:3.

A Heart for Praise (vv. 3-5)
The Lord had told His people that one day there would be a central place where they would worship (Ex. 23:14-19; Deut. 12:5-7, 11-14, 17-19; 14:23; 16:2, 16), and that place was Jerusalem. The Lord instructed David that the place on Mount Moriah where he had built the altar was to be the site for the temple (1 Chron. 21-22), and He also gave David the plans for

the structure (1 Chron. 28). Jerusalem had been a Jebusite stronghold before David captured it and made it his capital city, "the city of David" (2 Sam. 5:6-10). His choice was a wise one, for not only was Mount Zion an almost impregnable citadel, but it was located on the border of Judah and Benjamin and helped to bind the northern and southern tribes together. King Saul was from Benjamin, and David was from Judah.

When the psalmist looked at the city, he thought of unity and security. Just as the stones of the walls and houses were "bound firmly together," so the people were bound together in their worship of the Lord and their respect for the throne. The twelve separate tribes, plus the tribe of Levi, shared the same ancestors and history, participated in the same worship in the same holy city, and were governed by the same divine laws. The church today already has spiritual unity (Eph. 4:1-6), but we must endeavor to maintain it and demonstrate it before a watching world (John 17:20-23). As for security, Jesus promised that the very forces of hell could not stand before the onward march of His church (Matt. 16:18).

But it was the praise of Jehovah that was central (v. 4). God had commanded that His people go to Jerusalem for the feasts of Passover, Pentecost, and Tabernacles (Ex. 23:14-19; John 4:20-21), and the people went as worshipers and not sightseers. Yes, there was much to see in Jerusalem, but giving thanks to the Lord was their most important task and their greatest privilege. At the same time, the people were giving allegiance to the dynasty of David, for the same Lord who assigned the feasts also established the throne. In Romans 13, Paul makes it clear that the Lord established the system of governmental authority that we have,

and we must respect the offices even if we cannot always respect the officers. Though there is a separation of church and state in modern democracies, there must never be a separation of God and country. Regardless of our political affiliation, our most important civic duty is to pray for those in authority (1 Tim. 2:1-6).

A Heart for Prayer (vv. 6-9)

The name "Jerusalem" means "foundation of peace," and yet the city has been a center of conflict for centuries. If we understand biblical prophecy correctly, there can be no peace in Jerusalem or on earth until the Prince of Peace reigns on David's throne (Isa. 9:6-7; Luke 1:26-33). So, when we pray for the peace of Jerusalem, we are actually praying, "Thy kingdom come" (Matt. 6:10) and "Even so, come, Lord Jesus" (Rev. 22:20). Jesus wept over the city because they were ignorant of the peace God had for them (Luke 19:41-48) and had rejected their own Messiah (John 11:47-48). But our intercession must not be perfunctory prayers; they must come from our heart because we love God and love His people. Note the fruit of the Spirit in this psalm: love (v. 6), joy (v. 1), and peace (vv. 6-8; Gal. 6:22).

The "prosperity" mentioned in verse 6 does not refer to material wealth but primarily to the spiritual enrichment that comes to those who love God, His Son (born a Jew), His Word (a Jewish book), and His chosen people. "Salvation is of the Jews" (John 4:22). To promise that all who pray for the peace of Jerusalem will become wealthy is to misunderstand the promise. Paul prayed for his people (Rom. 10:1) and yet was a poor man materially (2 Cor. 6:10). Christian believers have a debt to Israel for the untold spiritual wealth they have given us (Rom.

15:25-27). It is selfish to want personal prosperity when the emphasis here is on the city of God, the chosen people of God (vv. 6-8), and the house of God (v. 9). But there is an application to believers today, for we are God's people, citizens of the heavenly country, and we must pray for one another and for the ministry of the churches. We belong to each other, we need each other, and we must help each other. We must pray for peace within and among the churches. We must pray for the needs of "our brothers and friends," and surely we must pray for the lost.

A heart for God will surely be a heart filled with praise and prayer.

Psalm 123

It is not until we read verse 4 that we discover the burden of the writer: the constant persecution of the people of Israel, being treated with scorn and contempt. In Psalm 124, Israel was almost swallowed up, drowned, and imprisoned in a trap. Captivity is the theme of 126, and 129 compares their suffering to a farmer plowing their backs. Has any nation ever suffered the way Israel has suffered? Of course, God's people today are also suffering because of their commitment to Christ (John 16:30). According to missiologists, more Christians were martyred in the twentieth century than in all the previous centuries combined! Some students assign this psalm to the time of King Hezekiah, when the Assyrians were attacking Jerusalem and making humiliating speeches about the Jews (Isa. 36-37). But during the post-exilic years, Israel also suffered the ridicule and scorn of their Gentile neighbors (Neh. 2:19; 4:1-4, 7ff). This psalm speaks about the God who is enthroned in heaven whose hand

would work for His people, and you find both of these themes in Ezra and Nehemiah. The "hand of God" is found in Ezra 7:6, 9, 28; 8:18, 22, 31 and Nehemiah 2:8, 18. "The God of heaven" is mentioned in Ezra 1:2; 5:11-12; 6:9-10; 7:12, 21, 23 and Nehemiah 1:4; 2:4. The psalm begins in the first person singular (I, my), but then changes to the plural (we, our, us). Perhaps this was a communal prayer, begun by a priest or Levite (v. 1), continued by a choir (v. 2), and closed by the congregation (vv. 3-4).

When we find ourselves among the slandered, ridiculed, and persecuted, where do we turn for help? The psalm gives three answers to that question.

We Look by Faith to God's Throne (v. 1)

Of course, with our human eyes, we cannot see God on His throne, but with the eyes of faith we see Him as we believe the Word. "My eyes are toward the Lord" (25:15, NKJV). To look toward the Lord means to trust Him and turn our problems over to Him by faith. "Looking unto Jesus, the author and finisher of our faith" (Heb. 12:2, NKJV). God's throne is mentioned often in the book of Psalms (9:4, 7; 11:4; 45:6; 47:8; 93:2; 97:2; 103:9), and to believers today, His throne is a throne of grace (Heb. 4:14-16). The life of faith begins by looking to the Lord by faith and trusting Him for salvation (Isa. 45:22). The life of faith continues as we keep our eyes of faith on Jesus (Heb. 12:2), and it will climax with faith becoming sight and we'll see Jesus in His glory (1 John 3:1-2).

We Look by Faith to God's Hand (v. 2)

In eastern countries, masters often commanded their servants by means of hand signals, so the servants kept their eyes on the master's hand. This is what gave them direction for their work. But the master's hand was also the source of their provision, what they needed for their daily sustenance. Finally, the master's hand protected them in times of danger. The *New Jewish Publication Society* translation reads "they follow their master's hand." So it is with God's people today: our direction, provision, and protection all come from our Master's hand and His hand never fails. Even the heart of a king is in the hands of the Lord (Prov. 21:1), so God's feeble remnant in Jerusalem did not have to fear the nations around them.

We Look for God's Mercy and Grace (vv. 3-4)

The exiles from Israel had spent seventy years in Babylon. Most of the older ones died and at least two new generations were born. Now, about 50,000 of these people were trying to rebuild their temple, restore their city, and revitalize their nation. This was not an easy task, and the nations around them did not want Israel back on the scene again. The Persian rulers who had promised to help them did not always keep their promises, or the local Persian officers interfered with the announced plans. It was another evidence of the hatred the Gentiles had for the Jews. "We have endured much contempt" (v. 3). (See 31:11, 18; 44:13; 119:22, 141; Neh. 2:19; 4:1-4, 7ff; Lam. 3:15, 30.) But God chooses and uses the despised things of this world (1 Cor. 1:28). After all, our salvation was purchased by One who was "despised and rejected of men" (Isa. 53:3).

We are not only subjects of the King (v. 1) and servants of the Master (vv. 2-3), we are also the children of a gracious Father who hears the cries of His children and comes to their aid. He has grace and mercy for each situation. In those post-exilic times, God's chosen people were being maligned, ridiculed, and opposed, but God gave them the grace they needed to finish the temple and restore the worship. The enemy was smug and complacent, but God was not at work in their midst. The nation of Israel continued, and one very special day, the promised Messiah was born into the human race in the little town of Bethlehem. If you find yourself laughed at and criticized because you belong to Jesus Christ, you are part of a very elite group, *and you do not have to be embarrassed or start looking for a place to hide!* There is grace available at the throne of grace from the God of all grace, so lift your eyes of faith to Him.

Psalm 124

The contempt and ridicule of Psalm 123 has now been mixed with anger (v. 3) and become open hostility. When David began his reign in Jerusalem, the Philistines attacked him twice, and the Lord gave David great deliverance (2 Sam. 5:17-25). This psalm may have been his song of thanksgiving to the Lord. Note the "flood" image in 2 Samuel 5:10 and 124:4-5. However, when Nehemiah and the people were repairing the walls and gates of Jerusalem, the surrounding nations ridiculed them (Neh. 2:19-20; 4:1-5) and then threatened to attack them (Neh. 4:7-23). Nehemiah's words "Our God will fight for us" (Neh. 4:20) remind us of 124:1-2 and 8. We may not have entire nations and armies opposing us, but we do face emergencies that are more than we can handle. That is when we turn to the Lord for help, because He is on our side and helps us with these emergencies.

The Sudden Attack (vv. 1-2)

The phrase "rose up" gives the image of a sudden ambush, a sneak attack that might have defeated Israel, except the Lord was on their side. "If God is for us, who can be against us?" (Rom. 8:31, NKJV; Ps. 56:9; 118:6; Gen. 31:42). Our enemy Satan does not give advance warning of his attacks; therefore, we must be sober and vigilant (1 Peter 5:8), put on the whole armor of God (Eph. 6:10-18), and be alert in our praying. God promised His chosen people that He would curse those who cursed them (Gen. 12:3), and He has kept that promise. The invading armies, such as Assyria and Babylon, did not conquer the Jews because their armies were too great for God, but because God's people were great sinners and the Lord had to chasten them. If we are walking with the Lord, we need not feel unprepared for the enemy's sudden attacks.

The Deepening Flood (vv. 3-5)

Here is a situation where we stand helpless as the problem gets worse and worse. During the rainy season, and when the mountain snow melts, the dry riverbeds in Israel quickly become filled with water and flash floods threaten houses and people. Jeremiah compared the enemy invasions to sudden floods (Jer. 47:1-4), and Job 27:19-20 uses the same image on a personal level. (See also 18:4, 16; 32:6; 69:1-2, 15; 88:17.) This image of the persecution of the Jews is also seen in Revelation 12:13-17. The psalmist feared that the raging waters of persecution would sweep over him and his people and that they would be swallowed up forever. Jeremiah pictured the Babylonian captivity of Israel as Nebuchadnezzar swallowing the nation (Jer. 51:34, 44). But if the Lord is on our side, He will provide a way of escape.

The Menacing Beast (v. 6)

A sudden attack by a wild beast is a biblical picture of persecution (7:1-2; 10:8-11; 27:1-2; 57:4). There are twelve words in the Hebrew language for lions, which indicates that the Jewish people in that day took wild beasts seriously. Jeremiah compared Babylon to a lion (Jer. 4:7; 51:38), and Peter compared Satan to a prowling lion (1 Peter 5:8). Like a cunning animal, Satan stalks us and waits until we have relaxed our guard, and then he pounces. But the Lord is stronger than Satan, and if we are abiding in Him, we can win the victory.

The Hidden Trap (vv. 7-8)

We must use the Word of God to throw light on our path so we can detect and avoid the devil's traps (119:105; 91:1-3; 1 Tim. 3:7; 6:9; 2 Tim. 2:24-26). The picture is that of a helpless bird who walked into the trap in order to eat the food. Satan always has fascinating bait to offer. The Lord may allow us to fall into a trap, but nobody can keep us when He wants us to be free. The Lord not only opened the trap but broke it so it cannot be used again! The death and resurrection of Jesus Christ has broken the dominion of sin and death and we can walk in freedom through Jesus Christ.

Praise God, we are not helpless! "Our help is in the name of the Lord" (v. 8).

Psalm 125

Three kinds of people are mentioned in this psalm: those who trust in the Lord (v. 1), who are also called righteous and good (vv. 3-4); those who compromise with the enemy (v. 3); and those who deliberately go on the wrong path (v. 5). We could probably call them the faithful, the backslidden, and the apostate. This psalm was probably composed during the post-exilic period of Ezra and Nehemiah. Nehemiah mentions all sorts of people who made his work difficult for him, beginning with Shemiah, the "secret informer," and Noadiah, the hireling prophetess (Neh. 6:10-14). Eliashib was a compromising high priest (Neh. 13:4-9), and one of his grandsons married into the family of an enemy of the Jews (Neh. 13:28). There were also many unnamed Jewish men who entered into mixed marriages that were contrary to God's law (Neh. 13:1-9, 23-31; Ezra 9-10). Thank God for the faithful who believe God and obey His Word! The psalm names the benefits that faith and faithfulness bring to God's people.

Faith Keeps Us Standing (vv 1-2)
Spiritual security and stability belong to those who walk by faith. The city of Jerusalem was firmly established and could not be shaken. For one thing, it was built on a solid foundation of rock that went deep into the ground. The city was surrounded by a number of hills and probably two sets of walls. Even more, Jerusalem was home to the holy temple of Jehovah and the throne of David. God's glory and God's authority dwelt among His people.

The writer did not say that God's people *should be* like Mount Zion but that they *are* like Mount Zion. We are built upon the solid Rock, Jesus Christ (1 Cor. 3:11; 1 Peter 2:4-8). He dwells within us and He surrounds us with His protection and mercy. As people of faith, we shall not be moved (16:8; 21:7; 62:6). Like Paul, we say, "None of these things move me" (Acts 20:24). We have a marvelous standing, for we stand in God's grace (Rom. 5:2; Gal. 5:1), and we stand by faith (Rom. 11:20). We take our stand on the truths of the Word of God (2 Thess. 2:15) and stand in

the will of God (Col. 4:12). It is God who enables us to stand (2 Cor. 1:21, 24), and because He does, we are able to accomplish the work He wants us to do (1 Cor. 15:58). When we begin to trust ourselves or other people, and we bypass the Lord, then we begin to waver, stumble, and fall.

Faith Keeps Us Obeying (v. 3)
The land of Israel belongs to the Lord and He allowed His people to dwell there as long as they obeyed His covenant (Lev. 25:2, 23, 38). The land was assigned by lot to the various tribes (Josh. 14-19) and was never to be sold to anyone outside the tribe. But over the years, their sins defiled the land and the Lord finally had to send the people to Babylon to give the land the rest and cleansing it needed. While the people were away, some of the land was taken over by strangers, including Gentiles from neighboring nations, and this had to be straightened out when the exiles returned. Israel was under Persian rule during the post-exilic years, and the Persian officers could do as they pleased. Some of the Jews became weary of this arrangement and capitulated to the Persians. "If you cannot whip them, join them." But the "scepter of wickedness" was wielded not only by Persians but also by greedy Israelites who disobeyed God's law and exploited their own people (Neh. 5). The prevalence of evil makes it easier for everybody to sin (Matt. 24:12), but the Lord will not permit this to go on forever. The people who trust God will obey His Word no matter what others may do, and they will not succumb to temptation (1 Cor. 10:13).

Faith Keeps Us Praying (v. 4)
Jesus taught us to keep on praying and not become discouraged if the answer is long in coming (Luke 18:1-8). The times

may be bad, but there are always good people in bad times, people who trust God and obey His will. No matter how depressing the times may be, people of faith pray and receive good things from the hand of their Father (Luke 11:9-13). To live by faith is to keep our eyes on the Lord (123:1; Heb. 12:1-2), rest on the promises of His Word, and do what is right no matter what others may say or do. Faith means living without scheming.

Faith Keeps Us Hoping (v. 5)

People of faith know that God will one day judge the disobedient, no matter how much they seem to get away with resisting God and abusing others. The future is your friend when Jesus is your Lord. It is not easy to walk on the narrow way, but it leads to life, while the broad way leads to destruction (Matt. 7:13-27). They may be enjoying the pleasures of sin now, but what will the outcome be? "Mark the blameless man, and observe the upright; for the future of that man is peace. But the transgressors shall be destroyed together; the future of the wicked shall be cut off" (37:37-38, NKJV).

The life of faith is not easy, but the life of unbelief is much harder—in this life and in the life to come.

Psalm 126

Some students connect this psalm with the sudden deliverance of Jerusalem from the Assyrian siege during the reign of Hezekiah (Isa. 36-37). But the Hebrew verb translated "turned again" in v. 1 (KJV; "brought back," NASB, NIV) and "turn again" or "restore" in verse 4, is also used to describe the return of the Jewish exiles from Babylon (Ezra 2:1; Neh. 7:6; Isa. 10:22; Jer. 22:10). Cyrus

gave his decree in 537 B.C., an event prophesied by Isaiah (44:24-45:7). Isaiah also prophesied the joy of the people at their liberation (Isa. 48:20; 49:8-13; 51:11; 54:1; 55:10-12) and the witness of this remarkable event to the other nations (Isa. 43:10-21; 44:8, 23; 52:7-10). But once the exiles were back in their land, their joy began to subside, for life is not always easy when you are making a new beginning after a time of discipline. But life is so arranged that we must often make new beginnings, and the Lord helps us by giving us special encouragements.

Within Us, the Joy of Freedom (vv. 1-3)

The generation of Jews that conquered the Promised Land was true to the Lord, and so were their children, but the third generation broke the covenant and turned to idols (Judg. 2:7-23). God punished His people *in the land* by allowing seven nations to invade, rob, and destroy. When Israel's rebellion became so great that the land itself was being defiled, God took them *out of the land* and sent them to Babylon for seventy years. Now they had been set free and they could not believe what was happening. Yes, they knew that both Isaiah and Jeremiah had promised this "second exodus," but it was too good to be true. During long years of waiting, they had dreamed of returning home, and now the dream had become reality. God in His grace had forgiven them (Isa. 40:1-2; 44:21-22) and they could make a new beginning. The Jews had lost their song in Babylon (137:1-5), but now they were shouting, laughing, and singing! What a witness of God's faithfulness to keep His promises!

The surrounding nations, some of whom hated Israel, were utterly astonished at this event and openly confessed that the God of Israel had done great things for them. The Jews replied that indeed He had done great things for them, and they gave God the glory. "If you can explain what is going on, God did not do it" (Dr. Bob Cook). This confession of the greatness of God was made by others in Scripture: Moses (Deut. 10:21), Job (Job 5:8-9), Samuel (1 Sam. 12:24), David (2 Sam. 7:21-23), the prophet Joel (Joel 2:21), Mary (Luke 1:49), and the unnamed demoniac whom Jesus healed (Luke 8:39). This ought to be the confession of every Christian and of every local church.

Around Us, the Promise of Life (v. 4)

"Turn again our captivity" (KJV) can also be translated "restore our fortunes." The captivity had ended and the Jews were praying for the blessing of the Lord on their life in the land. However, not all the Jews had left Babylon, for while many came during the reign of Cyrus (Ezra 1-3), others followed during the reigns of Darius (Ezra 6) and Artaxerxes (Ezra 7-8). It was important that the people return to their land and get to work, but it was also important that God bless their work (127:1-2). If the Lord did not keep His covenant and send the early and latter rains (Lev. 26:4; Deut. 11:10-12; 28:12), there would be no crops and their labors would have been in vain. Each raindrop was but a tiny thing, but when dropped on the earth, it was the promise of life. How gracious of the Lord to send "showers of blessing" (Ezek. 34:26) to His people! How important it is that God's people pray for His blessing and prepare themselves to receive it (2 Chron. 7:14; Mal. 3:8-12). In Scripture, water for drinking is a picture of the Spirit of God and the refreshing life that He brings to those who seek Him (John 7:37-38).

Before Us, the Challenge of Work (vv. 5-6)

"Faith without works is dead" (James 2:26), so after we have praised God and prayed, we must get to work, for work is a blessing, not a curse. God gave our first parents work to do in the garden before sin ever entered the human race (Gen. 2:15). In Scripture, the people God commissioned for special service were busy when He called them: Moses was caring for sheep (Ex. 3); Gideon was threshing wheat (Judg. 6); David was tending the family flock (1 Sam. 16); Nehemiah was serving the king (Neh. 1); Peter, Andrew, James, and John were busy in their fishing business (Luke 5:1-11); and Matthew was in his tax office (Matt. 9:9).

The returned remnant experienced some bad seasons (Hag. 1:9-11), but the promise came that God would send the rains and the harvests (Hag. 2:15-19). God would keep His covenant promises if His people would keep His covenant commands. The grain that the farmer sowed might have been used to make bread for his family, so it is no wonder he was weeping as he toiled. Tears and rejoicing often went together at that time (Ezra 3:8-13; 6:16, 22), but the farmer was trusting God to multiply the grain so that he would have both bread for his family to eat and seed to sow the next season (2 Cor. 9:10-11). In His covenant, God gave the promise of adequate food for the people (Deut. 28:1-14), and the sower was claiming that promise. It pleases the Lord when we water with our tears the seed of the Word that we sow. We cannot reap if we do not first sow the seed, and the seed must be watered with our tears and our prayers.

Some blessings God sends suddenly (vv. 1-3), some come in the course of time (v. 4), and some come as we patiently sow and weep (James 5:7). But His promise is secure: "in due season we shall reap if we do not lose heart" (Gal. 6:9, NKJV).

Psalm 127

No amount of human sacrifice or toil can accomplish much unless God's blessing is upon His people. That is the major message of this psalm. It is assigned to Solomon, who was both a builder and a father, but the message also seems to fit the post-exilic times of Nehemiah. The population of Jerusalem was small and the people had to build and repair the buildings. Houses were desperately needed for families or else the struggling Jewish nation had no future (Neh. 7:4). Surrounded by numerous enemies, Jerusalem needed strong gates and walls and watchmen on the alert day and night (Neh. 4:9ff; 7:3). Note that the psalm deals with the same elements Jeremiah wrote about in his letter to the Jewish exiles (Jer. 29:4-7). But the psalm also speaks to us today and reminds us of some privileges we have as the people of God in a dangerous and demanding world.

Building (v. 1a)

A wrecking crew or a demolition team can destroy in a few hours or days what it took engineers and builders months to plan and construct. Even a weak little child can heedlessly destroy something valuable, and some adults go through life just tearing things down. God had called us to build—our lives, our homes, our churches, and the kingdom of God around the world. Before commencing His public ministry, Jesus was a carpenter (Mark 6:3), and He is currently building His church in this world (Matt. 16:18). The apostle Paul saw himself as a builder (Rom. 15:20, 17), and he warned that it is a dangerous thing to destroy the local church (1 Cor. 3:11-17). Whether we are building structures with bricks and mortar and steel, or building lives, families, and churches with truth and love, we cannot succeed without the help of the Lord. Jesus said, "Without Me you can do nothing" (John 15:5, NKJV).

Guarding (1b)

Strong walls around the city and alert watchmen on those walls are essential if we are to protect what we have built—and how foolish it is to build and not protect! Many a child and many a ministry has been lost to the enemy because the watchmen did not stay awake and warn that the enemy was approaching. Building and battling go together; this is why Nehemiah's men had their tools in one hand and their swords at their side (Neh. 4:17-18). Jesus joined the two in Luke 14:25-33. The famous British preacher Charles Haddon Spurgeon called his publication *The Sword and The Trowel* because its purpose was to build believers and the church and to fight sin and false doctrine. As he awaited execution in a Roman prison, Paul encouraged Timothy to preach the Word and to be "watchful in all things" (2 Tim. 4:1-5). If parents, teachers, and church leaders do not courageously maintain the walls and guard against the enemy, our building will be in vain.

Enjoying (v. 2)

If verse 1 warns against overconfidence ("We can do it without God's help!"), verse 2 warns against overwork and anxious toil ("I have to do it all right now!"). This verse does not say it is wrong for people to get up early, work hard, and make sacrifices (see 2 Thess. 3:6-15). It only warns us that our work must be a blessing we enjoy and not a burden we endure. Yes, both physical and mental toil are a part of this fallen world (Gen. 3:17), but doing God's will is nourishment, not punishment. Work suited to our gifts and personalities is food for our souls (John 4:34), but the anxious laborer eats "the bread of sorrows"—sorrow while working and sorrow while trying to rest at night as he worries about the next day. God gives us "richly all things to enjoy" (1 Tim. 6:17), and this includes earning our daily bread. Note in Ecclesiastes how much Solomon had to say about enjoying life and labor (2:24; 3:12-15, 22; 5:18-20; 8:15; 9:7-10; 11:9-10).

God's special name for Solomon was "Jedidiah—beloved" (2 Sam. 12:25). But *all* of God's people are "God's beloved" (Rom. 1:7; Col. 3:12; 1 Thess. 1:4; 2 Thess. 2:13) because they are accepted and blessed in the Beloved One, Jesus Christ (Eph. 1:6, NASB; Matt. 3:17; 17:5). The last line of verse 2 is translated and interpreted several different ways, but the thrust of it seems clear. We get tired *in* God's work but we do not get tired *of* God's work, because the Lord who gives us the strength to work also gives us the rest we need. "The sleep of a laboring man is sweet" (Eccl. 5:12). But even as we sleep, God works for us in different ways, for He never slumbers or sleeps (see Mark 4:26-29). As we go to bed at night, we may look back at the day and wish we had worked better and harder, accomplished more and had fewer interruptions, but we can commit the day's work to the Lord and not fret. After a hard day's ministry, Jesus was able to go to sleep in a boat on the sea in a terrible storm! (Matt. 8:23-27).

Conserving (vv. 3-5)

It does no good to build and guard our houses and cities if there are no future generations to inherit them and keep the family, city, and nation going. There were few people living in Jerusalem in the post-exilic age (Neh. 7:4), and it was important that the young people marry and have families. Among the Jews, it was unheard of that a husband and wife not want children or that a child be aborted. "Children are *the* blessing for the Jew," writes Rabbi Leo Trepp. "Each child brings a blessing all his own, our ancestors would say. We rejoice in children because we are a people, a historical people" (*The Complete Book of Jewish Observance*, p. 217). Children are precious—a heritage—and make the home a treasury. But they are also useful—like fruit and arrows—and make the home a garden and an armory. If we do not raise our children to know and love the truth, who will plant the seeds of truth and fight the battles against lies and evil in the years to come? (For other comparisons, see 128:3 and 144:12.) The city gate was the place where important legal business was transacted (Deut. 21:19; Ruth 4:1ff; Amos 5:12), and it was helpful to have a godly family to back you up. Also, the enemy would try to enter at the city gate, and the more sons to fight at your side, the better was the opportunity for victory. It is in the family that we preserve the best of the past and invest it in the future. Every baby born is God's vote for the future of humankind and our opportunity to help make some new beginnings.

Not everyone is supposed to get married, nor are all married couples able to have children. But all adults can value the children, pray for them, be good examples to them, and see that they are protected and cared for and encouraged in their spiritual upbringing. Remember what Jesus said about this in Matthew 18:5-6.

Psalm 128

Because families traveled together to the annual feasts in Jerusalem, it is only right that another psalm be devoted to parents and their offspring. The previous psalm pictured children as a rich heritage and as arrows for defeating the enemy (127:3-5). This psalm uses agricultural images for both the wife and the children. In one form or another, the word "bless" is used four times, but it is the translation of two different Hebrew words. In verses 1-2, it is the word *asher* which is often translated "happy" (Gen. 30:12-13), and in verses 4-5, it is *barak*, which means "blessed of the Lord." The latter word is used by the Lord when He blesses people; the former word is used to describe the good that comes when people do that which pleases the Lord. Like 127 and Jeremiah 29:4-7, this psalm deals with protection (v. 1), working (v. 2), the family (vv. 3-4, 6), and God's blessing on Jerusalem (v. 5). While the writer includes all who fear the Lord (v. 1), the psalm is addressed especially to the man of the house (v. 3). We see a happy man and woman as they go through several stages in life.

Godly Believers (v. 1)
In the ancient Near East, marriages were arranged primarily by the parents, but the stories of Jacob (Gen. 28-30) and Ruth indicates that love was not entirely lacking in these marriages. Here we have a Jewish couple who truly feared the Lord and wanted to establish a home that Jehovah could bless. To fear the Lord means to reverence Him and seek to please Him by obeying His Word. In the background is the covenant God made with Israel (Lev. 26; Deut. 38-30). If they obeyed, God would meet their needs; if they disobeyed, He would chasten them.

This is the Old Testament version of Matthew 6:33. It takes three to form a happy marriage: a man and woman who love the Lord and each other, and the Lord who performed the first wedding back in the Garden of Eden.

Successful Workers (v. 2)
It is the Lord who gives His people "power to get wealth" (Deut. 8:18). How easy it is for us to think that our planning, skill, and hard work accomplished it all, but such is not the case. As we saw in the previous psalm, without the blessing of the Lord, all our labor is in vain. Each Jew was required to give tithes to the Lord, but the Lord wanted the workers to share the fruit of their labor. If the nation turned to other gods, one of the first places the Lord would send judgment was in the home and field (Lev. 26:14ff; Deut. 28:30-34).

Happy Parents (vv. 3-4)
Both the vine and the olive tree were important to the economy of Israel, the vine providing wine and the olive tree supplying fruit and oil (104:14-15). A husband's love for his wife is illustrated by the vine and the olive tree (Song. 7:6-9). Jewish couples wanted large families and considered each child a blessing from the Lord. The phrase "within your house" refers to the wife's apartment at the back of the tent, as far from the tent door as possible. The faithful wife is not unhappy in her own house, caring for children she dearly loved. The unfaithful wife leaves the safety and sanctity of her apartment and goes seeking for victims (Prov. 7:10-13). The olive shoots around the base of the parent tree, fresh and vigorous, picture the children around the family table. It takes patience to care for them as they grow, but the efforts are rewarding. How shocked those ancient families would be

if they visited a modern home and watched parents and children scattering in all directions and rarely eating a leisurely meal together.

Useful Citizens (v. 5)

The Jewish people are proud of their heritage and want to see God's very best blessings come to Jerusalem. They realize how enriched they are from Zion. They long for each of their children to bring honor to Israel, and they pray for the peace and prosperity of Israel and Jerusalem. Many of the psalms end with a prayer for the land and the city (14:7; 25:22; 72:18-19; 106:48; 130:7-8; 125:5; 131:3; 134:3; 135:21; 148:14). True patriotism begins in the home, where love of God, family, and country are bound together.

Contented Grandparents (v. 6)

From bride and groom to grandparents in just six verses! How time flies! Three generations are represented in the psalm, and all of them walking with the Lord. We are so prone to remember that God judges the succeeding generations if they imitate the sins of their ancestors, but we must remember that He also passes along the blessings when the ancestors have been godly (Ex. 34:67; Num. 14:18-19; Deut. 5:9-10). It is often the third generation that abandons the faith (Judg. 2), so we must pray much for our children and grandchildren, that the Lord will keep His good hand of blessing on their lives for His glory.

"Blessed is the nation whose God is the Lord" (33:12).

Psalm 129

The destruction of Jerusalem by the Babylonians was described by the prophets as "plowing" (vv. 3-4; Isa. 51:23;

Mic. 3:12; Jer. 26:17-18), so this psalm was probably written after the exiles returned to the land. There they were surrounded by enemy peoples who hated them, so the theme was appropriate. The psalmist speaks for the nation and states that, no matter how severe the persecution, nothing can destroy the people of Israel. But God's church has also suffered severe persecution throughout the centuries, and faithful individual Christians face personal hostility. "Yes, and all who desire to live godly in Christ Jesus will suffer persecution" (2 Tim. 3:12, NKJV). The psalm gives three instructions that we should follow when we find ourselves suffering for Jesus Christ.

Accept It (vv. 1-2)

Persecution is not something "strange" in the life of either Israel or the church (1 Peter 4:12). To ask, "Why, Lord?" is to confess our ignorance of the place of God's people in this present evil world. When the Lord called Abraham, He revealed that some would bless the Jews and others curse them (Gen. 12:1-3). Isaac was persecuted by Ishmael (Gen. 21:8-21; Gal. 4:21-31), and the Jews were terribly oppressed in Egypt (88:15; Hos. 11:1). However, the more they were persecuted, the more they increased (Ex. 1:9-14), and there the family of Jacob was molded into the nation of Israel. Israel has suffered more than any nation in history, *yet Israel has not been destroyed!*

Egypt tried to drown the Jews (Ex. 1:15-22), but the Lord drowned Egypt's crack troops (Ex. 14:19-31). The Assyrians tried to starve them into surrender, but God wiped out the Assyrian army (Isa. 37-38). Nebuchadnezzar, ruler of Babylon, tried to burn them up, but the Lord delivered them (Dan. 3). Belshazzar blasphemed the God of Israel and defiled the holy vessels of the temple, but that very night, the Medes and Persians killed him. The Persian soothsayers tried to throw Daniel to the lions, but God rescued him and the beasts killed the soothsayers instead (Dan. 6). Hitler killed over six million Jews in his gas chambers, but he was soundly defeated, and the nation of Israel was born a few years later. The church of Jesus Christ has experienced persecution, but it still stands and will stand until Jesus returns (Matt. 16:18). Every true believer can identify with Paul's testimony in 2 Corinthians 4:7-12. When it comes to suffering for the sake of the Lord, we must first of all accept it.

Benefit from It (vv. 3-4)

As you read these verses, you can almost feel the sharp cutting edges of the plow. *Their enemies treated Israel like dirt and walked on them!* (See Josh. 10:24 and Isa. 51:23.) Some students see in the plowing image a picture of prisoners being whipped, leaving long deep gashes on their backs. If that is a part of the picture, then our Lord endured the same suffering—and yet His stripes bring spiritual healing to those who trust Him! (Isa. 50:6; 53:5). The nation of Israel has been plowed long, deep, and often, but what a harvest of blessing it has brought to the world! The day came when God cut the cords that tied the oxen to the plow, and then Israel was free (see 124:7). The exiles returned to their homes wiser and better people because they had felt the pain of the plow. Instead of blaming God for their suffering, they confessed, "The Lord is righteous."

The plowing image is a good one for believers today, for it reminds us that there can be a glorious harvest, *but it depends on the seeds that we plant.* Of itself, suffering does not produce blessing. If we plant seeds of hatred and resentment, then suffering will produce bitterness. But if we plant faith, hope, love, and the precious promises of the Word, then the harvest will bless us and help others, and it will bring glory to God. (See 1 Peter 4:12-19.) God permits people to treat us like dirt, and we must accept it, but we have the privilege of transforming it by the grace of God into character that honors the Lord.

Commit to the Lord (vv. 5-8)

The harvest image continues, but moves from the fields to the housetops. Roofs were flat and usually composed of a mixture of mud and mortar, wood and thatching. It would be easy for windblown seeds to settle on the roofs, take root in the shallow soil, grow quickly, but not last. Jesus used this image in his parable about the sower (Matt. 13:5-6, 20-21). Where there has been no plowing, you will not get much of a harvest. The psalmist prayed that those who hated Zion would perish quickly like the useless grass on the roof. But why would anybody want to hate the Jews? Is this hatred born of envy? The most logical answer is that Satan hates Israel and has always been at war with her (see Rev. 12). Satan is also at war with the church (John 15:18-15; 17:14; 1 John 3:13).

Instead of returning evil for evil, the Jews committed the conflict to the Lord and trusted Him to vindicate His own people (Rom. 12:17-21). Jewish harvesters often blessed one another as they worked in the fields (Ruth 2:4), but no blessing would be given to Israel's enemies, for they were rebelling against the God of Israel. First, these enemies would be turned back in disgrace because they could not eradicate Israel, then they would wither away, and finally they would be mowed down and used for fuel. But the people of Israel can always say to the world, "We bless you in the name of the Lord," because Israel has brought to the world the knowledge of the true and living God, the Scriptures, and the Savior. "Salvation is of the Jews" (John 4:22).

When people treat you like dirt because you belong to Jesus, remember the ABCs of this psalm: accept it, benefit from it, commit it to the Lord.

Psalm 130

The sixth of the seven Penitential Psalms (see 6), Psalm 130 emphasizes what God does for helpless people who cry out to Him for mercy. Perhaps the Jewish pilgrims used this psalm to confess their sins and seek God's forgiveness and blessing as they made their way to the sanctuary. (See Heb. 10:19-25 for the kind of preparation believers today need when they approach the Lord.) No matter what our need, when we call upon the Lord in faith, He hears us and makes the changes needed in our lives.

From Death to Life (vv. 1-2)
The picture is that of a person drowning and unable to stand on the bottom or swim to safety. (See 40:2; 69:1-3, 13-15; Isa. 51:10; Ezek. 27:34.) The tense of the verb "cry" indicates that the writer had been crying in the past and continued to cry out as he wrote the psalm, because without God's merciful intervention, he would die. But he remembered the prayer of Solomon when the king dedicated the temple, and he knew that God's eyes were upon him and His ears open to his cries (2 Chron. 6:40; Ps. 34:15; 1 Peter 3:12). Five times he addressed Jehovah,

the God of the covenant (LORD) and three times Adonai, the Master (Lord). We can cry out to God from the depths of disappointment and defeat and from the depths of fear and perplexity. Like a heavy weight, sin drags its victims to the depths, but God made us for the heights (Isa. 40:31; Col. 3:1).

From Guilt to Forgiveness (vv. 3-4)
The psalmist moved from the sea to the courtroom, but there the sinner could not stand because of guilt. The only way we can get rid of the sin record is to come to God for His gracious forgiveness, and this forgiveness is made possible because of the work of Christ on the cross (32:1-2; Rom. 4:1-8). The word translated "mark" means "to observe and keep a record," and God is able to do that (90:8; 139:23-24; Jer. 2:22; 16:17; Ezek. 11:5; Hos. 7:2). Sinners cannot stand before the holy Judge and argue their own case (1:5; 143:2; Ezra 9:15; Nah. 1:6; Mal. 3:2). But God is ready to forgive (86:5; Neh. 9:17), and faith in the Savior brings forgiveness to the soul. God casts our sins behind His back and blots them out of His book (Isa. 38:17; 43:25; 44:22). He carries them away as far as the east is from the west (103:11-12), casts them into the sea (Mic. 7:19), and holds them against us no more (Jer. 31:34; Heb. 10:17). But forgiveness is not a blessing to be taken lightly, for it cost God His Son; therefore, we ought to love and fear God (76:7). If you take seriously the guilt of sin, you will take seriously the grace of forgiveness. Salvation is a serious and costly transaction.

From Darkness to Light (vv. 5-6)
From the courtroom we move to the city walls where the watchmen are alert as they peer through the darkness to detect the approach of any danger. Nothing they

do can make the sun come up any sooner, but when the day dawns, the guards rejoice that the city has been safe another night. When the Lord forgives sinners, it is for them the dawning of a new day as they move out of darkness into God's marvelous light (1 Peter 2:9; Luke 1:76-79; see comments on Ps. 27). The forgiven sinner is content to wait on the Lord for whatever He has planned for that day. This is not the waiting of *hopeless resignation* but of *hopeful anticipation,* for each new day brings new blessings from His hand (119:74, 81, 82; Lam. 3:22-26). If you find yourself forgiven but still in the darkness, wait on the Lord and trust His Word, but do not try to manufacture your own light (Isa. 50:10-11).

From to Bondage to Freedom (vv. 7-8)
Our final visit is to the slave market and the theme is *redemption*, which means "setting someone free by paying a price." Israel knew a great deal about God's redemption, for at the Exodus, God's power had set them free from Egyptian tyranny (Ex. 12-15). They had no hope and could not free themselves, but the Lord did it for them. He gave His people "abundant redemption" that included freedom from slavery, victory over their enemies, and a Promised Land for their home. The slave has no hope, but the child in the family looks forward to receiving an inheritance. All who trust Jesus Christ are children in God's family and not slaves, and their future is secure (Gal. 3:26-4:7). The psalmist saw a future redemption for the people of Israel, as did Paul (Rom. 11) and the prophets (Isa. 11, 60, 65-66; Zech. 12:10-14:21). Christian believers look forward to the coming of Christ and the redemption He will bring (Rom. 8:18-30).

Psalm 131

If anyone in Israel had reasons to be proud, it was David. The eighth son of a common citizen, he began as a humble shepherd and yet became Israel's greatest king. A courageous soldier, a gifted general and tactician, and a sincere man of God, it was David who defeated Israel's enemies, expanded her boundaries, and amassed the wealth that Solomon used to build the temple. He wrote nearly half of the psalms, and though (like all of us) he was guilty of disobeying the Lord, he was always repentant and sought God's merciful forgiveness. It was for David's sake that the Lord kept the light burning in Jerusalem during the years of Judah's decay, and it was from David's line that Jesus Christ came into this world. Except for a few lapses into selfishness and sin, David walked with the Lord in a humble spirit. In this brief psalm, he tells us the essentials of a life that glorifies God and accomplishes His work on earth.

Honesty—Accept Yourself (v. 1)
We move toward maturity when we honestly accept who we are, understand what we can do, accept both and live for God's glory. Rejecting or hating ourselves, fantasizing about ourselves, and envying others are marks of immaturity. David had seen some of this kind of behavior in his own son Absalom as well as in King Saul. A proud heart refuses to face reality, a high look covers up hidden inadequacy, and arrogant ambition ("going to and fro constantly") impresses some people but leads ultimately to embarrassing failure (Jer. 45:5). When you accept yourself and your lot and thank God for the way He made you, you do not need to impress people. They will see your worth and love you for who you are. (See 16:5-6; Prov. 18:12; Phil. 4:11-12; Heb. 13:5.) Spoiled

children want to be seen and heard and they get involved in things they cannot handle. David did not promote himself; it was all God's doing.

Humility—Accept God's Will (v. 2)

The simile of the weaned child is a beautiful picture of the meaning of humility and maturity. Hebrew children were weaned at ages three or four, and this experience marked the end of their infancy. But most children do not want to be deprived of mother's loving arms and satisfying breasts, and they feel rejected and unwanted. But after the crisis of birth, each child must eventually be weaned and learn the first lesson in the school of life: growing up involves painful losses that can lead to wonderful gains. The Hebrew word for "wean" means "to complete, to ripen, to treat kindly." The English word may be a contraction of the Scottish phrase "wee one," or it may come from a Teutonic word that means "to be accustomed." Maturing people know that life is a series of gains and losses, and they learn how to use their losses constructively. If children are to grow up and not just grow old, they must be able to function apart from mother. This means weaning, going to school, choosing a vocation, and probably marrying and starting a new home. They must learn that there is a difference between cutting the apron strings and cutting the heartstrings and that these separations do not rob them of mother's love.

God's goal for us is emotional and spiritual maturity (1 Cor. 13:11; 14:20; Eph. 4:13-15), and God sometimes has to wean us away from good things in order to give us better things. Abraham had to leave his family and city, send Ishmael away, separate from Lot, and put Isaac on the altar. Painful weanings! Joseph had to be separated from his father and his broth-

ers in order to see his dreams come true. Both Jacob and Peter had to be weaned from their own self-sufficiency and learn that faith means living without scheming. The child that David described wept and fretted but eventually calmed down and accepted the inevitable. The word describes the calming of the sea or the farmer's leveling of the ground after plowing (Isa. 28:25). Instead of emotional highs and lows, the child developed a steady uniform response, indicating a giant step forward in the quest for maturity. Successful living means moving from dependence to independence, and then to interdependence, always in the will of God. To accept God's will in the losses and gains of life is to experience that inner calm that is so necessary if we are to be mature people.

Hope—Anticipate the Future (v. 3)

Infants do not realize that their mother's decision is for their own good, for weaning sets them free to meet the future and make the most of it. The child may want to keep things as they are, but that way lies immaturity and tragedy. When we fret over a comfortable past, we only forfeit a challenging future. In the Christian vocabulary, hope is not "hope so." It is joyful anticipation of what the Lord will do in the future, based on His changeless promises. Like the child being weaned, we may fret at our present circumstances, but we know that our fretting is wrong. Our present circumstances are the womb out of which new blessings and opportunities will be born (Rom. 8:28).

Psalm 132

It is not likely that this is a post-exilic psalm. The ark is mentioned (v. 8), and after the destruction of the temple, the ark disappeared from the scene. Also, the writer referred in verse 10 to a king from David's dynasty, and there was no Davidic king after Zedekiah, until Jesus came to earth. Nobody in post-exilic Jerusalem was anointed as king. Since verses 8-10 are quoted by Solomon in his prayer at the dedication of the temple (2 Chron. 6:41-42), perhaps this psalm was written for that occasion. It could well have been a litany, with the worship leader opening (vv. 1-5) and the people responding (vv. 6-10). The leader then quoted God's words to David (vv. 10-12), and the people or a choir closed with a recital of God's promises to Israel (vv. 13-18). Note especially the references to David in Solomon's prayer (2 Chron. 6:3-11, 15-17). Psalm 132 also parallels Psalm 89 but is more optimistic in outlook. Note in 89 the use of anointed (v. 20; 132:10), enemy (vv. 22-23; 132:18), horn (v. 24; 132:17), and throne (v. 29). (For other "Zion psalms," see 24, 48, 68, and 89.) The completion of the temple was no assurance of God's blessing on Israel, for the important thing was that the people fulfill their responsibilities toward the Lord.

Give God His Rightful Place (vv. 1-5)

The ark represented God's throne on earth (80:1 and 99:1, NASB, NIV) and its rightful place was in the Holy of Holies of God's sanctuary. Unless God is on the throne of our lives, no enterprise we attempt can be really successful. The ark had been in several places before Solomon put it into the temple (2 Chron. 5). The ark went before the children of Israel as they followed the cloud and pillar of fire through the wilderness, and it also went before them into the water as the people crossed the Jordan River and entered Canaan. It is possible that the ark

was temporarily at Bethel (Judg. 20:27) and then Mizpah (Judg. 21:5), but it finally rested at Shiloh (1 Sam. 1-3). The wicked sons of Eli used the ark as a "good luck charm" and took it into battle against the Philistines, but the Philistines captured it (1 Sam. 4-5). Frightened by the judgments God sent, the Philistines returned the ark to the Jews, and for twenty years it rested in the house of Abinadab in Kirjath Jearim (1 Sam. 6:1-7:2). When David became king, he wanted the ark in Jerusalem and prepared a tent for it, but his first attempt failed (2 Sam. 6:1-11). The ark remained in the house of Obed-Edom for three months, and then David successfully brought God's throne to Jerusalem (2 Sam. 6:12-19; 1 Chron. 15-16). It appears that the tabernacle of Moses and its holy furniture were in Gibeon (1 Chron. 21:29).

David had two great ambitions: to bring the ark to Jerusalem and then to build a glorious temple to house it. He even made a vow to the Lord, and the Lord permitted him to fulfill the first desire but not the second (2 Sam. 7). David had gone through much hardship with reference to the building of the temple (v. 1; 1 Chron. 22:14), for the wealth he turned over to Solomon came from the spoils of his many battles. The worship leader called on God to "remember—pay attention to" what David had done, for humanly speaking, without David there would have been no temple. Even purchasing the property on which the temple was built cost David a great deal of pain (2 Sam. 24). The words spoken in verse 4 do not mean that David forsook sleep all those years but simply expressed the passion of his heart and the desire to accomplish his goal quickly (Prov. 6:4). "The Mighty One of Jacob" (vv. 2, 5) is an ancient name for Jehovah, for Jacob used it in his last words to his family (Gen. 49:24; and see Isa. 1:24; 49:26; 60:16).

Express to God Your Joyful Worship (vv. 6-9)

We get the impression that the ark was almost forgotten during the years it was in the house of Abinadab in Kirjath Jearim ("city of woods"). The city was only eight miles northwest of Jerusalem, so distance was no problem. Did some of the people in David's hometown of Bethlehem (Ephrathah—"fruitful land") "start the ball rolling" and encourage the king to act? At any rate, once the ark was back in Jerusalem, the people felt drawn to go on pilgrimage to the city. When Solomon put the ark into the Holy of Holies, the glory of God moved in, just as when Moses dedicated the tabernacle (1 Kings 8:1-11; Ex. 40). (On "footstool" see notes on 99:4-5.) The statement in verse 8 is taken from Numbers 10:33-36 and reminded the worshipers of God's guidance and power exhibited in the days of Moses. The prayer for the priests in verse 9 is answered in verse 16. A holy priesthood was important to the prosperity of Israel, but so was a nation dedicated to the Lord. The Lord could now "rest" in His house after many years of wandering from place to place (2 Sam. 7:6; 1 Chron. 28:2).

Remind God of His Faithful Covenant (vv. 10-12)

God's covenant with David (2 Sam. 7) assured Israel that one of David's descendants would sit on the throne, and now Solomon was king, "God's anointed." So it was for David's sake, not Solomon's, that God blessed the king and the people. The prophet Isaiah called this "the sure mercies of David" (Isa. 55:3). The psalmist reminded the Lord of His covenant, because he wanted someone from the Davidic dynasty to sit on the throne of Israel. Ultimately, this promise was fulfilled in Jesus Christ, the Son of David, whose throne and kingdom are forever (2 Sam. 7:11-17; Acts 13:26-39; Luke 1:30-33). If David's successors wanted the blessing of God, they needed to obey the law of God, and many of them did not. Believers today are united with the Lord in a new covenant that Jesus made in His own blood (Matt. 26:26-30; Heb. 12:24), and He will never break that covenant. The psalmist used David's name when he prayed to the Lord, but we pray in the name of Jesus (John 14:13-14; 15:16; 16:23-26). The Father is faithful to His Son, and the Son is faithful to the covenant He made in His own blood.

Trust God for His Bountiful Blessings (vv. 13-18)

God not only chose Israel to be His people and David and his descendants to be His kings, but He chose Zion to be the site of His temple and His throne (the ark). David had desperately wanted to build God a house, but was forbidden to do so, but he gathered the wealth needed, received the plans from the Lord, and bought the property on which the temple would stand. This purchase grew out of the sin David committed when he took a census of the people (2 Sam. 24). When the fire from heaven consumed his sacrifice, David knew that this was the place God had chosen. Other nations had temples, but none of those temples had the glory of the true and living God dwelling in them.

God spoke to the people in verses 14-18 and reaffirmed His covenant with Israel (Lev. 26; Deut. 27-30), for the people as well as the kings were obligated to obey the Lord if they expected to experience His blessing (v. 12). God promised to dwell with Israel, provide their food, bless their worship, and defeat their enemies. Two special images are seen here—the lamp and the sprouting horn (v. 17)—and both refer to David and to the promised Messiah, Jesus Christ. The burning lamp symbolized the king (2 Sam. 21:17), the preservation of life (18:28-30), and the perpetuation of the royal dynasty (1 Kings 11:36; 15:4; 2 Kings 8:19; 2 Chron. 21:7). The sins of some of David's successors deserved radical punishment, but for David's sake, the Lord allowed them to reign from David's throne. A horn is a symbol of power and strength, and the sprouting of the horn of David is a picture of the coming of the promised Messiah. The Hebrew word for "sprout" is translated "branch" in Isaiah 4:2, Jeremiah 23:5 and 33:15, and Zechariah 3:18 and 6:12, and refers to the Messiah, "the Branch." The word translated "flourish" or "shine" in verse 18 can also mean "to blossom," and is used that way in Numbers 17:8, the blossoming of Aaron's rod. This, too, is a Messianic image. So, the psalm ends by pointing to Jesus Christ.

The psalm concerns itself with David and God's covenant with him, but it points to David's greater Son, Jesus Christ, and His covenant with His church. The psalmist was concerned about the ark of the covenant, but the ark points to Jesus Christ who today is enthroned in the Holy of Holies in heaven. We see, not the earthly Zion, but the heavenly Zion (Heb. 12:22-24), and we rejoice that we are "a kingdom of priests" because of the grace of God (Rev. 1:5-6). Let us give God His rightful place, worship Him joyfully, rest on His faithful covenant, and trust Him for the promised blessings for those who willingly obey His will.

Psalm 133

David was king of Judah and Benjamin and ruled in Hebron for seven-and-a-half years. He inherited a divided nation and almost a civil war, but then the Lord gave him a united kingdom (2 Sam. 5; 1 Chron. 12:38-40). He could well have written this psalm when he began his reign in Jerusalem. The people usually journeyed to Jerusalem in family groups (see Luke 2:41-52), so this psalm perfectly suited the situation. It applies to individual believers and churches today, for we also have our "family quarrels" and need to learn to walk together in love. Maintaining the spiritual unity of God's people is the work of every believer, with the help of the Holy Spirit (Eph. 4:1-6), and three ministries of the Spirit are illustrated in this psalm.

We Are Born of the Spirit (v. 1)
When you read the Scriptures, you cannot help but discover that the "brothers" did not always live in unity. Cain killed Abel (Gen. 4), Lot quarreled with Abraham (Gen. 13), Joseph's brothers hated him and sold him for a slave (Gen. 37), and the brothers did not even get along among themselves! (Gen. 45:24). Miriam and Aaron criticized their brother Moses (Num. 12), and some of David's children turned against him (2 Sam. 13-18; and note 2 Sam. 12:10). Our Lord's own disciples frequently quarreled over which one of them was the greatest (Matt. 18:1ff; Mark 9:33ff; Luke 22:23ff), and Paul and Barnabas argued over John Mark and finally broke company and chose new ministry companions (Acts 15:36-41). The church began in visible unity (Acts 2:1, 44, 46), but when you read Paul's epistles, you find a sad story of rivalry and division, and it is not much better today.

It was one thing for the Jewish clans to spend a few days together while traveling to Jerusalem and quite something else to dwell together at home for the rest of the year! Yet they all had a common ancestor in Abraham; they spoke a common language; they worshiped the same God; they were children of the same covenant; they shared a common land; and they were governed by the same holy law. Christians today have experienced the same spiritual birth, worship the same God, declare the same gospel message, preach from the same Scriptures, and are headed for the same heavenly city, but, alas, there is often more division among us than unity! Yet all of us know that spiritual oneness in Christ (Gal. 3:26-29; Eph. 4:1-6) is both "good and pleasant." There is an artificial "unity" that is based on "least common denominator" theology and is more organizational uniformity than the kind of spiritual unity for which Jesus prayed (John 17:11, 21-23). This we must avoid. Those who have truly been "born of God" (1 John 2:29; 3:9; 4:7; 5:1, 4, 18) belong to the same family and need to love one another.

We Are Anointed by the Spirit (v. 2)

At his ordination, the high priest was anointed with the special oil that was compounded according to the directions God gave Moses (Ex. 30:22-33). He and the other priests were also sprinkled with the oil and the blood from the sacrifices (Ex. 29:1-9, 21). In Scripture, oil is a symbol of the Holy Spirit (Isa. 61:1-3; Zech. 4; Luke 4:17-19; Acts 10:38), for this anointing was given to priests, prophets, and kings, all of whom needed the Spirit's help to be able to minister effectively (1 Sam. 16:13). We often hear Christians pray for "an anointing of the Spirit" on God's servants, yet each true believer has already been anointed of God. This anointing establishes us so that we do not fall (2 Cor. 1:21-22) and enlightens us so that we do not go astray (1 John 2:20, 27). Every believer needs this strengthening and teaching ministry of God's Spirit.

When the high priest was anointed, the oil ran down his beard to the front of his body and over his collar. This suggests that the oil "bathed" the twelve precious stones that he wore on the breastplate over his heart, and this "bathing" is a picture of spiritual unity. When God's people walk in the Spirit, they forget about the externals and major on the eternal things of the Spirit. Externals divide us—gender, wealth, appearance, ethnic prejudices, social or political standing—while the Spirit brings us together and we glorify Christ.

We Are Refreshed by the Spirit (v. 3)

The Jews were basically an agricultural people and they depended on the early and latter rains and the dew to water their crops (Deut. 11:10-17). In Scripture, dew symbolizes the life-giving Word of God (Deut. 32:2), the blessing of God that brings fruitfulness (Gen. 27:28, 39; Deut. 33:13, 28), and God's special refreshing on His people (Hos. 14:5; Zech. 8:12). How often we need the refreshment of the Holy Spirit that comes silently but bountifully, like the dew upon the grass! When things are "dry," they begin to wither and fall apart, but when the dew comes, it brings new life and things hold together. Life means unity, death means decay, and the difference is the dew from heaven. Hebron in the far north was the highest of their mountains, nearly ten thousand feet, and Zion was one of the lesser mounts in the land. They were 200 miles apart, yet God sent His dew to both of them!

Travelers report that in some parts of the Holy Land, the morning dew is like a hard rain that fell in the night, saturating everything. The dew speaks of fruitfulness and the anointing oil speaks of fragrance, for the unity of God's people is both "good and pleasant."

What does the word "there" refer to in verse 3? Probably two things: (1) Zion and Jerusalem, for it is there God commanded His blessing (132:13-18; Lev. 25:21; Deut. 28:8), for "salvation is of the Jews" (John 4:22); and (2) where there is unity among His people (v. 1). The Holy Spirit is grieved by the sins that bring division (Eph. 5:25-32). Both images—the oil and the dew—remind us that unity is not something that we "work up" but that God sends down. When we get to the heavenly Zion (Heb. 12:18-29), there we will enjoy perfect unity "life forevermore." But why not seek to have that kind of unity today? "Will You not revive us again, that Your people may rejoice in You?" (85:6, NKJV)

Psalm 134

This last psalm of the "Songs of Ascents" series is quite brief, but it deals with a vast subject: worshiping the Lord and sharing His blessings with others. It is a short psalm—117 is the shortest—but it deals with a subject that could fill volumes. The psalm closes the collection with a benediction and leads into a series of psalms that emphasize praising the Lord. The inferences we draw from this psalm ought to encourage us in our own pilgrim journey and make us a blessing to others.

A God Who Never Sleeps (v. 1)

As you review these fifteen psalms, you see that the pilgrims had a variety of experiences on their journey, but they arrived safely in the Holy City, fulfilled their obligations, and were now preparing to return home. It was night and they wanted to make one last visit to the temple. Directed by the high priest, the temple priests and Levites were responsible to make sure everything was in order for the next day's ministry. They also checked the building to see that nothing dangerous or defiling had gotten past the doorkeepers and was hidden in the sacred precincts. The pilgrims heard a temple choir singing the praises of Jehovah, and their ministry would continue all night. Pagan temples were silent at night, because their gods had to rest (1 Kings 18:27), but "He who keeps you will not slumber. Behold, He who keeps Israel shall neither slumber nor sleep" (121:3-4, NKJV). The Lord gives sleep to His beloved people, but He stays awake and guards the city and watches over the family (127:1-2). He also hears the praises of His people.

"The Lord that made heaven and earth" (v. 3) also made the day and the night (Gen. 1:14-19), and the darkness and the light are both alike to Him (139:11-12). When we go to sleep, we know that the Father is caring for us, and when we awaken, He is there to greet us (91:1-6). If we awaken in the night, we can fellowship with Him and meditate on His Word (119:55, 62, 157-148). If God never slumbers nor sleeps, why should we stay awake all night, tossing and turning and fretting? "Be still, and know that I am God" (46:10).

A Worship That Never Ends (v. 2)

Visitors at churches sometimes ask, "When does the worship service end?" If you had asked that question of a priest or Levite in the temple in Jerusalem, he would have replied, "Never!" David arranged that the temple choirs praise the Lord day and night (92:1-2; 1 Chron. 9:33; 23:30). While you and I are asleep in our part of the world, somewhere else on the globe, believers are worshiping God. Even more, our High Priest in heaven intercedes for us and enables us to pray and to worship. Some people find it difficult to stay awake and alert during an hour's church service. What would they do if the Lord commanded them to praise Him all night long? "Any man can sing in the day," said Charles Spurgeon, "but he is the skillful singer who can sing when there is not a ray of light by which to read—who sings from his heart ... ."

God gives us "songs in the night" (42:8; 77:6; Job 35:10; Isa. 30:29), when circumstances are difficult and we cannot see our way. He gave David songs in the darkness of the cave when his life was in danger (142:7-11), and He gave Paul and Silas songs while they suffered in the Philippian jail (Acts 16:25). Our Lord sang a song in the night before He went out to Gethsemane and then Calvary (Matt. 26:30). The greatest responsibility and highest privilege of individual believers and of churches is to worship God, for everything that we are and do flows out of worship. Yet today, worship is often trivialized into cheap, clever entertainment, and the sanctuary has become a theater. As the choir in the temple lifted their hands to heaven (see on 28:2), they were pointing to the Source of all good things and praising Him for His mercy and grace. True worshipers lift "clean hands and a pure heart" to the Lord (24:4; James 4:8), for the Lord looks on the heart. We will worship God for all eternity (Rev. 4-5), so we had better start learning now.

A Blessing That Never Stops (v. 3)

As the pilgrims left the temple, a priest on duty called, "May the Lord bless you from Zion" (NASB; see 20:2; 128:5). The pronoun "you" is singular, for the blessing of God is for each of us personally. It is also singular in the priestly benediction found in Numbers 6:22-27. To leave God's house with God's blessing upon us is a great privilege, but it is also a great responsibility, for we must share that blessing with others. If it is a joy to *receive* a blessing, it is an even greater joy to *be* a blessing. Spiritually speaking, God blesses us from Zion, for "salvation is of the Jews" (John 4:22). From the day He called Abraham and gave him His covenant (Gen. 12:1-3), God has blessed the nations because of the Jewish people, for they have given us the knowledge of the true and living God as well as the gifts of the Word of God and the Savior. If God never sleeps and our worship never ends, then the blessing will not stop. Like the precious gift that Mary of Bethany gave to Jesus, the fragrance of the blessing will reach around the world (Mark 14:1-9).

Psalm 135

The emphasis of the psalm is on praising the Lord because of who He is and what He has done for His people. It opens with the command to "praise the Lord" repeated four times and concludes with the command to "bless the Lord," also repeated four times. "Jehovah" is found thirteen times in the psalm, and the familiar phrase "praise the Lord" ("hallelujah") is repeated eight times. The psalm has been called "a mosaic" because it contains numerous quotations from other parts of Scripture, no doubt collected by a temple liturgist who, led by the Spirit, put the material together for a special occasion of worship. Some students think that the occasion was the one described in Nehemiah 9, and the use of the phrase "our God" (vv. 2, 5) is characteristic of the book of Nehemiah (4:4, 20; 6:16; 9:32; 13:2). (See also Ex. 5:8; Deut. 31:7; 32:3; Josh. 24:18.) The Jewish people spoke of Jehovah as "our God" to affirm their separation from the false gods of the nations around them (vv. 15-18; 48:14; 67:6; 77:13; 115:3; 116:5). This psalm is an inspired statement of faith and believers today can shout a hearty "Amen!" to its affirmations.

The Lord Is Our God—He Chose Us (vv. 1-4)

It was God's election of Israel that set them apart from the rest of the nations, for they are "his people" (vv. 12, 14; 100:3; Deut. 32:9, 36, 43, 50). Israel is His treasured possession (v. 4; Ex. 19:5; Deut. 7:6; 14:2) and He gave them their land (v. 12). His temple stood in Jerusalem and His priests offered Him praise and sacrifices. The Jewish people were set apart to honor the name of the Lord and to bear witness to other nations that Jehovah is the one true God. Why did God choose Israel? Because "the Lord is good" (v. 3). The church today is an elect people, saved by the grace of God (Rom. 1:6; 8:30; Eph. 1:4) and called to glorify God (1 Peter 2:9-12). All believers are priests of the Lord and we must worship Him as He has instructed in His Word.

The Lord Is Sovereign—He Does What He Pleases (vv. 5-12)

The Lord is great (115:3; Ex. 15:11; 18:11), greater than the false gods of the nations. Their gods can do nothing (vv. 15-18), but Jehovah can do anything He wants to do! God showed His power over the gods of Egypt and Canaan by defeating their armies and giving Israel their possessions (vv. 8-12; Ex. 7-14; Num. 21:21-35). The Lord is ruler over all creation, from the heights of the heavens to the depths of the sea (Ex. 20:4). Even the weather is under His control (v. 7; 33:7; Job 38:22; Jer. 10:13; 51:16). Israel's exodus from Egypt is a fact of history, and Israel's faith is built on the revelation of the God of history, not the fantasies of the gods of mythology. The Christian faith is also built on solid historical facts (1 Cor. 15:1-8; 1 John 1:1-4).

The Lord Is Compassionate—He Vindicates His People (vv. 13-14)

The name of Jehovah is glorious and renowned; it is everlasting. Few people today think or speak about the gods of the past, but the name of the Lord God is still revered. One poet wrote, "The great god Ra whose shrines once covered acres / Is filler now for crossword puzzle makers." People who take comparative religions courses in school recognize the names of the ancient gods and goddesses, but one does not have to go to university to know the name of Jehovah God or of Jesus. Yet this glorious God, whose name will live forever, has compassion for lost sinners and for His people. Many times during their history, the Israelites were rescued and vindicated by the Lord as He put their enemies to shame. (See 102:12; Ex. 3:15; Deut. 32:26; and Heb. 10:30.)

The Lord Is the True and Living God—He Cares for Us (vv. 15-18)

With minor changes, these verses are quoted from 115:4-8. Dead idols cannot speak, see, hear, or breathe, and they cannot give life to their worshipers. Because Jehovah is the living God, He speaks to us in His Word, sees us in our every circumstance, hears our prayers, and comes to us when we need the help that only He can give. (See the comments on Ps. 115.)

The Lord Be Praised—He Is with Us (vv. 19-21)

Israel could praise the Lord because He was present with His people. No other nation could claim that distinction. His glory led Israel through the wilderness, and that glory resided in the sanctuary until God had to depart because of the nation's sins (Ezek. 7-11). What other nation had the glory of God dwelling in their midst (63:2; Rom. 9:4)? The Lord is not a distant God; He is "a very present help in trouble" (46:1). Jesus is "Immanuel—God with us" (Matt. 1:20-25; 28:20). "I will never leave you nor forsake you" (Heb. 13:5; Gen. 28:15; Josh. 1:5; Isa. 41:10, 17). Praise the Lord!

Psalm 136

This is an antiphonal psalm, prepared to be used by a worship leader and a choir, or a worship leader and the congregation, or perhaps two choirs. The rabbis called it "The Great Hallel" (praise). The psalm reviews God's dealings with His people and turns history into theology and theology into worship. If our worship is not based on history—what God had done in this world—then it lacks a theological message and is not true worship at all. The refrain is a familiar one. It was sung at the dedication of Solomon's temple (2 Chron. 7:3, 6) and also by King Jehoshaphat's singers when Judah was attacked by Moab and Ammon (2 Chron. 20:21). (See also 106:1; 107:1; and 118:1 and 29.) The divine title "the God of heaven" (v. 26) suggests a post-exilic date, for "God of heaven" was a title used frequently in that period (Ezra 1:2; 5:11-12;

6:9-10; 7:12, 21, 23; Neh. 1:4; 2:4; Dan. 2:18, 19, 44). The focus is on giving thanks to God for who He is and what He has done for His people.

The Creator—He Brings Forth (vv. 1-9)

The God of Israel is Jehovah, the God of the covenant, and He is good and merciful. The nations had their gods and lords (1 Cor. 8:5-6), but Jehovah alone is the God of gods and the Lord of lords. The dead gods of the nations (135:15-18) could never do the wonders that the Lord did, nor were they good and full of mercy (lovingkindness, covenant love, steadfast love). The apostle Paul joined mercy and grace in 1 Timothy 1:2, 2 Timothy 1:2, and Titus 1:4, and so did John (2 John 3) and Jude (Jude 2). God in His mercy does not give us what we do deserve, and in His grace, He gives us what we do not deserve, all for the sake of Jesus Christ. No wonder the psalmist gave thanks to the Lord!

The psalmist started at the beginning of time with the creation of the universe, recorded in Genesis 1. The Lord had the wisdom to plan creation and the power to execute that plan, and all He had to do was to speak the Word (33:6-9). Because humanity refused to be thankful for creation, mankind began that terrible descent into ignorance, idolatry, immorality, and ultimate judgment (Rom. 1:18ff). In the day or the night, whether we look up at the heavens or down at the earth and waters, we should see evidence of the hand of God and realize that a Creator brought it forth from nothing. In this creation is all that we need for life and work, so let us thank Him!

The Redeemer—He Brings Us Out (vv. 10-12)

The psalmist wrote nothing about Israel's years of suffering in Egypt, or the Lord's judgments against the gods of Egypt (Ex. 12:12), but focused on the Exodus. "Brought out" is a phrase the Jewish people used to describe their deliverance (Deut. 1:27; 4:20, 37; 5:6; 16:1). By the time Israel crossed the Red Sea, the land of Egypt, its firstborn sons, its religion, and its army had been destroyed by the power of God. The Exodus marked the birthday of the nation of Israel, and from that time, the Jews looked back each year at Passover and remembered what the Lord had done for them. The Exodus is also a picture of the redemption we have in Jesus Christ, the spotless lamb of God who shed His blood to set sinners free (1 Peter 1:18-19; John 1:29; Eph. 1:7; Col. 1:14; Heb. 9:12). God's mighty arm was revealed at the Exodus (Ex. 15:16), but it was revealed even more at the cross (Isa. 53:1ff; Luke 1:51).

The Shepherd—He Brings Us Through (vv. 13-16)

The Lord brought Israel through the sea (vv. 13-15) and through the wilderness (v. 16). A pillar of cloud guided them by day and a pillar of fire by night (Ex. 13:21-22). He led them to Sinai where they remained for over a year while Moses received and taught the divine law and supervised the construction of the tabernacle. The nation needed the discipline of the law and the delight of worship before they were ready to enter Canaan and take the land. Israel's unbelief and disobedience at Kadesh Barnea sent them back into the wilderness (Num. 13-14) where that rebellious generation died during the next thirty-eight years of wandering. Moses commanded the new generation to remember those wilderness years and obey the Word of God (Deut. 8). Indeed, the Lord Jesus Christ is our Shepherd in this life (23:1; 78:52-55; 80:1; John 10:11-

14; Heb. 13:20; 1 Peter 5:4) and throughout eternity (Rev. 7:17).

The Conqueror—He brings Us In (vv. 17-22)

As the forty years drew to a close, Moses led the people back to the gateway into the Promised Land, and on the way, Israel defeated great and mighty kings and took their lands (Num. 21). Reuben, Gad, and the half tribe of Manasseh claimed their inheritance east of the Jordan River (Num. 32; Josh. 18:7), but their men marched with Israel into Canaan and helped to conquer the enemy and claim the land (135:10-12; Josh. 22). The land belonged to the Lord but He gave it to Israel as their inheritance, and they would enjoy its blessings as long as they obeyed the covenant. Believers today have been delivered from sin through faith in Christ and are now in the "kingdom of the Son of His love" (Col. 1:13, NKJV). Canaan is not a picture of heaven, for there will be no wars in heaven. It pictures our present inheritance in Jesus Christ, an inheritance that we claim as we walk by faith and defeat Satan and his forces that want to keep us in bondage and spiritual poverty. This is the theme of Hebrews 1-4.

The Deliverer—He Brings Us Back (vv. 23-25)

These verses summarize Israel's failure to serve God and how the Lord brought seven nations into the land to punish them. The record is in the book of Judges. The people would turn to idols and the Lord would chasten them, as He promised He would. Then the situation would become so unbearable that the people would repent and cry out for mercy, and the Lord would "remember them" (see 132:1) and rescue them (Judg. 2:11-23). This was no way to live in the wonderful land God had given them, but it describes many professed believers today. When things are going well, they forget the Lord, but when things grow worse, they turn to Him for help. The mention of food in verse 24 reminds us that the nations that invaded Israel either destroyed the crops or took them, leaving the land impoverished (Judg. 6:1-6). If we are truly thankful for our food, and acknowledge that God provides it, then we are not likely to turn away from Him and worship other gods. The creatures of the earth look to God for what they need and thank the Lord by obeying His will and bringing Him glory (104:10-18).

There is only one way to end a psalm like this: "O give thanks to the God of heaven! For His mercy endures forever" (v. 26, NKJV).

Psalm 137

"Remember" and "forget" are used a total of five times in these nine verses. The American humorist Elbert Hubbard said, "A retentive memory may be a good thing, but the ability to forget is the true token of greatness." Sometimes we must remember to forget. A Jew, probably a Levite, wrote this psalm after he had returned home from Babylon with the remnant in 536 B.C. Twenty years later, Babylon was destroyed. The psalmist was with a group of former exiles (note the "we" and "us" in vv. 1-4), recalling some of their experiences, and from this encounter with the past, he learned some lessons about the human memory, himself, and the Lord.

Memory Can Open Wounds (vv. 1-4)
Sitting was the official position for mourning, and the Jewish exiles felt and acted like mourners at a funeral. The two major rivers were the Tigris and the Euphrates, but Babylon had a network of canals that helped to turn the desert into a garden. Perhaps the Jews gathered by the canals because they needed water for their religious rituals (Acts 16:13). Whatever else they may have left back in Judah, they brought their harps with them, for music was important to their worship of the Lord (81:1-3). Music was also one way of expressing their grief and seeking the help of the Lord "who gives songs in the night" (Job 35:10). These former exiles remembered the times their guards demanded that they entertain them by singing one of the "songs of Zion." What biting sarcasm! The Babylonians knew how the Jews honored Mount Zion and the city of Jerusalem, and how they boasted of Zion's strength and security (46:5, 7, 10, 11; 48; 76:1-3; 87), but now, the city and temple were in ruins. In their sarcasm, the guards were asking, "Where is your God? Why did He not deliver you?" (See 42:3, 10; 79:10; 115:2.)

The exiles had refused to obey; they did not sing for their captors. Why? For one thing, the Babylonians wanted "the Lord's song" (v. 4), and the Jewish people were not about to use sacred temple hymns to entertain the pagans. How tragic it is today when music stars use "Amazing Grace" or "The Lord's Prayer" to entertain pagan crowds that know neither the Lord nor His grace. What did Jesus say about throwing valuables to dogs and pigs (Matt. 7:6)? But even more—their hearts were not in giving a concert. Their captors wanted "songs of mirth," and the exiles had no joy. They had lost everything but God and their lives, and being normal people, they were deeply pained in their hearts. Their city, temple, and homes had been destroyed, their people had been deported, and the throne of David had been cast to the ground. But even worse, they had seen the Babylonian soldiers get great glee out of throwing Jewish babies against the walls and smashing their heads (v. 9). It was one way the Babylonians could limit the future generation of their enemies.

Yes, memories can bring pain, and the pain does not go away when we try to "bury" the memories. Denial usually makes things worse. But the fact that the exiles could talk about these painful things indicates that they were facing them honestly and learning how to process this pain in a mature way. It takes time for broken hearts to heal, and Jesus can heal them if we give Him all the pieces (147:3; Luke 4:18).

Memory Can Build Character (vv. 5-6)

Sometimes we have to lose things to really appreciate them. Here were the exiles in Babylon, mourning the loss of everything that was important to them, and asking themselves, "Did we really appreciate what the Lord gave us—our land, our city, the temple, our home, our children?" At least one man made a vow when he was in exile, that he would always remember Jerusalem and make it the highest priority and greatest joy in his life. By "Jerusalem," of course, he meant the Lord Jehovah, the temple and its ministry, the city and its people, and the ministry of Israel to the world. Before he wrote about God's judgments on Edom and Babylon (vv. 7-9), he judged himself for his own carelessness and even asked God to punish him if he failed to keep his vow. As we look back on life and evaluate our experiences, it is important that we learn our lessons and grow in godly character. "So teach us to number our days, that we may gain a heart of wisdom" (90:12, NKJV). "I will pay You my vows, which my lips have uttered ... when I was in trouble" (66:13-14, NKJV).

Memory Can Encourage Faith (vv. 7-9)

These three verses have been a serious problem for the unlearned and a target for the unbelieving who are at war with God and the Bible. However, once this passage is understood, it should encourage the faith of God's people in times of upheaval when the Lord seems to be shaking everything (Heb. 12:25-29). The Babylonian guards were taunting the Jewish exiles, wanting them to sing about their God *who had not rescued them* and their city, *which was now a heap of ruins.* This was not a matter of politics but theology, nor was it a personal vendetta but an issue between two nations. As individuals, we have the right to forgive an offender, but if the judge forgives every criminal who appears in his court, the foundations of society would be undermined and chaos would result.

The law God gave to Israel is based on the *lex talionis*—the law of retaliation—and retaliation is not revenge. It simply means "to pay back in kind." In short, the punishment must fit the crime, and our courts still follow that principle. In eighthteenth century England, there were over 200 capital crimes for which the culprit could be hanged, but no nation follows that pattern today. "Eye for eye, tooth for tooth" (Deut. 19:16-21) is not brutality; it is justice. A point that is often ignored is that, though Babylon was God's chosen instrument to discipline the Jews, *the Babylonians went too far and treated the Jews with brutality.* (See Isa. 47:1-7 and 51:22-23.) They abused the elderly, they murdered the babies and children, they violated the women, and they killed promiscuously. Though these practices may have been a normal part of ancient warfare (2 Kings 8:12; 15:16; Isa. 13:16; Nah. 3:10), Babylon went to the extreme in their inhumanity. But, let us be honest and admit that when nations today have done atrocious things—the Holocaust, for example—other nations have risen up in horror and demanded justice. If that response is correct for us, why is it wrong for the psalmist?

The psalmist knew from the prophets that God would judge Edom and Babylon, *so he prayed for the Lord to keep His promises.* Esau, father of the Edomites, was Jacob's brother (Gen. 25:30), and Esau's descendants should have shown mercy to their blood relatives. (On the future of Edom, see Isa. 63:1-6; Jer. 49:7-22; Ezek. 25:12-14 and 35:1ff; the book of Obadiah. As for Babylon's future, see Isa. 13, noting especially v. 16; and Jer. 50-51.) The psalmist knew these Scriptures and asked the Lord to fulfill them in His own time. "For the Lord is a God of recompense, He will surely repay" (Jer. 51:56, NKJV). Finally, the word "blessed" as used in verses 8-9 does not mean "happy" in the sense of Psalm 32:1, or even "favored by God" as in Psalm 1:1. It carries the meaning of "morally justified," as in Psalm 106:3—"Blessed are those who keep justice" (NKJV). It was not the Jewish people individually who punished Babylon but the God of Israel who answered their prayers and vindicated His people (Rom. 12:17-21). One day, He will vindicate His church and punish those who have persecuted and slain His servants (Rev. 6:9-17).

Psalm 138

This is the first of eight psalms attributed to David. They form a special collection just before the five "Hallelujah Psalms"

that climax the book. The psalm probably grew out of the opposition of the neighboring nations when David became king of a united Israel (2 Sam. 5; 8:1-14). It was God's plan that David reign over Israel (v. 8), but the Jebusites, Philistines, and Moabites wanted a divided Israel with a weak leader. David knew God's will, prayed for God's help (v. 3), trusted God for victory (vv. 7-8), and defeated the enemy. The psalm does not mention the Lord until verse 4, but it is obvious that Jehovah is the object of David's prayers and praise. The psalm helps us understand better what really happens when God answers prayer.

Answered Prayer Glorifies God's Name (vv. 1-3)

"The gods" are the false gods of the nations that attacked David (82:7). His victories over their armies were God's victories, and David wanted Jehovah to have the praise and glory (Jer. 50:1-2). The word translated "temple" means "sanctuary" and was applied to the tabernacle at Shiloh (see 1 Sam. 1:9; 3:3). The third line in verse 2 has been variously translated (except in the KJV and the NKJV) so as not to give the impression that God's Word is greater than God's character and reputation ("name"). The meaning seems to be: "I trusted your promises and prayed, and the Lord answered above and beyond anything that He promised." It is another way of expressing Ephesians 3:19-20. God gave David boldness to face his enemies and the strength to defeat them. God answered prayer and this brought glory to His name.

Answered Prayer Gives Witness to the Lost (vv. 4-5)

Jehovah is not only higher than the gods of the enemy, He is also greater than their rulers. David's victories proved that. However, there were Gentile kings who rejoiced that David had won the battles—rulers such as Hiram (2 Sam. 5:11) and Toi (2 Sam. 8:9). David prayed that the day would come when all the kings of the earth would hear God's Word and praise the Lord for His promises to Israel. Beginning with Egypt, every nation that has opposed and persecuted Israel has gone down in defeat, as God promised to Abraham (Gen. 12:1-3). (See 68:29-32; 72:8-11; 96:1, 3, 7-8; 102:15-17.) The Messianic hope of Israel is their only hope and the only hope of the world. Jesus has come; He is "the ruler of the kings of the earth" (Rev. 1:5) and the King of Kings and Lord of Lords (Rev. 19:16). What a great day that will be when the kings of the earth join together with God's people in praising the Lord!

Answered Prayer Accomplishes God's Purposes in Our Lives (vv. 6-8)

Jehovah is the Highest of the high and the Greatest of the great, but He is also willing to become the Lowest of the low and stoop down to meet our needs. To "look upon the lowly" means to pay attention to them and regard them with favor (11:4; 113:5-9; Isa. 57:15 and 66:2; Luke 1:47-55). The ultimate proof of this is the incarnation of Jesus Christ, for He became poor that we might become rich (2 Cor. 8:9) and became a servant that we might be set free (Phil. 2:1-12). He was lowly in His life and also in His death, for He who is perfect was treated like a criminal and nailed to a cross, and on that cross, He became sin for us (2 Cor. 5:21). David gave thanks that the Lord knew his need and came to his aid. In His covenant with David (2 Sam. 7), God revealed that He had a great purpose to fulfill through David's life, and He

would not allow the enemy to thwart that purpose. This is true of believers today (Phil. 1:6 and 2:13; Eph. 2:10 and 3:20; Col. 1:29), and He will not forsake us. It has well been said that the purpose of prayer is not to get man's will done in heaven but to get God's will done on earth, and this was demonstrated in David's life.

Psalm 139

What we think about God and our relationship to Him determines what we think about everything else that makes up our busy world—other people, the universe, God's Word, God's will, sin, faith, and obedience. Wrong ideas about God will ultimately lead to wrong ideas about who we are and what we should do, and this leads to a wrong life on the wrong path toward the wrong destiny. In other words, theology—the right knowledge of God—is essential to a fulfilled life in this world. David contemplated God and wrote for us a psalm whose message can only encourage us to be in a right relationship with Him.

God Knows Us Intimately—We Cannot Deceive Him (vv. 1-6)

The verb "search" means "to examine with pain and care." The Jewish people used this word to describe digging deep into a mine, exploring a land, and investigating a legal case. Our friends see the outside but God sees the heart, and we cannot deceive Him. Adam and Eve tried it (Gen. 3:7-24), Cain tried it (Gen. 4:1-15), and even David tried it (2 Sam. 11-12), and all of them discovered that God knew all about them. "Understand" in verse 2 means "to distinguish and discern with insight" and not just gather raw data.

"Compass" in verse 3 is a picture of winnowing grain, and "try" in verse 23 means "to test metal." The fact that God knows us intimately and exhaustively is asserted in verses 1, 2, 4, 14, and 23. He knows our actions, our locations, our thoughts and words, our ways, and our motives. "All things are naked and open to the eyes of Him to whom we must give account" (Heb. 4:13, NKJV). But even more, He knows what is best for us and does all He can to guide us that way. He hems us in behind and before and puts His hand on us to steady us and direct us. The word translated "beset" (KJV) or "enclosed" (NASB) means "to guard a valuable object," so God's knowledge and guidance are for our protection. What should be our response to this? We should be overwhelmed by the height and depth of God's knowledge and be thankful that He knows us perfectly. "I am not equal to it!" David exclaimed.

God Is with Us Constantly—We Cannot Escape Him (vv. 7-12)

If God knows so much about us, perhaps the wisest thing is to run away and hide, but all "escape routes" are futile. If we go up to heaven or down to sheol, the realm of the dead, God is there; if we travel the speed of light to the east or west (the Mediterranean Sea was west of Israel), His hand will catch us and tenderly lead us. We cannot hide even in the darkness, for to the Lord, the darkness is as the light. *God wants to walk with us and guide us, because His plan for us is the very best.* Why should we want to run away and hide? Adam and Eve tried it and failed (Gen. 3:8), and so did the prophet Jonah, who only went from bad to worse. We need God's presence with us if we want to enjoy His love and fulfill His purposes. (See Isa. 43:1-7; Ps. 23:4; Matt. 28:19-20.)

God Made Us Wonderfully—We Cannot Ignore Him (vv. 13-18)

This is one of the greatest passages in literature about the miracle of human conception and birth. "In the presence of birth," said Eugene Petersen, "we don't calculate—we marvel." David declared that God is present at conception and birth, because we are made in the image of God and God has a special purpose for each person who is born. We live in and with our bodies all our lives, and we know how amazing they are. God formed us as He wants us to be, and we must accept His will no matter how we feel about our genetic structure, our looks, or our abilities. The verb "covered" (v. 13, KJV) means "woven together" (see Isa. 32:12), and "intricately wrought" in verse 15 is translated "embroidered" in Exodus. In the mother's womb, the Lord weaves and embroiders a human being, and abortion interrupts this miracle. What a tragedy!

But the Lord did more than design and form our bodies; He also planned and determined our days (v. 16). This probably includes the length of life (Job 14:5) and the tasks He wants us to perform (Eph. 2:10; Phil. 2:12-13). This is not some form of fatalism or heartless predestination, for what we are and what He plans for us come from God's loving heart (33:11) and are the very best He has for us (Rom. 12:2). If we live foolishly, we might die before the time God has ordained, but God's faithful children are immortal until their work is done. How can we ignore God when He has given us such a marvelous body and planned for us a wonderful life? Life is not a prison, it is an exciting pilgrimage, and the Lord has prepared us for what He prepared for us. Our responsibility is to yield ourselves to Him daily, ponder His thoughts found in

His Word (92:5; Isa. 55:8-9), and walk in the Spirit. God thinks of us! (Jer. 29:11). Should we not think about Him?

God Judges Righteously—We Cannot Dispute Him (vv. 19-24)

If we cannot deceive God, escape God, or ignore God, is it not sensible to obey God? Yes, it is reasonable, but there are those who prefer to oppose God and dispute what He says about them in His Word. David called these people wicked, violent, liars, blasphemers, and rebels, and he grieved because of them. God also grieves over sinners—the Father does (Gen. 6:6), the Son does (Mark 3:5; Luke 19:41), and so does the Spirit (Eph. 4:30). Yes, it is difficult to love rebellious sinners and still hate their sins, but we need more "holy hatred" in this day when blatant sin is a popular form of entertainment. (See 11:5; 45:7; 97:10; Amos 5:14-15; Rom. 12:9, 19-21.) Whenever we pray "Thy kingdom come," we are asking the Lord to judge the wicked, and we leave the matter in His hands. But David closed with a prayer for God to search His heart, know his anxieties and concerns, forgive him, and lead him. We must be cautious as we examine ourselves because we do not even know our own hearts (Jer. 17:9). It is best to open the Word and let the Spirit search us and speak to us, for then we discover the truth. We must never dispute with God, for He loves us and wants only the very best for us.

Psalm 140

It seems likely that the circumstances behind this psalm occurred during David's years as a member of King Saul's official staff, when Saul's envy and paranoia were developing. In their attempt to please the king, some of Saul's officers spread lies about young David and even tried to set traps to make him look bad. God's people face similar situations today, for Satan is a murderer (John 8:44), a slanderer and accuser (Rev. 12:10), and a deceiver (2 Cor. 11:3). We learn four lessons from this psalm that encourage us to trust God and be faithful when Satan's servants oppose us.

What Sinners Do to God's People (vv. 1-5)

David's presence among Saul's leaders was like light in darkness (Eph. 5:8ff) and health in a hospital. When confronted by a godly man like David, Saul and his leaders either had to change their ways or get rid of him, and they chose the latter course. They were evil men (v. 1) who planned evil (v. 2), spoke evil (v. 3), and practiced evil (vv. 4-5). Note that verse 3b is quoted in Romans 3:13 as part of the evidence Paul assembled that proves the depravity of the human heart. The phrase "the evil man" (v. 1, KJV) is collective, for the pronouns in the psalm are plural (vv. 2-4, 6, 8). What David needed from the Lord was wisdom to avoid their traps and protection from their violent plans. You meet the "hunting metaphor" in 9:16, 31:4, 19:110, 141:9, and 142:3, and the "sharp tongue" image is found in 52:2, 55:21, 57:4, 59:7, and 64:3. As God's people in an evil world, we must expect the opposition of the enemy and trust the Lord to enable us to overcome (John 16: 33).

What God's People Should Do to Sinners (vv. 6-8)

First, we must affirm our faith in the Lord and not be ashamed to confess it openly. We must humbly ask Him for the help we need to live and work among difficult people who hate us and want to see us fail. Whenever David found himself in that kind of a situation, he gave himself to prayer and asked God for the wisdom to know what to do and the strength to do it. Here he asked God to put a helmet on his head and protect him from deception and danger (60:7; Eph. 6:17). He also prayed for his enemies, that their evil desires would change and their evil plans not succeed. If they succeeded, they would only become proud and go on to do greater evil. Our prayers for godless people must focus on changing their character, and not just stopping their persecution of believers. David obeyed Matthew 5:44.

What Sin Does to Sinners (vv. 9-11)

Our enemies think they are hurting us, but they are really hurting themselves. The trouble they cause us will only come right back on their own heads, for it is an inexorable law of God that people reap what they sow. They dropped burning coals on David's head, but God would return the same to them (see 11:6; 18:8; 120:4; Prov. 25:22; Gen. 19:24). The destructive fires they lit with their tongues would burn them, and they would fall into the pits they had dug for David (v. 10; see 7:15; 9:15; 35:7-8; Prov. 26:27). They hunted David and set traps for him, but evil would eventually hunt them down and destroy them (v. 11). "Be sure your sin will find you out" (Num. 32:23).

What God Does for His People (vv. 12-13)

We have read the whole story, so we know that God did maintain David's cause, defeat his enemies, and keep His promise to put him on the throne of Israel. David would establish a dynasty that would eventually bring the Savior into the world. He would write nearly half of the psalms, he would expand and defend

the borders of the kingdom, and he would make the preparations necessary for the building of the temple. What a great man he was because he trusted in the Lord! David was grateful to God for His intervention, and he determined to live to glorify the God of Israel. David wrote, "The Lord will accomplish what concerns me" (138:8, NASB), and God honored His faith. For God's devoted people, the best is yet to come. Yield to Him and He will accomplish what He has planned for you, and you will be satisfied.

Psalm 141

Even a casual reading of 140 and 141 reveals that the two are related and use a similar vocabulary—heart, tongue, hands, snares, the righteous, and so forth. The enemy was after David again and he needed immediate help. It has been suggested that David wrote this psalm after his cave experience with Saul (1 Sam. 24), but then he was not really in danger; or perhaps he wrote it when he was away from the sanctuary during Absalom's rebellion. Life is built on character and character is built on decisions. This psalm reveals David making a number of wise decisions as he faced the attacks of the enemy.

"I Will Seek the Lord's Help" (vv. 1-2)

Whenever the enemy caused trouble, David's first response was to pray. "The Lord is my light and my salvation; whom shall I fear? The Lord is the strength of my life; of whom shall I be afraid?" (27:1, NKJV). He was a man with spiritual insight who understood that he could pray and worship God even if he was away from the sanctuary and had no priest to assist him (40:6-8; 50:8-9; 51:16-

17; Isa. 1:11-17; Jer. 7:22-23; Hos. 6:6; Mic. 6:6-8; Mark 12:32-33). Each evening, the Jewish priest would offer a burnt offering on the brazen altar and also burn incense on the golden altar, but God accepted David's prayer and uplifted hands. Frankincense was usually included with the burnt offering. (See Ex. 30:1-10, 34-38; Lev. 2:2.) Incense is a picture of prayer going up to the Lord (Rev. 5:8; 8:4). David's hands were empty but his heart was full of love for the Lord and faith in His promises. Both Ezra (Ezra 9) and Daniel (Dan. 9) prayed at the time of the evening offering. After the second temple was built, this psalm was read when the evening sacrifices were offered and the lamps were lit in the holy place.

"I Will Keep Myself from Sin" (vv. 3-4)

David faced a great temptation to compromise with the enemy, and he knew this was wrong. But, they were slandering him so why should he not slander them? But the problem was with his heart, not his mouth, and he prayed for a heart that would not be inclined to approve of their sins and imitate them (Prov. 4:23). David pictured his temptation as "eating their delicacies" (see Prov. 4:14-17). Times of testing become times of temptation when we stop believing and start scheming, when we ask "*How* can I get out of this?" instead of "*What* can I get out of this?"

"I Will Gladly Accept Counsel" (v. 5)

"The righteous" can also be translated "the Righteous One," referring to the Lord; but either way, the message is the same. When we yield to God's will, the difficulties of life are tools that God uses to bring maturity to our lives. Often the Lord sends people to speak to us, and

their words hurt us, but they do not harm us (Prov. 9:8; 17:10; 19:25; 27:10). King Saul did not listen to rebuke and went from bad to worse. In the ancient world, honored guests at a meal were anointed with fragrant oil (Luke 7:44-46), but David knew that the enemy's delicacies and oil were but bait in the traps they had set for him (vv. 9-10). David would rather be admonished than anointed. As we face the problems and perils of the Christian life, it is important that we listen to wise counsel and obey it.

"I Will Let God Judge My Enemies" (vv. 6-7)

These two verses have puzzled translators and expositors, but the general message seems clear. David continued to pray for his enemies, and he saw a day coming when God would judge them and vindicate his own cause (138:8; 140:12). Perhaps it is best to translate the verbs "Let the judges be thrown down … let them learn that my words were true … let them say, 'As one plows … .'" To throw people from a cliff was a terrible form of execution (2 Chron. 25:12; Luke 4:29), but David is no doubt speaking in metaphorical language as in verses 1-5. When God has judged the leaders, their followers will agree that David's words were correct, especially when they see the unburied bones of those leaders bleaching in the sun. The scavenger birds and beasts will have stripped their corpses of flesh. If "they" in verse 7 refers to David's men, the idea may be that they are willing to die for David's cause and "plowed under," for this will eventually bring a harvest of righteousness to the land. The image is similar to that in 129:1-4. However, the first explanation is better.

"I Will Keep Going by Faith" (vv. 8-10)

Fixing one's eyes on the invisible Lord means living by faith in His Word (Isa. 45:22; Heb. 12:1-2). God had anointed David to be king of Israel and nothing but David's own disobedience could frustrate that plan. Unlike Peter when he walked on the water in the storm, David did not take his eyes of faith off the Lord (Matt. 14:22-33). God was David's refuge and he was immortal until his work was done. If David had worried about the traps and hidden snares the enemy had set, he would have been paralyzed with fear; but he committed himself to the Lord and walked safely through the battlefield. Four simple words declare his faith, "I pass by safely" (v. 10, NASB). This reminds us of our Lord's experience in the synagogue at Nazareth, when the people became angry at His message and tried to throw Him from a cliff, but "He went His way" (Luke 4:28-30). Life goes on and there is work to do, so we must not allow tough situations to paralyze us but to energize us in trusting the Lord. Life's trials are not excuses for doing nothing; they are opportunities for claiming God's promises and experiencing His miraculous power.

Psalm 142

This is the last of the psalms attributed to David that relate to the years in which he was fleeing from Saul (see 7, 34, 52, 54, 56, 57, and 59). Whether his "prison" (v. 7) was the cave of Adullam (1 Sam. 22) or a cave in En Gedi (1 Sam. 24), we cannot be sure, but it is obvious that he was in danger and was depressed and feeling abandoned. But he did what God's people must always do in times of crisis: he looked to the Lord for help. He knew very little about Saul and his plans, but he did know about Jehovah and His great promises, and because of his faith in these assurances, he triumphed over his feelings and his foes.

The Lord Hears Our Prayers (vv. 1-2)

David not only cried aloud with his voice, but he cried earnestly from his heart. He was a godly young man who had faithfully served the Lord and his king, and yet there he was in a cave, hiding like a guilty criminal. Later in life, David would understand more fully that during those fugitive years in the wilderness, God was equipping him for the work he would do the rest of his life, but at the time, his situation was miserable. His feelings were so pent up within him that he "poured out" his troubles (43:4; 62:8; 102 title) and his inner turmoil ("complaint"). God knew David's difficult situation better than he did, but the Lord has ordained that our prayers are a part of His providential answers. When we need bread, our heavenly Father wants us to come and ask (Luke 11:9-13). The word "trouble" means "in a tight place, in narrow straits" (120:1; 138:7; 143:11). David would learn that those dangerous narrow places usually led to wider places and greater opportunities (18:18-19; 4:1; 25:17).

The Lord Knows Our Circumstances (vv. 3-4)

In verse 3, the pronoun changes from "him" to "you" (see 23:4). David was a great warrior, but he was "feeling faint" within and was overwhelmed by all that was happening to him (77:3; 143:4; Jonah 2:7; Lam. 2:12). But what life does to us depends on what life finds in us, and David was a man with faith in his heart. He trusted God to show him the way to go and to protect him on the path. One day he would look back and realize that God's "goodness and mercy" had attended his way throughout his life (23:6). Were there hidden traps before him? Then the Lord would guide and protect him (140:5; 141:9). He had no bodyguard at his right hand, and nobody seemed to care whether he lived or died, but the Lord cared and stood at his right hand (16:8; 109:31; 110:5; 121:5). No matter the circumstances around us or the feelings within us, God cares for us (1 Peter 5:7). We can be confident that He is working all things together for His glory and our good (Rom. 8:28).

The Lord Meets Our Needs (5-7)

He is our "refuge and strength" (46:1), so we have all the protection we need. The cave may have been his temporary home, but David knew that the Lord was his Rock and his fortress (90:1; 91:1-2). But the Lord was also his portion (16:5; 73:26), so his desperate situation really deprived him of nothing. In the Lord, we always have all that we need. The Lord was his deliverer, and time after time, often in the nick of time, David would behold the hand of God rescuing him from the hands of the enemy. As David prayed, he realized that it was the name and purposes of the Lord that were really important and not his personal safety, comfort, or promised kingship. He prayed to be delivered so that he might praise God and glorify Him. He looked forward to the day when prayer would give way to praise, and the people would gather around him and welcome him as their king. It would be a long and difficult journey, but the Lord would perfect what He had planned for him (138:8). Eventually, David was delivered and the nation surrounded him and received him as God's chosen ruler. The

Lord gives bountifully to His children (13:6; 116:7; 119:17; Eph. 1:3). When He gave us Jesus Christ, He gave us all that we will ever need.

Psalm 143

This is the seventh and last of the "penitential psalms" (see on Ps. 6). It is included primarily because David felt he needed to confess sins that were keeping him from enjoying God's help and blessing (vv. 1-2). He had concluded that the suffering he was experiencing from the attacks of the enemy were actually God's chastening, so he asked God for mercy. It is true that the Lord can use painful circumstances and difficult people to bring us to repentance, but sometimes those very things are God's "tools" to polish and mature us, not to punish us. In this psalm, David presents many requests to the Lord, all of which may be summarized in two prayers: "Hear me" (vv. 1-6) and "Answer me" (vv. 7-12). This kind of praying is a good example for us to follow.

"Hear Me"—Tell God Your Situation (vv. 1-6)

The basis for David's prayer was the character of God, His faithfulness and righteousness, attributes that are mentioned again in verse 11. God is righteous in all that He does because He is holy, and He is faithful to His covenant and His promises. We plead these same attributes when we confess our sins to the Lord and claim His forgiveness (1 John 1:9). By calling himself God's servant (vv. 2, 12), David affirmed that he was a son of the covenant and could plead on the basis of God's Word. He also affirmed his own sinfulness (130:3-4; Job 9:32; 22:4; and see Rom. 3:20 and Gal. 2:16).

After focusing on God's character and his own needs, David told the Lord what he was enduring because of his enemies. The reference is probably to King Saul's relentless persecution during David's exile years. His vivid description almost helps us to feel the pain that David and his men were experiencing. They were crushed to the ground, lying in a dark grave like a corpse (v. 7; 7:5; 74:20; 88:5-6; Lam. 3:6), discouraged by a fainting ("stunned") heart that wants to give up, and wrapped up in a depressed spirit that is appalled and devastated. Those who believe that God's people never have their dark days and difficult weeks need to ponder this passage carefully.

What made this even more difficult was David's memory of "the good old days" (v. 5; see 77:5, 11-12). Was he remembering the peaceful days he spent as a shepherd, caring for his father's flock? But a lion and a bear attacked the flock (1 Sam. 17:34-36), so perhaps the "good old days" were not that good! Did he recall the days he served in Saul's court, playing the harp for the paranoid king and leading his soldiers out to victory? But Saul tried to kill David and even commanded his men to kill him. No, David remembered the great works of God recorded in the Scriptures—the Creation ("the works of His hands"), the call of Abraham, the pilgrimage of Jacob, the life of Joseph (from suffering to glory), the exodus from Egypt and the conquest of Canaan. David had his own "Hebrews 11" to encourage his faith. He stood in the cave and made it into a Holy of Holies as he lifted his hands expectantly to the Lord in praise and prayer. (See 28:2; 44:20; 63:4; 77:2; 88:9; 141:2.) The Hebrew text of verse 6 reads "My soul—for Thee," for there is no verb. The image of the parched land suggests the verb "thirsts," used by the

King James Version and the *New International Version*, and the *New American Standard Bible* reads "longs for Thee." The idea is the same: David's hands were raised to God because he longed for Him and thirsted for fellowship with Him (42:2; 63:1; 84:2; 107:9; John 7:37-39; Rev. 21:6; 22:17). When we reach out to the Lord, it is because He has first reached out for us.

"Answer Me"—Wait for the Answer in Expectation (vv. 7-12)

What were the answers for which David was waiting anxiously? The same answers we want to receive today. For one thing, *we want to see God's face (v. 7).* David had often heard the priestly benediction declare that God's face would shine upon His people in gracious blessing (Num. 6:22-27), but if He was displeased, He would hide His face from them (10:1; 13:1; 69:17; 102:2). To know the shining of His face means to walk in the light of His countenance and enjoy the smile of God upon our lives, but the absence of that blessing was like a living death (28:1).

We also want *to hear God's Word (v. 8).* To see His smile and hear His voice gives us the strength we need to overcome the enemy. David moved from the darkness (v. 3) to the morning and the dawning of a new day (5:3; 30:5; 59:16; 88:13; 130:6; 90:14). The Word reminded him of God's unfailing love, and the Word strengthened his faith (Rom. 10:17) and gave him guidance on the dangerous path he had to take from the cave to the crown.

We also want the blessing of *experiencing the protection of God (v. 9).* Jehovah was David's "Rock" (18:2, 31, 46; 19:14), and he hid himself in "the cleft of the Rock" (Ex. 33:22) and was safe from the enemy. "Rock of ages / Cleft for me / Let me hide myself in Thee." Another answer we receive from the Lord is *a knowledge of the will of God (v.10)*. His good Spirit (Neh. 9:20) teaches us from the Word and shows us the path we should take (119:105). A knowledge of God's will gives us confidence in the difficulties of life; it keeps us going when the going gets tough. Finally, God answers prayer by helping us *bring glory to His great name (vv. 11-12)*. "For thy name's sake" was the great motivation of David's life and ministry (see 1 Sam. 17:26, 36, 45-47). "Hallowed be Thy name" is the first request in the Lord's Prayer, and it ought to be the motivation of all our prayers. David knew that he had a great work to do for the Lord, and he depended on the Lord to help him accomplish it and bring honor to His name.

Psalm 144

David wrote this psalm to "bless the Lord" (vv. 1, 15) and honor Him for making him a successful warrior and king, and to pray for His continued blessing of his people. He was concerned about dangers around them (vv. 6-7, 11) and needs within the land (vv. 12-14). In writing this psalm, he used material from Psalm 18, his great song of victory when he became king, so perhaps 144 was written about that same time (1 Sam. 5, 8). During his years of exile, David had learned much about himself and about the Lord. In this psalm, he gave witness to Jehovah, the God of Israel, and reminded his people that their God was not like the gods of their neighbors.

The Loving God Who Cares for Us Personally (vv. 1-4)

David had been a fugitive for perhaps ten years and then he reigned over Judah for seven years and six months. By the time he became king of all the tribes and made Jerusalem his capital, he had seen many battles and would fight many more. But God prepares and equips His leaders, and David had no fear of the future (18:34, 45; 55:21; 78:9). (For the image of God as Rock and fortress, see 18:2, and as shield, see 3:3.) The phrase "my goodness" (KJV) is translated "my lovingkindness" in the *New American Standard Bible* and "my loving God" in the *New International Version*. (See 18:2, 47.) The associating of love and war is unusual, but "You who love the Lord, hate evil" (97:10, NKJV). David inherited twelve tribes that did not always get along with each other, and during the years immediately following the death of King Saul, tribal rivalry and conflict created numerous problems. But God brought about political unity within the nation and gave David victory against the enemies outside the nation (18:47-48).

David's position and reputation did not go to his head, for he asked, "Who am I that God should do this for me?" The statements in verses 3-4 remind us of 8:4, and this is a reminder that we need, especially when we think we can handle life without trusting God. The Hebrew word translated "breath" is *habel*, the name of one of Adam's sons (Abel), and the word translated "vanity" thirty-eight times in Ecclesiastes. (See also 39:4-6, 22; 62:9; 78:33; 94:11.) The "shadow" image is found in 102:11, 109:23, Job 8:9 and 14:2, and Ecclesiastes 6:12 and 8:13. How helpless we are without the Lord!

The Mighty God Who Delivers Us Victoriously (vv. 5-11)

David used these same vivid images in 18:8-9, 14-17, 45, and 50. The Jewish people did not forget God's dramatic appearance at Mount Sinai (Ex. 19:18-25 and 20:18-21), but here the mountains and "great waters" seem to stand for the enemies of Israel (104:32; Isa. 8:7; 59:19; 64:1-5; Mic. 1:4; Nah. 1:5; and Hab. 3:10). The "strange children" of verse 7 (KJV) are the outsiders who attacked Israel, the "aliens and foreigners." Some of them also tried to get into the nation and cause trouble (v. 11). They told lies and took oaths they never meant to keep. When they lifted their right hand in an oath, it was only deception. As he contemplated God's power and mercy, David sang a new song to the Lord (see 33:3), for he had experienced God's help in a new way, learned afresh the wonderful character of the Lord, and was making a new beginning as king of the nation. The plural "kings" refers to David's successors.

The Gracious God Who Blesses Us Abundantly (vv. 12-15)

David never engaged in war just for the sake of conquest. His goal was to defend the land so the people could live peaceful and profitable lives. The people of Israel were God's people, and they had a work to accomplish on the earth. Therefore, they had to have children (v. 12), the necessities of life (v. 13), and peace in the land (v. 14). All of these blessings were promised to them in God's covenant (Deut. 28:1-14) if the people and their rulers obeyed the laws of the Lord. David mentioned the home and family first, for as goes the home, so goes the nation. He compared the sons to strong growing plants (127:3-5; 128:3) and the daughters to beautiful graceful statues that could support buildings. Then he moved to the fields to behold bountiful crops and multiplying flocks and herds. Once again, these blessings are all mentioned in God's covenant. Translations of verse 14 differ. Are the oxen heavy with young or bearing heavy loads because the fields are so

fruitful? Is the picture that of a family of animals giving birth without losing any of their young, or was David describing a battle scene with the enemy breaking through the walls and the people crying out in the streets? "Breaking in" could describe the enemy coming through the walls, and "going out" the captives being led out as the people weep and express their sorrow. In His covenant with Israel, God promised them victory over the enemy, peace, prosperity, and a happy life. It is unfortunate that the nation rebelled against Jehovah and lost all those blessings in Babylonian captivity. "How blessed are the people whose God is the Lord!" for He cares for us personally, delivers us victoriously, and blesses us bountifully.

Psalm 145

This is the last psalm in the book attributed to David, and it is also an acrostic. The Hebrew letter *nun* (our letter *n*) is missing at verse 14, although some early versions based on the Septuagint have a verse starting with *nun*. (See NIV marginal note.) This is the only psalm called "A psalm of praise." David mentioned several attributes of God, among them His greatness (v. 3), His grace, goodness and compassion (vv. 8-9), His glory and might (v. 11), His righteousness and kindness (v. 17), and His providential care (v. 20). Who could not praise a God with these wonderful characteristics? But along with telling us why we should praise the Lord, David tells us when we should praise Him.

Praise God from Day to Day (vv. 1-2)

In heaven, we shall praise the Lord forever and forever, but now is the time to get prepared as we praise Him from day to day. No matter how dark and difficult the day may be, there is always something for which we can praise the Lord—even if it is only that the situation is not always this bad! Our universe operates a day at a time as the heavenly bodies move in orbit around the sun, and we are foolish to try to live two days at a time. "As your days, so shall your strength be" (Deut. 33:25, NKJV), and some of that strength comes from praising and thanking the Lord.

Praise God from Generation to Generation (vv. 3-7)

One of the important obligations of the older generation is to pass on to the younger generation the truth about the Lord. Whether we admit it or not, every local church is one generation short of extinction, and we must obey 2 Timothy 2:2. (See 48:13; 71:18; 78:6; 79:13; 102:18; Ex. 3:15; 12:14, 17, 42; Judg. 2:10.) God is so great that the human mind cannot fathom Him (Isa. 40:28; Job 5:9; 9:10; 11:7; Rom. 11:33; Eph. 3:8), but the human heart can love Him and tell others how great He is. God's character and God's awesome works furnish us with more material than we could ever exhaust, and we will have all of eternity to keep learning more! But David was not writing only about theology; he was also writing about personal witness, what the Lord has done in our own lives. "Come, you children, listen to me; I will teach you the fear of the Lord" (34:11, NKJV). The older generation must reach back into their lives and "utter the memory" of God's great goodness (v. 7). The word translated "utter" means "to pour forth like a bubbling spring" (19:2; 59:7; 94:4; 119:17).

Praise God from Nation to Nation (vv. 8-13a)

David knew his basic theology (v. 8; Ex. 34:6; Num. 14:18; Neh. 9:17), but he also knew that this wonderful truth must be shared with others. Jonah knew it but would not share it (Jonah 4). "All" is one of the key words of this psalm. God is good to all (v. 9) and His throne lasts for all generations (v. 13). He upholds all who fall (v. 14) and the eyes of all creatures look to God for their food (v. 15). He satisfies every living thing (v. 16) and helps all who call on Him (v. 18). One day all flesh will praise Him (v. 21). "Salvation is of the Jews" (John 4:22), but the message of salvation was not supposed to remain with the Jews. It was not sufficient for the people of Israel to praise God and teach their children to praise Him. They were obligated to share the truth about the Lord with their Gentile neighbors and let their light shine (Isa. 42:6). The psalm begins "I will extol Thee" but ends "All flesh will bless His name" (v. 21). The church today has a similar obligation and privilege. All of God's works in creation praise Him around the world, but for some reason, His own people do not follow this example. God has compassion on all—God loves a lost world (John 3:16)—and we keep it to ourselves! The glory and wonder of God's spiritual kingdom must be proclaimed from nation to nation as well as from house to house. (Note that v. 13 is quoted in Dan. 4:3.)

Praise God from Need to Need (vv. 13b-16)

Our great God is not an "absentee landlord" who collects rent but never repairs the roof. He knows our every need and He is there to help those who call on Him—those who fall, those carrying back-breaking burdens, those who hunger, and certainly those who want to be saved from their sins (Acts 2:21). We toil for our daily bread, but all God has to do is open His hand when He hears our cries and meet whatever needs we have. When He supplies one need, we must praise Him, and we must praise Him when He supplies the next need! "Casting all your care upon Him, for He cares for you" (1 Peter 5:7, NKJV). (See 104:27-28 and Matt. 6:26.)

Praise God from Prayer to Prayer (vv. 17-21)

The emphasis here is on calling on the Lord. "Yet you do not have because you do not ask" (James 4:2, NKJV). God is righteous, so we want to come with clean hands and a pure heart (66:18), but God is also loving, so we should love Him and obey Him. Prayer is not just a creature coming to the Creator, or a servant coming to the Master; it is a child coming to the heavenly Father, knowing that He will meet the need (Luke 11:1-13). He hears us, watches over us, and supplies our every need (Phil. 4:19). When He answers prayer, we must praise Him, and when He answers another prayer, we must praise Him. "My mouth will speak the praise of the Lord," wrote David, and we must follow his example. The sad thing about the wicked, whom God will destroy, is that they have nobody to thank when a blessing comes their way! We need to tell them about our wonderful Lord who died for them and desires to save them.

Psalm 146

The last five psalms are the "Hallelujah Psalms" that focus our attention on praising the Lord. This psalm begins with a vow to praise God throughout life. The next psalm tells us it is "good and pleasant" to praise the Lord, and 148 reminds us that when we praise God, we join with all creation, for heaven and earth praise Him. In 149, God's people are admonished to worship joyfully, and the last psalm tells us where and why and how "everything that has breath" should praise the Lord. These five psalms are a short course in worship, and God's people today would do well to heed their message. Sanctuaries are turning into religious theaters and "worship" is becoming more and more entertainment. The author of this psalm understood that God was not just a part of life but the heart of life. Paul had the same conviction (Phil. 1:21; Col. 3:4).

Life Means Praising God (vv. 1-2)

God gives us life and breath (Acts 17:25), so it is only right that we use that life and breath to praise Him (150:6). To receive the gifts and ignore the Giver is the essence of idolatry. The writer promised God he would praise Him all of his life, and certainly this is wise preparation for praising Him for eternity (104:33). To live a life of praise is to overcome criticism and complaining, to stop competing against others and comparing ourselves with them. It means to be grateful in and for everything (1 Thess. 5:18; Eph. 5:20) and really believe that God is working all things together for our good (Rom. 8:28). A life of praise is free from constant anxiety and discouragement as we focus on the Lord, who is mentioned eleven times in this psalm.

Life Means Trusting God (vv. 3-6)

Most people trust in "flesh and blood," themselves and others, instead of trusting the Lord to use "flesh and blood" to accomplish His will (118:5-9; 44:4-8). What nobody else can do, God can do for us and through us. These verses suggest that the psalmist was concerned that Israel's leaders not enter into ungodly alliances, but that they turn to God for help. Beginning with Abraham (Gen. 12:10ff) and the exodus generation (Ex. 14:10-14; 16:1-3; Num. 14:1-10), the people of Israel turned to Egypt for help instead of trusting the Lord, and this was true even during the days of Isaiah (Isa. 31) and Jeremiah (Jer. 2:18; 37:1-10; 42-43). To trust in human wisdom and strength is to depend on that which cannot last, for all people die, and the brilliant ideas of one leader are replaced by the not-so-brilliant ideas of a new leader. In the Hebrew text, "man" is *adam*, which comes from the word *adamah* which means "earth." We came from the earth and return to the earth (Gen. 3:19).

"But will the Lord help me, as weak and failing as I am?" many believers ask. Well, He is "the God of Jacob" (v. 5), a title used at least a dozen times in The Psalms. (See 20:1; 24:6; 46:7, 11.) Jacob was far from being perfect, yet God honored his faith and helped him in times of need. Jacob trusted God's promises, for his hope was in the Lord, but too often he depended on his own schemes to see him through. The beatitude in verse 5 is the last of twenty-five in the book of Psalms, starting with 1:1. But Jehovah is not only the God of Jacob, He is also the "God who made heaven and earth" (v. 6; 115:5; 121:2; 124:8; 134:3; Ezra 5:11) and has the power to act on behalf of His people. When we pray, we come to the throne of the universe to ask our Father for what we need. Finally, He is the God who "keeps faith forever" (v. 6, NASB). Israel knows Him as the God of the covenant, and Christian believers today know Him as the God and Father of our Lord Jesus Christ who initiated a new covenant by giving His life on the cross. Jehovah is a God who can be trusted to keep His Word.

Life Means Loving God (vv. 7-9)

This list of God's gracious ministries to needy people has at its heart "The Lord loves" (v. 8). He loves the church (Eph. 5:25), a lost world (John 3:16), and His people Israel (Deut. 4:37), and the greatest proof of that love is the cross (Rom. 5:8). Paul wrote, "He loved me and gave Himself for me" (Gal. 2:20, NKJV). All of the sins that help to produce these sad conditions were dealt with on the cross, but their existence in society is proof that the law of sin and death is reigning in this world (Rom. 5:12-21). During His ministry on earth, Jesus revealed God's love by helping people who were hungry, sick, crippled, blind, bowed down, and otherwise unable to help themselves (Luke 4:16-21; Isa. 61:1-3). We love God because He first loved us (1 John 4:19), and if we truly love God, we will love those who need God's help and will do all we can to help them (1 John 3:10-24; James 2:14-26). Living in love means more than enjoying God's love for us (John 14:21-24). It also means sharing God's love with others. We may not be able to perform miracles to heal the afflicted, but we can help them in other ways.

Life Means Reigning with God (v. 10)

This statement comes from the song of victory that Israel sang at the Exodus: "The Lord shall reign forever and ever" (Ex. 15:18). "The Lord reigns" is found in 93:1, 96:10, 97:1, and 99:1. Think of it: the sovereign Lord of the universe is our loving heavenly Father! Not only does the Lord reign over the nations (47:8), but we can "reign in life" through Jesus Christ as we yield to Him and walk in the Spirit (Rom. 5:17). We are now seated with

Christ in the heavenlies (Eph. 1:18-23; 2:4-10; Col. 3:1-4), and the throne of the universe is to us a throne of grace (Heb. 4:14-16). We "reign in life" as, by faith, we draw upon our spiritual resources in Christ and together with Him make decisions and exercise ministry. We do not need to wait for the kingdom to come to start reigning with Christ (Matt. 19:28; Rev. 22:5), for God's grace is reigning (Rom. 5:20-21), and we can reign with Christ today (Rom. 5:21). Then we can have a life of praising God, trusting God, and loving God, a life that will glorify God.

Psalm 147

When Nehemiah and his people finished rebuilding the walls of Jerusalem, restoring the gates, and resettling the people, they called a great assembly for celebration and dedication, and it is likely that this psalm was written for that occasion (vv. 2, 12-14; Neh. 12:27-43). The verb "gather together" in verse 2 is used in Ezekiel 39:28 for the return of the captives to Judah, and the word "outcasts" in verse 2 is used for these exiles (Neh. 1:9). One of the unique characteristics of this psalm is the large number of present participles in it—"building, healing, binding, counting, lifting up," and so on—all of which speak of the constant and dynamic working of the Lord for His people. The psalm presents three reasons why the people should praise the Lord, and each section is marked off by the command to praise God (vv. 1, 7 and 12).

Praise the Lord—His People Have Been Restored (vv. 1-6)
The Medes and Persians captured Babylon in 539 B.C., and in 537 B.C. Cyrus

issued a decree permitting the Jews to return to their land. Led by Zerubbabel, a large band of exiles went back to Judah the next year and the temple was rebuilt. Nehemiah came in 444 B.C. to restore the walls and gates of Jerusalem. Both Isaiah and Jeremiah had predicted the captivity of the Jews as well as their release and return, and God's prophetic Word proved true, as it always does. But the psalmist did not simply notice the event; he also noticed the way the Lord tenderly cared for His people. Many lost loved ones in the invasion and during the time in Babylon, and all returned to a devastated land and ruined houses. No wonder they were brokenhearted (34:18; Isa. 61:1). The "wounds" (v. 3; "sorrows") were in their hearts, not their bodies, for many had repented and confessed their sins to the Lord, and through the Word, the Lord gave them the comfort they needed (107:20; Isa. 40). Our God is so great that He knew each person and each need (John 10:14, 27-28). The God of the galaxies, who knows the name of every star, is also the God who heals the broken hearts of His people (Luke 4:16-21). He builds up Jerusalem and lifts up His people, for nothing is too hard for Him. (See 20:8; 146:9; and Isa. 40:26-29.)

Sing to the Lord—the Land Has Been Refreshed (vv. 7-11)
The exiles returned to a land that had been left a war zone for seven decades, and they needed the early and latter rains in order to get a harvest. The Lord gathered the clouds over the land and emptied their life-giving rain on the newly planted seed. He even caused grass to grow on the mountains where nobody had planted any seed! He gave food to the wild beasts so they would not attack the humans, and He even sent food for the

noisy young ravens. (See 104:1-24.) The ancients believed that young ravens were abandoned by the parent birds and had to find their own food (Luke 12:24). It was essential that the men and their farm animals stay healthy so they could work toward a harvest and be able to feed themselves and their families. But as important as that was, the most important thing was trusting the Lord, fearing the Lord, and giving Him delight as He beheld their devotion and obedience (33:16-17; 146:3-4; Matt. 6:33). It is an awesome thought that we can bring pleasure to the heart of the heavenly Father (35:27; 37:23; 149:4).

Extol the Lord—the Word Has Been Revealed (vv. 12-20)

God's prophetic Word made possible the rebuilding of Jerusalem (Neh. 3:3, 6, 13-15; 7:1-4; Lam. 2:9), and then the Lord added His blessing to the city and its people. In the Hebrew language, "peace" (*shalom)* is much more than the absence of war. It describes total well being, including material prosperity and physical and spiritual health. Peace at the borders means peace in the nation, for invaders have to cross the borders before they can attack. Peaceful borders, strong walls, locked gates—it adds up to safety and security. Because of their disobedience, the nation had forfeited the "finest of the wheat" (81:16; Deut. 32:13-14), but now the Lord would give His people the very best. After all, the Lord controls the weather with a word (33:9) and He can do as He pleases. Hail storms and snowstorms are very infrequent in the Holy Land, except in the higher altitudes, but the Word of God accomplishes what He purposes. The Word brings the winter and then it brings the springtime, for all creation obeys the will of the Lord.

This truth prepares the way for the final thrust of the psalm: God gave His Word to Israel, and they must obey it even as creation obeys it (vv. 19-20; Deut. 4:7-8, 32-34; Rom. 3:1-2; 9:4). What a privilege it was for the people of Israel to be the bearers of God's Holy Word and to share it with the world! After the fall of Jerusalem, Jeremiah wrote, "The Law is no more" (Lam. 2:9), but God's Word was not destroyed with the city and temple. God's Word endures forever (1 Peter 1:25). The church today is blessed by having the Word of God, but we must obey it and share with a lost world. The Jewish nation took great care to protect the manuscripts of God's Word and their scholars carefully counted the letters and words, but they did not look beyond the text into the truth being taught (John 5:38-40). When their Messiah came, they did not recognize Him (John 1:26; 1 Cor. 2:6-12). How easy it is for us to respect the Word of God, bind it in expensive leather, and explain it with exhaustive notes, *and yet not obey what it tells us to do!* "Every Bible should be bound in shoe leather," said evangelist D. L. Moody, which is another way of saying "faith without works is dead" (James 2:14-26).

Psalm 148

The word "praise" is used thirteen times in these fourteen verses. The psalm begins in the highest heavens and ends with the little nation of Israel. If any psalm reveals the glory and grandeur of the worship of the Lord, it is this one, for it is cosmic in its dimensions and yet very personal in its intentions. How anyone could trivialize the privilege and responsibility of worship after pondering this psalm is difficult to understand.

The Heavens Praise the Lord (vv. 1-6)

We do not praise a god who was manufactured on earth; we praise the one true and living God who reigns from the highest heavens, the God who created all things. Solomon was right when he said, "Behold, heaven and the heaven of heavens cannot contain You" (1 Kings 8:27, NKJV; see Deut. 10:14; Neh. 9:6; 2 Cor. 12:2). The "hosts [armies] of heaven" include the angels (103:20-21) and the stars and planets (Deut. 4:19), all of which praise the Lord. He is "Lord of Sabaoth—the Lord of Hosts" (Rom. 9:29; Isa. 1:9; James 5:4). Scripture gives us a few descriptions of worship in heaven (Isa. 6; Dan. 7:9-10; Rev. 5:11-14), and we are cautioned not to worship the angels (Col. 2:18; Rev. 22:8-9). The sun, moon, and stars also praise God simply by doing what they were commanded to do (8:1-3; 19:1-6; 89:36-37; 136:7-9). We cannot see the angels in heaven, but we can see the heavenly bodies by day and night, and they tell us that there is a God and that He is wise, powerful, and glorious (Rom. 1:18-20). The pagan nations worshiped the creation instead of the Creator and Israel often fell into the same sin. The waters above and below take us back to Genesis 1:6-7 and 7:11, and see Psalm 104:3. Why should the hosts of heaven praise the Lord? Simply because He made them and gave them the privilege of serving Him and His people and bringing glory to His name. We have many more reasons for praising Him, and yet too often, we do not do it.

The Earth Praises the Lord (vv. 7-13)

The sea creatures from the ocean depths head the list (104:6; Gen. 1:21), followed by the demonstrations of God's power in the atmosphere (107:25). Remember David's psalm about the storm (29)?

"Fire" in verse 8 is probably lightning, although some opt for volcanic disturbances. Lightning often accompanied hail storms in the Holy Land. To us, the storms are unpredictable and seem out of control as they do extensive damage, but we are assured that they are accomplishing God's will. The psalmist then moved from the sea and atmosphere into the land where God placed trees for food and trees for building, wild animals and domestic animals, small creatures ("creeping things"), and birds. But men and women are the highest creatures in God's creation, because they were made in the image of God (Gen. 1:26-28). If any of God's creation has good reason to praise the Lord, it is mankind, because we have the privilege of knowing God more intimately, and we have the promise of one day being like Christ. Angels rejoice when sinners are saved, but they cannot experience the grace of God (Luke 15:7, 10). We wonder how many world leaders take time to thank and praise God. Whether we are male or female, young or old, famous or unknown, we can all know the Lord and praise the Lord. *We know His name!* What a privilege to be a child of the King!

The People of Israel Praise the Lord (v. 14)

In Scripture, a "horn" is a symbol of power and dignity, a king or a kingdom. To "take away the horn" means to deprive a nation or person of authority and prestige (79:10; see also 89:17, 24; 132:17; Ezek. 29:21). When the Lord brought His people back from exile in Babylon, He "raised up a horn" for them. This cannot refer to a king, for David's dynasty had ended with the capture of Zedekiah and the returned remnant had no king. But they did have a nation, a temple, and a priesthood, and they had preserved the sacred Word that the Lord had given them through their prophets (147:19-20). But Luke 1:69 gives us the right to apply this image to Jesus Christ, the Son of David, for He is the only person qualified to sit on David's throne (Luke 1:30-33). "Salvation is of the Jews" (John 4:22), and the Jews are a people who are still dear to the Lord (Ex. 19:6; Num. 16:5; Deut. 4:1-8).

If you read this psalm again with Jesus in mind, you can see how much greater He is than anything or anyone mentioned, for He is the Creator of all things (John 1:1-3; Col. 1:16-17). He is Captain of the hosts of the Lord (Josh. 5:14), the Sun of Righteousness (Mal. 4:2; Luke 1:78) and the Morning Star (Rev. 22:16). When ministering here on earth, He demonstrated power over storms (Matt. 8:23-27; 14:23-33), trees (Matt. 21:18-22), and wild and domestic animals (Mark 1:13; 11:1-3). He is far above the angels (Heb. 1; Eph. 1:18-23 and 3:10-11). He revealed the Father's name (John 17:6) and glorified that name in all He was, said, or did (John 1:14; 2:11; 11:4, 40; 12:28; 14:13; 17:4). In all things, Jesus Christ has the preeminence (Col. 1:18).

Psalm 149

Everything that God's people do in serving and glorifying the Lord must flow out of worship, for without Him we can do nothing (John 15:5). The most important activity of the local church is the worship of God, for this is the activity we will continue in heaven for all eternity. This psalm is a primer on worship and gives us the basic instructions we need.

Worship the Lord Intelligently (vv. 1-2)

Worship is something that we must learn to do, and we will be learning all of our lives. In times of corporate worship, the saints do minister to one another (Eph. 5:19; Col. 3:16), but the primary focus must be on the Lord, glorifying and extolling Him. Yes, we may worship the Lord in solitude, and we should (v. 5), but we must not forsake the assembly of the saints (Heb. 10:25). As members of the body of Christ (1 Cor. 12:12-13, 27), we belong to each other, affect each other, and need each other. We need both the old songs and the new songs (see on 33:3), which suggests an intelligent balance in worship. The church family has young and old, new believers, and seasoned saints (1 Tim. 5:1-2; Titus 2:1-8; 1 John 2:12-14), and nobody should be ignored. The old songs bear witness to our steadfastness in keeping the faith, but the new songs give evidence that we are maturing in the faith as we grow in the knowledge of His Word and His grace (2 Peter 3:18). A maturing faith demands mature expressions of worship, just as a maturing marriage demands new expressions of devotion, but we do not abandon the old and major only on the new. "Let us press on to maturity" (Heb. 6:1, NASB). The old and the new must be integrated or we will not be balanced believers (Matt. 13:51-52). We must walk in the Spirit (Eph. 5:18-21) and grow in knowledge of the Word (Col. 3:16), learning new truths about the old truths and having new experiences of blessing from both.

The church today can join with Israel in saying, "God is our Maker and our King" (95:6; 100:3; 10:16; 24:7-10; Eph. 2:10; Rev. 15:3; 19:16). How He has made us is His gift to us, and what we do with it is our gift to Him. We must remind ourselves that we came from the dust, but because of God's grace, we are destined for glory! "Soon and very soon / We're going to see the King."

Worship the Lord Fervently (vv. 3-4)

A very expressive people, the Jews used musical instruments, songs, and dances in their worship of the Lord. The dances, of course, were not modern ballroom or disco dances but rather interpretive dances that pointed to the Lord and not some person's talent (see Ex. 15:20; Jude 11:34; 1 Sam. 18:6; Jer. 31:4). We find no evidence that the New Testament church patterned its worship after the Jewish temple. Their pattern seems to have been the local synagogue worship, with its emphasis on prayer, the reading of the Word, exposition and exhortation, and singing hymns. However, spiritual fervency must not be confused with fleshly enthusiasm. There are false worshipers as well as true worshipers (John 4:22-24; Col. 2:16-23), and some people who think they are filled with the Spirit are really being fooled by the spirits. Bringing false fire into the sanctuary can lead to death (Lev. 10:1-11). Our purpose is not to please ourselves or to demonstrate how "spiritual" we are. Our purpose is to delight the Lord (147:11), and humility is one virtue that brings Him great joy (Isa. 66:1-2). The Lord gives spiritual beauty to those whose worship brings Him delight. Worship ought to be beautiful, for we are beholding the beauty of the Lord (27:4; 29:2; 90:17; 96:9) and becoming more like the Lord (2 Cor. 3:18). Worship must focus on God, not on us, and it must be enrichment, not entertainment. The experience of true worship can help us experience deliverance from the bondage of sin and the world.

Worship the Lord Gratefully (v. 5)

"Let the saints rejoice in this honor" is the *New International Version* translation, the "honor" being the privilege of worshiping the true and living God. God gave His Word and His glory only to the nation of Israel (147:19-20; Rom. 9:1-5), and this Word and glory have peen passed on to the church (John 17:8, 14, 22). When the believer's private worship and the church's corporate worship become routine, the Spirit is grieved and the blessing is gone. Worship ought to mean so much to us that we sing even on our beds! The word is "couches" and could refer to someone reclining at the table or resting in bed. Singing at the table or in our bed can bring joy to the Lord. Instead of the bed "swimming" with tears (6:6, NKJV), it is filled with "songs in the night" (42:8; 77:6). Even while lying in a sickbed, we can look up to God and worship Him. Without private worship, we are but hypocrites at public worship.

Worship the Lord Triumphantly (vv. 6-9)

Worship and warfare go together, as the book of Revelation makes very clear.[26] Satan has always wanted to be worshiped (Isa. 14:12-15), and he is willing to pay for it (Matt. 4:8-11). Satan is constantly at work enticing the world to worship him (Rev. 13), for he does not mind if people are "religious" so long as they leave out Jesus Christ and the truth of the gospel. In recent years, some denominations have eliminated the "militant songs" from their hymnals and their worship, and this is disappointing. Whether we like it or not, the church is an army, this world is a battlefield, and there is a struggle going on for the souls of lost sinners (Matt. 16:17-18; Eph. 6:10ff; 2 Tim. 2:3-4; 2 Cor. 10:3-5). Jesus Christ, the Prince of Peace (Isa. 9:6), is also the Conquering Warrior (45:3-7; Rev. 19:11-21), and like the workers in Nehemiah's day, we must have both tools for building and swords for battling (Neh. 4:17-18). Our weapons are prayer, the sword of the Spirit, the Word of God (Eph. 6:17; Heb. 4:12), and hymns of praise to the Lord. Worship is warfare, for we are singing soldiers! Did not our Lord sing before He went out to the cross to do battle against the devil? (See Matt. 26:30; John 12:31-32; and Col. 2:13-15.)

God has declared in writing that "the day of the Lord" will come when He will send judgment to a world that has rejected Christ and chosen to worship Satan (Rev. 6-19). God's people will appear to be the losers, but in the end, they will conquer the enemy and reign with Christ (Rev. 19:11ff). Today, the sword belongs to human government and its agents (Rom. 13), and God's servants do not wield it (John 18:10-11, 36-37). But the day of the Lord will come "as a thief in the night" (1 Thess. 5:2ff), and then Christ will "gird His sword ... and ride prosperously" (45:3-5). Until then, the church must take worship very seriously and realize that worship is a part of the believer's spiritual warfare. To ignore worship, trivialize it, turn it into entertainment, or make it a routine activity is to play right into the hands of the enemy. It is an honor to serve in the Lord's army of worshiping warriors!

Psalm 150

When you read and study the psalms, you meet with joys and sorrows, tears and trials, pains and pleasures, *but the book of Psalms closes on the highest note of praise!* Like the book of Revelation that closes the New Testament, this final psalm says to God's people, "Don't worry—this is the way the story will end. We shall all be praising the Lord!" The word "praise" is used thirteen times in this psalm, and ten of those times, we are *commanded* to "Praise Him." Each of the previous four Books of Psalms ends with a benediction (41:13; 72:18-19; 89:52; 106:48), but the final Book ends with a whole psalm devoted to praise. Like the previous psalm, it gives us a summary of some essentials of true worship.

The Focus of Worship: The Lord (1a, 6b)

"Hallelu Yah"—hallelujah—"Praise the Lord!" Jehovah (or Yah, for Yahweh) is the covenant name of the Lord. It reminds us that He loves us and has covenanted to save us, keep us, care for us, and eventually glorify us, because of the sacrifice of Jesus Christ, His Son, on the cross. The new covenant was not sealed by the blood of animal sacrifices but by the precious blood of Christ. "God" is the "power name" of God (El, Elohim), and this reminds us that whatever He promises, He is able to perform. Worship is not about the worshiper and his or her needs; it is about God and His power and glory. Certainly we bring our burdens and needs with us into the sanctuary (1 Peter 5:7), but we focus our attention on the Lord.

The Places of Worship: Heaven and Earth (v. 1b)

The "firmament" is the great expanse of heaven (11:4; 148:1; Gen. 1:6) where the angels and "spirits of just men made perfect" (148:1-7; Heb. 12:23) worship the Lord. The "sanctuary" was the Jewish tabernacle or temple where the priests and Levites led the people in praising God. We know that the Lord does not live in the structures that we design and build

(Acts 7:48-50; 17:24-25), but there is nothing sinful about setting aside a place totally dedicated to worshiping the Lord. The early church met in the temple, in upper rooms, in private homes, and even in synagogues, and when persecution began, they met in caves and underground burial chambers. People who excuse themselves from public worship because they "worship God in nature" need to be reminded that the God of nature has revealed Himself in Jesus Christ and commanded us to gather together with other believers (Heb. 10:25). We can lift our hearts to the Lord from any geographic location, for our God fills heaven and earth.

The Themes of Worship: God's Acts and Attributes (v. 2)

The Old Testament is a record of "the mighty acts of God" as performed for the nation of Israel, the chosen people of God. Especially notable are the exodus from Egypt, the conquest of the Promised Land, the expansion of the Davidic kingdom, the deliverance of the Jews from Babylon, and the restoring of the nation. In the four Gospels we see the acts of God as done by Jesus Christ, the Son of God, and in the Acts and Epistles, we have the record of the Holy Spirit's mighty acts accomplished through the people of God. The acts of God reveal the character of God, His holiness, love, wisdom, power, grace, and so on—what the psalmist called "His excellent greatness" (NASB). The nation of Israel had a calendar of special feasts to help them remember who God was and what God had done (Lev. 23), and there is nothing wrong with the church having a similar calendar for the great events in the ministry of Christ. However, we must beware lest the routine use of the calendar becomes more important than the meaning of the days, or that the observing of these days is a means of salvation (Rom. 14:1-15:13; Gal. 4:8-10; Col. 2:16-17). We cannot plumb the depths of all that God is or all that He has done (106:2; 145:4, 11, 12). This is why our eternal worshiping of God will never become boring!

The Means of Worship: Musical Instruments and Human Voices (vv. 3-6)

When it is used correctly, by God's grace and for God's glory, the human voice is the most perfect musical instrument in the world, but we find no prohibitions in Scripture against using man-made instruments in the worship of God. Instruments will be used in heaven (Rev. 5:8; 8:6-12), and there will also be singing (Rev. 5:9-14; 6:12; 11:16-18; 15:1-4; 16:5-7; 19:1-9). The psalmist seems to be describing an orchestra that has string instruments, percussion instruments, and wind instruments. The trumpet was the *shofar* or ram's horn that the priests and Levites used (47:6; 98:6) along with the harp and lyre (1 Chron. 25:1). The timbrel was probably what we know today as a tambourine. It was usually played by the women to accompany their sacred dances (Ex. 15:20-21). There were two kinds of cymbals, smaller ones that gave a clear sound and larger ones that gave a loud sound. But the final verse sums it up. Whether you can play an instrument or not, no matter where you live or what your ethnic origin, male or female, young or old—"Let everything that has breath praise the Lord!" After all, that breath comes from the Lord (Acts 17:25), and if things that do not have breath can praise the Lord (148:8-9), surely we can, too!

Praise the Lord!

ENDNOTES

BOOK I

1. The word "man" is generic and includes both men and women.

2. The Hebrew word *letz* means "to mock, to scorn." In modern Hebrew, *letzen* means "a clown."

3. V. 1 can be translated "has not walked ... has not stood ... has not sat." The only person who ever lived that way on earth was Jesus Christ, and in Him, we have the righteousness of God (2 Cor. 5:21).

4. See Gen. 18:19, Ex. 33:12, 2 Sam. 7:20 and 2 Tim. 2:19 for other examples of this meaning of the word "know."

5. The word for "Son" is *bar*, which is Aramaic, and not the familiar *ben*, which is Hebrew. But the Spirit is speaking to Gentile nations outside the nation of Israel.

6. The "communal laments" are 36, 44, 60, 74, 79, 80, 83, 90, 112, 137.

7. In The Psalms, the Lord is also called "God of my salvation" (27:9), "God of my strength" (27:9), "God of my mercy" (59:17), "God of my praise" (109:1) and "God of my life" (42:8).

8. For other "intrigue" psalms, see 17, 25, 27-28, 31, 35, 41, 52, 54-57, 59, 63, 64, 71, 86, 109, 140, 141. These involved the plots of either King Saul or Absalom.

9. Since they deal with similar themes, Pss. 9 and 10 have parallel statements. See 9:10/10:1, 18; 9:20-21/10:12,18; 9:13/10:4, 12-13; 9:19/10:11; 9:6/10:16.

10. See *Double-Speak* by William Lutz (1989) and *The New Double-Speak* (1996), both published by HarperCollins.

11. *Earth and Altar* (IVP, 1985), p. 111.

12. For a comparison of Matt. 5-7 and Ps. 15, see Appendix 70 of *The Companion Bible*, by E. W. Bullinmger (London: Lamp Press.)

13. *Dialogues of Alfred North Whitehead*, compiled by Lucien Price (New American Library, 1964), pp. 223-224.

14. *Critique of Practical Reason*, p. 2.

15. *Reflections on The Psalms* (NY: Harcourt Brace Jovanovich, 1958), p. 63.

16. *The Future of Life* (NY: Alfred A. Knopf, 2002), chapter 1.

17. Some interpret the picture as the bridegroom leaving the marriage pavilion after consummating the marriage, rejoicing that now "two had become one." Either way, David saw the sunrise as a time of joy as he faced the day, and also as a time of determination to reach the goals set for the day.

18. This may explain why Ps. 19 is appointed in the church lectionary to be read on Christmas Day.

19. *The Road Less Traveled* (NY: Simon and Schuster, 1978), p. 15.

20. For other important "one thing" statements in Scripture, see Josh. 23:14; Ecc. 3:19; Mark 10:21; Luke 10:42; 18:22; John 9:25; Phil. 3:13.

21. David said "I have sinned" more than once (2 Sam. 12:13; 24:10, 17; 1 Chron. 21:8, 17; Ps. 41:4 and 51:4). For others who also said "I have sinned," some of them insincerely, see: Ex. 9:27; 10:16; Num. 22:34; Josh. 7:20; 1 Sam. 15:24, 30; 26:21; Matt. 27:4; Luke 15:18, 21.

22. London: Geoffrey Bles, 1950; page 81.

23. *The Journals of Jim Elliot*, edited by Elizabeth Eliot (Revell, 1978), p. 174.

BOOK IV

24. Heb. 4:7 ascribes this psalm to David. The NIV and NASB both read "through David," while the KJV and NKJV both read "in David," that is, "in the Psalter." This is the preferable translation.

BOOK V

25. Some students connect these "degrees" with the fifteen degrees on King Hezekiah's sundial (Isa. 38:8; 2 Kings 20:9-10). See *Old Testament Problems* by J. W. Thirtle (Morgan & Scott, 1916); Appendix 67 of *The Companion Bible*; and chapter ten of *Mark These Men* by J. Sidlow Baxter. There are some interesting parallels between Isa. 36-38 and Pss. 120-134, but modern evangelical scholarship has not accepted Thirtle's interesting theory.

26. See chapters 13-15 of my book *Real Worship: Playground, Battleground or Holy Ground?* (Baker Books) for a more detailed discussion of Satan's desire for worship.

PROVERBS

CHAPTER ONE
DON'T JUST MAKE A LIVING, MAKE A LIFE!

Introduction to the Book of Proverbs

My wife, Betty, is the navigator in our household. For more than forty years, I've depended on her to plan our ministry trips and our occasional holidays and to direct me when I'm driving. She knows that I don't have a good sense of direction and have even been known to get lost just a few miles from home. But the Lord gave her built-in radar, and I've learned to trust her, whether we're in the big city, the African bush, or the English countryside.

I need a similar "spiritual radar" to guide me when I'm embarking on a "study journey" through a book of the Bible. That radar is provided by the Holy Spirit who guides us into God's truth (John 16:13) and, if we let Him, keeps us from going on unprofitable detours. But if I begin my journey by answering some basic questions about the book I'm studying, the Holy Spirit will find me better prepared for His teaching ministry. The questions I ask myself are:

(1) What is the major theme of the book?
(2) Who wrote the book and how is it written?
(3) What is the key verse that helps "unlock" the message of the book?
(4) What does this book say about Jesus Christ?
(5) What must I do to get the most out of this book?

Let's get prepared for our pilgrimage through Proverbs by answering these five questions.

1. What Is the Major Theme of the Book of Proverbs?

One word answers the question: *wisdom.* In Proverbs, the words *wise* and *wisdom* are used at least 125 times, because the aim of the book is to help us *acquire* and *apply* God's wisdom to the decisions and activities of daily life.

The book of Proverbs belongs to what scholars call the "wisdom literature" of the Old Testament, which also includes Job and Ecclesiastes.[1] The writers of these books wrestled with some of the most difficult questions of life as they sought to understand life's problems from God's point of view. After all, just because you're a believer and you walk by faith, it doesn't mean you put your mind on the shelf and stop thinking. The Lord expects us to apply ourselves intellectually and do some serious thinking as we study His Word. We should love the Lord with our minds as well as with our hearts and souls (Matt. 22:37).

Wisdom was an important commodity in the ancient Near East; every ruler had his council of "wise men" whom he consulted when making important decisions. Joseph was considered a wise man in Egypt, and Daniel and his friends were honored for their wisdom while serving in Babylon. God wants His children today to "walk circumspectly [carefully], not as fools but as wise" (Eph. 5:15, NKJV). Understanding the book of Proverbs can help us do that. It isn't enough simply to be educated and have knowledge, as important as education is. We also need wisdom, which is the ability to use knowledge. Wise men and women have the competence to grasp the meaning of a situation and understand what to do and how to do it in the right way at the right time.

To the ancient Jew, wisdom was much more than simply good advice or successful planning. I like Dr. Roy Zuck's definition: "Wisdom means being skillful and successful in one's relationships and responsibilities ... observing and following the Creator's principles of order in the moral universe."[2] In that definition you find most of the important elements of biblical wisdom, the kind of wisdom we can learn from the book of Proverbs.

Biblical wisdom begins with a right relationship with the Lord. The wise person believes that there is a God, that He is the Creator and Ruler of all things, and that He has put within His creation a divine order that, if obeyed, leads ultimately to success. Wise people also assert that there is a moral law operating in this world, a principle of divine justice which makes sure that eventually the wicked are judged and the righteous are rewarded. Biblical wisdom has little if any relationship to a person's IQ or education, because it is a matter of moral and spiritual understanding. It has to do with character and values; it means looking at the world through the grid of God's truth.

In the Old Testament, the Hebrew word for "wise" (*hakam*) is used to describe people skillful in working with their hands, such as the artisans who helped build the tabernacle (Ex. 28:3; 35:30-36:2) and Solomon's temple (1 Chron. 22:15). Wisdom isn't something theoretical, it's something very practical that affects every area of life. It gives order and purpose to life; it gives discernment in making decisions; and it provides a sense of fulfillment in life to the glory of God.

Wisdom keeps us in harmony with the principles and purposes that the Lord has built into His world so that as we obey God, everything works for us and not against us. This doesn't mean we don't experience trials and difficulties, because trials and difficulties are a normal part of life. But it means we have the ability to deal with these adversities successfully so that we grow spiritually and the Lord is glorified.

People with wisdom have the skill to face life honestly and courageously, and to manage it successfully so that God's purposes are fulfilled in their lives. That's why I called the original Be series book on Proverbs *Be Skillful*, because we're seeking to learn from Proverbs the divine principles that can make us skillful, not in making a living, but in making a life. The pages of history are filled with the names of brilliant and gifted people who were *smart* enough to become rich and famous but not *wise* enough to make a successful and satisfying life. Before his death, one of the world's richest men said that he would have given all his wealth to make one of his six marriages succeed. It's one thing to make a living, but quite something else to make a life.

2. Who Wrote the Book of Proverbs and How Is It Written?

Author. In 1:1, 10:1, and 25:1, we're told that King Solomon is the author of the proverbs in this book. God gave Solomon great wisdom (1 Kings 3:5-15), so that people came from the ends of the earth to listen to him and returned home amazed (4:29-34; Matt. 12:42). He spoke 3,000 proverbs, most of which are not included in this book. The Holy Spirit selected only those proverbs that the people of God should understand and obey in every age.[3]

But other servants, guided by God's Spirit, were also involved in producing this book. "The men of Hezekiah" (Prov. 25:1) were a group of scholars in King Hezekiah's day (700 B.C.) who compiled the material recorded in chapters 25-29, and in Proverbs 30 and 31, you meet "Agur the son of Jakeh" and "King Lemuel," although many scholars think "Lemuel" was another name for Solomon. Most of the material in this book came from King Solomon, so it's rightly called "the proverbs of Solomon" (1:1).

As every Bible reader knows, Solomon began his reign as a man of wisdom but ended his life practicing the greatest folly (1 Kings 11; Deut. 17:14-20). In order to achieve his political goals and keep the kingdom in peace, Solomon allied himself to other nations by marrying hundreds of women, and these heathen princesses gradually turned his heart away from loyalty to the Lord. How tragic that Solomon didn't even obey the precepts he wrote in his own book!

Approach. "Always do right—this will gratify some and astonish the rest." Mark Twain said that, and President Harry S. Truman liked the quotation so much he had it framed and placed on the wall behind his desk in the Oval Office.

Whether or not they tell the whole truth, clever sayings like Twain's are like burrs that stick in your mind. You find yourself recalling them and quoting them. This is especially true of proverbs, some of which are now so ancient they've become clichés. I once had to tell a pastor that my schedule wouldn't allow me to accept his kind invitation to speak at his church. He replied, "Oh, well, nothing ventured, nothing gained." The proverb he quoted has been around a long time. Chaucer quoted a version of it in one of his poems—in 1385!

Almost every tribe and nation has its share of proverbs expressed in ways that make it easy to "hang" proverbial wisdom in the picture gallery of your memory. "Every invalid is a physician," says an Irish proverb, and a Serbian proverb reads, "If vinegar is free, it is sweeter than honey." A proverb from Crete is a favorite of mine: "When you want a drink of milk, you don't buy the whole cow." Centuries ago, the Romans smiled at timid politicians and soldiers and said to each other, "The cat would eat fish, but she doesn't want to get her feet wet."

As an intellectual exercise, I challenge you to expand those four proverbs into four paragraphs of explanation. If you do, you'll learn to appreciate the brevity and richness of good proverbs. Proverbs are pithy statements that summarize in a few choice words practical truths relating to some aspect of everyday life. The Spanish novelist Cervantes defined a proverb as "a short sentence based on long experience." From a literary point of view, that isn't a bad definition.

Some people think that our English word *proverb* comes from the Latin *proverbium,* which means "a set of words put forth," or, "a saying supporting a point." Or, it may come from the Latin *pro* ("instead of," "on behalf of") and *verba* ("words"); that is, a short statement that takes the place of many words. The proverb "Short reckonings make long friendships" comes across with more power than a lecture on forgiving your friends. One of my junior high school teachers, when she heard the low murmur of pupils talking in class, would say, "Empty barrels make the most noise," and that would take care of the problem.

The Hebrew word *mashal* is translated "proverb," "parable," and even "allegory," but its basic meaning is "a comparison." Many of Solomon's proverbs are comparisons or contrasts (see 11:22; 25:25; 26:6-9), and some of his proverbs present these comparisons by using the word "better" (see 15:16-17; 16:19, 32; 17:1; 19:1).

Throughout the centuries, familiar maxims and proverbial sayings have been compiled into books, but no collection is more important than the Old Testament book of Proverbs. For one thing, the book of Proverbs is a part of Scripture and therefore is inspired by the Spirit of God (2 Tim. 3:16-17). Proverbs contains much more than clever sayings based on man's investigation and interpretation of human experience. Because God inspired this book, it is a part of divine revelation and relates the concerns of human life to God and the eternal. The book of Proverbs is quoted in the New Testament[4]

and therefore has a practical application to the lives of believers today.

According to 2 Timothy 3:16-17, "All Scripture is... profitable" in four ways: for *doctrine*—that's what's right; for *reproof*—that's what's not right; for *correction*—that's how to get right; and for *instruction in righteousness*—that's how to stay right. You will find all four of these purposes fulfilled in the book of Proverbs. These inspired sayings teach us about God, man, sin, creation, and a host of other doctrinal topics. These proverbs rebuke and reprove sinners for their lying, laziness, drunkenness, sexual sins, and other personal failures. But Proverbs doesn't stop with conviction; the book also administers correction, telling us how to turn from sin and mend our ways. It shows us how to stay on the path of wisdom and not stray again.

My friend Dr. Bob Cook, now home with the Lord, told me that he started reading Proverbs regularly when he was just a boy. There are thirty-one chapters in Proverbs, so if you read a chapter a day, you can read the book through once a month. Bob's father promised to give him a dollar every time he faithfully finished reading the book, so every year Bob gained spiritual treasure and earned twelve dollars just by reading Proverbs.

Traditional man-made proverbs don't always agree with each other and aren't always right, but you can trust the book of Proverbs. "Look before you leap" advises caution, while, "He who hesitates is lost" warns you not to miss your golden opportunity. Which maxim do you follow? "Many hands make light work" is contradicted by, "Too many cooks spoil the broth." However, the proverbs in Scripture are consistent with each other and with the total pattern of divine truth given in the Bible.

Furthermore, the children of God have the Holy Spirit to guide them as they seek for God's wisdom in God's Word, because the Holy Spirit is "the Spirit of wisdom" (Isa. 11:2; Eph. 1:17).

But we still have to answer the important question, "Why did Solomon use proverbs and not some other kind of literary approach as he recorded these divine truths?" Keep in mind that, apart from kings, prophets, and priests, the average Jewish adult didn't own copies of their sacred books and had to depend on memory to be able to meditate on God's truth and discuss it (Deut. 6:1-9). If Solomon had written a lecture on pride, few people would remember it, so he wrote a proverb instead: "Pride goes before destruction, a haughty spirit before a fall" (Prov. 16:18, NIV). There are only seven words in the original Hebrew, and even a child could memorize seven words!

Because proverbs are brief and pictorial, they are easy to memorize, recall, and share. Edward Everett's two-hour oration at the Gettysburg battlefield is written in American history books, but Abraham Lincoln's two-minute "Gettysburg Address" is written on the hearts of millions of people. Believers who learn the key proverbs in this book will have at their disposal the wisdom they need for making right decisions day after day. The truths found in Proverbs touch upon every important area of human life, such as acquiring and using wealth, making and keeping friends, building a happy home, avoiding temptation and trouble, controlling our feelings, disciplining the tongue, and building godly character.

Analysis. But why didn't the Holy Spirit direct the authors to arrange these proverbs in topical fashion, so we could quickly find what we need to know? Derek Kidner reminds us that the book of Proverbs, "is no anthology, but a course of education in the life of wisdom."[5] As we read Proverbs chapter by chapter, the Spirit of God has the freedom to teach us about many subjects, and we never know from day to day which topic we'll need the most. Just as the Bible itself isn't arranged like a systematic theology, neither is Proverbs. What Solomon wrote is more like a kaleidoscope than a stained-glass window: We never know what the next pattern will be.

The first nine chapters of Proverbs form a unit in which the emphasis is on "wisdom" and "folly," personified as two women. (The Hebrew word for wisdom is in the feminine gender.) In chapters 1, 8, and 9, Wisdom calls to men and women to follow her and enjoy salvation, wealth,[6] and life. In chapters 5, 6, and 7, Folly calls to the same people and offers them immediate satisfaction, but doesn't warn them of the tragic consequences of rejecting Wisdom: condemnation, poverty, and death. Chapters 10–15 form the next unit and present a series of *contrasts* between the life of wisdom and the life of folly. The closing chapters of the book (16–31) contain a variety of proverbs that give us *counsel* about many important areas of life.

As you survey Solomon's approach, you can see how wise God was in arranging the book this way. Wisdom isn't some abstract treasure that's so far away we can't grasp it. Through His Word and by His Spirit, God is every day calling us to the life of wisdom. If we want to live wisely, *we must begin with commitment to Jesus Christ*, who is "the wisdom of God" (1 Cor. 1:30). Wisdom and Folly each want to control our lives, and we must make the choice.

After we have committed ourselves to the Lord and His wisdom, we must recognize that there are consequences to the decisions we make. The proverbs in chapters 10-15 depict so vividly the contrasts that exist between the life of wisdom and the life of folly, between faith and unbelief, obedience and disobedience. We can't compromise and expect God to bless. The final section of the book (chapters 16-31) contains the further counsels we need for developing spiritual discernment and making wise decisions.

3. What Is the Key Verse That Helps "Unlock" the Book?

I suggest that 1:7 is the key verse we're looking for: "The fear of the Lord is the beginning [chief part] of knowledge: but fools despise wisdom and instruction." This statement is amplified in 9:10—"The fear of the Lord is the beginning of wisdom: and the knowledge of the holy [Holy One] is understanding." (See also Job 28:28 and Psalm 111:10.)

There are at least eighteen references to "the fear of the Lord" in Proverbs (1:7, 29; 2:5; 3:7; 8:13; 9:10; 10:27; 14:2, 26-27; 15:16, 33; 16:6; 19:23; 22:4; 23:17; 24:21; 31:30). If you read all these verses carefully, you'll get a good idea of what this important biblical phrase means.

If we truly "fear the Lord," we acknowledge from our hearts that He's the Creator, we're the creatures; He's the Father, we're His children; He's the Master, we're the servants. It means to respect God for who He is, to listen carefully to what He says, and to obey His Word, knowing that our disobedience displeases Him, breaks our fellowship with Him, and invites His chastening. It's not the servile fear of the slave before the master but the reverential and respectful fear of the child before the parent. Children fear not only because their parents can hurt them, but also because *they*

can hurt their parents. Proverbs 13:13 admonishes us to fear God's commandments, which suggests that the way we treat our Bible is the way we treat God.

"But what is this fear of the Lord?" asks Charles Bridges, and he answers the question adequately: "It is that affectionate reverence by which the child of God bends himself humbly and carefully to his Father's law. His wrath is so bitter, and His love so sweet; that hence springs an earnest desire to please Him, and—because of the danger of coming short from his own weakness and temptations—a holy watchfulness and *fear,* 'that he might not sin against Him.'" [7]

The six verses that precede this key verse (1:7) explain why the book of Proverbs was written: to give us wisdom, instruction, understanding, subtlety (prudence), knowledge, discretion, learning, and counsel. Everything depends on wisdom; the other seven words are practically synonymous with it.

Louis Goldberg says that wisdom means exhibiting "His [God's] character in the many practical affairs of life."[8] *Instruction* carries the idea of discipline, a parent's correction that results in the building of the child's character. *Understanding* means the ability to grasp a truth with insight and discernment. *Prudence* ("subtlety") is the kind of intelligence that sees the reasons behind things. People with prudence can think their way through complex matters and see what lies behind them, and thereby make wise decisions about them. (In a negative sense, the word translated "prudence" means craftiness. It is used to describe Satan in Gen. 3:1.)

The word translated *knowledge* comes from a Hebrew root that describes skill in hunting (Gen. 25:27), sailing (2 Chron. 8:18), and playing a musical instrument (1

Sam. 16:16). Knowledge involves the ability to distinguish; the Latin equivalent gives us our English word *science*. *Discretion* is the ability to devise wise plans after understanding a matter. The negative meaning is "to devise a plot."

The Hebrew root for *learning* means "to lay hold of, to grasp, to acquire or buy." When we grasp something with the mind, then we have learned it. The word translated *counsel* is related to the verb "to steer a ship." Counsel is wise guidance that moves one's life in the right direction.

You'll find these eight words repeated often in the book of Proverbs; when you put them together, you have a summary of what Solomon means by wisdom.

4. What Does Proverbs Say about Jesus Christ?

In Jesus Christ "are hid all the treasures of wisdom and knowledge" (Col. 2:3), and He is our wisdom (1 Cor. 1:24, 30). Solomon was the wisest ruler who ever lived, and yet Jesus Christ is "greater than Solomon" in both His wisdom and His wealth (Matt. 12:42). Certainly all the beautiful qualities of wisdom described in Proverbs are seen in Jesus Christ, and His earthly walk is a pattern for God's people to follow (1 John 2:6).

The description of wisdom in Proverbs 8:22-31 suggests Jesus Christ as the eternal wisdom of God, but that isn't the main thrust of the passage. Solomon personifies wisdom as the joyful son of a father, a master craftsman, and reminds us that wisdom is one of God's eternal attributes. God magnified His wisdom in the way He created the universe. The "laws of nature" that form the basis for modern science were "built into" the universe by the wisdom of God. When we honestly study creation, no matter what branch of science we follow, we're only

thinking God's thoughts after Him. Jesus Christ, the eternal creative Word, was there in the beginning (John 1:1-5; Heb. 1:1-4; Col. 1:15-17).[9] Wise people learn the eternal "wise principles" of life built into creation and seek to obey them.

5. What Must We Do to Get the Most out of This Book?

Solomon often uses the phrase, "my son" (Prov. 1:8, 10, 15; 2:1; 3:1, 11, 21; 4:10, 20; 5:1, 20; 6:1, 3, 20; 7:1; 19:27; 23:15, 19, 26; 24:13, 21; 27:11), which suggests that Proverbs contains truths that loving godly parents would pass along to their children[10] (see 1 Chron. 29:1). As God's children, we need His loving counsel, and He gives it to us in this book. So, the first essential for an effective study of Proverbs is *faith in Jesus Christ so that you can honestly call God your Father.* You can't *make* a life until you first *have* life, and this life comes through faith in Jesus Christ (John 3:16, 36).

What applies to the study of Proverbs applies to the study of any book in the Bible: Unless we are spiritually prepared, diligent, disciplined in study, and obedient to what God tells us, we won't really understand very much of God's Word. A willingness to obey is essential (John 7:17). F.W. Robertson said that, "obedience is the organ of spiritual knowledge." The Holy Spirit teaches the serious, not the curious.

At least a dozen times in Proverbs you find the imperatives "hear" or "hearken"[11] (Prov. 1:8; 4:1, 10; 5:7; 7:24; 8:6, 32-33; 19:20; 22:17; 23:19, 22); many other verses explain the blessings that come to those who obey (who hear and heed) the Word of God (1:5, 33; 8:34; 12:15; 15:31-32). In fact, Solomon warns us not to listen to instruction that will lead us astray (19:27; see Ps. 1:1). This doesn't mean that

Christian students can't study the classics and books written by nonbelievers, but they must be careful to read them in the light of the Scriptures. The counsel of godly Robert Murray M'Cheyne is helpful: "Beware the atmosphere of the classics," he wrote to a friend in college. "True, we ought to know them; but only as chemists handle poisons—to discover their qualities, not to infect their blood with them."[12]

As you study, keep in mind that Hebrew proverbs are generalized statements of what is usually true in life, and they must not be treated like promises. "A friend loves at all times" (Prov. 17:17, NKJV), but sometimes even the most devoted friends may have disagreements. "A soft answer turns away wrath" (15:1, NKJV) in most instances, but our Lord's lamblike gentleness didn't deliver Him from shame and suffering. The assurance of life for the obedient is given often (3:2, 22; 4:10, 22; 8:35; 9:11; 10:27; 12:28; 13:14; 14:27; 19:23; 21:21; 22:4) and generally speaking, this is true. Obedient believers will care for their bodies and minds and avoid substances and practices that destroy, but some godly saints have died very young while more than one godless rebel has had a long life. David Brainerd, missionary to the American Indians, died at thirty. Robert Murray M'Cheyne died just two months short of his thirtieth birthday. Henry Martyn, missionary to India and Persia, died at thirty-two. William Whiting Borden, who gave his fortune to God's work, was only twenty-five years old when he died in Egypt on his way to China.

"The righteous man is rescued from trouble, and it comes on the wicked instead" (11:8, NIV) certainly happened to Mordecai (Est. 7) and Daniel (Dan. 6), but millions of Christian martyrs testify to the fact that the statement isn't an absolute in this life. In fact, in Psalm 73, Asaph concludes that the wicked get the upper hand in this world, but the godly have their reward for eternity. The book of Proverbs has little to say about the life to come; it focuses on this present life and gives guidelines for making wise decisions that help to produce a satisfying life.

God calls us to receive His wisdom and be skillful, so that we can make a life that will glorify Him. The important thing isn't how long we live but how we live, not the length but the depth of life. Fools wade in the shallows, but wise people launch out into the deep and let God give them His very best.

CHAPTER TWO
IS ANYBODY LISTENING?
Proverbs 1: 7-33; 8–9

Three hundred years before Christ, the Greek philosopher Zeno made a statement that he never dreamed would become a powerful weapon for parents everywhere. No doubt your parents quoted Zeno's words to you whenever as a child you talked too much: "The reason why we have two ears and only one mouth is that we may listen the more and talk the less."

If ancient Greece had been as noisy as our world today, Zeno might have changed his mind and covered his ears. The Greeks didn't have the necessities of life that we have, like radios and televisions (both stationary and portable), amplified rock music (120 decibels), telephones and pesky solicitation calls, movies, camcorders and VCRs, and all the other devices that have invaded modern life. Zeno never heard a jet plane (140 decibels) or a power mower (100 decibels), nor did he ever stop his car next to a vehicle inhabited by sinister stereo speakers emitting sounds so loud that the vehicle was shaking. Zeno never spent the night in a motel room with tissue paper walls separating him from the room next door where a TV set was being ignored by a guest who was obviously deaf.

"Listen more and talk less." Bah, humbug! There are times when about the only way you can protect your sanity and your hearing is to open your mouth and say something, even if it's only a primal scream.

But the greatest tragedy of life isn't that people invade our privacy, get on our nerves, and help destroy our delicate hearing apparatus. The greatest tragedy is that there's so much noise that *people can't hear the things they really need to hear.* God is trying to get through to them with the voice of wisdom, but all they hear are the confused communications clutter, foolish voices that lead them farther away from the truth. Even without our modern electronic noisemakers, a similar situation existed in ancient Israel when Solomon wrote Proverbs, because there's really nothing new under the sun. God was speaking to people in Solomon's day, but they weren't listening.

If you'll refer to the suggested outline of Proverbs, you'll see that the first nine chapters present two women—Wisdom and Folly personified—as they seek to win the attention and obedience of people in the city streets and squares. In this chapter, I want to focus on Wisdom's calls, and then in the next chapter we'll

listen to Folly and learn what she has to offer.

1. Wisdom's Call to Salvation (Prov. 1:8-33)

This paragraph records three voices that the person reading Proverbs needs to identify.

The voice of instruction (vv. 8-10, 15-19). This is the voice of a godly father, urging his son to listen to Wisdom and obey what he hears. Note that both the father and the mother have been involved in teaching the boy,[1] and they both warn him not to abandon what he's been told. These parents have obeyed the instructions of Moses (Deut. 6:6-9) and have faithfully taught their family the Word of God. But what will their children do with all this teaching?

The parents' desire is that the children obey what they have learned, so that God's truth will become a lovely ornament to beautify their lives, like a crown on a king or a necklace on a queen. Paul told Christian servants to "adorn the doctrine of God our Savior in all things" (Titus 2:10), which simply means to make the Bible beautiful to others by living a godly life. Peter exhorted Christian wives to win their lost husbands by focusing on the imperishable beauty of Christian character rather than the artificial beauty of manmade glamour (1 Peter 3:3-4).

In Proverbs 1:15-19, the father tells his son how to avoid yielding to temptation. First, he says, check carefully the path you're on and don't walk with the wrong crowd. (This sounds very much like Ps. 1:1 and 2 Cor. 6:14-18.) If you're walking with the wrong crowd, you'll end up doing the wrong things. Second, don't play with temptation, because temptation always leads to a trap (Prov. 1:17). Birds don't take bait when they can plainly see the trap, and people ought to be smarter than birds.[2]

Third, when you disobey God by harming others, you only harm yourself (vv. 18-19). You're free to take what you want from life, but eventually you'll have to pay for it, and the price you pay is higher than the value you gain. You end up sacrificing the permanent for the immediate, and that's a bad investment.

The voice of temptation (vv. 11-14). Anybody who makes it easy for us to disobey God certainly isn't a friend. The offer they made sounded exciting, but it only led to disaster. How tragic that a group of people would actually find enjoyment in doing evil, and how foolish of them to think their loot would satisfy their desires. They rejected the eternal treasures of wisdom (3:14-16; 16:16) for the cheap trinkets of this world, and they lost their souls in the bargain.

The voice of salvation (vv. 20-33). How does Wisdom speak? In a loud ringing voice that everybody can hear! Through both creation (Rom. 10:18; Ps. 19:1-4) and conscience (Rom. 2:14-16), "what may be known of God is manifest in them [the lost world], for God has shown it to them" (Rom. 1:19, NKJV). The church's task is to proclaim the Gospel message so everybody can hear, believe, and be saved. Like Wisdom, we must herald the Word in an uncompromising way.

Where does Wisdom speak? In the crowded streets and public places where busy people gather to take care of the business of life. The message of God's truth is made for the marketplace, not the ivory tower; we must share it "at the head of the noisy streets" (Prov. 1:21, NIV). Wisdom even went to the city gate where the leaders were transacting official business. No matter where people are, they need to hear Wisdom's call.

To whom does Wisdom speak? To three classes of sinners: the simple ones, the scorners (scoffers, mockers, NIV), and the fools[3] (v. 22). The *simple* are naive people who believe anything (14:15) but examine nothing. They're gullible and easily led astray. *Scorners* think they know everything (21:24) and laugh at the things that are really important. While the simple one has a blank look on his face, the scorner wears a sneer. *Fools* are people who are ignorant of truth because they're dull and stubborn. Their problem isn't a low IQ or poor education; their problem is a lack of spiritual desire to seek and find God's wisdom. Fools enjoy their foolishness but don't know how foolish they are! The outlook of fools is purely materialistic and humanistic. They hate knowledge and have no interest in things eternal. I'll have more to say about each of these in a later chapter.

What does wisdom say to them? First, she brings an *indictment* against them (1:22) and asks how long they plan to remain in their dangerous spiritual condition. Wisdom has spoken to them time and time again, but they have refused to listen, and this will make their judgment even more severe. Then Wisdom issues an *invitation* that they turn from their evil ways and receive her gifts (v. 23). This is a call to repentance and faith. She promises to change their hearts and teach them the wisdom of God from the Word of God.

How do the simple, the scorners, and the fools respond to Wisdom? They refuse to obey her voice; they won't take hold of her outstretched hand; they laugh at her warnings; and they mock her words. Note the word "also" in verse 26. Because they laughed at Wisdom, one day Wisdom will also laugh at them. Because they mocked her, she will mock them. Wisdom sees a storm of judgment coming that will bring distress and anguish to all who reject God's invitation.

When that judgment arrives, sinners will call upon the Lord but it will be too late. "Seek the Lord while He may be found, call upon Him while He is near" (Isa. 55:6, NKJV). Sinners will reap what they have sown. "Therefore they shall eat the fruit of their own way, and be filled to the full with their own fancies" (Prov. 1:31, NKJV). They turned away their ears from hearing the truth (v. 32; see 2 Tim. 4:4) and were complacently comfortable with believing lies. In contrast to the judgment promised to unbelievers, wisdom promises security and peace to those who will listen to her and believe (Prov. 1:33).

2. Wisdom's Call to True Wealth (Prov. 8:1-36)

In His mercy, the Lord continues to call to sinners because He is "long-suffering toward us, not willing that any should perish but that all should come to repentance" (2 Peter 3:9, NKJV). Wisdom returns to the crowded places of the city and calls out so everyone may hear. But note that she addresses the simple and the fools *but not the scorners* (compare Prov. 1:22 with 8:5). They had laughed at her message and turned away from the truth, so their opportunities were over, not because God wasn't speaking but because their hearts were too hard to hear. "Today, if you will hear His voice, do not harden your hearts" (Heb. 4:7-8, NKJV). "See that you do not refuse Him who speaks" (12:25, NKJV).

Wisdom's second message has three very clear points, followed by a call to decision.

"You can trust my words" (vv. 6-9). Five adjectives are used here to describe the character of the message Wisdom declares. Her words are "excellent" (v. 6),

a word that is often translated "captain" or "ruler" in the Old Testament. The *New International Version* reads "worthy things," and other translations use "noble" or "princely." Since God's message is the Word of the King, it is indeed noble and princely.

The message also contains "right things" (vv. 6, 9), a word that describes something straight. The English word "right" comes from the Latin *rectus* which means "straight." This root is also seen in words like "direct" and "correct." God's Word is also true (v. 7) and righteous (v. 8). Folly uses deceptive and "crooked" words to achieve her purposes, language that George Orwell called "newspeak" in his novel *Nineteen Eighty-Four* and that we would today call "double-speak." Whatever God's Word says about anything is right and can be trusted (Ps. 119:128). "The judgments of the Lord are true and righteous altogether" (19:9, NKJV).

Wisdom's words are plain, spoken clearly and openly so that there can be no confusion. Of course, those who reject the Lord don't understand what God is saying (1 Cor. 2:12-16), but this isn't because the Word of God is confusing or unclear. It's because sinners are spiritually blind and deaf (Matt. 13:14-15). The problem is with the hearer, not the speaker. Mark Twain is supposed to have said, "It isn't what I don't understand about the Bible that worries me, but what I do understand."

"You can receive true wealth" (vv. 10-21). This passage deals with enrichment, not riches in the material sense. Wisdom isn't promising to put money in the bank for us; she's urging us to seek eternal wealth instead of gold, silver, and precious stones (see vv. 18-19 as well as 2:4; 3:13-15 and 1 Cor. 3:12). This is an Old

Testament version of Matthew 6:33: "But seek first the kingdom of God and His righteousness, and all these things shall be added to you" (NKJV).

Some Israelites during the Old Testament era had the idea that wealth was a sign of God's blessing while poverty and trouble were evidences that you were out of His favor. Because Job's friends held to a "prosperity theology," they concluded that Job was a great sinner or he wouldn't be suffering so much. When Jesus said it was hard for a rich man to enter God's kingdom, His astounded disciples asked, "Who then can be saved?" (Matt. 19:23-26) If rich people don't make it to heaven, who will?

But Wisdom has better gifts to offer than perishable riches—blessings like prudence, knowledge, discretion ("witty inventions," Prov. 8:12), the fear of the Lord, humility, godly speech, wise counsel, understanding, guidance on life's path, strength for the journey, and "durable riches." A life that's enriched by God may be poor in this world's goods, but it is rich in the things that matter most. It's good to enjoy the things that money can buy, provided you don't lose the things that money can't buy. *What Wisdom has to offer can't be purchased anywhere, no matter how rich you are.*

How do we secure this satisfying and enduring wealth? Hear the Word of God (v. 6), receive instruction (v. 10), love truth and wisdom (vv. 17, 21), and seek God and His wisdom daily (v. 17). Many of God's people have discovered how important it is to start each day with the Lord, meditating on His Word, praying and worshiping Him. (See Ps. 57:8 and 63:11; Gen. 19:27; Ex. 24:4; and Mark 1:35.)

"You can see My works" (vv. 22-31). We touched upon this in chapter 1 and found it to be an explanation of the wisdom of God at work in the creation of the universe. While it isn't a description of Jesus Christ, for the eternal Son of God was never created, it does foreshadow Christ as the creative Word that brought everything into being (John 1:1-4; Col. 2:3).

One of the lessons of this paragraph is that the power and splendor of God, seen all around us in creation, are evidence of what God's wisdom can do. The same God who worked in the "old creation" also wants to work in our lives in the "new creation" (2 Cor. 5:17; Eph. 2:10; 4:24; Col. 3:10). The Lord Jesus Christ, who holds the universe together and causes it to fulfill His will, can hold our lives together and accomplish His purposes for His glory.

When we belong to Jesus Christ and walk in His wisdom, all of creation works for us; if we rebel against His wisdom and will, things start to work against us, as Jonah discovered when he tried to run away from the Lord.

"You must make a decision!" (vv. 32-36) Having declared God's truth, Wisdom now calls for a decision, as all faithful heralds must do. How people respond to God's message is a matter of life or death (vv. 35-36), and it's impossible to be neutral. Wisdom calls for a sincere life-changing decision that involves turning from sin (repentance) and turning to Christ (faith). If the decision is real, it will result in a commitment to the Lord that leads to meeting with Him daily, like a servant at the master's door.

Those who reject God's truth sin against their own souls. Those who hate God's truth are heading for eternal death (Rev. 20:11-15).

3. Wisdom's Call to Life (Prov. 9:1-18)

Instead of going to the busy places of the

city, Wisdom now remains at home and serves as hostess of a grand feast.

Preparation (vv. 1-2). In the previous chapter, we saw Wisdom at work in creation, but here we see her having built a spacious house ("seven pillars") where she prepares a sumptuous banquet. The Jewish people didn't use their flocks and herds for food, so opportunities to eat roast beef or lamb were infrequent and welcomed. The table would be spread with delectable foods as well as wine to drink. "Mingled" (mixed) wine could mean diluted with water (usually three parts water) or mixed with spices. However, the presence of wine on the table must not be interpreted as a divine endorsement of alcoholic beverages. Wine was a normal part of a Jewish meal, but nowhere does the Bible approve of drunkenness (see 20:1; 23:29-35; 31:4-7). More on this topic in a later chapter.

Invitation (vv. 3-9). Instead of going out herself as in the previous two "calls," Wisdom now sends her lovely maidens to the highest places of the city to invite people to the feast. It was customary in those times for a host or hostess to issue two invitations. The first one, given some days in advance, notified the guests of the day and hour of the feast; the second one, given the day of the feast, ascertained who was actually coming (see Luke 14:16-24; Matt. 22:1-14). Knowing the approximate number of the guests, the cooks could then prepare sufficient meat so that there was plenty for everybody and nothing would be wasted. We don't read here of any preliminary invitation. The maidens are simply saying, "Come right now!"

Note that they are inviting one class of people: the simple (Prov. 9:4). Wisdom's first call was to the simple, the scorners, and the fools (1:22). The scorners laughed at her, so in her second call she invited only the simple and the fools (8:5). But the fools didn't want God's wisdom, so in this third call she invites only the simple ones to come to her feast. It's a dangerous thing to reject God's invitation; you never know when it may be your last one (Luke 14:24).

Of course, when the simple people accept the invitation, it means leaving the old crowd, and the fools and scoffers will try to talk them into staying (Prov. 9:6-8). Sinners don't want to be rebuked and reproved, but wise people will accept and benefit from both. Fools, scoffers, and the simple like to have their own way and be told they're doing fine, but wise men and women want the truth. Teach wise people and they'll accept the truth and become wiser; try to teach fools and they'll reject the truth and become even greater fools.

Celebration (vv. 10-12). When you respond to Wisdom's invitation and attend the feast, what will you receive? For one thing, you'll have a greater respect for the Lord and a deeper knowledge of the Holy One (v. 10). The better you know God, the keener will be your knowledge and discernment when it comes to the decisions of life.

Once again, Wisdom promises to give us long life (v. 11) and to fill our days and years with rich experiences of God's grace. God wants to add years to our life and life to our years, and He will do it if we obey His wisdom. Verse 12 reminds us that the Lord wants to build godly character into our lives, and we can't borrow character from others or give our character to them. This is an individual matter that involves individual decisions. Belonging to a fine family, attending a faithful church, or studying in an excellent school can't guarantee the building of our character. Character is built on decisions, and bad decisions will create bad character.

Condemnation (vv. 13-18). The chapter closes with a quick glimpse of the prostitute (Folly) as she calls to the same simple ones and invites them to her house. But if they accept her invitation, they'll be attending a funeral and not a feast— and it will be their own funeral!

In 5:15-18, Solomon compared the joys of married love to drinking pure water from a refreshing fountain, but Folly (the adulteress) offers "stolen water" from somebody else's fountain. God ordained marriage to be a "fence" around the fountain so that nobody will pollute it. "Thou shalt not commit adultery" (Ex. 20:14) has never been removed from God's Law.

When it comes to possessing eternal life and living so as to please God, it's an either/or situation. Either we accept the invitation or we reject it; either we obey His wisdom or we reject it. Those who claim to be neutral are rejecting His Word as much as those who turn away from it completely. "He that is not with Me is against Me," said Jesus (Matt. 12:30).

What will it be in your life, the feast or the funeral?

CHAPTER THREE
THE PATH OF WISDOM AND LIFE
Proverbs 2–4

A newspaper cartoon shows an automobile balancing precariously over the edge of a cliff, with an embarrassed husband at the wheel and his disgusted wife sitting next to him. Meekly, he says to his wife, "Honey, there's got to be a lesson here somewhere."

There's a lesson there all right, and it's this: *The only way to end up at the right destination is to choose the right road.* If you've ever made a wrong turn in a strange place and found yourself lost, then you know how important that lesson is.

The metaphor of life as a journey is a familiar one; it is found in the Bible as well as in classical literature. *The Odyssey* of Homer describes Ulysses' ten-year journey from Troy to his home in Ithaca, and Bunyan's *Pilgrim's Progress* is an account of Christian's journey from the City of Destruction to the heavenly city. The Bible frequently exhorts us to choose the right path, but the contemporary world thinks there are "many ways to God" and any path you sincerely follow will eventually take you there.

Jesus made it clear that in this life we can take only one of two ways, and each of them leads to a different destination. Everybody has to choose either the crowded road that leads to destruction or the narrow road that leads to life (Matt. 7:13-14). There's no middle way.

In the book of Proverbs, the words "path" and "way" (and their plurals) are found nearly 100 times (KJV). Wisdom is not only a person to love, but wisdom is also a path to walk, and the emphasis in chapters 2, 3, and 4 is on the blessings God's people enjoy when they walk on Wisdom's path. The path of Wisdom leads to life, but the way of Folly leads to death; when you walk on the path of Wisdom, you enjoy three wonderful assurances: Wisdom *protects* your path (chap. 2), *directs* your path (chap. 3), and *perfects* your path (chap. 4).

1. Wisdom Protects Your Path (Prov. 2)
The key verse in chapter 2 is verse 8: "He guards the paths of justice, and preserves the way of His saints" (NKJV). The repeti-

tion of the phrase "my son" (2:1; 3:1, 11, 21; 4:10, 20; and see 4:1, "my children") reminds us that the book of Proverbs records a loving father's wise counsel to his family. The British statesman Lord Chesterfield said, "In matters of religion and matrimony I never give any advice; because I will not have anybody's torments in this world or the next laid to my charge." But Jewish fathers were *commanded* to teach their children wisdom (Deut. 6:1-9); if the children were smart, they paid attention and obeyed. Life is dangerous. It is wise to listen to the counsel of godly people who have walked the path before us.

Three different "walks" are described in this chapter.

Walking with God (vv. 1-9). Chapters 2-4 all begin with an admonition to listen to God's words and take them to heart (3:1-12; 4:1-9), because that's the only way we can walk with God and live skillfully. Eight imperatives in this paragraph reveal our responsibilities toward God's truth: *receive* (accept) God's words and *hide* them (store them up) in our minds and hearts; *incline* the ear and *apply* the heart; *cry after* knowledge and *lift up the voice* for understanding; *seek* for wisdom and *search after* it. If you want wisdom, you must listen to God attentively (Matt. 13:9), obey Him humbly (John 7:17), ask Him sincerely (James 1:5), and seek Him diligently (Isa. 55:6-7), the way a miner searches for silver and gold.

Obtaining spiritual wisdom isn't a once-a-week hobby, it is the daily discipline of a lifetime. But in this age of microwave ovens, fast foods, digests, and numerous "made easy" books, many people are out of the habit of daily investing time and energy in digging deep into Scripture and learning wisdom from the Lord. Thanks to television, their attention

span is brief; thanks to religious entertainment that passes for worship, their spiritual appetite is feeble and spiritual knowledge isn't "pleasant to [their] soul" (Prov. 2:10). It's no wonder fewer and fewer people "take time to be holy" and more and more people fall prey to the enemies that lurk along the way.

If we do our part, God will keep His promise and protect us from the enemy (vv. 7-8): "He holds victory in store for the upright, He is a shield to those whose walk is blameless, for He guards the course of the just and protects the way of His faithful ones" (NIV). "Your word I have hidden in my heart, that I might not sin against You" (Ps. 119:11, NKJV).

People are willing to work diligently in their jobs because they know they'll earn a paycheck, but what about applying themselves diligently to God's Word in order to gain spiritual riches that are more valuable than gold and silver and jewels, riches that will last forever? (See 2:4; 3:13-15; 8:10-21; 16:16.) There's a price to pay if we would gain spiritual wisdom, but there's an even greater price to pay if we don't gain it. We must walk with God through the study of His Word.

Walking with the wicked (vv. 10-19). Here we meet "the evil man" and "the strange woman," two people who are dangerous because they want to lead God's children away from the path of life. The evil man is known for his perverse ("froward," KJV; crooked) words (see vv. 12, 14; 6:14; 8:13; 10:31-32; and 16:28, 30). He walks on the dark path of disobedience and enjoys doing that which is evil. He belongs to the crowd Solomon warns us about in 1:10-19. The person who walks in the way of wisdom would immediately detect his deceit and avoid him.

The "strange woman" is the adulteress, the wayward wife described so vividly in

7:1-27. If the evil man uses *perverse* words to snare the unwary, the adulteress uses *flattering* words. Someone has said that flattery isn't communication, it is manipulation; it's people telling us things about ourselves that we enjoy hearing and wish were true. The strange woman knows how to use flattery successfully. She has no respect for God, because she breaks His law (Ex. 20:14); she has no respect for her husband because she violates the promises she made to him when she married him. She no longer has a guide or a friend in the Lord or in her husband, because she has taken the path of sin. Anyone who listens to her words and follows her path is heading for the cemetery.

Walking with the righteous (vv. 20-22). Note the argument that Solomon gives in this chapter that begins with the "if" of verse 1 and continues with the "then" of verse 9 and the "thus" of verse 20. *If* we receive God's words and obey them, *then* we will have wisdom to make wise decisions, and *thus* God will keep His promise and protect us from the evil man and the strange woman. When you obey God, you have the privilege to "walk in the ways of good men" (v. 20, NIV). *If you follow the Word of God, you will never lack for the right kind of friends.*

The wicked may appear to be succeeding, but their end is destruction (Ps. 37). The godly will be rooted in the place of God's blessing (Ps. 1:3), but the ungodly will be uprooted from the land. The safest and most satisfying path is the path of wisdom, the path of life.

2. Wisdom Directs Our Path (Prov. 3)

The key verses in this chapter are verses 5-6, a promise God's people have often claimed as they have sought the Lord's direction for their lives. And this promise has never failed them—if they have obeyed the conditions God has laid down in verses 1-12. God keeps His promises when we obey His precepts, because our obedience prepares us to receive and enjoy what He has planned for us.

Conditions to meet (vv. 1-12). The first condition for receiving God's guidance is that we *learn God's truth* (vv. 1-4). The will of God is revealed in the Word of God (Col. 1:9-10), and the only way to know His will is to study His Word and obey it. By receiving the Word within our hearts, we experience growth in godly character so that mercy and truth ("love and faithfulness," NIV) become beautiful ornaments in our lives (Prov. 3:3; 1:9). It isn't enough for believers to carry the Bible in their hands; they must let the Holy Spirit write it on their hearts (3:3; 7:3; 2 Cor. 3:1-3). Obedience to the Word can add years to your life and life to your years.

Second, we must *obey God's will (vv. 5-8).* "He shall direct your paths" (v. 6, NKJV) is the promise, but the fulfillment of that promise is predicated on our obedience to the Lord. We must trust Him with all our heart and obey Him in all our ways. That means total commitment to Him (Rom. 12:1-2). The word translated "trust" in verse 5 means "to lie helpless, facedown." It pictures a servant waiting for the master's command in readiness to obey, or a defeated soldier yielding himself to the conquering general.

The danger, of course, is that we lean on our own understanding and thereby miss God's will. This warning doesn't suggest that God's children turn off their brains and ignore their intelligence and common sense. It simply cautions us not to depend on our own wisdom and experience or the wisdom and experience of others. Abraham did this when he went to Egypt (Gen. 12:10-20) and so did Joshua when he attacked the little town of Ai

(Josh. 7). When we become "wise in [our] own eyes" (Prov. 3:7), then we're heading for trouble.

Share God's blessings (vv. 9-10) is the third condition we must meet if we want God to direct our paths. There's no such thing as "spiritual" and "material" in the Christian life, for everything comes from God and belongs to God. The Old Testament Jews brought the Lord the firstlings of their flocks (Ex. 13:1-2) and the firstfruits of their fields (Lev. 23:9-14), and in this way acknowledged His goodness and sovereignty. The New Testament parallel is seen in Matthew 6:33.

If we don't faithfully give to the Lord, we don't really trust the Lord. Of course, our tithes and offerings aren't "payment" for His blessings; rather, they're evidence of our faith and obedience. Christian industrialist R.G. LeTourneau used to say, "If you give because it pays, it won't pay." Giving is heart preparation for what God wants to say to us and do for us. "For where your treasure is, there your heart will be also" (Matt. 6:21, NKJV).

Our fourth responsibility is to *submit to God's chastening (Prov. 3:11-12)*. Chastening is a part of God's plan to help His sons and daughters mature in godly character (Heb. 12:1-11). God chastens us, not as a judge punishes a criminal, but as a parent disciplines a child. He acts in love and His purpose is that we might become "partakers of His holiness" (Heb. 12:10). Sometimes He chastens because we have rebelled and need to repent; other times He chastens to keep us from sinning and to prepare us for His special blessing. No matter how much the experience *hurts us,* it will never *harm us,* because God always chastens in love (Deut. 8:2-5).

Blessings to enjoy (vv. 13-35). If we trust and obey, our Father will direct our path into the blessings He has planned

for us; the first of these blessings is the *true wealth that comes from wisdom (vv. 13-18).* Some people know the price of everything but the value of nothing; consequently, they make unwise choices and end up with shoddy merchandise. An acquaintance of mine, thinking he was getting a bargain, bought a box of white shirts from a street vendor for just a few dollars. When he opened the box at home, he discovered they weren't shirts at all: they were dickeys made to be used on corpses. So much for his bargain. You take what you want from life, and you pay for it.

It's good to have the things money can buy, provided you don't lose the things money can't buy. What good is an expensive house if there's no happy home within it? Happiness, pleasantness, and peace aren't the guaranteed by-products of financial success, but they are guaranteed to the person who lives by God's wisdom. Wisdom becomes a "tree of life" to the believer who takes hold of her, and this is a foretaste of heaven (Rev. 22:1-2).

Another blessing is *harmony with God's creation (Prov. 3:19-20).* The person who walks according to God's wisdom can sing, "This is my Father's world," and really mean it. The wisdom of God brought everything into being (8:22ff), including what science calls "the laws of nature." Obey these laws and creation will work with you; disobey them and creation will work against you. People in the so-called "New Age" movement try to be "at one" with creation, but they're doomed to fail because they reject the wisdom of God. Christians who live by God's wisdom will be good stewards of His creation and will use His gifts for His glory.

A third blessing is *the Father's providential care (3:21-26).* Because God *directs* our path, He is able to *protect* our path. The

Lord isn't obligated to protect His children when they willfully go their own way. They're only tempting Him, and that's a dangerous thing to do. Back in the early '40s an angry unbeliever asked a pastor friend of mine, "Why doesn't God stop this terrible war?" My friend quietly replied, "He doesn't stop it because He didn't start it." It was started by people who rejected God's wisdom and pursued their own selfish plans.

When you surrender yourself to God, every part of your body belongs to Him and will be protected by Him. He will help you keep your *eyes* from wandering (v. 21), your *neck* from turning your face away from God's path (vv. 22; see Luke 9:53), your *feet* walking on the right path (Prov. 3:23, 26), and even your *backbone* safe while you're sleeping (v. 24). If something frightening suddenly happens, you won't be afraid (v. 25; see Pss. 112:7; 121:3-6), because the Lord is protecting you. How we sleep is sometimes evidence of how much we trust the Lord (Pss. 4–5).

A positive relationship with others (Prov. 3:27-35) is a fourth blessing the believer enjoys when he or she walks in the wisdom of God. Wise Christians will be generous to their neighbors and live peaceably with them (vv. 27-30), doing their best to avoid unnecessary disagreements (Rom. 12:18). After all, if we truly love God, we will love our neighbor as we would want him to love us.

On the other hand, if our neighbor is a perverse person who scoffs at our faith (Prov. 3:31-35), the Lord will guide us in letting our light shine and His love show so that we will influence him but he won't lead us astray. Sometimes it takes a great deal of patience, prayer, and wisdom to rightly relate to people who don't want Christians in the neighborhood, but perhaps that's why God put us there.

It's possible to have a godly home in the midst of an ungodly neighborhood, for God "blesses the home of the righteous" (v. 33, NIV). We are the salt of the earth and the light of the world, and one dedicated Christian in a neighborhood can make a great deal of difference and be a powerful witness for the Lord.

3. Wisdom Perfects Our Path (Prov. 4)

The key verse in chapter 4 is verse 18, "But the path of the just is like the shining light, that shineth more and more unto the perfect day." The picture is that of the sunrise ("the first gleam of dawn," NIV) and the increasing of the light on the pilgrim path as the day advances. If we walk in the way of God's wisdom, the path gets brighter and brighter and there is no sunset! When the path ends, we step into a land where the light never dims, for "there shall be no night there" (Rev. 22:5).

God has a plan for each of His children (Eph. 2:10), and if we walk in His wisdom, we can confidently say, "The Lord will perfect that which concerns me" (Ps. 138:8, NKJV). Our path may not be an easy one, but it will always be a fulfilling one as we walk in the will of the Father. This involves three responsibilities on our part: knowing God's Word (Prov. 4:19), trusting God's providence (vv. 10-19), and obeying God's will (vv. 20-27).

Knowing God's Word (vv. 1-9). Some children don't like to hear Dad say, "Now, back when I was a boy..." but they might learn a lot if they paid attention and listened. He learned wisdom from his father and now he's passing it on to the next generation. This is the primary way God has ordained for His truth to be preserved and invested from generation to generation (Deut. 6:3-9; Eph. 6:1-4; 2 Tim. 1:3-5; 2:2; 3:14-17). Children who have godly parents and grandparents ought to give thanks to the Lord for their rich heritage, instead of scoffing at that heritage and abandoning it for the way of the world.

"Get wisdom" (Prov. 4:5) suggests, "buy wisdom," because the Hebrew word carries the idea of a commercial transaction. There's a price to pay if you want to know God's truth and obey it. "Buy the truth, and sell it not" (23:23). Parents and grandparents can teach us, but only *we* can receive the Word into our hearts, cherish it, and pay the price to obey it.

The father tells his sons to treat wisdom the way they would treat their mother, sister, or wife: love her, honor her, embrace her, exalt her! The bumper sticker that asks, "Have you hugged your children today?" ought to be balanced with, "Have you hugged wisdom today?" In Proverbs, Wisdom is personified as a beautiful woman who invites us to her lavish banquet, while Folly is the adulteress or prostitute who tempts us to poverty and death. The one you love is the one who will control your life. Embrace Wisdom and you will have security (4:6), honor (v. 8), and beauty (v. 9).

Trusting God's providence (vv. 10-19). When you receive God's truth into your heart, God renews your mind (Rom. 12:2) and enables you to think wisely. This helps you make right decisions and experience the guidance of God day by day. God in His loving providence directs us and prepares the path for us. Augustine said, "Trust the past to the mercy of God, the present to His love, and the future to His providence." But King David said it better long before Augustine: "You will show me the path of life; in Your presence is fullness of joy; at Your right hand are pleasures forevermore" (Ps. 16:11, NKJV).[1]

If you are willing to do God's will, you will have God's guidance (John 7:17), but if you treat God's will like a buffet lunch, choosing only what pleases you, He will never direct you. As I've said before, the will of God isn't for the curious; it's for the serious. As we look back on more than forty years of marriage and ministry, my wife and I can testify to God's providential leading in our lives in ways that we never suspected He would use.

But God's children can't expect God's leading if they shuttle back and forth between the path of wisdom and the path of the wicked (Prov. 4:14-17). Stay as far away from that path as you can! Don't enter it! Avoid it! Don't go near it! Go as far from it as you can! Certainly we must witness to unsaved people whom the Lord brings to us, but we must never adopt their lifestyle or imitate their ways. *God doesn't guide His children when they're walking in darkness.* When you're living in the will of God, the path gets brighter and brighter, not darker and darker (1 John 1:5-10).

The danger is that we let the lessons of wisdom slip through our fingers and we lose them. "Take fast hold of instruction; let her not go" (Prov. 4:13). Hold on to wisdom the way a child holds a parent's hand and trusts Mother or Father to guide and protect. God is able to keep us from stumbling (Jude 24) if we'll keep ourselves in His wisdom.

Obeying God's will (vv. 20-27). This is a wonderful paragraph to us as a personal spiritual inventory to see if we're really living in obedience to the Lord. Let's ask ourselves:

"What comes into my ears?" (v. 20) Whatever enters my ears will ultimately influence my mind, my heart, and my decisions, so I'd better be careful what I listen to. Paul warns us to beware of "obscenity, foolish talk or coarse joking" (Eph. 5:4, NIV), and Psalm 1:1 tells us to avoid ungodly counsel. When people speak, we must be able to identify God's

voice (John 10:3-5, 16) and obey what He says.

"What is within my heart?" (v. 23) Whatever the heart loves, the ears will hear and the eyes will see. When our children were small, no matter where we were driving, they could usually find the ice cream shops and the toy stores; I must confess that I managed to locate the bookstores! "Above all else, guard your heart, for it is the wellspring of life" (v. 23, NIV). If we pollute that wellspring, the infection will spread; before long, hidden appetites will become open sins and public shame.

The Bible warns us to avoid a double heart (Ps. 12:2), a hard heart (Prov. 28:14), a proud heart (21:4), an unbelieving heart (Heb. 3:12), a cold heart (Matt. 24:12), and an unclean heart (Ps. 51:10). "Search me, O God, and know my heart" (139:23).

"What is upon my lips?" (v. 24) Whatever is in the heart will ultimately come out of the mouth (Matt. 12:33-34). God's children must be careful to have "sound speech that cannot be condemned" (Titus 2:8), speech that's gracious and "seasoned with salt" (Col. 4:6, NKJV). The ancient Romans, listening to one of their orators, would look at each other, smile, and say, "Cum grano salis"—"Take it with a grain of salt." But Christians are supposed to *put the salt into their speech* and keep their words pure and honest.

As we shall see in a later chapter, Proverbs has a great deal to say about human speech; in fact, the word "mouth" is used over fifty times and the word "lips" over forty times in the *Authorized Version*. Among other things, Solomon warns us about perverse lips (Prov. 4:24), lying lips (12:22), flattering lips (20:19), deceptive lips (24:28), and undisciplined lips (10:19). "He who guards his lips guards his life, but he who speaks rashly will come to ruin" (13:3, NIV).

"What is before my eyes?" (v. 25) Outlook determines outcome. Abraham was the friend of God because he walked by faith and "looked for a city ... whose builder and maker is God" (Heb. 11:10). Lot became a friend of the world because he walked by sight and moved toward the wicked city of Sodom (Gen. 13:10, 12). Everybody has some vision before them that helps to determine their values, actions, and plans. We would all be wise to imitate David who said, "I will set no wicked thing before mine eyes" (Ps. 101:3), and the writer of Psalm 119 who prayed, "Turn my eyes away from worthless things" (v. 37, NIV). If you are "looking unto Jesus" (Heb. 12:2) as you walk the path of life, then keep that posture of faith. If you look back (Luke 9:62) or around (Matt. 14:30), you may go on a detour.

"What is beyond my path?" (vv. 26-27) The Hebrew word translated "ponder" means "to weigh" or "to make level." It is related to a word that means "scales" (16:11). In his final speech before he drank the hemlock, Socrates said, "The unexamined life is not worth living"; Paul wrote, "Examine yourselves as to whether you are in the faith. Test yourselves" (2 Cor. 13:5, NKJV). The Lord is weighing our ways (Prov. 5:21) and our hearts (21:2), as well as our actions (1 Sam. 2:3), and we had better do the same. Life is too short and too precious to be wasted on the temporary and the trivial.

If we're walking in the way of wisdom, God promises to protect our path, direct our path, and perfect our path.

All folly can offer us is danger, detours, and disappointments, ultimately leading to death.

It shouldn't be too difficult to make the right choice!

CHAPTER FOUR
THE PATH OF FOLLY AND DEATH
Proverbs 5–7

You shall not commit adultery." The Lord God spoke those words at Mount Sinai, and we call what He said the Seventh Commandment (Ex. 20:14). It declares that sexual intimacy outside the bonds of marriage is wrong, even if "between consenting adults."[1] This law specifically mentions adultery, but the commandment includes the sexual sins prohibited elsewhere in Scripture (Lev. 18; Rom. 1:18-32; 1 Cor. 6:9-20; Eph. 5:1-14). God invented sex and has every right to tell us how to use it properly.

However, on hearing the Seventh Commandment, many people in contemporary society smile nonchalantly and ask, "What's wrong with premarital or extramarital sex, or any other kind, for that matter?" After all, they argue, many people indulge in these things and seem to get away with it. Furthermore, these activities are more acceptable today than they were in Solomon's day; why make a big issue out of it? "Life is a game in which the rules are constantly changing," says a contemporary writer; "nothing spoils a game more than those who take it seriously."[2] So, the verdict's in: sex is fun, so don't take it too seriously.

It's true that some well-known people have indulged in sexual escapades and even bragged about it, including government officials, Hollywood stars, sports heroes, and (alas!) preachers, but that doesn't make it right. Sexual sin is one of the main themes of numerous movies, TV programs, novels, and short stories; yet popularity is no test of right and wrong. Many things that the law says are legal, the Bible says are evil, and there won't be a jury sitting at the White Throne Judgment (Rev. 20:11-15; 21:27; 22:15).

Why worry about sexual sins? These three chapters of Proverbs give us three reasons why we should worry if we break God's laws of purity: because sexual sin is eventually disappointing (Prov. 5), gradually destructive (chap. 6), and ultimately deadly (chap. 7). That's why God says, "You shall not commit adultery."

1. Sexual Sin Is Eventually Disappointing (Prov. 5)

When married people honor and respect sex as God instructs them in His Word, they can experience increasing enjoyment and enrichment in their intimacy. But when people break the rules, the result is just the opposite. They experience disappointment and disillusionment and have to search for larger "doses" of sexual adventure in order to attain the imaginary pleasure level they're seeking.

God created sex not only for reproduction but also for enjoyment, and He didn't put the "marriage wall" around sex to *rob us* of pleasure but to *increase* pleasure and *protect* it. In this chapter, Solomon explains the disappointments that come when people violate God's loving laws of sexual purity.

Their experience goes from sweetness to bitterness (vv. 1-6). We've met "the strange woman" before (2:16; NIV, "adulteress") and she'll be mentioned again (5:20; 6:24; 7:5; 20:16; 22:14; 23:27; 27:13). The word translated "strange" basically means "not related to." The "strange woman" is one to whom the man is not related by marriage, and therefore any sexual liaison with her is evil. The beginning of this sinful alliance may be exciting and sweet, because the kisses and words from her lips drip like honey (7:13-20), but in the end, the "sweetness" turns to bitterness and the honey becomes poison (5:4).

The book of Proverbs emphasizes the importance of *looking ahead to see where your actions will lead you* (see 5:11; 14:12-14; 16:25; 19:20; 20:21; 23:17-18, 32; 24:14, 20; 25:8). The wise person checks on the destination before buying a ticket (4:26), but modern society thinks that people can violate God's laws and escape the consequences. They're sure that whatever has happened to others will never happen to them. Sad to say, their ignorance and insolence can never neutralize the tragic aftermath that comes when people break the laws of God. "Oh, that they were wise, that they understood this, that they would consider their latter end!" (Deut. 32:29)

Their experience goes from gain to loss (vv. 7-14). Temptation always includes hopeful promises; otherwise, people would never take the devil's bait. For a time, it seems like these promises have been fulfilled, and sinners bask in the sunshine of pleasant experiences and false assurances. This is what family counselor J. Allan Petersen calls, "the myth of the greener grass."[3] People who commit sexual sins think their problems are solved ("She understands me so much better than my wife does!") and that life will get better and better. But disobedience to God's laws always brings sad consequences and sinners eventually pay dearly for their brief moments of pleasure.

When you read verses 9-14, you hear the words of a suffering sinner lamenting the high cost of disobeying God's laws, because *the most expensive thing in the world is sin.* He discovers that the woman's husband is a cruel man who demands that he pay for what he's done, so the adulterer ends up giving his strength to others and

toiling away to pay his debt. Instead of luxury, the sinner has misery; instead of riches, poverty; instead of success, ruin; and instead of a good reputation, the name of an adulterer. He looks back and wishes he had listened to his parents and his spiritual instructors, but his wishes can't change his wretched situation. Yes, God in His *grace* will forgive his sins if he repents, but God in His *government* sees to it that he reaps what he sows.

Their experience goes from purity to pollution (vv. 15-20). Solomon compares enjoying married love to drinking pure water from a fresh well, but committing sexual sin is like drinking polluted water from the gutter or sewer. Sex within marriage is a beautiful river that brings life and refreshment, but sex outside marriage is a sewer that defiles everything it touches. To commit sexual sin is to pour this beautiful river into the streets and the public squares. What waste! If you "drink deep" of the wrong kind of love (7:18, NIV) it will destroy you.

The commitment of marriage is like the banks of the river that keep the river from becoming a swamp. God's holy law confines the waters within the banks, and this produces power and depth. Extramarital and premarital affairs don't satisfy because they're shallow, and it doesn't take much to stir up shallow water. A man and woman pledged to each other in marriage can experience the growing satisfaction that comes with love, commitment, depth, and purity.

But there's something else involved here. Solomon admonishes the husband to be "ravished" with his wife's love (5:19-20); the word translated "ravished" also means "intoxicated" or "infatuated."[4] The adulterer watches the river turn into a sewer, but the faithful husband sees the water become wine! I think it's significant that Jesus turned water into wine at a wedding feast, as though He were giving us an object lesson concerning the growing delights of marriage (John 2:1-11).

When a husband and wife are faithful to the Lord and to each other, and when they obey Scriptures like 1 Corinthians 7:1-5 and Ephesians 5:22-33, neither of them will look for satisfaction anywhere else. If they love each other and seek to please each other and the Lord, their relationship will be one of deepening joy and satisfaction; they won't look around for "the greener grass."

Their experience goes from freedom to bondage (vv. 21-23). Freedom of choice is one of the privileges God has given us, but He instructs us and urges us to use that freedom wisely. The laws of God are guideposts to lead us on the path of life, and He watches the decisions we make and the roads we take. "The eyes of the Lord are in every place, beholding the evil and the good" (15:3).

As long as we use our freedom wisely, we will mature in Christian character, and God can trust us with more freedom. But if we abuse our freedom and deliberately disobey His Word, our freedom will gradually become bondage, the kind of bondage that can't easily be broken. "The evil deeds of a wicked man ensnare him; the cords of his sin hold him fast" (5:22, NIV). Those words could have been used as an epitaph for Samson (Judg. 13–16).

It's impossible to sin without being bound. One of the deceitful things about sin is that it promises freedom but only brings slavery. "Most assuredly, I say to you, whoever commits sin is a slave of sin" (John 8:34, NKJV). "Do you not know that to whom you present yourselves slaves to obey, you are that one's slaves whom you obey, whether of sin leading to

death, or of obedience leading to righteousness?" (Rom. 6:16, NKJV)

The cords of sin get stronger the more we sin, yet sin deceives us into thinking we're free and can quit sinning whenever we please. As the invisible chains of habit are forged, we discover to our horror that we don't have the strength to break them. Millions of people in our world today are in one kind of bondage or another and are seeking for deliverance, but the only One who can set them free is Jesus Christ. "Therefore if the Son makes you free, you shall be free indeed" (John 8:36, NKJV).

No wonder the father warns his children to stay away from the adulteress. "Remove your way far from her, and do not go near the door of her house" (Prov. 5:8, NKJV). "Her house is the way to hell, going down to the chambers of death" (7:27).

2. Sexual Sin Is Gradually Destructive (Prov. 6)

Chapter 6 deals with three enemies that can destroy a person financially, physically, morally, or spiritually: unwise financial commitments (vv. 1-5), laziness (vv. 6-11), and lust (vv. 20-35). It is not unusual for one person to be guilty of all three, because laziness and lust often go together; people who can easily be pressured into putting up security for somebody can be pressured into doing other foolish things, including committing adultery. "For where your treasure is, there will your heart be also" (Matt. 6:21).

We will consider Proverbs 6:1-11 in our study of wealth and work. Verses 12-19 will be included in chapter 5, in our study of "the wicked people" mentioned in the book of Proverbs. In verses 20-35, Solomon deals with adultery and points out what people will lose who commit this heinous sin.

They lose the Word of God (vv. 20-24). In chapters 5-7, each of the warnings against adultery is prefaced by an admonition to pay attention to the Word of God (5:1-2; 6:20-24; 7:1-5). It is by our trusting and obeying His truth that God keeps us from believing the enemy's lies. Certainly children have the obligation to honor their father and mother (6:20; see 1:8), and God's children have the responsibility and privilege of bringing glory to their Father's name. "Marriage is honorable among all, and the bed undefiled; but fornicators and adulterers God will judge" (Heb. 13:4, NKJV).

The Word should be bound to the heart (Ps. 119:11), because the heart is "the wellspring of life" (Prov. 4:23, NIV).[5] God's truth should also control the neck, because a man might be tempted to turn his head and look at a beautiful woman for the purpose of lusting (Matt. 5:27-30). He may not be able to avoid seeing the woman the first time, but it's looking the second time that gets him into trouble.

The Word of God in the mind and heart is like a guide who leads us on the safe path and protects us from attacks. It's also like a friend who talks to us and counsels us along the way (Prov. 6:22). We walk in the light because the Word is a lamp (v. 23; Ps. 119:105, 130). If we listen to God's voice in His Word, we won't fall for the enemy's flattery (Prov. 6:24).

Read 1 John 1:5-10 and note that "walking in the light" assures us of hearing the Word of God, while "walking in darkness" causes us to lose His Word. If we disobey Him, we don't *do* the truth (Prov. 6:6), we don't *have* the truth (v. 8), and *His Word is not in us* (v. 10). There is a gradual erosion of the spiritual life, from light to darkness, and with this erosion comes a deterioration of Christian character.

They lose wealth (vv. 25-26). This parallels 5:7-14, and see 29:3. To be "brought to a piece of bread" means to be degraded to the lowest level of poverty (see Luke 15:13-16, 30). If the adultery results in scandal, a lawsuit, and a divorce, the price will not be cheap; in this day of AIDS and other sexually transmitted diseases, the adulterer is taking chances with his health and his life.

They lose enjoyment (vv. 27-31). Fire is a good thing if it's confined and controlled. It can keep us warm, cook our food, drive our turbines, and manufacture our electricity. Sex is a good gift from God, but like fire, if it gets out of control, it becomes destructive. What begins as a "warm" experience soon becomes a burning experience, like holding a torch in your lap or walking on burning coals.

"But sex is a normal desire, given to us by God," some people argue. "Therefore, we have every right to use it, even if we're not married. It's like eating: If you're hungry, God gave you food to eat; if you're lonely, God gave you sex to enjoy." Some of the people in the Corinthian church used this argument to defend their sinful ways: "Foods for the stomach and the stomach for foods" (1 Cor. 6:13, NKJV). But Paul made it clear that the believer's body belonged to God and that the presence of a desire wasn't the same as the privilege to satisfy that desire (vv. 12-20).

Solomon used a similar approach in Proverbs 6:30-31. Certainly hunger is a strong force in human life, and the only way to satisfy hunger is to eat, but if you steal the bread that you eat, you're breaking the law. You'll end up paying more for that bread than if you'd gone out and bought a loaf at the bakery. As you sit in jail or stand in court, the enjoyment you had from that bread will soon be forgotten.

Adultery is stealing. "For this is the will of God, your sanctification; that is, that you abstain from sexual immorality … and that no man transgress and defraud his brother in the matter" (1 Thess. 4:3, 6, NASB). When adultery enters a marriage, everybody loses.

They lose their good sense (v. 32). King David was a brilliant strategist on the battlefield and a wise ruler on the throne, but he lost his common sense when he gazed at his neighbor's wife and lusted for her (2 Sam. 12). He was sure he could get away with his sin, but common sense would have told him he was wrong. Every stratagem David used to implicate Bathsheba's husband failed, so he ended up having the man killed. Surely David knew that we reap what we sow, and reap he did, right in the harvest field of his own family.

They lose their peace (vv. 33-35). The angry husband will use every means possible to avenge himself, for a loving husband would rather that his neighbor steal his money than steal his wife. "For love is as strong as death, its jealousy unyielding as the grave. It burns like blazing fire, like a mighty flame" (Song. 8:6, NIV). The offender will have no peace, and no amount of money he offers the husband will be accepted. The adulterer loses his reputation in the community and might actually suffer physical punishment. Of course, he and the woman were supposed to be stoned to death (Lev. 20:10; Deut. 22:22), but we're not sure this penalty was always exacted.

In today's society, if a person has enough money and "clout," he or she might be able to survive an adulterous scandal, but life is still never quite the same. Whether in this life or the next, sinners can be sure that their sins will find them out. Indulging in sexual sin is always a losing proposition.

3. Sexual Sin Is Ultimately Deadly (Prov. 7)

For the third time, Solomon calls the young person back to the Word of God (vv. 1-5), because keeping God's commandments is a matter of life or death. The adulteress lives on a dead-end street: "Her house is the way to hell, going down to the chambers of death" (v. 27).

The familiar phrase "apple of your eye" (v. 2) refers to the pupil of the eye which the ancients thought was a sphere like an apple. We protect our eyes because they're valuable to us, and so should we honor and protect God's Word by obeying it. Sexual sin often begins with undisciplined eyes and hands (Matt. 5:27-30), but the heart of the problem is … the heart (Prov. 7:2-3). If we love God's wisdom as we love those in our family, we wouldn't want to visit the house of the harlot.

This chapter vividly describes a naive young man who falls into the trap of the adulteress. Note the steps that lead to his destruction.

He tempts himself (vv. 6-9). You get the impression that this young man is either terribly dumb or very proud, convinced that he can play with sin and get away with it. But he's only tempting himself and heading for trouble. To begin with, he's out at night ("walking in darkness"—see 2:13; John 3:19-21; 1 John 1:5-7), and he's deliberately walking near the place of temptation and danger. He didn't heed the wise counsel of the Lord, "Remove your way far from her, and do not go near the door of her house" (5:8, NKJV). God's Word wasn't controlling his feet (3:26; 4:27).

During more than forty years of ministry, I've listened to many sad stories from people who have indulged in sexual sin and suffered greatly; in almost every instance, the people deliberately put themselves into the place of temptation and danger. Unlike Job, they didn't make "a covenant with [their] eyes not to look lustfully at a girl" (Job 31:1, NIV), nor did they follow the example of Joseph and flee from temptation (Gen. 39:7ff; 2 Tim. 2:22). We can't help being tempted, but we can certainly help tempting ourselves.

He is tempted by the woman (vv. 10-20). Like the deadly spider in the web, the woman was watching at the window, ready to pounce on her prey. She was a man's wife, but when he was out of town, she dressed like a prostitute so she could attract the men who were searching for her services (Gen. 38:14-15; Ezek. 16:16). While her husband was away, she saw no reason why she shouldn't make some money and enjoy herself at the same time. She'd been in the streets, looking for victims (Prov. 7:11-12), but now one was coming right to her door!

She caught him (Gen. 39:12), kissed him (Prov. 5:3), and convinced him that it was an opportune time for him to visit her. Before leaving town, her husband had gone with her to the temple where he'd sacrificed a peace offering (Lev. 7:11-21), and she had some of the meat at home. She would prepare him a feast that he would never forget. "This is the way of an adulterous woman: She eats and wipes her mouth, and says, 'I have done no wickedness' " (Prov. 30:20, NKJV).

She appeals to the young man's male ego as she flatters him and makes him think he's very special to her. What she's offering to him she would never offer to anyone else! She appeals to his imagination as she describes her beautiful bed and the expensive spices that perfume it. She assures him that nobody will find out about it (except that somebody's watching, 7:6) and that her husband won't be home for many days. They have plenty of time to enjoy themselves.

He tempts the Lord (vv. 21-27). When we pray, "Lead us not into temptation" (Matt. 6:13), we know that God doesn't tempt us (James 1:13-16); yet we may tempt ourselves, tempt others, and even tempt God (Ex. 17:1-7; Num. 14:22; Deut. 6:16; Ps. 78:18, 56; 1 Cor. 10:9). We tempt God when we deliberately disobey Him and put ourselves into situations so difficult that only God can deliver us. It's as though we "dare Him" to do something.

The youth made a sudden decision to follow the woman, and when he did, he began to act like an animal. He was no longer a young man, made in the image of God, but an ox going to the slaughter or a bird walking into the trap. Human beings are the only creatures in God's creation who can choose what kind of creatures they want to be. God wants us to be sheep (Ps. 23:1; John 10; 1 Peter 2:25), but there are other options, such as horses or mules (Ps. 32:9), or even hogs and dogs (2 Peter 2:22). When we live outside the will of God, we lose our privileges as human beings made in His divine image.

By going to her house, her table, and her bed, the young man willfully disobeyed God's Law, *but the Lord didn't intervene.* He allowed the youth to indulge in his sensual appetites and suffer the consequences. God could have stopped him, but He didn't, because the Word says, "You shall not tempt [put to the test] the Lord your God" (Matt. 4:7; Deut. 6:16). If instead of tempting the Lord, the youth had *looked up* to the Lord and remembered His Word (Prov. 7:24), *looked within* and kept his heart focused on God's truth (v. 25), and *looked ahead* to see the terrible consequences of his sin (vv. 26-27), he would have turned around and fled from the harlot's clutches.

Society today not only smiles at sexual sin, it actually approves it and encourages it. Perversions the very mention of which would have shocked people fifty years ago are openly discussed today and are even made the subject of novels, movies, and TV dramas. What Paul saw in his day and described in Romans 1:18-32 is now apparent in our own day, but people resent it if you call these practices "sin." After all, "Everybody's doing it."

But the Gospel is still "the power of God unto salvation" (Rom. 1:16) and Christ can still change people's lives (1 Cor. 6:9-11). It isn't enough for Christians to protest the evil; we must also practice the good (Matt. 5:13-16) and proclaim the good news that sinners can become new creatures in Christ (2 Cor. 5:17).

If the world had more light, there would be less darkness.

If the world had more salt, there would be less decay.

If the world heard more truth, there would be less deception.

We have a job to do!

INTERLUDE

From this chapter on, we'll be studying the book of Proverbs *topically*, bringing together texts that deal with the same subjects and showing how they relate to each other and to your personal Christian life today. In a sense, we'll be studying what the Bible teaches about practical Christian living, using the book of Proverbs as our point of reference.

No classification of texts is inspired or final, and many verses could be put into several different categories. The psalmist was right when he said, "To all perfection I see a limit, but Your commands are boundless" (Ps. 119:96, NIV). Since I won't be quoting every relevant verse, be sure to look up and read the references that I give. It's important that you ponder these Scriptures if you want to get the full benefit of your study.

The easiest way to *study* Proverbs is by topics, but the best way to *read* Proverbs is chapter by chapter, just the way it's written. Why? Because each chapter presents a variety of truths, and you never know which one you will need for any given day. In fact, some verses are repeated so that we'll be sure to get the message.

"The fear of the Lord is the beginning of knowledge" (Prov. 1:7), so keep your heart reverent before Him, and be willing to obey what He says to you.

CHAPTER FIVE
PEOPLE, WISE AND OTHERWISE—PART I
(The Wise and the Wicked)

If you carefully watch the crowds in a shopping mall, you'll discover that there are all kinds of people in this world; no doubt the crowds are coming to the same conclusion as they look at you. Playwright George Bernard Shaw said, "If the other planets are inhabited, they're using the earth for their insane asylum." No wonder Charles M. Schulz has his comic strip character Linus exclaim, "I love mankind. It's people I can't stand!"

The book of Proverbs is basically about different kinds of people, what they believe and do, and how they interact with one another. People create circumstances that are good and bad, and you and I have to deal with people and circumstances as we go through life. Solomon's aim in writing this book is to help us become skillful in relating to both people and circumstances so that we can make a success out of life to the glory of God.

During our survey of Proverbs 1-9, we casually met five different kinds of people: the wise, the wicked, the fool, the simple, and the scorner. Now it's time to get better acquainted with these people and learn what it really means to be wise.

1. The Wise

The entire book of Proverbs is a guide to attaining wisdom, but here and there Solomon points out several important characteristics of the wise man and woman. Of course, the first step toward wisdom is *saving faith in Jesus Christ*. Wise people are "wise unto salvation" (2 Tim. 3:15) before they gain wisdom about anything else, because Jesus Christ is the Wisdom of God (Col. 2:3; 1 Cor. 1:30). Educated and trained people who ignore or reject Christ can succeed in making a good *living*, but without Him they can never succeed in making a good *life*—one that glorifies God. The wisest thing a person can do is to trust Christ and live in obedience to Him.

Let's consider some of the important characteristics of wise people.

Wise people listen to wise instruction, especially the Word of God. "A wise man[1] will hear, and will increase learning" (1:5). Wise people pay attention to spoken instruction as well as to the written Word of God (22:17-21). Jesus warns us to take heed *what* we hear (Mark 4:24) and *how* we hear (Luke 8:18). "Stop listening to instruction, my son, and you will stray from the words of knowledge" (Prov. 19:27, NIV). "Buy the truth, and do not sell it, also wisdom and instruction and understanding" (23:23, NKJV). It costs to acquire wisdom, but it's worth it!

This means that we must diligently spend time reading and studying the Word of God, appropriating its truths into our hearts, and obeying what God commands (2:1-9). It isn't enough to own a study Bible and read books about the Bible, helpful as they are. It's one thing to know about the Bible and quite something else to hear God speak through His Word and teach us His wisdom so that we become more like Jesus Christ. During my many years of ministry, I've met a few people whose knowledge of Scripture was phenomenal, but who failed to manifest the fruit of the Spirit (Gal. 5:22-23). "Knowledge puffs up, but love builds up" (1 Cor. 8:1, NIV).

But there's a negative side to this as well: Wise people don't waste their time listening to foolishness and lies. Wise people are careful about what they read, what they hear and see, and what they talk about in daily conversation. They're diligent to keep trash out of their minds and hearts, because "garbage in" ultimately means "garbage out" (see Prov. 4:23). For this reason, they carefully control the radio and television and they are selective in their reading.

Those who are wise profit from rebuke (9:8-9; 10:17; 17:10) and from advice (13:10; 12:15; 19:20). They don't think so highly of themselves that they can't learn from others (3:7; 26:12). If we're "wise in our own eyes," we certainly won't be wise in God's eyes!

Wise people fear the Lord. "The fear of the Lord is the beginning of wisdom" (1:7). "Do not be wise in your own eyes; fear the Lord and depart from evil" (3:7). We've already learned that "fearing the Lord" means respecting Him so that we obey His will and seek to honor His name. Fearing the Lord is the opposite of tempting the Lord by deliberately disobeying Him and then daring Him to intervene. "Work out your own salvation with fear and trembling" (Phil. 2:12). "Serve the Lord with fear, and rejoice with trembling" (Ps. 2:11).

The fear of the Lord is "a fountain of life" (Prov. 14:27) and leads to life (19:23). It gives security (14:26), hope (23:17-18), and the promise of long life (10:27). When you fear the Lord, you keep your priorities straight. "Better is a little with the fear of the Lord, than great treasure with trouble" (15:16, NKJV). You also steer clear of evil (8:13; 16:6; see also 14:2).

Wise people associate with wise people. "He who walks with wise men will be wise, but the companion of fools will be destroyed" (13:20, NKJV). As we read and study Scripture, we associate with the wise men and women of Bible history and learn from them. By spending time with godly friends, we can learn wisdom and grow in our knowledge of Christ. As I look back over my Christian pilgrimage, I thank God for the many people the Lord brought into my life to help me better understand the wisdom and ways of the Lord. "A righteous man is cautious in friendship, but the way of the wicked leads them astray" (12:26, NIV).

One of the best ways to "walk with the wise" is to read church history and Christian biography. I have hundreds of volumes of biography and autobiography in my library, some of which I have read many times, and these books have greatly enriched my life. I didn't have the privilege of knowing personally J. Hudson Taylor, Amy Carmichael, St. Augustine, Dwight L. Moody, Billy Sunday, G. Campbell Morgan, Fanny Crosby, or Robert Murray M'Cheyne, but by reading their biographies and autobiographies,

sermons and letters, I've benefited from their walk with the Lord.

Wise people preserve what they've gained and they use it. "Wise people store up knowledge, but the mouth of the foolish is near destruction" (10:14, NKJV). If wisdom is stored in the heart, then we'll say the right thing at the right time, and people will be helped. But fools lose whatever wisdom they may have picked up, and their words only bring destruction.

A parallel text is 12:27: "The lazy man does not roast his game, but the diligent man prizes his possessions" (NIV). The Scottish preacher George Morrison has a powerful sermon on this text entitled "Wasted Gains."[2] (The very title is a sermon!) What a tragedy it is when people waste their gains by failing to use their education, the sermons and Bible lessons they've heard, or the books they've read. Truly wise people treasure the knowledge and skills they've worked hard to acquire and use this treasure to the glory of God.

I recall hearing some of my student friends say at seminary graduation, "Thank the Lord, no more Greek and Hebrew!" They had spent several years learning to use the Bible languages, and now they were selling their valuable language tools and thereby wasting their gains.

Over the years, I have made good use of wide-margin Bibles in which I've written the things God's taught me and that I've learned from others. Many times while preparing a sermon or writing a book, I have turned to these notes and "invested" my gains. When I read a good book, I underline important sentences, write notes in the margins, and compile my own index of ideas at the back of the book. My copier gets plenty of use because I copy material from books and put it into file folders for future use. This way I'm not wasting my gains.

Wise people flee from sin. "A wise man fears and departs from evil, but a fool rages and is self-confident" (14:16, NKJV). If we fear the Lord, we will hate evil (8:13; see Ps. 97:10; Rom. 12:9). The self-confident person isn't wise. Joshua was self-confident and lost a battle (Josh. 7); Samson was self-confident and became a prisoner (Judg. 16:20ff); Peter was self-confident and betrayed the Lord three times (Luke 22:33-34). "Therefore let him who thinks he stands take heed lest he fall"(1 Cor. 10:12, NKJV).

Wise people don't take unnecessary chances and experiment to see how close they can get to the precipice without falling off. When Joseph was confronted with evil, he fled (Gen. 39:7ff). I heard about a handsome assistant pastor who was being pursued by several young ladies in the church, and the senior minister warned him to be careful.

"Oh, there's safety in numbers," the young man replied rather flippantly, defending himself. To which the senior minister wisely replied, "Yes, there's safety in numbers; but sometimes there's more safety in exodus." Paul would have agreed with the older pastor, for he wrote to Timothy, "Flee youthful lusts" (2 Tim. 2:22).

Wise people discipline their speech. "A wise man's heart guides his mouth, and his lips promote instruction" (Prov. 16:23, NIV). "In the multitude of words sin is not lacking, but he who restrains his lips is wise" (10:19, NKJV). Proverbs has so much to say about the dynamics and dangers of human speech that we'll devote an entire chapter to this topic. Suffice it to say now that the wise person realizes the power of the tongue and keeps it under God's control. "The fruit of the Spirit is ... self-control" (Gal. 5:22-23; see James 3). The speech of wise people will instruct and inspire, and you're nourished as you listen; the talk of fools only tears down and leaves you empty and discouraged (note Eph. 5:1-7).

Wise people are diligent in their work. "Lazy hands make a man poor, but diligent hands bring wealth. He who gathers crops in summer is a wise son, but he who sleeps during harvest is a disgraceful son" (Prov. 10:4, NIV). Diligence and laziness are key topics in Proverbs, and we'll study them later in greater detail. Solomon makes it clear that God has nothing good to say about careless, lazy people. Wise people are working people, people who make the most of their opportunities and who carry their share of the load. My friend Dr. Bob Cook used to say that hard work is a thrill and a joy when you're doing the will of God; Scottish novelist George MacDonald said, "It's our best work that He wants, not the dregs of our exhaustion."

Wise people seek to influence others to trust the Lord. "The fruit of the righteous is a tree of life, and he who wins souls is wise" (11:30, NKJV). The word translated "wins" means "to capture," as a hunter captures his prey. Wise people seek to capture the ignorant and disobedient by sharing God's wisdom with them. Jesus told His fishermen disciples that they would be "catching men" instead of catching fish (Luke 5:10). Wisdom leads to righteousness, and righteousness produces fruit ("a tree of life"), and this fruit "entices" those who are hungry for what is real and eternal. By both their lives and their words, wise people seek to lead others to the Lord.

As we continue our study of Proverbs, we'll discover other personal characteristics of those who are wise; I trust we'll seek to imitate them. After all, God promises that the wise will inherit glory (3:35), bring joy to others (10:1; 15:20), bring help from God (12:18), never be in want (21:10), and have strength to wage war (24:5-6). The way of wisdom is the way of true life.

2. The Wicked

The wicked and their wickedness are mentioned at least 100 times in Proverbs, usually in contrast to the good and the righteous. Proverbs 6:12-19 is somewhat of a summary statement that describes the evil person and the hateful[3] sins that he commits.

The wicked are "naughty," that is, worth nothing (naught), without profit. It's the Hebrew word *belial (beli* without; *yaal,* profit), used to describe worthless people (Deut. 13:13; Judg. 19:22; 1 Sam. 25:25; 1 Kings 21:10, 13). Sin is not only destructive, it's also unproductive.

Every part of the wicked person's anatomy is devoted to evil and his "body language" communicates evil (see Rom. 3:10-18). His mouth is perverse ("froward," KJV) a word that means "crooked, twisted." He can't be trusted. When he wants to signal his confederates that it's time to do evil, he winks his eye, shuffles his feet, and motions with his fingers; they get the message. The cause of all this evil is the perversity of his inner person, for it is out of the heart that evil comes (Mark 7:14-23; Jer. 17:9). He's skillful at plotting evil and the result is dissension. He's a troublemaker who sows discord, but judgment is certain and will come when he least expects it. How much better it is when the whole body is yielded to God (Rom. 12:12) and controlled by His Word (Prov. 4:20-27)!

You see these sinful characteristics manifested in the specific sins described in Proverbs 6:16-19, sins that God hates.

First on the list is *pride,* because pride is usually the basic motivation for all other sins. It was pride that turned Lucifer into Satan (Isa. 14:12-14) and that led Eve to disobey God and eat the forbidden fruit (Gen. 3:1-6; note "you shall be as God"). "The fear of the Lord is to hate evil; pride and arrogance and the evil way and the perverse mouth I hate" (Prov. 8:13).

God also hates a *lying tongue,* for God is a God of truth (Deut. 32:4; John 14:6; 1 John 5:6), and His Law says, "Thou shalt not bear false witness" (Ex. 20:16). God sees a lie, not as an act of speech but as a deadly force that goes to work in society and divides and destroys. When we lie, we open the door for Satan to work, for he is a liar (John 8:44); when we speak truth, we give opportunity for the Spirit to work (Eph. 4:14-25). There is a place reserved in hell for liars (Rev. 21:8, 27; see 2 Thess. 2:10).

The third sin God hates is *murder,* "hands that shed innocent blood." His commandment is, "Thou shalt not kill [murder]" (Ex. 20:13). God permits the government to exercise capital punishment and strengthen justice in the land (Gen. 9:5-6; Rom. 13:1-7), but the shedding of innocent blood pollutes the land (Num. 35:30-34). Murderers have their part in the lake of fire (Rev. 21:8; 22:15).

A heart that devises wicked schemes (NIV) is hateful to God because it's a misuse of the great gift of imagination that He has given us. (See Gen. 6:5; 8:21; Jer. 23:17; Rom. 1:21.) The imagination is the "womb" out of which either evil or good is born. People who can plan evil things that hurt others can also plan good things that will help others. The imagination needs to be cleansed and kept pure before God so He can use it in His service. Only God can change the sinful heart (Jer. 31:33-34; Heb. 10:14-18; Ps. 51:10), and God's people must take care to guard their hearts against evil (Prov. 4:23).

Sinners have *feet that are swift in running to mischief [evil]* because they want to fulfill their schemes quickly and enjoy their pleasures immediately. God's people should have cleansed feet (John 13:1-17; 1 John 1:9), beautiful feet (Rom. 10:14-15), prepared feet (Eph. 6:15), and obedient feet (Gen. 13:17; Josh. 1:3; 3:15). If we do, we'll bring blessing. But the wicked use their feet to get involved in sin: meddling as busybodies (2 Thess. 3:11; 1 Tim. 5:13), tempting others into sin (Prov. 5:5 and 7:11), and breaking God's laws (1:10-16). If the saints were "on their feet" and as eager to obey the Lord as sinners are to disobey, the lost world would soon be evangelized!

God has called His people to be witnesses to the truth (Acts 1:8), but the wicked person is *a false witness who speaks lies*. Bearing false witness is a violation of the Ninth Commandment (Ex. 20:16). Without truth, things start to fall apart; when people "lie officially," the foundations of society begin to crumble. Whether it's a statement from a government official, a clause in a contract, a deposition in court, or a promise at the marriage altar, truth cannot be violated without society ultimately suffering. The British poet John Dryden wrote, "Truth is the foundation of all knowledge and the cement of all societies."

The last of the seven sins that God hates is *sowing discord among brethren.* "Behold, how good and how pleasant it is for brethren to dwell together in unity" (Ps. 133:1). The wicked person destroys that unity by sowing "seeds" that produce a bitter and divisive harvest. Some of these seeds are: pride (Prov. 13:10; see 3 John 9-10), gossip (Prov. 16:28; 17:9; 18:8; 26:20), anger and hatred (10:12; 15:18; 29:22), a quarrelsome spirit (17:14, 19; 25:8; 26:21), and foolish questions (1 Tim. 6:3-5; 2 Tim. 2:14, 23).

The truly godly person sows seeds of unity and peace, not seeds of division (James 3:17-18). Discord and division in the church are terrible sins because they are contrary to the spiritual unity that Jesus prayed for (John 17:21) and that the Spirit was given to produce in the body (Eph. 4:1-6). How can lost sinners ever believe that God loves *them* when God's children don't even love *one another?*

All it takes is one stubborn troublemaker to wreck the unity in a family, a Bible study group, or a church. "Drive out the mocker, and out goes strife; quarrels and insults are ended" (Prov. 22:10, NIV). In one of the churches I pastored, we had such a man. When the Lord finally removed him, the new atmosphere in the fellowship was exhilarating. Official meetings that used to consume hours were considerably shortened, and there was a new freedom in discussion and decision.

It is enlightening to contrast this description of the wicked person with Christ's description of the godly person in Matthew 5:1-16. Jesus begins with humility, "the poor in spirit" (Matt. 5:3), while Solomon starts with "a proud look" (Prov. 6:17). "When pride comes, then comes shame; but with the humble is wisdom" (11:2). The seventh characteristic of the wicked is sowing discord among brethren, while the seventh beatitude is "Blessed are the peacemakers" (Matt. 5:9).

There is a wisdom from above that brings peace and purity to God's people, and there is a wisdom from beneath that brings strife and shame (James 3:13-18). There is a wisdom of this world that destroys the church and a wisdom from God that builds the church (1 Cor. 3:16-23).

"To the law and to the testimony! If they do not speak according to this word, it is because there is no light in them" (Isa. 8:20, NKJV).

CHAPTER SIX
PEOPLE, WISE AND OTHERWISE—PART 2
(The Simple, Scorner, and Fool)

While much more could be said about both the wise and the wicked, we need to move on and get better acquainted with "the terrible trio"—the simple, the scorners, and the fools. You will meet these three frequently as you read the book of Proverbs.

You'll recall that in her first invitation, Wisdom called to all three of them (Prov. 1:22), but in her second invitation, she called only to the simple and the fools (8:5). The scorner wasn't even interested in listening; he had dropped out of the picture. Then, in her third invitation, Wisdom called only to the simple (9:4), because the fools had turned away and joined the scorners. *It's a dangerous thing to reject God's invitation to walk the path of wisdom and of life. You may never get another opportunity.*

1. The Simple

The simple are the naive people who believe everything, because they don't have convictions about anything. What they think is sophisticated "tolerance" is only spiritual ignorance, because they lack the ability to discriminate between truth and error. "A simple man believes anything, but a prudent man gives thought to his steps" (14:15, NIV). Charles R. Bridges writes, "To *believe every word* of God is faith. To *believe every word* of man is credulity."[1]

We're living at a time when people who have convictions are considered bigots if not ignoramuses. It's popular and politically correct to be open-minded and uncritical of what other people think or believe. Except when it comes to cashing a check when they're broke, getting a prescription filled when they're sick, or asking directions when they're lost, most people don't believe in absolutes. They insist that there's no such thing as objective truth. According to them, whatever "feels good" down inside is truth for you; nobody has the right to criticize you for what you believe. Apply that philosophy to money, medicine, mechanics, or maps and see how successful you will be!

In his comments on Groundhog's Day, Brooks Atkinson writes: "People everywhere enjoy believing things they know are not true. It spares them the ordeal of thinking for themselves and taking responsibility for what they know."[2] The old saying, "What you don't know won't hurt you," is false, as any physician or auto mechanic can tell you. What you don't know could kill you! "For the turning away [waywardness] of the simple shall slay them" (1:32).

The simple are simple because they reject the truth of God's Word that gives "prudence [common sense] to the simple" (v. 4, NIV). The tragedy is that simple people actually love their simplicity (v. 22) and have no desire to change. Because they don't take a stand for anything, they fall for everything; this saves them the trouble of thinking, studying, praying, and asking God for wisdom. Instead of working hard to dig into the mines of God's wisdom (2:1-9), the simple prefer to take it easy and pick up whatever cheap trinkets they can find on the surface.

It was a simple young man who listened to the prostitute and ended up an animal led to the slaughter (7:7ff). "The simple inherit folly, but the prudent are crowned with knowledge" (14:18). Sometimes the simple will learn when they see others punished for their sins

(19:25; 21:11). The wise person learns from instruction, but the simpleton has to see a living example before he or she will learn. Wise people see danger coming and avoid it, but the simple ones walk right into it (22:3; 27:12). Some people have to learn the hard way.

All of us are ignorant in many things, but simpletons are ignorant of their ignorance and are unwilling to learn. They follow the philosophy, "Where ignorance is bliss, 'tis folly to be wise."[3] But when there's a Bible to read, a life to build, and an eternity to prepare for, it is folly to be ignorant.

2. The Scorner

Scorners think they know everything, and anybody who tries to teach them is only wasting time. "Proud and haughty scorner [scoffer] is his name" (21:24). Scorners can't find wisdom even if they seek for it (14:6), because learning God's truth demands a humble mind and an obedient will. What scorners lack in knowledge they make up for in arrogance. Instead of sensibly discussing a matter with those who could teach them, they only sneer at truth and deny it. My Hebrew lexicons describe them as "frivolous and impudent." Having no intellectual or spiritual ammunition, the scorner depends on ridicule and contempt to fight his enemies.

Scorners show how ignorant they are by the way they respond to advice and reproof. "He who reproves a scoffer gets shame for himself ... . Do not reprove a scoffer, lest he hate you; rebuke a wise man, and he will love you" (9:7-8, NKJV). "A wise son heeds his father's instruction, but a scoffer does not listen to rebuke" (13:1, NKJV). "A scoffer does not love one who corrects him, nor will he go to the wise" (15:12, NKJV). When you try to teach

a scorner, you're just casting pearls before swine. The scorner knows everything! The tragedy is that scorners cause all kinds of trouble wherever they go. Whether in the neighborhood, on the job, or in the church, the scorner is toxic and spreads infection. "Cast out the scorner, and contention shall go out; yea, strife and reproach shall cease" (22:10). Scorners can even create problems for a whole city. "Mockers [scorners] stir up a city, but wise men turn away anger" (29:8, NIV). The Hebrew verb translated "stir up" conveys the image of somebody stirring up a fire or blowing on a flame to make it burn more vigorously. By their contemptible words and attitudes, they add fuel to a fire that ought to be allowed to die out.

The pages of both religious and political history are stained by the records of the deeds of proud mockers who wouldn't listen to wise counsel but impulsively rushed into matters too high for them (Ps. 131). Their tongues were "set on fire of hell" James 3:6); they defiled and damaged families, churches, cities, and entire nations. Churches can be quickly divided and destroyed by arrogant people who laugh at biblical truth and seek to have their own way. All spiritual leaders need to read and heed Acts 20:28-31 and James 3:13-18.

Scoffers are "an abomination to men" (Prov. 24:9) and to God. In fact, the Lord "scorns the scornful, but gives grace to the humble" (3:34, NKJV). This verse is quoted both by James (4:6) and Peter (1 Peter 5:5). "Judgments are prepared for scoffers" (Prov. 19:29), and because scorners mock God, God mocks the scorners. Consider what the Lord did to the builders at Babel (Gen. 11), to Pharaoh at the Red Sea (Ex. 14), to Nebuchadnezzar in Babylon (Dan. 4), to Herod Agrippa in Judea (Acts 12:20-25), and a host of others who defied His will.

3. The Fool

The English words "fool" and "folly" come from the Latin *follis*, which means "bellows." It also described a person's puffed-up cheeks. *Follis* indicates that a fool is a windbag, somebody full of air but lacking in substance. Fools may look like giants, but when the wind is taken out of them, they shrink dramatically and reveal what they really are—pygmies.

In Proverbs, three different Hebrew words are translated "fool": *kesyl*, the dull, stupid fool who is stubborn; *ewiyl*, the corrupt fool who is morally perverted and unreasonable; and *nabal*, the fool who is like a stubborn animal, the brutish fool. (See 1 Sam. 25.) In this summary of the characteristics of the fool, we'll combine the verses and not distinguish the three different types. After all, fools are fools, no matter what name we give them!

Fools won't learn from God's Word. "The fear of the Lord is the beginning [controlling principle] of knowledge: but fools despise wisdom and instruction" (1:7). The problem with fools isn't low IQ or deficient education. Their big problem is their heart: They won't acknowledge the Lord and submit to Him. "There is no fear of God before their eyes" (Rom. 3:18).

A fool's own father can't instruct him (Prov. 15:5), and if you try to debate with him, it will only lead to trouble (29:9). Why? Because fools actually enjoy their folly and think they're really living! "Folly is a joy to him who is destitute of discernment" (15:21, NKJV; see 1:22; 12:15; 18:2). Warn them about sin and they laugh at you (14:9).

One reason fools don't learn wisdom is because they can't keep their eyes focused on what's important. "A discerning man keeps wisdom in view, but a fool's eyes wander to the ends of the earth" (17:24, NIV). Instead of dealing with reality, the fool lives in a faraway fantasy world. God's Word helps people keep their feet on the ground and make wise decisions in this difficult world in which we live.

Fools can't control their speech. "The tongue of the wise uses knowledge rightly, but the mouth of fools pours forth foolishness" (15:2, NKJV; see 13:16). The fool's speech is proud and know-it-all (14:3), and fools have a tendency to speak before they know what they're saying or what's being discussed (18:13). "Do you see a man hasty in his words? There is more hope for a fool than for him" (29:20, NKJV). "The way of a fool is right in his own eyes, but he who heeds counsel is wise" (12:15, NKJV). You can't warn fools or tell them anything they need to know because they already know everything!

Fools do a lot of talking, but they never accomplish what they've talked about. "The wise in heart will receive commandments: but a prating fool shall fall" (10:8; see v. 10). The word translated "prating" means "to babble and talk excessively," and is related to the word "prattle." It's much easier to talk about things than to hear God's Word and obey it.

Lies and slander are what fools specialize in (10:18), and the wise person won't stay around to listen (14:7-8). "The lips of the wise disperse knowledge, but the heart of the fool does not do so" (15:7, NKJV). "Excellent speech is not becoming to a fool" (17:7, NKJV). All of us must be careful what kind of conversation we listen to, because Jesus said, "Take heed what you hear" (Mark 4:24). Furthermore, when fools are speaking, what they say could start a fight! (18:6-7)

Fools can't control their temper. "A fool's wrath is known at once, but a prudent man covers shame" (12:16, NKJV).

"He who is slow to wrath has great understanding, but he who is impulsive exalts folly" (14:29, NKJV). "Even a fool is counted wise when he holds his peace; when he shuts his lips, he is considered perceptive" (17:28, NKJV). "A fool vents all his feelings, but a wise man holds them back" (29:11, NKJV).

When business is being transacted in the city gate (Ruth 4), fools should keep quiet if they want to appear wise (Prov. 24:7)! It's unfortunate that some people think they must always speak at meetings, even when they have nothing to say.

Don't incur the wrath of a fool unless you want to carry a terrible burden. "A stone is heavy, and the sand weighty, but a fool's wrath is heavier than them both" (27:3). Once a fool is angry with you, he or she will carry on the war to the bitter end and do a great deal of damage. That's why we must exercise discernment when we disagree with fools or try to counsel them. "Do not answer a fool according to his folly, or you will be like him yourself. Answer a fool according to his folly, or he will be wise in his own eyes" (26:4-5, NIV). Sometimes fools deserve only a deaf ear; other times they must be rebuked and their folly answered from the Word. It takes wisdom to know which response is correct, lest we end up casting pearls before swine.

Fools are proud and self-confident. "He who trusts in his own heart is a fool, but whoever walks wisely will be delivered" (28:26, NKJV). "Do you see a man wise in his own eyes? There is more hope for a fool than for him" (26:12). We hear people saying, "Well, if I know my own heart..." but God warns us that we don't know our own hearts and we can't always trust what our hearts say to us. "The heart is deceitful above all things, and desperately wicked; who can know it?" (Jer. 17:9)

Many people today believe what Emerson wrote: "Trust thyself: every heart vibrates to that iron string."[4] Or they may follow William Ernest Henley's philosophy as expressed in his famous poem, "Invictus": "I am the master of my fate/I am the captain of my soul." These expressions of proud human achievement sound very much like Satan's offer in Eden: "You will be like God" (Gen. 3:5, NKJV), which is the basis of the New Age movement. Whatever exalts man will ultimately fail; whatever glorifies God will last forever.[5]

Because of their proud self-confidence, fools like to meddle, especially when there's something to argue about: "It is an honor for a man to cease from strife: but every fool will be meddling" (Prov. 20:3). Anybody can start a quarrel, but it takes a wise person to be able to stop one or, better yet, to avoid one (30:32-33). Fools think that fighting over minor disagreements will bring them honor, but it only makes them greater fools.

While waiting for a Sunday morning worship service to begin at a church where I was to be the guest preacher, I sat in an adult Sunday school class that met in the church sanctuary. One man in that class questioned almost everything the teacher said and really made a nuisance of himself quibbling about minor things. He wanted to appear wise, but he only convinced us that he was a fool. As I sat there listening, I thought of 1 Timothy 6:4-5: "He is proud, knowing nothing, but is obsessed with disputes and arguments over words, from which come envy, strife, reviling, evil suspicions, useless wranglings" (NKJV).

Fools create problems and bring sorrow, especially to their parents. "A wise son makes a glad father, but a foolish son is the grief of his mother" (Prov. 10:1, NKJV; see 15:20; 17:21, 25). Every godly father says to his son, "Be wise, my son, and bring joy to my heart" (27:11, NIV), but the pages of the Bible record the sorrow that foolish sons brought to their parents.

Cain grieved his parents when he killed his brother Abel (Gen. 4). Esau deliberately married heathen women just to provoke his father Isaac (Gen. 28:6-9). Jacob's sons lied to him about their brother Joseph and broke his heart (Gen. 37). Samson grieved his parents by living with pagan women and fraternizing with the enemies of Israel (Judg. 13-16). David's sons broke his heart with their evil ways. Amnon violated his half sister Tamar and Absalom killed him for doing it (2 Sam. 13). Then Absalom rebelled against David and seized the kingdom (2 Sam. 15-18).

Can anything be done to change foolish children into wise men and women? "Though you grind a fool in a mortar, grinding him like grain with a pestle, you will not remove his folly from him" (Prov. 27:22, NIV). Women in the ancient world ground grain in a bowl (mortar) using a hard tool (pestle) with which they could crack and pulverize the kernels. The image is clear: no amount of pressure or pain will change a fool and make anything useful out of him. Wise parents should discipline foolish children to give them hope (22:15),[6] but a foolish adult can be changed only by the grace of God. Unless fools repent and turn to the Lord, they will live as slaves (11:29) and "die without instruction" (5:23).

Fools don't know how to use wealth properly. "In the house of the wise are stores of choice food and oil, but a foolish man devours all he has" (21:20, NIV). Fools may know the price of everything, but they know the value of nothing; they waste their wealth on things stupid and sinful. "Whoever loves wisdom makes his father rejoice, but a companion of harlots wastes his wealth" (29:3, NKJV). This verse reminds us of our Lord's Parable of the Prodigal Son (Luke 15:11-24). "The crown of the wise is their riches, but the foolishness of fools is [yields] folly" (Prov. 14:24). The wise have something to leave to their children, but fools waste both their wealth and their opportunities to increase it. "Luxury is not fitting for a fool" (19:10).

Fools can't be trusted with responsibility. "As snow in summer and rain in harvest, so honor is not fitting for a fool" (26:1, NKJV). The word *honor* in the Hebrew *(kabod)* means "heavy, weighty," and can refer to the glory of God and the special respect given to people. A fool doesn't have what it takes to handle responsibility successfully and win the respect of others. Giving honor to a fool is about as fitting as snow in summer or as helpful as rain during harvest! Both mean disaster.

In 26:3-12, Solomon elaborates on this theme by presenting a number of vivid pictures of the fool and what happens when you give him a job to do. For one thing, you'll have to treat him like a dumb animal and use a whip to motivate him (v. 3; see Ps. 32:9). Try to give him orders and explain what he's to do and you're in danger of becoming like him (Prov. 26:4-5). Send him on an important mission and you might as well cripple yourself, and be prepared for trouble (v. 6).[7] As a lame person's legs are useless to take him anywhere, so a fool can't "get anywhere" with a proverb (v. 7). He not only confuses others, but he harms himself, like a drunk punctured by a thorn (v. 9). Don't ask a fool to teach the Bible because he won't know what he's talking about and it's painful to listen to him. And don't ask a fool to wage war because he ties the stone in the sling (v. 8) !

The original text of verse 10 is very difficult and there are many varied translations. "Like an archer who wounds everyone, so is he who hires a fool or who hires those who pass by" (NASB). "Like an archer who wounds at random is he who hires a fool or any passer-by" (NIV). "Like an archer who wounds everybody is he who hires a passing fool or drunkard" (RSV). Note that the emphasis is on the one doing the hiring and not on the fool. If you hire a fool (or just anybody who passes by) and give him or her responsibility, you might just as well start shooting at random, because the fool will do a lot of damage. Of course, nobody in his right mind would start shooting at random, so, nobody in his right mind would hire a fool.

Fools don't learn from their mistakes but go right back to the same old mess, like a dog returning to eat his vomit (v. 11). Experience is a good teacher for the wise, but not for fools. This verse is quoted in 2 Peter 2:22 as a description of counterfeit believers who follow false teachers. Like a sow that's been washed, they look better on the outside; and like a dog that's vomited, they feel better on the inside; but they're still not sheep! They don't have the divine new nature; consequently, they go right back to the old life. Obedience and perseverance in the things of the Lord are proof of conversion.

What will happen to the fool? "A man's own folly ruins his life, yet his heart rages against the Lord" (Prov. 19:3, NIV). This reminds us of Pharaoh in Exodus 5-15, who saw his country ruined by God's plagues and yet wouldn't give in to the Lord. He raged against Jehovah and Moses and even pursued the Jews to take them back, only to see his best sol-diers drowned in the Red Sea. God's discipline helps a wise person obey the Word, but punishment only makes a foolish person more wicked. The same sun that melts the ice hardens the clay.

Because they "feed on foolishness" (Prov. 15:14), fools have no moral strength. "The lips [words] of the righteous feed many, but fools die for lack of wisdom" (10:21). They not only lack spiritual and intellectual nourishment, but they also lack refreshing water: "Understanding is a fountain of life to those who have it, but folly brings punishment to fools" (16:22, NIV). The image of words and God's Law as "a fountain of life" is also found in 10:11; 13:14; 14:27, and 18:4. Follow Wisdom and you live on a fruitful oasis; follow Folly and your home is an arid desert.

The fool will "die without instruction" (5:23). "The wise shall inherit glory: but shame shall be the promotion of fools" (3:35). They will hear God's voice say, "Fool! This night your soul will be required of you" (Luke 12:20, NKJV), but then it will be too late.

The only fools who are "wise fools" are Christians, because they're "fools for Christ's sake" (1 Cor. 4:10). The world calls them fools, but in trusting Jesus Christ and committing their lives to Him, they've made the wisest decision anybody can make.

I read about a man who bore witness to his faith in a busy shopping area by wearing a sandwich board which read: I'M A FOOL FOR JESUS CHRIST. WHOSE FOOL ARE YOU?

A wise question! Be sure you can give a wise answer.

CHAPTER SEVEN
"RICH MAN, POOR MAN, BEGGAR MAN, THIEF"

Money isn't everything," said a wit, "but it does keep you in touch with your children." ... On a more serious level, Paul summarized the Christian philosophy of wealth when he wrote: "Let him who stole steal no longer, but rather let him labor, working with his hands what is good, that he may have something to give him who has need" (Eph. 4:28, NKJV).

According to Paul, you can get wealth in three ways: by stealing it, earning it, or receiving it as a gift, which would include getting it as an inheritance. Stealing is wrong (Ex. 20:15), labor is honorable (Ex. 20:9) and, "It is more blessed to give than to receive" (Acts 20:35).

In the book of Proverbs, King Solomon tells us a great deal about these three kinds of people—the thieves, the workers, and the poor who need our help. (Among the thieves, I'm including "the sluggard," the lazy person who never works but expects others to take care of him. That's being a thief, isn't it?) However, wealthy as he was (1 Kings 4; 10), King Solomon emphasized that *God's wisdom is more important than money.* "How much better is it to get wisdom than gold! and to get understanding rather to be chosen than silver!" (Prov. 16:16; see 2:1-5; 3:13-15; 8:10-21) This is Solomon's version of Matthew 6:33; he's reminding us that while it is good to have the things money can buy, be sure you don't lose the things money can't buy.

1. The Thieves

The book of Proverbs opens with a stern warning against participating in get-rich-quick schemes that involve breaking the Law (Prov. 1:10-19). These schemes are self-destructive and lead to bondage and possibly the grave. Beware of people who promise to make you wealthy without asking you to work or take any risks. "Wealth obtained by fraud dwindles, but the one who gathers by labor increases it" (13:11, NASB). "A man with an evil eye hastens after riches, and does not consider that poverty will come upon him" (28:22, NKJV). "Ill gotten treasures are of no value, but righteousness delivers from death" (10:2, NIV).

Proverbs 21:5-7 points out three ways *not* to get wealth: following hasty schemes (v. 5), lying to people (v. 6), and robbing (v. 7). Most if not all get-rich-quick schemes involve some kind of deception and are nothing but scams.[1] Unfortunately, even God's people have been duped by scam artists, and more than one trusting soul has lost his or her life savings in a "sure thing" that turned out to be a sure loser. However, scams wouldn't succeed if there weren't people eager to get rich as quickly and easily as possible. But, as the old adage puts it, "There are no free lunches." You take what you want from life, but eventually you pay for it.

God demands that we be honest in all our business dealings. Dishonesty is robbery. "Dishonest scales are an abomination to the Lord, but a just weight is His delight" (11:1, NKJV; see 16:11; 20:10, 23). Moses commanded in the Law that the people use honest weights and measures (Lev 19:35-36; Deut. 25:13-16); since Israel didn't have an official Department of Standards to check on these things, the law wasn't always obeyed. Amos accused the merchants in his day of "skimping the measure, boosting the price and cheating with dishonest scales" (Amos 8:5, NIV); Micah asked "Shall I count them pure with the wicked balances, and with the bag of deceitful weights?" (Mic. 6:11)

Another dishonest way to get wealth is to use your resources selfishly and disregard the needs of others. "A generous man will prosper; he who refreshes others will himself be refreshed. People curse the man who hoards grain, but blessing crowns him who is willing to sell" (Prov. 11:25-26, NIV). In times of drought and famine, a prosperous farmer could corner the grain market and become rich at the expense of his needy neighbors (see Neh. 5). We need to realize that everything we have comes from God (1 Cor. 4.7; John 3:27) and that we are but stewards of His wealth. While everyone expects that a businessman will make a profit, nobody wants him to "make a killing" and hurt others.

The biggest thieves of all are the lazy people who could work but won't, the people who consume what others produce but produce nothing for others to use. The "sluggard" and the "slothful man" are mentioned at least seventeen times in Proverbs, and nothing good is said about them.

We need to recognize the fact that *work is not a curse.* God gave Adam work to do in the Garden even before sin entered the scene (Gen. 2:15). Before He began His public ministry, Jesus worked as a carpenter (Mark 6:3); the apostle Paul was a tentmaker (Acts 18:1-3). In that day, rabbis had vocations and supported themselves but didn't accept payment from their students. When we engage in honorable employment we're cooperating with God in caring for and using His creation, we're helping to provide for others, and we're growing in character. The work God has called us to do ought to nourish us (John 4:34), not tear us down; "the laborer is worthy of his hire" (Luke 10:7; 1 Tim. 5:18).

What are some of the marks of sluggards? For one thing, *they love to sleep.* "How long will you lie there, you sluggard? When will you get up from your sleep?" (Prov. 6:9, NIV) "As a door turns on its hinges, so does the lazy man on his bed" (26:14). Lots of motion—but no progress!

Sleep is a necessary element for a healthy life, but too much sleep is destructive. Wise people enjoy sleep that's "sweet" (3:24) because they know they're in God's will, and the laborer's sleep is "sweet" because he or she has worked hard (Eccl. 5:12), but the sleep of the sluggard is a mark of selfishness and laziness. "Laziness could run a competitive race for the most underrated sin," write Ronald Sailler and David Wyrtzen in *The Practice of Wisdom* (Chicago: Moody, 1992). "Quietly it anesthetizes its victim into a lifeless stupor that ends in hunger, bondage and death" (p. 82).

Put the sluggard to work and *he's more of a nuisance than a help.* "As vinegar to the teeth, and as smoke to the eyes, so is the sluggard to them that send him" (Prov. 10:26). Vinegar on the teeth and smoke in the eyes aren't necessarily lethal, but they do irritate you; so does a sluggard who won't get the job done. All he does is dream about the things he wants to enjoy, but he won't work hard enough to earn them. "The sluggard's craving will be the death of him, because his hands refuse to work" (21:25, NIV). Dreams become nightmares if you don't discipline yourself to work.

Another mark of the sluggard is a *know-it-all attitude.* "The lazy man is wiser in his own eyes than seven men who can answer sensibly" (26:16, NKJV). He lives in a fantasy world that prevents him from being a useful part of the real world (13:4; 21:25-26), but he can tell everybody else what to do. He's never succeeded at anything in his own life, but he can tell others how to succeed.

Sluggards are good at *making excuses.* Either the weather is too cold for plowing (20:4), or it's too dangerous to go out of the house (22:13; 26:13). "The way of the sluggard is blocked with thorns, but the path of the upright is a highway" (15:19, NIV). The diligent man or woman can always find a reason to work, but the sluggard always has an excuse for not working. Evangelist Billy Sunday defined an excuse as, "the skin of a reason stuffed with a lie," and he was right. People who are good at making excuses are rarely good at doing anything else.

What finally happens to the sluggard? For one thing, unless others care for them, *sluggards live in poverty and hunger.* "Laziness casts one into a deep sleep, and an idle person will suffer hunger" (19:15, NKJV; see 10:4; 13:4). "If any would not work, neither should he eat" was the standard for the New Testament church (see 2 Thess. 3:6-15). The saints were happy to care for those who needed help and couldn't care for themselves, but they had no time for freeloaders who lived by the sacrifices of others (Acts 2:44-47; 1 Tim. 5:3-16). The sluggard gets so lazy, he won't feed himself even when the food is brought right to him (Prov. 19:24; 26:15)!

The sluggard *loses his freedom and is enslaved to others.* "The hand of the diligent will rule, but the lazy man will be put to forced labor" (12:24, NKJV). His debts accumulate to the point where he has to become a slave and work off what he owes (see Lev. 25:39-55; Deut. 15:12-18). The "easy life" of leisure turns out to be very costly as the sluggard exchanges

his pillow for a plow and has to work off his debts the hard way.

The sluggard *wastes God-given resources.* "He also that is slothful in his work is brother to him that is a great waster" (Prov. 18:9). The lazy person may be "working" but not doing a very good job. Consequently, what's done will either have to be thrown out or done over; this means it will cost twice as much.

The sluggard also wastes *God-given opportunities.* "He who gathers in summer is a wise son; he who sleeps in harvest is a son who causes shame" (10:5, NKJV). When the fields are ready for harvest, the reapers have to go to work, because the opportunity won't be there forever (John 4:27-38). Diligent people are alert to their God-given opportunities and seek to make the most of them.

2. The Poor and Needy
Had the nation of Israel obeyed God's laws, their land would have remained fruitful and there would have been very little poverty or oppression of the poor. Every seventh day was a Sabbath, when the people rested and gave their land and farm animals rest. Every seventh year was a Sabbatical Year, when the land and workers were allowed to rest for the entire year. Every fiftieth year was a Year of Jubilee, when the land not only lay fallow but was returned to its original owners (Lev. 25:1-34). By this means, the Lord sought to restore the fertility of the land regularly and also prevent wealthy people from amassing huge farms and thus controlling the economy. According to 2 Chronicles 36:20-21, the nation didn't obey these special laws for the land; God had to send the people to Babylon to give the land a rest.

What are the causes of poverty and need? Some people are poor simply because they won't work. Work is available but they prefer not to know about it. "Lazy hands make a man poor, but diligent hands bring wealth" (Prov. 10:4, NIV). "Do not love sleep, lest you come to poverty" (20:13, NKJV). Or perhaps the enemy is pleasure: "He who loves pleasure will be a poor man; he who loves wine and oil will not be rich" (21:17, NKJV). Of course, the drunkard and the glutton are usually among the poor (23:21). Time, energy, money, and opportunity are wasted when leisure and pleasure control a person's life.

Unfortunately, some people weren't disciplined when young and taught the importance of work. "He who ignores discipline comes to poverty and shame, but whoever heeds correction is honored" (13:18, NIV). Listening to orders and obeying them, paying attention to correction and reproof and not repeating mistakes, and respecting supervision are essential to success in any job. It's worth noting that the Prodigal's first request was, "Father, give me!" But when he returned home, his desire was, "Make me one of your servants" (Luke 15:12, 19). He'd learned the value of his father's discipline and the joy of hard work.

Some people are needy because *they like to talk but never act*. "In all labor there is profit, but idle chatter leads only to poverty" (Prov. 14:23, NKJV). This reminds us of our Lord's parable about the two sons (Matt. 21:28-32).

People can become poor because of *unwise financial dealings*. Rush impulsively into a "good deal" and you may lose everything (Prov. 21:5), and beware of signing notes and assuming other people's debts (6:1-5), especially strangers (11:15). "A man devoid of understanding shakes hands in a pledge, and becomes surety for his friend" (17:18, NKJV; see 22:26-27). The Jews were permitted to loan money to other Jews, but they were not to charge interest (Lev. 25:35-38; Ex. 22:25). They were permitted to charge interest to Gentiles (Deut. 23:20). However, they were warned against "going surety" and assuming debts larger than they could pay (Prov. 22:7).

There are also times when people become poor because of *people and events over which they have no control*. "A poor man's field may produce abundant food, but injustice sweeps it away" (13:23, NIV; see 18:23; 28:8). The prophets condemned wicked rulers and businessmen who crushed the poor and seized what little they had (Isa. 3:13-15; 10:1-4; Amos 2:6-7; 4:1; 5:11-12; 8:4-10). When there's justice in the land and people fear the Lord, then the poor have a voice and protection from oppression.

Oppressing the poor is condemned by God. "He who oppresses the poor reproaches his Maker, but he who honors Him has mercy on the needy" (Prov. 14:31, NKJV). God doesn't respect the rich more than He respects the poor. "The rich and the poor have this in common, the Lord is the maker of them all" (22:2, NKJV). The poor are made in the image of God, so the way we treat the poor is the way we treat God. Churches that show deference to the rich and ignore the poor have forgotten the royal law, "Thou shalt love thy neighbor as thyself" (James 2:1-8).

How do we help the poor? To begin with, we ought not to look down on the poor because of their troubles, thinking we are better than they. "He who despises his neighbor sins; but he who has mercy on the poor, happy is he" (Prov. 14:21, NIV). God has a special concern for the poor and needy, and in exploiting them we will find ourselves fighting the Lord. "Rob not the poor, because he is poor: neither oppress the afflicted in the gate: for the Lord will plead their cause, and spoil [plunder] the soul of those that spoiled them" (22:22-23; see Deut. 15:7; 24:12).

Christian citizens ought to see to it that laws are written fairly and enforced justly. "The righteous care about justice for the poor, but the wicked have no such concern" (Prov. 29:7, NIV). "A ruler who oppresses the poor is like a driving rain that leaves no crops" (28:3, NIV). "Speak up and judge fairly; defend the rights of the poor and needy" (31:9, NIV). "The king who judges the poor with truth, his throne will be established forever" (29:14). These are solemn statements indeed!

When we assist the poor, we are investing with the Lord, and He will see to it that we get our dividends at the right time.[2] "He who has pity on the poor lends to the Lord, and He will pay back what he has given" (19:17; see 11:24; 22:9). Before the church helps, however, the family has an obligation to assist their own needy (1 Tim. 5:4, 8). This leaves the church free to help those who have no one to share their burdens. If we shut our ears to the cries of the poor, God will shut His ears to our prayers (Prov. 21:13).

Having pastored three churches, I know some of the problems congregations can have with "con artists" who pose as "believers passing through town who need help." In over forty years of ministry, I recall very few instances when strangers we helped wrote and thanked us when they got home or even repaid the gift. Certainly pastors and deacons must exercise caution and wisdom lest they do more harm than good, but we must also remember that we're helping truly needy people for Jesus' sake (Matt. 25:34-40). Bernard of Clairvaux, composer of "Jesus, the Very Thought of Thee," gave wise counsel when he said, "Justice seeks out the merits of the case, but pity only

regards the need." If our Lord dealt with us today only on the basis of justice, where would we be?

3. The Diligent

Diligent hands are directed by a diligent heart, and this means *the discipline of the inner person.* "Keep your heart with all diligence, for out of it springs the issues of life" (Prov. 4:23, NKJV). When we cultivate the inner person through prayer, meditation on the Word, and submission to the Lord, then we can experience the joys of a disciplined and diligent life. "The fruit of the Spirit is ... self-control" (Gal. 5:22-23).

The reward for faithful hard work is— more work! "Well done, good and faithful servant; you were faithful over a few things, I will make you ruler over many things" (Matt. 25:21, NKJV; see Luke 19:16-19). "Do you see a man who excels in his work? He will stand before kings; he will not stand before unknown men" (Prov. 22:29, NKJV).

One of the blessings of diligent labor is the joy of developing the kind of ability and character that others can trust, thereby fitting ourselves for the next responsibility God has prepared for us. Joseph was faithful in suffering and service, and this prepared him to rule Egypt. David faithfully cared for a few sheep, and God gave him an entire nation to shepherd (Ps. 78:70-72). Joshua was faithful as Moses' helper and became Moses' successor. "Wisdom is the principal thing. ... Exalt her, and she will promote you" (Prov. 4:7-8, NKJV). "The wise shall inherit glory: but shame shall be the promotion of fools" (3:35).

There's no substitute for hard work. "Lazy hands make a man poor, but diligent hands bring wealth" (10:4, NIV). "All hard work brings a profit, but mere talk leads only to poverty" (14:23, NIV). A new college graduate was asked if he was looking for work. He thought for a minute and then replied, "No, but I would like to have a job." That seems to be the attitude of too many people today. Poet Robert Frost said, "The world is full of willing people: some willing to work and the rest willing to let them."

Diligent people *plan their work and work their plan.* "The plans of the diligent lead surely to plenty, but those of everyone who is hasty, surely to poverty" (21:5, NKJV). "Commit your works to the Lord, and your thoughts will be established" (16:3, NKJV; see 24:27). Thomas Edison said, "I never did anything worth doing by accident, nor did any of my inventions come by accident; they came by work." More than one scientific breakthrough seemed to be discovered by accident, but there was still a great deal of hard work put into the project before the breakthrough came. Benjamin Franklin wrote in his *Poor Richard's Almanack,* "Diligence is the mother of good luck, and God gives all things to industry."

God blesses the labors of people who are *honest.* "Wealth gained by dishonesty will be diminished, but he who gathers by labor will increase" (13:11, NKJV). God expects "a just weight and a just balance" (16:11; see 20:10, 23). He also expects us to be honest in our words as we deal with people in our work. "Lying lips are an abomination to the Lord, but those who deal truthfully are His delight" (12:22, NKJV).

God blesses diligent people for their *generosity.* "There is one who scatters, yet increases more; and there is one who withholds more than is right, but it leads to poverty. The generous soul will be made rich, and he who waters will also be watered himself" (11:24-25, NKJV). "He who has a generous eye will be blessed, for he gives of his bread to the poor" (22:9,

NKJV). Mark the difference between the diligent worker and the slothful person: "The desire of the lazy man kills him, for his hands refuse to labor. He covets greedily all day long, but the righteous gives and does not spare" (21:25-26, NKJV).

Diligent people are *careful not to incur debts they can't handle.* "The rich rules over the poor, and the borrower is servant to the lender" (22:7, NKJV). While a certain amount of honest debt is expected in today's world, and everybody wants to achieve a good credit rating, we must be careful not to mistake presumption for faith. As the familiar adage puts it, "When your outgo exceeds your income, then your upkeep is your downfall."

It's a dangerous thing for people to become greedy for more and more money and to overextend themselves to acquire it. Each of us must discover at what financial level God wants us to live and be content with it. "Two things I ask of you, O Lord; do not refuse me before I die: Keep falsehood and lies far from me; give me neither poverty nor riches, but give me only my daily bread. Otherwise, I may have too much and disown You and say, 'Who is the Lord?' Or I may become poor and steal, and so dishonor the name of my God" (30:7-9, NIV).

I was a "depression baby" and the text my sister and two brothers and I learned to live by was, "Use it up, wear it out; make it do, or do without." Our parents taught us the difference between luxuries and necessities, and they didn't try to impress the neighbors by purchasing things they didn't need with money they couldn't afford to spend. But that philosophy of life seems to have almost disappeared. Today if you talk about hard work, wise stewardship, the dangers of debt, and the importance of accountability before God, somebody is bound to smile (or laugh out loud) and tell you that times have changed.

Our Heavenly Father knows that His children have needs that must be met (Matt. 6:32); in our modern society, this means we must have money to procure them. But our most important task isn't to earn money; our most important task is to be the kind of people God can trust with money, people who are faithful in the way we use what God gives us. "But seek first the kingdom of God and His righteousness, and all these things shall be added to you" (Matt. 6:33, NKJV).

"The real measure of our wealth," said John Henry Jowett, "is how much we'd be worth if we lost all our money." Character is more important than position, and wisdom than possessions. God doesn't glorify poverty, but neither does He magnify affluence. "There is one who makes himself rich, yet has nothing; and one who makes himself poor, yet has great riches" (Prov. 13:7, NKJV).

We must not think that the way of the wealthy is always easy,[3] because there are also perils that accompany wealth and success in life. Wealthy people face problems that people of ordinary means don't face, for an increase in wealth usually means an increase in decision-making, risk-taking, and possibly physical danger. "A man's riches may ransom his life, but a poor man hears no threat" (13:8, NIV). Kenneth Taylor aptly paraphrases this verse, "Being kidnapped and held for ransom never worries the poor man!" (TLB) Thieves will break into a mansion but not a hovel.

One of the subtle dangers of wealth is *a false sense of security.* "He who trusts in his riches will fall, but the righteous will flourish like foliage" (11:28). After all, riches won't save the sinner on the day of judgment (11:4); they can't buy peace (15:16-17) or a good name (22:1). Riches have a tendency to fly away when we least expect it (23:4-5; 27:23-24).

If God blesses our diligent work with success, *we must be careful not to become proud.* "The wealth of the rich is their fortified city; they imagine it an unscalable wall" (18:11, NIV). This reminds us of the rich farmer in our Lord's parable (Luke 12:13-21). If successful people aren't careful, they'll start mistreating people (Prov. 14:21; 18:23) and becoming a law to themselves (28:11). "By humility and the fear of the Lord are riches, and honor, and life" (22:4). Rich people have many friends (14:20; 19:4, 6), but will those friends remain faithful if the rich become poor? (19:7) Wealth is a wonderful servant for humble people but a terrible master for the proud.

The wrong attitude toward money can *wreck friendships and even destroy a home.* "He who is greedy for gain troubles his own house, but he who hates bribes will live" (15:27, NKJV). The man or woman who thinks only of getting rich will put money ahead of people and principles, and soon they start to neglect the family in their frantic pursuit of wealth. Expensive gifts to the children become substitutes for the gift of themselves; before long, values become twisted and the family falls apart. How many families have been destroyed because of the distribution of an estate! As a lawyer friend of mine used to say, "Where there's a will, there's relatives."

In connection with that problem, wealthy people have to worry about *what their children will do with their wealth.* "For riches are not forever, nor does a crown endure to all generations" (27:24, NKJV). Solomon discussed this problem in Ecclesiastes 2:18-26 and came to the conclusion that the best thing rich people can do is enjoy their wealth while they're able and not worry about their heirs. Perhaps their will should read, "Being of sound mind and body, I spent it all!"[4]

"Rich man, poor man, beggar man, thief." God has a word for all of them. Are they willing to receive it?

CHAPTER EIGHT
FAMILY, FRIENDS, AND NEIGHBORS

In 1937, the number one fiction bestseller in the United States was Margaret Mitchell's *Gone with the Wind*. The number one nonfiction title was Dale Carnegie's *How to Win Friends and Influence People*, and since then, millions of copies have been sold around the world. Why? Because just about everybody has "people problems" and wants to know how to solve them. Getting along with other people is an important part of life.

The book of Proverbs is the best manual you'll find on people skills, because it was given to us by the God who made us, the God who can teach us what we need to know about human relationships, whether it's marriage, the family, the neighborhood, the job, or our wider circle of friends and acquaintances. If we learn and practice God's wisdom as presented in Proverbs, we'll find ourselves improving in people skills and enjoying life much more.

1. Husbands and Wives

According to Scripture, God established three human institutions in the world: marriage and the home (Gen. 2:18-25), human government (Gen. 9:1-6; Rom. 13),

and the local church (Acts 2); of the three, the basic institution is the home. As goes the home, so go the church and the nation. The biblical views of marriage and the family have been so attacked and ridiculed in modern society that it does us good to review what the Creator of the home has to say about His wonderful gift of marriage.

Marriage. King Solomon had 700 wives and 300 concubines (1 Kings 11:3), and in so doing he disobeyed God's Law—by multiplying wives (Deut. 17:17), and by taking these wives from pagan nations that didn't worship Jehovah, the true and Living God (Ex. 34:16; Deut. 7:1-3). Eventually, these women won Solomon over to their gods, and the Lord had to discipline Solomon for his sins (1 Kings 11:4ff).

In contrast to this, the book of Proverbs magnifies the kind of marriage that God first established in Eden: one man married to one woman for one lifetime (Gen. 2:18-25; Matt. 19:19).[1] The husband is to love his wife and be faithful to her (Prov. 5). The wife is not to forsake her husband and seek her love elsewhere (2:17). They are to enjoy one another and grow in their love for each other and for the Lord.

In ancient days, marriages were arranged by the parents. Our modern "system" of two people falling in love and getting married would be foreign to their thinking and their culture. In that day, a man and woman got married and then learned to love each other; they expected to stay together for life. Today, a man and woman learn to love each other, then they get married, and everybody hopes they'll stay together long enough to raise the children.

The husband. A man can inherit houses and lands, but "a prudent wife is from the Lord" (19:14, NIV).[2] "He who finds a wife finds a good thing, and obtains favor from the Lord" (18:22, NKJV). Blessed is that marriage in which the husband acknowledges God's goodness to him in giving him his wife! When a husband takes her for granted, he grieves both her and the Lord. He should love her and be loyal to her all the days of his life.

The book of Proverbs places on the husband the responsibility of guiding the home according to the wisdom of God, but as we shall see in chapter 31, the wife also plays an important part. Where two people love the Lord and love each other, God can guide and bless them. It's not a "fifty-fifty" arrangement, because "two become one." Rather, it's a 100 percent devotion to each other and to the Lord.

The wife. Every wife will either build the home or tear it down (14:1). If she walks with the Lord, she will be a builder; if she disobeys God's wisdom, she will be a destroyer. She must be faithful to her husband, for "A wife of noble character is her husband's crown, but a disgraceful wife is like decay in his bones" (12:4, NIV). A crown or a cancer: What a choice! And beauty isn't the only thing he should look for; it's also important that a wife have wisdom and discretion (11:22).

Husbands occasionally create problems for their wives, but Solomon doesn't mention any of them. However, he does name some of the problems a wife might create for her husband. "The contentions of a wife are a continual dripping" (19:13). A wife who quarrels constantly creates the kind of atmosphere in a home that would tempt her husband to look for attention elsewhere. "Better to live on the corner of a roof than share a house with a quarrelsome wife" (21:9, NIV; see 21:19; 25:24; 27:15-16). But let's be fair and admit that the situation might be reversed and the husband be the culprit. God hates family discord (6:19), and we should do everything we can to practice in the home the kind of love that produces unity and harmony.

The finest description of the ideal wife is found in 31:10-31. This poem is an acrostic with the initial words of the twenty-two verses all beginning with successive letters of the Hebrew alphabet (see Ps. 119). This acrostic form was a device to help people commit the passage to memory. Perhaps Jewish parents instructed their sons and daughters to memorize this poem and use it as a guide for their lives and in their homes. What kind of wife is described here?

First of all, *she is a woman of character* (Prov. 31:10-12). Just as wisdom is more important than wealth (3:15), so character is more important than jewels. Peter gave this same counsel to Christian wives in his day (1 Peter 3:1-6). *Marriage doesn't change a person's character.* If there are character weaknesses in either the husband or the wife, marriage will only reveal and accentuate them. A husband or wife who hopes to change his or her spouse after the honeymoon is destined for disappointment.

If the husband and wife trust each other, there will be harmony in the home. Her husband has no fears or suspicions as she is busy about her work, because he knows she has character and will do nothing but good for him and their children. If brides and grooms take seriously the vows of love and loyalty they repeat to each other and to God at the altar, they will have a wall of confidence around their marriage that will keep out every enemy.

She's a woman *who isn't afraid to work* (Prov. 31:13-22, 24). Whether it's going to the market for food (vv. 14-15), buying real estate (v. 16a), or planting a vineyard

(v. 16b), she's up early and busy with her chores. You get the impression that the night before she makes a list of "things to do" and doesn't waste a minute in idleness. "She sets about her work vigorously" (v. 17, NIV), whether spinning thread, helping the poor, or providing a wardrobe for her children. She prepares the very best for her family and they have no reason to be ashamed.

She is a *generous* person (v. 20). As she ministers to her family, she keeps her eyes open for people who have needs, and she does what she can to help them. Happiness comes to those who have mercy on the poor (14:21), and nothing given to the Lord for them will ever be lost (19:17).

This wife *makes it easy for her husband to do his work* (v. 23). The city gate was the place where civic business was transacted, so her husband was one of the elders in the community (Ruth 4). While no such restrictions exist today, it would have been unthinkable in that day for a woman to sit on the "city council." But this loyal wife didn't want to take his place; she just did her work and made it easier for him to do his.

A husband and wife should complement each other as they each seek to fulfill their roles in the will of God. Wise is that husband who recognizes his wife's strengths and lets her compensate for his weaknesses. Doing this isn't a sign of personal failure, nor is it rebellion against the divine order (1 Cor. 11:3). Both leadership and submission in a home are evidences of love and obedience, and the one doesn't nullify the other.

She is confident as she faces the future (Prov. 31:25). In the Bible, to be "clothed" with something means that it is a part of your life and reveals itself in your character and conduct. (See 1 Tim. 2:9-10; Col.

3:8-14.) This wife can laugh at future problems and troubles because she has strength of character and she's prepared for emergencies. She is a woman of faith who knows that God is with her and her family.

This wife is a capable *teacher of wisdom* (Prov. 31:26). She certainly teaches her children the wisdom of God, especially the daughters, preparing them for the time when they will have homes of their own. But it's likely that she also shares her insights with her husband, and he's wise enough to listen. Remember that earlier in the book, Solomon used a beautiful woman to personify wisdom; this godly wife does the same.

She is an *attentive overseer of the household* (v. 27). She isn't idle, and nothing in the household escapes her notice, whether it's food, finances, clothing, or school lessons. Managing the household is an exacting job, and she does her work faithfully day and night. Any husband and father who thinks that his wife "has it easy" should take her responsibilities for a week or two and discover how wrong he is!

She's a woman *worthy of praise* (vv. 28-29). It's a wonderful thing when husband and children can praise wife and mother for her faithful ministry in the home. The suggestion here is that this praise was expressed regularly and spontaneously and not just on special occasions. (They didn't have Mother's Day in Israel. Every day should be Mother's Day and Father's Day!) It's tragic when the members of a family take each other for granted and fail to show sincere appreciation. The father ought to set the example for the children and always thank his wife for what she does for the family. He should see in her the woman who surpasses them all!

The secret of her life is that *she fears the Lord* (v. 30). It's wonderful if a wife has charm and beauty; the possession of these qualities is not a sin. But the woman who walks with the Lord and seeks to please Him has a beauty that never fades (1 Peter 3:1-6). The man who has a wife who daily reads the Word, meditates, prays, and seeks to obey God's will, has a treasure that is indeed beyond the price of rubies.

Finally, *her life is a testimony to others* (Prov. 31:31). Her husband and children acknowledge her value and praise her, but so do the other people in the community. Even the leaders in the city gate recognize her good works and honor her. "A kindhearted woman gains respect" (11:16, NIV). God sees to it that the woman who faithfully serves Him and her family is properly honored, and certainly she will have even greater honor when she stands before her Lord.

This beautiful tribute to the godly wife and mother tells every Christian woman what she can become if she follows the Lord. It also describes for every Christian man the kind of wife for whom he ought to be looking and praying. But it also reminds the prospective husband that he'd better be walking with the Lord and growing in his spiritual life so that he will be worthy of such a wife if and when God brings her to him.

2. Parents and Children

In ancient Israel, a Jewish husband and wife would no more consider aborting a child than they would consider killing each other. Their philosophy was, "Behold, children are a heritage from the Lord, the fruit of the womb is a reward" (Ps. 127:3). To them, marriage was a "bank" into which God dropped precious children who were His investment for the future, and it was up to the father and mother to raise those children in the fear of God. Children were rewards not pun-

ishments, opportunities not obstacles. They aren't burdens; they're investments that produce dividends.

Along with the basic necessities of physical life, what should the godly home provide for the children?

Example. "The righteous man leads a blameless life; blessed are his children after him" (Prov. 20:7, NIV), and we've already considered the influence of the godly mother's example (31:28). British statesman Edmund Burke called example "the school of mankind," and its first lessons are learned in the home even before the children can speak. Benjamin Franklin said that example was "the best sermon," which suggests that the way parents act in the home teaches their children more about God than what the children hear in Sunday School and church.

When parents walk with God, they give their children a heritage that will enrich them throughout their lives. Godliness puts beauty within the home and protection around the home. "He who fears the Lord has a secure fortress, and for his children it will be a refuge" (14:26, NIV). The world wants to penetrate that fortress and kidnap our children and grandchildren, but godly parents keep the walls strong and the spiritual weapons ready.

Instruction. "My son, hear the instruction of your father, and do not forsake the law of your mother" (1:8, NKJV; 6:20). The book of Proverbs is primarily the record of a father's instructions to his children, instructions that they were to hear and heed all their lives. "Cease listening to instruction, my son, and you will stray from the words of knowledge" (19:27, NKJV). "My son, keep my words, and treasure my commands within you" (7:1, NKJV).

The man who deliberately walked into the trap of the adulteress did so because he ignored what his parents had taught him. "How I have hated instruction, and my heart despised correction! I have not obeyed the voice of my teachers, nor inclined my ear to those who instructed me!" (5:12-13) As we get older, it's remarkable how much more intelligent our parents and teachers become!

The Bible is the basic textbook in the home. It was once the basic textbook in the educational system, but even if that were still true, the Bible in the school can't replace the Bible in the home. I note that many modern parents sacrifice time and money to help their children excel in music, sports, and social activities; I trust they're even more concerned that their children excel in knowing and obeying the Word of God.

Every parent should pray and work so that their children will have spiritual wisdom when the time comes for them to leave the home. "A wise son makes a glad father, but a foolish son is the grief of his mother" (10:1, NKJV; see 15:20; 23:15-16, 24-25; 27:11; 29:3). "A wise son heeds his father's instruction, but a scoffer does not listen to rebuke" (13:1, NKJV). In my pastoral ministry, I have often had to share the grief of parents and grandparents whose children and grandchildren turned their backs on the Word of God and the godly example given in the home. In some instances, the children, like the Prodigal Son, "came to themselves" and returned to the Lord, but they brought with them memories and scars that would torture them for the rest of their lives.

Loving discipline. Many modern educators and parents revolt against the biblical teaching about discipline. They tell us that, "Spare the rod and spoil the child" is nothing but brutal prehistoric pedagogy that cripples the child for life.[3] But nowhere does the Bible teach blind brutality when it comes to disciplining children. The emphasis is on love, because this is the way God disciplines His own children. "My son, do not despise the chastening of the Lord, nor detest His correction; for whom the Lord loves He corrects, just as a father the son in whom he delights" (3:11-12, NKJV; 13:24). Do we know more about raising children than God does?

Discipline has to do with correcting character faults in a child while there is still time to do it (22:15). Better the child is corrected by a parent than by a law enforcement officer in a correctional institution. "Chasten your son while there is hope, and do not set your heart on his destruction" (19:18, NKJV). I prefer the *New International Version* translation of the second clause: "do not be a willing party to his death." A vote against discipline is a vote in favor of premature death. (See 23:13-14.)

What a tragedy when children are left to themselves, not knowing where or what the boundaries are and what the consequences of rebellion will be! I may be wrong, but I have a suspicion that many people who can't discipline their children have a hard time disciplining themselves. If you want to enjoy your children all your life, start by lovingly disciplining them early. "The rod and rebuke give wisdom, but a child left to himself brings shame to his mother" (29:15, NKJV). "Correct your son, and he will give you rest; yes, he will give delight to your soul" (29:17, NKJV).

Proverbs 22:6 is a religious "rabbit's foot" that many sorrowing parents and grandparents desperately resort to when children stray from the Lord: "Train up a child in the way he should go: and when he is old, he will not depart from it." They interpret this to mean, "they will stray away for a time but then come back," but that isn't what it says. It says that if they're raised in the wisdom and way of the Lord, *they won't stray away at all.* Even in old age, they will follow the wisdom of God.

Certainly it's true that children raised in the nurture and admonition of the Lord can stray from God, but they can never get away from the prayers of their parents or the seed that's been planted in their hearts. Parents should never despair but keep on praying and trusting God to bring wayward children to their senses. But that isn't what Proverbs 22:6 is speaking about. Like the other proverbs, it's not making an ironclad guarantee but is laying down a general principle.[4]

In the autumn of 1993, we replaced a pin oak that a tornado had ripped out of our front yard, and the nursery people attached three guy-wires to the trunk of the new tree to make sure it would grow straight. They also taped metal rods to two limbs that were growing down instead of straight out. If you don't do these things while the tree is young and pliable, you'll never be able to do it at all. "As the twig is bent, so is the tree inclined," says an old proverb, a paraphrase of Proverbs 22:6.

God has ordained that parents are older and more experienced than their children and should therefore lovingly guide their children and prepare them for adult life. If any of their children end up sluggards (10:5), gluttons (28:7), fornicators (29:3), rebels (19:26; 20:20; 30:11-12, 17; see Deut. 21:18-21) and robbers (28:24), it should be *in spite of* the parents' training and not *because of* it.

3. Friends and Neighbors

G.K. Chesterton said that God commanded us to love both our enemies and our neighbors because usually they were the same people. My wife and I have always been blessed with wonderful neighbors whom we consider friends; that seems to be the biblical ideal, for the Hebrew word *(ra'a)* can mean "friend" or "neighbor." In this survey, we'll include both meanings; for what's true of friends ought to be true of neighbors.

The basis for friendship. Proverbs makes it clear that true friendship is based on love, because only love will endure the tests that friends experience as they go through life together. "A friend loves at all times, and a brother is born for adversity" (17:17, NKJV). It's possible to have many companions and no real friends. "A man of many companions may come to ruin, but there is a friend who sticks closer than a brother" (18:24, NIV). Friendship is something that has to be cultivated, and its roots must go deep.

God's people must be especially careful in choosing their friends. "The righteous should choose his friends carefully, for the way of the wicked leads them astray" (12:26, NKJV). "He who walks with wise men will be wise, but the companion of fools will be destroyed" (13:20). Friendships that are based on money (6:1-5; 14:20; 19:4, 6-7) or sin (16:29-30; 1:10-19) are destined to be disappointing. So are friendships with people who have bad tempers (22:24-25), who speak foolishly (14:7), who rebel against authority (24:21-22, NIV), or who are dishonest (29:27). Believers need to heed Psalm 1:1-2 and 2 Corinthians 6:14-18.

The qualities of true friendship. I've already mentioned *love,* and true love will produce *loyalty.* "A friend loves at all times" (Prov. 17:17, NIV) and "there is a friend who sticks closer than a brother" (18:24, NIV). Sometimes our friends do more for us in an emergency than our relatives do! By the way, this loyalty ought to extend to our parents' friends. "Do not forsake your friend and the friend of your father" (27:10, NIV). Long-time family friends can be a blessing from one generation to the next.

True friends know how to *keep a confidence.* "If you argue your case with a neighbor, do not betray another man's confidence, or he who hears it may shame you and you will never lose your bad reputation" (25:9-10, NIV). If you have a disagreement with somebody, don't bring another person into the discussion by betraying confidence, because you'll end up losing both your reputation ("You can't trust him with anything confidential!") and your friend who trusted you with his private thoughts. "A gossip betrays a confidence, but a trustworthy man keeps a secret" (11:13, NIV; see 20:19). If we aren't careful, gossip can ruin a friendship (16:28), so the wise thing to do is to cover offenses with love (17:9; 1 Peter 4:8).

This leads to the next important quality for true friends and good neighbors: *the ability to control the tongue.* "With his mouth the godless destroys his neighbor, but through knowledge the righteous escape" (Prov. 11:9, NIV). Don't believe the first thing you hear about a matter, because it may be wrong (18:17); remember that "a man of understanding holds his tongue" (11:12, NIV). If your neighbor or friend speaks falsely of you, talk to him about it privately, but don't seek to avenge yourself by lying about him (24:28-29; 25:18). And beware of people who cause trouble and then say, "I was only joking" (26:18-19).

Friends and neighbors must be *lovingly honest with one another.* "Faithful are the wounds of a friend; but the kisses of an enemy are deceitful" (27:6). True friendship in the Lord can't be built on deception; even if "the truth hurts," it can never harm if it's given in love. Better that

we "speak the truth in love" (Eph. 4:15), because the Spirit can use truth and love to build character, while the devil uses lies and flattery to tear things down (Prov. 29:5). "He who rebukes a man will find more favor afterward than he who flatters with the tongue" (28:23). It has well been said that flattery is manipulation, not communication; what honest person would want to manipulate a friend?

We must never take our friends for granted and think that they will immediately forgive our offenses, even though forgiveness is the right thing for Christians. "A brother offended is harder to win than a strong city, and contentions are like the bars of a castle" (18:19). It's strange but true that some of God's people will forgive offenses from unbelievers that they would never forgive if a Christian friend committed them. It takes a diamond to cut a diamond, and some Christians have a way of putting up defenses that even the church can't break through. Matthew 18:15-35 gives us the steps to take when such things happen, and our Lord warns us that an unforgiving spirit only puts us into prison!

Faithful friends and neighbors *counsel and encourage each other.* "Ointment and perfume delight the heart, and the sweetness of a man's friend gives delight by hearty counsel" (Prov. 27:9, NKJV). The images of oil and perfume are fine when the discussion is pleasant, but what's it like when friends disagree? "As iron sharpens iron, so a man sharpens the countenance of his friend" (27:17). If we're not disagreeable, we usually learn more by disagreeing than by giving in and refusing to say what we really think, "speaking the truth in love" (Eph. 4:15).

Friends and neighbors must *exercise tact and be sensitive to each other's feelings.* If we spend too much time together, we may wear out our welcome. "Seldom set foot in your neighbor's house, lest he become weary of you and hate you" (Prov. 25:17, NKJV). I've known people who spent so much time with each other that they eventually destroyed their friendship. If we're going to grow, we need space; space comes from privacy and solitude. Even husbands and wives must respect each other's privacy and not be constantly together if their love is to mature.

"He who blesses his friend with a loud voice, rising early in the morning, it will be counted a curse to him" (27:14, NKJV). Beware the "friend" who loudly and frequently praises you and tells you what a good friend you are, because true friendship doesn't depend on such antics—especially if he wakes you up to do it! Love is sensitive to other people's feelings and needs, and true friends try to say the right thing at the right time in the right way (25:20).

A happy family, encouraging friends, and good neighbors: What blessings these are from the Lord! Let's be sure we do our part to make these blessings a reality in our lives and the lives of others.

CHAPTER NINE
A MATTER OF LIFE OR DEATH
(Human Speech)

A judge speaks some words and a guilty prisoner is taken to a cell on death row. A gossip makes a phone call and a reputation is blemished or perhaps ruined. A cynical professor makes a snide remark in a lecture and a student's faith is destroyed.

Never underestimate the power of words. For every word in Hitler's book *Mein Kampf*, 125 people died in World War II.[1] Solomon was right: "Death and life are in the power of the tongue" (Prov. 18:21). No wonder James compared the tongue to a destroying fire, a dangerous beast, and a deadly poison (James 3:5-8). Speech is a matter of life or death.

When you summarize what Proverbs teaches about human speech, you end up with four important propositions: (1) speech is an awesome gift from God; (2) speech can be used to do good; (3) speech can be used to do evil; and (4) only God can help us use speech to do good.

1. Speech Is an Awesome Gift from God

Our older daughter's first complete sentence was, "Where Daddy go?" Considering how full my schedule was in those days, it was an appropriate question for her to ask. But, who taught Carolyn how to understand and speak those words? And who explained to her how to put together a sentence that asked a question?

"The ability [to speak] comes so naturally that we are apt to forget what a miracle it is," writes Professor Steven Pinker. "Language is not a cultural artifact that we learn the way we learn to tell time or how the federal government works. Instead, it is a distinct piece of the biological makeup of our brains."[2] Christian believers would say that when God created our first parents, He gave them the ability to speak and understand words. Made in the image of a God who communicates, human beings have the wonderful gift of speech. "The answer of the tongue is from the Lord" (16:1).

God spoke to Adam and gave him instructions about life in the Garden, which he later shared with Eve; they both understood what God told them (Gen. 2:15-17; 3:2-3). Adam was able to name the animals (2:18-20) and to give a descriptive name to his bride (vv. 22-24). Satan used words to deceive Adam and Eve (3:1-5), and Eve must have used words to persuade her husband to eat (v. 6). The Garden of Eden was a place of communication because God gave Adam and Eve the ability to understand and use words.

The images used in Proverbs for human speech indicate the value of this divine gift that we not only take for granted but too often waste and abuse. Wise words are compared to *gold and silver.* "The tongue of the just is like choice silver: the heart of the wicked is little worth" (Prov. 10:20). "A word aptly spoken is like apples of gold in settings of silver. Like an earring of gold or an ornament of fine gold is a wise man's rebuke to a listening ear" (25:11-12, NIV). Our words ought to be as balanced, beautiful, and valuable as the most precious jewelry; we ought to work as hard as the craftsman to make them that way. (See Eccl. 12:9-11.)

Words are also like *refreshing water.* "The mouth of a righteous man is a well [fountain] of life" (Prov. 10:11). "The words of a man's mouth are deep waters; the wellspring of wisdom is a flowing brook" (18:4, NKJV). When we listen to and appropriate the words of a godly person, it's like taking a drink of refreshing water. "The law of the wise is a fountain of life" (13:14), and "the fear of the Lord is a fountain of life" (14:27). But it isn't enough for the wise to speak to us; we must be prepared to listen. "Understanding is a wellspring of life to him who has it" (16:22, NKJV). The soil of the heart must be pre-

pared and the seed of the Word planted, or the water won't do us much good.

Right words are like *nourishing, health-giving food.* "The tongue that brings healing is a tree of life, but a deceitful tongue crushes the spirit" (15:4, NIV). What a wonderful thing it is to say the right words and help to heal a broken spirit! The phrase, "tree of life," means "source of life" and goes back to Genesis 2:9.[3] "The lips of the righteous feed many" (Prov. 10:21; see 18:20). "Pleasant words are like a honeycomb, sweetness to the soul and health to the bones" (16:24, NKJV; see Ps. 119:103). "Reckless words pierce like a sword, but the tongue of the wise brings healing" (Prov. 12:18, NIV; see 12:14; 13:2).

The apostle Paul considered biblical doctrine to be "healthy doctrine" ("sound doctrine," KJV)[4] that nourishes the believer's spiritual life. He warned Timothy to beware of anything that was "contrary to sound [healthy] doctrine" (1 Tim. 1:10), and he reminded him that the time would come when professed Christians wouldn't "endure sound [healthy] doctrine" (2 Tim. 4:3). Spiritual leaders are to use sound doctrine to exhort the careless and rebuke the deceivers (Titus 1:9-10; 2:1). The words of Jesus are "wholesome [healthy] words," but the words of false teachers are "sick" (1 Tim. 6:3-4, see NIV). "Their teaching will spread like gangrene" (2 Tim. 2:17, NIV), but God's words are "life to those who find them, and health to all their flesh" (Prov. 4:22, NKJV).

The Christian who recognizes how awesome is the gift of speech will not abuse that gift but will dedicate it to the glory of God. The New Testament scholar Bishop B.F. Westcott wrote, "Every year makes me tremble at the daring with which people speak of spiritual things." We all need to heed the words of

Solomon: "Do not be rash with your mouth, and let not your heart utter anything hastily before God. For God is in heaven, and you on earth; therefore let your words be few" (Eccl. 5:2, NKJV).

2. Speech Can Be Used to Do Good

No matter what may be wrong with us physically, when the doctor examines us, he or she often says, "Stick out your tongue!" This principle applies to the Christian life, for what the tongue does reveals what the heart contains. Inconsistent speech bears witness to a divided heart, for it is "out of the abundance of the heart" that the mouth speaks (Matt. 12:34). "Out of the same mouth proceedeth blessing and cursing," wrote James. "My brethren, these things ought not so to be" (James 3:10).

What we say can help or hurt other people. When we reviewed some of the images of speech found in Proverbs, we learned that our words can bring beauty and value, nourishment, refreshment, and healing to the inner person. But the awesome power of words reveals itself in other positive ways.

Our words can bring peace instead of war. "A soft [gentle] answer turns away wrath, but a harsh word stirs up anger" (Prov. 15:1, NKJV). "A hot-tempered man stirs up dissension, but a patient man calms a quarrel" (v. 18, NIV).[5] Solomon isn't advising us to compromise the truth and say that what's wrong is really right. Rather, he's counseling us to have a gentle spirit and a conciliatory attitude when we disagree with others. This can defuse the situation and make it easier for us to settle the matter peacefully.

Once again, the key issue is the condition of the heart. If there's war in the heart, then our words will be destructive missiles instead of healing medicines.

"But if you have bitter envy and self-seeking in your hearts, do not boast and lie against the truth" (James 3:14, NKJV). Earthly wisdom advises us to fight for our rights and make every disagreement a win/lose situation, but heavenly wisdom seeks for a win/win situation that strengthens the "unity of the Spirit in the bond of peace" (Eph. 4:3). "But the wisdom that is from above is first pure, then peaceable, gentle, willing to yield,[6] full of mercy and good fruits, without partiality and without hypocrisy" (James 3:17, NKJV). Applying this wisdom means taking the attitude that's described in Philippians 2:1-12, the attitude that was practiced by Jesus Christ.

Our words can help restore those who have sinned. "As an earring of gold, and an ornament of fine gold, so is a wise reprover upon an obedient [listening] ear" (Prov. 25:12). It isn't easy to reprove those who are wrong, and we need to do it in a meek and loving spirit (Gal. 6:1); yet it must be done. To flatter those who are disobeying God's Word will only confirm them in their sin and make us their accomplices. "He who rebukes a man will find more favor afterward than he who flatters with the tongue" (28:23, NKJV). "He who keeps instruction is in the way of life, but he who refuses reproof goes astray" (10:17, NKJV).

In Matthew 18:15-20 Jesus explains the procedure for helping restore a sinning brother or sister. First, we must talk to the offender personally and confidentially, trusting God to change the heart. If that fails, we must try again, this time taking witnesses with us. If even that fails, then what was confidential must become public as we share the matter with the church. If the offender fails to hear the church, then he or she must be excluded from the church as though they were not believers at all. Of course, during this whole procedure, we must be much in prayer, seeking the Lord's help for ourselves and for those we're trying to help.

Our words can instruct the ignorant. "The lips of the wise disperse knowledge" (Prov. 15:7). "The wise in heart are called discerning, and pleasant words promote instruction" (16:21, NIV). While there are many good and helpful things to learn in this brief life that we have on earth, the most important is the wisdom of God found in the Word of God (8:6-8). "Wisdom is the principal thing; therefore get wisdom. And in all your getting, get understanding" (4:7, NKJV). After we acquire wisdom, we must share it with others, for "wisdom is found on the lips of the discerning" (10:13, NIV).

Whether it's parents teaching their children (Deut. 6:1-13), older women teaching the younger women (Titus 2:3-5), or spiritual leaders in the church teaching the next generation of believers (2 Tim. 2:2), accurate instruction is important to the ongoing of the work of God. Every local church is but one generation short of extinction; if we don't teach the next generation the truth of God, they may not have a church.

In spite of all the books and periodicals that are published and all the Christian programs that are broadcast, we're facing today a famine of God's Word (Amos 8:11). People attend church services and special meetings of all kinds, purchase Bibles and books, and listen to Christian radio and TV. But there seems to be little evidence that all this "learning" is making a significant difference in families, churches, and society as a whole. Many professed believers are "spiritually illiterate" when it comes to the basics of the Christian life. We desperately need men who will obey 2 Timothy 2:2 and women who will obey Titus 2:3-5, or we will end up with an uninstructed church.

Our words can rescue the perishing "A true witness delivers souls, but a deceitful witness speaks lies" (Prov. 14:25, NKJV). While this verse can be applied to our own personal witness for Christ in rescuing the lost (Acts 1:8), the context is that of a court of law. An accused criminal in Israel could be condemned on the testimony of two or three witnesses; if the case involved a capital crime, the witnesses had to be the first to cast the stones (Deut. 17:6-7). The law forbade the bearing of false witness (Ex. 20:16; 23:2; Deut. 5:20), and anyone found guilty of perjury was given the punishment that the accused would have received (Deut. 19:16-18).

If my testimony could save an innocent person from death, and I refused to speak, then my silence would be a terrible sin. "Deliver those who are drawn toward death, and hold back those stumbling to the slaughter. If you say, 'Surely we did not know this,' does not He who weighs the hearts consider it? He who keeps your soul, does He not know it? And will He not render to each man according to his deeds?" (Prov. 24:11-12, NKJV) Whether it's rescuing prisoners from execution or lost sinners from eternal judgment, we can't plead ignorance if we do nothing.

Our words can encourage those who are burdened. "Anxiety in the heart of man causes depression, but a good word makes it glad" (12:25, NKJV). "A man finds joy in giving an apt reply—and how good is a timely word!" (15:23, NIV) When we're walking in the Spirit daily and being taught by the Lord, we'll know how "to speak a word in season to him who is weary" (Isa. 50:4). "Pleasant words are a honeycomb, sweet to the soul and healing to the bones" (Prov. 16:24, NIV).

The Royal British Navy has a regulation which reads, "No officer shall speak discouragingly to another officer in the discharge of his duties." We need to practice that regulation in our homes and churches! Each of us needs to be a Barnabas, a "son of encouragement" (Acts 4:36-37). Near the close of his ministry, a famous British preacher of the Victorian Age said, "If I had my ministry to do over, I would preach more to broken hearts." Jesus came, "to heal the brokenhearted" (Luke 4:18), and we can continue that ministry today with words of encouragement and hope.

3. Speech Can Be Used to Do Evil

From Satan's speech to Eve in Genesis 3 to the propaganda of the false prophet in the book of Revelation, the Bible warns us that words can be used to deceive, control, and destroy. It is estimated that the average American is exposed to over 1,500 "promotion bites" in the course of a day, some of them subliminal and undetected, but all of them powerful. Whether it's political "double-speak,"[7] seductive advertising, or religious propaganda, today's "spin doctors" know how to manipulate people with words.

But it isn't only some of the professional promoters who are guilty. There are many ways that you and I can turn words into weapons and damage others.

We hurt others by lying. "Truthful lips endure forever, but a lying tongue lasts only a moment" (Prov. 12:19, NIV). "Lying lips are an abomination to the Lord, but they that deal truly are His delight" (12:22; and see 6:16-17). Solomon warns us against bearing false witness and violating the Ninth Commandment (Ex. 20:16). (See Prov. 14:5, 25; 19:5, 9, 28; 21:28; 24:28.) When words can't be trusted, then society starts to fall apart. Contracts are useless, promises are vain, the judicial system becomes a farce, and all personal relationships are suspect. "Like a club or a sword or a sharp arrow is the man who gives false testimony against his neighbor" (25:18, NIV).

One of the marks of liars is that they enjoy listening to lies. "A wicked man listens to evil lips; a liar pays attention to a malicious tongue" (17:4, NIV). It's a basic rule of life that the ears hear what the heart loves, so beware of people who have an appetite for gossip and lies.

"An honest answer is like a kiss on the lips" (24:26, NIV; see 27:6). A kiss is a sign of affection and trust, and God wants His people to "[speak] the truth in love" (Eph. 4:15). It has well been said that love without truth is hypocrisy and truth without love is brutality, and we don't want to be guilty of either sin. The world affirms, "Honesty is the best policy," but as the British prelate Richard Whateley said, "He who acts on that principle is not an honest man." We should be honest because we're honest people in our hearts, walking in the fear of the Lord, and not because we're shrewd bargainers who follow a successful policy.

We hurt others by gossiping. "You shall not go about as a talebearer among your people" (Lev. 19:16, NKJV). "Talebearer" is the translation of a Hebrew word that means "to go about," and is probably derived from a word meaning "merchant." The talebearer goes about peddling gossip! "A talebearer reveals secrets, but he who is of a faithful spirit conceals a matter" (Prov. 11:13, NKJV). Gossips flatter people by sharing secrets with them, but to be one of their "customers" is dangerous. "He who goes about as a talebearer reveals secrets; therefore do not associate with one who flatters with his lips" (20:19, NKJV).

The gossip "eats" and enjoys his secrets like you and I eat and enjoy food. "The words of a gossip are like choice morsels; they go down to a man's inmost parts" (18:8, NIV; see 26:22). People who feed on gossip only crave more, and the only remedy is for them to develop an appetite for God's truth (2:10). We must beware of gossips because they do a great deal of damage. "An ungodly man digs up evil, and it is on his lips like a burning fire. A perverse man sows strife, and a whisperer separates the best of friends" (16:27-28, NKJV; see 17:9). "Where there is no wood, the fire goes out; and where there is no talebearer, strife ceases" (26:20, NKJV).

We hurt others by flattery. The English word "flatter" comes from a French word that means "to stroke or caress with the flat of the hand." Flatterers compliment you profusely, appealing to your ego, but their praise is far from sincere. They pat you on the back only to locate a soft spot in which to stick a knife! "A man who flatters his neighbor spreads a net for his feet" (29:5, NKJV).

"A lying tongue hates those who are crushed by it, and a flattering mouth works ruin" (26:28, NKJV). Satan flattered Eve when he said, "You shall be as God" (Gen. 3:5). In Proverbs, the prostitute seduces her prey by using flattery (Prov. 5:3; 7:5, 21). Some people flatter the rich because they hope to get something from them (14:20; 19:4, 6).

Most of us secretly enjoy flattery and dislike rebuke, yet rebuke does us more good (27:6; 28:23). There is certainly a place for honest appreciation and praise, to the glory of God (1 Thess. 5:12-13), but we must beware of people who give us insincere praise with selfish motives, especially if they begin their flattery first thing in the morning (Prov. 26:24-25). If it weren't for our pride, flattery wouldn't affect us. We privately enjoy hearing somebody agree with what we think of ourselves!

We hurt others by speaking in anger. "An angry man stirs up dissension, and a hot-tempered one commits many sins" (29:22, NIV). Angry people keep adding fuel to the fire (26:21) instead of trying to find ways to put the fire out. Many people carry anger in their hearts while they outwardly pretend to be at peace with their friends, and they cover their anger with hypocritical words. "Fervent lips with a wicked heart are like earthenware covered with silver dross" (26:23, NKJV). If we're inwardly angry at people, all our profuse professions of friendship are but a thin veneer over common clay. "Speak when you are angry," wrote Ambrose Bierce, "and you will make the best speech you will ever regret."

Instead of covering our anger with cheap dross, we should cover others' sins with sincere love. "Hatred stirs up strife, but love covers all sins" (10:12, NKJV; 1 Peter 4:8). Love doesn't *condone* sin or encourage sinners to try to hide their sins from the Lord (Prov. 28:13; 1 John 1:9), but love doesn't tell the sin to others. (See Gen. 9:18-29.) If I'm angry with someone and he sins, I'll be tempted to spread the news as a way of getting even.

We hurt others by impetuous speech. "Do you see a man hasty in his words? There is more hope for a fool than for him" (Prov. 29:20, NKJV). "He who answers a matter before he hears it, it is folly and shame to him" (18:13, NKJV; note v. 17). "The heart of the righteous studies how to answer, but the mouth of the wicked pours forth evil" (15:28, NKJV; see 10:19). "Reckless words pierce like a sword" (12:18, NIV). But reckless words not only hurt others, they can also hurt us because we utter them. "Whoever guards his mouth and tongue keeps his soul from troubles" (21:23, NKJV; see 13:3). This is especially true when we make rash promises to the Lord or to others (20:25; 22:26-27; see Eccl. 5:1-5).

We hurt others by talking too much. "In the multitude of words sin is not lacking, but he who restrains his lips is wise" (Prov. 10:19, NKJV). "The mouth of fools pours forth foolishness" (15:2). People who discipline their tongue can control their whole body (James 3:1-2). There is "a time to keep silence, and a time to speak" (Eccl. 3:7), and the wise know how to hold their peace (Prov. 11:12-13; 17:28).

We hurt others by talking instead of working. "All hard work brings a profit, but mere talk leads only to poverty" (14:23, NIV). Mankind seems to be divided into three classes: *dreamers* who have great ideas but never accomplish much, *talkers* who exercise their jaw muscles and vocal cords but not their hands and feet, and *doers* who talk little but with God's help turn their dreams into realities.

4. Only God Can Help Us Use the Gift of Speech for Good

When David prayed, "Set a watch, O Lord, before my mouth; keep the door of my lips" (Ps. 141:3), he was doing a wise thing and setting a good example. All of God's people need to surrender their bodies to the Lord (Rom. 12:1), and this includes the lips and the tongue. We must also yield our hearts to the Lord, because what comes out of the mouth originates in the heart.

Proverbs 16:1 has been a great help to me, especially when I've been called upon to give counsel: "To man belong the plans of the hearts, but from the Lord comes the reply of the tongue" (NIV). When you couple this with 19:21, it gives you great encouragement: "Many are the plans in a man's heart, but it is the Lord's purpose that prevails" (NIV). On many occasions, I've had to make decisions about complex matters, and the Lord has given me just the words to speak. However, if my heart had not been in touch with His Word and yielded to His will, the Spirit might not have been able to direct me. If we make our plans the best we can and commit them to the Lord, He'll guide us in what we say and do.

God also gives us "spiritual radar" so that we can assess a situation and make the right reply. "The lips of the righteous know what is acceptable" (10:32). "A man has joy by the answer of his mouth, and a word spoken in due season, how good it is" (15:23, NKJV; see Isa. 50:4-6). "The heart of the righteous studies how to answer, but the mouth of the wicked pours forth evil" (Prov. 15:28, NKJV). There is beauty and value in the "word fitly spoken" (25:11-12).

People who speak wisely, saying the right thing at the right time in the right way, are people who store God's truth in their hearts. "Wisdom is found on the lips of him who has understanding" (10:13, NKJV), and that understanding comes from the Word of God. "Wise people store up knowledge" (10:14, NKJV); they are "filled richly" with the Word of God (Col. 3:16). "The heart of the wise teaches his mouth, and adds learning to his lips" (Prov. 16:23, NKJV). If we devote our hearts to serious study of the Word, even while we're sharing the truth with others, God will teach us more of His truth. I have had this happen while ministering the Word, and it's a wonderful experience of God's goodness.

One of my school teachers used to say, "Empty barrels make the most noise," and she was right. Too often in church board meetings and business meetings, those who talk the most have the least to say. People who don't prepare their hearts for such meetings are making themselves available to become the devil's tools for hindering God's work. If we're filled with the Word and led by the Spirit, we'll be a part of the answer and not a part of the problem.

Have you heard the fable of the king and the menu? A king once asked his cook to prepare for him the best dish in the world, and he was served a dish of tongue. The king then asked for the worst dish in the world, and again was served tongue.

"Why do you serve me the same food as both the best and the worst?" the perplexed monarch asked.

"Because, your majesty," the cook replied, "the tongue is the best of things when used wisely and lovingly, but it is the worst of things when used carelessly and unkindly."

"Death and life are in the power of the tongue" (18:21, NKJV).

"The mouth of the righteous is a fountain of life" (10:11, NIV).

Choose life!

CHAPTER TEN
MAKE WAY FOR THE RIGHTEOUS!

Those who obey the wisdom taught in God's Word will become more skillful in handling the affairs of life. But we must not think that this wisdom is a set of rules or a collection of "success formulas" that anyone can occasionally apply as he or she pleases. Following God's wisdom is a fulltime endeavor. *His Word must first*

work within our hearts and transform our character before we can become the kind of people God can guide and bless. You don't need godly character these days to be a success in making money. Many Hollywood celebrities, dishonest businessmen, and deceptive politicians have proved that. But if you're concerned with making a *life*, you must major on building godly character.

This explains why the words *righteous* and *righteousness* are used so often in Proverbs. Wisdom leads, "in the way of righteousness" (8:20), and "in the way of righteousness is life" (12:28). "The prospect of the righteous is joy, but the hopes of the wicked come to nothing" (10:28, NIV). The wicked have hopes, but they're false hopes, so it behooves us to examine our own hearts to make sure we're among the righteous who truly have hope, and that we're the kind of people the Lord can trust with His blessings.

1. The God of Righteousness

The Hebrew words in Proverbs that are translated "righteous," "righteousness," "upright," and "uprightness" describe ethical conduct that conforms to God's standards and moral character that comes from a right relationship to the Lord and His Word. True righteousness isn't just toeing the line and obeying the rules. As Jesus teaches in the Sermon on the Mount, it is possible for us to obey the law outwardly while cultivating sin inwardly. It isn't enough for us not to kill or not to commit adultery; we must also not harbor hatred and lust in our hearts (Matt. 5:21-48).

Our God is a righteous God. His character is holy and without sin (1 John 1:5), and all that He says and does is right and just. "He is the Rock, His work is perfect; for all His ways are justice, a God of truth and without injustice; righteous and upright is He" (Deut. 32:4, NKJV). "For the Lord is righteous, He loves righteousness; His countenance beholds the upright" (Ps. 11:7, NKJV).

God's Word is righteous. "I open my lips to speak what is right. ... All the words of my mouth are just; none of them is crooked or perverse. To the discerning all of them are right; they are faultless to those who have knowledge" (Prov. 8:6, 8-9, NIV; see Ps. 119:138). The Word of God reveals the God of the Word; His Word, like His character, can be trusted.

Other nations had their gods, temples, priests, and sacrifices, but only the people of Israel worshiped the living God *who spoke to them and gave them His Word.* "Did any people ever hear the voice of God speaking out of the midst of the fire, as you have heard, and live? ... Out of heaven He let you hear His voice, that He might instruct you; on earth He showed you His great fire, and you heard His words out of the midst of the fire" (Deut. 4:33, 36, NKJV).

However, the privilege of *hearing* God's Word brings with it the responsibility of *obeying* what He commands. "You shall therefore keep His statutes and His commandments which I command you today, that it may go well with you and with your children after you, and that you may prolong your days in the land which the Lord your God is giving you for all time" (Deut. 4:40, NKJV). "See that you do not refuse Him who speaks" (Heb. 12:25, NKJV).

God's acts are righteous. "I am the Lord, who exercises kindness, justice and righteousness on earth, for in these I delight" (Jer. 9:24, NIV). "The Lord our God is righteous in everything He does" (Dan. 9:14, NIV). We may question God's plans and even accuse Him of being unfair, but nobody can succeed in proving that God has ever done anything wrong. "The Lord is righteous in her midst, He will do no unrighteousness. Every morning He brings His justice to light; He never fails" (Zeph. 3:5, NKJV).

God wants His people to be righteous. It is unthinkable that a righteous God would violate His own nature and disobey His own Word by asking His people to be less than righteous. Before He gave Israel His Law, God said: "Now therefore, if you will indeed obey My voice and keep My covenant, then you shall be a special treasure to Me above all people.... and you shall be to Me a kingdom of priests and a holy nation" (Ex. 19:5-6, NKJV). Jesus echoed this divine desire when He said, "Therefore you shall be perfect, just as your Father in heaven is perfect" (Matt. 5:48, NKJV).

The problem, of course, is that people are—people. And that means that they're sinners. "Every way of a man is right in his own eyes, but the Lord weighs the hearts" (Prov. 21:2, NKJV). "There is not a righteous man on earth who does what is right and never sins" (Eccl. 7:20, NIV). "There is none righteous, no, not one" (Rom. 3:10; see Ps. 14:1-3). How can sinners ever be righteous before a righteous God?

When you read Proverbs, you discover that God mentions many different sins that people committed in ancient Israel and still commit in our communities today, sins like anger, deception, thievery, murder, slander, gossip, drunkenness, adultery, bribery, jealousy, rebellion against parents, and a host of other things that all of us would recognize. Proverbs makes it very clear that people are sinners.

God provides righteousness for those who will accept it. How can a guilty sinner ever become righteous enough to please a holy God? If God is going to be just, all He can do is condemn the wicked and accept the righteous, but there are no righteous people for Him to accept! We certainly don't become righteous by being religious. "To do righteousness and justice is more acceptable to the Lord than sacrifice" (Prov. 21:3). Disobedient King Saul learned that lesson from Samuel (1 Sam. 15:22), and this important principle was repeated by several other prophets (Isa. 1:11-17; Jer. 7:22-23; Mic. 6:68). In fact, Isaiah said that our righteousnesses were "as filthy rags" in God's sight (Isa. 64:6)—so what must our *sins* look like to Him?

"He who justifies the wicked, and he who condemns the just, both of them alike are an abomination to the Lord" (Prov. 17:15, NKJV). *But that's exactly what the Lord God did!* His Son, Jesus Christ, died for the sins of the world, "the just for the unjust" (1 Peter 3:18); the judgment that should have been ours was laid on Him (2:24). God justifies (declares righteous) the ungodly, not when they do good works but when they put their faith in Christ. "But to him who does not work [for righteousness] but believes on Him who justifies the ungodly, his faith is accounted for righteousness" (Rom. 4:5, NKJV).[1]

"The wicked shall be a ransom for the righteous," wrote Solomon, "and the transgressor for the upright" (Prov. 21:18), but that wasn't true at Calvary. There the Righteous One became a ransom for the wicked when Jesus was numbered with the transgressors and died for our sins (Isa. 53:4-6, 12). The only way to be righteous before God is to trust Jesus Christ and receive His righteousness as God's free gift (Rom. 5:17; 2 Cor. 5:21).[2] Then we can begin to walk "the path of righteousness" and enjoy the blessings of the Lord.

Not everybody who claims to be among the righteous is truly a child of God. God's people *understand righteousness* (Prov. 2:9) because they meditate on His Word and seek to obey it. They do *righteousness* (1:3; 25:26) because true faith always leads to works (James 2:14-26). They *speak righteousness* (Prov. 10:11; 12:6, 17; 13:5; 15:28; 16:13) and their words can be trusted, and they *pursue righteousness* and make it the passion of their hearts. "The Lord detests the way of the wicked, but He loves those who pursue righteousness" (15:9, NIV). "Blessed are they who hunger and thirst for righteousness; for they shall be filled" (Matt. 5:6).

When people are right with God, He leads them in "right paths" (Prov. 4:11), and teaches them "right things" (8:6). Their minds and hearts are filled with right thoughts (12:5), and their lips speak right words (23:16). Their work is right (21:8), because God works in them and through them to accomplish His will (Phil. 2:12-13).

2. The Path of Righteousness

In our study of Proverbs 2-4, we learned that following the way of wisdom is compared to a pilgrim walking a path. As we follow His wisdom, God protects, directs, and perfects our path. God's desire for us is that we "walk in the way of goodness, and keep to the paths of righteousness" (2:20). We're warned not to listen to evil men "who leave the paths of uprightness to walk in the ways of darkness" (v. 13, NKJV); nor should we heed the seductive words of the evil woman whose "house leads down to death, and her paths to the dead" (v. 18, NKJV).

I read about a dirt-road intersection in the prairies of Canada where somebody had posted this sign: "Be careful what rut you take—you'll be on it a long time!" Each of us must choose to travel one of two paths, and the path we choose determines the destination we'll reach (Matt. 7:13-14). It also determines the quality of life we'll experience along the way. Solomon points out some of the blessings that come to those who walk the path of life and wisdom.

To begin with, God's people experience His *direction*. "The righteousness of the blameless will direct his way aright, but the wicked will fall by his own wickedness" (Prov. 11:5, NKJV). The Lord directs the paths of those who trust and obey (3:5-6), because God wants His children to know His will (Acts 22:14) and enjoy doing it (Eph. 6:6). The Lord reveals His will only to those who are willing to obey it (John 7:17).

On the path of the righteous, God's people also experience *deliverance*. "The righteousness of the upright shall deliver them, but transgressors shall be taken in their own naughtiness" (Prov. 11:6). Godly people certainly have their share of trials and testings, but the Lord promises to help them and make these experiences turn out for good (Rom. 8:28). "The righteous cry out, and the Lord hears, and delivers them out of all their troubles" (Ps. 34:17). Obedience to the Lord keeps us from many of the troubles that sinners experience, but when the Lord permits us to suffer, He promises to bring us through. "The wicked is snared by the transgression of his lips, but the just shall come out of trouble" (Prov. 12:13).

We have God's *provision* for all we need if we're walking in His wisdom. "I walk in the way of righteousness, along the paths of justice, bestowing wealth on those who love me and making their treasuries full" (8:20-21, NIV). This isn't an encouragement for us to jump on the "health-wealth-and-success" bandwagon. Proverbs was originally written for Jews under the Old Covenant; under that covenant, material blessing was a part of God's promise to Israel (Deut. 28:1-14). Believers today can be sure of God's provision for their every need as they obey His will (Phil. 4:19; Matt. 6:24-34). It sometimes looks to us as though the righteous are suffering and the wicked prospering, but faith sees beyond today and considers where the godless end up (Ps. 73). "Better is a little with righteousness than great revenues without right [with injustice]" (Prov. 16:8). Our real prosperity isn't here on earth but in glory when we see the Lord. "Misfortune pursues the sinners, but prosperity is the reward of the righteous" (13:21, NIV).

3. The Influence of Righteousness

The life of righteousness must not become a solitary and selfish experience. *When God blesses the righteous, He does it so they can share the blessing with others.* "I will bless you," God promised Abraham, "and you shall be a blessing" (Gen. 12:2, NKJV). The "blessed man" of Psalm 1 is "like a tree" that produces fruit for *others* to enjoy (Ps. 1:3). "The righteous will thrive like a green leaf ... . The fruit of the righteous is a tree of life" (Prov. 11:28, 30, NIV).

Let's trace the circles of influence that radiate from the lives of men and women of God who walk on His paths.

They are blessed in their character. The eminent American preacher Phillips Brooks said that the purpose of life was the building of character through truth. Christian character is one thing we'll take to heaven with us. We'll all have glorified bodies like that of our Lord (Phil. 3:20-21; 1 John 3:1-3), and we'll all be happy in His presence, but we will not all immediately have the same capacity for appreciating spiritual things. Every vessel will be filled, but not all vessels will be the same size. Those who have walked closely with their Lord will be delighted to see Him (2 Tim. 4:8), but others will be "ashamed before Him at His coming" (1 John 2:28).

The righteous desire the very best from the Lord, and He grants it to them (Prov. 10:24; 11:23). When we delight ourselves in the Lord, we will want the things that delight Him (Ps. 37:4). The developing of spiritual perception, a godly appetite, and the ability to choose the best (Phil. 1:9-11), is one of the blessed byproducts of a holy walk with God. The more we become like Christ, the less we enjoy the "entertainment" of this world and long for the enrichment of the world to come.

Of course, godly character comes from feeding on the Word and taking time to be holy. "Give instruction to a wise man, and he will be yet wiser; teach a just man, and he will increase in learning" (Prov. 9:9). Even reproof helps the godly person to mature. "Do not correct a scoffer, lest he hate you; rebuke a wise man, and he will love you" (v. 8, NKJV).

The righteous are kind and generous (21:26) and show their kindness, not only in the way they treat people (29:7) but also in the way they treat animals. "A righteous man regards the life of his animal, but the tender mercies of the wicked are cruel" (12:10, NKJV).

They are blessed in their home. "The Lord's curse is on the house of the wicked, but He blesses the home of the righteous" (3:33, NIV). "The house of the wicked will be overthrown, but the tent of the upright will flourish" (14:11, NKJV). The wicked may live in houses, and the righteous have only tents, but with the blessing of the Lord, the righteous person's tent will be a palace! "The wicked are overthrown, and are not: but the house of the righteous shall stand" (12:7).

In the Hebrew culture, "house" refers to the family as well as the structure in which the family dwells (2 Sam. 7:16, 25, 27), which means that the children of the godly are included in the blessing. "The righteous man walks in his integrity; his children are blessed after him" (20:7, NKJV). "Through wisdom a house is built, and by understanding it is established; by knowledge the rooms are filled with all precious and pleasant riches" (24:3-4; see 14:1).

One of the greatest rewards in life is to be a blessing to your children and grandchildren. "I have been young, and now am old; yet I have not seen the righteous forsaken, nor his descendants begging bread" (Ps. 37:25, NKJV). This blessing includes material things (Prov. 13:22), but it applies even more to spiritual treasures.

When I was born, a doctor told my parents that I wouldn't live beyond the age of two; yet the Lord enabled them to raise me, even though I wasn't a robust child. Why did I survive? Partly because of a great grandfather who had prayed years before that there would be a preacher of the Gospel in every generation of our family—and there has been! "The memory of the just is blessed: but the name of the wicked shall rot" (10:7).

"Like a bird that strays from its nest is a man who strays from his home" (27:8, NIV). In our contemporary American society, about 17 percent of the population relocates each year, but in ancient Israel, people stayed close to home. The extended family was the norm, with children and grandchildren learning to revere their ancestors and respectfully learning from them. The person who strayed from home was either up to no good or had to leave because of family problems.

But the verse applies spiritually as well as geographically: We must not stray from the example of our godly ancestors or the spiritual treasures they left us. How tragic it is when children and grandchildren ridicule and reject the spiritual heritage of their family and turn instead to the ways of the world.

They are blessed as citizens and leaders. "When it goes well with the righteous, the city rejoices; and when the wicked perish, there is jubilation. By the blessing of the upright the city is exalted, but it is overthrown by the mouth of the wicked" (11:10-11, NKJV). "When the righteous are in authority, the people rejoice; but when a wicked man rules, the people groan" (29:2, NKJV).

Israel was a monarchy and the king was expected to rule in the fear of the Lord (20:8, 26). "It is an abomination to kings to commit wickedness: for the throne is established by righteousness" (16:12). "Take away the wicked from before the king, and his throne shall be established in righteousness" (25:5). God cast out the Canaanite nations because their sins were abominable to Him (Deut. 12:29-32), and He chastened Israel when they imitated the sins of those nations (Judg. 2). God would not tolerate the sin of idolatry.

By turning away from God's Law, wicked rulers led the way for the nation to become evil. Whenever the nation had a godly king, such as David, Josiah, or Hezekiah, God blessed His people. But when an ungodly king ascended the throne, the Lord withdrew His blessing and left them to their own devices. Eventually, the Northern Kingdom of Israel was taken over by Assyria, the Southern Kingdom of Judah was exiled in Babylon, and Jerusalem and the temple destroyed.

During times of spiritual decay, it was the godly remnant of righteous people who maintained the flickering flame of spiritual life in the nation. When false prophets, greedy priests, and ruthless kings joined together to lead the nation away from the true God, it was the faithful remnant that served as salt and light in the land. "Then they that feared the Lord spake often one to another: and the Lord hearkened, and heard it, and a book of remembrance was written before Him for them that feared the Lord, and that thought upon His name" (Mal. 3:16).

Israel is the only nation that has a special covenant relationship with God, but the principle of Proverbs 14:34 still stands: "Righteousness exalts a nation, but sin is a disgrace to any people" (NIV). Deuteronomy 12, Amos 1-2, and Romans 1:18-32 make it clear that God judges the Gentile nations for their sins even though He didn't give them the same law that He gave to Israel (Ps. 147:19-20). National leaders can't escape the judgment of God when they lead the people away from God's holy standards. Legalizing sin doesn't make it right. No wonder Thomas Jefferson wrote, "Indeed I tremble for my country when I reflect that God is just."

Godly parents can raise godly children, and godly children can provide godly influence in their communities and in the nation. In a democracy, where leadership is elected and not inherited, the Lord's remnant must exert as much influence for righteousness as possible; certainly every believer ought to pray for those in authority (1 Tim. 2:1-8). I have ministered the Word in hundreds of churches and conferences in the United States, and I confess that rarely have I heard government leaders mentioned in the pulpit prayers. If the church obeyed the Word and prayed, national leaders would have to take God into account in their deliberations. "The king's heart is in the hand of the Lord; He directs it like a watercourse wherever He pleases" (Prov. 21:1, NIV).

I occasionally hear people lamenting the state of the nation, but most of them fail to point out the main cause: *The church collectively and believers individually aren't doing their job in spreading righteousness.* If the righteous remnant were spreading more salt and light, there would be less decay and darkness (Matt. 5:13-16). Christians have a job to do: praying for all in authority, winning the lost, living godly lives, and raising godly children.

And it would help if we humbled ourselves and sought God's face (2 Chron. 7:14); for apart from the deep working of God's Spirit in hearts, there is no hope for any nation.

"Blessed is the nation whose God is the Lord, the people He chose for His inheritance" (Ps. 33:12, NIV).

CHAPTER ELEVEN ENJOYING GOD'S GUIDANCE

Mention the phrase, "the will of God," and you'll get different responses from different people, not all of them positive.

Some people will say, "Not that again!" They remember their adolescent years when it seemed like every lesson and sermon they heard hammered away on knowing and doing God's will, and it all seemed so impractical to them at that time.

Others will smile knowingly, recalling the difficult "valley experiences" of life when the only thing that kept them going was depending on the will of God. The

will of God wasn't always easy, but it was always good and right.

Perhaps some people will say nothing, but they'll feel a hidden inward pain as they remember how they deliberately disobeyed God's will and suffered for it. They had to learn the hard way how to delight in the will of God.

No matter how we may feel personally about the topic, if we're going to be skillful in life, we have to understand what God's will is and how it works in our everyday experiences. In the book of Proverbs, Solomon shares with us the essentials for knowing, doing, and enjoying the will of God.

1. Faith

"Trust in the Lord with all your heart, and lean not on your own understanding; in all your ways acknowledge Him, and He shall direct your paths" (Prov. 3:5-6, NKJV). These two verses have encouraged believers everywhere in their quest for God's guidance, and for those who have sincerely met the conditions, the promise has never failed. But when we say, "I'm trusting in the Lord," what are we really affirming?

That we belong to God. No unbeliever could honestly rest on the words of Proverbs 3:5-6. While a sovereign God can rule and overrule in the life of any person, saved or lost,[1] it is clear that the life of the unsaved person is motivated and energized by the world, the flesh, and the devil (Eph. 2:1-3). Only a believer can have the guidance of the indwelling Holy Spirit or understand the teachings of the Scriptures, and only a believer would really *want* to understand and obey the will of God.

That God has a plan for our lives. "Many are the plans in a man's heart, but it is the Lord's purpose that prevails"

(Prov. 19:21, NIV). It is inconceivable that our loving Heavenly Father would give His Son to die for us, and then abandon us to our own ways! We are not our own because we have been purchased by God (1 Cor. 6:19-20), so it's reasonable that our Master should have a perfect plan for us to fulfill for His glory. Ephesians 2:10 assures us that the good works God wants us to accomplish have already been determined; in Philippians 2:12-13, God assures us that He works in us to accomplish His good pleasure. The talents we were born with (Ps. 139:13-18) and the gifts we received at conversion (1 Cor. 12:1-11) are brought together by the Holy Spirit so that we can do what God has called us to do.

That this plan is the best thing for us. How could a holy God will for His children anything less than His best, and how could a loving God plan anything that would harm us? We have no reason to fear the will of God, because His plans come from His heart. "The counsel of the Lord stands forever, the plans of His heart to all generations" (Ps. 33:11, NKJV). Unless we see the will of God as the expression of the love of God, we'll resist it stubbornly, or do it grudgingly, instead of enjoying it. Faith in God's love and wisdom will transform our attitude and make the will of God nourishment instead of punishment (John 4:34).

That the Father will reveal His will in His time. It's through "faith and patience" that we receive what God promises (Heb. 6:12, 15), and it's as dangerous to run ahead of the Lord as it is to stubbornly lag behind. "It is not good to have zeal without knowledge, nor to be hasty and miss the way" (Prov. 19:2, NIV). "Be not like the horse or like the mule" (Ps. 32:9). The horse rushes ahead and the mule won't budge, and both attitudes are wrong. Even the great apostle Paul didn't always know exactly the way God was guiding, and he had to pause in his work and wait for divine direction (Acts 16:6-10). Our times are in His hand (Ps. 31:15), and the Father is always on schedule (John 11:6-10).

2. Commitment

Knowing and obeying the will of God can't be a halfhearted endeavor on our part, a hobby we indulge in when there's an emergency or when we "feel like it." God wants us to trust Him with *all* our heart and acknowledge Him in *all* our ways. Knowing and doing the will of God isn't a "spiritual technique" that we use occasionally; it's a committed lifestyle that involves everything we do.

Successful athletes make winning their full-time pursuit, and this shows up in the way they eat, sleep, exercise, and relate to their coaches and teammates. The word for this is commitment, and commitment involves obedience. "He who scorns instruction will pay for it, but he who respects a command is rewarded" (Prov. 13:13, NIV).

In the book of Proverbs, the wise father repeatedly gives his son loving calls to obedience. "My son, do not forget my law, but let your heart keep my commands" (3:1, NKJV). "My son, keep your father's command, and do not forsake the law of your mother" (6:20, NKJV). "My son, keep my words, and treasure my commands within you" (7:1, NKJV). *The will of God isn't a curiosity for us to study, it's a command for us to obey; God isn't obligated to reveal His will unless we're willing to do it.* "If anyone wants to do His will, he shall know concerning the doctrine, whether it is from God or whether I speak on My own authority" (John 7:17, NKJV). As F. W. Robertson said, "Obedience is the organ of spiritual knowledge."

This commitment is spelled out in Romans 12:1-2, another familiar passage about the will of God. Before I can "prove by experience" what God's will is, and discover that His will is "good, pleasing and perfect" (NIV), I must give Him my body, my mind, and my will, a total commitment of my total being. This is a once-for-all presentation, but it needs to be renewed daily as we meet with the Lord in worship and prayer.

A pastor friend of mine once said to me, "There are too many 'cafeteria Christians' in our congregation. Instead of letting God plan the whole meal and accepting it, they pick and choose what they want, and they miss the best dishes He fixes for them!" God wants all of our heart, and He expects us to obey all of His will in all of our ways. If Jesus Christ gave His all for us, how can we do less than give our all to Him?

The Hebrew word translated "acknowledge" in Proverbs 3:6 carries with it the idea of intimate communion and is used to describe the marriage relationship (Gen. 4:1; 19:8). Whenever I find myself distant from my Father, then I know that I've allowed something to enter my life that is not in the sphere of His will. Since the will of God comes from the heart of God, it ought to draw my heart closer to Him.

3. Instruction

"A wise son heeds his father's instruction" (Prov. 13:1, NIV). "Take firm hold of instruction, do not let go; keep her, for she is your life" (4:13, NKJV). "Give instruction to a wise man, and he will be yet wiser: teach a just man, and he will increase in learning" (9:9).

In order to "trust in the Lord," we must have His Word to instruct us, because "faith comes by hearing, and hearing by the word of God" (Rom. 10:17, NKJV). Scripture is "the word of faith" (Rom. 10:8) which generates and nourishes faith in our hearts, and we can depend on His Word. "Every word of God is pure; He is a shield to those who put their trust in Him" (Prov. 30:5, NKJV; see 22:17-21).

To deliberately act apart from the instruction of the Scriptures is to rebel against the revealed will of God. "He who despises the word will be destroyed, but he who fears the commandment will be rewarded" (13:13, NKJV; see 19:16). To ignore the Word of God is to deprive ourselves of the guidance we need for making the decisions of life. "Stop listening to instruction, my son, and you will stray from the words of knowledge" (19:27, NIV).

Most of the situations, opportunities, and decisions the average person encounters in life are already dealt with in the Word of God. Consult a topical index to the Bible, or even to the book of Proverbs, and you'll see how thoroughly Scripture deals with the practical affairs of life. Of course, we can't expect the Bible to specifically tell us the name of the person we should marry, which job we should accept, what car we should buy, or where to spend our vacation, but if we're saturated with God's wisdom and sincerely seeking His will, we'll be ready for Him to guide us by His Spirit and the providential circumstances of life.

"A man's steps are of the Lord; how then can a man understand his own way?" (20:24, NKJV) God overruled Joseph's brothers' envy and used their evil deeds to build Joseph's faith and save Jacob's family (Gen. 50:20). At the time, nobody could understand what the Lord was doing, but He was working out His perfect plan. In the school of faith, sometimes we don't know what the lesson is until we've passed—or failed—the examination!

When we studied Proverbs 1-4, we learned that it is necessary for us to *apply ourselves* to God's Word if we hope to receive His instruction. According to Proverbs 2:1-4, our responsibility is to receive the Word, treasure it, listen to it, apply our heart to it, cry out for it, and search for it the way a miner searches for treasure; *then* we will "understand the fear of the Lord, and find the knowledge of God" (2:5, NKJV).

Reading and meditating on God's Word ought to be a daily habit with us. "Blessed is the man who listens to me," says Wisdom, "watching daily at my gates, waiting at the posts of my doors" (8:34, NKJV). If you want your faith and spiritual discernment to mature, there's no substitute for the disciplined, systematic reading of the whole Word of God. "Wise people store up knowledge" (10:14, NKJV), because you never know when you'll need some truth from the Bible to help you overcome a temptation or make a decision.

But there's another factor involved, and that's *prayer,* because the Word of God and prayer go together (John 15:7; Acts 6:4; Eph. 6:17-18). "If anyone turns a deaf ear to the law, even his prayers are detestable" (Prov. 28:9, NIV; see 15:8). The word translated "law" in this verse is *torah,* which means "instruction." If I won't listen to God's instruction, why should God listen to my petition?

4. Counsel

"Plans are established by counsel; by wise counsel wage war" (20:18, NKJV). If experienced generals seek counsel as they wage war, shouldn't we seek counsel for the battles of life? It's dangerous to rely on our own wisdom and experience and to ignore the wisdom and experience of other believers who have successfully walked with the Lord. "The way of a fool is right in his own eyes, but he who heeds counsel is wise" (12:15, NKJV).

The first source of wise counsel is *Christian parents.* "Listen to your father who begot you, and do not despise your mother when she is old" (23:22, NKJV; see 6:20-23). "A wise son heeds his father's instruction" (13:1, NKJV). Not everybody has the privilege of being raised in a godly home, but even then, the Lord often provides "substitute parents" who can share the wisdom of the Lord.

Christian friends can also listen, counsel, and pray. "Ointment and perfume delight the heart, and the sweetness of a man's friend gives delight by hearty counsel" (27:9, NKJV). *The Living Bible* paraphrases the verse, "Friendly suggestions are as pleasant as perfume," but sometimes a friend's counsel may not be perfume! It may be acid! Even then, we have nothing to lose; for "as iron sharpens iron, so a man sharpens the countenance of his friend" (27:17, NKJV). The sparks may fly, but God will give us the light that we need. "Faithful are the wounds of a friend, but the kisses of an enemy are deceitful" (27:6).

How we accept and apply rebuke is a test of how devoted we are to truth and wisdom and how sincere we are in wanting to know God's will. "He who listens to a life-giving rebuke will be at home among the wise" (15:31, NIV). "He who disdains instruction despises his own soul, but he who heeds rebuke gets understanding" (v. 32, NKJV). Friends who flatter us and avoid telling us the truth are only doing us harm. "He who rebukes a man will in the end gain more favor than he who has a flattering tongue" (28:23, NIV; see 29:5).

Not every friend is a good counselor, so we must choose wisely. "The purposes of a man's heart are deep waters, but a man of understanding draws them out" (20:5, NIV). We don't know our own hearts (Jer. 17:9), and only God's Word can honestly reveal "the thoughts and intents [motives] of the heart" (Heb. 4:12). It takes a counselor with loving patience and a discerning spirit to help us see what lies deep within our hearts.

While it's usually true that "a multitude of counselors" assures a wise decision (Prov. 11:14; 15:22; 24:6; see Ex. 23:2), at the same time, we must avoid running from friend to friend asking for advice. This may indicate that we're trying to find somebody who will tell us what we want to hear! "A man of many companions may come to ruin, but there is a friend who sticks closer than a brother" (Prov. 18:24, NIV).[2] It isn't enough to have friends; we must have *a friend* who will "speak the truth in love" (Eph. 4:15).

Often in my conference ministry, people will approach me with personal problems and ask for advice. I try to avoid giving counsel for several reasons: I don't know the people; I'm not going to be there long enough to continue a counseling relationship; a quick chat after a meeting isn't counseling; and I don't want to take the place of a faithful local pastor.

"Have you discussed this matter with your pastor?" I ask, and I carefully listen to the reply. No matter what the words are, the reply often indicates, "I talked to him, but it didn't do any good" (meaning possibly, "I didn't get my way") or, "I've talked to him and a dozen other ministers and guest speakers!" Then I know that anything I say will probably do little good.

In seeking counsel, we must be sincere, because a loving and wise friend can often see dangers and detours that are hidden from us. It's best to be accountable to another believer and submit to the authority of the spiritual leaders in our church. During more than forty years of ministry, I've witnessed the painful downfalls of several "Lone Ranger" Christians who thought they didn't need anybody's counsel. "A man who isolates himself seeks his own desire; he rages against all wise judgment" (Prov. 18:1, NKJV). Christians are God's sheep, and we need to flock together. As members of Christ's spiritual body (1 Cor. 12), we belong to each other, and we need each other.

5. Plans

We must never think that in determining the will of God, the believer is passive and only the Lord is active. "Let go and let God" is a clever motto, but I'm not sure it applies to every area of the Christian life.[3] If all we do is exercise faith, commit our way to the Lord, read the Bible, and counsel with our friends, we may never get much done for the Lord. You can't steer a car when it's in neutral, and "faith without works is dead" (James 2:26).

But doesn't Proverbs 3:5 warn us against leaning on our own understanding? Yes, it does, but the word "leaning" means "to rely on," and our faith must be in God's Word and not in our own wisdom. It's the same word used of a king who leans on the arm of an officer (2 Kings 5:18; 7:2, 17) or a person who leans on a staff (18:21).

As we seek to know God's will, we must gather all the facts we can and assess them, because our decision must be based on knowledge and not hearsay. "Every prudent man acts out of knowledge, but a fool exposes his folly" (Prov. 13:16, NIV). "He who answers a matter before he hears it, it is folly and shame to him" (18:13, NKJV). This applies whether we're answering somebody else or answering the Lord. "The wisdom of the prudent is to give thought to their ways, but the folly of fools is deception" (14:8, NIV). We must take time for an honest look at facts.

God expects us to use our brains and make plans, but He also expects us to submit those plans to Him and let Him make the final decision. "To man belong the plans of the heart, but from the Lord comes the reply of the tongue" (16:1, NIV). "Commit to the Lord whatever you do, and your plans will succeed" (v. 3, NIV). If we're yielded to the Lord and our plans are not His plans, He will show us what's right and steer us away from what's wrong. "And if on some point you think differently, that, too, God will make clear to you" (Phil. 3:15, NIV). "In his heart a man plans his course, but the Lord determines his steps" (Prov. 16:9, NIV).

It is when we rebel against the Lord and want to go our own way that we get into trouble. "There is no wisdom nor understanding nor counsel against the Lord" (21:30). That's why we must begin our search for God's will by reading His Word and obeying it, because the Scriptures reveal the character and the purposes of God. The will of God will never contradict either the purposes of God or the character of God, so we must wait before the Lord, because "the plans of the diligent lead to profit as surely as haste leads to poverty" (21:5, NIV). If we're walking by faith, we won't rush ahead, for, "whoever believes will not act hastily" (Isa. 28:16, NKJV).

So, when we have a decision to make, we gather all the facts and seek wise counsel, we make our plans, we commit ourselves and our plans to the Lord, we

listen to His Word, and we wait before Him for His leading. Sometimes God leads us through a Bible promise or warning; sometimes while we're at worship with God's people, He speaks through a song or Scripture reading; or He may direct us through providential circumstances. More than once in my own life, His disciplines have turned out to be His directions (Prov. 3:11-12; Heb. 12:1-11).

6. Obedience

"In all your ways acknowledge Him" (Prov. 3:6) means, "Do God's will in every area of life. Seek to honor Him in everything." Note verse 7, "Do not be wise in your own eyes; fear the Lord and depart from evil" (NKJV). Pride and disobedience in any area of life can get us on dangerous detours, so we must stay humble before Him. "When pride comes, then comes shame; but with the humble is wisdom. The integrity of the upright will guide them, but the perversity of the unfaithful will destroy them" (11:2-3, NKJV).

The assurance is, "and He shall direct your paths." Dr. G. Campbell Morgan said: "Not always in easy or pleasant paths, but always in right paths. Not always in those I would have chosen, but always in paths which lead to success … . The paths that He directs lead always through mist and mystery, through battle and through bruising, to the fulfillment of the meaning of life."[4]

Some people live only for entertainment and try to escape the burdens of life. Others live for enjoyment and try to make the most of life. God's dedicated people live for enrichment and discover fulfillment in life as they do the will of God from the heart.

Which one are you?

CHAPTER TWELVE
POPULAR SINS (DRUNKENNESS, DISRESPECT, ILLUSION, GREED, PRIDE)

T hanks to worldwide media coverage and the constant pressure for higher program ratings, sin has become an important part of international entertainment. Evil activities that we ought to be weeping over are now sources of entertainment; they are vividly displayed on movie and TV screens and discussed in depth in newspapers and magazines. The all-seeing camera moves into the bedroom, the barroom, and the courtroom and enables excited viewers to enjoy sin vicariously. Movies and TV are instructing generation after generation of children how to ridicule virginity, laugh at sobriety, challenge authority, and reject honesty. Actors, actresses, and advertisers have convinced them that "having fun," "feeling good," and "getting away with it" are now the main goals in life.

The book of Proverbs has something to say about popular sins that are weakening our homes, threatening the peace of our communities, and destroying lives.

1. Drunkenness

Alcohol is a narcotic, not a food; Proverbs warns us about alcohol abuse. We need to heed that warning today. Paying for the tragic consequences of drug and alcohol abuse in the United States drains $200 billion annually out of the economy, which averages out to approximately $800 per citizen per year. About 50,000 people a year are killed by drunk drivers, and millions of work hours are lost because of alcohol related absences and work accidents. The United States consumes 60 percent of the world's illicit drugs (alcohol is a legal drug), and drug users spend $150 billion in the United States just on cocaine![1]

Wine and Israel. Wine is mentioned nearly 150 times in the Old Testament. The people of Israel considered it a gift from God, along with oil and bread (Ps. 104:15). When Isaac blessed Jacob, he asked God to give him "the dew of heaven, and the fatness of the earth, and plenty of corn [grain] and wine" (Gen. 27:28; see also Deut. 7:13). However, milk and water, not wine, were the usual daily drinks at Jewish tables; like meat, wine was usually kept for special festive occasions. The Jews also had "strong drink," which was brewed from fermented grain or fruit.

While drunkenness is condemned by the Law and the Prophets,[2] the use of wine was not forbidden, except to priests serving in the holy precincts (Lev. 10:8-10) and to people under a Nazirite vow (Num. 6:1-12). Wine was used as a drink offering to the Lord (Ex. 29:38-41; Num. 15:1-15), and could be brought as part of the Jews' tithes (Neh. 10:36-39), so wine itself wasn't considered sinful. The problem was what wine *did* to people. The Old Testament doesn't demand total abstinence, although certainly it recommends it.[3]

Wine and wisdom. "Wine is a mocker, intoxicating drink arouses brawling, and whoever is led astray by it is not wise" (Prov. 20:1, NKJV). This is the first of several passages in Proverbs that warn against what today we call "alcohol abuse." Alcohol mocks people by creating in them a thirst for more while not satisfying that thirst. The more people drink, the less they enjoy it. The drinker becomes a drunk and then a brawler. In spite of what the slick advertising says about the charm of drink, it just isn't a smart thing to do. As a Japanese proverb puts it, "First the man takes a drink; then the drink takes a drink; then the drink takes the man."

Alcohol also mocks people by giving them a false sense of happiness and strength, and this is what often leads to fights. The weakling thinks he's a superman so he challenges anybody who gets in his way. The grade-school dropout thinks he's the wisest person in town and argues with anybody who disagrees with him.

As I was writing this chapter, I read an item in the newspaper that illustrates my point. According to the Associated Press, a British charter plane had to make an emergency landing in Munich because a drunken passenger slugged his girlfriend and started brawling with other passengers. German police had to handcuff the man and drag him off the plane. After sobering up in an airport security cell, the man discovered that the airport had charged him $3,000 for the emergency landing and extra jet fuel. Those were expensive drinks![4]

Addiction to alcohol can lead to poverty (21:17), so it's wise to stay away from the people who encourage you to drink (23:20-21). Proverbs 23:29-35 is the most vivid description of the tragic consequences of drunkenness you will find anywhere in Scripture,[5] including delirium, sorrow, strife, bruises, and bloodshot eyes;[6] "and in the end it bites like a snake and poisons like a viper" (23:32, NIV). You'd think that after having this frightening experience, the drinker would want to become a total abstainer for life, but alas, he's a slave! "When will I wake up so I can find another drink?" (v. 35, NIV)

Alcohol and civic responsibilities don't mix, according to Proverbs 31:1-9;[7] yet the alcohol flows freely under capitol domes and at embassies. A resident of Washington, D.C., said to me, "There are three parties in this city: the Republican Party, the Democratic Party, and the cocktail party."

King Lemuel's mother warned him to stay away from wine so that he would be capable of serving others. "Woe to you, O land, when your king is a child, and your princes feast in the morning! Blessed are you, O land, when your king is the son of nobles, and your princes feast at the proper time—for strength and not for drunkenness" (Eccl. 10:16-17, NKJV; see Hos. 7:5). "Woe to those who are heroes at drinking wine and champions at mixing drinks, who acquit the guilty for a bribe, but deny justice to the innocent" (Isa. 5:22, NIV). That's what the queen mother was warning her son to avoid.

Proverbs 31:6-7 seems to suggest that there are times when wine should be used to help people, such as encouraging the dying or comforting the suffering so they can forget their troubles. I think verses 6-7 are spoken in irony and not as a commandment, because nobody's problems are solved by forgetting them, and who wants to spend his or her last minutes of life on earth drunk? When Jesus faced death on the cross, He refused to accept the wine sedative that was offered Him (Matt. 27:33-34). If it's wrong for the king to drink wine because it prevents him from helping people, then it's wrong for needy people to drink wine *because it prevents them from helping themselves!* The dying person needs help in preparing to meet God, and the suffering person needs help in solving life's problems; drinking alcohol will accomplish neither one.[8]

We help people, not by deadening them to their problems and pains, but by encouraging them to trust the Lord and lean on His Word. We certainly must stand up for the oppressed (Prov. 31:8-9), but they also need to be in shape to stand up for themselves, something alcohol won't supply.

Wine and today's believer. The New Testament clearly warns today's Christians about the sin of drunkenness. "Let us walk properly, as in the day, not in revelry and drunkenness, not in lewdness and lust, not in strife and envy" (Rom. 13:13, NKJV; see 1 Thess. 5:7; Luke 21:34). Galatians 5:21 names drunkenness as one of the works of the flesh, and 1 Peter 2:11 admonishes us to "abstain from fleshly lusts which war against the soul."

Passages like Romans 14:1-15:13 and 1 Corinthians 8-10 instruct us to: (1) receive other Christians and not make differences about diets and special days a test of fellowship or spirituality; (2) avoid being a stumbling block to others; (3) seek to build one another up in Christian maturity; and (4) avoid being obstinate and defensive about our own personal convictions so that they become a cause of disunity in the church. Christians with a weak conscience stumble easily and need to be built up, but stronger Christians are sometimes quick to criticize and look down on others. Both groups need love, patience, and the help of the Spirit.

My wife and I have traveled enough to know that there's such a thing among God's people as "cultural Christianity." Practices that are acceptable in one place may be classified as sins in another place, and this includes the use of alcohol as a beverage. Christians everywhere should deplore drunkenness, but not all of us agree on total abstinence or even on what "moderation" is.

Our conviction is total abstinence, but we haven't made it a test of fellowship or spirituality. As far as I know, we've never created problems ministering in different cultures, even in the homes of people who disagreed with our views. Other Christians have respected us because we've respected them and tried to manifest Christian love. But by not using alcoholic beverages, my wife and I have not been tempted to get drunk; we've also been examples to believers who might stumble if we did drink. These two blessings are worth more to us than whatever pleasure there may be in drinking alcoholic beverages.[9]

2. Disrespect

"The eye that mocks his father, and scorns obedience to his mother, the ravens of the valley will pick it out, and the young eagles will eat it" (Prov. 30:17, NKJV). The child who looks at his or her parents with contempt and disrespect will one day be treated like an unburied corpse, and to be left unburied was a great reproach in Israel. As I read the newspapers and news magazines, I become more and more convinced that we're living in the generation described in Proverbs 30:11-14 with its pride, greed, violence, and lack of appreciation for parents.

Disrespect for parents usually begins with disrespect for the Word of God that parents seek to teach to their children. "A fool despises his father's instruction" (15:5). "He who despises the word will be destroyed, but he who fears the commandment will be rewarded" (13:13). Sometimes children go off to college or a university and get poisoned by ideas that are contrary to Scripture, and then they come home to tell everybody how stupid and old-fashioned their parents are. If children maintain this haughty attitude, they'll eventually rob their parents (28:24), curse their parents (20:20), and bring shame to their parents (19:26).

Under the Old Covenant, children who disobeyed their parents and broke the law were in danger of losing their lives. I'm not advocating that disrespect for parents be made a capital crime today, but passages like Deuteronomy 21:18-21 and Leviticus 20:9 show how seriously God takes the Fifth Commandment: "Honor your father and your mother, that your days may be long upon the land which the Lord your God is giving you" (Ex. 20:12, NKJV; see Eph. 6:1-4). Children who don't respect godly, loving parents aren't likely to respect teachers, policemen, or any other authority symbol in society.

3. Illusion

We live in a world of illusion, with people trying to impress each other. "One man pretends to be rich, yet has nothing; another pretends to be poor, yet has great wealth" (Prov. 13:7). Worth is measured by wealth, not by character and conduct; as long as people have money and fame, they're considered important. To be "rich and famous" is the ambition of millions of people; until they reach that goal, they enjoy riches and fame vicariously as they follow the career of their favorite celebrity.

Wise people believe God's truth and live for reality and not for illusion. "The wisdom of the prudent is to give thought to their ways, but the folly of fools is deception" (14:8, NIV). Some of the deceptive illusions people are foolishly clinging to today are:

"There are no consequences, so do as you please."
"If it feels good, it is good."

"The important thing in life is to have fun."
"There are no absolutes." (What about this statement?)
"The older generation can't teach you anything."
"Commitment is enslavement. Stay free."

Those of us who have had to counsel disillusioned people, some of whom were contemplating suicide, know how damaging these lies can be in the human life. A life that's built on lies is bound to be disappointing and will eventually fall apart. It's only when we build on God's truth that we can withstand the storms of life (Matt. 7:24-29).

To trust Jesus Christ is to know reality, because He is the truth (John 14:6). To know and obey God's Word is to know the truth (17:17), and to be empowered by the Holy Spirit is to experience truth (1 John 5:6). God is a God of truth, and those who know Him by faith have no desire to frolic in the senseless illusions of the world system (2:15-17).

4. Greed

"He who is greedy for gain troubles his own house" (Prov. 15:27, NKJV). "Hell and Destruction are never full; so the eyes of man are never satisfied" (27:20, NKJV).

A 1994 *Money* magazine survey indicates that Americans are a greedy lot and will even cheat to "make money." Twenty-four percent said they wouldn't correct a waiter who undercharged them, up from 15 percent in 1987; 9 percent said they'd keep money found in a wallet, up from 4 percent in their 1987 survey.[10] Here's the saddest of all: Twenty-three percent said they'd be willing to commit a crime to "get $10 million" if they knew they wouldn't get caught! The love of money is still a root of all kinds of evil (1 Tim. 6:10).

God calls covetousness idolatry (Eph. 5:5; Col. 3:5) because a covetous heart puts something else in the place that God rightfully should occupy in our lives. But the modern business society applauds covetousness and calls it "ambition" and "the first step to success." Business magazines praise the "pyramid climbers" who get to the top, no matter how they got there. Unfortunately, this contemporary view of success has invaded the church, and some Christian workers have thrown ethics and godliness aside in their quest to become important and successful.

An Arabian proverb says, "Covetousness has for its mother unlawful desire, for its daughter injustice, and for its friend violence." Is it any wonder that our modern covetous society witnesses so much injustice and violence? The only cure is to change the heart and replace desire for things with devotion to God, and only Jesus Christ can perform that miracle.

If believers today would read John Bunyan's *Pilgrim's Progress,* they'd meet Mr. Hold-the-World, Mr. Save-All, and Mr. Money-Love; they'd discover what Bunyan thought about Demas, the one-time associate of Paul who fell in love with "this present world" (Col. 4:14; Phile. 24; 2 Tim. 4:10). While it isn't a sin to be wealthy—Abraham and David were both wealthy men and yet godly men—it is a sin to want more than we really need and to keep what we ought to give. Covetousness is like cancer: It grows secretly and robs us of spiritual health, and the only remedy is to cut it out.

In chapter 7 of this book, we studied what Proverbs says about wealth, and there's no need to repeat it. The emphasis in Proverbs is on seeing material possessions as the gift of God, thanking

Him for them, and using them for the glory of God and the good of others. John Wesley, founder of the Methodist Church, taught his people:

Do all the good you can,
By all the means you can,
In all the ways you can,
In all the places you can,
At all the times you can,
To all the people you can,
As long as you ever can.

If ever there was a prescription for curing greed, that's it!

5. Pride

Many theologians believe that pride is the "sin of all sins," for it was pride that changed an angel into the devil (Isa. 14:12-15). Lucifer's, "I will be like the Most High" (v. 14) challenged the very throne of God; in the Garden of Eden, it became, "You will be like God" (Gen. 3:5). Eve believed it, and you know the rest of the story. "Glory to man in the highest" is the rallying cry of proud, godless humanity that's still defying God and trying to build heaven on earth (11:1-9; Rev. 18).

"The proud and arrogant man— 'Mocker' is his name; he behaves with overweening pride" (Prov. 21:24, NIV). "Before his downfall a man's heart is proud, but humility comes before honor" (18:12, NIV; see 29:23). God hates "a proud look" (6:16-17) and promises to destroy the house of the proud (15:25). Just about every Christian can quote Proverbs 16:18, but not all of us heed it: "Pride goes before destruction, and a haughty spirit before a fall" (NKJV).

The saintly Scottish preacher James Denney said, "No man can bear witness to Christ and to himself at the same time. No man can give the impression that he himself is clever and that Christ is mighty to save." That quotation should be printed in large letters and displayed in every church sanctuary and conference auditorium where God's people gather. It might humble some of the preachers and musicians who call so much attention to themselves that the hungry sheep can't see Jesus. If the greatest sin is the corruption of the highest good, then people who use the Christian religion to promote themselves are guilty of great transgression.

Solomon illustrated our desire for recognition and praise by writing about honey. "It is not good to eat much honey; so to seek one's own glory is not glory" (25:27, NKJV). Balance this with 25:16: "Have you found honey? Eat only as much as you need, lest you be filled with it and vomit" (25:16). If honey represents praise, then beware of trying to digest too much of it! More than one celebrity has admitted being "sick of it all" and wishing he or she could just enjoy life as a normal average citizen. I think it was the late radio comedian Fred Allen who defined celebrities as "people who work hard to be famous so they have to wear dark glasses so as not to be recognized."

"The pride of life" is one of the commodities that the world system offers (1 John 2:15-17), and most people will pay anything to acquire it. Bible commentator William Barclay said, "Pride is the ground in which all the other sins grow, and the parent from which all the other sins come." If we're going to get rid of the poisonous fruit, we have to attack the dangerous root; that's a painful thing to do. For the believer, the answer is found in obeying the Christ described in John 13:1-17 and Philippians 2:1-18.

The five "popular sins" I've discussed—drunkenness, disrespect, illusion, greed, and pride—have been with

mankind since the days of the Flood, but for some reason, they seem to be even more prevalent today. Perhaps it's because the news coverage is better. Or maybe it's because we're in the last days. We expect to find these sins prevalent among lost people, but we don't expect to find them in the church. If the church ever hopes to witness to the lost world, it must be different from the lost world.

Paul learned that believers at Corinth were getting drunk at their church meetings (1 Cor. 11:21), and he warned them that drunkards would not inherit the kingdom of God (6:10; see 5:11).

Some children in the Ephesian church were not respecting and obeying their parents, and Paul reminded them that the Fifth Commandment still applied (Eph. 6:1-3).

The apostle John warned the saints to whom he sent his first epistle that the world was passing away, with all of its illusions, and that they had better keep themselves from idols (1 John 2:15-17; 5:21).

Jesus warned His disciples, "Take heed, and beware of covetousness" (Luke 12:15); Paul wrote to the Colossian believers that covetousness was idolatry (Col. 3:5).

Paul cautioned the churches not to appoint young Christians to places of spiritual leadership, "lest being lifted up with pride [they] fall into the condemnation of the devil" (1 Tim. 3:6). And John had to deal with proud Diotrephes who was running the church and wouldn't submit to the authority of God's apostle (3 John 9-11).

Alas, these sins *are* found in the church!

James was right: "My brethren [and sisters], these things ought not to be so" (James 3:10).

CHAPTER THIRTEEN
"THIS GOD IS OUR GOD"

We study the Word of God so that we might better know the God of the Word. The better acquainted we are with God, the more we become like Him and acquire the skills we need for life and service. "The fear of the Lord is the beginning of wisdom, and the knowledge of the Holy One is understanding" (Prov. 9:10, NKJV). You can make a living without knowing many things, but you can't make a life without knowing God.

"It is impossible to keep our moral practices sound and our inward attitudes right while our idea of God is erroneous or inadequate," writes A.W. Tozer. "If we would bring back spiritual power to our lives, we must begin to think of God more nearly as He is."[1]

If we read the book of Proverbs, or any book in the Bible, seeking only for doctrinal truth but ignoring God Himself, we'll miss what the Holy Spirit wants to say to us and do for us. It would be like a child devoting hours to studying the family album but not spending time with his family, getting to know them personally. If we have no growing acquaintance with God, then what we think we know about Him may be misleading; this hinders us from building a godly life. To quote Tozer again: "The essence of idolatry is the entertainment of thoughts about God that are unworthy of Him."[2] If that's true, and I believe it is, then it's possible to be a Bible student and also an idolater!

The book of Proverbs reveals to us the wonderful God whom we should trust, obey, love, and get to know in a deeper way. As we grow in our intimacy with God, we will develop the wisdom and skills we need to be successful in making a life.

1. A Holy God

According to Proverbs 9:10 and 30:3, God is "the Holy One"; the word translated "holy" means "utterly different, wholly other." God's very nature is holy: "You shall be holy, for I am holy" (Lev. 11:44-45; 19:2; 20:7, 26; 21:8, 15; 22:9, 16, 32; 1 Peter 1:16).[3] "God is light and in Him is no darkness at all" (1 John 1:5).

But we must not think of God's holiness simply as the absence of defilement, like a sterilized surgical instrument. Nor is God's holiness an inert, negative attribute. It's something positive and active, His perfect nature accomplishing His perfect will. It's like the "sea of glass mingled with fire" that John saw before the throne of God in heaven (Rev. 15:2). "For our God is a consuming fire" (Heb. 12:29; see Deut. 4:24).

Because He is holy, God hates sin (Prov. 6:17-19). Evangelists remind us that "God hates sin but He loves sinners," and certainly nobody will question God's love for a lost world (John 3:16; Rom. 5:8). But people can willfully sin so much that they become abominable to God. The perverse man is an abomination to God (Prov. 3:32; 11:20), and so are the proud (16:5), liars (12:22), cheats (11:1; 20:10, 23), hypocrites (15:8; 21:27; 28:9), and the unjust (17:15). Sin becomes so identified with the sinner that the very person becomes reprehensible to the Lord. This doesn't negate His love, but we must keep in mind that God's love is a *holy* love as well as a sacrificing love. It's a dangerous thing to play with sin and defy the living God. "He who is often rebuked, and hardens his neck, will suddenly be destroyed, and that without remedy" (29:1, NKJV).

Proverbs 21:12 calls God "the Righteous One" (NIV) or "the righteous God" (NKJV) and states that He judges the wicked for their wickedness. A holy God must be righteous in all His ways and just in all His dealings (24:11-12). "The curse of the Lord is on the house of the wicked, but He blesses the home of the just" (3:33, NKJV). Sometimes God sends immediate judgment on the wicked (2:22), but sometimes He merely takes away His restraining hand and allows the sinners' sins to judge them. "The evil deeds of a wicked man ensnare him; the cords of his sin hold him fast" (5:22, NIV; see Rom. 1:18ff).

2. A Sovereign God

The fact that God is holy and just assures us that there are righteous principles that govern the universe and His dealings with us. As Dr. A. T. Pierson put it, "History is His story." "The Lord works out everything for His own ends— even the wicked for a day of disaster" (Prov. 16:4, NIV). "Many are the plans in a man's heart, but it is the Lord's purpose that prevails" (19:21, NIV). The Christian believer remembers Colossians 1:16: "All things were created by Him [Christ], and for Him." Jesus Christ is the Alpha and the Omega, the beginning and the end of all things.

The proud mind of sinful man rebels against the very thought of the sovereignty of God and affirms, "I am the master of my fate: I am the captain of my soul."[4] Charles Spurgeon said, "No doctrine in the whole Word of God has more excited the hatred of mankind than the truth of the absolute sovereignty of God. The fact that 'the Lord reigneth' is indisputable, and it is this fact that arouses the utmost opposition of the unrenewed human heart."[5]

Divine sovereignty doesn't destroy human responsibility and turn humans into robots. "To man belong the plans of the heart, but from the Lord comes the reply of the tongue" (16:1, NIV). "The lot is cast into the lap, but its every decision is from the Lord" (v. 33, NKJV). "A man's heart plans his way, but the Lord directs his steps" (v. 9, NKJV). God expects us to study, think, weigh possibilities, and make decisions, but we dare not "lean on [our] own understanding" (3:5). God promises to give wisdom to those who ask (James 1:5) and to direct those who are willing to obey (Prov. 3:5-6).

Because He is the Creator of all things, God is sovereign in nature (3:19-20; 8:22-31; 30:4). He's also sovereign in history and geography, controlling the rise and fall of rulers and nations (Acts 17:22-28; Dan. 4:17, 34-35). "By Me kings reign, and rulers decree justice" (Prov. 8:15). "The king's heart is in the hand of the Lord, like the rivers of water; He turns it wherever He wishes" (21:1, NKJV). "There is no wisdom or understanding or counsel against the Lord" (v. 30, NKJV).

Keep in mind that the God who decrees the end—His purposes—also decrees the means to the end. If He determines to overthrow Pharaoh and deliver Israel from Egypt, He also decrees that Moses and Aaron go to Egypt to confront Pharaoh. If He purposes to bring Israel into the Promised Land, He also decrees that Joshua shall be trained to lead them. If He purposes to win lost souls, He also decrees that a witness will share the Gospel. "And how shall they hear without a preacher? And how shall they preach unless they are sent?" (Rom. 10:14-15, NKJV)

The sovereignty of God is one of the greatest motivations for Christian life and service, because *we know that God is on the throne and controls all things.* His commandments are His enablements, and "we know that all things work together for good to those who love God, to those who are the called according to His purpose" (Rom. 8:28, NKJV). Instead of being a deterrent to evangelism, an understanding of divine sovereignty is a stimulus to biblical evangelism; for we are sure that God is "taking out" a "people for His name" (Acts 15:14, NKJV; see 18:1-11) and that His Word will not return void (Isa. 55:10-11). God is "not willing that any should perish" (2 Peter 3:9) but desires all people to be saved (1 Tim. 2:4), and Jesus commanded us to go into all the world with the message of salvation (Matt. 28:18-20). Our task is to obey and share the message; His responsibility is to save those who believe.

As sovereign Ruler over all things, the Lord sees and knows what's happening, the thoughts, actions, words, and motives of all people. "For a man's ways are in full view of the Lord, and He examines all his paths" (Prov. 5:21, NIV). "The eyes of the Lord are everywhere, keeping watch on the wicked and the good" (15:3, NIV). "The Lord weighs the hearts" (21:2, NKJV; see 17:3 and 24:12). When God judges, He judges justly, whether He's punishing the wicked or rewarding the righteous.

It's encouraging to know that "the Lord reigns" (Ps. 93:1) and that His righteous purposes will be fulfilled. Let's be sure that we're walking with Him on the path of life, surrendered to His will and seeking to honor His name.

3. A Compassionate God

God's tender compassion and concern are seen in His care of the poor and needy. Widows and orphans in Israel were especially vulnerable to exploitation and abuse, and God warned His people in His Law to beware of mistreating them (Ex. 22:22; Deut. 10:18; 14:29; 26:12; 27:19).

"He who oppresses the poor reproaches his Maker, but he who honors Him has mercy on the needy" (Prov. 14:31, NKJV; see 17:5). "The rich and the poor have this in common, the Lord is the maker of them all" (22:2, NKJV). When the Savior came to earth, He identified with the poor and the outcasts (Luke 4:16-21; 2 Cor. 8:9), and God wants to show His compassion for them through His people. To harm the needy is to give pain to the heart of God.

"Do not rob the poor because he is poor, nor oppress the afflicted at the gate; for the Lord will plead their cause, and plunder the soul of those who plunder them" (Prov. 22:22-23, NKJV). "The gate" was ancient Israel's equivalent of our modern courtroom, for there the elders met to settle village disputes. The poor might not be able to afford a lawyer, but God would come to their defense (23:10-11).[6]

Stealing the property of the poor was one way to get rich quick, even though the Law commanded that the ancient landmarks not be moved (22:28; Deut. 19:14; 27:17; Isa. 1:23; Hos. 5:10). God owned the land (Lev. 25:23) and loaned it to His people, and they were to keep their property within the tribes and clans. Family farms were marked off by stones, not fences; these ancient landmarks were to be honored and protected. "The Lord will destroy the house of the proud: but He will establish the border of the widow" (Prov. 15:25). The Lord keeps an eye on the property lines.

We can sin against the poor by neglect as well as by oppression. "Whoever shuts his ears to the cry of the poor will also cry himself and not be heard" (21:13, NKJV). "He who gives to the poor will not lack, but he who hides his eyes will have many curses" (28:27, NKJV). If we shut our ears and close our eyes, pretending to be ignorant of their plight, God will take note of it and shut His eyes to our needs and His ears to our prayers—and so will other people. We will reap what we sow. (See Deut. 15:7-11.)

"He who has pity on the poor lends to the Lord, and He will pay back what he has given" (Prov. 19:17, NKJV). When we give to help others, we're actually giving to the Lord; He puts it on account and pays rich dividends (Phil. 4:15-17). "Inasmuch as you did it to one of the least of these My brethren, you did it to Me" (Matt. 25:40, NKJV). By the way, this principle also applies to the way we treat our enemies (Prov. 20:22; 25:21-22; Rom. 12:18-21).

God is a shield to those who trust Him (Prov. 30:5) and a strong tower for those who run to Him for help (18:10). "The name of the Lord" in verse 10 signifies all the glorious attributes of the Lord. Because of who He is and what He is, those who trust Him don't have to worry—because He is always their refuge and strength (Ps. 46:1).

One of God's compassionate ministries to us is that of *divine guidance.* Proverbs 3:5-6 is a promise God's people have been claiming for centuries, and it has never failed. As I said earlier in this book, God expects us to assess a situation and get all the facts we can, but we must never lean on our own understanding. We must humble ourselves before Him and seek His direction in all things, and we must be sure that our motives are right.

But what if we make a mistake, as we're all prone to do, and start to move in the wrong direction? "In his heart a man plans his course, but the Lord determines his steps" (16:9, NIV). "Many are the plans in a man's heart, but it is the Lord's purpose that prevails" (19:21, NIV; see 16:33). If we sincerely want to know and obey God's plan, the Lord will direct us and providentially guide our steps in ways that we may not understand. "A man's steps are of the Lord; how then can a man understand his own way?" (20:24, NKJV)

The Danish philosopher Sören Kierkegaard said, "Life can only be understood backward, but it must be lived forward." One day we shall look back and say with David, "Surely [only] goodness and mercy [have followed] me all the days of my life" (Ps. 23:6).[7] Knowing that God lovingly guides our steps as we seek to follow Him is a great encouragement when we don't know which way to go. "Who is the man that fears the Lord? Him shall He teach in the way He chooses" (25:12, NKJV). Even the great apostle Paul wasn't always sure of the next step, but the Lord guided him (Acts 16:6-10).

4. A Wise God

Theologians tell us that God's wisdom refers to His ability to devise perfect means to attain perfect ends. Nobody has to teach God anything. "For who has known the mind of the Lord? Or who has become His counselor?" (Rom. 11:34, NKJV; Isa. 40:13; Jer. 23:18). And nobody can ever say that God made a mistake, because in His wisdom, He does all things well (Rom. 8:28; 9:20-21). No wonder Paul called Him "God only wise" (16:27).

God has revealed His wisdom in creation. "By wisdom the Lord laid the earth's foundations, by understanding He set the heavens in place; by His knowledge the deeps were divided, and the clouds let drop the dew" (Prov. 3:19-20, NIV). The astronomer watching a comet through a telescope and the biologist peering at a cell through a microscope are both discovering God's wisdom, for scientific study is but the act of thinking God's thoughts after Him.

While seeking to witness to a university student whose religion was science, I noticed that he kept using the word "universe."

"Why do you say 'universe' and not 'multiverse'?" I asked.

Puzzled, the student said, "I don't understand what you mean."

"Well," I replied, "the word 'universe' implies that everything around us is one, a unity. If that's the case, where did this unity come from? What instituted the laws that you're studying in your science classes? Why do all these things work together and produce a 'universe' instead of a 'multiverse'?"

He saw which way the conversation was going and quickly changed the subject!

But my question is a valid one. If there weren't wisdom and order built into the universe (what most people call "scientific laws"), the farmer couldn't expect a harvest, the astronomer couldn't predict an eclipse, the scientist couldn't safely conduct an experiment, the pilot wouldn't be able to fly his plane, and nobody on earth would know from one moment to another what the stars and planets would do next! Isaac Watts said it perfectly:

I sing the wisdom that ordained
The sun to rule the day;
The moon shines full at His command,
And all the stars obey.[8]

God's wisdom is also seen in His *providential ordering of events*, not only for

nations but also for individuals. "There is no wisdom, no insight, no plan that can succeed against the Lord" (21:30, NIV). "To God belong wisdom and power; counsel and understanding are His" (Job 12:13, NIV). The English word "providence" comes from the two Latin words *video*, "to see," and *pro*, "before." God in His wisdom "sees before," that is, plans in advance and "sees to it" that His will is accomplished.

Providence doesn't mean that God simply "foresees" what lies ahead and "adjusts" Himself accordingly. God alone knows and controls future events. The Baptist theologian Augustus Hopkins Strong calls providence, "that continuous agency of God by which he makes all the events of the physical and moral universe fulfill the original design with which he created it."[9] Without violating man's ability to choose, God "works all things according to the counsel of His will" (Eph. 1:11, NKJV) and rules and overrules in all things. "The Lord does whatever pleases Him, in the heavens and on the earth, in the seas and all their depths" (Ps. 135:6, NIV).

God wants to share His wisdom with us, which, of course, is the emphasis of the book of Proverbs. "For the Lord gives wisdom; from His mouth come knowledge and understanding; He stores up sound wisdom for the upright" (2:6-7). *The first step in receiving God's wisdom is trusting Jesus Christ and becoming a child of God.* The world is frantically seeking the wisdom to know what to do and the power to be able to do it, and these are found only in Jesus Christ, "the power of God, and the wisdom of God" (1 Cor. 1:24).

The Gospel of salvation sounds like a foolish message to the lost world, for it seems foolish to commit your life to somebody who died on a cross in weakness and shame. But the preaching of that cross releases the power of God to change lives! (Rom. 1:16) "For the message of the cross is foolishness to those who are perishing, but to us who are being saved it is the power of God" (1 Cor. 1:18, NKJV).

After you trust Christ and become a child of God (John 1:11-13), the next step is to ask God to give you His wisdom in the ordering of your life (James 1:5). "The fear of the Lord teaches a man wisdom, and humility comes before honor" (Prov. 15:33, NIV). As you read His Word, meditate and pray, and seek to glorify Him, He will direct your steps (3:5-6). The way may not always be easy, but it will be the best way (Rom. 8:28). Remember that the will of God comes from the heart of God (Ps. 33:11), so you don't have to worry.

When you have decisions to make, take time to pray and meditate on the Word. Ask God to direct you and, if necessary, seek wise counsel from friends who are mature in the faith. At the start of each day, ask God to guide you in every decision you must make, big or small; a wrong "small" decision could lead to disturbing "big" decisions. As you grow in the wisdom and knowledge of God, and as you walk by faith, seeking to honor the Lord, you will increase in spiritual discernment and live skillfully.

"The path of the righteous is like the first gleam of dawn, shining ever brighter till the full light of day. But the way of the wicked is like deep darkness; they do not know what makes them stumble" (Prov. 4:18-19, NIV).

To quote A.W. Tozer again: "With the goodness of God to desire our highest welfare, the wisdom of God to plan it, and the power of God to achieve it, what do we lack? Surely we are the most favored of all creatures."[10]

ENDNOTES

PREFACE

1. T.S. Eliot, *Collected Poems 1909-1962* (New York: Harcourt Brace and World, 1963), 147.

CHAPTER 1

1. There are also "wisdom psalms": 1, 19, 32, 34, 37, 49, 73, 78, 112, 119, 127-128, 133.

2. Roy Zuck, *Biblical Theology of the Old Testament* (Chicago: Moody, 1991), 232.

3. Among the Jews, proverbs were a popular and accepted way to digest and preserve wisdom. (For proverbs outside the book of Proverbs see 1 Sam. 10:11-12; 24:13; Ezek. 12:22-23; 16:44; 18:1-2. See also Matt. 9:12, 17; 24:18; John 4:35, 37; 9:4; 1 Cor. 6:13; 14:8; 15:33.)

4. Proverbs 3:11-12 is quoted in Hebrews 12:5-6; 3:34 in James 4:6 and 1 Peter 5:5; 11:31 in 1 Peter 4:18; 25:21-22 in Romans 12:20; and 26:11 in 2 Peter 2:22.

5. Derek Kidner, *Proverbs* in *Tyndale Old Testament Commentaries* (Downers Grove, Ill.: InterVarsity, 1964), 22.

6. Keep in mind that "wealth" means much more than possessing material things. The Bible doesn't promise that obedient Christians will all be healthy, wealthy, and successful. It does promise that they will have godly character, enjoy their Father's generous gifts to meet all their needs, and escape many of the physical and emotional pains and problems that the ungodly usually suffer. God's covenant with the Jews promised special blessings if they obeyed and chastisement if they disobeyed (see Deut. 27-28), but the book of Proverbs also emphasizes the "true riches" of the spiritual life that are summarized in Christ's beatitudes. It has well been said that true happiness lies, not in the greatness of your possessions, but in the "fewness" of your wants.

7. Charles Bridges, *Exposition of the Book of Proverbs* (Grand Rapids: Zondervan, 1959), 3-4.

8. L.C. Harris, Gleason Archer, and Bruce Watke, *Theological Wordbook of the Old Testament*, vol. 1 (Chicago: Moody, 1980), 283.

9. The phrase, "the beginning of the creation of God" in Revelation 3:14 (KJV) cannot mean that Jesus was the first thing God

created, since the Son of God was with the Father before there was a creation (John 1:15). The Greek word *arche* can mean either "first in time" or "first in rank"; therefore the NIV translates the phrase, "the ruler of God's creation." The familiar title, "firstborn" can also refer to rank. As "the firstborn of every creature" (Col. 1:15, KJV), Jesus is the head of creation ("the firstborn over all creation," NIV).

10. Remember that the Hebrew society was strongly masculine and that primarily the fathers trained the sons while the mothers trained the daughters. The masculine emphasis in Scripture must not be interpreted as a sexist bias but rather as a characteristic of the Jewish culture of that day, a characteristic that should no longer persist in the light of the Gospel (Gal. 3:26-29).

11. The Hebrew word for *hear is shema*. The Jewish confession of faith in Deuteronomy 6:4-5 is called "The Shema." Implied in the word "hear" is receiving and obeying God's Word.

12.. Andrew A. Bonar, *Memoir and Remains of Robert Murray M'Cheyne* (London: Banner of Truth, 1966), 29.

CHAPTER 2

1. The father's statement, "my son," is found forty-one times in Proverbs, but the influence of the mother isn't ignored. See 1:8; 4:3; 6:20; 10:1; 15:20; 19:26; 20:20; 23:22; 23:25; 28:24; 30:11, 17; 31:1ff.

2. James 1:14 uses the images of hunting and fishing to get the same point across. The verbs "drawn away" and "enticed" carry the idea of "luring with bait," whether baiting a trap or a fishing hook. Temptation is the bait, and Satan wants us to think we can grab the bait and avoid the consequences (Gen. 3:5). Alas, it never works that way.

3. In Proverbs, three Hebrew words are translated "fool": *kesyl*, the dull, stupid fool; *ewiyl*, the corrupt fool who is morally perverted; *nabal*, the stubborn, brutish fool whose mind is made up and won't be convinced. For a vivid example of this third variety of fool, see 1 Samuel 25.

CHAPTER 3

1. This has been my life verse since 1948 when I entered seminary to prepare for ministry, and I can bear witness that it has never

failed me. When you walk on God's path, you delight in God's presence and enjoy God's pleasures. You have life, joy, and pleasure—and it gets better and better as life progresses!

CHAPTER 4

1. I realize that modern psychology considers to be "sexual" many if not most of our human responses to one another; for, after all, we are sexual beings and not robots. However, the phrase "sexual intimacy outside the bonds of marriage" refers specifically to intercourse and forms of sexual relationship that substitute for intercourse. Our Lord spoke of "fornications" (plural) in Matthew 15:19; the edict of the Jerusalem conference mentioned "fornication," which certainly included the sexual sins condemned by the Law of Moses (Acts 15:20; Lev. 18). It appears that in some contexts the words "adultery" and "fornication" are inclusive of various forms of sexual sins.

2. Quentin Crisp wrote this in *Manners from Heaven*, chapter 7.

3. *The Myth of the Greener Grass*, by J. Allan Petersen (Wheaton, Ill.: Tyndale, 1983), is one of the best books from a biblical point of view on understanding and preventing extramarital affairs and healing marriages that have been violated by them. As every pastor knows, more of this kind of sin goes on in local churches than we dare openly admit.

4. The basic meaning of the Hebrew word is "to go astray, to err" and can describe the results of drinking too much alcohol (20:1; Isa. 28:7). It's translated "go astray" in Proverbs 5:23 (KJV); in verses 19-20, it means "to be ravished, intoxicated."

5. The command to bind God's Word to various parts of the body was taken literally by the Pharisees (3:3; 6:21; 7:3; Deut. 6:8-9); this was the origin of the "phylactery" (Matt. 23:5), a small leather case containing four portions of the Old Testament (Ex. 13:1-10 and 11-16, and Deut. 6:4-9 and 11:13-21) written on parchment. When attending public prayers, the orthodox Jew tied one phylactery to his forehead and the other to his left arm. They also put a phylactery at the door of their house. "Phylactery" is a word that comes from the Greek and means "to watch over, to safeguard." It was

their belief that wearing God's Word like an amulet would protect them from evil.

CHAPTER 5

1. Let me remind you that the book of Proverbs has a definite masculine focus because in the ancient Jewish society daughters usually weren't educated for the affairs of life. Most of them were kept secluded and prepared for marriage and motherhood. For the most part, when you read "man" in Proverbs, interpret it generically and read "person," whether male or female. Proverbs isn't a sexist book, but it was written in the context of a strongly male-oriented society.

2. George Morrison, *Sunrise: Addresses from a City Pulpit* (London: Hodder and Stoughton, 1903), 169-77. Kregel Publications has embarked on the project of reprinting all of George Morrison's books, and I recommend them to you. He was a peerless preacher.

3. Some contemporary theology so emphasizes God's love that it loses sight of the fact that God also hates. God has no pleasure in sin (Ps. 5:4). Sin grieves the Father (Gen. 6:6), the Son (Mark 3:5), and the Spirit (Eph. 4:30). Love and hatred can exist in the same heart (see Ps. 97:10, Amos 5:14-15, Ps. 45:7, and Rom. 12:9). If God's people loved holiness more, they would hate sin more. God is love (1 John 4:8, 16), but He is also light (1 John 1:5) and a consuming fire (Heb. 12:29).

CHAPTER 6

1. Charles R. Bridges, *Exposition of the Book of Proverbs* (Grand Rapids: Zondervan, 1959), 179.

2. Brooks Atkinson, *Once around the Sun* (New York: Harcourt, Brace, 1951), 37.

3. This oft-quoted statement is the last line of Thomas Gray's poem, "Ode on a Distant Prospect of Eton College," but its message is usually misunderstood. In the poem, Gray contrasts the joyful innocence of children in school to the difficulties they will have when they reach adulthood. He asks us not to rob them of their youthful pleasures too soon. There will be time enough for them to learn that life isn't always fun and games. We expect a certain amount of naive innocence in children, but not in adults.

4. Ralph Waldo Emerson, *Essays: First and Second Series* (New York: E.P. Dutton, 1938), 31. Emerson was one of the preachers of the "success philosophy" that has become the unofficial civil religion of the United States. His essay, "Self-Reliance," is the "Bible" of the under-believers and overachievers in the business world, and some of its humanistic ideas have infiltrated the church and produced a "success theology" that is unbiblical. I enjoy reading Emerson, but I carefully separate the wheat from the chaff.

5. There is a "sanctified self-confidence" that's based on faith, energized by the Holy Spirit, and glorifies God. Paul expressed it when he wrote, "I can do all things through Christ who strengthens me" (Phil. 4:13, NKJV); David gave testimony to it in Psalm 18:29-39.

6. Isaac's favoritism toward Esau (Gen. 25:28), Jacob's pampering of Joseph (Gen. 37:3), and David's failure to discipline his sons properly all helped to create the family problems I've mentioned.

7. Some commentators translate the phrase "drink violence" ("damage") as "to be stripped bare." In other words, send a fool on an important mission and you'll end up crippled and humiliated!

CHAPTER 7

1. The origin of the word "scam" is obscure. It comes from carnival jargon and may be a variation of the word "scheme." Before the law stepped in to control such things, some carnival workers were notorious at fleecing the unsuspecting public with get-rich-quick offers. Alas, what was once confined to carnivals is now found on Wall Street.

2. Of course, we don't give to others in order to get something back, because that would be selfish. We must be motivated by love and a desire to honor the Lord.

3. The story of "King Midas and the Golden Touch" is supposed to teach this important lesson. As the king acquired more and more gold, he discovered the hard way the things that were really important to him.

4. I wrote that in jest, of course, but only to get your attention and remind you of your accountability before God. Christians will want their last will and testament also to be a last will and *testimony*. How we dispose of the wealth God gives us, whether it be little or much, tells other people what is

really important to us. It's frightening how many professed believers don't even have a will! Where is their sense of stewardship?

CHAPTER 8

1. In marriage, two people become one flesh (Gen. 2:24); therefore, if one partner dies, the marriage is dissolved (Rom. 7:1-3) and the living partner may remarry "in the Lord" (1 Cor. 7:39). The book of Proverbs doesn't whitewash the problems that can be faced in marriage, but nowhere does it deal with divorce. It magnifies God's original plan for marriage and the home, and that's what we should do today. People who get married with one hand on an escape hatch aren't likely to have a happy home.

2. Jesus makes it clear in Matthew 19:11-12 that not everybody is supposed to get married, and Paul states that singleness is a gift from God just as much as is marriage (1 Cor. 7:7). I once heard the gifted Christian educator Henrietta Mears say that the only reason she wasn't married was because the apostle Paul was dead!

3. The proverb, "Spare the rod and spoil the child" goes back to the days of Rome (Qui parcit virge, odit filium = "Who spares the rod, hates [his] son") and has been in English literature since the year 1000. Those exact words aren't found in Scripture, but Proverbs 13:24 comes closest: "He that spareth his rod hateth his son: but he that loveth him chasteneth him betimes [early]." The Roman proverb no doubt comes from the Hebrew proverb, which is much older.

4. In The New American Commentary, Duane A. Garrett translates the verse, "Train up a child in a manner befitting a child, and even as he grows old he will not turn from it" (Nashville: Broadman Press, 1993), vol. 14, 188. See also Gleason Archer's explanation in The Encyclopedia of Bible Difficulties (Grand Rapids: Zondervan, 1982), 252-53. We don't know how much spiritual instruction Solomon received from his father David, but when Solomon was old, he turned away from the Lord (1 Kings 11:1-8). Some students think that Ecclesiastes is his "confession of faith," written after he returned to the Lord, but the book doesn't say so and it isn't wise to speculate.

CHAPTER 9

1. Robert B. Downs, Books That Changed the World (New York: New American Library, 1956), 129.

2. Steven Pinker, The Language Instinct (New York: William Morrow, 1994), 15, 18. Dr. Pinker is professor and director of the Center for Cognitive Neuroscience at the Massachusetts Institute of Technology. In his book The Difference of Man and the Difference It Makes, philosopher Mortimer J. Adler calls human speech "the pivotal fact." He says that "man is the only talking, the only naming, declaring or questioning, affirming or denying, the only arguing, agreeing or disagreeing, the only discursive, animal" (New York: World Publishing Co., 1968), 112. That is what makes us different from the "other animals."

3. According to Genesis 3:1-7, Satan tempted Eve to eat of the forbidden tree so she would become like God, "knowing good and evil." But it isn't necessary to disobey God to develop discernment; His divine wisdom instructs us concerning good and evil, and is our "tree of life" (See Prov. 3:18).

4. The Greek word translated "sound" (hugiaino) gives us the English word "hygiene," and means, "to be sound in health."

5. The Hebrew word translated "quarrel" has legal overtones and can refer to a lawsuit (Ex. 23:2-3, NIV). Solomon's counsel is wise: it's better to keep cool and speak calmly than to argue with your opponent and end up with an expensive lawsuit that nobody really wins.

6. The Greek word translated "willing to yield" ("easy to be entreated") speaks of a conciliatory attitude and not a compromising bargain that seeks for "peace at any price." Conciliatory people are willing to hear all sides of a matter and honestly seek for areas of agreement. They are open to "yielding to persuasion." Some people mistake prejudice and stubbornness for conviction and faithfulness.

7. In his novel Nineteen Eighty-Four, George Orwell warned us about "newspeak"; in his book Double-Speak (New York: Harper & Row, 1989), William Lutz explains today's version of what Orwell predicted half a century ago. It's frightening!

CHAPTER 10

1. Paul is referring to Abraham's faith in Genesis 15:6. Some people have the idea that sinners during the Old Testament era were saved by good works while sinners today are saved by faith in Christ, but this idea is wrong. *Anybody who has ever been saved has been saved by faith, because nobody can be saved by good works (Eph. 2:8-9).* Hebrews 11 informs us that Old Testament saints were saved by faith, and Habakkuk 2:4 states, "The just shall live by his faith." This verse is quoted in Romans 1:17, Galatians 3:11, and Hebrews 10:38; these three epistles make it very clear that salvation is by faith in Jesus Christ and faith alone.

2. Justification is the gracious act of God whereby He *declares* the believing sinner righteous in Jesus Christ and gives us a righteous standing in His sight. Sanctification is the divine process whereby God *makes* His children more like Jesus Christ as we walk in the Spirit and yield to His will. The person who is justified will want to reject sin and obey God because justification involves sharing the life of God as well as having a right standing before God (Rom. 5:18). A right position before the Lord leads to a right practice in daily life.

CHAPTER 11

1. God never violates any person's freedom, but He works so that His purposes are accomplished even through the lives of people who don't know Him or won't acknowledge Him. This was true of Cyrus (2 Chron. 36:22; Isa. 44:28-45:1), Nebuchadnezzar (Jer. 25:9; 27:6), and Pharaoh (Ex. 9:16; Rom. 9:14-18).

2. The KJV reads "A man who hath friends must show himself friendly," and the margin of the NKJV reads "A man who has friends may come to ruin." The idea seems to be that having many companions *but no real friends* could lead a person to ruin, for there's nobody who cares enough about him to rebuke him. The original text is difficult, but the NIV seems to say it best.

3. Psalm 46:10 says, "Be still, and know that I am God"; the phrase "be still" literally means "take your hands off," or "stop your striving." There are times when we prove our faith simply by waiting on the Lord and allowing Him to work. Naomi's advice to Ruth was excellent: "Sit still, my daughter" (Ruth 3:18), and so was Moses' instruction to Israel at the Red Sea: "Stand still!" (Ex. 14:13) But when it's time to act, no amount of devotion will substitute for obedience. See Josh. 7:10ff; 1 Samuel 16:1ff; 1 Kings 19:15ff.

4. *The Westminster Pulpit,* vol. IV (London: Pickering and Inglis), 147.

CHAPTER 12

1. Arnold M. Washton and Donna Boundy, *Willpower's Not Enough* (New York: Harper & Row, 1989), 7-18.

2. See Habakkuk 2:15; Isaiah 5:11-22; 28:1-3; Amos 6:3-6; Deuteronomy 21:20.

3. I haven't been able to learn when the Jews added wine to their Passover meal, although some authorities claim the custom goes back to the days of the first temple. Wine isn't mentioned in Exodus 12:11-27, but by the time you get to the New Testament, wine is a part of the meal (Matt. 26:26-30). Would they use unleavened bread and leavened (fermented) wine? Since four different cups of wine were used in the ceremony, the wine was diluted.

4. *The Lincoln (Neb.) Star,* July 15, 1994.

5. It's worth noting that immorality is closely associated with drunkenness (Prov. 23:27-28), for the two often go together.

6. The Hebrew word translated "redness" in the KJV and "bloodshot" in the NIV, means "dullness, dimness." The drunkard's vision is blurred so that he doesn't see clearly what is there and claims he sees what isn't there. Too much alcohol can produce bloodshot eyes as well as a ruddy face. Some expositors think that the word suggests "blacked eyes," i.e., as the result of a fight; yet true as it is, that probably isn't what the writer had in mind.

7. Lemuel means "devoted to God" and may have been another name for King Solomon. God's special name for Solomon was Jedidiah, which means "beloved of Jehovah." We don't know for sure who King Lemuel and his mother were and it's useless to speculate.

8. In Paul's day, wine was used for medicinal purposes (1 Tim. 5:23), but this doesn't give us license to make an ancient practice into a

modern norm. Many people seize this one verse but reject everything else Paul wrote in this epistle. If we're going to obey one admonition, why not obey all of them?

9. A report issued by the Commission on Substance Abuse at Colleges and Universities, sponsored by Columbia University, states that drinking is a serious problem on American campuses. Ninety-five percent of violent crime on campus is alcohol-related. Sixty percent of the female students who had sexually transmitted diseases were "under the influence of alcohol at the time of intercourse," and alcohol was involved in 90 percent of all campus rapes. At the time of the survey, 42 percent of the students (men and women) admitted "binge drinking" within the previous two weeks. One-third of the students drink primarily to get drunk. Students who live in fraternity and sorority houses drink more than other students. One ponders the future of the nation if the next generation of leaders is already suffering from "bottle fatigue."

10. Twenty-one percent of the people ages eighteen to thirty-four would keep the money, but only two percent of the people sixty-five and older would do so. Where is our younger generation getting its ethical standards?

CHAPTER 13

1. A.W. Tozer, *The Knowledge of the Holy* (New York: Harper and Brothers, 1961), 7. This is one of the finest devotional studies of the attributes of God in print. See also Richard L. Strauss, *The Joy of Knowing God* (Neptune, N.J.: Loizeaux, 1984).

2. ibid., 11.

3. For a fuller treatment of the subject, see *Be Holy*, my exposition of Leviticus (Wheaton, Ill.: Victor Books, 1994).

4. The quotation is from "Invictus" by William Ernest Henley. The word *invictus* is Latin for "invincible, unconquered." Henley suffered from tuberculosis of the bones and bravely endured at least twenty operations, but one wishes he had given the Lord credit for some of the determination that kept him going. We admire any person's courage in the face of seeming defeat, and his poem is an inspiring clarion call to personal courage, but the Christian believer would

prefer 2 Corinthians 12:7-10.

5. These were the opening words of his sermon preached at the Metropolitan Tabernacle, London, on Sunday evening, February 4, 1866. See vol. 58 of *The Metropolitan Tabernacle Pulpit*, 13.

6. The word translated "redeemer" in Proverbs 23:11 is *goel* and refers to the kins-man-redeemer, such as Boaz in the book of Ruth. For the law governing the redemption of property, see Leviticus 25:47-55. The *goel* had to be a close relative who was willing to pay and able to pay. He is a picture of Jesus Christ, who in His incarnation took upon Himself flesh and blood (Heb. 2:14) that He might redeem us from our spiritual bankruptcy and sin. See my book *Be Committed* for an exposition of Ruth and an explanation of the law of the kinsman-redeemer.

7. Most scholars believe that Psalm 23 was a product of David's latter years and not the poem of a young shepherd. It's possible that it grew out of the insurrection caused by his wicked son Absalom (2 Sam. 15-19). David had experienced many difficulties in his long life, yet he saw only God's goodness and mercy.

8. The hymn we call, "I Sing the Mighty Power of God," Isaac Watts entitled, "Praise for Creation and Providence." It was originally written for children. For some reason, we've lost one verse from some of our hymnals:

His hand is my perpetual guard,
He guides me with His eye;
Why should I then forget the Lord,
Whose love is ever nigh?

Paul used divine creation as part of his proof that the Gentiles, who were never given the revelation of God's Law, are still guilty before God and will be judged by Him (Rom. 1:18ff).

9. A.H. Strong, *Systematic Theology*, one-volume edition (Philadelphia: The Judson Press, 1949), 419. Strong goes on to say, "Providence does not exclude, but rather implies the operation of natural law, by which we mean God's regular way of working ... . Prayer without the use of means is an insult to God" (p. 439).

10. Tozer, *The Knowledge of the Holy*, 70.

ECCLESIASTES

OUTLINE

Key theme: Is life really worth living?
Key verses: 1:1–3; 12:13–14

I. THE PROBLEM DECLARED. 1–2

Life is not worth living! Consider:
1. The monotony of life. 1:4–11
2. The vanity of wisdom. 1:12–18
3. The futility of wealth. 2:1–11
4. The certainty of death. 2:12–23
Enjoy life. 2:24

II. THE PROBLEM DISCUSSED 3–10

He considers each of the above arguments:
1. The monotony of life. 3:1–5:9
    (1) Look up. 3:1–8
    (2) Look within. 3:9–14
    (3) Look ahead. 3:15–22
    (4) Look around. 4:1–5:9
Enjoy life. 3:12–15, 22

2. The futility of wealth. 5:10–6:12
    (1) Employing wealth. 5:10–17
    (2) Enjoying wealth. 5:18–6:12
Enjoy life. 5:18–20

3. The vanity of wisdom. 7:1–8:17
    (1) We make life better. 7:1–10
    (2) We see life clearer. 7:11–18
    (3) We face life stronger.

7:19–8:17
Enjoy life. 8:15
4. The certainty of death. 9:1–10:20
    (1) Death is unavoidable.
    9:1–10
    (2) Life is unpredictable.
    9:11–18
    (3) Beware of folly. 10:1–20
Enjoy life. 9:7–10

III. THE PROBLEM DECIDED 11–12

1. Live by faith. 11:1–6
2. Enjoy life now. 11:7–12:8
3. Prepare for judgment. 12:9–14
Enjoy life. 11:9–10

CONTENTS

Introduction to the Book of Ecclesiastes

When I was asked to launch an Old Testament series of BE books, I could think of no better book to start with than Ecclesiastes. And I could think of no better title than *Be Satisfied*, because that's what Ecclesiastes is about.

"Life is filled with difficulties and perplexities," King Solomon concluded, "and there's much that nobody can understand, let alone control. From the human point of view, it's all vanity and folly. But life is God's gift to us and He wants us to enjoy it and use it for His glory. So, instead of complaining about what you don't have, start giving thanks for what you do have—and be satisfied!"

Our Jewish friends read Ecclesiastes at the annual Feast of Tabernacles, a joyful autumn festival of harvest. It fits! For Solomon wrote, "There is nothing better for a man, than that he should eat and drink, and that he should make his soul enjoy good in his labor. This also I saw, that it was from the hand of God" (Eccl. 2:24). Even the apostle Paul (who could hardly be labeled a hedonist) said that God gives to us "richly all things to enjoy" (1 Tim. 6:17).

Life without Jesus Christ is indeed "vanity and vexation of spirit" (Eccl. 1:14). But when you know Him personally, and live for Him faithfully, you experience "fullness of joy [and] pleasures forever more" (Ps. 16:11).

CHAPTER ONE
IS LIFE WORTH LIVING?
Ecclesiastes 1:1-3

Vanity of vanities," lamented Solomon, "all is vanity!" Solomon liked that word "vanity"; he used it thirty-eight times in Ecclesiastes as he wrote about life "under the sun." The word means "emptiness, futility, vapor, that which vanishes quickly and leaves nothing behind."

From the human point of view ("under the sun"), life does appear futile; and it is easy for us to get pessimistic. The Jewish writer Sholom Aleichem once described life as "a blister on top of a tumor, and a boil on top of that." You can almost *feel* that definition!

The American poet Carl Sandburg compared life to "an onion—you peel it off one layer at a time, and sometimes you weep." And British playwright George Bernard Shaw said that life was "a series of inspired follies."

When you were studying English literature in school, you may have read Matthew Arnold's poem "Rugby Chapel" in which he includes this dark description of life:

Most men eddy about
Here and there—eat and drink,
Chatter and love and hate,
Gather and squander, are raised
Aloft, are hurl'd in the dust,
Striving blindly, achieving
Nothing; and then they die—

What a relief to turn from these pessimistic views and hear Jesus Christ say, "I am come that they might have life, and that they might have it more abundantly" (John 10:10). Or to read Paul's majestic declaration, "Therefore, my beloved brethren, be steadfast, unmovable, always abounding in the work of the Lord, knowing that your labor is not in vain in the Lord" (1 Cor. 15:58, NKJV).

Life is "not in vain" if it is lived according to the will of God, and that is what Solomon teaches in this neglected and often misunderstood book.

Before we embark on a study of Ecclesiastes, let's first get acquainted with the author and his aim in writing the book. We also want to get an overview of the book so we can better understand his approach to answering the question, "Is life really worth living?"

1. The Author

Nowhere in this book did the author give his name, but the descriptions he gave of himself and his experiences would indicate that the writer was King Solomon. He called himself "son of David" and "king in Jerusalem" (1:1, 12), and he claimed to have great wealth and wisdom (2:1-11, and 1:13; see 1 Kings 4:20-34 and 10:1ff). In response to Solomon's humble prayer, God promised him both wisdom and wealth (1 Kings 3:3-15); and He kept His promise.

Twelve times in Ecclesiastes the author mentioned "the king," and he made frequent references to the problems of "official bureaucracy" (4:1-3; 5:8; 8:11; 10:6-7). Keep in mind that Solomon ruled over a great nation that required a large standing army and extensive government agencies. He carried on many costly building projects and lived in luxury at court (1 Kings 9:10-28 and 10:1ff; 2 Chron. 1:13-17). Somebody had to manage all this national splendor, and somebody had to pay for it!

Solomon solved the problem by ignoring the original boundaries of the twelve tribes of Israel and dividing the nation into twelve "tax districts," each one managed by an overseer (1 Kings 4:7-19). In time, the whole system became oppressive and corrupt, and after Solomon died, the people begged for relief (2 Chron. 10). As you study Ecclesiastes, you sense this background of exploitation and oppression.

King Solomon began his reign as a humble servant of the Lord, seeking God's wisdom and help (1 Kings 3:5-15). As he grew older, his heart turned away from Jehovah to the false gods of the many wives he had taken from foreign lands (1 Kings 11:1ff). These marriages were motivated primarily by politics, not love, as Solomon sought alliances with the nations around Israel. In fact, many of the things Solomon did that seemed to bring glory to Israel were actually contrary to the Word of God (Deut. 17:14-20).

No amount of money or authority could stop the silent but sure ripening of divine judgment. The famous Scottish preacher Alexander Whyte said that "the secret worm...was gnawing all the time in the royal staff upon which Solomon leaned." The king's latter years were miserable because God removed His hand of blessing (1 Kings 11) and maintained Solomon's throne only because of His promise to David. After Solomon's death, the nation divided, and the house of

David was left with but two tribes, Judah and Benjamin.

Ecclesiastes appears to be the kind of book a person would write near the close of life, reflecting on life's experiences and the lessons learned. Solomon probably wrote Proverbs (Prov. 1:1; 1 Kings 4:32) and the Song of Solomon (1:1) during the years he faithfully walked with God, and near the end of his life, he wrote Ecclesiastes. There is no record that King Solomon repented and turned to the Lord, but his message in Ecclesiastes suggests that he did.

He wrote Proverbs from the viewpoint of a wise teacher (1:1-6), and Song of Solomon from the viewpoint of a royal lover (3:7-11), but when he wrote Ecclesiastes, he called himself "the Preacher" (1:1, 2, 12; 7:27; 12:8-10). The Hebrew word is *Koheleth* (ko-HAY-leth) and is the title given to an official speaker who calls an assembly (see 1 Kings 8:1). The Greek word for "assembly" is *ekklesia*, and this gives us the English title of the book, Ecclesiastes.

But the Preacher did more than call an assembly and give an oration. The word Koheleth carries with it the idea of *debating*, not so much with the listeners as with himself. He would present a topic, discuss it from many viewpoints, and then come to a practical conclusion. Ecclesiastes may appear to be a random collection of miscellaneous ideas about a variety of topics, but Solomon assures us that what he wrote was orderly (12:9).

Let's consider now the aim and the development of the book.

2. The Aim

Solomon has put the key to Ecclesiastes right at the front door: "Vanity of vanities, saith the Preacher, vanity of vanities; all is vanity. What profit hath a man of all his labor which he taketh under the sun?" (1:2-3). Just in case we missed it, he put the same key at the back door (12:8). In these verses, Solomon introduces some of the key words and phrases that are used repeatedly in Ecclesiastes, so we had better get acquainted with them.

Vanity of vanities. We have already noted that Solomon used the word "vanity" thirty-eight times in this book. It is the Hebrew word *hevel*, meaning "emptiness, futility, vapor." The name "Abel" probably comes from this word (Gen. 4:2). Whatever disappears quickly, leaves nothing behind and does not satisfy is *hevel*, vanity. One of my language professors at seminary defined *hevel* as "whatever is left after you break a soap bubble."

Whether he considers his wealth, his works, his wisdom, or his world, Solomon comes to the same sad conclusion: all is "vanity and vexation of spirit" (2:11). However, this is not his final conclusion, nor is it the only message that he has for his readers. We will discover more about that later.

Under the sun. You will find this important phrase twenty-nine times in Ecclesiastes, and with it the phrase "under heaven" (1:13; 2:3; 3:1). It defines the outlook of the writer as he looks at life from a human perspective and not necessarily from heaven's point of view. He applies his own wisdom and experience to the complex human situation and tries to make some sense out of life. Solomon wrote under the inspiration of the Holy Spirit (12:10-11; 2 Tim. 3:16), so what he wrote was what God wanted His people to have. But as we study, we must keep Solomon's viewpoint in mind: he is examining life "under the sun."

In his *Unfolding Message of the Bible*, G. Campbell Morgan perfectly summarizes Solomon's outlook: "This man had been living through all these experiences under the sun, concerned with nothing above the sun...until there came a moment in which he had seen the whole of life. And there was something over the sun. It is only as a man takes account of that which is over the sun as well as that which is under the sun that things under the sun are seen in their true light" (Fleming H. Revell Company, 1961, p. 229).

Profit. The Hebrew word *yitron*, usually translated "profit," is used ten times in Ecclesiastes (1:3; 2:11, 13 [excelleth]; 3:9; 5:9, 16; 7:12 [excellency]; 10:10, 11 [better]). It is used nowhere else in the Old Testament, and its basic meaning is "that which is left over." It may be translated "surplus, advantage, gain." The word "profit" is just the opposite of "vanity." Solomon asks, "In the light of all the puzzles and problems of life, what is the advantage of living? Is there any gain?"

Labor. At least eleven different Hebrew words are translated "labor" in our Authorized Version, and this one is *amal*, used twenty-three times in Ecclesiastes. It means "to toil to the point of exhaustion and yet experience little or no fulfillment in your work." It carries with it the ideas of grief, misery, frustration, and weariness. Moses expressed the meaning of this word in Deuteronomy 26:7 and Psalm 90:10. Of course, looked at only "under the sun," a person's daily work might seem to be futile and burdensome, but the Christian believer can always claim 1 Corinthians 15:58 and labor gladly in the will of God, knowing his labor is "*not* in vain in the Lord."

Man. This is the familiar Hebrew word *adam* (Gen. 1:26; 2:7, 19) and refers to man as made from the earth (*adama* in the Hebrew: Gen. 2:7; 3:19). Of course, man is made in the image of God, but he came from the earth and returns to the earth after death. Solomon used the word forty-nine times as he examined "man under the sun."

These are the basic words found in the opening verses of Ecclesiastes, but there are a few more key words that we need to consider.

Evil. This word is used thirty-one times and in the *King James Version* (KJV) is also translated "sore" (1:13; 4:8), "hurt" (5:13; 8:9), "mischievous" (10:13), "grievous" (2:17), "adversity" (7:14), "wickedness" (7:15), and "misery" (8:6). It is the opposite of "good" and covers a multitude of things: pain, sorrow, hard circumstances, and distress. It is one of King Solomon's favorite words for describing life as he sees it "under the sun."

Joy. In spite of his painful encounters with the world and its problems, Solomon does not recommend either pessimism or cynicism. Rather, he admonishes us to be realistic about life, accept God's gifts and enjoy them (2:24; 3:12-15, 22; 5:18-20; 8:15; 9:7-10; 11:9-10). After all, God gives to us "richly all things to enjoy" (1 Tim. 6:17). Words related to joy (enjoy, rejoice, etc.) are used at least seventeen times in Ecclesiastes. Solomon does not say, "Eat, drink, and be merry, for tomorrow you die!" Instead, he advises us to trust God and enjoy what we *do* have rather than complain about what we *don't* have. Life is short and life is difficult, so make the most of it while you can.

Wisdom. Since it is one of the Old Testament wisdom books, Ecclesiastes would have something to say about both wisdom and folly. There are at least thirty-two references to "fools" and "folly" and at least fifty-four to "wisdom." King Solomon was the wisest of men (1 Kings 4:31) and he applied this wisdom as he sought to understand the purpose of life "under the sun." The

Preacher sought to be a philosopher, but in the end, he had to conclude, "Fear God, and keep His commandments" (12:13).

God. Solomon mentions God forty times and always uses "Elohim" and never "Jehovah." Elohim ("God" in the English Bible) is the Mighty God, the glorious God of creation who exercises sovereign power. Jehovah ("LORD" in the English Bible) is the God of the covenant, the God of revelation who is eternally self-existent and yet graciously relates Himself to sinful man. Since Solomon is dealing exclusively with what he sees "under the sun," he uses Elohim.

Before we leave this study of the vocabulary of Ecclesiastes, we should note that the book abounds in personal pronouns. Since it is an autobiography this is to be expected. Solomon was the ideal person to write this book, for he possessed the wealth, wisdom, and opportunities necessary to carry out the "experiments" required for this investigation into the meaning of life. God did not make King Solomon disobey just so he could write this book, but He did use Solomon's experiences to prepare him for this task.

3. The Analysis

Refer back to the Outline of Ecclesiastes, at the beginning of this study on Ecclesiastes, and note the places where Solomon admonished us to enjoy life and be satisfied with what God has assigned to us.

In Ecclesiastes 12:8-12, Solomon explained how he wrote this book: he sought out the best words and arranged them in the best order. As he wrote, he included "goads" to prod us in our thinking and "nails" on which to hang some practical conclusions. Keep this in mind as you study. His work was inspired by God because he was guided by the "One Shepherd" (Ps. 80:1).

4. The Application

What is the practical application of this book for us today? Is Ecclesiastes nothing but an interesting exhibit in a religious museum, or does it have a message for people in the Space Age?

Its message is for today. After all, the society which Solomon investigated a millennium before the birth of Christ was not too different from our world today. Solomon saw injustice to the poor (4:1-3), crooked politics (5:8), incompetent leaders (10:6-7), guilty people allowed to commit more crime (8:11), materialism (5:10), and a desire for "the good old days" (7:10). It sounds up-to-date, doesn't it?

If you have never trusted Jesus Christ as your Savior, then this book urges you to do so without delay. Why? Because no matter how much wealth, education, or social prestige you may have, life without God is futile. You are only "chasing after the wind" if you expect to find satisfaction and personal fulfillment in the things of the world. "For what shall it profit a man, if he should gain the whole world, and lose his own soul?" asked Jesus (Mark 8:36).

Solomon experimented with life and discovered that there was no lasting satisfaction in possessions, pleasures, power, or prestige. He had everything, yet his life was empty! There is no need for you and me to repeat these experiments. Let's accept Solomon's conclusions and avoid the heartache and pain that must be endured when you experiment in the laboratory of life. These experiments are costly and one of them could prove fatal.

When you belong to the family of God through faith in the Son of God, life is not monotonous: it is a daily adventure that builds character and enables you to serve others to the glory of God. Instead of making decisions on the basis of the vain wisdom of this world, you will have God's wisdom available to you (James 1:5).

As far as wealth and pleasure are concerned, God gives to us "richly all things to enjoy" (1 Tim. 6:17). "The blessing of the Lord makes one rich, and He adds no sorrow with it" (Prov. 10:22, NKJV). The wealth and pleasures of the world do not satisfy, and the quest for power and position is futile. In Jesus Christ we have all that we need for life and death, time and eternity.

If there is one truth that Solomon emphasizes in this book, it is the certainty of death. No matter what Solomon enjoyed or accomplished, the frightening shadow of death was always hovering over him. But Jesus Christ has defeated death and is "the resurrection and the life" (John 11:25). The victory of His resurrection means that our "labor is not in vain in the Lord" (1 Cor. 15:58).

If you don't know Jesus Christ as your Savior, then all that you work for and live for will ultimately perish; and you will perish too. But faith in Jesus Christ brings you the gift of eternal life and the privilege of serving Him and investing your years in that which is eternal.

So, the first message of Ecclesiastes is: turn from the futility of sin and the world, and put your faith in Jesus Christ (John 3:16; Eph. 2:8–10).

But if you are a believer in Jesus Christ and have received the gift of eternal life, then Solomon asks you, "Are you living for the Lord or for the things of the world?" Remember, Solomon knew God and was greatly blessed by Him, yet he turned from the Lord and went his own way. No wonder he became pessimistic and skeptical as he looked at life! He didn't have God's perspective because he wasn't living for God's purposes.

More than one professed Christian has followed Solomon's bad example and started living for the things of this world. Paul wrote about one of his associates in ministry, "Demas hath forsaken me, having loved this present world" (2 Tim. 4:10). The apostle John warned, "Love not the world, neither the things that are in the world" (1 John 2:15), and James admonished us to keep ourselves "unspotted from the world" (1:27).

When you start living for the world instead of for the will of God, you begin to look at life from the wrong perspective: "under the sun" and not "above the sun." Instead of seeking those things which are above (Col. 3:1ff), you start majoring on the things that are below. This wrong vision soon causes you to adopt wrong values and you stop living for the eternal. The result is disappointment and defeat; the only remedy is repentance and confession of sin (1 John 1:9).

Ecclesiastes also contains a message for the faithful believer who wants to serve the Lord and have a fulfilled life in Jesus Christ. Solomon says, "Don't bury your head in the sand and pretend that problems don't exist. They do! Face life honestly, but look at life from God's perspective. Man's philosophies will fail you. Use your God-given wisdom, but don't expect to solve every problem or answer every question. The important thing is to obey God's will and enjoy all that He gives you. Remember, death is coming— so, be prepared!"

Perhaps this message is best summarized in the prayer of Moses: "So teach us to number our days, that we may apply our hearts unto wisdom" (Ps. 90:12).

I opened this chapter by quoting some metaphors that describe "life," and I want to quote one more. It's from the popular American novelist Peter De Vries: "Life is a crowded superhighway with bewildering cloverleaf exits on which a man is liable to find himself speeding back in the direction he came."

That need not happen to you! King Solomon has already explored the road exhaustively and given us a dependable map to follow. And if we follow God's Word, we will be satisfied.

Are you ready for the journey?

What will life be for you: vanity or victory?

CHAPTER TWO
LIVING IN CIRCLES
Ecclesiastes 1:4-18

Everything an Indian does is in a circle," said Black Elk, the Sioux religious leader. "Even the seasons form a great circle in their changing and always come back again to where they were. The life of a man is a circle from childhood to childhood...."

You would think Black Elk had been studying the first chapter of Ecclesiastes, except for one fact: for centuries, wise men and women in different nations and cultures have been pondering the mysteries of the "circles" of human life. Whenever you use phrases like "life cycle," or "the wheel of fortune," or "come full circle," you are joining Solomon and Black Elk and a host of others in taking a cyclical view of life and nature.

But this "cyclical" view of life was a burden to Solomon. For if life is only part of a great cycle over which we have no control, is life worth living? If this cycle is repeated season after season, century after century, why are we unable to understand it and explain it? Solomon pondered these questions as he looked at the cycle of life "under the sun," and he came to three bleak conclusions: nothing is changed (1:4-7), nothing is new (1:8-11), and nothing is understood (1:12-18).

1. Nothing Is Changed (Eccl. 1:4-7)

In this section, Solomon approached the problem as a scientist and examined the "wheel of nature" around him: the earth, the sun, the wind, and the water. (This reminds us of the ancient "elements" of earth, air, fire, and water.) He was struck by the fact that generations of people came and went while the things of nature remained. There was "change" all around, yet nothing really changed. Everything was only part of the "wheel of nature" and contributed to the monotony of life. So, Solomon asked, "Is life worth living?"

Solomon presented four pieces of evidence to prove that nothing really changes.

The earth (v. 4). From the human point of view, nothing seems more permanent and durable than the planet on which we live. When we say that something is "as sure as the world," we are echoing Solomon's confidence in the permanence of planet Earth. With all of its diversity, nature is uniform enough in its operation that we can discover its "laws" and put them to work for us. In fact, it is this "dependability" that is the basis for modern science.

Nature is permanent, but man is transient, a mere pilgrim on earth. His pilgrimage is a brief one, for death finally claims him. At the very beginning of his book, Solomon introduced a topic frequently mentioned in Ecclesiastes: the brevity of life and the certainty of death.

Individuals and families come and go, nations and empires rise and fall, but nothing changes, for the world remains the same. Thomas Carlyle called history "a mighty drama, enacted upon the theater of time, with suns for lamps and eternity for a background." Solomon would add that the costumes and sets may occasionally change, but the actors and the script remain pretty much the same; and that's as sure as the world.

The sun (v. 5). We move now from the cycle of birth and death on earth to the cycle of day and night in the heavens. "As sure as the world!" is replaced by "As certain as night follows day!" Solomon pictures the sun rising in the east and "panting" (literal translation) its way across the sky in pursuit of the western horizon. But what does it accomplish by this daily journey? To what purpose is all this motion and heat? As far as the heavens are concerned, one day is just like another, and the heavens remain the same.

The wind (v. 6). From the visible east-west movement of the sun, Solomon turned to the invisible north-south movement of the wind. He was not giving a lecture on the physics of wind. Rather, he was stating that the wind is in constant motion, following "circuits" that man cannot fully understand or chart. "The wind blows where it wishes," our Lord said to Nicodemus, "and you ... cannot tell where it comes from and where it goes" (John 3:8, NKJV).

Solomon's point is this: the wind is constantly moving and changing directions, and yet it is still—the wind! We hear it and feel it, and we see what it does, but over the centuries, the wind has not changed its cycles or circuits. Man comes and goes, but the changeless wind goes on forever.

The sea (v. 7). Solomon described here the "water cycle" that helps to sustain life on our planet. Scientists tell us that, at any given time, 97 percent of all the water on earth is in the oceans, and only .0001 percent is in the atmosphere, available for rain. (That's enough for about ten days of rain.) The cooperation of the sun and the wind makes possible the evaporation and movement of moisture, and this keeps the water "circulating." But the sea never changes! The rivers and the rains pour water into the seas, but the seas remain the same.

So, whether we look at the earth or the heavens, the winds or the waters, we come to the same conclusion: nature does not change. There is motion but not *promotion*. No wonder Solomon cites *the monotony of life* as his first argument to prove that life is not worth living (1:4-11).

All of this is true *only if you look at life "under the sun"* and leave God out of the picture. Then the world becomes a closed system that is uniform, predictable, unchangeable. It becomes a world where there are no answers to prayer and no miracles, for nothing can interrupt the cycle of nature. If there is a God in this kind of a world, He cannot act on our behalf because He is imprisoned within the "laws of nature" that cannot be suspended.

However, God *does* break into nature to do great and wonderful things! He does hear and answer prayer and work on behalf of His people. He held the sun in place so Joshua could finish an important battle (Josh. 10:6-14), and He moved the sun back as a sign to King Hezekiah (Isa. 38:1-8). He opened the Red Sea and the Jordan River for Israel (Ex. 14; Josh. 3–4). He "turned off" the rain for Elijah (1 Kings 17) and then "turned it on" again (James 5:17-18). He calmed the wind and the waves for the disciples (Mark 4:35-41), and in the future, will use the forces of nature to bring terror and judgment to people on the earth (see Revelation 6ff).

When, by faith, you receive Jesus Christ as your Savior, and God becomes your Heavenly Father, you no longer live in a "closed system" of endless monotonous cycles. You can gladly sing, "This is my Father's world!" and know that He will meet your every need as you trust Him (Matt. 6:25-34). Christians live in this world as pilgrims, not prisoners, and therefore they are joyful and confident.

2. Nothing Is New (Eccl. 1:8-11)

If nothing changes, then it is reasonable to conclude that nothing in this world is new. This "logical conclusion" might have satisfied people in Solomon's day, but it startles us today. After all, we are surrounded by, and dependent on, a multitude of marvels that modern science has provided for us—everything from telephones to pacemakers and miracle drugs. How could anybody who watched Neil Armstrong walk on the moon agree with Solomon that nothing is new under the sun?

In this discussion, Solomon stopped being a scientist and became a historian. Let's follow the steps in his reasoning.

Man wants something new (v. 8). Why? Because everything in this world ultimately brings weariness, and people long for something to distract them or deliver them. They are like the Athenians in Paul's day, spending their time "in nothing else, but either to tell, or to hear some new thing" (Acts 17:21). But even while they are speaking, seeing, and hearing these "new things," they are still dissatisfied with life and will do almost anything to find some escape. Of course, the entertainment industry is grateful for this human hunger for novelty and takes advantage of it at great profit.

In Ecclesiastes 3:11, Solomon explains why men and women are not satisfied with life: God has put "eternity in their heart" (NIV, NASB, KNJV) and nobody can find peace and satisfaction apart from

Him. "Thou hast made us for Thyself," prayed St. Augustine, "and our hearts are restless until they rest in Thee." The eye cannot be satisfied until it sees the hand of God, and the ear cannot be satisfied until it hears the voice of God. We must respond by faith to our Lord's invitation, "Come unto me...and I will give you rest" (Matt. 11:28).

The world provides nothing new (vv. 9-10). Dr. H.A. Ironside, longtime pastor of Chicago's Moody church, used to say, "If it's new, it's not true; and if it's true, it's not new." Whatever is new is simply a recombination of the old. Man cannot "create" anything new because man is the creature, not the Creator. "That which hath been is now, and that which is to be hath already been" (3:15). Thomas Alva Edison, one of the world's greatest inventors, said that his inventions were only "bringing out the secrets of nature and applying them for the happiness of mankind."

Only God can create new things, and he begins by making sinners "new creatures" when they trust Jesus Christ to save them (2 Cor. 5:17). Then they can walk "in newness of life" (Rom. 6:4), sing a "new song" (Ps. 40:3), and enter into God's presence by a "new and living way" (Heb. 10:20). One day, they will enjoy "a new heaven and a new earth" (Rev. 21:1) when God says, "Behold, I make all things new" (Rev. 21:5).

Why we think things are new (v. 11). The answer is simple: we have bad memories and we don't read the minutes of the previous meeting. (See 2:16, 4:16, and 9:5.) It has well been said that the ancients have stolen all of our best ideas, and this is painfully true.

A young man approached me at a conference and asked if he could share some new ideas for youth ministry. He was very enthusiastic as he outlined his program, but the longer I listened, the more familiar his ideas became. I encouraged him to put his ideas into practice, but then told him that we had done all of those things in Youth for Christ before he was born, and that YFC workers were still doing them. He was a bit stunned to discover that there was indeed nothing new under the sun.

Solomon wrote, of course, about the basic principles of life and not about methods. As the familiar couplet puts it: Methods are many, principles are few / methods always change, principles never do. The ancient thinkers knew this. The Stoic philosopher Marcus Aurelius wrote, "They that come after us will see nothing new, and they who went before us saw nothing more than we have seen." The only people who really think they have seen something new are those whose experience is limited or whose vision can't penetrate beneath the surface of things. Because something is recent, they think it is new; they mistake novelty for originality.

3. Nothing Is Understood (Eccl. 1:12-18)

The historian now becomes the philosopher as Solomon tells how he went about searching for the answer to the problem that vexed him. As the king of Israel, he had all the resources necessary for "experimenting" with different solutions to see what it was that made life worth living. In the laboratory of life, he experimented with enjoying various physical pleasures (2:1-3), accomplishing great and costly works (2:4-6), and accumulating great possessions (2:7-10) only to discover that all of it was only "vanity and grasping for the wind" (v. 14, NKJV).

But before launching into his experiments, Solomon took time to try to think

the matter through. He was the wisest of all men and he applied that God-given wisdom to the problem. He devoted his mind wholly to the matter to get to the root of it ("seek") and to explore it from all sides ("search"). Dorothy Sayers wrote in one of her mystery novels, "There is nothing you cannot prove if only your outlook is narrow enough." Solomon did not take that approach.

Here are some of his tentative conclusions:

Life is tough, but it is the gift of God (v. 13). He described life as a "sore travail" ("grievous task," NKJV) that only fatigues you ("may be exercised", NKJV). Of course, when God first gave life to man, the world had not been cursed because of sin (Gen. 3:14ff). Since the fall of man, "the whole creation groans and labors with birth pangs" (Rom. 8:22, NKJV); this is one reason why life is so difficult. One day, when our Lord returns, creation will be delivered from this bondage.

While sitting in my backyard one evening, I heard a robin singing merrily from atop a TV aerial. As I listened to him sing, I preached myself a sermon:

> Since early dawn, that bird has done nothing but try to survive. He's been wearing himself out hiding from enemies and looking for food for himself and his little ones. And yet, when he gets to the end of the day, *he sings about it!*
>
> Here I am, created in the image of God and saved by the grace of God, and I complain about even the little annoyances of life. One day, I will be like the Lord Jesus Christ; for that reason alone, I should be singing God's praises just like that robin.

Life doesn't get easier if you try to run away from it (v. 14). All the works that are done "under the sun" never truly satisfy the heart. They are but "vanity and grasping for the wind" (v. 14, NKJV). Both the workaholic and the alcoholic are running away from reality and living on substitutes, and one day the bubble of illusion will burst. We only make life harder when we try to escape. Instead of running away from life, we should run to God and let Him make life worth living.

The ultimate door of escape is suicide, and Solomon will have something to say about man's desire for death. Some specialists claim that 40,000 persons commit suicide in the United States annually, and an estimated 400,000 make the attempt. But once you have *chosen to live* and have rightly rejected suicide as an option, then you must choose *how* you are going to live. Will it be by faith in yourself and what you can do, or by faith in the Lord?

Not everything can be changed (v. 15). It is likely that Solomon, who was an expert on proverbs (1 Kings 4:32), quoted a popular saying here in order to make his point. He makes a similar statement in 7:13. If we spend all our time and energy trying to straighten out everything that is twisted, we will have nothing left with which to live our lives! And if we try to spend what we don't have, we will end up in bankruptcy.

In short, Solomon is saying, "The past can't always be changed, and it is foolish to fret over what you might have done." Ken Taylor paraphrases verse 15, "What is wrong cannot be righted; it is water over the dam; and there is no use thinking of what might have been" (TLB).

We must remind ourselves, however, that God has the power to straighten out what is twisted and supply what is lacking. He will not change the past, but He can change the way that the past affects us. For the lost sinner, the past is a heavy anchor that drags him down; but for the child of God, the past—even with its sins and mistakes—is a rudder that guides him forward. Faith makes the difference.

When He was ministering here on earth, our Lord often straightened out that which was twisted and provided that which was lacking (Luke 13:11-17; Matt. 12:10-13, 15:29-39; John 6:1-13). Man cannot do this by his own wisdom or power, but "with God nothing shall be impossible" (Luke 1:37). Solomon was looking at these problems from a vantage point "under the sun," and that's why they seemed insoluble.

Wisdom and experience will not solve every problem (vv. 16-18). Those who go through life living on explanations will always be unhappy for at least two reason. First, this side of heaven, there are no explanations for some things that happen, and God is not obligated to explain them anyway. (In fact, if He did, we might not understand them!) Second, God has ordained that His people live by *promises* and not by explanations, by faith and not by sight. "Blessed are they that have not seen, and yet have believed" (John 20:29).

If anybody was equipped to solve the difficult problems of life and tell us what life was all about, Solomon was that person. He was the wisest of men, and people came from all over to hear his wisdom (1 Kings 4:29-34). His wealth was beyond calculation so that he had the resources available to do just about anything he wanted to do. He even experienced "madness and folly" (the absurd, the opposite of wisdom) in his quest for the right answers. Nothing was too hard for him.

But these advantages didn't enable Solomon to find all the answers he was seeking. In fact, his great wisdom only *added* to his difficulties, for wisdom and knowledge increase sorrow and grief. People who never ponder the problems of life, who live innocently day after day, never feel the pain of wrestling with God in seeking to understand His ways. The more we seek knowledge and wisdom, the more ignorant we know we are. This only adds to the burden. "All our knowledge brings us nearer to our ignorance," wrote T. S. Eliot in "Choruses From `The Rock.'" An old proverb says, "A wise man is never happy."

All of this goes back to the Garden of Eden and Satan's offer to Eve that, if she ate of the fruit, she would have the knowledge of good and evil (Gen. 3). When Adam and Eve sinned, they did get an experiential knowledge of good and evil; but since they were alienated from God, this knowledge only *added* to their sorrows. It has been that way with man ever since. Whether it be jet planes, insecticides, or television, each advance in human knowledge and achievement only creates a new set of problems for society.

For some people, life may be monotonous and meaningless, but it doesn't have to be. For the Christian believer, life is an open door, not a closed circle; there are daily experiences of new blessings from the Lord. True, we can't explain everything; but life is not built on explanations: it's built on promises—and we have plenty of promises in God's Word!

The scientist tells us that the world is a closed system and nothing is changed.

The historian tells us that life is a closed book and nothing is new.

The philosopher tells us that life is a deep problem and nothing is understood.

But Jesus Christ is "the power of God and the wisdom of God" (1 Cor. 1:24), and He has miraculously broken into history to bring new life to all who trust Him.

If you are "living in circles," then turn your life over to Him.

CHAPTER THREE
DISGUSTED WITH LIFE?
Ecclesiastes 2

There is but one step from the sublime to the ridiculous." Napoleon is supposed to have made that statement after his humiliating retreat from Moscow in the winter of 1812. The combination of stubborn Russian resistance and a severe Russian winter was too much for the French army, and its expected sublime victory was turned into shameful defeat.

As part of his quest for "the good life," King Solomon examined everything from the sublime to the ridiculous. In the great laboratory of life, he experimented with one thing after another, always applying the wisdom that God had given him (vv. 3, 9). In this chapter, Solomon recorded three stages in his experiments as he searched for a satisfying meaning to life.

1. He Tested Life (Eccl. 2:1-11)
Solomon had the means and the authority to do just about anything his heart desired. He decided to test his own heart to see how he would respond to two very common experiences of life: enjoyment (1-3) and employment (4-11).

Enjoyment (2:1-3). The Hebrew people rightly believed that God made man to enjoy the blessings of His creation (Ps. 104, and note 1 Tim. 6:17). The harvest season was a joyful time for them as they reaped the blessings of God on their labor.

At the conclusion of his book, Solomon admonished his readers to enjoy God's blessings during the years of their youth, before old age arrived and the body began to fall apart (12:1ff). Eight times in Ecclesiastes, Solomon used the Hebrew word meaning "pleasure," so it is obvious that he did not consider God a celestial spoilsport who watched closely to make certain nobody was having a good time.

Solomon specifically mentioned wine and laughter as two sources of pleasure used in his experiment. It takes very little imagination to see the king in his splendid banquet hall (1 Kings 10:21), eating choice food (1 Kings 4:22-23), drinking the very best wine, and watching the most gifted entertainers (2:8b). But when the party was over and King Solomon examined his heart, it was still dissatisfied and empty. Pleasure and mirth were only vanity, so many soap bubbles that quickly burst and left nothing behind.

Perhaps many of the king's servants envied Solomon and wished to change places with him, but the king was unhappy. "Even in laughter the heart is sorrowful," he wrote in Proverbs 14:13, "and the end of that mirth is heaviness."

Today's world is pleasure-mad. Millions of people will pay almost any amount of money to "buy experiences" and temporarily escape the burdens of life. While there is nothing wrong with innocent fun, the person who builds his or her life only on seeking pleasure is bound to be disappointed in the end.

Why? For one thing, pleasure-seeking usually becomes a selfish endeavor; and selfishness destroys true joy. People who live for pleasure often exploit others to get what they want, and they end up with broken relationships as well as empty hearts. *People are more important than things and thrills.* We are to be channels, not reser-voirs; the greatest joy comes when we share God's pleasures with others.

If you live for pleasure alone, enjoyment will decrease unless the intensity of the pleasure increases. Then you reach a point of diminishing returns when there is little or no enjoyment at all, only bondage. For example, the more that people drink, the less enjoyment they get out of it. This means they must have more drinks and stronger drinks in order to have pleasure; the sad result is desire without satisfaction. Instead of alcohol, substitute drugs, gambling, sex, money, fame, or any other pursuit, and the principle will hold true: when pleasure alone is the center of life, the result will ultimately be disappointment and emptiness.

There is a third reason why pleasure alone can never bring satisfaction: it appeals to only part of the person and ignores the total being. This is the major difference between shallow "entertainment" and true "enjoyment," for when the whole person is involved, there will be both enjoyment and enrichment. Entertainment has its place, but we must keep in mind that it only helps us to escape life temporarily. True pleasure not only brings delight, but it also builds character by enriching the total person.

Employment (2:4-11). Next, Solomon got involved in all kinds of projects, hoping to discover something that would make life worth living. He started with *great works* (4-6), including houses (1 Kings 7), cities (2 Chron. 8:4-6), gardens, vineyards, orchards and forests (1 Kings 4:33), and the water systems needed to service them. Of course, Solomon also supervised the construction of the temple (1 Kings 5ff), one of the greatest buildings of the ancient world.

He not only had works, but he also had *workers* (7a). He had two kinds of slaves: those he purchased and those born in his household. He might have added that he "drafted" 30,000 Jewish men to work on various projects (1 Kings 5:13-18). His father David had conscripted the strangers in the land (1 Chron. 22:2), but Solomon drafted his own people, and the people resented it (see 1 Kings 12).

Of course, Solomon accumulated *wealth* (7b-8a), in flocks and herds (1 Kings 8:63) as well as gold and silver (1 Kings 4:21 and 10:1ff). He was the wealthiest and wisest man in the whole world, yet he was unhappy because activity alone does not bring lasting pleasure.

There can be joy in the *doing* of great projects, but what happens when the task is finished? Solomon found delight *in* all his labor (2:10); but *afterward,* when he considered all his works, he saw only "vanity and vexation of spirit" (2:11). The journey was a pleasure, but the destination brought pain. "Success is full of promise until men get it," said the American preacher Henry Ward Beecher, "and then it is a last-year's nest from which the birds have flown."

We must not conclude that Solomon was condemning work itself, because work is a blessing from God. Adam had work to do in the Garden even before he sinned. "The Lord God took the man and put him in the Garden of Eden to work it and take care of it" (Gen. 2:15, NIV). In the book of Proverbs, Solomon exalted diligence and condemned laziness; for he knew that any honest employment can be done to the glory of God (1 Cor. 10:31). But work *alone* cannot satisfy the human heart, no matter how successful that work may be (Isa. 55:2).

This helps us to understand why many achievers are unhappy people. Ambrose Bierce called achievement "the death of endeavor and the birth of disgust." This is often the case. The overachiever is often a person who is trying to escape himself or herself by becoming a workaholic, and this only results in disappointment. When workaholics retire, they often feel useless and sometimes die from lack of meaningful activity.

Solomon tested life, and his heart said, "Vanity!"

Solomon Hated Life (Eccl. 2:12-23)

"I turned myself to behold" simply means, "I considered things from another viewpoint." What he did was to look at his wisdom (12-17) and his wealth (18-23) *in light of the certainty of death.* What good is it to be wise and wealthy if you are going to die and leave everything behind?

The certainty of death is a topic Solomon frequently mentioned in Ecclesiastes (1:4; 2:14-17; 3:18-20; 5:15-16; 6:6; 8:8; 9:2-3, 12; 12:7-8). He could not easily avoid the subject as he looked at life "under the sun," for death is one of the obvious facts of life. The French essayist Montaigne wrote, "Philosophy is no other thing than for a man to prepare himself to death." Only that person is prepared to live who is prepared to die.

He considered his wisdom (2:12-17). Since both the wise man and the fool will die, what is the value of wisdom? For one thing, we can leave our wisdom for the guidance of the next generation, but how can we be sure they will value it or follow it? "What can the man do that cometh after the king?" suggests that it is folly for successive generations to make the same "experiments" (and mistakes) when they can learn from their forefathers, *but they do it just the same!* There is nothing new under the sun (1:9); they can only repeat what we have already done.

In spite of the fact that all men must die, wisdom is still of greater value than folly. They are as different as night and day! *The wise man sees that death is coming and lives accordingly, while the fool walks in darkness and is caught unprepared.* However, being prepared for death does not necessarily relieve Solomon of his burden about life; for it takes a person a long time to learn how to live, and then life ends. All of this seems so futile.

Both the wise man and the fool die, and both the wise man and the fool are forgotten (v. 16). Solomon's fame has remained, of course (1 Kings 4:29-34; Matt. 6:28-30); but most "famous" people who have died are rarely mentioned in ordinary conversation, although their biographies are found in the encyclopedias. (I note that some of these biographies get smaller from edition to edition.)

"So I hated life!" concluded Solomon, but he was not contemplating suicide; for death was one thing he wanted to avoid. "I hate life and yet I am afraid to die!" said the French humanist Voltaire; Solomon would agree with him. Life seemed irrational and futile to Solomon, and yet it was still better than death. We might paraphrase his statement, "Therefore, I was disgusted with life!"

The healthy Christian believer certainly would not hate life, no matter how difficult the circumstances might be. It is true that some great men have wanted to die, such as Job (Job 3:21–7:15), Moses (Num. 11:15), Elijah (1 Kings 19:4), and Jonah (Jonah 4:3), but we must not take these special instances as examples for us to follow. All of these men finally changed their minds.

No, the Christian should "love life" (1 Peter 3:10, quoted from Ps. 34:12ff), seeking to put the most into it and getting the most out of it, to the glory of God. We may not enjoy everything in life, or be able to explain everything about life, but

that is not important. We live by promises and not by explanations, and we know that our "labor is not in vain in the Lord" (1 Cor. 15:58).

He considered his wealth (2:18-23). Not only did Solomon hate life, but he hated the wealth that was the result of his toil. Of course, Solomon was born wealthy, and great wealth came to him because he was the king. But he was looking at life "under the sun" and speaking for the "common people" who were listening to his discussion. He gave three reasons why he was disgusted with wealth.

First, *you can't keep it* (v. 18). The day would come when Solomon would die and leave everything to his successor. This reminds us of our Lord's warning in the parable of the Rich Fool (Luke 12:13-21) and Paul's words in 1 Timothy 6:7-10. A Jewish proverb says, "There are no pockets in shrouds."

Money is a medium of exchange. Unless it is spent, it can do little or nothing for you. You can't eat money, but you can use it to buy food. It will not keep you warm, but it will purchase fuel. A writer in *The Wall Street Journal* called money "an article which may be used as a universal passport to everywhere except heaven, and as a universal provider of everything except happiness."

Of course, you and I are *stewards* of our wealth; God is the Provider (Deut. 8:18) and the Owner, and we have the privilege of enjoying it and using it for His glory. One day we will have to give an account of what we have done with His generous gifts. While we cannot take wealth with us when we die, we can "send it ahead" as we use it today according to God's will (Matt. 6:19-34).

Second, *we can't protect it* (vv. 19-20). It's bad enough that we must leave our wealth behind, but even worse that we might leave it to somebody who will waste it! Suppose he or she is a fool and tears down everything we have built up? Solomon didn't know it at the time, but his son Rehoboam would do that very thing (1 Kings 11:41—12:24).

Many people have tried to write their wills in such a way that their estates could not be wasted, but they have not always succeeded. In spite of the instruction and good example they may give, the fathers and mothers have no way of knowing what the next generation will do with the wealth that they worked so hard to accumulate. Solomon's response was to walk about and simply resign himself ("despair" v. 20) to the facts of life and death. As the rustic preacher said, "We all must learn to cooperate with the inevitable!"

Third, *we can't enjoy it as we should* (vv. 21-23). If all we do is think about our wealth and worry about what will happen to it, we will make our lives miserable. We do all the work and then leave the wealth to somebody who didn't even work for it (v. 21). Is that fair? We spend days in travail and grief and have many sleepless nights, yet our heirs never experience any of this. It all seems so futile. "What does a man get for all the toil and anxious striving with which he labors under the sun?" (v. 22, NIV)

At this point, Solomon appears to be very pessimistic, but he doesn't remain that way very long. In a step of faith he reaches the third stage in his experiment.

3. He Accepted Life (2:24-26)

This is the first of six "conclusions" in Ecclesiastes, each of which emphasizes the importance of accepting life as God's gift and enjoying it in God's will (3:12-15, 22; 5:18-20; 8:15; 9:7-10; 11:9-10). Solomon is not advocating "Eat, drink and be merry, for tomorrow we die!" That is the philosophy of fatalism not faith. Rather, he is saying, "Thank God for what you do have, and enjoy it to the glory of God." Paul gave his approval to this attitude when he exhorted us to trust "in the living God, who gives us richly all things to enjoy" (1 Tim. 6:17, NKJV).

Solomon made it clear that not only were the blessings from God, but even the *enjoyment of the blessings* was God's gift to us (v. 24). He considered it "evil" if a person had all the blessings of life from God but could not enjoy them (6:1-5). It is easy to see why the Jewish people read Ecclesiastes at the Feast of Tabernacles, for Tabernacles is their great time of thanksgiving and rejoicing for God's abundant provision of their needs.

The translation of verse 25 in the *King James Version* is somewhat awkward; the *New American Standard Bible* is better: "For who can eat and who can have enjoyment without Him?" The farmer who prayed at the table, "Thanks for food and for good digestion" knew what Solomon was writing about.

The important thing is that we seek to please the Lord (v. 26) and trust Him to meet every need. God wants to give us wisdom, knowledge, and joy; these three gifts enable us to appreciate God's blessings and take pleasure in them. *It is not enough to possess "things"; we must also possess the kind of character that enables us to use "things" wisely and enjoy them properly.*

Not so with the sinner. (The Hebrew word means "to fall short, to miss the mark.") The sinner may heap up all kinds of riches, but he can never truly enjoy them because he has left God out of his life. In fact, his riches may finally end up going to the righteous. This is not always the case, but God does make it happen that "the wealth of the sinner is laid up for the just"

(Prov. 13:22). At their exodus from Egypt, the Israelites spoiled their Egyptian masters (Ex. 3:22; 12:36), and throughout Jewish history their armies took great spoil in their many conquests. In fact, much of the wealth that went into the temple came from David's military exploits.

It is "vanity and vexation of spirit" ("meaningless, a chasing after wind," NIV) for the sinner to heap up riches and yet ignore God. Apart from God, there can be no true enjoyment of blessings or enrichment of life. It is good to have the things that money can buy, *provided* you don't lose the things that money can't buy.

This completes the first section of Ecclesiastes—*The Problem Declared.* Solomon has presented four arguments that seem to prove that life is really not worth living: the monotony of life (1:4-11), the vanity of wisdom (1:12-18), the futility of wealth (2:1-11), and the certainty of death (2:12-23). His argument appears to be true *if* you look at life "under the sun," that is, only from the human point of view.

But when you bring God into the picture, everything changes! (Note that God is not mentioned from 1:14 to 2:23.) Life and death, wisdom and wealth, are all in His hands; He wants us to enjoy His blessings and please His heart. If we rejoice in the gifts, but forget the Giver, then we are ungrateful idolaters.

In the next eight chapters, Solomon will consider each of these four arguments and refute them. At the end of each argument he will say, "Enjoy life and be thankful to God!" (See the outline on pages 475–476.) In his discussions, he will face honestly the trials and injustices of life, the things that make us cry out, "Why, Lord?" But Solomon is not a shallow optimist wearing rose-tinted glasses, nor is he a skeptical pessimist wearing

blinders. Rather, he takes a balanced view of life and death and helps us look at both from God's eternal perspective.

"Life isn't like a book," says Chuck Colson, founder of Prison Fellowship ministry. "Life isn't logical, or sensible, or orderly. Life is a mess most of the time. And theology must be lived in the midst of that mess."

Solomon will provide us with that theology.

It's up to us to live it—and *be satisfied!*

CHAPTER FOUR
TIME AND TOIL
Ecclesiastes 3

Ponder these quotations from two famous professors: "Why shouldn't things be largely absurd, futile, and transitory? They are so, and we are so, and they and we go very well together." That's from philosopher George Santayana, who taught at Harvard from 1889 to 1912.

"There is no reason to suppose that a man's life has any more meaning than the life of the humblest insect that crawls from one annihilation to another." That was written by Joseph Wood Krutch, professor of English at Columbia University from 1937 to 1952.

Both of these men were brilliant in their fields, but most of us would not agree with what they wrote. We believe that something grander is involved in human life than mere transitory existence. We are *not* like insects. Surely Dr. Krutch knew that insects have *life cycles,* but men and women have *histories.* One bee is pretty much like another bee, but people are unique and no two stories are the same. You can write *The*

Life of the Bee, but you can't write *The Life of the Man* or *The Life of the Woman.*

If we as individuals are not unique, then we are not important; if we are not important, then life has no meaning. If life has no meaning, life isn't worth living. We might as well follow the Epicurean philosophy: "Let us eat and drink, for tomorrow we die."

Solomon has presented four arguments proving that life was nothing but grasping broken soap bubbles and chasing after the wind. But he was too wise a man to let his own arguments go unchallenged, so in Ecclesiastes 3–10, he reexamined each of them carefully. His first argument was *the monotony of life* (1:4-11), and he examined it in Ecclesiastes 3:1–5:9. He discovered four factors that must be considered before you can say that life is monotonous and meaningless.

First, he saw something *above* man, a God who was in control of time and who balanced life's experiences (3:1-8). Then he saw something *within* man that linked him to God—eternity in his heart (3:9-14). Third, Solomon saw something *ahead of* man—the certainty of death (3:15-22). Finally, he saw something *around* man— the problems and burdens of life (4:1–5:9).

So, The Preacher asked his listeners to look up, to look within, to look ahead, and to look around, and to take into consideration time, eternity, death, and suffering. These are the four factors God uses to keep our lives from becoming monotonous and meaningless. We will consider three of these factors in this chapter and the fourth in our next study.

1. Look Up: God Orders Time (Eccl. 3:1-8)

You don't have to be a philosopher or a scientist to know that "times and seasons" are a regular part of life, no matter where you live. Were it not for the dependability of God-ordained "natural laws," both science and daily life would be chaotic, if not impossible. Not only are there times and seasons in this world, but there is also an overruling providence in our lives. From before our birth to the moment of our death, God is accomplishing His divine purposes, even though we when always understand what He is doing.

In fourteen statements, Solomon affirmed that God is at work in our individual lives, seeking to accomplish His will. All of these events come from God and they are good *in their time.* The inference is plain: if we cooperate with God's timing, life will not be meaningless. Everything will be "beautiful in His time" (v. 11), even the most difficult experiences of life. Most of these statements are easy to understand, so we will examine only those that may need special explanation.

Birth and death (v. 2). Things like abortion, birth control, mercy killing, and surrogate parenthood make it look as though man is in control of birth and death, but Solomon said otherwise. Birth and death are not human accidents; they are divine appointments, for God is in control. (Read Gen. 29:31-30:24 and 33:5; Josh. 24:3; 1 Sam. 1:9-20; Pss. 113:9 and 127; Jer. 1:4-5; Luke 1:5-25; Gal. 1:15 and 4:4.) Psalm 139:13-16 states that God so wove us in the womb that our genetic structure is perfect for the work He has prepared for us to do (Eph. 2:10). We may foolishly hasten our death, but we cannot prevent it when our time comes, unless God so wills it (Isa. 38). "All the days ordained for me were written in Your book" (Ps. 139:16, NIV).

Planting and plucking (v. 2). Being an agricultural people, the Jews appreciated the seasons. In fact, their religious calendar was based on the agricultural year

(Lev. 23). Men may plow and sow, but only God can give the increase (Ps. 65:9-13). "Plucking" may refer either to reaping or to pulling up unproductive plants. A successful farmer knows that nature works for him only if he works with nature. This is also the secret of a successful life: learn God's principles and cooperate with them.

Killing and healing (v. 3). This probably refers, not to war (v. 8) or self-defense, but to the results of sickness and plague in the land (1 Sam. 2:6). God permits some to die while others are healed. This does not imply that we should refuse medical aid, for God can use both means and miracles to accomplish His purposes (Isa. 38).

Casting away stones and gathering stones (v. 5). Tour guides in Israel will tell you that God gave stones to an angel and told him to distribute them across the world—and he tripped right over Palestine! It is indeed a rocky land and farmers must clear their fields before they can plow and plant. If you wanted to hurt an enemy, you filled up his field with stones (2 Kings 3:19, 25). People also gathered stones for building walls and houses. Stones are neither good nor bad; it all depends on what you do with them. If your enemy fills your land with rocks, don't throw them back. Build something out of them!

Embracing and refraining from embracing (v. 5). People in the Near East openly show their affections, kissing and hugging when they meet and when they part. So, you could paraphrase this, "A time to say hello and a time to say goodbye." This might also refer to the relationship of a husband and wife (Lev. 15:19-31; and see 1 Cor. 7:5).

Getting and losing (v. 6). "A time to search and a time to give it up for lost" is another translation. The next phrase gives biblical authority for garage sales: a time to keep and a time to clean house!

Tearing and mending (v. 7). This probably refers to the Jewish practice of tearing one's garments during a time of grief or repentance (2 Sam. 13:31; Ezra 9:5). God expects us to sorrow during bereavement, but not like unbelievers (1 Thess. 4:13-18). There comes a time when we must get out the needle and thread and start sewing things up!

Loving and hating (v. 8). Are God's people allowed to hate? The fact that the next phrase mentions "war and peace" suggests that Solomon may have had the nation primarily in mind. However, there are some things that even Christians ought to hate (2 Chron. 19:2; Ps. 97:10; Prov. 6:16-19; Rev. 2:6, 15).

Life is something like a doctor's prescription: taken alone, the ingredients might kill you; but properly blended, they bring healing. God is sovereignly in control and has a time and a purpose for everything (Rom. 8:28). This is not fatalism, nor does it rob us of freedom or responsibility. It is the wise providence of a loving Father Who does all things well and promises to make everything work for good.

2. Look Within: Eternity Is in Your Heart (Eccl. 3:9-14)

The Preacher adjusted his sights and no longer looked at life *only* "under the sun." He brought God into the picture and this gave him a new perspective. In verse 9, he repeated the opening question of 1:3, "Is all this labor really worth it?" In the light of "new evidence," Solomon gave three answers to the question.

First, *man's life is a gift from God (v. 10)*. In view of the travail that we experience from day to day, life may seem like a strange gift, but it is God's gift just the same. We "exercise" ourselves in trying to explain life's enigmas, but we don't always succeed. If we believingly accept life as a gift, and thank God for it, we will have a better attitude toward the burdens that come our way. If we grudgingly accept life as a burden, then we will miss the gifts that come our way. Outlook helps to determine outcome.

Second, *man's life is linked to eternity (v. 11).* Man was created in the image of God, and was given dominion over creation (Gen. 1:26-28); therefore, he is different from the rest of creation. He has "eternity ["the world," KJV] in his heart" and is linked to heaven. This explains why nobody (including Solomon) can be satisfied with his or her endeavors and achievements, or is able to explain the enigmas of life (1:12–2:11). God accomplishes His purposes in His time, but it will not be until we enter eternity that we will begin to comprehend His total plan.

Third, *man's life can be enjoyable now (vv. 12-14).* The Preacher hinted at this in 2:24 and was careful to say that this enjoyment of life is the gift of God (see 3:13; 6:2; and 1 Tim. 6:17). "The enjoyment of life" is an important theme in Ecclesiastes and is mentioned in each of the four sections of chapters 3–10. (Review the outline on pages 479–480.) Solomon is encouraging not pagan hedonism, but rather the practice of enjoying God's gifts as the fruit of one's labor, no matter how difficult life may be. Life appears to be transitory, but whatever God does is forever, so when we live for Him and let Him have His way, life is meaningful and manageable. Instead of complaining about what we don't have, let's enjoy what we do have and thank God for it.

When the well-known British Methodist preacher William Sangster learned that he had progressive muscular atrophy and could not get well, he made four resolutions and kept them to the end: (1) I will never complain; (2) I will keep the home bright; (3) I will count my blessings; (4) I will try to turn it to gain. This is the approach to life that Solomon wants us to take.

However, we must note that Solomon is not saying, "Don't worry—be happy!" He is promoting faith in God, not "faith in faith" or "pie in the sky by and by." Faith is only as good as the *object* of faith, and the greatest object of faith is the Lord. He can be trusted.

How can life be meaningless and monotonous for you when God has made you a part of His eternal plan? You are not an insignificant insect, crawling from one sad annihilation to another. If you have trusted Jesus Christ, you are a child of God being prepared for an eternal home (John 14:1-6; 2 Cor. 4). The Puritan pastor Thomas Watson said, "Eternity to the godly is a day that has no sunset; eternity to the wicked is a night that has no sunrise."

The proper attitude for us is the fear of the Lord (v. 14), which is not the cringing of a slave before a cruel master, but the submission of an obedient child to a loving parent. (See 5:7; 7:18; 8:12-13; and 12:13.) If we fear God, we need not fear anything else for He is in control.

3. Look Ahead: Death Is Coming to All (Eccl. 3:15-22)
Solomon already mentioned the certainty of death in 2:12-23, and he will bring the subject up several times before he ends his book (4:8; 5:15-16; 6:6; 8:8; 9:2-3, 12; 12:7-8). Life, death, time, and eternity: these are the "ingredients" that make up our brief experience in this world, and they must not be ignored.

Verse 15 helps us recall 1:9-11 and gives us the assurance that God is in control of the "cycle of life." The past seems to repeat itself so that "there is no new thing under the sun" (1:9), but God can break into history and do what He pleases. His many miracles are evidence that the "cycle" is a pattern and not a prison. His own Son broke into human life through a miraculous birth. He then died on a cross and rose again, thus conquering the "life-death cycle." Because Jesus Christ broke the "vicious circle," He can make us a part of a new creation that overcomes time and death (2 Cor. 5:17-21).

Solomon added a new thought here: "and God will call the past to account" (v. 15, NIV). Scholars have a difficult time agreeing on the translation of this phrase. It literally says "God seeks what hurries along." Solomon seems to say that time goes by swiftly and gets away from us; but God keeps track of it and will, at the end of time, call into account what we have done with time (12:14). This ties in with verses 16-17 where Solomon witnessed the injustices of his day and wondered why divine judgment was delayed.

"How can God be in control when there is so much evil in our world, with the wicked prospering in their sin and the righteous suffering in their obedience?" Solomon was not the first to raise that question, nor will he be the last. But once again, he comforted himself with two assurances: God has a time for everything, including judgment (see 8:6, 11), and God is working out His eternal purposes in and through the deeds of men, even the deeds of the wicked.

Yes, God will judge when history has run its course, *but God is judging now* (v. 18). In the experiences of life, God is testing man. (The word is "manifest" in the KJV. The Hebrew word means "to sift, to

winnow.") God is revealing what man is really like; He is sifting man. For, when man leaves God out of his life, he becomes like an animal. (See Ps. 32:9; Prov. 7; 2 Peter 2:19-20.) He lives like a beast and dies like a beast.

We must be careful not to misinterpret verses 19-20 and draw the erroneous conclusion that there is no difference between men and animals. Solomon merely pointed out that men and beasts have two things in common: they both die and their bodies return to the dust (Gen. 2:7; 3:19). Being made in the image of God, man has a definite advantage over animals as far as life is concerned, but when it comes to the fact of death, man has no special advantage: he too turns to dust. Of course, people who are saved through faith in Christ will one day be resurrected to have glorified bodies suitable for the new heavenly home (1 Cor. 15:35ff).

The Bible says that death occurs when the spirit leaves the body (James 2:26, and see Gen. 35:18 and Luke 8:55). In verse 21, Solomon indicates that men and animals do not have the same experience at death, even though they both turn to dust after death. Man's spirit goes to God (see 12:7), while the spirit of a beast simply ceases to exist. You find a similar contrast expressed in Psalm 49.

The Preacher closed this section by reminding us again to accept life from God's hand and enjoy it while we can (v. 22). Nobody knows what the future holds; and even if we did know, we can't return to life after we have died and start to enjoy it again. (See 6:12; 7:14; 9:3.) Knowing that God is in sovereign control of life (3:1), we can submit to Him and be at peace.

God holds the key of all unknown,
And I am glad;
If other hands should hold the key,

Or if He trusted it to me,
I might be sad.

I cannot read His future plans,
But this I know:
I have the smiling of His face,
And all the refuge of His grace,
While here below.

(J. Parker)

Faith learns to live with seeming inconsistencies and absurdities, for we live by promises and not by explanations. We can't explain life, but we must experience life, either enduring it or enjoying it.

Solomon calls us to accept life, enjoy it a day at a time, and be satisfied. *We must never be satisfied with ourselves,* but we must be satisfied with what God gives to us in this life. If we grow in character and godliness, and if we live by faith, then we will be able to say with Paul, "I have learned to be content whatever the circumstances" (Phil. 4:11, NIV).

CHAPTER FIVE
LIFE JUST ISN'T FAIR
Ecclesiastes 4

When Solomon first examined life "under the sun," his viewpoint was detached and philosophical (1:4-11); his conclusion was that life was meaningless and monotonous. But when he examined the question again, he went to where people really lived and discovered that life was not that simple. As he observed real people in real situations, the king had to deal with some painful facts, like life and death, time and eternity, and the final judgment.

Phillips Brooks, Anglican Bishop of Massachusetts a century ago, told ministerial students to read three "books": the Book of books, the Bible; the book of nature; and the book of mankind. The ivory tower investigator will never have a balanced view of his subject if he remains in his ivory tower. Learning and living must be brought together.

In this chapter, Solomon recorded his observations from visiting four different places and watching several people go through a variety of experiences. His conclusion was that life is anything but monotonous, for we have no idea what problems may come to us on any given day. No wonder he wrote, "Do not boast about tomorrow, for you do not know what a day may bring forth" (Prov. 27:1, NKJV).

1. In the Courtroom (Eccl. 4:1-3)

"Politics" has been defined as "the conduct of public affairs for private advantage." The nation of Israel had an adequate judicial system (Ex. 18:13-27; Deut. 17; 19), based on divine Law; but the system could be corrupted just like anything else (5:8). Moses warned officials to judge honestly and fairly (Lev. 19:15; Deut. 1:17), and both the prophet and the psalmist lashed out against social injustice (Ps. 82; Isa. 56:1; 59:1ff; Amos 1–2). Solomon had been a wise and just king (1 Kings 3:16-28), but it was impossible for him to guarantee the integrity of every officer in his government.

Solomon went into a courtroom to watch a trial, and there he saw innocent people being oppressed by power-hungry officials. The victims wept, but their tears did no good. Nobody stood with them to comfort or assist them. The oppressors had all the power, and their victims were helpless to protest or ask for redress.

The American orator Daniel Webster once called justice "the ligament which holds civilized beings and ... nations together." The "body politic" in Solomon's day had many a torn ligament!

The king witnessed three tragedies: (1) oppression and exploitation in the halls of justice; (2) pain and sorrow in the lives of innocent people; and (3) unconcern on the part of those who could have brought comfort. So devastated was Solomon by what he saw that he decided it was better to be dead than to be alive and oppressed. In fact, one was better off never having been born at all. Then one would never have to see the evil works of sinful man.

Why didn't Solomon do something about this injustice? After all, he was the king. Alas, even the king couldn't do a great deal to solve the problem. For once Solomon started to interfere with his government and reorganize things, he would only create new problems and reveal more corruption. This is not to suggest that we today should despair of cleaning out political corruption. As Christian citizens, we must pray for all in authority (1 Tim. 2:1-6) and do what we can to see that just laws are passed and fairly enforced. But it's doubtful that a huge administrative body like the one in Israel would ever be free of corruption, or that a "crusader" could improve the situation.

Edward Gibbon, celebrated author of *The Decline and Fall of the Roman Empire,* said that political corruption was "the most infallible symptom of constitutional liberty." Perhaps he was right; for where there is freedom to obey, there is also freedom to disobey. Some of Solomon's officials decided they were above the law, and the innocent suffered.

2. In the Marketplace (Eccl. 4:4-8)

Disgusted with what he saw in the "halls of justice," the king went down to the marketplace to watch the various laborers at work. Surely he would not be disappointed there, for honest toil is a gift from God. Even Adam had work to do in the Garden (Gen. 2:15), and our Lord was a carpenter when He was here on earth (Mark 6:3). Solomon considered four different kinds of men.

The industrious man (v. 4). It was natural for Solomon first to find a laborer who was working hard. For, after all, had not the king extolled the virtues of hard work in the book of Proverbs? The man was not only busy, but he was skillful in his work and competent in all he did. He had mastered the techniques of his trade.

So much for the worker's *hands;* what about his *heart?* It was here that Solomon had his next disappointment. The only reason these people perfected their skills and worked hard at their jobs was to compete with others and make more money than their neighbors. The purpose of their work was not to produce beautiful or useful products, or to help people, but to stay ahead of the competition and survive in the battle for bread.

God did not put this "selfishness factor" into human labor; it's the result of sin in the human heart. We covet what others have; we not only want to have those things, but we want to go beyond and have even more. Covetousness, competition, and envy often go together. Competition is not sinful of itself, but when "being first" is more important than being honest, there will be trouble. Traditional rivalry between teams or schools can be a helpful thing, but when rivalry turns into riots, sin has entered the scene.

The idle man (vv. 5-6). Solomon moved from one extreme to the other and began to study a man who had no ambition at all. Perhaps the king could learn about life by examining the antithesis, the way scientists study cold to better understand heat. It must have been difficult for him to watch an idle man, because Solomon had no sympathy for lazy people who sat all day with folded hands and did nothing. (See Prov. 18:9; 19:15; 24:30-34.)

Solomon learned nothing he didn't already know: laziness is a slow comfortable path toward self-destruction. It may be pleasant to sleep late every morning and not have to go to work, but it's unpleasant not to have money to buy the necessities of life. "'Let me sleep a little longer!' Sure, just a little more! And as you sleep, poverty creeps upon you like a robber and destroys you; want attacks you in full armor" (Prov. 6:10-11, TLB). Paul stated it bluntly: "If any would not work, neither should he eat" (2 Thess. 3:10).

The industrious man was motivated by competition and caught in the rat race of life. He had no leisure time. The idle man was motivated by pleasure and was headed for ruin. He had no productive time. Is there no middle way between these two extremes? Yes, there is.

The integrated man (v. 6). Here was a man whose life was balanced: he was productive in his work, but he was also careful to take time for quietness. He did not run in the rat race, but neither did he try to run away from the normal responsibilities of life. A 1989 Harris survey revealed that the amount of leisure time enjoyed by the average American had shrunk 37 percent from 1973. This suggests that fewer people know how to keep life in balance. They are caught in the rat race and don't know how to escape.

Why have both hands full of profit if that profit costs you your peace of mind and possibly your health? Better to have gain in one hand and quietness in the other. When a heart is controlled by envy and rivalry, life becomes one battle after another (James 3:13–4:4, and see Prov. 15:16). Paul's instructions about money in 1 Timothy 6 is applicable here, especially verse 6, "But godliness with contentment is great gain."

The industrious man thinks that money will bring him peace, but he has no time to enjoy it. The idle man thinks that doing nothing will bring him peace, but his lifestyle only destroys him. The integrated man enjoys both his labor and the fruit of his labor and balances toil with rest. You can take what you want from life, *but you must pay for it.*

The independent man (vv. 7-8). Then Solomon noticed a solitary man, very hard at work, so he went to question him. The king discovered that the man had no relatives or partners to help him in his business, nor did he desire any help. He wanted all the profit for himself. But he was so busy, he had no time to enjoy his profits. And, if he died, he had no family to inherit his wealth. In other words, all his labor was in vain.

The Greek philosopher Socrates said, "The unexamined life is not worth living." But the independent man never stopped long enough to ask himself: "For whom am I working so hard? Why am I robbing myself of the enjoyments of life just to amass more and more money?" The industrious man was at least providing employment for people, and the idle man was enjoying some leisure, but the independent man was helping neither the economy nor himself.

Solomon's conclusion was, "This, too, is meaningless—a miserable business!" (v. 8, NIV) God wants us to labor, but to labor in the right spirit and for the right reasons. Blessed are the balanced!

3. On the Highway (Eccl. 4:9-12)

Solomon's experience with the independent man caused him to consider the importance of friendship and the value of people doing things together. He may have recalled the Jewish proverb, "A friendless man is like a left hand bereft of the right." Perhaps he watched some pilgrims on the highway and drew the conclusion, "Two are better than one."

Two are certainly better than one when it comes to *working* (v. 9) because two workers can get more done. Even when they divide the profits, they still get a better return for their efforts than if they had worked alone. Also, it's much easier to do difficult jobs together because one can be an encouragement to the other.

Two are better when it comes to *walking* (v. 10). Roads and paths in Palestine were not paved or even leveled, and there were many hidden rocks in the fields. It was not uncommon for even the most experienced traveler to stumble and fall, perhaps break a bone, or even fall into a hidden pit (Ex. 21:33-34). How wonderful to have a friend who can help you up (or out). But if this applies to our *physical* falls, how much more does it apply to those times when we stumble in our *spiritual* walk and need restoration (Gal. 6:1-2)? How grateful we should be for Christian friends who help us walk straight.

Two are better than one when it comes to *warmth* (v. 11). Two travelers camping out, or even staying in the courtyard of a public inn, would feel the cold of the Palestinian night and need one another's warmth for comfort. The only way to be "warm alone" is to carry extra blankets and add to your load.

Finally, two are better than one when it comes to their *watchcare,* especially at night (v. 12). "Though one may be over-

powered, two can defend themselves" (v. 12, NIV). It was dangerous for anyone to travel alone, day or night; most people traveled in groups for fellowship and for safety. Even David was grateful for a friend who stepped in and saved the king's life (2 Sam. 21:15-17).

Solomon started with the number *one* (v. 8), then moved to *two* (v. 9), and then closed with *three* (v. 12). This is typical of Hebrew literature (Prov. 6:16; Amos 1:3, 6, 9, etc.). One cord could be broken easily; two cords would require more strength; but three cords woven together could not be easily broken. If two travelers are better than one, then three would fare even better. Solomon had more than numbers in mind; he was also thinking of the unity involved in three cords woven together—what a beautiful picture of friendship!

4. In the Palace (Eccl. 4:13-16)

This is Solomon's fourth "better" statement (4:3, 6, 9), introducing a story that teaches two truths: the instability of political power and the fickleness of popularity. The king in the story had at one time heeded his counselors' advice and ruled wisely, but when he got old, he refused to listen to them. The problem was more than pride and senility. He was probably surrounded by a collection of "parasites" who flattered him, isolated him from reality, and took from him all they could get. This often happens to weak leaders who are more concerned about themselves than about their people.

There is a hero in the story, a wise youth who is in prison. Perhaps he was there because he tried to help the king and the king resented it. Or maybe somebody in the court lied about the youth. (That's what happened to Joseph. See Gen. 39.) At any rate, the youth got out of prison and became king. Everybody cheered the underdog and rejoiced that the nation at last had wise leadership.

Consider now what this story says. The young man was born poor, but he became rich. The old king was rich, but it didn't make him any wiser, so he might just as well have been poor. The young man was in prison, but he got out and took the throne. The old king was imprisoned in his stupidity (and within his circle of sycophants) and lost his throne. So far, the moral of the story is: Wealth and position are no guarantee of success, and poverty and seeming failure are no barriers to achievement. The key is wisdom.

But the story goes on. Apparently the young man got out of prison and took the throne because of popular demand. "I have seen all the living under the sun throng to the side of the second lad who replaces him" [the old king] (v. 15, NASB). It looked like the new young king had it made, but alas, his popularity didn't last. "He can become the leader of millions of people and be very popular. But, then, the younger generation grows up around him and rejects him!" (v. 16, TLB) The new crowd deposed the king and appointed somebody else.

Oliver Cromwell, who took the British throne away from Charles I and established the Commonwealth, said to a friend, "Do not trust to the cheering, for those persons would shout as much if you and I were going to be hanged." Cromwell understood crowd psychology!

Once again, Solomon drew the same conclusion: it is all "vanity and vexation of spirit" (see vv. 4 and 8).

No matter where Solomon went, no matter what aspect of life he studied, he learned an important lesson from the Lord. When he looked up, he saw that God was in control of life and balanced its varied experiences (3:1-8). When he looked within, he saw that man was made for eternity and that God would make all things beautiful in their time (3:9-14). When he looked ahead, he saw the last enemy, death. Then as he looked around (4:1-16), he understood that life is complex, difficult, and not easy to explain. One thing is sure: No matter where you look, you see trials and problems and people who could use some encouragement.

However, Solomon was not cynical about life. Nowhere does he tell us to get out of the race and retreat to some safe and comfortable corner of the world where nothing can bother us. Life does not stand still. Life comes at us full speed, without warning, and we must stand up and take it and, with God's help, make the most of it.

If this chapter teaches us anything, it is that we need one another because "two are better than one." Yes, there are some advantages to an independent life, but there are also disadvantages, and we discover them painfully as we get older.

The chapter also emphasizes balance in life. "Better is a handful with quietness than both hands full, together with toil and grasping for the wind" (v. 6, NKJV). It's good to have the things that money can buy, provided you don't lose the things that money can't buy. What is it really costing you *in terms of life* to get the things that are important to you? How much of the permanent are you sacrificing to get your hands on the temporary?

Or, to quote the words of Jesus: "For what shall it profit a man, if he shall gain the whole world, and lose his own soul? Or what shall a man give in exchange for his soul?" (Mark 8:36-37).

CHAPTER SIX
STOP, THIEF!
Ecclesiastes 5

The magazine cartoon showed a dismal looking man walking out of a bank manager's office with the manager saying to his secretary, "He suffers from back problems: back taxes, back rent, and back alimony."

Many people today suffer from similar "back problems." They refuse to heed the warning Bill Earle gave many years ago: "When your outgo exceeds your income, your upkeep will be your downfall."

The wealthy King Solomon knew something about money. Some of this wisdom he shared in the book of Proverbs, and some he included here in Ecclesiastes. After all, he couldn't discuss "life under the sun" and ignore money!

But he goes beyond the subject of mere money and deals with the *values* of life, the things that really count. After all, there is more than one way to be rich and more than one way to be poor. In this chapter, Solomon issues three warnings that relate to the values of life.

1. Don't Rob the Lord (Eccl. 5:1-7)
Solomon had visited the courtroom, the marketplace, the highway, and the palace. Now he paid a visit to the temple, that magnificent building whose construction he had supervised. He watched the worshipers come and go, praising God, praying, sacrificing, and making vows. He noted that many of them were not at all sincere in their worship, and they left the sacred precincts in worse spiritual condition than when they had entered. What was their sin? They were robbing God of the reverence and honor that He

deserved. Their acts of worship were perfunctory, insincere, and hypocritical.

In today's language, "Keep thy foot!" means "Watch your step!" Even though God's glorious presence doesn't dwell in our church buildings as it did in the temple, believers today still need to heed this warning. *The worship of God is the highest ministry of the church and must come from devoted hearts and yielded wills.* For God's people to participate in public worship while harboring unconfessed sin is to ask for God's rebuke and judgment (Isa. 1:10-20; Amos 5; Ps. 50).

Solomon touched on several aspects of worship, the first of which was *the offering of sacrifices (v. 1).* God's people today don't offer animals to the Lord as in Old Testament times, because Jesus Christ has fulfilled all the sacrifices in His death on the cross (Heb. 10:1-14). But as the priests of God, believers today offer up spiritual sacrifices through Him: our bodies (Rom. 12:1-2); people won to the Savior (Rom. 15:16); money (Phil. 4:18); praise and good works (Heb. 13:15-16); a broken heart (Ps. 51:17); and our prayers of faith (Ps. 141:1-2).

The important thing is that the worshiper "be more ready to hear," that is, to obey the Word of God. Sacrifices are not substitutes for obedience, as King Saul found out when he tried to cover up his disobedience with pious promises (1 Sam. 15:12-23). Offerings in the hands without obedient faith in the heart become "the sacrifice of fools," because *only a fool thinks he can deceive God.* The fool thinks he is doing good, but he or she is only doing evil. And God knows it.

Then Solomon issued a warning about *careless praying (vv. 2-3).* Prayer is serious business. Like marriage, "it must not be entered into lightly or carelessly, but soberly and in the fear of God." If you and

I were privileged to bring our needs and requests to the White House or to Buckingham Palace, we would prepare our words carefully and exhibit proper behavior. How much more important it is when we come to the throne of Almighty God. Yet, there is so much flippant praying done by people who seem to know nothing about the fear of the Lord.

When you pray, watch out for both *hasty words* and *too many words* (Matt. 6:7). The secret of acceptable praying is a prepared heart (Ps. 141:1-2), because the mouth speaks what the heart contains (Matt. 12:34-37). If we pray only to impress people, we will not get through to God. The author of *Pilgrim's Progress,* John Bunyan, wrote: "In prayer, it is better to have a heart without words, than words without a heart."

Verse 3 presents an analogy: Just as many dreams show that the person sleeping is a hard worker, so many words show that the person praying is a fool (Prov. 29:20). I recall a church prayer meeting during which a young man prayed eloquently and at great length, but nobody sensed the power of God at work. When an uneducated immigrant stood up and stammered out her brief prayer in broken English, we all said a fervent "Amen!" We sensed that God had heard her requests. Spurgeon said, "It is not the length of our prayers, but the strength of our prayers, that makes the difference."

Solomon's third admonition had to do with *making vows to the Lord (vv. 4-7).* God did not require His people to make vows in order to be accepted by Him, but the opportunity was there for them to express their devotion if they felt led to do so (see Num. 30; Deut. 23:21-23; Acts 18:18).

The Preacher warned about two sins. The first was that of making the vow with no intention of keeping it, in other words, lying to God. The second sin was making the vow but delaying to keep it, hoping you could get out of it. When the priest ["angel" = messenger] came to collect the promised sacrifice or gift, the person would say, "Please forget about my vow! It was a mistake!"

God hears what we say and holds us to our promises, unless they were so foolish that He could only dismiss them. If providence prevents us from fulfilling what we promised, God understands and will release us. If we made our vows only to impress others, or perhaps to "bribe" the Lord ("If God answers my prayer, I will give $500 to missions!"), then we will pay for our careless words. Many times in my pastoral ministry I have heard sick people make promises to God as they asked for healing, only to see those promises forgotten when they recovered.

People make empty vows because they live in a religious "dream world"; they think that *words* are the same as *deeds* (v. 7). Their worship is not serious, so their words are not dependable. They enjoy the "good feelings" that come when they make their promises to God, but they do themselves more harm than good. They like to "dream" about fulfilling their vows, but they never get around to doing it. They practice a make-believe religion that neither glorifies God nor builds Christian character.

"I will go into thy house with burnt offerings; I will pay thee my vows, which my lips have uttered, and my mouth hath spoken, when I was in trouble" (Ps. 66:13-14). When we rob the Lord of the worship and honor due to Him, we are also robbing ourselves of the spiritual blessings He bestows on those who "worship Him in spirit and in truth" (John 4:24).

2. Don't Rob Others (Eccl. 5:8-9)

Solomon left the temple and went to the city hall where he again witnessed corrupt politicians oppressing the poor (3:16-17; 4:1-3). The government officials violated the law by using their authority to help themselves and not to serve others, a practice condemned by Moses (Lev. 19:15; Deut. 24:17).

The remarkable thing is that Solomon wrote, "Don't be surprised at this!" He certainly did not approve of their unlawful practices, but he knew too much about the human heart to expect anything different from the complicated bureaucracy in Israel.

The *New International Version* translation of verse 8 gives a vivid description of the situation: "One official is eyed by a higher one, and over them both are others higher still." Instead of the poor man getting a fair hearing, "the matter is lost in red tape and bureaucracy" (v. 8, TLB), and the various officials pocket the money that should have gone to the innocent poor man.

Verse 9 is difficult, and major translations do not agree. The general idea seems to be that in spite of corruption in the bureaucracy, it is better to have organized government, and a king over the land, than to have anarchy. A few dishonest people may profit from corrupt practices, but *everybody* benefits from organized authority. Of course, the ideal is to have a government that is both honest and efficient, but man's heart being what it is, the temptation to dishonest gain is always there. Lord Acton wrote to Bishop Mandell Creighton in 1887, "Power tends to corrupt; absolute power corrupts absolutely." Solomon's investigation bears this out.

3. Don't Rob Yourself (Eccl. 5:10-20)

Solomon had already discussed "the futility of wealth" in 2:1-11, and some of those ideas are repeated here. What he did in this section was demolish several of the myths that people hold about wealth. Because they hold to these illusions, they rob themselves of the blessings God has for them.

Wealth brings satisfaction (v. 10). Some people treat money as though it were a god. They love it, make sacrifices for it, and think that it can do anything. Their minds are filled with thoughts about it; their lives are controlled by getting it and guarding it; and when they have it, they experience a great sense of security. What faith in the Lord does for the Christian, money does for many unbelievers. How often we hear people say, "Well, money may not be the number one thing in life, but it's way ahead of whatever is number two!"

The person who loves money cannot be satisfied no matter how much is in the bank account—because the human heart was made to be satisfied only by God (3:11). "Take heed and beware of covetousness," warned Jesus, "for one's life does not consist in the abundance of the things which he possesses" (Luke 12:15, NKJV). First the person loves money, and then he loves *more* money, and the disappointing pursuit has begun that can lead to all sorts of problems. "For the love of money is a root of all kinds of evil" (1 Tim. 6:10, NKJV).

Money solves every problem (v. 11). There is no escaping the fact that we need a certain amount of money in order to live in this world, but money *of itself* is not the magic "cure-all" for every problem. In fact, an increase in wealth usually creates new problems that we never even knew existed before. Solomon mentioned one: relatives and friends start showing up and enjoying our hospitality. All we can do is watch them eat up our wealth. Or perhaps it is the tax agent who visits us and decides that we owe the government more money.

John Wesley, cofounder of the Methodist Church, told his people, "Make all you can, save all you can, give all you can." Wesley himself could have been a very wealthy man, but he chose to live simply and give generously.

Wealth brings peace of mind (v. 12). The late Joe Louis, world heavyweight boxing champion, used to say, "I don't like money actually, but it quiets my nerves." But Solomon said that possessing wealth is no guarantee that your nerves will be calm and your sleep sound. According to him, the common laborer sleeps better than the rich man. The suggestion seems to be that the rich man ate too much and was kept awake all night by an upset stomach. But surely Solomon had something greater in mind than that. *The Living Bible* expresses verse 12 perfectly: "The man who works hard sleeps well whether he eats little or much, but the rich must worry and suffer insomnia."

More than one preacher has mentioned John D. Rockefeller in his sermons as an example of a man whose life was almost ruined by wealth. At the age of fifty-three, Rockefeller was the world's only billionaire, earning about a million dollars a week. But he was a sick man who lived on crackers and milk and could not sleep because of worry. When he started giving his money away, his health changed radically and he lived to celebrate his ninety-eighth birthday!

Yes, it's good to have the things that money can buy, provided you don't lose the things that money can't buy.

Wealth provides security (vv. 13-17). The picture here is of two rich men. One hoarded all his wealth and ruined himself by becoming a miser. The other man made some unsound investments and

lost his wealth. He was right back where he started from and had no estate to leave to his son. He spent the rest of his days in the darkness of discouragement and defeat, and he did not enjoy life. Like all of us, he brought nothing into the world at birth, and he took nothing out of the world at death (see Job 1:21; Ps. 49:17; 1 Tim. 6:7).

This account makes us think of our Lord's parable about the Rich Fool (Luke 12:13-21). The man thought all his problems were solved when he became rich, but immediately he was faced with providing bigger barns for his wealth. He thought he was safe and secure for years to come, but that night he died! His money provided no security whatsoever.

Keep in mind that Solomon was advocating neither poverty nor riches, because both have their problems (Prov. 30:7-9). The Preacher was warning his listeners against the love of money and the delusions that wealth can bring. In the closing verses of the chapter (vv. 18-20), he affirmed once again the importance of accepting our station in life and enjoying the blessings that God gives to us.

The thing that is "good and fitting" (v. 18, NKJV) is to labor faithfully, enjoy the good things of life, and accept it all as the gracious gift of God. Solomon gave us this wise counsel before in 2:24, 3:12-13, and 3:22, and he will repeat it at least three more times before he ends his "sermon."

There are three ways to get wealth: we can work for it, we can steal it, or we can receive it as a gift (see Eph. 4:28). Solomon saw the blessings of life as God's gift to those who work and who accept that work as the favor of God. "To enjoy your work and to accept your lot in life—that is indeed a gift from God" (v. 19, TLB).

Solomon added another important thought: the ability to *enjoy* life's blessings is also a gift from God. Solomon will expand on this thought in the next chapter and point out the unhappiness of people who possess wealth but are not able to enjoy it. We thank God for food, but we should also thank Him for healthy taste buds and a digestive system that functions correctly. A wealthy friend, now in heaven, often took me and my wife to expensive restaurants, but he was unable to enjoy the food because he couldn't taste it. All of his wealth could not purchase healing for his taste buds.

Verse 20 may mean that the person who rejoices in God's daily blessings will never have regrets. "The person who does that will not need to look back with sorrow on his past, for God gives him joy" (TLB). The time to start storing up happy memories is *now*. "So teach us to number our days, that we may apply our hearts unto wisdom" (Ps. 90:12).

It may also mean that the believer who gratefully accepts God's gifts today will not fret and worry about how long he or she will live. It is an established fact that the people who have the most birthdays live the longest, but if they keep complaining about "getting old" they will have very little to enjoy. People who are thankful to God "will not dwell overmuch upon the passing years," as the *New English Bible* translates verse 20. They will take each day as it comes and use it to serve the Lord.

In chapter 6, Solomon will conclude his discussion of "the futility of wealth." He might well have chosen Matthew 6:33 as the text for his message, "But seek first the kingdom of God and His righteousness, and all these things shall be added to you" (NKJV). The important thing is that we love the Lord, accept the lot He assigns us, and enjoy the blessings He graciously bestows.

If we focus more on the gifts than on the Giver, we are guilty of idolatry. If we accept His gifts, but complain about them, we are guilty of ingratitude. If we hoard His gifts and will not share them with others, we are guilty of indulgence. But if we yield to His will and use what He gives us for His glory, then we can enjoy life and be satisfied.

CHAPTER SEVEN
IS LIFE A DEAD-END STREET?
Ecclesiastes 6

It's interesting to read the different expressions people use to picture *futility*. Solomon compared the futility of life to a soap bubble ("vanity of vanities") and to "chasing after the wind." I have read statements like: "As futile as watering a post," "As futile as plowing the rocks," "As futile as singing songs to a dead horse" (or "singing twice to a deaf man"), and "As futile as pounding water with a mortar" (or "carrying water in a sieve").

In his poem *The Task*, the hymn writer William Cowper ("There Is a Fountain") pictured futility this way:

> The toil of dropping buckets into
>   empty wells,
> and growing old in drawing nothing
>   up.

If Cowper were alive today, he might look at our "automobile society" and write:

> As futile as blind men driving cars
> down crowded dead-end streets.

Is life a dead-end street? Sometimes it seems to be, especially when we don't reach our goals or when we reach our goals but don't feel fulfilled in our achievement. More than one person in the Bible became so discouraged with life that he either wanted to die or wished he had never been born. This includes Moses (Num. 11:15), Elijah (1 Kings 19:4), Job (3:21; 7:15), Jeremiah (8:3; 15:10), and Jonah (4:3). Even the great apostle Paul despaired of life during a particularly tough time in his life (2 Cor. 1:8-11).

Perhaps the basic problem is that life confronts us with too many mysteries we can't fathom and too many puzzles we can't solve. For life to be truly satisfying, it has to make sense. When it doesn't make sense, we get frustrated. If people can't see a purpose in life, especially when they go through deep suffering, they start to question God and even wonder if life is worthwhile.

In Ecclesiastes 6, Solomon discussed three of life's mysteries: riches without enjoyment (1-6), labor without satisfaction (7-9), and questions without answers (10-12).

1. Riches Without Enjoyment (Eccl. 6:1-6)

What a seeming tragedy it is to have all the resources for a satisfying life and yet not be able to enjoy them for one reason or another. More than one person has worked hard and looked forward to a comfortable retirement only to have a heart attack and become either an invalid or a statistic. Or perhaps the peace of retirement is shattered by a crisis in the family that begins to drain both money and strength. Why do these things happen?

Solomon mentioned this subject in 5:19 and hinted at it in 3:13. To him, it was a basic principle that nobody can truly

enjoy the gifts of God apart from the God who gives the gifts. To enjoy the gifts without the Giver is idolatry, and this can never satisfy the human heart. Enjoyment without God is merely entertainment, and it doesn't satisfy. But enjoyment with God is enrichment and it brings true joy and satisfaction.

Verse 2 may describe a hypothetical situation, or it might have happened to somebody Solomon knew. The fact that God gave Solomon riches, wealth, and honor (2 Chron. 1:11) made the account even more meaningful to him. How fortunate a person would be to lack nothing, but how miserable if he or she could not enjoy the blessings of life.

What would prevent this person from enjoying life? Perhaps trouble in the home (Prov. 15:16-17; 17:1), or illness, or even death (Luke 12:20). The person described in verse 2 had no heir, so a stranger acquired the estate and enjoyed it. It all seems so futile.

What is Solomon saying to us? "Enjoy the blessings of God *now* and thank Him for all of them." Don't *plan* to live—start living now. Be satisfied with what He gives you and use it all for His glory.

Verses 3-6 surely deal with a hypothetical case, because nobody lives for two thousand years, and no monogamous marriage is likely to produce a hundred children. (Solomon's son Rehoboam had eighty-eight children, but he had eighteen wives and sixty concubines—like father, like son. (See 2 Chronicles 11:21.) The Preacher was obviously exaggerating here in order to make his point: No matter how much you possess, if you don't possess the power to enjoy it, you might just as well never have been born.

Here is a man with abundant resources and a large family, both of which, to an Old Testament Jew, were marks of God's special favor. But his family does not love him, for when he died, he was not lamented. That's the meaning of "he has no burial" (see Jer. 22:18-19). His relatives stayed around him only to use his money (5:11), and they wondered when the old man would die. When he finally did die, his surviving relatives could hardly wait for the reading of the will.

The rich man was really poor. For some reason, perhaps sickness, he couldn't enjoy his money. And he couldn't enjoy his large family because there was no love in the home. They didn't even weep when the man died. Solomon's conclusion was that it were better for this man had he never been born, or that he had been still-born (see Job 3).

Among the Jews at that time, a still-born child was not always given a name. That way, it would not be remembered. It was felt that this would encourage the parents to get over their sorrow much faster. "It [the child] comes without meaning, it departs in darkness, and in darkness its name is shrouded" (v. 4, NIV). In my pastoral ministry, broken-hearted parents and grandparents have sometimes asked, "Why did God even permit this child to be conceived if it wasn't going to live?" Solomon asked, "Why did God permit this man to have wealth and a big family if the man couldn't enjoy it?"

Some would argue that existence is better than nonexistence and a difficult life better than no life at all. Solomon might agree with them, for "a living dog is better than a dead lion" (9:4). But the problem Solomon faced was not whether existence is better than nonexistence, but whether there is any purpose behind the whole seemingly unbalanced scheme of things. As he examined life "under the sun," he could find no reason why a person should

be given riches and yet be deprived of the power to enjoy them.

The ability to enjoy life comes from within. It is a matter of character and not circumstances. "I have learned, in whatsoever state I am, therewith to be content," Paul wrote to the Philippians (4:11). The Greek word *autarkes*, translated "content," carries the idea of "self-contained, adequate, needing nothing from the outside." Paul carried *within* all the resources needed for facing life courageously and triumphing over difficulties. "I can do all things through Christ who strengthens me" (Phil. 4:13, NKJV).

The 2,000-year-old man and the still-born baby both ended up in the same place—the grave. Once again, the Preacher confronted his listeners with the certainty of death and the futility of life without God. He was preparing them for "the conclusion of the matter" when he would wrap up the sermon and encourage them to trust God (11:9–12:14).

2. Labor Without Satisfaction (Eccl. 6:7-9)

Solomon had spoken about the rich man; now he discusses the situation of the poor man. Rich and poor alike labor to stay alive. We must either produce food or earn money to buy it. The rich man can let his money work for him, but the poor man has to use his muscles if he and his family are going to eat. But even after all this labor, the appetite of neither one is fully satisfied.

Why does a person eat? So that he can add years to his life. But what good is it for me to add years to my life *if I don't add life to my years?* I'm like the birds that I watch in the backyard. They spend all their waking hours either looking for food or escaping from enemies. (We have cats in our neighborhood.) These birds are not really *living;* they are only *existing.* Yet they are fulfilling the purposes for which the Creator made them—and they even sing about it!

Solomon is not suggesting that it's wrong either to work or to eat. Many people enjoy doing both. But if life consists *only* in working and eating, then we are being controlled by our appetites and that almost puts us on the same level as animals. As far as nature is concerned, self-preservation may be the first law of life, but we who are made in the image of God must live for something higher (John 12:20-28). In the new creation (2 Cor. 5:17), self-preservation may well be the first law of death (Mark 8:34-38).

Both questions in verse 8 are answered by "None!" If all you do is live to satisfy your appetite, then the wise man has no advantage over the fool, nor does the poor man have any advantage trying to better his situation and learning to get along with the rich. Solomon is not belittling either education or self-improvement. He is only saying that these things of themselves cannot make life richer. We must have something greater for which to live.

A century ago, when the United States was starting to experience prosperity and expansion, the American naturalist Henry David Thoreau warned that men were devising "improved means to unimproved ends." He should see our world today. We can send messages around the world in seconds, but do we have anything significant to say? We can transmit pictures even from the moon, but our TV screens are stained with violence, sex, cheap advertising, and even cheaper entertainment.

Verse 9 is Solomon's version of the familiar saying, "A bird in the hand is worth two in the bush." This proverb has been around for a long time. The Greek biographer Plutarch (46–120) wrote, "He is a fool who lets slip a bird in the hand for a bird in the bush." Solomon is saying, "It's better to have little and really enjoy it than to dream about much and never attain it." Dreams have a way of becoming nightmares if we don't come to grips with reality.

Is Solomon telling us that it's wrong to dream great dreams or have a burning ambition to accomplish something in life? Of course not, but we must take care that our ambition is motivated by the glory of God and not the praise of men. We must want to serve others and not promote ourselves. If we think our achievements will automatically bring satisfaction, we are wrong. True satisfaction comes when we do the will of God from the heart (Eph. 6:6). "My food," said Jesus, "is to do the will of Him who sent Me, and to accomplish His work" (John 4:34, NASB).

Yes, in the will of God there can be riches with enjoyment and labor with satisfaction. But we must accept His plan for our lives, receive His gifts gratefully, and enjoy each day as He enables us. "Thou wilt show me the path of life. In thy presence is fullness of joy; at thy right hand there are pleasures for evermore" (Ps. 16:11).

3. Questions Without Answers (Eccl. 6:10-12)

Thus far, Solomon has said that life is a dead-end street for two kinds of people: those who have riches but no enjoyment and those who labor but have no satisfaction. But he has tried to point out that true happiness is not the automatic result of making a good living; it is the blessed by-product of making a good life. If you devote your life only to the pursuit of happiness, you will be miserable; however, if you devote your life to doing God's will, you will find happiness as well.

The British essayist and poet Joseph Addison (1672–1718) wrote, "The grand essentials to happiness in this life are something to do, someone to love, and something to hope for." Addison probably didn't have Christianity in mind when he wrote that, but we have all three in Jesus Christ!

The Preacher was not finished. He knew that life was also a dead-end street for a third kind of person—the person who required answers to all of life's questions. Solomon was not condemning honest inquiry, because Ecclesiastes is the record of his own investigation into the meaning of life. Rather, Solomon was saying, "There are some questions about life that nobody can answer. But our ignorance must not be used as an excuse for skepticism or unbelief. Instead, our ignorance should encourage us to have faith in God. After all, we don't live on explanations; we live on promises."

It's been my experience in pastoral ministry that most explanations don't solve personal problems or make people feel better. When the physician explains an X-ray to a patient, his explanation doesn't bring healing, although it is certainly an essential step toward recovery. Suffering Job kept arguing with God and demanding an explanation for his plight. God never did answer his questions, because knowledge in the mind does not guarantee healing for the heart. That comes only when we put faith in the promises of God.

Without going into great detail, in verses 10-12 Solomon touches on five questions that people often ask.

Since "what's going to be is going to be," why bother to make decisions? Isn't it all predestined anyway? "Whatever exists has already been named, and what man is has been known" (v. 10a, NIV). To the Jewish

mind, giving a name to something is the same as fixing its character and stating what the thing really is. During the time of creation, God named the things that He made, and nobody changed those designations. "Light" is "light" and not "darkness"; "day" is "day" and not "night." (See Isa. 5:20.)

Our name is "man"—Adam, "from the earth" (Gen. 2:7). Nobody can change that: we came from the earth and we will return to the earth (Gen. 3:19). "Man" by any other name would still be "man," made from the dust and eventually returning to the dust.

The fact that God has named everything does not mean that our world is a prison and we have no freedom to act. Certainly God can accomplish His divine purposes with or without our cooperation, but He invites us to work with Him. We cooperate with God as we accept the "names" He has given to things: sin is sin; obedience is obedience; truth is truth. If we alter these names, we move into a world of illusion and lose touch with reality. This is where many people are living today.

We are free to decide and choose our world, *but we are not free to change the consequences.* If we choose a world of illusion, we start living on substitutes, and there can be no satisfaction in a world of substitutes. "And this is eternal life, that they may know Thee, the only true God, and Jesus Christ whom Thou hast sent" (John 17:3, NASB). "And we know that the Son of God has come, and has given us understanding, in order that we might know Him who is true, and we are in Him who is true, in His Son Jesus Christ. This is the true God and eternal life" (1 John 5:20, NASB).

Why disagree with God? We can't oppose Him and win, can we? "...neither may he contend with him that is mightier than he" (v. 10b). The word translated "contend" also means "dispute." Solomon seems to say, "It just doesn't pay to argue with God or to fight God. This is the way life is, so just accept it and let God have His way. You can't win, and even if you do think you win, you ultimately lose."

But this is a negative view of the will of God. It gives the impression that God's will is a difficult and painful thing that should be avoided at all cost. Jesus said that God's will was the food that nourished and satisfied Him (John 4:32-34). It was meat, not medicine. The will of God comes from the heart of God and is an expression of the love of God. (See Ps. 33:11.) What God wills for us is best for us, because He knows far more about us than we do.

Why would anyone want to have his or her "own way" just for the privilege of exercising "freedom"? Insisting on having our own way isn't freedom at all; it's the worst kind of bondage. In fact, the most terrible judgment we could experience in this life would be to have God "give us up" and let us have our own way (Rom. 1:24, 26, 28).

God is free to act as He sees best. He is not a prisoner of His attributes, His creation, or His eternal purposes. You and I may not understand how God exercises His freedom, but it isn't necessary for us to know all. Our greatest freedom comes when we are lovingly lost in the will of God. Our Father in heaven doesn't feel threatened when we question Him, debate with Him, or even wrestle with Him, so long as we love His will and want to please Him.

What do we accomplish with all these words? Does talking about it solve the problem? (v. 11). In fact, there are times when it seems like the more we discuss a subject, the less we really understand it. Words don't always bring light; sometimes they produce clouds and even darkness. "The more the words, the less the meaning"(v. 11, NIV). But this is where we need the Word of God and the wisdom He alone can give us. If some discussions appear useless and produce "vanity," there are other times when conversation leads us closer to the truth and to the Lord.

Who knows what is good for us? (v. 12). God does! And wise is the person who takes time to listen to what God has to say. Yes, life may seem to be fleeting and illusive, like a soap bubble ("vain") or a shadow, but "he who does the will of God abides forever" (1 John 2:17, NKJV).

Does anybody know what's coming next? (v. 12b). In spite of what the astrologers, prophets, and fortune-tellers claim, nobody knows the future except God. It is futile to speculate. God gives us enough information to encourage us, but He does not cater to idle curiosity. One thing is sure: death is coming, and we had better make the best use of our present opportunities. That is one of the major themes in Ecclesiastes.

Solomon has discussed two of his arguments that life is not worth living: the monotony of life (3:1–5:9) and the futility of wealth (5:10–6:12). He has discovered that life "under the sun" can indeed be monotonous and empty, but it need not be *if we include God in our lives*. Life is God's gift to us, and we must accept what He gives us and enjoy it while we can (3:12–15, 22; 5:18–20).

Solomon will next take up his third argument, the vanity of man's wisdom (7:1–8:17), and discuss whether or not wisdom can make life any better. Though wisdom can't explain all the problems or answer all the questions, it is still a valuable ally on the journey of life.

CHAPTER EIGHT
HOW TO BE BETTER OFF
Ecclesiastes 7

Where ignorance is bliss, 'tis folly to be wise." Thomas Gray wrote those oft-quoted words in his poem "Ode on a Distant Prospect of Eton College." He pictured the students on the playing field and in the classroom, enjoying life because they were innocent of what lay ahead.

> Alas, regardless of their doom,
> The little victims play!
> No sense have they of ills to come,
> Nor care beyond today.

His conclusion was logical: at that stage in life, it is better to be ignorant and happy, because there will be plenty of time later to experience the sorrows that knowledge may bring.

> Yet ah! why should they know their
> fate?
> Since sorrow never comes too late,
> And happiness too swiftly flies.
> Thought would destroy their para-
> dise.
> No more; where ignorance is bliss,
> 'Tis folly to be wise.

Solomon had come to a similar conclusion when he argued in 1:12-18 that wisdom did not make life worth living. "For in much wisdom is much grief," he wrote in 1:18, "and he that increaseth knowledge, increaseth sorrow."

But then the king took a second look at the problem and modified his views. In Ecclesiastes 7 and 8, he discussed the importance of wisdom in life ("wisdom" is found fourteen times in these two chapters); and he answered the question asked in 6:12, "For who knoweth what is good for man in this life?" The Preacher concluded that, though wisdom can't explain all of life's mysteries, it can make at least three positive contributions to our lives.

1. Wisdom Can Make Life Better (Eccl. 7:1-10)

"Better" is a key word in this chapter; Solomon used it at least eleven times. His listeners must have been shocked when they heard Solomon describe the "better things" that come to the life of the person who follows God's wisdom.

Sorrow is better than laughter (7:1-4). If given the choice, most people would rather go to a birthday party than to a funeral, but Solomon advised against it. Why? Because sorrow can do more good for the heart than laughter can. (The word "heart" is used four times in these verses.) Solomon was certainly not a morose man with a gloomy lifestyle. After all, it was King Solomon who wrote Proverbs 15:13, 15; 17:22—*and* the Song of Solomon! Laughter can be like medicine that heals the broken heart, but sorrow can be like nourishing food that strengthens the inner person. It takes both for a balanced life, but few people realize this. There is "a time to laugh" (Eccl. 3:4).

Let's begin with Solomon's bizarre statement that the day of one's death is better than the day of one's birth (v. 1). This generalization must not be divorced from his opening statement that a person's good reputation (name) is like a fragrant perfume. (There is a play on words here: "name" is *shem* in the Hebrew and "ointment" is *shemen*.) He used the same image in 10:1 and also in Song of Solomon 1:3.

Solomon was not contrasting *birth* and *death*, nor was he suggesting that it is better to die than to be born, because you can't die unless you have been born. He was contrasting two significant days in human experience: the day a person receives his or her name and the day when that name shows up in the obituary column. The life lived between those two events will determine whether that name leaves behind a lovely fragrance or a foul stench. "His name really stinks!" is an uncouth statement, but it gets the point across.

If a person dies with a good name, his or her reputation is sealed and the family need not worry. In that sense, the day of one's death is better than the day of one's birth. The life is over and the reputation is settled. (Solomon assumed that there were no hidden scandals.) "Every man has three names," says an ancient adage; "one his father and mother gave him, one others call him, and one he acquires himself."

"The memory of the just is blessed, but the name of the wicked shall rot" (Prov. 10:7, and see Prov. 22:1). Mary of Bethany anointed the Lord Jesus with expensive perfume and its fragrance filled the house. Jesus told her that her name would be honored throughout the world, and it is. On the other hand, Judas sold the Lord Jesus into the hands of the enemy; and his name is generally despised (Mark 14:1-11). When Judas was born, he was given the good name "Judah," which means "praise." It belonged to the royal tribe in Israel. By the time Judas died, he had turned that honorable name into something shameful.

In verses 2-4, Solomon advised the people to look death in the face and learn from it. He did not say that we should be *preoccupied* with death, because that could be abnormal. But there is a danger that we might try to avoid confrontations with the reality of death and, as a result, not take life as seriously as we should. "So teach us to number our days, that we may apply our hearts unto wisdom" (Ps. 90:12).

The Preacher is not presenting us with an either/or situation; he is asking for balance. The Hebrew word for "laughter" in verse 3 can mean "the laughter of derision or scorn." While there is a place for healthy humor in life, we must beware of the frivolous laughter that is often found in "the house of mirth" (v. 4). When people jest about death, for example, it is usually evidence that they are afraid of it and not prepared to meet it. They are running away.

The late Dr. Ernest Becker wrote in his Pulitzer Prize-winning book *The Denial of Death*, "...the idea of death, the fear of it, haunts the human animal like nothing else; it is a mainspring of human activity—activity designed largely to avoid the fatality of death, to overcome it by denying in some way that it is the final destiny for man" (Free Press, 1975, p. ix). King Solomon knew this truth centuries ago!

Rebuke is better than praise (7:5-6). King Solomon compared the praise of fools to the burning thorns in a campfire: you hear a lot of noise, but you don't get much lasting good. (Again, Solomon used a play on words. In the Hebrew, "song" is *shir*, "pot" is *sir*, and "thorns" is *sirim*.) If we allow it, a wise person's rebuke will accomplish far more in our lives than will the flattery of fools. Solomon may have learned this truth from his father (Ps. 141:5), and he certainly emphasized it when he wrote the book of Proverbs (10:17; 12:1; 15:5; 17:10; 25:12; 27:5, 17; 29:1, 15).

The British literary giant Samuel Johnson was at the home of the famous actor David Garrick, and a "celebrated lady" persisted in showering Johnson with compliments. "Spare me, I beseech you, dear madam!" he replied; but as his biographer Boswell put it, "She still laid it on." Finally Johnson silenced her by saying, "Dearest lady, consider with yourself what your flattery is worth, before you bestow it so freely."

The "long haul" is better than the shortcut (7:7-9). Beware of "easy" routes; they often become expensive detours that are difficult and painful. In 1976, my wife and I were driving through Scotland, and a friend mapped out a "faster" route from Balmoral Castle to Inverness. It turned out to be a hazardous one-lane road that the local people called "The Devil's Elbow," and en route we met a bus and a cement truck! "Watch and pray" was our verse for that day.

Bribery appears to be a quick way to get things done (v. 7), but it only turns a wise man into a fool and encourages the corruption already in the human heart. Far better that we wait patiently and humbly for God to work out His will than that we get angry and demand our own way (v. 8). (See also Prov. 14:17; 16:32; and James 1:19.)

"Better is the end of a thing than the beginning" applies when we are living according to God's wisdom. The beginning of sin leads to a terrible end—death (James 1:13-15), but if God is at the beginning of what we do, He will see to it that we reach the ending successfully (Phil. 1:6; Heb. 12:2). The Christian believer can claim Romans 8:28 because he knows that God is at work in the world, accomplishing His purposes.

An Arab proverb says, "Watch your beginnings." Good beginnings will usually mean good endings. The Prodigal Son started with happiness and wealth, but ended with suffering and poverty (Luke 15:11-24). Joseph began as a slave but ended up a sovereign! God always saves "the best wine" until the last (John 2:10), but Satan starts with his "best" and then leads the sinner into suffering and perhaps even death.

Today is better than yesterday (7:10). When life is difficult and we are impatient for change, it is easy to long for "the good old days" when things were better. When the foundation was laid for the second temple, the old men wept for "the good old days" and the young men sang because the work had begun (Ezra 3:12-13). It has been said that "the good old days" are the combination of a bad memory and a good imagination, and often this is true.

Yesterday is past and cannot be changed, and tomorrow may not come, so make the most of today. *"Carpe diem!"* wrote the Roman poet Horace. "Seize the day!" This does not mean we shouldn't learn from the past or prepare for the future, because both are important. It means that we must live *today* in the will of God and not be paralyzed by yesterday or hypnotized by tomorrow. The Victorian essayist Hilaire Belloc wrote, "While you are dreaming of the future or regretting the past, the present, which is all you have, slips from you and is gone."

2. Wisdom Helps Us See Life Clearly (Eccl. 7:11-18)

One of the marks of maturity is the ability to look at life in perspective and not get out of balance. When you have God's wisdom, you will be able to accept and deal with the changing experiences of life.

Wealth (7:11-12). Wisdom is better than a generous inheritance. Money can lose its value, or be stolen, but true wisdom keeps its value and cannot be lost, unless we become fools and abandon it deliberately. The person who has wealth but lacks wisdom will only waste his fortune, but the person who has wisdom will know how to get and use wealth. We should be grateful for the rich treasure of wisdom we have inherited from the past, and we should be ashamed of ourselves that we too often ignore it or disobey it. Wisdom is like a "shelter" to those who obey it; it gives greater protection than money.

Providence (7:13). The rustic preacher who said to his people, "Learn to cooperate with the inevitable!" knew the meaning of this verse. *The Living Bible* paraphrases it, "See the way God does things and fall into line. Don't fight the facts of nature." This is not a summons to slavish fatalism; like Ecclesiastes 1:15, it is a sensible invitation to a life yielded to the will of God. If God makes something crooked, He is able to make it straight; and perhaps He will ask us to work with Him to get the job done. But if He wants it to stay crooked, we had better not argue with Him. We don't fully understand all the works of God (11:5), but we do know that "He hath made everything beautiful in its time" (3:11). This includes the things we may think are twisted and ugly.

While I don't agree with all of his theology, I do appreciate the "Serenity Prayer" written in 1934 by Reinhold Niebuhr. A version of it is used around the world by people in various support groups, such as Alcoholics Anonymous, and it fits the lesson Solomon teaches in verse 13:

O God, give us
Serenity to accept what cannot be
changed,
Courage to change what should be
changed,
And wisdom to distinguish the one
from the other.

Adversity and prosperity (7:14). Wisdom gives us perspective so that we aren't discouraged when times are difficult or arrogant when things are going well. It takes a good deal of spirituality to be able to accept prosperity as well as adversity, for often prosperity does greater damage (Phil. 4:10-13). Job reminded his wife of this truth when she told him to curse God and die: "What? Shall we receive good at the hand of God, and shall we not receive evil [trouble]?" (2:10). Earlier, Job had said, "The Lord gave, and the Lord hath taken away; blessed be the name of the Lord" (1:21).

God balances our lives by giving us enough blessings to keep us happy and enough burdens to keep us humble. If all we had were blessings in our hands, we would fall right over, so the Lord balances the blessings in our hands with burdens on our backs. That helps to keep us steady, and as we yield to Him, He can even turn the burdens into blessings.

Why does God constitute our lives in this way? The answer is simple: to keep us from thinking we know it all and that we can manage our lives by ourselves. "Therefore, a man cannot discover anything about his future" (v. 14, NIV). Just about the time we think we have an explanation for things, God changes the situation, and we have to throw out our formula. This is where Job's friends went wrong: they tried to use an old road map to guide Job on a brand new journey, and the map didn't fit. No matter how much experience we have in the Christian life, or how many books we read, we must still walk by faith.

Righteousness and sin (7:15-18). If there is one problem in life that demands a mature perspective, it is "Why do the righteous suffer and the wicked prosper?" The good die young while the wicked seem to enjoy long lives, and this seems contrary to the justice of God and the Word of God. Didn't God tell the people that the obedient would live long (Ex. 20:12; Deut. 4:40) and the disobedient would perish? (Deut. 4:25-26; Ps. 55:23).

Two facts must be noted. Yes, God did promise to bless Israel in their land if they obeyed His law, but He has not given those same promises to believers today under the new covenant. Francis Bacon (1561–1626) wrote, "Prosperity is the blessing of the Old Testament; adversity is the blessing of the New." Our Lord's opening words in the Sermon on the Mount were not "Blessed are the rich in substance" but "Blessed are the poor in spirit" (Matt. 5:3, and see Luke 6:20).

Second, the wicked appear to prosper *only if you take the short view of things.* This was the lesson Asaph recorded in Psalm 73 and that Paul reinforced in Romans 8:18 and 2 Corinthians 4:16-18. "They have their reward" (Matt. 6:2, 5, 16), and that reward is all they will ever get. They may gain the whole world, but they lose their own souls. This is the fate of all who follow their example and sacrifice the eternal for the temporal.

Verses 16-18 have been misunderstood by those who say that Solomon was teaching "moderation" in everyday life: don't be too righteous, but don't be too great a sinner. "Play it safe!" say these cautious philosophers, but this is not what Solomon wrote.

In the Hebrew text, the verbs in verse 16 carry the idea of reflexive action. Solomon said to the people, "Don't claim to be righteous and don't claim to be wise." In other words, he was warning them against *self-righteousness and the pride that comes when we think we have*

"arrived" and know it all. Solomon made it clear in verse 20 that there are no righteous people, so he cannot be referring to true righteousness. He was condemning the self-righteousness of the hypocrite and the false wisdom of the proud, and he warned that these sins led to destruction and death.

Verse 18 balances the warning: we should take hold of true righteousness and should not withdraw from true wisdom, and the way to do it is to walk in the fear of God. "The fear of the Lord is the beginning of wisdom" (Prov. 9:10), and Jesus Christ is to the believer "wisdom and righteousness" (1 Cor. 1:30), so God's people need not "manufacture" these blessings themselves.

3. Wisdom Helps Us Face Life Stronger (Eccl. 7:19-29)

"Wisdom makes one wise man more powerful than ten rulers in a city" (v. 19, NIV). The wise person fears the Lord and therefore does not fear anyone or anything else (Ps. 112). He walks with the Lord and has the adequacy necessary to face the challenges of life, including war (see 9:13-18).

What are some of the problems in life that we must face and overcome? Number one on the list is *sin*, because nobody on earth is sinless *(v. 20, and note 1 Kings 8:46).* We are all guilty of both sins of omission ("doeth good") and sins of commission ("sinneth not"). If we walk in the fear of God and follow His wisdom, we will be able to detect and defeat the wicked one when he comes to tempt us. Wisdom will guide us and guard us in our daily walk.

Another problem we face is *what people say about us (vv. 21-22).* The wise person pays no attention to the gossip of the day because he has more important matters which to attend. Charles Spurgeon told his pastoral students that the minister ought to have one blind eye and one deaf ear. "You cannot stop people's tongues," he said, "and therefore the best thing to do is to stop your own ears and never mind what is spoken. There is a world of idle chitchat abroad, and he who takes note of it will have enough to do" (*Lectures to My Students;* Marshall, Morgan, and Scott reprint edition, 1965, p. 321). Of course, if we are honest, we may have to confess that we have done our share of talking about others! (See Ps. 38 and Matt. 7:1-3.)

A third problem is *our inability to grasp the meaning of all that God is doing in this world (vv. 23-25, and see 3:11 and 8:17).* Even Solomon with all his God-given wisdom could not understand all that exists, how God manages it, and what purposes He has in mind. He searched for the "reason [scheme] of things" but found no final answers to all his questions. However, the wise man knows that he does not know, and this is what helps to make him wise!

Finally, the wise person must deal with *the sinfulness of humanity in general (vv. 26-29).* Solomon began with the sinful woman, the prostitute who traps men and leads them to death (v. 26, and see Prov. 2:16-19; 5:3-6; 6:24-26; and 7:5-27). Solomon himself had been snared by many foreign women who enticed him away from the Lord and into the worship of heathen gods (1 Kings 11:3-8). The way to escape this evil woman is to fear God and seek to please Him.

Solomon concluded that the whole human race was bound by sin and one man in a thousand was wise—and not one woman! (The number 1,000 is significant in the light of 1 Kings 11:3.) We must not think that Solomon rated women as less intelligent than men, because this is not the case. He spoke highly of women in Proverbs (12:4; 14:1; 18:22; 19:14; and 31:10ff), Ecclesiastes (9:9), and certainly in the Song of Solomon. In the book of Proverbs, Solomon even pictured God's wisdom as a beautiful woman (1:20ff; 8:1ff; 9:1ff). But keep in mind that women in that day had neither the freedom nor the status that they have today, and it would be unusual for a woman to have learning equal to that of a man. It was considered a judgment of God for women to rule over the land (Isa. 3:12, but remember Miriam and Deborah, two women who had great leadership ability).

God made man (Adam) upright, but Adam disobeyed God and fell, and now all men are sinners who seek out many clever inventions. Created in the image of God, man has the ability to understand and harness the forces God put into nature, but he doesn't always use this ability in constructive ways. Each forward step in science seems to open up a Pandora's box of new problems for the world, until we now find ourselves with the problems of polluted air and water and depleted natural resources. And besides that, man has used his abilities to devise alluring forms of sin that are destroying individuals and nations.

Yes, there are many snares and temptations in this evil world, but the person with godly wisdom will have the power to overcome. Solomon has proved his point: wisdom can make our lives better and clearer and stronger. We may not fully understand all that God is doing, but we will have enough wisdom to live for the good of others and the glory of God.

CHAPTER NINE
WHAT ABOUT THE WICKED?
Ecclesiastes 8

As King Solomon continued to investigate the value of wisdom, he came face to face with the problem of evil in the world, a problem that no thinking person can honestly avoid. It is not *unbelief* that creates this problem, but *faith*. If there is no God, then we have nobody to blame but ourselves (or fate) for what happens in the world. But if we believe in a good and loving God, we must face the difficult question of why there is so much suffering in the world. Does God know about it and yet not care? Or does He know and care but lack the power to do anything about it?

Some people ponder this question and end up becoming either agnostics or atheists, but in so doing, they create a whole new problem: "Where does all the *good* come from in the world?" It's difficult to believe that matter *alone* produced the beautiful and enjoyable things we have in our world, even in the midst of so much evil.

Other people solve the problem by saying that evil is only an illusion and we shouldn't worry about it, or that God is in the process of "evolving" and can't do much about the tragedies of life. They assure us that God will get stronger and things will improve as the process of evolution goes on.

Solomon didn't deny the existence of God or the reality of evil, nor did he limit the power of God. Solomon solved the problem of evil by affirming these factors *and seeing them in their proper perspective.* We must not forget that one major source of evil in this world is fallen man and his "many devices," both good and evil, that have helped to create problems of one kind or another (7:29, NASB). God certainly can't be blamed for that!

During the darkest days of World War II, somebody asked a friend of mine, "Why doesn't God stop the war?" My friend wisely replied, "Because He didn't start it in the first place." Solomon would have agreed with that answer.

The Preacher explored the problem of evil in the world by examining three key areas of life.

1. Authority (Eccl. 8:1-9)

Beginning with Nimrod (Gen. 10:8-9) and continuing over the centuries through Pharaoh, Sennacherib, Nebuchadnezzar, Darius, the Caesars, and the latest petty dictator, millions of good people have been oppressed in one way or another by bad rulers. The Jews often suffered at the hands of foreign oppressors, and Solomon himself had been guilty of putting his own people under a heavy yoke of bondage (1 Kings 4:7-28; 12:1ff).

Keep in mind that Eastern rulers in that day held the power of life and death in their hands and often used that power capriciously. They were not elected by the people nor were they answerable to them. Some leaders ruled as benevolent dictators, but for the most part rulers in the ancient East were tyrannical despots who permitted nothing to stand in the way of fulfilling their desires.

Solomon described an officer in the royal court, a man who had to carry out the orders of a despotic ruler. The officer had wisdom; in fact, it showed on his face (v. 1, and see Neh. 2:1ff and Prov. 15:13). Suppose the king commanded the servant to do something evil, something that the servant did not want to do? What should the servant do? Here is where wisdom comes to his aid. His wisdom told him that there were four possible approaches he could take to this problem.

Disobedience. But Solomon's admonition was, "Keep the king's commandment" *(v. 2).* Why? To begin with, the officer must be true to his oath of allegiance to the king and to God, who is the source of all authority in this world (Rom. 13). To disobey orders would mean breaking his promise to the ruler and to God, and that has serious consequences.

The king's word would have more power than the word of his servant (v. 4) and was bound to prevail, even if the king had to eliminate the opposition. Nobody could safely question the ruler's decisions because "the king can do no wrong." There was no law that could find the king guilty.

Third, the officer should obey orders so that he might avoid punishment (v. 5a). After all, his disobedience could lead to his death (see Dan. 4). Paul used a similar argument in Romans 13:3-4. We all have enough misery, so why add to it (v. 7)? Furthermore, since nobody can predict the future, we don't know how the king will respond to our decisions.

One thing is sure: a day is coming when wickedness will be judged (v. 8b), and even kings will not escape. Nobody can control the wind or prevent the day of his death ("wind" and "spirit" are the same word in the Hebrew), and nobody can get discharged from the army when a war is on. Likewise, nobody can stop the inexorable working of God's law, "Whatever a man sows, that he will also reap" (Gal. 6:7, NKJV). "Be sure your sin will find you out" (Num. 32:23).

But suppose the servant simply cannot obey his master? Then the servant must consider the other possibilities.

Desertion (v. 3a). You can just see the officer leaving the king's presence in disgust and giving up his position in court. Even this action may not be safe since the king might be offended and punish the man anyway. But more than one person has quit a job or resigned from office in order to maintain his or her integrity. I recall chatting with a Christian press operator who left a fine job with a large printing firm because the company had decided to start printing pornographic magazines. He lost some income, but he kept his character.

Defiance (v. 3b). "Do not stand up for a bad cause" (NIV) can mean "Don't promote the king's evil plan" or "Don't get involved in a plan to overthrow the king." I prefer the second interpretation because it goes right along with the first admonition in verse 3. The officer rushes from the king's presence, finds others who are opposed to the king's plans, and with them begins to plot against the crown. Solomon did not approve of this approach.

Is there ever a place for "civil disobedience" in the life of the believer? Do law-abiding citizens have the right to resist authority when they feel the law is not just? Thomas Jefferson wrote, "Resistance to tyrants is obedience to God." Was he right?

When it comes to matters of conscience and the law, devoted believers have pretty much agreed with Peter: "We ought to obey God rather than men" (Acts 5:29). Christian prisoners and martyrs down through the ages testify to the courage of conscience and the importance of standing up for what is right. This doesn't mean we can resist the law on every minor matter that disturbs us, but it does mean we have the obligation to obey our conscience. How we express our disagreement with the authorities demands wisdom and grace; this is where the fourth possibility comes in.

Discernment (vv. 5b-6). The wise servant understands that "time and judgment [procedure, NASB]" must be considered in everything we do, because it takes discernment to know the right procedure for the right time. The impulsive person who overreacts and storms out of the room (v. 3) is probably only making the problem worse. Wisdom helps us understand people and situations and to figure out the right thing to do at the right time. "The wise heart will know the proper time and procedure" (v. 5b, NIV).

This is illustrated beautifully in the lives of several Old Testament believers. Joseph didn't impulsively reveal to his brothers who he was, because he wanted to be sure their hearts were right with their father and their God. Once he heard them confess their sins, Joseph knew it was the right time to identify himself. His handling of this delicate matter was a masterpiece of wisdom (see Gen. 43–45).

Nehemiah was burdened to rebuild the walls of Jerusalem, but he was not sure the king would release him for the task (Neh. 1–2). He waited and watched and prayed, knowing that God would one day open the way for him. When the opportune hour came, Nehemiah was ready and the king granted him his request. Nehemiah knew how to discern "time and procedure."

A prisoner of war in a Gentile land, Daniel refused to eat the unclean food set before him, but he didn't make a big scene about it. Instead, he exercised gentleness and wisdom by suggesting that the guards permit the Jews to experiment with a different diet. The plan worked and Daniel and his friends not only kept themselves ceremonially clean, but they were promoted in the king's court (see Dan. 1).

The apostles exercised spiritual discernment when they were arrested and persecuted (Acts 4–5). They showed respect toward those in authority even though the religious leaders were prejudiced and acted illegally. The apostles were even willing to suffer for their faith, and the Lord honored them.

We have the options of disobeying, running away, defying orders, and even fighting back. But before we act, we must first exercise wisdom and seek to discern the right "time and procedure." It's not easy to be a consistent Christian in this complicated evil world, but we can ask for the wisdom of God and receive it by faith (James 1:5; 3:17-18).

2. Inequity (Eccl. 8:10-14)

Solomon summarized his concern in verse 14: "righteous men who get what the wicked deserve, and wicked men who get what the righteous deserve" (NIV). In spite of good laws and fine people who seek to enforce them, there is more injustice in this world than we care to admit. A Spanish proverb says, "Laws, like the spider's web, catch the fly and let the hawks go free." According to famous trial lawyer F. Lee Bailey, "In America, an acquittal doesn't mean you're innocent; it means you beat the rap." His definition is a bit cynical, but poet Robert Frost defined a jury as "twelve persons chosen to decide who has the better lawyer."

In verse 10, Solomon reported on a funeral he had attended. The deceased was a man who had frequented the temple ("the place of the holy") and had received much praise from the people, but he had not lived a godly life. Yet he was given a magnificent funeral, with an eloquent eulogy, while the truly godly people of the city were ignored and forgotten.

As he reflected on the matter, Solomon

realized that the deceased man had continued in his sin because he thought he was getting away with it (v. 11). God is indeed longsuffering toward sinners and doesn't always judge sin immediately (2 Peter 3:1-12). However, God's mercy must not be used as an excuse for man's rebellion.

The Preacher concluded that the wicked will eventually be judged and the righteous will be rewarded (vv. 12-13), so it is better to fear the Lord and live a godly life. The evil man may live longer than the godly man. He may appear to get away with sin after sin, but the day of judgment will come and the wicked man will not escape. It is wisdom that points the way; for "the fear of the Lord is the beginning of wisdom" (Prov. 9:10).

No matter how long or full the wicked man's life may seem to be, it is only prolonged like a shadow and has no substance (v. 13). In fact, the shadows get longer as the sun is setting. Solomon may be suggesting that the long life of the wicked man is but a prelude to eternal darkness. What good is a long life if it is only a shadow going into the blackness of darkness forever (Jude 13)?

How should the wise person respond to the inequities and injustices in this world? Certainly we should do all we can to encourage the passing of good laws and the enforcement of them by capable people, but even this will not completely solve the problem. Until Jesus Christ sets up His righteous kingdom, there will always be injustices in our world. It is one of the "vanities" of life, and we must accept it without becoming pessimistic or cynical.

3. Mystery (Eccl. 8:15-17)

The person who has to know everything, or who thinks he knows everything, is destined for disappointment in this world. Through many difficult days and sleepless nights, the Preacher applied himself diligently to the mysteries of life. He came to the conclusion that "man cannot find out the work that is done under the sun" (v. 17; see 3:11; 7:14, 24, 27-28). Perhaps we can solve a puzzle here and there, but no man or woman can comprehend the totality of things or explain all that God is doing.

Historian Will Durant surveyed human history in his multivolume *Story of Civilization* and came to the conclusion that "our knowledge is a receding mirage in an expanding desert of ignorance." Of course, this fact must not be used as an excuse for stupidity. "The secret things belong unto the Lord our God, but those things which are revealed belong unto us and to our children forever, that we may do all the words of this law" (Deut. 29:29). God doesn't expect us to know the unknowable, but He does expect us to learn all that we can and obey what He teaches us. In fact, the more we obey, the more He will teach us (John 7:17).

A confession of ignorance is the first step toward true knowledge. "And if anyone thinks that he knows anything, he knows nothing yet as he ought to know" (1 Cor. 8:2, NKJV). The person who wants to learn God's truth must possess honesty and humility. Harvard philosopher Alfred North Whitehead said, "Not ignorance, but ignorance of ignorance, is the death of knowledge."

The French philosopher Blaise Pascal wrote in his famous *Pensees* (#446): "If there were no obscurity, man would not feel his corruption; if there were no light, man could not hope for a cure. Thus it is not only right but useful for us that God should be partly concealed and partly revealed, since it is equally dangerous for man to know God without knowing his own wretchedness as to know his wretchedness without knowing God."

For the fourth time, Solomon told his congregation to enjoy life and delight in the fruit of their labors (v. 15; see 2:24; 3:12-15; and 5:18-20). Remember, this admonition is not the foolish "eat, drink, and be merry" philosophy of the unbelieving hedonist. Rather, it is the positive "faith outlook" of God's children who accept life as God's special gift and know that He gives us "all things richly to enjoy" (1 Tim. 6:17). Instead of complaining about what we don't have, we give thanks for what we do have and enjoy it.

This ends Solomon's re-examination of "the vanity of wisdom" (1:12-18). Instead of rejecting wisdom, the king concluded that wisdom is important to the person who wants to get the most out of life. While wisdom can't explain every mystery or solve every problem, it can help us exercise discernment in our decisions. "Yes, there is a time and a way for everything" (8:6, TLB), and the wise person knows what to do at just the right time.

CHAPTER TEN
MEETING YOUR LAST ENEMY
Ecclesiastes 9

"Oh why do people waste their breath
Inventing dainty names for death?"

John Betjeman, the late Poet Laureate of England, wrote those words in his poem "Graveyards." Every honest person can answer the question, as Betjeman did in his poem: we invent "dainty names" because we don't want

to face up to the reality of death. Sociologist Ernest Becker claimed "that of all things that move men, one of the principal ones is his terror of death" (*The Denial of Death*, p. 11).

During many years of pastoral ministry, I have seen this denial in action. When visiting bereaved families, I have noticed how often people deliberately avoid the word "death" and substitute phrases like "left us," "went home," "went to sleep," or "passed on." Of course, when a Christian dies, he or she does "go to sleep" and "go home," but this assurance should not make death any less real in our thinking or our feeling. The person who treats death lightly may fear death the most. If we take life seriously—and we should—then we can't treat death flippantly.

This is not the first time the subject of death has come into Solomon's discourse, nor will it be the last. (See 1:4; 2:14-17; 3:18-20; 4:8; 5:15-16; 6:6; 8:8; 12:1-7.) After all, the only way to be prepared to live is to be prepared to die. Death is a fact of life, and Solomon examined many facets of life so that he might understand God's pattern for satisfied living. Robert E. Lee's last words were, "Let the tent be struck!" Unless Jesus Christ returns and takes us to heaven, we will one day "strike our tent" (2 Cor. 5:1-8) and leave the battlefield for a better land. We must be ready.

In this chapter, Solomon drew two conclusions: death is unavoidable (1-10) and life is unpredictable (11-18). That being the case, the best thing we can do is trust God, live by faith, and enjoy whatever blessings God gives us.

1. Death Is Unavoidable (Eccl. 9:1-10)

"I'm not afraid to die;" quipped Woody Allen, "I just don't want to be there when it happens." But he *will* be there when it happens, as must every human being, because there is no escaping death when your time has come. Death is not an accident, it's an appointment (Heb. 9:27), a destiny that nobody but God can cancel or change.

Life and death are "in the hand of God" (v. 1), and only He knows our future, whether it will bring blessing ("love") or sorrow ("hatred"). Solomon was not suggesting that we are passive actors in a cosmic drama, following an unchangeable script handed to us by an uncaring director. Throughout this book, Solomon has emphasized our freedom of discernment and decision. But only God knows what the future holds for us and what will happen tomorrow because of the decisions we make today.

"As it is with the good man, so with the sinner." (v. 2, NIV). If so, why bother to live a godly life?" someone may ask. "After all, whether we obey the Law or disobey, bring sacrifices or neglect them, make or break promises, we will die just the same." Yes, we share a common destiny on earth—death and the grave—*but we do not share a common destiny in eternity.* For that reason, everybody must honestly face "the last enemy" (1 Cor. 15:26) and decide how to deal with it. Christians have trusted Jesus Christ to save them from sin and death, so, as far as they are concerned, "the last enemy" has been defeated (Rom. 6:23; John 11:25-26; 1 Thess. 4:13-18; 1 Cor. 15:51-58). Unbelievers don't have that confidence and are unprepared to die.

How people deal with the reality of death reveals itself in the way they deal with the realities of life. Solomon pointed out three possible responses that people make to the ever-present fear of death.

Escape (v. 3). The fact of death and the fear of death will either bring out the best in people or the worst in people; and too often it is the worst. When death comes to a family, it doesn't *create* problems; it *reveals* them. Many ministers and funeral directors have witnessed the "X-ray" power of death and bereavement as it reveals the hearts of people. In facing the death of others, we are confronted with our own death, and many people just can't handle it.

"The heart of the sons of men is full of evil," and that evil is bound to come out. People will do almost *anything but repent* in order to escape the reality of death. They will get drunk, fight with their relatives, drive recklessly, spend large amounts of money on useless things, and plunge into one senseless pleasure after another, all to keep the Grim Reaper at arm's length. But their costly endeavors only distract them from the battle; they don't end the war, because "the last enemy" is still there.

Those of us who were privileged to have the late Joseph Bayly as our friend know what a positive attitude he had toward death. He and his wife had been through the valley many times and God used them to bring comfort and hope to other sorrowing pilgrims. His book *The Last Thing We Talk About* (David C. Cook Pub. Co.) is a beautiful testimony of how Jesus Christ can heal the brokenhearted. "Death is the great adventure," said Joe, "beside which moon landings and space trips pale into insignificance."

You don't get that kind of confidence by trying to run away from the reality of death. You get it by facing "the last enemy" honestly, turning from sin and trusting Jesus Christ to save you. Have you done that?

Endurance (vv. 4-6). When confronted by the stern fact of death, not everybody dives into an escape hatch and shouts,

"Let's eat, drink, and be merry, for tomorrow we die!" Many people just grit their teeth, square their shoulders, and endure. They hold on to that ancient motto, "Where there's life, there's hope!" (That's a good paraphrase of v. 4.)

That motto goes as far back as the third century B.C. It's part of a conversation between two farmers who are featured in a poem by the Greek poet Theokritos. "Console yourself, dear Battos," says Korydon. "Things may be better tomorrow. While there's life there's hope. Only the dead have none." Shades of Ecclesiastes!

Solomon would be the last person to discourage anybody from hoping for the best. Better to be a living dog (and dogs were despised in that day) than a dead lion. All that the Preacher asked was that we have some common sense along with our hope, lest too late we find ourselves grasping a false hope.

To begin with, let's keep in mind that one day we shall die (v. 5). The Christian believer has "a living hope," not a "dead" hope, because the Savior is alive and has conquered death (1 Peter 1:3-5; 2 Tim. 1:10). A hope that can be destroyed by death is a false hope and must be abandoned.

What Solomon wrote about the dead can be "reversed" and applied to the living. The dead do not know what is happening on earth, but the living know and can respond to it. The dead cannot add anything to their reward or their reputation, but the living can. The dead cannot relate to people on earth by loving, hating, or envying, but the living can. Solomon was emphasizing the importance of seizing opportunities while we live, rather than blindly hoping for something better in the future, because death will end our opportunities on this earth.

"The human body experiences a powerful gravitational pull in the direction of hope," wrote journalist Norman Cousins, who himself survived a near-fatal illness and a massive heart attack. "That is why the patient's hopes are the physician's secret weapon. They are the hidden ingredients in any prescription."

We endure because we hope, but "hope in hope" (like "faith in faith") is too often only a kind of self-hypnosis that keeps us from facing life honestly. While a patient may be better off with an optimistic attitude, it is dangerous for him to follow a *false hope* that may keep him from preparing for death. That kind of hope is hopeless. When the end comes, the patient's *outlook* may be cheerful, but the *outcome* will be tragic.

Life is not easy, but there is more to life than simply enduring. There is a third response to the fact of death, a response that can be made only by those who have trusted Jesus Christ as their Savior.

Enjoyment (vv. 7-10). This has been one of Solomon's recurring themes (2:24; 3:12-15, 22; 5:18-20; 8:15), and he will bring it up again (11:9-10). His admonition "Go thy way!" means: "Don't sit around and brood! Get up and live!" Yes, death is coming, but God gives us good gifts to enjoy so enjoy them!

Solomon didn't urge us to join the "jet set" and start searching for exotic pleasures in far away places. Instead, he listed some of the common experiences of home life: happy leisurely meals (v. 7), joyful family celebrations (v. 8), a faithful, loving marriage (v. 9), and hard work (v. 10). What a contrast to modern society's formula for happiness: fast food and a full schedule, the addictive pursuit of everything new, "live-in marriages," and shortcuts guaranteed to help you avoid work but still get rich quick.

In recent years, many voices have united to call us back to the traditional values of life. Some people are getting tired of the emptiness of living on substitutes. They want something more substantial than the "right" labels on their clothes and the "right" names to drop at the "right" places. Like the younger brother in our Lord's parable (Luke 15:11-24), they have discovered that everything that's really important is back home at the Father's house.

Enjoy your meals (v. 7). The average Jewish family began the day with an early snack and then had a light meal ("brunch") sometime between 10:00 and noon. They didn't eat together again until after sunset. When their work was done they gathered for the main meal of the day. It consisted largely of bread and wine, perhaps milk and cheese, with a few vegetables and fruit in season, and sometimes fish. Meat was expensive and was served only on special occasions. It was a simple meal that was designed to nourish both the body and the soul, for eating together ("breaking bread") was a communal act of friendship and commitment.

King Solomon sat down to a daily feast (1 Kings 4:22-23), but there is evidence that he didn't always enjoy it. "Better a meal of vegetables where there is love than a fattened calf with hatred" (Prov. 15:17, NIV). "Better a dry crust with peace and quiet than a house full of feasting, with strife" (Prov. 17:1, NIV). The most important thing on any menu is *family love*, for love turns an ordinary meal into a banquet. When the children would rather eat at a friend's house than bring their friends home to enjoy their mother's cooking, it's time to take inventory of what goes on around the table.

Enjoy every occasion (v. 8). Life was difficult in the average home, but every family knew how to enjoy special occasions such as weddings and reunions. That's when they wore their white garments (a symbol of joy) and anointed themselves with expensive perfumes instead of the usual olive oil. These occasions were few, so everybody made the most of them.

But Solomon advised the people to wear white garments *always* and to anoint themselves *always* with special perfume. Of course, his congregation didn't take his words literally, because they knew what he was saying: make every occasion a special occasion, even if it's ordinary or routine. We must not express our thanksgiving and joy only when we are celebrating special events. "Rejoice in the Lord always. Again I will say, rejoice!" (Phil. 4:4, NKJV).

Among other things, this may be what Jesus had in mind when He told His disciples to become like little children (Matt. 18:1-6). An unspoiled child delights in the simple activities of life, even the routine activities, while a pampered child must be entertained by a variety of expensive amusements. It's not by searching for special things that we find joy, but by making the everyday things special.

Enjoy your marriage (v. 9). Solomon knew nothing about "live-in couples" or "trial marriages." He saw a wife as a gift from God (Prov. 18:22; 19:14), and marriage as a loving commitment that lasts a lifetime. No matter how difficult life may be, there is great joy in the home of the man and woman who love each other and are faithful to their marriage vows. Solomon would agree with psychiatrist M. Scott Peck who calls *commitment* "the foundation, the bedrock of any genuinely loving relationship" (*The Road Less Traveled*, p. 140).

It's too bad Solomon didn't live up to his own ideals. He forsook God's pattern for marriage and then allowed his many wives to seduce him from the Lord (1 Kings 11:1-8). If he wrote Ecclesiastes later in life, as I believe he did, then verse 9 is his confession, "Now I know better!"

Enjoy your work (v. 10). The Jewish people looked upon work, not as a curse, but as a stewardship from God. Even their rabbis learned a trade (Paul was a tentmaker) and reminded them, "He who does not teach a son to work, teaches him to steal." Paul wrote, "If any would not work, neither should he eat" (2 Thess. 3:10).

"Do it with all your might"(NASB) suggests two things: Do your very best, and do it while you still have strength. The day may come when you will have to lay down your tools and make way for a younger and stronger worker. Colossians 3:17 applies this principle to the New Testament Christian.

The things that make up employment in this life will not be present in the grave (sheol, the realm of the dead), so make the most of your opportunities now. One day our works will be judged, and we want to receive a reward for His glory (1 Cor. 3:10ff; Col. 3:23-25).

If we fear God and walk by faith we will not try to escape or merely endure life. We will enjoy life and receive it happily as a gift from the Lord.

2. Life Is Unpredictable (Eccl. 9:11-18)

Anticipating the response of his listeners (and his readers), Solomon turned from his discussion of death and began to discuss life. "If death is unavoidable," somebody would argue, "then the smartest thing we can do is major on our strengths and concentrate on life. When death comes, at least we'll have the satisfaction of knowing we worked hard and achieved some success."

"Don't be too sure of that!" was Solomon's reply. "You can't guarantee what will happen in life, because life is unpredictable."

To begin with, our *abilities* are no guarantee of success *(vv. 11-12)*. While it is generally true that the fastest runners win the races, the strongest soldiers win the battles, and the smartest and most skillful workers win the best jobs, it is also true that these same gifted people can fail miserably because of factors out of their control. The successful person knows how to make the most of "time and procedure" (8:5), but only the Lord can control "time and chance" (v. 11).

Solomon already affirmed that God has a time for everything (3:1-8), a purpose to be fulfilled in that time (8:6), and "something beautiful" to come out of it in the end (3:11). The word "chance" simply means occurrence or event. It has nothing to do with gambling. We might say, "I just happened to be in the right place at the right time, and I got the job. Ability had very little to do with it!"

Of course, Christians don't depend on such things as "luck" or "chance," because their confidence is in the loving providence of God. A dedicated Christian doesn't carry a rabbit's foot or trust in lucky days or numbers. Canadian humorist Stephen Leacock said, "I'm a great believer in luck. I find that the harder I work, the more I have of it." Christians trust God to guide them and help them in making decisions, and they believe that His will is best. They leave "time and chance" in His capable hands.

Who knows when trouble will arrive on the scene and wreck all our great plans (v. 12)? When they least expect it, fish are caught in the net and birds are caught in the trap. So men are snared in "evil times," sudden events that are beyond their control. That's why we should take to heart the admonition against boasting (James 4:13-17).

Second, our *opportunities* are no guarantee of success *(vv. 13-18)*. It is not clear whether the wise man actually delivered the city, or whether he could have saved it, and was asked but did not heed. I lean toward the second explanation because it fits in better with verses 16-18. (The Hebrew allows for the translation "could have"; see the verse 15 footnote in the NASB). The little city was besieged and the wise man could have delivered it, but nobody paid any attention to him. Verse 17 suggests that a ruler with a loud mouth got all of the attention and led the people into defeat. The wise man spoke quietly and was ignored. He had the opportunity for greatness but was frustrated by one loud ignorant man.

"One sinner [the loud ruler] destroys much good" (v. 18, NKJV) is a truth that is illustrated throughout the whole of Scripture, starting with Adam and his disobedience to God (Gen. 3; Rom. 5). Achan sinned and brought defeat on the army of Israel (Josh. 7). David's sin brought trouble to Israel (2 Sam. 24), and the revolt of Absalom led the nation into a civil war (2 Sam. 15ff).

Since death is unavoidable and life is unpredictable, the only course we can safely take is to yield ourselves into the hands of God and walk by faith in His Word. We don't live by explanations; we live by promises. We don't depend on luck but on the providential working of our loving Father as we trust His promises and obey His will.

As we walk by faith, we need not fear our "last enemy," because Jesus Christ has conquered death. "Fear not; I am the first and the last; I am He that liveth, and was dead; and, behold, I am alive for evermore" (Rev. 1:17-18). Because He is alive, and we live in Him, we don't look at life and say, "Vanity of vanities, all is vanity!"

Instead, we echo the confidence expressed by the apostle Paul: "But thanks be to God, who gives us the victory through our Lord Jesus Christ. Therefore, my beloved brethren, be steadfast, immovable, always abounding in the work of the Lord, knowing that your labor is not in vain in the Lord" (1 Cor. 15:57-58, NKJV).

CHAPTER ELEVEN
A LITTLE FOLLY IS DANGEROUS
Ecclesiastes 10

Before he concluded his message, Solomon thought it wise to remind his congregation once again of the importance of wisdom and the danger of folly. (The word "folly" is used nine times in this chapter.) In verse 1, he laid down the basic principle that folly creates problems for those who commit it. He had already compared a good name to fragrant perfume (7:1), so he used the image again. What dead flies are to perfume, folly is to the reputation of the wise person. The conclusion is logical: Wise people will stay away from folly!

Why is one person foolish and another wise? It all depends on the inclinations of the heart (v. 2). Solomon was not referring to the physical organ in the body, because everybody's heart is in the same place, except for those who might have some birth defect. Furthermore, the physical organ has nothing to do with wisdom or folly. Solomon was referring to the center of one's life, the "master control" within us that governs "the issues of life" (Prov. 4:23).

In the ancient world, the right hand was the place of power and honor, while the left hand represented weakness and rejection (Matt. 25:33, 41). Many people considered the left side to be "unlucky." (The English word "sinister" comes from a Latin word that means "on the left hand.") Since the fool doesn't have wisdom in his heart, he gravitates toward that which is wrong (the left) and gets into trouble (see 2:14). People try to correct him, but he refuses to listen, and this tells everybody that he is a fool (v. 3).

Having laid down the principle, Solomon then applied it to four different "fools."

1. The Foolish Ruler (Eccl. 10:4-7)

If there is one person who needs wisdom, it is the ruler of a nation. When God asked Solomon what gift he especially wanted, the king asked for wisdom (1 Kings 3:3-28). Lyndon B. Johnson said, "A president's hardest task is not to *do* what's right, but to *know* what's right." That requires wisdom.

If a ruler is *proud*, he may say and do foolish things that cause him to lose the respect of his associates *(v. 4)*. The picture here is of a proud ruler who easily becomes angry and takes out his anger on the attendants around him. Of course, if a man has no control over himself, how can he hope to have control over his people? "He who is slow to anger is better than the mighty and he who rules his spirit than he who takes a city" (Prov. 16:32, NKJV). "Whoever has no rule over his own spirit is like a city

broken down, without walls" (Prov. 25:28, NKJV).

However, it isn't necessary for his servants to act like fools! In fact, that's the worse thing they can do (8:3). Far better that they control themselves, stay right where they are and seek to bring peace. "Through patience a ruler can be persuaded, and a gentle tongue can break a bone" (Prov. 25:15, NIV). "A king's wrath is a messenger of death, but a wise man will appease it" (Prov. 16:14, NIV).

To be sure, there is a righteous anger that sometimes needs to be displayed (Eph. 4:26), but not everything we call "righteous indignation" is really "righteous." It is so easy to give vent to jealousy and malice by disguising them as holy zeal for God. Not every religious crusader is motivated by love for God or obedience to the Word. His or her zeal could be a mask that is covering hidden anger or jealousy.

But if a ruler is too *pliable*, he is also a fool *(vv. 5-7)*. If he lacks character and courage, he will put fools in the high offices and qualified people in the low offices. The servants will ride on horses while the noblemen will walk (see Prov. 19:10 and 30:21-22). If a ruler has incompetent people advising him, he is almost certain to govern the nation unwisely.

Solomon's son Rehoboam was proud and unyielding, and this led to the division of the kingdom (1 Kings 12:1-24). Instead of following the advice of the wise counselors, he listened to his youthful friends. He made the elders walk and he put the young men on the horses. On the other hand, more than one king in Jewish history has been so pliable that he turned out to be nothing but a figurehead. The best rulers (and leaders) are men and women who are tough-minded but tenderhearted, who put the best people on the horses and don't apologize for it.

2. Foolish Workers (Eccl. 10:8-11)

Students are not agreed on what Solomon's point is in this graphic section. Was he saying that every job has its occupational hazards? If so, what lesson was he teaching, and why did he take so much space to illustrate the obvious? His theme is *folly,* and he certainly was not teaching that hard work is foolish because you might get injured! Throughout the book, Solomon emphasized the importance of honest labor and the joys it can bring. Why would he contradict that message?

I believe Solomon was describing people who attempted to do their work and suffered *because they were foolish.* One man dug a pit, perhaps a well or a place for storing grain, but fell into the pit himself. Why? Because he lacked wisdom and failed to take proper precautions. Frequently Scripture uses this as a picture of just retribution, but that doesn't seem to be the lesson here. (See Ps. 7:15; 9:15-16; 10:2; 35:8; 57:6; Prov. 26:27; 28:10.)

Another man broke through a hedge [wall, fence], perhaps while remodeling his house, and a serpent bit him. Serpents often found their way into hidden crevices and corners, and the man should have been more careful. He was overconfident and did not look ahead.

Verse 9 takes us to the quarries and the forests, where careless workers are injured cutting stones and splitting logs. Verse 10 pictures a foolish worker *par excellence:* a man who tried to split wood with a dull ax. The wise worker will pause in his labors and sharpen it. As the popular slogan says, "Don't work harder—work smarter!"

Snake charmers were common as entertainers in that day (v. 11, and see Ps. 58:4-5 and Jer. 8:17). Snakes have no external ears; they pick up sound waves primarily through the bone structure of the head. More than the music played by the charmer, it is the man's disciplined actions (swaying and "staring") that hold the snake's attention and keep the serpent under control. It is indeed an art.

Solomon described a performer who was bitten by the snake before the man had opportunity to "charm" it. Besides risking his life, the charmer could not collect any money from the spectators (see v. 11, NIV). They would only laugh at him. He was a fool because he rushed and acted as though the snake was charmed. He wanted to collect his money in a hurry and move to another location. The more "shows" he put on, the bigger his income. Instead, he made no money at all.

Some charmers had a mongoose available that "caught" the snake just at the right time and "saved" the man from being bitten. If for some reason the mongoose missed his cue, the serpent might attack the charmer, and that would be the end of the show. Either way, the man was foolish.

The common denominator among these "foolish workers" seems to be presumption. They were overconfident and ended up either hurting themselves or making their jobs harder.

3. Foolish Talkers (Eccl. 10:12-15)

In the book of Proverbs, Solomon had much to say about the speech of fools. In this paragraph, he pointed out four characteristics of their words.

First, they are **destructive** words *(v. 12).* The wise person will speak gracious words that are suited to the listeners and the occasion (Prov. 10:32; 25:11). Whether in personal conversation or public ministry, our Lord always knew the right thing to say at the right time (Isa. 50:4). We should try to emulate Him. But the fool blurts out whatever is on his mind and doesn't stop to consider who might be hurt by it. In the end, it is the fool himself who is hurt the most: "a fool is consumed by his own lips" (Eccl. 10:12, NIV).

In Scripture, destructive words are compared to weapons of war (Prov. 25:18), a fire (James 3:5-6), and a poisonous beast (James 3:7-8). We may try to hurt others with our lies, slander, and angry words, but we are really hurting ourselves the most. "He who guards his mouth preserves his life, but he who opens wide his lips shall have destruction" (Prov. 13:3, NKJV). "Whoever guards his mouth and tongue keeps his soul from troubles" (Prov. 21:23, NKJV).

Second, they are *unreasonable* words *(v. 13)*. What he says doesn't make sense. And the longer he talks, the crazier it becomes. "The beginning of his talking is folly, and the end of it is wicked madness" (NASB). He would be better off to keep quiet, because all that he says only lets everybody know that he is a fool (5:3). Paul called these people "unruly and vain talkers" (Titus 1:10), which J.B. Phillips translates "who will not recognize authority, who talk nonsense" (PH).

Occasionally in my travels, I meet people who will talk about anything anybody brings up, as though they were the greatest living experts on that subject. When the Bible or religion comes into the conversation, I quietly wait for them to hang themselves, and they rarely disappoint me. The Jewish writer Shalom Aleichem said, "You can tell when a fool speaks: he grinds much and produces little."

Third, they are *uncontrolled* words *(v. 14a)*. The fool is "full of words" without realizing that he is saying nothing. "In the multitude of words, sin is not lacking, but he who restrains his lips is wise" (Prov. 10:19, NKJV). The person who can control his or her tongue is able to discipline the

entire body (James 3:1-2). Jesus said, "But let your `Yes' be `Yes' and your `No' be `No.' For whatever is more than this is from the evil one" (Matt. 5:37, NKJV).

Finally, they are *boastful* words *(14b-15)*. Foolish people talk about the future as though they either know all about it or are in control of what will happen. "Do not boast about tomorrow, for you do not know what a day may bring forth" (Prov. 27:1, NKJV). Several times before, Solomon has emphasized man's ignorance of the future (3:22; 6:12; 8:7; 9:12), a truth that wise people receive but fools reject. (See James 4:13-17.)

There is a bit of humor here. The fool boasts about his future plans and wearies people with his talk, but he can't even find the way to the city. In Bible times, the roads to the cities were well-marked so that any traveler could find his way, but the fool is so busy talking about the future that he loses his way in the present. "He can't find his way to the city" was probably an ancient proverb about stupidity, not unlike our "He's so dumb, he couldn't learn the route to run an elevator."

4. Foolish Officers (Eccl. 10:16-20)

Solomon has already described foolish rulers. Now he exposes the folly of the officers who work under those rulers, the bureaucrats who were a part of the machinery of the kingdom. He gave four characteristics of these foolish men.

Indulgence (vv. 16-17). If the king is immature, the people he gathers around him will reflect that immaturity and take advantage of it. But if he is a true nobleman, he will surround himself with noble officers who will put the good of the country first. Real leaders use their authority to build the nation, while mere officeholders use the nation to build their authority. They use public funds for their own selfish purposes, throwing parties and having a good time.

It is a judgment of God when a people are given immature leaders (Isa. 3:1-5). This can happen to a nation or to a local church. The term "elder" (Titus 1:5ff) implies maturity and experience in the Christian life, and it is wrong for a believer to be thrust into leadership too soon (1 Tim. 3:6). Age is no guarantee of maturity (1 Cor. 3:1-4; Heb. 5:11-14), and youth sometimes outstrips its elders in spiritual zeal. Oswald Chambers said, "Spiritual maturity is not reached by the passing of the years, but by obedience to the will of God." The important thing is maturity, not just age.

The *New International Version* translates verse 16, "Woe to you, O land whose king was a servant." The suggestion is that this servant became king with the help of his friends (cf. 4:13-14). Now he was obligated to give them all jobs so he could remain on the throne. In spite of their selfish and expensive indulgence, these hirelings could not be dismissed, because the king's security depended on them. To the victor belong the spoils!

Incompetence (v. 18). These foolish officers are so busy with enjoyment that they have no time for employment, and both the buildings and the organization start to fall apart. "He also who is slothful in his work is brother to him that is a great waster" (Prov. 18:9). There is a difference between those who *use* an office and those who merely *hold* an office (1 Tim. 3:10). Immature people enjoy the privileges and ignore the responsibilities, while mature people see the responsibilities as privileges and use them to help others.

Woodrow Wilson wrote, "A friend of mine says that every man who takes office in Washington either grows or swells; when I give a man an office, I watch him carefully to see whether he is swelling or growing."

Indifference (v. 19). This verse declares the personal philosophy of the foolish officers: Eat all you can, enjoy all you can, and get all you can. They are totally indifferent to the responsibilities of their office or the needs of the people. In recent years, various developing nations have seen how easy it is for unscrupulous leaders to steal government funds in order to build their own kingdoms. Unfortunately, it has also happened recently to some religious organizations.

"For the love of money is a root of all kinds of evil" (1 Tim. 6:10, NKJV). The prophet Amos cried out against the wicked rulers of his day who trampled on the heads of the poor and treated them like the dust of the earth (Amos 2:7, and see 4:1; 5:11-12). The courts might not catch up with all the unscrupulous politicians, but God will eventually judge them, and His judgment will be just.

Indiscretion (v. 20). The familiar saying "A little bird told me" probably originated from this verse. You can imagine a group of these officers having a party in one of their private rooms and, instead of toasting the king, they are cursing ["making light of"] him. Of course, they wouldn't do this if any of the king's friends were present, but they were sure that the company would faithfully keep the secret. Alas, somebody told the king what was said, and this gave him reason to punish them or dismiss them from their offices.

Even if we can't respect the person in the office, we must respect the office (Rom. 13:1-7; 1 Peter 2:13-17). "You shall not revile God, nor curse a ruler of your people" (Ex. 22:28).

These hirelings were certainly indiscreet when they cursed the king, for they should have known that one of their number would use this event either to intimidate his friends or to ingratiate himself with the ruler. A statesman asks, "What is best for my country?" A politician asks, "What is best for my party?" But a mere officeholder, a hireling, asks, "What is safest and most profitable for me?"

This completes Solomon's review of his fourth argument that life is not worth living, "the certainty of death" (2:12-23). He has concluded that life is indeed worth living, even though death is unavoidable (9:1-10) and life is unpredictable (9:11-18). What we must do is avoid folly (ch. 10) and live by the wisdom of God.

This also concludes the second part of his discourse. He has reviewed the four arguments presented in chapters 1 and 2, and has decided that life was really worth living after all. The best thing we can do is to trust God, do our work, accept what God sends us, and enjoy each day of our lives to the glory of God (3:12-15, 22; 5:18-20; 8:15; 9:7-10). All that remains for the Preacher is to conclude his discourse with a practical application, and this he does in chapters 11 and 12. He will bring together all the various strands of truth that he has woven into his sermon, and he will show us what God expects us to do if we are to be satisfied.

CHAPTER TWELVE
WHAT LIFE IS ALL ABOUT
Ecclesiastes 11

I s life worth living?"
That was the question the Preacher raised when he began the discourse that we call Ecclesiastes.

After experimenting and investigating "life under the sun," he concluded, "No, life is *not* worth living!" He gave four arguments to support his conclusion: the monotony of life, the vanity of wisdom, the futility of wealth, and the certainty of death.

Being a wise man, Solomon reviewed his arguments and this time brought God into the picture. What a difference it made. He realized that life was not monotonous but filled with challenging situations from God, each in its own time and each for its own purpose. He also learned that wealth could be enjoyed and employed to the glory of God. Though man's wisdom couldn't explain everything, Solomon concluded that it was better to follow God's wisdom than to practice man's folly. As for the certainty of death, there is no way to escape it; and it ought to motivate us to enjoy life now and make the most of the opportunities God gives us.

Now Solomon was ready for his conclusion and personal application. What he did was present *four pictures of life* and attach to each picture a practical admonition for his listeners (and readers) to heed. The development looks like this:

Life is an ADVENTURE—live by faith (11:1-6)
Life is a GIFT—enjoy it (11:7–12:8)
Life is a SCHOOL—learn your lessons (12:9-12)
Life is a STEWARDSHIP—fear God (12:13-14)

These four pictures parallel the four arguments that Solomon had wrestled with throughout the book. Life is not monotonous; rather, it is an adventure of faith that is anything but predictable or tedious. Yes, death is certain, but life is a gift from God and He wants us to enjoy it. Are there questions we can't answer and problems we can't solve? Don't despair. God teaches us His truth as we advance in "the school of life," and He will give us wisdom enough to make sensible decisions. Finally, as far as wealth is concerned, all of life is a stewardship from God; and one day He will call us to give an account. Therefore, "fear God, and keep His commandments" (12:13).

1. Life Is an Adventure: Live by Faith (Eccl. 11:1-6)

When I was a boy, I practically lived in the public library during the summer months. I loved books, the building was cool, and the librarians gave me the run of the place since I was one of their best customers. One summer I read nothing but true adventure stories written by real heroes like Frank Buck and Martin Johnson. These men knew the African jungles better than I knew my hometown! I was fascinated by *I Married Adventure*, the autobiography of Martin Johnson's wife, Osa. When Clyde Beatty brought his circus to town, I was in the front row watching him "tame" the lions.

Since those boyhood days, life has become a lot calmer for me, but I trust I haven't lost that sense of adventure.

In fact, as I get older, I'm asking God to keep me from getting set in my ways in a life that is routine, boring, and predictable. "I don't want my life to end in a swamp," said British expositor F.B. Meyer. I agree with him. When I trusted Jesus Christ as my Savior, "I married adventure"; and that meant living by faith and expecting the unexpected.

Solomon used two activities to illustrate his point: the merchant sending out his ships (vv. 1-2), and the farmer sowing his seed (vv. 3-6). In both activities, a great deal of faith is required, because neither the merchant nor the farmer can control the circumstances. The ships might hit a reef, meet a storm, or be attacked by pirates, and the cargo lost. Bad weather, blight, or insects might destroy the crop, and the farmer's labor would be in vain. However, if the merchant and the farmer waited until the circumstances were ideal, they would never get anything done! Life has a certain amount of risk to it, and that's where faith comes in.

The merchant (vv. 1-2). "Cast thy bread upon the waters" may be paraphrased, "Send out your grain in ships." Solomon himself was involved in various kinds of trade, so it was natural for him to use this illustration (1 Kings 10:15, 22). It would be months before the ships would return with their precious cargo; but when they did, the merchant's faith and patience would be rewarded. Verse 2 suggests that he spread out his wealth and not put everything into one venture. After all, true faith is not presumption.

"For you do not know" is a key phrase in this section (vv. 2, 5, 6). Man is ignorant of the future, but he must not allow his ignorance to make him so fearful that he becomes either careless or paralyzed. On the contrary, not knowing the future should make us more careful in what we plan and what we do. Verse 2 can be interpreted, "Send cargo on seven or eight ships, because some of them are bound to bring back a good return on the investment." In other words, "Don't put all your eggs in one basket."

The farmer (vv. 3-6). Daniel Webster called farmers "the founders of civilization," and Thomas Jefferson said they were "the chosen people of God." Farming has never been easy work, and this was especially true in the Holy Land in Bible days. The Jews tilled a rocky soil, and they depended on the early and latter rains to nourish their seed. Nobody can predict the weather, let alone control it, and the farmer is at the mercy of nature.

Verse 3 contrasts the clouds with the tree. Clouds are always changing. They come and go, and the farmer hopes they will spill their precious water on his fields. Trees are somewhat permanent. They stand in the same place, unless a storm topples them; and then they lie there and rot. The past [the tree] cannot be changed, but the present [the clouds] is available to us, and we must seize each opportunity.

But don't sit around waiting for ideal circumstances (v. 4). The wind is never right for the sower, and the clouds are never right for the reaper. If you are looking for an excuse for doing nothing, you can find one. Billy Sunday said that an excuse was "the skin of a reason stuffed with a lie." Life is an adventure and often we must launch out by faith, even when the circumstances seem adverse.

Just as nobody knows "the way of the wind" (v. 5, NKJV, and see John 3:8) or how the fetus is formed in the womb (Ps. 139:14-15), so nobody knows the works of God in His creation. God has a time and a purpose for everything (3:1-11), and we must live by faith in His Word. Therefore, use each day wisely (v. 6). Get up early and sow your seed, and work hard until evening. Do the job at hand and "redeem the time" (Eph. 5:15-17), trusting God to bless at least some of the tasks you have accomplished. Just as the merchant sends out more than one ship, so the farmer works more than one crop.

Life is an adventure of faith, and each of us is like a merchant, investing today in that which will pay dividends tomorrow. We are like the farmer, sowing various kinds of seeds in different soils, trusting God for the harvest (Gal. 6:8-9; Ps. 126:5-6; Hos. 10:12). If we worried about the wind toppling a tree over on us, or the clouds drenching us with rain, we would never accomplish anything. "Of course, there is no formula for success," said famous concert pianist Arthur Rubinstein, "except perhaps an unconditional acceptance of life and what it brings."

2. Life Is a Gift: Enjoy It (Eccl. 11:7–12:8)

This is Solomon's sixth and final admonition that we accept life as a gift and learn to enjoy all that God shares with us (see 2:24; 3:12-15, 22; 5:18-20; 8:15; 9:7-10). In order to do this, we must obey three instructions: rejoice (11:7-9), remove (11:10), and remember (12:1-8).

Rejoice (11:7-9). What a joy it is to anticipate each new day and accept it as a fresh gift from God! I confess that I never realized what it meant to live a day at a time until I was nearly killed in an auto accident back in 1966. It was caused by a drunk driver careening around a curve between eighty and ninety miles per hour. By the grace of God, I had no serious injuries; but my stay in the Intensive Care Ward, and my time of recuperation at home, made me a firm believer in Deuteronomy 33:25, "As thy days, so shall thy strength be." Now when I awaken early each morning, I thank God for the new day; and I ask Him to help me use it wisely for His glory and to enjoy it as His gift.

Solomon especially instructed the young people to take advantage of the days of youth before the "days of darkness" would arrive. He was not suggesting that young people have no problems or that older people have no joys. He was simply making a generalization that youth is the time for enjoyment, before the problems of old age start to reveal themselves.

My middle name is Wendell; I'm named after Wendell P. Loveless, who was associated for many years with the Moody Bible Institute in Chicago, especially radio station WMBI. He lived into his nineties and was alert to the very end. During one of our visits with him, he told me and my wife, "I don't go out much now because my parents won't let me—Mother Nature and Father Time!"

Young people have to watch their hearts and their eyes, because either or both can lead them into sin (Num. 15:39; Prov. 4:23; Matt. 5:27-30). "Walk in the ways of your heart" (NKJV) is not an encouragement to go on a youthful fling and satisfy the sinful desires within (Jer. 17:9; Mark 7:20-23). It is rather a reminder for young people to enjoy the special pleasures that belong to youth and can never be experienced again in quite the same way. Those of us who are older need to remember that God expects young people to act like young people. The tragedy is that too many older people are trying to act like young people!

Solomon's warning is evidence that he doesn't have sinful pleasures in mind: "God will bring you into judgment."

God does give us "all things richly to enjoy" (1 Tim. 6:17), but it is always wrong to enjoy the pleasures of sin. The young person who enjoys life in the will of God will have nothing to worry about when the Lord returns.

Remove (v. 10). Privileges must be balanced by personal responsibilities. Young people must put anxiety out of their hearts (Matt. 6:24-34) and evil away from their flesh (2 Cor. 7:1). The word translated "sorrow" means "vexation, inner

pain, anxiety." If we are living in the will of God, we will have the peace of God in our hearts (Phil. 4:6-9). The sins of the flesh only destroy the body and can bring eternal judgment to the soul.

The phrase "childhood and youth are vanity" does not mean that these stages in life are unimportant and a waste of time. Quite the opposite is true! The best way to have a happy adult life and a contented old age is to get a good start early in life and avoid the things that will bring trouble later on. Young people who take care of their minds and bodies, avoid the destructive sins of the flesh, and build good habits of health and holiness, have a better chance for happy adult years than those who "sow their wild oats" and pray for a crop failure.

The phrase means "childhood and youth are transient." These precious years go by so quickly, and we must not waste our opportunities for preparing for the future. The Hebrew word translated "youth" can mean "the dawning" or "blackness of hair" (as opposed to gray hair). Youth is indeed the time of "dawning," and before we know it, the sun will start to set. Therefore, make the most of those "dawning years," because you will never see them again. "Youthful sins lay a foundation for aged sorrows," said Charles Spurgeon, and he was right.

Remember (12:1-8). This third instruction means more than "think about God." It means "pay attention to, consider with the intention of obeying." It is Solomon's version of Matthew 6:33, "But seek first the kingdom of God and His righteousness" (NKJV). How easy it is to neglect the Lord when you are caught up in the enjoyments and opportunities of youth. We know that dark days (11:8) and difficult [evil] days (12:1) are coming, so we had better lay a good spiritual foundation as early in life as possible. During our youthful years, the sky is bright (11:7), but the time will come when there will be darkness and one storm after another.

Verses 3-7 give us one of the most imaginative descriptions of old age and death found anywhere in literature. Students don't agree on all the details of interpretation, but most of them do see here a picture of a house that is falling apart and finally turns to dust. A dwelling place is one biblical metaphor for the human body (Job 4:19; 2 Cor. 5:1-2 [a tent]; 2 Peter 1:13 [a tent]), and taking down a house or tent is a picture of death. The meaning may be:

keepers of the house—Your arms and hands tremble.

strong men—Your legs, knees, and shoulders weaken and you walk bent over.

grinders—You start to lose your teeth.

windows—Your vision begins to deteriorate.

doors—Either your hearing starts to fail, or you close your mouth because you've lost your teeth.

grinding—You can't chew your food, or your ears can't pick up the sounds outdoors.

rise up—You wake up with the birds early each morning, and wish you could sleep longer.

music—Your voice starts to quaver and weaken.

afraid—You are terrified of heights and afraid of falling while you walk down the street.

almond tree—If you have any hair left, it turns white, like almond blossoms.

grasshopper—You just drag yourself along, like a grasshopper at the close of the summer season.

desire—You lose your appetite, or perhaps your sexual desire.

long home—You go to your eternal [long] home and people mourn your death.

Verse 6 describes a golden bowl—a lamp—hanging from the ceiling on a silver chain. The chain breaks and the bowl breaks. The fragile "cord of life" is snapped and the light of life goes out. Only wealthy people could have such costly lamps, so Solomon may be hinting that death is no respecter of persons.

The verse also pictures a well with a windlass for bringing up a pitcher filled with water. One day the wheel breaks, the pitcher is shattered, and the end comes. The fountain of water was an ancient image for life (Ps. 36:8-9; Rev. 21:6). When the machinery of life stops working, the water of life stops flowing. The heart stops pumping, the blood stops circulating, and death has come. The spirit leaves the body (James 2:26; Luke 23:46; Acts 7:59), the body begins to decay, and eventually it turns to dust.

For the last time in his discourse, the Preacher said, "Vanity of vanities...all is vanity." The book closes where it began (1:2), emphasizing the emptiness of life without God. When you look at life "under the sun," everything does seem vain; but when you know Jesus Christ as your Savior, "your labor is not in vain in the Lord" (1 Cor. 15:58).

3. Life Is a School: Learn Your Lessons (Eccl. 12:9-12)

Someone has said that life is like a school, except that sometimes you don't know what the lessons are until you have failed the examination. God teaches us primarily from His Word; but He also teaches us through creation, history, and the various experiences of life. Solomon explained the characteristics of his own work as a teacher of God's truth.

To begin with, his teaching was *wise* (*v. 9*); for Solomon was the wisest of men (1 Kings 3:3-28). The king studied and explored many subjects, and some of his conclusions he wrote down in proverbs.

His teaching was also **orderly** (*v. 9*). After studying a matter, he weighed his conclusions carefully, and then arranged them in an orderly fashion. His whole approach was certainly scientific. We may not always see the pattern behind his arrangement, but it is there just the same.

Solomon sought to be *careful* in his teaching, so he used "acceptable words." This means "pleasing" or "gracious" words (10:12) that would win the attention of his listeners and readers. However, at no time did he dilute his message or flatter his congregation. He always used *upright words of truth.* (See Prov. 8:6-11.) Like our Lord Jesus Christ, the king was able to combine "grace and truth" (John 1:17; Luke 4:16-32).

The Preacher claimed that his words were **inspired**, given by God, the One Shepherd (*v. 11*). Inspiration was the special miracle ministry of the Holy Spirit that enabled men of God to write the Word of God as God wanted it written, complete and without error (2 Tim. 3:16-17; 2 Peter 1:20-21).

He compared his words to "goads" and "nails" (v. 11), both of which are necessary if people are to learn God's truth. The "goads" prod the people to pay attention and to pursue truth, while the "nails" give them something on which to hang what they have learned. Good teaching requires both: the students must be motivated to study, and the instructors must be able to "nail things down" so that the lessons make sense.

On the surface, verse 12 seems to be a negative view of learning; but such is not the case. The statement is a warning to the student not to go beyond what God has written in His Word. Indeed, there are many books, and studying them can be a wearisome chore. But don't permit man's books to rob you of God's wisdom. "Be warned, my son, of anything in addition to them [the words of the wise]" (v. 12, NIV). These "nails" are sure and you can depend on them. Don't test God's truth by the "many books" written by men; test men's books by the truth of God's Word.

Yes, life is a school, and we must humble ourselves and learn all we can. Our textbook is the Bible, and the Holy Spirit is our Teacher (John 14:26; 15:26; 16:12-15). The Spirit can use gifted human teachers to instruct us, but He longs to teach us personally from His Word (Ps. 119:97-104). There are always new lessons to learn and new examinations to face as we seek to grow in grace and in the knowledge of our Savior (2 Peter 3:18).

4. Life Is a Stewardship: Fear God (Eccl. 12:13-14)

We don't own our lives, because life is the gift of God (Acts 17:24-28). We are stewards of our lives, and one day we must give an account to God of what we have done with His gift. Some people are only spending their lives; others are wasting their lives; a few are investing their lives. Corrie ten Boom said, "The measure of a life, after all, is not its duration but its donation." If our lives are to count, we must fulfill three obligations.

Fear God (*v. 13*). Ecclesiastes ends where the book of Proverbs begins (Prov. 1:7), with an admonition for us to fear the Lord. (See 3:14; 5:7; 7:18; and 8:12-13.) The "fear of the Lord" is that attitude of reverence and awe that His people show to

Him because they love Him and respect His power and His greatness. The person who fears the Lord will pay attention to His Word and obey it. He or she will not tempt the Lord by deliberately disobeying or by "playing with sin." An unholy fear makes people run away from God, but a holy fear brings them to their knees in loving submission to God.

"The remarkable thing about fearing God," wrote Oswald Chambers, "is that, when you fear God, you fear nothing else; whereas, if you do not fear God, you fear everything else." The prophet Isaiah says it perfectly in Isaiah 8:13, and the psalmist describes such a man in Psalm 112.

Keep His commandments (v. 13). God created life and He alone knows how it should be managed. He wrote the "manual of instructions" and wise is the person who reads and obeys. "When all else fails, read the instructions!"

The fear of the Lord must result in obedient living, otherwise that "fear" is only a sham. The dedicated believer will want to spend time daily in Scripture, getting to know the Father better and discovering His will. "The fear of the Lord is the beginning of knowledge, but fools despise wisdom and instruction" (Prov. 1:7).

The last phrase in verse 13 can be translated "this is the end of man" (i.e., his purpose in life), or "this is for all men." Campbell Morgan suggests "this is the whole of man." He writes in *The Unfolding Message of the Bible*, "Man, in his entirety, must begin with God; the whole of man, the fear of God" (p. 228). When Solomon looked at life "under the sun," everything was fragmented and he could see no pattern. But when he looked at life

from God's point of view, everything came together into one whole. If man wants to have wholeness, he must begin with God.

Prepare for final judgment (v. 14). "God shall judge the righteous and the wicked" (3:17). "But know that for all these God will bring you into judgment" (11:9, NKJV). Man may seem to get away with sin (8:11), but their sins will eventually be exposed and judged righteously. Those who have not trusted the Lord Jesus Christ will be doomed forever.

"The eternity of punishment is a thought which crushes the heart," said Charles Spurgeon. "The Lord God is slow to anger, but when he is once aroused to it, as he will be against those who finally reject his Son, he will put forth all his omnipotence to crush his enemies."

Six times in his discourse, Solomon told us to enjoy life while we can; but at no time did he advise us to enjoy sin. The joys of the present depend on the security of the future. If you know Jesus Christ as your Savior, then your sins have already been judged on the cross; and "there is therefore now no condemnation to them who are in Christ Jesus" (Rom. 8:1 and see John 5:24). But if you die having never trusted Christ, you will face judgment at His throne and be lost forever (Rev. 20:11-15).

Is life worth living? Yes, *if you are truly alive through faith in Jesus Christ.* Then you can be satisfied, no matter what God may permit to come to your life.

"He who has the Son has life; he who does not have the Son of God does not have life" (1 John 5:12, NKJV).

You can receive life in Christ and—*be satisfied!*

SONG OF SOLOMON

CONTENTS AND SUGGESTED OUTLINE OF SONG OF SOLOMON

Introduction to the Song of Solomon

Author. Jewish tradition and most evangelical scholarship both assign this book to King Solomon, although some students believe an anonymous author wrote the book but assumed the persona of Solomon. This seems strange when the Shulamite (the bride) does most of the speaking. The book is about love and marriage, and during the week of the marriage celebration, the Jewish bride and groom are treated like a king and queen. Solomon is mentioned in 1:1, 5; 3:7, 9, 11; and 8:11, 12. Solomon was both a king (1:4, 12; 3:9, 11; 7:5) and a shepherd (1:7-8, 2:16; 6:2-3), for in Old Testament days, rulers were called "shepherds" (Jer. 23; Ezek. 34). The eastern sheik was the father of a household, the shepherd of a flock, and the king over a realm (see Luke 12:32). The key female character in Song of Solomon worked as a shepherdess (1:8) and the keeper of a vineyard (1:6).

Name. Solomon wrote 1,005 songs (1 Kings 4:32), but this one is "the song of songs" (1:1), that is, the greatest of all songs. Just as the "Holy of Holies" is the holiest place and the "King of kings" is the highest of all kings, so the "song of songs" is the greatest of all songs. The theme of the book is love, and the greatest virtue is love (1 Cor. 13:13). During his period of skepticism, Solomon wrote Ecclesiastes with its doleful theme of "vanity of vanities," a phrase he used thirty-eight times. But in his younger days, before he became entangled with the gods of his many pagan wives (1 Kings 11:1-8), Solomon understood the joys and virtues of married love and

wrote this beautiful book. He ultimately had 700 wives and 300 concubines (1 Kings 11:3) and in so doing violated the law of the Lord (Deut. 17:17). He married many of his princess wives mainly to establish peaceful and profitable relations with their fathers.[1]

Theme. There are many theological overtones to this book, but the major theme is the excitement and enjoyment of God's gifts of sex, love, and marriage. Unlike some religions that condemn physical pleasures in general and sex in particular, both Jews and Christians see life and its physical pleasures as the gifts of God. This is especially true of marriage and the intimate love of husband and wife. Sex and marriage were taken very seriously in the Jewish culture. Engagement was a binding relationship that could be severed only by divorce, and premarital sin and adultery were dealt with severely. Weddings were joyful occasions that lasted a week, and the union was expected to last a lifetime. The Jews gladly accepted God's gifts of sex and marriage and were not embarrassed to admit it. The Jews also saw their nation "married to Jehovah" (Isa. 50:1; 54:4-5; Jer. 3; Ezek. 16 and 23; Hos. 1–3), and for this reason they read the Song of Solomon annually on the eighth day of Passover. God delivered them from Egypt because He loved them (Deut. 7:7-8), and He was "married" to them at Mount Sinai when Israel accepted His covenant (Ex. 18-24). Reading the Song of Solomon reminded them to love the Lord their God with all their heart (Deut. 6:4-5; Matt. 22:37). Since the church is the bride of Christ, and Solomon is a type of Christ (Matt. 12:42), believers today can also learn many important spiritual lessons from this unusual book.

Story. Unlike modern novels, this book doesn't present an obvious story line, but it seems to have a definite plot which is "discovered" as you read the book carefully. The cast of characters is small: King Solomon; the lovely woman (the "Shulamite," a feminine form of the name Solomon) who becomes his wife; the Shulamite's brothers (1:5-6; 8:8-10); and "the daughters of Jerusalem" who function as a background chorus. It is the Shulamite who does most of the speaking in the book.

The Shulamite's brothers were employed by Solomon to care for his vineyards, but they put their sister to work in them as well (8:11-14). King Solomon, disguised as a shepherd, visited his vineyards, saw the Shulamite, and fell in love with her (1:1-2:7). She pictures their times together as a rich banquet. The next spring, he came to her and proposed marriage, and she accepted, but he had to go away for a time, promising to come back. While he was absent, she dreamed about him (3:1-5). Then he returned and revealed that he was King Solomon. They married and consummated their marriage on their wedding night (3:6-5:1). The remainder of the book describes the celebration of their love as they experienced various adventures together.

Most current translations and study Bibles identify the speakers, although not everybody agrees on these identifications. However, the disagreements are relatively few and minor and don't greatly affect the interpretation.

This book has a great deal to teach us about God's gift to men and women of the pleasures of love and sex. But it also presents the divine standards God has set for marriage, illustrating the joyful privileges and serious obligations husbands and wives have toward God and each other (see 1 Cor. 7:1-5; Eph. 5:22-33; 1 Peter 3:1-7). The Jews called the Song of Solomon "the Holy of Holies" of Scripture and wouldn't allow it to be read by the young and immature. In today's world, with its emphasis on the sensual pleasures of indiscriminate lust and not on the pure pleasures of sex in marriage, our young people could use a good course based on the Song of Solomon.

The Song of Solomon is an "outdoor book," using many images from nature—gardens, fields, mountains, flocks, birds, flowers, spices, and animals—and the love of the man and woman fits right into this context. All nature is God's gift to us and should be used for His glory, including human nature and the wonderful gift of sexuality. When a husband and wife have a beautiful and holy relationship, their whole world becomes beautiful and holy. Without dodging reality or defiling God's gifts, the book deals quite frankly with human sexuality and shows how it can be sanctified and used for God's glory. It is a book of metaphors and similes that uses many literary devices to show us the wonder and glory of divine and human love. Like the book of Esther, the Song of Solomon doesn't mention God's name, but understanding this book will certainly make the Lord much more real to you, whether you are married or single.

Interpretation. The Jewish rabbis saw the Song of Solomon as a book extolling human love and the proper use of sex in marriage. They also saw the book as an illustration of God's love for His people Israel and His desire to share a deeper love with His people. Christian interpreters take the same approach, seeing in Song of Solomon the love relationship between Christ and His church. The New

Testament pictures the church as a bride and Christ as the Bridegroom (Matt. 9:15; John 3:29; 2 Cor. 11:1-4; Eph. 5:22-33; Rev. 19:7; 21:2, 9; 22:17). The Holy Spirit wants to bring to us a deeper fellowship with the Father and the Son as we commune with the Lord in His Word and obey His will (John 14:19-27). Worship and fellowship are to be much more than religious rituals and doctrines we agree with intellectually. There can be a deeper work of the Spirit in our lives that reveals the heavenly Bridegroom in a fuller way, and we should not be satisfied with a mere surface acquaintance with the Lord.

While the Song of Solomon illustrates the deepening love we can have with Christ, we must be careful not to turn the story into an allegory and make everything mean something. All things are possible to those who allegorize—and what they come up with is usually heretical. It's almost laughable to read some of the ancient commentaries (and their modern imitators) and see how interpreters have made Solomon say what they want him to say. The language of love is imaginative and piles one image on top of another to convey its message. But to make the bride's breasts represent the two ordinances, or the garden stand for the local church, or the voice of the turtledove mean the Holy Spirit speaking, is to obscure if not destroy the message of the book. Other texts in the Bible may support the ideas expressed by these fanciful interpreters, but their ideas didn't come from what Solomon wrote.

"Greater than Solomon." Whatever Solomon was, had, or did, Jesus far surpassed him, for He is indeed "greater than Solomon" (Matt. 12:42). Solomon was known for his great wisdom (1 Kings 4:29; 5:12), but Jesus Christ *is* the wisdom of God (1 Cor. 1:24), and in Him all of God's wisdom dwells (Col. 2:3). Solomon was also known for his wealth (1 Kings 10), but in Jesus Christ there are "unsearchable riches" (Eph. 3:8; see Phil. 4:19). Solomon disobeyed God and married many wives, but Jesus obeyed the Father and died on the cross that He might have a spotless bride for all eternity (Eph. 5:25-27; Rev. 21:2, 9ff). The relationship described between Solomon and the Shulamite pictures to us the love between Christ and His bride, and when Jesus returns and takes His people to heaven, the bride will become His wife. Solomon built a temple that was ultimately destroyed, but Jesus is building His temple, the church (Matt. 16:18), and it will glorify Him forever (Eph. 2:20-22).

ANTICIPATION: THE COURTSHIP

Song of Solomon 1:1-3:5

With no explanation of who she is or what wonderful things have happened to her, the Shulamite launches into a statement about her love for the king.

True love is like a banquet (1:2-2:7). First she speaks *of* him and then she speaks *to* him. She yearns for expressions of his love (kisses; 8:1) and confesses that his love[2] is better than wine. The effects of wine are shallow and temporary, but the enrichment that comes from true love is deep and lasting. Note that the expressions of love include touch (kisses), taste (wine), and smell (ointment). No wonder she cries out to him, "Take me with you!" It is his love that draws her to his chambers where a great banquet has been prepared. The women of Jerusalem approve her choice and her decision to go with him. There are four parties involved in marriage: the bride, the groom, society, and the Lord. Other people don't choose our mates for us, but the approval of godly friends is a great encouragement. The women express their approval of the king and run after them as they go to the banquet in the king's chambers.

The Shulamite rejoices that he has chosen her and repeats her statement about his love being better than wine. But then she suddenly feels unworthy of such an honor and describes herself as "dark but still lovely" (1:5). She had been tanned by the hot eastern sun as she worked for her brothers in the vineyard. She kept their vineyards but neglected to care for her own vineyard—herself. The tents of Kedar were made out of the hair of black goats, and she felt that she looked just like them! She speaks to the shepherd-king and offers to go care for his flocks instead of attending the banquet. Otherwise, she would have to veil her face, and then the other guests would take her for a prostitute (Gen. 38:14-15). He didn't reply to her question, but the women of Jerusalem suggested she follow the flocks of the other shepherds, for shepherds often pastured their sheep together.

But Solomon would have none of her confessions of unworthiness and ugliness! In 1:9-11, he extols her beauty[3] and calls her "my love" (see 1:15; 2:2, 10, 13; 4:1, 7; 5:2; 6:4). If today a man compared his wife or girlfriend to a mare pulling a chariot, he would probably be in trouble, but the lovely Shulamite knew what Solomon meant. No sensible charioteer would ever put a mare among stallions! But Solomon was only saying, "You are unique—one among many, unique, very special." A noble horse is indeed a beautiful creature, and Solomon was an expert

on horses (1 Kings 10:25ff). Furthermore, the king's horses wore exquisite ornaments, something his beloved didn't need because her own beauty was sufficient (see 1 Peter 3:3-4). The daughters of Jerusalem offered to make her special jewelry to please the king (1:11), but Solomon wouldn't permit it. Our Lord Jesus is today using His Word to beautify His bride (Eph. 5:26-27), and as we obey Him, we are preparing ourselves for the great heavenly wedding (Rev. 19:7-9).

The company arrives at the banquet hall where they recline at the table with the king and his beloved (1:12). Frequently in the Song of Solomon you find love compared to the enjoyment of food and drink, such as fruit (2:3-4), wine (1:2; 5:1), and honey and milk (5:1). Scripture compares the future reign of Christ to a great marriage feast (Isa. 25:6; Matt. 8:11; Luke 13:29 and 14:15; Rev. 19:6-9). The beloved Shulamite wears perfume that attracts her lover; in fact, she sees him as a sachet of myrrh over her heart and as a cluster of beautiful flowers from the rich oasis of En Gedi. She tells him this, and he responds by telling her she is beautiful, especially her eyes. She also tells him that he is handsome and uses two images to assure him that their love would last: their couch (not "bed") at the table was green, like a verdant garden or field, and their rafters were strong. The roof wasn't about to fall down!

But then she lapses back into abasing herself, for she compares herself to a common crocus (rose) from Sharon and an ordinary hyacinth (lily) of the fields (2:1).[4] In spite of what a familiar Gospel song says, it is the Shulamite who makes this comparison of herself and not the king who make this comparison of himself. But the king responds by using the image of the lily and comparing her to a lily among thorns! She then responds by comparing him to a beautiful apple tree in a forest, under which she could sit down and find protection from the sun (1:6) and fruit for her sustenance. It would be unusual to find an apple tree in a common forest, so she is saying that he is "one in a million."

Solomon was not ashamed of his love for her and displayed it like the banner of an army. "He must love me," muses the Shulamite, "because he brought me to this banquet and wasn't ashamed to be associated with me." But the very thought of being loved by so great a person left her faint, and she asked for apples and cakes of raisins so she could regain her strength. In 2:6, she anticipates the consummation of their marriage ("O that his left hand were under my head and his right hand embracing me!"), but she knows she must wait for the right time. That's why she admonishes the women from Jerusalem who accompanied her not to rush into love and marriage but to wait for the right time. Even Solomon would write, "There is a time to love" (Eccl. 3:8). She gives this "charge" again in 3:5, 5:8, and 8:4. True love isn't something we work up; it's something the Lord sends down within us when we meet the right person at the right time.[5]

True love is like an adventure in the country (2:8-17). After the banquet, the king left the scene, and we assume that his courtiers escorted the Shulamite safely home. She went back to her normal life, but her eyes and ears were always open as she anticipated his return. Then it happened! One day as she was in her brothers' home, she heard his voice and saw him coming toward her like a beautiful gazelle or a noble stag, bounding across every barrier that stood between him and his beloved. He stopped at the wall that protected the house and looked at her through the lattice window. Then he spoke to her and twice invited her to "come away" (vv. 10, 13).[6] This invitation would be repeated in 4:8, and the Shulamite herself would extend this invitation to her lover (7:11; 8:14).

"Come" is the great word of the Gospel of God's grace. It is God's loving invitation to the weary who need rest (Matt. 11:28-30), the sin-stained who need cleansing (Isa. 1:18), the hungry who need nourishment (Luke 14:17), and all who thirst for the water of life (Rev. 22:17). But "come" is also His invitation to His own people: "Come and see" (John 1:39), "Come and drink" (John 7:37-38), "Come and dine" (John 21:12). In this text, the king invited his beloved to leave her home and her work and go with him to enjoy an adventure in the country.

Love is not only a banquet of delights, but love is also an adventure. There must be spontaneous expressions of affection if love is to thrive. It was the early springtime and the latter rains had stopped. The flowers were blooming, the birds were singing, and the trees and vines were sprouting. New life was everywhere and abounding! But it seems that his beloved would rather stay home, in the place of security, like a dove in the clefts of the rocks on the mountainside. He wanted to hear her voice and see her face, but she preferred to stay quietly at home. To grow in their love for each other, they needed to be together and have different experiences in different places. This is how we learn more about ourselves and our potential mates. But this principle also applies to our love for the Lord. We must go with Him into new and challenging experiences that will deepen our love and strengthen our faith.

The "little foxes" (2:15) represent those things that quietly destroy relationships. Foxes get into vineyards to feed on the grapes, and the keepers must prop up the branches so the foxes can't reach them. The Shulamite was still trying to "keep her own vineyard" (1:6)—develop her own personality and prepare for her future—and her unwillingness to go with the king was robbing her of opportunities for maturity. The fruit of their relationship was still tender and needed to be both protected and encouraged.[7] But she makes it clear that her hesitation doesn't alter her relationship with her lover, because they belong to each other and she knows where he is and what he's doing (v. 16). "Feed" in verse 16 means "to pasture a flock." Just as he came to her as a bounding deer (vv. 8-9), so he will come back, and she will welcome him (v. 17).

True love brings dreams of the one you love (3:1-5). The beloved goes to bed and has a dream about her lover. After all, she refused an invitation to spend time with him, and perhaps her conscience was bothering her. In her dream, she left the security of her home and at night searched for him in the city. The watchmen couldn't help her, but she persisted and eventually found him and wouldn't let him go. Her desire was for them to get married, so she brought him to her mother's house and into the very room where she herself had been conceived. Isaac had brought his wife Rebekah into his mother's tent and there consummated their marriage (Gen. 24:67). This is the first mention of the Shulamite's mother, but nothing is said about her father. (See 3:4,11; 6:9; 8:2, 5.)

At some point in this dream, or perhaps the next day, she gave her usual admonition to the daughters of Jerusalem

to let the Lord direct in their lives and not run ahead of His will (v. 5)—even in their dreams!

CONSUMMATION: THE WEDDING

Song of Solomon 3:6–5:1

At last the day arrived for the Shulamite to wed her beloved! Not only would he claim her as his wife, but she would discover that her husband was the king!

Claiming the bride (3:6-11). The glorious procession appears on the horizon. It is Solomon being carried in his richly decorated palanquin, surrounded by sixty of his bravest soldiers, with a cloud of fragrant incense above him.[8] He wears a wedding crown given to him by his mother. The daughters of Jerusalem get excited and sing to each other, "Go forth, O daughters of Zion!" The bride has her attendants, the king has joy in his heart, and the time has finally come for the wedding to take place. Today's Christians would see in this a reminder of the coming of the King of kings to claim His bride, the church.

Extolling her beauty (4:1-7). In modern marriages, the bride is the center of attention, and "What did the bride wear?" is the big question. But the king is more concerned with her own beauty than with her attire. He has claimed her for himself and it is now their wedding night. She will lay aside her veil as a symbol that she belongs to him and she has nothing to hide.[9] (See Gen. 24:65.) His speech opens and closes with, "You are beautiful!" The images the king uses to describe her beauty may seem strange to us, but measures of beauty change from age to age and culture to culture.

Doves' eyes would reflect peace and depth. The bride's teeth were clean, even, and beautiful. When you remember that ancient peoples didn't quite understand dental hygiene, this is an admirable trait. Healthy teeth would also affect her breath (7:8). She had a queenly neck and a posture with it that exuded control, power, and stability. She was a tower of strength! The "mountains of myrrh" refer to her breasts, which he would enjoy all night until the dawn would break, and she would also enjoy his expressions of love.

Consummating the marriage (4:8-5:1). Beginning in verse 8, six times he calls her his "spouse" or his bride. After the marriage is consummated, she is no longer a bride but a wife. They are enjoying a "mountaintop experience" as they share their love (v. 8), and he tells her how beautiful she is. "Thy love" in verse 10 refers to her words and actions and not just her feelings. It could be translated "love-making."

He rejoices that his bride is a virgin, "a garden locked up, a spring enclosed and a fountain sealed" (v. 12). This is another evidence that the Lord wants both the man and the woman to stay sexually pure. Conjugal love is pictured in terms of satisfying thirst (v. 15; see Prov. 5:15-23) and exploring a beautiful and fruitful garden that never grows old. The bride is the garden, and the bridegroom prays that the winds of life will make her even more beautiful and desirable. We may not appreciate the north wind, but even it can help us mature in our love.

With this lovely preparation completed, the bride is now ready, and she invites her husband to come into his garden and drink the living water and eat the nourishing fruits. He accepts her loving invitation and then says, "I have come into my garden!" They had feasted at the beginning of their relationship (1:2-2:7), but it was nothing like this! They now had truly tasted the fruits and enjoyed the wine, milk, and fragrant spices.

Who speaks in verse 5b? Is it the bride telling her husband-lover that he may visit the garden often? "Drink deeply" ("drink your fill") suggests that there is always more to learn and enjoy as the marriage progresses. But the noun "beloved" is plural and can be translated "lovers." Surely the daughters of Jerusalem aren't there at that private sacred moment! It's been suggested that this may be God speaking to the couple and through them encouraging all married couples to enjoy the blessings of married love, for He created sex for pleasure as well as for procreation.

CELEBRATION: THE MARRIAGE

Song of Solomon 5:2-8:14

During the week following a Jewish wedding, family and friends treated the newlyweds like royalty. Modern couples have a "honeymoon" and usually travel to some special place where they will be left alone.[10] But eventually the couple has to return to life with its problems and duties, and so did Solomon and his wife.

The quest for her husband (5:2-9). The Shulamite had another disturbing dream. (See 3:1-4.) She heard her husband calling to her (note that he doesn't call her his "bride") and asking her to let him in. Apparently she had locked the door and gone to bed without him. But she had bathed and was comfortable in bed and didn't want to be disturbed. Perhaps she wasn't in the mood for romance. She didn't respond to his voice, but she did respond when she saw his hand come through the opening for the door latch and when she smelled the fragrant perfume on his hand. The king didn't force his way in, but surely he was disappointed when his beloved rejected him.

Realizing her mistake, the Shulamite went to the door, but when she did, she discovered that he was gone. Her heart sank, for love is a delicate thing, easily misunderstood and quickly hurt. She called, but he didn't answer, so she went in search of him. This time the city guards didn't cooperate with her; instead, they wounded her and took her cloak. Did they think she was a prostitute out looking for business? The beloved seemed to have most of her trouble in the night and not when she was walking in the daytime with her king. First John 1:5-10 comes to mind. She told the daughters of Jerusalem that she was faint from love (2:5), for she was learning that there's a price to pay in marriage if we want to mature in our affection. They asked her what made her beloved so special, and her reply was another description of how handsome he was.

The beauty of her husband (5:10-16). Perhaps if she had told him this on their wedding night, he wouldn't have left her temporarily or been so quick to leave before she could open the door. "Love is patient, love is kind" (1 Cor. 13:4, NIV), but love needs to be nourished with kind words and actions. Again, the measures she used to describe his attractiveness are different from those we use today, but they do convey the right message. "White and ruddy" describes a man radiant with health and strength, just like David (1 Sam. 16:12; 17:42). "Ruddy" comes from a word that means "red," which could suggest a red tint to the hair or perhaps the "bronzed" complexion of the person who has an active life outdoors.

A head like fine gold means a valuable head; that is, his brains were worth something. A body like ivory and marble speaks of beauty and strength. "Like Lebanon" also suggests beauty and strength, but this time she points to the famous and valuable cedars of Lebanon. The beautiful phrase "altogether lovely" says it all. Over the years, our bodies change and we get old, but the husband and wife who grow in their appreciation and evaluation of each other will never cultivate a critical attitude. "Young in heart" is the secret of a long and happy marriage.

Their meeting in the garden (6:1-13). It's now daylight and the women of Jerusalem offer to help her to find her husband, but the Shulamite knows him well and knows where he has gone. One of the important elements in a marriage is getting to know each other so well that we can "read each other's minds" and anticipate actions and words. "I am my beloved's and my beloved is mine" expresses it perfectly (6:3; see 2:16 and 7:10). Solomon was not lost to her even though they weren't together. He was feeding his flock in the garden and she knew where to go.

The moment he saw her, he welcomed her and began to extol her virtues. He didn't scold her for keeping him outside the door or for walking about the city alone at night and getting bruised by the watchmen. Tirzah was the capital of the northern kingdom of Israel after the nation divided. "You are fit for a king!" is what he was saying. The Jews thought that Jerusalem was the most beautiful of all cities (Ps. 48; Ps. 50:2; Lam. 2:15). "Terrible" means "awesome, majestic." Remember, he is speaking about a woman and comparing her to an impressive army on the march. Her eyes alone captivated him and overcame him. He used a number of the similes that she had used in 4:10-16, although he wasn't present to hear her words. They are starting to become very much alike, something that often happens in marriages.

The number of queens and concubines in his harem was much lower than in his later years (6:8; 1 Kings 11:3), so this was written very early in his reign. But of all the women in his life, the Shulamite was his favorite as well as the favorite of her mother and the other queens in the palace. In the eyes of the Shulamite, Solomon was "altogether lovely [beautiful]" (5:16), and in Solomon's eyes, his wife was "the only one of her kind—unique" (6:9). Even the daughters of Jerusalem praised the Shulamite for her beauty. They had been with her at night and saw her as fair as the moon, and now that it was morning, she looked as lovely as the dawn. As the sun ascended, she looked as awesome as an army, a phrase the king had used (v. 4). Some see verse 10 describing the king and his wife riding off in the royal palanquin.

The beloved wife decided she wanted to visit their garden to see if the spring had brought new growth to the trees and vines, so there was a temporary separation from her husband. But then a remarkable thing happened: she found herself "among the chariots of the people of the prince" (v. 12, NIV margin). Her husband's army was arriving, and the garden looked like a battlefield. But gardens are for beauty and nourishment, not for battles. Is there a suggestion here that marriage should be neither a battleground nor a playground, but a garden that is carefully cultivated and thoroughly enjoyed? The first marriage took place in a perfect garden (Gen. 2:18-25), and mar-

riage ought to be like a garden. This takes work, but it's worth it! Noticing her absence, the daughters of Jerusalem call for her to return so they can gaze upon her beauty, but in her modesty, she asks, "Why look at me? What is there to look at?" Solomon answers the question from 6:13c to 7:9.

They express their mutual love (7:1-8:4). "When you look at me and my wife," replied Solomon, "you are seeing two armies!" The Hebrew is *mahanaim* and takes us back to the time Jacob was about to meet his brother Esau and was very much afraid (Gen. 32:1ff). God gave him a vision of an army of angels sent from heaven to protect him, so Jacob called the name of the place "Mahanaim" because he saw two armies—the army of God above him and his own army of retainers around him. The wrong kind of military language is often used with reference to marriage, such as, "My wife is a battleaxe!" or "My husband's on a campaign to buy a boat!" But the Song of Solomon sees the wife and husband like two armies marching together, each helping and defending the other (6:4, 10). They don't battle with each other, but they attack anything that will threaten their marriage.

Most of the similes in 7:1-9 have been used before in the book, but a few are new. He describes her beauty from foot (v. 1) to head (vv. 5 and 9). Both food and drink are referenced in 7:2, describing the intimate area of her body, and this suggests that the husband is nourished by the love of his wife. Oriental "fish pools" were beautiful and peaceful, even though filled with life, and so were her eyes (v. 4). Previously, Solomon had been so smitten by her look that he was overcome (6:5), but now he can watch her eyes and find beauty and excitement. If today you compared a woman's neck or nose to a tower, you would offend her, but not so in that day. The reference isn't to size or prominence but to proportion and fitness. Like a tower on the city wall, or even standing alone in the land, it was in the right setting and had its own beauty. Hair "like purple" isn't referring to dyed hair but to royal curtains or tapestries. Whereas the king had been transfixed by her eyes (6:5), now it's her hair that captures him.

In verses 6-9, he introduces a fascinating new metaphor. He sees his lovely wife as a palm tree, beautiful and fruitful, and their intimate love as his climbing the tree and eating its fruits. ("Grapes" in v. 7, KJV should be "fruit," referring to dates.) Kissing her was like drinking wine, and he told her so. Her reply was that she hoped the wine would flow gently over his lips and teeth and please him. Again she assures him of their mutual love and devotion (v. 10; see 2:16 and 6:3). "His desire is toward me" reminds us of Genesis 3:16, where the Lord said that Eve's desire would be for her husband. Sexual attraction in marriage must be a mutual experience, and the husband and wife must work at making themselves desirable.

Now the bride wants to make a visit to the country, something Solomon had wanted to do before and she had refused (2:8-17). Sometimes visiting another place gives a freshness to marriage relationships, and she promised to give him her love (7:12). A husband and wife have conjugal obligations to each other (1 Cor. 7:1-7), but they shouldn't look upon married love as a dutiful responsibility. It is also a gift they share with each other, as they shared the feast and the joys of visiting the garden. Mandrakes have long been associated with sexual passion (Gen.

30:14), although there's no evidence that they work as a sexual stimulant. The Shulamite enjoys fruit that is both new and old, suggesting that they're brave enough to try something new but wise enough not to abandon what they know really works.

As she closes her monologue, she expresses regret that she can't show her love to him spontaneously, as a sister can do to a brother (8:1-4). In that society at that time, for a wife to kiss her husband in public would be considered uncouth, so they had to wait until they were alone. She wanted to be a "big sister" to him and kiss him, take him home to her mother, and learn from her mother how to treat him. Once again, the image of food and drink is used to describe their love: he would embrace her and she would provide the wine and pomegranate juice. The seeds of the pomegranate are found in sacs that contain a tasty juice.

They pledge unending love and faithfulness (8:5-14). The daughters of Jerusalem see the couple returning home from their honeymoon trip to the villages, and they note that in the royal carriage she is leaning on her husband in love. (See 3:6 for a parallel picture.) As they come to her native village, they see a prominent apple tree, and the king reminds her that she had been sleeping under that tree, weary from work, when first he saw her. Then he pointed to her girlhood home and reminded her that there she had been conceived and delivered.

But those days were ended. Now they belonged to each other and needed to be true to each other. He asked her to make him the seal on her heart and arm, for a seal speaks of ownership and protection. Their love brought them together and their love would keep them together. The grip of death and the grave can't be broken, and neither can the hold of love. A husband and wife aren't envious of each other but they are jealous over one another, and that jealousy is powerful, like the very fire of God.[11] The bride picks up this image of the fire and says that such love can't be put out by water, and it's not for sale! Any man who offered to buy love would be scorned and rejected. By speaking in this way, the king and his wife affirm their unending love for each other.

Verses 8-14 form an appendix to the story. As the Shulamite returns to her girlhood home with her husband, she remembers what her brothers said about her when she was younger. They didn't think she was ready for marriage because she hadn't yet matured. The images of the wall and the door have to do with the girl's virginity. If she was a door, a woman of easy access, then she would not be fit to be a bride, but if she kept herself pure, behind a wall, as it were, then they could give her away to the man who asked for her. The Shulamite boldly stated that she was a wall and entered the marriage bed a pure virgin. But in spite of her brothers' sneers, she developed physically and had breasts that her husband admired (4:5-6; 7:3, 7-8).

Now that she is married, her brothers will not be able to enlist her help in caring for the vineyard. But Solomon owns the vineyard and, as his wife, she has a share in it! Verses 11-12 seem to speak about a new "work contract" she negotiated between her husband and her brothers, providing them with more money for their labors. They might be able to hire extra help to replace their sister.

The book closes with the Shulamite in her garden, chatting with some friends, and her husband calls to her because he wants to hear her voice. Where there is love, the husband and wife want to be together and share their ideas and feelings. Yes, there's a place for other companions, but nobody must replace the mate God gives to us. How does the beloved respond to his call? She tells him to hurry up and leave with her, because the "mountains of spices" (her breasts, 4:5-6) are awaiting his touch. Of course, her companions in the garden don't understand this code word, so she doesn't embarrass anybody. Husbands and wives frequently have a secret language of love that others don't understand.

Observations

The presence of immature people in a congregation would make it difficult to preach from this book, but a series of lessons from the Song of Solomon would be very helpful to a class of engaged couples or newlyweds. The book would be ideal as a basis for premarital counseling. If in our teaching and preaching we do allegorize some portions, we must first of all give the basic interpretation. Since the relationship of Christ and His church is like that of a husband and wife, there are certain applications that we can make.

In using this book in public ministry, we must be wise as serpents and harmless as doves and not allow our good works to be classified as evil. Some people are against anything in the pulpit that deals with sex, while others wonder where they can get the help that they desperately need. Wise is the minister and teacher who can keep the right balance.

ENDNOTES

1. It's interesting to compare and contrast what Solomon wrote about marriage in Proverbs, Ecclesiastes, and Song of Solomon. Proverbs extols monogamy and the enjoyment of married love (Prov. 5:15-20) and also warns against fornication, adultery, and "the strange woman" (Prov. 2:16ff; 5:1ff; 6:20-35; 7:1-27; 22:14; 23:27-28; 30:20). Several times in Proverbs, Solomon admonishes the young man to choose the right wife and thereby avoid having to live with a nagging critical woman! Ecclesiastes also admonishes the man to "live joyfully" with the wife of his youth (9:9). In spite of his many wives and concubines, Solomon realized that true pleasure in marriage was the result of a lifetime of devotion to one mate, during which they grow together and learn to love each other more.

2. The word "love" is in the plural in 1:2 and 4, 4:10, and 7:12, and can be translated "love-making," the king's actions and not just his feelings toward her. However, the Shulamite and the king do not consummate their love until after they are married (4:12-5:1). Premarital sex was not acceptable in Israel. If the bride was accused of premarital sin, she and her parents had to provide public proof of her virginity (Deut. 22:13-21).

3. Solomon calls her beautiful (lovely, fair) in 1:10 and 15, 2:10 and 13, 4:1 and 7, 6:4, and 7:1 and 6. This is a good example for husbands to follow!

4. She is not speaking about the rose as we know it today. The image of the lily (hyacinth) appears also in 2:16, 4:5, 5:13, 6:2-3 and 7:2.

5. This repeated admonition to the unmarried daughters of Jerusalem is a warning against premarital sex. The Shulamite wants them to remain pure in mind and body so they will enter into the full joy of married love at the right time and with the right person. No matter what society does and the law permits, the Bible knows nothing of unmarried couples living together as though married. Some things are legal that may not be biblical.

6. The Shulamite here reports what her lover said to her. It's important that loving husbands and wives remember what they say to each other, and that believers remember the Word of their King.

7. Some students think that v. 15 is spoken by the Shulamite as a defense of her unwillingness to have an adventure with the king. Others think that her brothers may have interrupted the dialogue and reminded her of her responsibilities in the vineyard.

8. The word "this" in v. 6 is feminine and some apply it to the bride, but the text can be translated "What is that," referring to the scene or to Solomon's carriage, which is feminine in Hebrew.

9. In modern weddings, the lifting of the bride's veil is symbolic of the sexual consummation of the marriage that will later take place. "I am his and he is mine."

10. "Honeymoon" came into the English vocabulary in the 16th century to identify the first month after marriage when the newlyweds showed special tenderness and love toward each other. Their new relationship was as sweet as honey, but it might end with the changing of the moon. Married people have their ups and downs, but there's no reason why their relationship should decay instead of develop.

11. This phrase can be translated "the very flame of the Lord." See NIV margin. If this is the correct translation, then this is the only place that the name of the Lord is mentioned in the Song of Solomon.

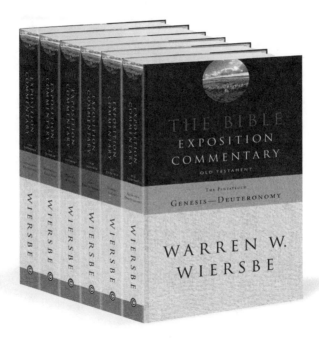